ENVIRONMENTAL LAW AND GOVERNANCE FOR THE ANTHROPOCENE

The era of eco-crises signified by the Anthropocene trope is marked by rapidly intensifying levels of complexity and unevenness, which collectively present unique regulatory challenges to environmental law and governance. This volume sets out to address the currently under-theorised legal and consequent governance challenges presented by the emergence of the Anthropocene as a possible new geological epoch. While the epoch has yet to be formally confirmed, the trope and discourse of the Anthropocene undoubtedly already confront law and governance scholars with a unique challenge concerning the need to question, and ultimately re-imagine, environmental law and governance interventions in the light of a new socio-ecological situation, the signs of which are increasingly apparent and urgent. This volume does not aspire to offer a univocal response to Anthropocene exigencies and phenomena. Any such attempt is, in any case, unlikely to do justice to the multiple implications and characteristics of Anthropocene forebodings. What it does is to invite an unrivalled group of leading law and governance scholars to reflect upon the Anthropocene and the implications of its discursive formation in an attempt to trace some initial, often radical, future-facing and imaginative implications for environmental law and governance.

Environmental Law and Governance for the Anthropocene

Edited by
Louis J Kotzé

·HART·
PUBLISHING
OXFORD AND PORTLAND, OREGON
2017

Hart Publishing
An imprint of Bloomsbury Publishing Plc

Hart Publishing Ltd	Bloomsbury Publishing Plc
Kemp House	50 Bedford Square
Chawley Park	London
Cumnor Hill	WC1B 3DP
Oxford OX2 9PH	UK
UK	

www.hartpub.co.uk
www.bloomsbury.com

Published in North America (US and Canada) by
Hart Publishing
c/o International Specialized Book Services
920 NE 58th Avenue, Suite 300
Portland, OR 97213-3786
USA

www.isbs.com

**HART PUBLISHING, the Hart/Stag logo, BLOOMSBURY and the
Diana logo are trademarks of Bloomsbury Publishing Plc**

First published 2017

British Library Cataloguing-in-Publication Data
A catalogue record for this book is available from the British Library.

ISBN:	HB:	978-1-50990-656-7
	ePDF:	978-1-50990-654-3
	ePub:	978-1-50990-655-0

Library of Congress Cataloging-in-Publication Data

Names: Kotzé, Louis J., editor.

Title: Environmental law and governance for the anthropocene / edited by Louis Kotzé.

Description: Oxford [UK] ; Portland, Oregon : Hart Publishing, 2017. | Includes bibliographical
references and index.

Identifiers: LCCN 2017004607 (print) | LCCN 2017004792 (ebook) | ISBN 9781509906567
(hardback : alk. paper) | ISBN 9781509906550 (Epub)

Subjects: LCSH: Environmental law, International. | Climatic changes—Effect of human beings on. |
Climatic changes—Law and legislation. | Sustainable development—Law and legislation. |
Philosophical anthropology. | Geology, Stratigraphic—Anthropocene.

Classification: LCC K3585.5 . E58 2017 (print) | LCC K3585.5 (ebook) | DDC 344.04/6—dc23

LC record available at https://lccn.loc.gov/2017004607

Typeset by Compuscript Ltd, Shannon
Printed and bound in Great Britain by Lightning Source UK Ltd

To find out more about our authors and books visit www.hartpublishing.co.uk. Here you will find extracts,
author information, details of forthcoming events and the option to sign up for our newsletters.

For Anél du Plessis; a lifelong companion.

PREFACE: DISCOMFORTING CONVERSATIONS IN THE ANTHROPOCENE*

There is persuasive evidence suggesting that planetary systems are on the brink of human-induced ecological disaster that could change life on Earth as we know it. This evidence underlies scientists' recent suggestion that the Earth system has entered a period in which humanity has emerged as a geological force triggering an epoch called the Anthropocene. The term 'Anthropocene' was first introduced in a publication by Eugene Stoermer and Paul Crutzen as a term of art expressing the geological significance of anthropogenic change.[1] The use of the term 'Anthropocene' suggests that the Earth is rapidly moving into a critically unstable state, with the Earth system gradually becoming less predictable, non-stationary and less harmonious as a result of the growing global human imprint on the biosphere. In the geo-ecological context, the term 'Anthropocene' therefore denotes a new period when human beings dominate the Earth by acting as the major driving force in modifying the biosphere.

A proposal to formalise the Anthropocene as an epoch of the geological timescale is currently being prepared by the Anthropocene Working Group, for consideration by the International Commission on Stratigraphy. With its formal acceptance pending, the Anthropocene trope has meanwhile managed to grab the attention of a growing trans-disciplinary cohort of scholars and has become a major academic enterprise. The growing trans-disciplinary and global interest that the Anthropocene is attracting suggests that it is steadily becoming a popular lens through which to consider the scientific and increasingly the social aspects of past, present and future global environmental change. In tandem with its instigating this trans-disciplinary scientific confluence, the term 'Anthropocene' is rapidly transcending its initial use as a mere rhetorical device, permitting deeper epistemological and ontological enquiries into regulatory interventions that govern human behaviour on Earth. The notion of the Anthropocene is thus increasingly deployed to assist the broader scientific community and could serve a future-facing role in, among other things: solidifying the idea of humanity as an Earth system driver; aiding understanding of anthropogenic Earth system processes; fostering deeper

* This preface is based on chapter abstracts submitted by the authors. Their contributions are acknowledged with thanks.
[1] P Crutzen and E Stoermer 'The "Anthropocene"' 2000 (41) *IGBP Newsletter* 17–18.

political, social and cultural awareness of human-induced environmental change; and—the subject of this volume—instigating highly critical interrogations of the (mostly unsuccessful and ineffective) regulatory interventions used thus far to mediate the human-environment interface.

To this end, the idea of the Anthropocene is noticeably beginning to infiltrate contemporary legal and governance discourse, potentially providing a new perspective from which scholars can consider the role of law and governance in mediating the human-environment interface. In particular, realising that environmental law and governance are deeply implicated in the systems that have caused the Anthropocene allows an opening up, as it were, of hitherto prohibitive closures in the law, and of legal and regulatory discourse more generally. It invites fresh critical engagement with the world order that the law operatively maintains, and movement towards other understandings of global environmental change and ways to mediate this change through law and governance structures that will be more attuned to the challenges of the Anthropocene.

There is a steady realisation that existing legal and governance systems cannot continue to rely on the assumption, never adequately questioned owing to our experience so far, that the present relatively stable conditions of the Holocene will last indefinitely. To be sure, environmental law and governance cannot continue to rest comfortably on foundations that evolved under the Holocene, simply because under the emerging biospheric conditions of the Anthropocene traditional notions of environmental law and governance will be unable to maintain the type of societal ordering it would typically have sought to achieve under 'normal' Holocene conditions. The Anthropocene is therefore not only a possible new formal geological epoch: for environmental law and governance scholars specifically, the Anthropocene provides a unique opportunity to converse about the type of law and governance interventions capable of responding to the exigencies and complexities of a new and increasingly urgent socio-ecological reality. These conversations will be discomforting, as they go to the core of humans' place in the Earth and its systems, human responsibility for causing the socio-ecological crisis and human responsibility to address this crisis.

Accepting that the Anthropocene could be formally declared a new geological epoch in the near future (and even if it were not, it will likely remain an increasingly powerful discursive category), this volume seeks to provide the first collective, critical, and most importantly, *radical* exploration of future visions of law and governance for the Anthropocene. It endeavours to begin to trace out questions, issues and future-facing dilemmas fundamental to the search for an answer to the question: *how could environmental law and governance be reimagined to better mediate the human-environment interface in the Anthropocene?* In answering this question, this volume endeavours to provide a consolidated point of departure for the architects of future environmental law and governance.

Contributors to the volume were requested to be as critical of the regulatory status quo as they needed to be; to be as radical as they wished to be in their critique and proposals; to be unrestrained in their explorations of future projections and visions of what they see as an ideal vision for environmental law and governance for the Anthropocene; to be as imaginative as possible in doing so; and to prise open the existing closures of a hegemonic world and regulatory order that produces limits and a stifling sense of monolithic ideology closing down the space for other modes of being and thinking. The contributions in this volume therefore neither seek to uncritically restate the regulatory status quo, nor do they present an opportunity to embark on unimaginatively positivistic black-letter law analysis. Instead, the point of departure is that a wholesale regulatory change is required as a result of the Anthropocene and that a different mode of thinking about environmental law and governance is urgently needed; in short, a different way of thinking about the entire human-environment interface, which centrally includes a reorientation and/or redesign of environmental law and its concomitant governance arrangements.

The volume is divided into four parts that are centred on distinct but related themes. The chapters in Part 1 focus on the limits and potential of law and governance in the Anthropocene. The authors of the three chapters in this part take us back to basics, as it were, by critiquing some of the foundational aspects upon which much of environmental law and governance have been fashioned for decades. Taking the Earth system governance metaphor and the planetary boundaries paradigm as a point of departure, in Chapter 1 Jonathan Verschuuren discusses the question: 'What is the current and future role of sustainable development and the associated principles of environmental law in the Anthropocene?' He critically interrogates the current impact of the principles of environmental law (such as the no harm principle, the cooperation principle, the integration principle and the precautionary principle), and then reflects on what might be required for the future. A major insight is that although the concept of sustainable development and the principles of environmental law are having a growing impact, their role remains weak. In theory, these existing principles could steer governance alongside the evolving Earth system approach by focusing on remaining within planetary boundaries, provided that a radically stronger normative and legal force with respect to the principles is established, and that they are safeguarded by all legal institutions at all levels of governance across the planet. Importantly, new principles, such as the principles of resilience and enhancement, are urgently needed in the light of the realisation that we are crossing critical planetary boundaries at an alarming pace.

Tim Stephens argues in Chapter 2 that the Anthropocene's new geological terminology is primarily descriptive, but that it nonetheless invites profound normative questions, among them being what purpose international environmental law should serve in an era in which human and natural forces are intermixed and inseparable. Like Verschuuren, he notes that researchers have begun to consider the implications of the Anthropocene and sought to identify principles and institutions of Earth system governance that can maintain the long-term stability of geobiophysical systems. Earth system governance literature has been strongly influenced by the work of Earth systems scientists who have proposed nine planetary boundaries that define the 'safe operating space' for human development. However, with some exceptions there has been limited analysis of the implications of the Anthropocene for international environmental law, the body of international law devoted to addressing environmental challenges having transboundary or global dimensions. In an initial effort to address this gap, his analysis seeks to highlight the strengths and weaknesses of international environmental regimes in preventing the transgression of planetary boundaries. The chapter also offers reflections on how international environmental law demands fundamental reimagining if it is to maintain its role and relevance in the Anthropocene.

Benjamin Richardson concludes Part 1 by reflecting in Chapter 3 on the temporalities of environmental law. He argues that environmental degradation is associated with misalignments between humankind's contrived social time and the Earth's timescales. The time frame and tempo of the modern economy reflect a mechanistic, invariant, industrial clock time that has commodified and accelerated time, thereby distancing human society from the temporalities found in nature, such as those associated with biological, ecological, evolutionary and climatic processes. He indicates how the law is complicit in these trends, accelerating the depletion of natural resources such as through fast-track development legislation and resource governance regimes premised on unsustainable time frames of exploitation. Furthermore, the law habitually embeds temporal inertia in environmental regulation, such as the limited scope for relicensing development, which limits its capacity to respond flexibly to changing circumstances. An equally serious temporal failure of environmental law is its insouciance about past ecological damage and the importance of its repair and restoration. Without the restoration of former ecological characteristics, sustainable development may be unattainable, because prevailing conditions are already too degraded. Taking a multijurisdictional approach, Richardson's analysis advances a more holistic view of time into environmental law.

Authors in Part 2 of the volume convene around ontological and epistemological questions confronting law and governance in the Anthropocene. Anna Grear commences this predominantly theoretical part by bringing together, in Chapter 4, critical scholarship concerning environmental law and its subject with Donna Haraway's reflections on the Anthropocene, as well as insights from New Materialism, in order to trouble some counter-productive and eco-destructive assumptions haunting the 'Anthropos' of the Anthropocene. She uses these reflections to suggest potential lines of thought for the re-imagination of environmental law's 'subjects' and for moving beyond the trajectories and tropes underlying environmental law in its manifestation as an intensifying form of neoliberal governmentality.

Vito De Lucia argues in Chapter 5 that science has arguably entered a postnormal state, where a plurality of 'knowledges' co-exists and makes competing claims to truth. Environmental law, closely intertwined with epistemological, axiological and material problematics, is itself an increasingly complex and contested field of law and its traditional reference categories no longer seem to offer critical purchase. Against this background De Lucia explores what he terms the 'double register' of the Anthropocene, in the light of which he offers a biopolitical read-ing of environmental law, with a view to further advancing the project tentatively called 'critical environmental law'.

Firmly embedded within the idea of 'critical environmental law', Andreas Philippopoulos-Mihalopoulos argues in Chapter 6 that it is important to embrace the responsibility that comes with the Anthropocene, which, in terms of envi-ronmental law, requires nothing less than a radical revisiting of its basic tenets. He examines 'critical environmental law' from three angles: grammar, theoretical perspective and methodology. Grammar refers to the need for a new, anthropo-cenic vocabulary that will deal with the challenges of the Anthropocene. To this effect, he suggests some terms, such as continuum/rupture, human/nonhuman/inhuman, as well as geologic immersion and planetary withdrawal. Theoretical perspective refers to the way current thinking changes or at least is affected by the Anthropocene—indeed, how current environmental legal thinking is *turning* in order to accommodate the needs of the new epoch. Finally, methodology refers to the way the Anthropocene changes the way we seek knowledge and the epistemo-logical presuppositions of the limits of such knowledge. The chapter finally offers four theses in the form of suggestions on how 'critical environmental law' needs to adapt methodologically in order to integrate the anthropocenic grammar and perspective.

Saskia Vermeylen concludes Part 2 by offering critical perspectives on material-ity and the ontological turn in the Anthropocene in Chapter 7. In an attempt to establish a dialogue between law, anthropology and eco-philosophy, she demon-strates how law is perceived as being deeply anthropocentric. The central position of the human subject in the juridical order as both agent and beneficiary on the one hand, and on the other the natural world, which has gradually been reduced to an object, may no longer be tenable. Such a realisation asks us to think about the ecology of the Anthropocene. In pursuit of such an endeavour, she explores the challenges and opportunities of the Anthropocene for environmental law. Through a closer reading of anthropology and eco-philosophy, a new legal terrain is (re)discovered wherein the laws of nature dictate a new contract between living and non-living entities in the universe as an 'ultimate' attempt to save the Earth and all its living and non-living inhabitants.

The penultimate part of the volume focuses on ways to reimagine selected issues surrounding planetary stewardship and global justice; both critical con-siderations in the Anthropocene. Maria Ivanova and Natalia Escobar-Pemberthy reflect in Chapter 8 on the role of global goals as a strategic global policy frame-work in global environmental governance in the Anthropocene. They indicate that the United Nations, as the main global governance institution, has for many years delivered along three main dimensions: peace and security, economic and social affairs and, more recently, environmental concerns. Predominantly driven by the United Nations, the Millennium Development Goals and the recently proclaimed Sustainable Development Goals, have expressed expectations and committed countries to policies and targets to enhance development while promoting sustainability. The authors specifically analyse these global goals, and their two dimensions, articulation and implementation, as a key global governance instrument in the Anthropocene. To this end, they argue that the Anthropocene demands both action and accountability and requires that we approach the implementation of the new Sustainable Development Goals based on those lessons we have learned from the past.

In Chapter 9 I offer views on what a constitutionalised global environmental law and governance order could look like. Departing from the idea that constitutionalism offers a potentially powerful narrative and, more importantly, normative order, I attempt to understand and describe the potential of constitutionalism as an apex regulatory institution for mediating the human-environment interface in the Anthropocene. These insights are then transplanted to the global regulatory domain where I seek traces of global constitutionalism in the current (mostly defunct) global environmental law and governance space. I focus for this purpose on determining if, and the extent to which, global environmental constitutionalism exists in the form of a global environmental constitution, the global rule of environmental law, the separation of global environmental powers, the global environmental judiciary, global environmental constitutional supremacy, global environmental democracy and, finally, global environmental rights.

Carmen Gonzales focuses on the critical aspect of global justice in Chapter 10. Her premise is that the failure of international law and institutions to address global environmental degradation has significant implications for law and society as the planet's ecosystems approach irreversible tipping points. She shows how the environmental problems of the Anthropocene are inextricably intertwined with patterns of trade, finance, investment and production that have created an enormous and growing economic gap between and within affluent and poor countries; the Global North and the Global South. Grounded in colonialism, these North-South divisions have often paralysed international lawmaking, resulting in deadlocks in environmental treaty negotiations and agreements characterised by ambiguity, lack of ambition and inadequate compliance and enforcement mechanisms. International environmental law is a field in crisis because the problems it currently confronts are deeply embedded in the existing economic order and cannot be adequately addressed by simply tinkering on the margins. By interrogating the North-South divide in international environmental law, Gonzales offers several strategies to bridge the divide and create a more just and sustainable economic order grounded in a robust conception of environmental justice for the Anthropocene.

Klaus Bosselmann concludes Part 3 with Chapter 11 where he argues that ecological integrity must be a fundamental legal norm for a new 'world system' in the Anthropocene. He indicates that while the Anthropocene presents us with great challenges and uncertainties, it will possibly also prompt a significant reconfiguration of values in relation to the current status quo. In the Anthropocene, the Earth appears as a single system with socio-economic systems and ecological systems jointly determining its dynamics. To stay within planetary boundaries, humanity's socio-economic systems must ideally be governed in a way that preserves the integrity of ecological systems. He examines possibilities of conceptualising ecological integrity jurisprudentially as a fundamental norm, or *Grundnorm*, to function as a 'universal acid' affecting all areas of law and governance, beyond traditional environmental tools and policies. Fundamentally, once embedded, ecological integrity could guide governance systems of successful communities; failure to do so will be a counter survival tactic.

The final part of the volume explores possible futures in critical regulatory, geographical and institutional 'spaces', notably those related to the human-nature space through the lens of the ecosystem approach; the corporation and corporate governance space; the adjudication space; the emerging normative space of transnational environmental law; and the regional European environmental law and governance space. Karen Morrow offers a critical examination in Chapter 12 of human responsibility in the context of the human-environment relationship and ecosystems in the Anthropocene. She indicates that the Anthropocene has not emerged from the ether. Rather, it is both the fledging product of an exploitative conception of the relationship between humanity and the environment, and ultimately the signal of the end to the illusion of control that is integral to the paradigm of mastery that informs it. Morrow examines the urgent need for and possibility of fundamental change in the human-environment relationship, employing transformational ecological thinking, and considers the treatment of ecosystems as a case in point. Having discussed the emergence of ecosystems approaches to environmental governance as currently realised, and their limitations, she then reflects on the potential contribution of other approaches to refashioning the human-ecosystem relationship. She contemplates the role that various notions of rights might play in this regard: individual rights, and (more radically) collective rights, and (more ambitiously still) rights for nature; and argues the crucial potential of the concomitant yet relatively neglected concept of human responsibility. Morrow concludes by urging an environmental enlightenment, in which the true position of humanity as both enmeshed in the environment and in a unique position to shape its future is recognised and acted upon.

Sally Wheeler offers a particularly critical account in Chapter 13 of the corporation in the Anthropocene. She shows how the corporation, with its own heritage of anthropomorphic descriptions, is one of the key creations of the Anthropocene epoch. The analysis sets the rise of the corporate form as the primary method for wealth accumulation in the Anthropocene epoch. Wheeler suggests that the corporate form, as it is currently constituted, is not capable of addressing the acute environmental challenges so vividly evident in the Anthropocene, despite the activities of corporations being largely responsible for these challenges. Corporate social responsibility and stakeholding are examined as two possible ways of ameliorating corporate activities, but ultimately they are rejected in favour of an ethics for the corporation based on the work of Emmanual Levinas.

In Chapter 14 Lynda Collins turns the focus towards the judiciary and critically reflects on the issue of transformative adjudication in the Anthropocene. She argues that to meet the daunting challenges of our current era, human communities will arguably need to transform at every level. This will require engagement and mobilisation by all actors in society, but some enjoy a unique power to catalyse the necessary shift away from environmentally destructive modes of living and towards long-term sustainability. She argues that the judiciary has a crucial role to play in transforming systems and societies around the world to secure our common future. Judges can both improve and transcend inadequate environmental legislation, acting as a life-saving safety net to protect people and ecosystems from regulatory failure. In particular, judges can reinvent environmental law for the Anthropocene through progressive adjudication in civil actions for damages, the public trust doctrine, constitutional environmental rights and indigenous environmental law.

Jolene Lin argues in Chapter 15 that the concept of the Anthropocene invites us to think more critically about law and environmental governance and whether environmental law is sufficiently equipped to respond to the challenges of the Anthropocene. In the exploration for alternative forms of governance to supplement traditional inter-state lawmaking, the concept of the 'transnational' has gained traction in environmental law scholarship. She explores how a shift from international environmental law to transnational environmental law may provide us with a more nuanced approach as we consider how we should deal with the effects of global human-induced environmental change. To explore the potential of transnational environmental law to provide a more appropriate response to the complex challenges of the Anthropocene, she employs the European Union's sustainable biofuels regulatory regime as a case study to illustrate how transnational environmental law works in practice and what its regulatory potential could be in the Anthropocene.

Finally, and staying with the focus on European Union environmental law, Han Somsen argues in Chapter 16 that measured against the challenges posed by the Anthropocene, European Union environmental law is dysfunctional and is set to remain so unless comprehensively reformed. Like Bosselmann, he believes that reform must target the absence of a high-order ecological *Grundnorm* capable of fettering the Union's institutions' boundless discretion and of redressing an exclusive focus on human dignity that legitimates the systematic collateralisation of ecological imperatives. He suggests that such a foundational reordering must also come to discipline environmental enhancement initiatives that are qualitatively fundamentally different from conventional environmental improvement measures.

While these contributions do not and cannot offer the final word on any ideal vision for law and governance in the Anthropocene, individually and collectively they attempt to open up existing systemic closures, and to critically revisit the epistemic assumptions and normative and regulatory limits and deficiencies of the law and its regulatory domain as they relate to the human-environment interface. At the same time, the volume serves as an invitation to fellow epistemic travellers to contribute to this critically important and growing area of scholarly interrogation.

Louis J Kotzé

ACKNOWLEDGEMENTS

This collected volume is the result of several years of close interaction and collaboration with numerous colleagues around the world. All of the contributors to this volume have in one way or another enriched me, both professionally and personally. I am exceptionally fortunate and grateful for this privilege and for the honour to have been able to convene such an illustrious group of scholars around the theme of environmental law and governance in the Anthropocene. I am deeply grateful and indebted to each of them for responding swiftly to numerous editorial requests; for delivering exceptionally strong contributions the first time round; and for their continued support of this project. The stellar people at Hart Publishing have been as efficient and professional as they always are. In particular, thank you to Sinead Moloney, Emily Braggins, Mary Mahoney and Tom Adams for a truly unrivalled publishing experience. Finally, my thanks to the South African National Research Foundation for its financial support.

Louis J Kotzé
Potchefstroom, November 2016

CONTENTS

LIST OF CONTRIBUTORS

(in alphabetical order)

Klaus Bosselmann is Professor of Law at the University of Auckland.

Lynda Collins is Professor of Law at the University of Ottawa.

Vito De Lucia is a Post-doctoral Fellow at the KG Jebsen Centre for the Law of the Sea, UiT Arctic University of Norway.

Natalia Escobar-Pemberthy is a PhD candidate at the Center for Governance and Sustainability, University of Massachusetts, Boston, and Assistant Professor at Universidad EAFIT, Colombia.

Carmen Gonzalez is Professor of Law at Seattle University School of Law.

Anna Grear is Professor of Law and Theory at the University of Cardiff.

Maria Ivanova is Associate Professor of Global Governance at the John W McCormack Graduate School of Policy and Global Studies, University of Massachusetts, Boston.

Louis J Kotzé is Research Professor of Law at North-West University.

Jolene Lin is Associate Professor of Law at the University of Hong Kong.

Karen Morrow is Professor of Environmental Law at Swansea University.

Andreas Philippopoulos-Mihalopoulos is Professor of Law and Theory at the University of Westminster.

Benjamin J Richardson is Professor of Environmental Law at the University of Tasmania.

Han Somsen is Professor of Law at Tilburg University.

Tim Stephens is Professor of International Law and Australian Research Council Future Fellow at the University of Sydney.

Saskia Vermeylen is Senior Lecturer at the University of Strathclyde.

Jonathan Verschuuren is Professor of Law at Tilburg University.

Sally Wheeler is Professor of Law at Queen's University.

Part 1

Back to Basics: The Limits and Potential of Law and Governance in the Anthropocene

1

The Role of Sustainable Development and the Associated Principles of Environmental Law and Governance in the Anthropocene

JONATHAN VERSCHUUREN

I. Introduction

In our current efforts to formally determine a new human-dominated geological epoch called the Anthropocene, we acknowledge that humans have changed and are changing many of the basic Earth systems. By not living in harmony with the Earth's natural systems, humans have been inflicting Earth systems changes for centuries. Explicated most clearly by global climate change, we are witnessing the truly global impacts of our actions. We have started to interact with some of the basic processes of the planet; becoming one with them, as it were, and we are now able to change these processes in dramatic ways as geological agents. Scientists distinguish nine planetary boundaries that are to be respected should human societies be able to develop and be prosperous in the future.[1] Three of the seven boundaries that can be quantified at a global level have already been crossed (nitrogen, phosphorus and genetic diversity), and two more are at risk (climate change and land system change), as a consequence of which abrupt or irreversible environmental changes are occurring.[2] By crossing planetary boundaries, humans are not only jeopardising themselves, but the planet as we know her as well.

In order to avoid crossing planetary boundaries, we need to better utilise regulatory institutions such as international environmental law. To do that, we need to have a fresh look at the foundations of international environmental law, such as

---

[1] W Steffen and others, 'Planetary Boundaries: Guiding Human Development on a Changing Planet' (2015) 347 *Science* 6223. This article builds on J Rockström and others, 'Planetary Boundaries: Exploring the Safe Operating Space for Humanity' (2009) 14 *Ecology and Society* 32.
[2] ibid.

its principles upon which it is based and through which it has developed over the years. More particularly in the Anthropocene, what is the role of the well-known concept of sustainable development and associated environmental law principles, such as the no harm principle and the precautionary principle? These principles have, at least in theory, formed the basis of international, regional and national environmental law across the globe for the last two to three decades. Looking back, how do we assess the impact of these principles? A critical view would be that they were ineffective, or at last did not prevent the planetary boundaries from being crossed or from being placed at risk.[3] On the other hand, one might argue that the large-scale use of chemical fertilisers and massive emission of greenhouse gases started well before the concept of sustainable development was adopted as a leading legal and governance principle. After all, the events that led to the Anthropocene have already existed well before the adoption of most of the principles. In an effort to address this issue, part II of this chapter assesses the current impact and meaning of the concept of sustainable development and the principles of environmental law, with a view to establishing their contribution to keeping humanity within the safe operating space on the planetary boundaries.[4] This section therefore looks back, primarily focusing on sustainable development, with reference to other principles such as the no harm and prevention principle, the cooperation principle and the precautionary principle. This assessment of the current impact of the principles of environmental law will enable me to discuss, in part III, to what extend current principles of environmental law can and should play a role in the Anthropocene.

Looking forward, what does the concept of sustainable development and environmental law principles (still?) mean in the era of the Anthropocene? Some of the authors who first presented the nine planetary boundaries have argued for a much more drastic transformation of basic human processes towards sustainable development. They argue that we need an energy transformation, a food security transformation, an urban sustainability transformation, a population transformation, a biodiversity management transformation and a private and public governance transformation.[5] Interestingly, these authors think that the latter transformation is one of the most difficult to achieve:

> One of the most difficult but important challenges will be the governance transformation. In an age of planetary boundaries public policy decisions must be made on the

---

[3] See on the ineffectiveness of international environmental in general and the concept of sustainability in particular, LJ Kotzé, 'Rethinking Global Environmental Law and Governance in the Anthropocene' (2014) 32(2) *Journal of Energy & Natural Resources Law* 121, 136; and more generally LJ Kotzé, *Global Environmental Constitutionalism in the Anthropocene* (Oxford, Hart 2016).

[4] This section is largely based on, and uses parts of, a recent chapter by the author investigating the current legal status of the concept of sustainable development: J Verschuuren, 'The Growing Significance of the Principle of Sustainable Development as a Legal Norm' in D Fisher (ed), *Research Handbook on Fundamental Concepts of Environmental Law* (Cheltenham, Edward Elgar, 2016) 276–305.

[5] J Rockström, JD Sachs, MC Öman, G Schmidt-Traub, 'Sustainable Development and Planetary Boundaries' Background paper for the High-Level Panel of Eminent Persons on the Post-2015 Development Agenda, Prepared by the co-chairs of the Sustainable Development Solutions Network (2013).

basis of scientific evidence. Environmental degradation is often aggravated by lack of transparency and accountability of local and national governments. When public institutions are weak or corrupt, when they do not respect the rule of law, then the public goods of sound environmental management tend to be massively underprovided. Improving governance at local, provincial and national levels is of course very complex and takes a long time.[6]

This chapter looks at one of the central elements of the governance system, the concept of sustainable development and the main legal principles of environmental law that underpin the governance system. When we accept that the nine planetary boundaries are the Earth system boundaries that have to be respected, then perhaps these boundaries need to be more central in environmental law and should reflect in the way these principles are explained and applied, so that they can really push the necessary transformations. Should environmental law principles perhaps then be amended, and if so, how? Do they offer a legal anchor point in an otherwise boundless era, where humans decide about the planet as they see fit? Once we accept that humans indeed have the capability to alter the environment according to this species' wishes, everything is possible: an engineered climate, modified crops, a sea conveniently changed into a lake and the reintroduction of species that once were extinct. We probably need some anchor points to guide the decision-making process on these matters. If so, are the current principles and the way they play out legally suited to fulfil that task? Are we in need of new environmental law principles, such as the principle of restoration or enhancement, ie law aimed at bringing the Earth's systems (back) to a new equilibrium, and that fully respects the natural processes of the planet or at least the nine planetary boundaries? These questions are dealt with in part III.

II. The Impact of Principles of Environmental law in the Holocene: The Rise of Sustainable Development

There is substantial literature on sustainable development in a wide range of disciplines. Legal scholarship usually researches the roots of sustainable development and the legal status: is it a political aspirational goal (*Leitmotif*), a value, a concept, a legal principle, or a legal rule? It is not my aim to contribute to that debate with this chapter.[7] For this chapter, I start from the assumption that

---

[6] ibid, 16.

[7] For that discussion, see my contribution, 'The Growing Significance of the Principle of Sustainable Development as a Legal Norm' (n 4), and, among many others, K Bosselmann, *The Principle of Sustainability. Transforming Law and Governance* (Farnham, Ashgate, 2013); MC Cordonier Segger, A Khalfan, *Sustainable Development Law: Principles, Practices and Prospects* (Oxford, Oxford University Press, 2004); G Handl, 'Sustainable Development: General Rules versus Specific Obligations' in

sustainable development plays an important role in the law and policy debates on the relationship between economic development and the environment. When looking at policies of governments at all levels, and at policies of businesses, the concept of sustainable development probably has had the biggest impact of all environmental law principles. Government authorities around the world, from local to international, have adopted policies aimed at achieving sustainable development. Many business corporations, both small and medium-sized enterprises and large multinationals, have integrated sustainable development or, more briefly, 'sustainability' considerations into their business strategies. This worldwide focus on sustainable development can be attributed to the 1987 report of the World Commission on Environment and Development (WCED) 'Our Common Future'. In this report, sustainable development was described as 'a process of change in which the exploitation of resources, the direction of investments, the orientation of technological development and institutional change are all in harmony and enhance both current and future potential to meet human needs and aspirations'.[8] The work of the WCED was inspired by an urgent call from the General Assembly of the United Nations to 'help define shared perceptions of long-term environmental issues and the appropriate efforts needed to deal successfully with the problems of protecting and enhancing the environment, a long-term agenda for action during the coming decades and aspirational goals for the future'.[9] The WCED clearly came up with such an aspiration by holding humans responsible for the continuation of life on Earth and by stating that, unless drastic behavioural changes comes about, today's generation may not fulfil its needs while endangering the possibility for future generations to fulfil their needs.[10] Let us first have a look at how the concept of sustainable development, since 1987, has been translated into binding international law (part II.A) and then assess whether and how some courts used this and other principles in their judgments (part II.B).

W Lang (ed), *Sustainable Development and International Law* (London, Graham & Trotman, 1995); P Malanczuk, 'Sustainable Development: Some Critical Thoughts in the Light of the Rio Conference' in K Ginther, E Denters and PJIM de Waart (eds),*Sustainable Development and Good Governance* (Leiden, Martinus Nijhoff, 1995); Y Matsui, 'The Road to Sustainable Development: Evolution of the Concept of Sustainable Development in the UN' in K Ginther, E Denters, and PJIM de Waart (eds), *Sustainable Development and Good Governance* (Leiden, Martinus Nijhoff 1995); Ph Sands, J Peel, A Fabra and R MacKenzie,*Principles of International Environmental Law*, 3rd edn (Cambridge, Cambridge University Press, 2012); N Schrijver, *The Evolution of Sustainable Development in International Law: Inception, Meaning and Status* (The Hague, Hague Academy of International Law, 2008); J Verschuuren, *Principles of Environmental Law. The Ideal of Sustainable Development and the Role of Principles of International, European, and National Environmental Law* (Baden-Baden, Nomos, 2003); Ch Voigt, *Sustainable Development as a Principle of International Law. Resolving Conflicts between Climate Measures and WTO Law* (Leiden, Martinus Nijhoff, 2009).

[8] WCED, *Our Common Future* (Oxford, Oxford University Press, 1987) 46.
[9] ibid, ix.
[10] ibid, 8.

A. Sustainable Development in International Environmental Agreements

Given the influence of the WCED's report, especially in UN circles, it is not remarkable that sustainable development emerged as the key underlying concept during the 1992 UN Conference on Environment and Development (UNCED) in Rio de Janeiro.[11] The Rio Declaration on Environment and Development explicitly mentions the sustainable development 12 times, including in its principle 1: '[H]uman beings are at the centre of concerns for sustainable development. They are entitled to a healthy and productive life in harmony with nature'. Another example is principle 4, which codifies the integration principle as follows: '[I]n order to achieve sustainable development, environmental protection shall constitute an integral part of the development process and cannot be considered in isolation from it'. Here, sustainable development is presented as the goal of the integration principle. At the same conference, the concept of sustainable development also emerged in binding international law documents. The two legally binding conventions adopted at the Rio Conference, the Convention on Biological Diversity (CBD)[12] and the UN Framework Convention on Climate Change[13] (UNFCCC) and their associated protocols, refer to sustainable development throughout their burgeoning provisions.

In the CBD, 'sustainable use' is defined as 'the use of components of biological diversity in a way and at a rate that does not lead to the long-term decline of biological diversity, thereby maintaining its potential to meet the needs and aspirations of present and future generations'.[14] Almost all provisions of the CBD show that policies and measures have to be aimed at achieving a measure of sustainable use. Article 6, for example, lists the 'general measures for conservation and sustainable use', whereas Article 10 lays down the duties of the parties on the sustainable use of components of biological diversity. The Cartagena Protocol to the CBD contains multiple references to 'the conservation and sustainable use of biological diversity' in several of its specific binding rules, such as the rule that the state of import may review its decision regarding a transboundary movement of a living genetically modified organism at any time, 'in light of new scientific information on potential adverse effects on the conservation and sustainable use of biological diversity'.[15] The same goes for the Nagoya Protocol, which provides among others

---

[11]　Distr Gen A/Conf 151/5/Rev. 1, Rio de Janeiro, 13 June 1992.

[12]　The Convention on Biological Diversity (Rio de Janeiro, 5 June 1992), (1992) 31 ILM 818, entered into force 29 December 1993.

[13]　United Nations Framework Convention on Climate Change (New York, 9 May 1992), (1992) 31 ILM 849, entered into force 21 March 1994.

[14]　CBD, Art 2. This definition was later copied in other conventions, such as the Agreement for the Conservation of African-Eurasian Migratory Waterbirds (The Hague, 16 June 1995), (1995) 6 YIEL 504, entered into force 16 June 1995.

[15]　Art 12 of the Cartagena Protocol on Biosafety to the Convention on Biological Diversity (Cartagena, 29 January 2000), (2000) 39 ILM 1027, entered into force 11 September 2003.

'[t]he Parties shall encourage users and providers to direct benefits arising from the utilization of genetic resources towards the conservation of biological diversity and the sustainable use of its components'.[16]

In Article 2, the UNFCCC sets as the objective of the Convention the stabilisation of greenhouse gas concentrations with the aim to 'enable development to proceed in a sustainable manner'. Article 3 is titled 'principles'. It primarily codifies the principle of common-but-differentiated responsibilities by referring to both elements of the definition of sustainable development by the WCED, ie intergenerational and intra-generational equity.[17] The provision states: '[P]arties have a right to, and should, promote sustainable development'.[18] From a legal point of view, the latter is a somewhat peculiar provision, entailing both a right and a duty for states parties, albeit in the article on 'principles', thus mixing up no less than three different types of legal norms in one short sentence: it introduces a legal right, a legal duty and a legal principle! Article 3 also codifies the cooperation principle, again with the aim to achieve sustainable economic development.[19] Article 4 lists the specific obligations of states, such as the duty for all states to 'promote sustainable management (…) of sinks and reservoirs of all greenhouse gases (…), including biomass, forests and oceans as well as other terrestrial, coastal and marine ecosystems'.[20] National mitigation policies in developed countries have to aim at maintaining strong and sustainable economic growth.[21]

The Kyoto Protocol, the instrument that set binding reduction targets for the countries listed in Annex I to the UNFCCC, extensively refers to sustainable development.[22] The occurrence of sustainable development in the provision on the Clean Development Mechanism (CDM) is especially significant. This instrument allows Annex I states to achieve part of their emission reduction targets through projects in developing countries, as long as these projects, besides achieving a reduction in greenhouse gas emissions, achieve sustainable development in the developing country hosting the CDM-project.[23] There is an extensive approval process, part of which focuses on the requirement that sustainable development must be achieved: the project developer must obtain confirmation from the competent authority in the developing country that the project activity assists in

---

[16] Art 9 of the Nagoya Protocol on Access to Genetic Resources and the Fair and Equitable Sharing of Benefits Arising from their Utilization to the Convention on Biological Diversity (Nagoya, 29 October 2010), UNEP/CBD/COP/DEC/X/1, entered into force 12 October 2014.

[17] UNFCCC, Art 3(1) and (2) respectively.

[18] Art 3(4).

[19] Art 3(5) reads: 'The Parties should cooperate to promote a supportive and open international economic system that would lead to sustainable economic growth and development in all Parties'.

[20] UNFCCC, Art 4(1)(d).

[21] UNFCCC, Art 4(2)(a).

[22] Kyoto Protocol to the United Nations Convention on Climate Change, UN Doc FCCC/CP/1997/7/Add. 1 (Kyoto, 10 December 1997), (1998) 37 ILM 22, entered into force 16 February 2005.

[23] KP, Art 12(2): 'The purpose of the clean development mechanism shall be to assist Parties not included in Annex I in achieving sustainable development and in contributing to the ultimate objective of the Convention'.

achieving sustainable development.[24] This requirement has met much criticism after clearly unsustainable projects leading to, among others, human rights violations, were carried out.[25] In an effort to better ensure that the projects lead to sustainable development, in 2014, the CDM Executive Board launched a voluntary online tool for highlighting the sustainable development benefits of the CDM in a 'structured, consistent, comparable and robust manner', primarily by asking the project developers to respond to a checklist of predefined sustainability indicators (the so-called 'SD Tool').[26]

In the area of the marine environment, the term 'sustainable yield' is extensively used in relation to fisheries and preserving fish stocks, a term that dates back to the 1930s.[27] Since 1992, however, the broader concept of sustainable development has been infiltrating fisheries-related conventions. A prominent example is the 1995 Agreement on the Conservation and Management of Straddling Fish Stocks and Highly Migratory Fish Stocks.[28] Sustainable development is the overarching objective of the Agreement and is the basis for more specific obligations for the parties such as: adopting measures to ensure long-term sustainability of fish stocks.[29]

Other than these, various other environmental conventions concluded since 1992 refer to the concept of sustainable development. The Stockholm Convention on Persistent Organic Pollutants, for example, allows developing country parties to give precedence to sustainable economic and social development over full and effective implementation of their commitments under the Convention.[30] The UN Convention on the Law of the Non-navigational Uses of International Watercourses recognises sustainable utilisation as its main objective.[31] The Protocol on Strategic Environmental Assessment to the Espoo Convention on Environmental

---

[24] Distr Gen FCCC/KP/CMP/2005/8/Add.1, 30 March 2006, Decision 3/CMP.1, Modalities and procedures for a clean development mechanism as defined in Art 12 of the Kyoto Protocol, Annex at 15.

[25] There has been much research into this issue. By way of example, I refer to Sutter and Parreño, who concluded: 'While a large part (72%) of the total portfolio's expected Certified Emission Reductions (CERs) are likely to represent real and measurable emission reductions, less than 1% are likely to contribute significantly to sustainable development in the host country'; Ch Sutter, JC Parreño, 'Does the Current Clean Development Mechanism (CDM) Deliver its Sustainable Development Claim? An Analysis of Officially Registered CDM Projects' (2007) 84 *Climatic Change* 75. Authors used 3 sustainability criteria for their assessment: employment generation, distribution of CER returns, improvement in local air quality.

[26] See UNFCCC's website at http://climate-l.iisd.org/news/unfccc-publishes-tool-for-elaborating-cdms-sustainable-development-benefits/.

[27] Maximum sustainable yield is a theoretical concept used extensively in fisheries science and management since the 1930s; MN Maunder, 'Maximum Sustainable Yield' (2008) 5 *Encyclopedia of Ecology* 2292.

[28] Agreement for the Implementation of the Provisions of the United Nations Convention on the Law of the Sea of 10 December 1982 relating to the Conservation and Management of Straddling Fish Stocks and Highly Migratory Fish Stocks (New York, 4 August 1995), (2003) 2167 UNTS 3, entered into force 11 December 2001.

[29] ibid, Art 2.

[30] Art 13(4) of the Convention on Persistent Organic Pollutants (Stockholm, 22 May 2001), (2001) 40 ILM 532, entered into force on 17 May 2004.

[31] Art 5 of the UN Convention on the law of the non-navigational uses of international watercourses (New York, 21 May 1997), (1997) 36 ILM 700, entered into force on 17 August 2014.

Impact Assessment in a Transboundary Context has as its objective to integrate, through a strategic assessment, environmental and health concerns into measures and instruments designed to further sustainable development.[32]

It should be noted, though, that there are also important post-1992 international environmental instruments that do not refer to sustainable development. One example is the Convention on Civil Liability for Damage Resulting from Activities Dangerous to the Environment.[33] Others only refer to sustainable development in their preambles, such as the London Protocol on the Prevention of Marine Pollution by Dumping of Wastes and Other Matter,[34] and the Aarhus Convention on Access to Information, Public Participation and Decision-Making and Access to Justice in Environmental Matters.[35]

B. Sustainable Development in Regional Environmental Law and Governance Regimes

Most regional organisations have adopted sustainable development as one of their core aims. One of the objectives of the African Union, laid down in the Constitutive Act of the African Union, is to 'promote sustainable development at the economic, social and cultural levels as well as the integration of African economies'.[36] The Organisation of American States has soft-law instruments aimed at achieving sustainable development;[37] most importantly the Inter-American Program on Sustainable Development (PIDS),[38] and the Declaration of Santo Domingo for the Sustainable Development of the Americas.[39] Within the Association of Southeast Asian Nations (ASEAN), soft-law instruments mainly address sustainable development, especially the Declaration on Environmental Sustainability.[40]

---

[32] Art 1 of the Protocol on Strategic Environmental Assessment to the Espoo Convention on Environmental Impact Assessment in a Transboundary Context (Kiev, 21 May 2003), (2003) UN Doc. ECE/MP.EIA/2003/2, 85, entered into force on 11 July 2010.

[33] The Convention on Civil Liability for Damage Resulting from Activities Dangerous to the Environment (Lugano, 21 June 1993), (1993) 32 ILM 1228, not yet entered into force.

[34] Protocol to the Convention on the Prevention of Marine Pollution by Dumping of Wastes and Other Matter (London, 7 November 1996), (1997) 36 ILM 1, entered into force 24 March 2006.

[35] The Convention on Access to Information, Public Participation and Decision-Making and Access to Justice in Environmental Matters (Aarhus, 25 June 1998), (1999) 38 ILM 517, entered into force on 30 October 2001.

[36] Art 3(j) of the Constitutive Act of the African Union, adopted by the 36th ordinary session of the assembly of heads of state, Lomé (Togo), 11 July 2000.

[37] For a full overview, see CS de Windt, MA Orellana, 'Introduction to Environmental Law in the Americas' in W Scholtz, J Verschuuren (eds), *Regional Environmental Law* (Cheltenham, Edward Elgar, 2015) 131.

[38] Inter-American Program for Sustainable Development, adopted 11 May 2007, OEA/XLIII.1.

[39] Declaration of Santo Domingo for the Sustainable Development of the Americas, adopted 19 November 2010, OEA/Ser.K/XVIII.2.

[40] ASEAN Declaration on Environmental Sustainability, adopted 20 November 2007; see http://environment.asean.org/asean-declaration-on-environmental-sustainability/.

In the European Union, sustainable development received a firm place in legally binding instruments.[41] Currently, sustainable development is embedded in the EU's constitutive treaties: the Treaty on the European Union (TEU), the Treaty on the Functioning of the European Union (TFEU) and the Charter of Fundamental Rights. The preamble to the TEU refers to the 'principle of sustainable development'.[42] Article 3 then mentions sustainable development as the main goal of the EU's internal market: the EU 'shall work for the sustainable development of Europe'.[43] A similar goal has to be achieved with the EU's external relations policies.[44] Finally, Article 21 on the EU's foreign policy states that this policy has to foster the sustainable economic, social and environmental development of developing countries and has to help develop international measures to preserve and improve the quality of the environment and the sustainable management of global natural resources, in order to ensure sustainable development.[45]

Given the very broad and general wording of these provisions in the TEU, it is generally thought that the concept of sustainable development in these provisions cannot be regarded as a normative-legal concept,[46] nor can precise obligations be deduced on the basis of Article 3.[47] The provision rather serves as a guideline to policy drafting. To be sure, in the EU's sustainable development strategies of 2001[48] and 2006,[49] as well as the 2009 review by the European Commission (EC) of these strategies, sustainable development is characterised as 'the overarching long-term goal' of the EU.[50] The latter review shows that, despite the arguably weak legal character of Article 3, the adoption of sustainable development as an overarching policy goal has been successful. In recent years, the EU has demonstrated its clear commitment to sustainable development. The EC believes that the EU

has successfully mainstreamed this sustainability dimension into many policy fields. The EU's climate change and energy policies are evidence of the impact that sustainable development strategy [sic] has had on the political agenda. The EU has started to integrate the sustainability dimension in many other policy fields also.[51]

---

[41] Sustainable development was first acknowledged as an overarching objective of EU policies in the Treaty of Amsterdam amending the Treaty establishing the European Community [1997] OJ C 340/173, introducing this objective in Art 2 of the EC-Treaty.

[42] Consolidated version of the Treaty on European Union [2012] OJ C 326, 13.

[43] TEU, Art 3(3).

[44] TEU, Art 3(5).

[45] TEU, Art 21(2)(d) and (f) respectively.

[46] JH Jans, HHB Vedder, *European Environmental Law after Lisbon*, 4th edn (Groningen, Europa Law Publishing, 2012) 8.

[47] A Epiney, 'Environmental Principles' in R Macrory (ed), *Reflections on 30 Years of EU Environmental Law. A High Level of Protection?* (Groningen, Europa Law Publishing, 2006) 27.

[48] European Commission, 'A Sustainable Europe for a Better World: A European Union Strategy for Sustainable Development' COM(2001)264 final.

[49] European Council, DOC 10917/06.

[50] European Commission, 'Mainstreaming Sustainable Development into EU Policies: 2009 Review of the European Union Strategy for Sustainable Development' COM(2009) 400 final. For an overview and links to all relevant EU documents on the sustainable development strategy; seehttp://ec.europa.eu/environment/archives/eussd/index.htm.

[51] ibid, 3.

The current general strategy for the EU, towards 2020 ('Europe 2020'), has sustainable development as a central theme, with a strong emphasis on resource efficiency and the achievement of a low carbon economy.[52]

The TFEU has more specific provisions on the various policy areas of the EU, such as environmental policy. It codified a series of legal principles that play an important role in EU environmental law and policy. The integration principle was codified in Article 11 TFEU. This provision makes it clear that the achievement of sustainable development is the ultimate aim of integrating environmental considerations in all EU policies:[53] '[e]nvironmental protection requirements must be integrated into the definition and implementation of the Union's policies and activities, in particular with a view to promoting sustainable development'. In the provision that lists the principles of EU environmental law, however, sustainable development is not mentioned. Here only the principles of 'high level of protection', the precautionary principle, the prevention principle, the principle that environmental damage should be rectified at source, and the polluter pays principle are referred to.[54] Interestingly, the 2006 Sustainable Development Strategy referred to earlier, lists some of these principles as 'policy guiding principles', including the precautionary principle and the polluter pays principle.[55] This shows that these legal principles are considered important to give legal meaning to the concept of sustainable development, and that it is not useful, and indeed not possible, to apply sustainable development as a lone-standing principle of environmental law.

Many other EU-legal instruments refer to the principles mentioned in the treaties, including the principle of sustainable development, both in the recitals and in the provisions. The Environmental Liability Directive, for example, states in recital 2: '[t]he prevention and remedying of environmental damage should be implemented through the furtherance of the "polluter pays" principle, as indicated in the Treaty and in line with the principle of sustainable development'.[56] The Strategic Environmental Assessment Directive, in Article 1, sets out its objective:

> to provide for a high level of protection of the environment and to contribute to the integration of environmental considerations into the preparation and adoption of plans and programmes with a view to promoting sustainable development, by ensuring that, in accordance with this Directive, an environmental assessment is carried out of certain plans and programmes which are likely to have significant effects on the environment.[57]

---

[52] European Commission, 'Europe 2020. A Strategy for Smart, Sustainable and Inclusive Growth' COM(2010) 2020.

[53] Consolidated version of the Treaty on the Functioning of the European Union [2012] OJ C 326, 47.

[54] TFEU, Art 191(2).

[55] European Council, DOC 10917/06 (n 49) 5. These principles were copied from the European Commission's Draft Declaration on Guiding Principles for Sustainable Development, COM(2005) 218 final.

[56] Directive 2004/35/EC of 21 April 2004 on environmental liability with regard to the prevention and remedying of environmental damage [2004] OJ L 143/56.

[57] Directive 2001/42/EC of 27 June 2001 on the assessment of the effects of certain plans and programmes on the environment [2001] OJ L 197/30.

C. Sustainable Development in Court

Given the widespread use of the concept of sustainable development in international law since 1992, it is not surprising that courts and tribunals have also started to refer to the concept in their case law. In its most detailed and far-reaching judgment in an environmental case thus far, the International Court of Justice (ICJ) heavily relied on 'the objective of sustainable development'.[58] In the *Pulp Mills* case between Argentina and Uruguay decided in 2010, the Court had to interpret the meaning of Article 27 of the 1975 Statute of the River Uruguay, which stipulates:

> [t]he right of each party to use the waters of the river, within its jurisdiction, for domestic, sanitary, industrial and agricultural purposes shall be exercised without prejudice to the application of the procedure laid down in Articles 7 to 12 when the use is liable to affect the regime of the river or the quality of its waters.[59]

Argentina argued that a range of legal principles has to be applied to interpret the 1975 Statute, including 'the principles of sustainable development, prevention, precaution and the need to carry out an environmental impact assessment'.[60] Following its 1997 decision in the *Gabčikovo-Nagymaros* case, the ICJ first referred to its order in that case, in which it argued that use of the river 'should allow for sustainable development which takes account of "the need to safeguard the continued conservation of the river environment and the rights of economic development of the riparian States"'.[61] In the *Gabčikovo-Nagymaros* judgment, the ICJ stated that there is a need to reconcile economic development with protection of the environment, as 'aptly expressed in the concept of sustainable development'.[62] Based on these earlier references to sustainable development, the Court found in the *Pulp Mills* case that the formulation of Article 27 of the 1975 Statute reflects

> the need to strike a balance between the use of the waters and the protection of the river consistent with the objective of sustainable development. (…) Consequently, it is the opinion of the Court that Article 27 embodies this interconnectedness between equitable and reasonable utilization of a shared resource and the balance between economic development and environmental protection that is the essence of sustainable development.[63]

This is a remarkable and far-reaching move by the Court. It basically inserts the 'objective' of sustainable development into the text of the 1975 Statute, thus

---

[58] For a much broader overview of the ICJ's case law, see N Schrijver, 'An Overview of the Jurisprudence of the International Court of Justice' in MC Cordonier Segger, Y Saito, CG Weeramantry (eds), *Sustainable Development Principles in the Decisions of International Courts and Tribunals 1992–2012* (Abingdon-on-Thames, Routledge, 2015).

[59] *Pulp Mills on the River Uruguay (Argentina/Uruguay)* Judgment, ICJ Reports 2010, 14.

[60] ibid at [55].

[61] ibid at [75].

[62] *Gabčikovo-Nagymaros Project (Hungary/Slovakia)* Judgment, ICJ Reports 1997, 78, [140]–[141].

[63] *Pulp Mills on the River Uruguay (Argentina/Uruguay)* Judgment, ICJ Reports 2010, 14 at [177].

adding content to a legal document that predates the emergence of sustainable development as a dominant policy goal.[64]

Probably the most developed case law on principles of environmental law at the regional level is that of the Court of Justice of the EU (CJEU). This will not come as a surprise considering that environmental principles have been firmly embedded in the various EU Treaties.[65] A review of case law on these principles, however, shows that practically all of them are decided by relying on the more specific principles, such as the prevention principle and the precautionary principle, as opposed to the more general principle of sustainable development.[66] The CJEU often refers to sustainable development (a search in the database shows 52 hits),[67] but almost always these are references to treaty texts or texts of directives or regulations that refer to sustainable development, without any meaningful further substantive discussion on the meaning of the principle or the impact that the principle has in the specific case.[68] Nevertheless, the Court sometimes does refer to sustainable development as laid down either in the treaties or in more specific legal instruments of the EU (ie directives or regulations) to underpin its interpretation of specific obligations. An example is the recent Green Network case where the Court stated:

> it is also important to consider that (…) that directive seeks to promote an increase in the contribution of renewable energy sources to electricity production in the internal market for electricity. Recital 1 [of Directive 2001/77/EC of the European Parliament and of the Council of 27 September 2001 on the promotion of electricity produced from renewable energy sources in the internal electricity market] (…) recognises the need to promote renewable energy sources as a priority measure, given that their exploitation contributes to environmental protection and sustainable development and can, in addition, also create local employment, have a positive impact on social cohesion, contribute to security of supply and make it possible to meet Kyoto targets more quickly.[69]

In an older case, the Advocate General to the Court argued that the objective of sustainable development requires the authorities to integrate environmental protection requirements into decisions that may harm biodiversity.[70]

---

[64] See in more detail, D Tladi, 'The Principles of Sustainable Development in the Case Concerning Pulp Mills on the River Uruguay' in MC Cordonier Segger, Y Saito, CG Weeramantry (eds), *Sustainable Development Principles in the Decisions of International Courts and Tribunals 1992–2012* (n 58).

[65] See II.A above.

[66] eg Avilés, although he sets out to discuss case law on the 'principle of sustainable development', in fact only discusses case law on other principles, LA Avilés, 'Sustainable Development and the Legal Protection of the Environment in Europe' (2012) 12(3) *Sustainable Development Law & Policy* 29, 32–33.

[67] Text search on 'sustainable development' in all judgments by the CJEU (excluding opinions of the Advocate General), 31 July 2015 through the CJEU case law search form, http://curia.europa.eu/juris. Note that not all judgments are available in English, so the search does not cover all judgments.

[68] Recent examples are: Case C-369/14 *Sommer Antriebs- und Funktechnik v Rademacher Geräte-Elektronik*, 16 July 2015, ECLI:EU:C:2015:491; Case C-461/13 *Bund für Umwelt und Naturschutz Deutschland v Bundesrepublik Deutschland*, 1 July 2015, ECLI:EU:C:2015:433.

[69] Case C-66/13, *Green Network*, 26 November 2014, ECLI:EU:C:2014:2399.

[70] Case C-371/98, *First Corporate Shipping*, 7 March 2000, ECLI:EU:C:2000:600.

There are many countries in which courts have relied on the concept of sustainable development, such as Brazil,[71] Argentina,[72] New Zealand[73] and Pakistan.[74] In the Netherlands, a recent example is the *Urgenda* case, as decided by a Dutch District Court in a 2015 tort case against the Netherlands state. This case shows how the concept of sustainable development can influence judicial outcomes, for instance on the issue of standing.[75] Urgenda is a citizens' platform, legally a foundation with the aim 'to stimulate and accelerate the transition processes to a more sustainable society, beginning in the Netherlands'.[76] In a public interest suit, the foundation sued the State of Netherlands and asked the court to rule that current Dutch policies to reduce greenhouse gases are not strict enough, and to order the state to achieve a larger reduction by 2020. Because of the occurrence of the word 'sustainable society' in the foundation's by-laws and because the claim was partly done on behalf of future generations, the Court, when deciding on the foundation's standing, had to deal with sustainable development. The Court did not label sustainable development in any specific way; not as a principle, nor otherwise. In my view, this indicates that courts often are reluctant to give 'sustainable development' the status of a principle of law. On the other hand, it is also clear that courts can no longer ignore the notion of sustainable development. The court relied on the UNFCCC's focus on sustainable development (in Articles 2 and 3(4)),[77] and on the definition of 'sustainability' in the Brundtland Report.[78] The Court accepted Urgenda's standing in this case by stating:

> In defending the right of not just the current but also the future generations to availability of natural resources and a safe and healthy living environment, it [the citizen's platform Urgenda] also strives for the interest of a sustainable society. This interest of a sustainable society is also formulated in the legal standard invoked by Urgenda for the protection against activities which, in its view, are not 'sustainable' and threaten to lead to serious threats to ecosystems and human societies.[79]

D. Interim Conclusion: Impact of Sustainable Development and the Associated Principles of Environmental Law

This brief survey of references to the principles of environmental law, with a more elaborate focus on the concept of sustainable development, shows that they are

---

[71] I Sarlet, T Fensterseifer, 'Brazil' in LJ Kotzé, AR Paterson (eds), *The Role of the Judiciary in Environmental Governance. Comparative Perspectives* (Alphen aan den Rijn, Wolters Kluwer, 2009) 249, 257.

[72] J Carballo, 'Argentina' in Kotzé, Paterson (eds), *The Role of the Judiciary in Environmental Governance. Comparative Perspectives* (n 71) 270, 283.

[73] K Bosselmann, 'New Zealand' in Kotzé, Paterson (n 71) 354, 368.

[74] P Hassan, J Hassan, 'Pakistan' in Kotzé, Paterson (n 71) 381, 396.

[75] *Urgenda Foundation v the State the Netherlands*, District Court The Hague, 24 June 2015, ECLI:NL:RBDHA:2015:7196.

[76] ibid at [2.2].

[77] ibid at [2.38].

[78] ibid at [4.8].

[79] ibid.

slowly emerging in binding legal texts and court decisions. Although the concept of sustainable development and more concrete legal principles that are increasingly used to give specific content to the concept of sustainable development at first glance seem important basic legal norms that may steer environmental governance, their overall impact unfortunately remains weak. They do not effectively determine the direction and content of all relevant policies and laws. Until now, environmental law has largely focused on regulating local and regional impacts by setting emission limits so that human health and ecosystems are not endangered, and by setting limits to land-use change so that biodiversity, at least in some areas, is preserved. In some regions of the world, this has been a successful approach that has led to a satisfactory quality of the environment. For Europe, for example, a recent outlook concludes:

> [l]ooking back on the last 40 years, implementation of environment and climate policies has delivered substantial benefits for the functioning of Europe's ecosystems and for the health and living standards of its citizens. In many parts of Europe, the *local environment* is arguably in as good a state today as it has been since the start of industrialisation. Reduced pollution, nature protection and better waste management have all contributed.[80]

Current environmental law, however, seems insufficient to deal with the new challenges that we face in the Anthropocene; challenges that do not arise at the local level but at the global level, at the level of the Earth system. The same outlook for Europe finds:

> '[d]espite the environmental improvements of recent decades, the challenges that Europe faces today are considerable. European natural capital is being degraded by socio-economic activities such as agriculture, fisheries, transport, industry, tourism and urban sprawl. And global pressures on the environment have grown at an unprecedented rate since the 1990s, driven not least by economic and population growth, and changing consumption patterns.[81]

The question is, how should environmental law and governance change so as to more effectively deal with these global challenges? This question will be addressed in the remainder of this chapter.

III. The Anthropocene: A Focus on Earth Systems

The authors of the influential *Science* article on planetary boundaries argue that in addition to local and regional environmental impacts,

> we now face constraints at the planetary level where the magnitude of the challenge is vastly different. The human enterprise has grown so dramatically since the mid-20th

---

[80] European Environment Agency, *The European Environment. State and Outlook 2015*. Synthesis Report (Copenhagen, EEA, 2015) 9. Own emphasis.
[81] ibid, 9–10.

century that the relatively stable, 11,700-year long Holocene epoch, the only state of the planet that we know for certain can support contemporary human societies, is now being destabilized.[82]

They continue to argue that the precautionary principle implies that we should not drive the Earth system substantially away from a Holocene-like condition.[83] Ultimately, this would require people to respect nine planetary boundaries that are fundamental to Earth system functioning: climate change, biosphere integrity, stratospheric ozone depletion, atmospheric aerosol loading, ocean acidification, biogeochemical flows, land-system change, freshwater use, introduction of novel entities.[84]

These nine planetary boundaries have emerged from Earth Systems science. Scientists from a range of disciplines now work together because they have come to realise that 'everything is connected to everything else'.[85] Earth systems refer to

> the organizational structure and processes through which different component systems of Earth's physical world work. These component systems include the water (hydrological) cycle, weather and climate system, biogeochemical cycles (including carbon, nitrogen, phosphorus, sulphur), biosphere and sediment system. All of these components are driven through the movement of mass and energy over different spatial and temporal scales.[86]

Knight shows that these processes have low predictability as they are characterised by non-linearity and complexity, and therefore are inherently difficult to manage, either individually or in combination.[87]

Following Biermann, it is clear that acknowledgement of the Anthropocene and the associated reorientation of science towards the Earth systems should have a significant impact on governance and law.[88] As Rowan puts it:

> [The Anthropocene] is thus not a new factor that can be accommodated within existing conceptual frameworks, including those within which policy is developed, but signals a profound shift in the human relation to the planet that questions the very foundations of these frameworks themselves. (…) The Anthropocene is therefore not simply a disputed designation in geological periodization but a philosophical event that has struck like an earthquake, unsettling the tectonic plates of conceptual convention.[89]

What impact does this metaphorical 'earthquake' have on environmental law and governance in general and on the principles of environmental law and governance

---

[82] Steffen and others, 'Planetary Boundaries' (n 1) at 1.

[83] ibid, 2.

[84] Steffen and others (n 1).

[85] As is playfully explained to the wider audience by AD Sills, *Barron's E-Z Earth Science* (Hauppauge, Barron's, 2010) 12.

[86] J Knight, 'Anthropocene Futures: People, Resources and Sustainability' (2015) 2(2) *The Anthropocene Review* 153–54.

[87] ibid, 154.

[88] F Biermann, 'Planetary Boundaries and Earth System Governance: Exploring the Links' (2012) 81 *Ecological Economics* 4–9.

[89] R Rowan in E Johnson, H Morehouse (eds), 'After the Anthropocene: Politics and Geographic Inquiry for a New Epoch' (2014) 38(3) *Progress in Human Geography* 1–18, 9.

in particular? While many Anthropocene-related articles and books have emerged over the past two-three years, there is hardly any juridical scholarship addressing the impact of the Earth Systems approach on environmental law.[90] I will now undertake a first attempt to find some elements of the answer to the question above. It will become clear from the discussion below that at least three considerations are important: first, it seems that the nine planetary boundaries should be integrated in environmental law and governance more explicitly as thresholds within which we have to remain (part III.A). Secondly, the current fragmentation of environmental law needs to be addressed (part III.B). Thirdly, environmental law will have to move beyond protection and preservation and focus more on restoration and enhancement (part III.C).

A. Integrating the Nine Planetary Boundaries into Sustainable Development and the Associated Principles of Environmental Law and Governance

Saying that it is difficult to rethink environmental law from an Earth systems or planetary boundaries perspective is an understatement. Law (even international law) is tied to jurisdictions of individual countries. These individual countries, when drafting and implementing environmental law, tend to keep a sharp eye on their own economic and social interests. The world's legal systems, in addition to this focus on self-interest, have an inherent shortcoming as well, as they are tied to some 200 individual states that are delimited by inter-state boundaries. As a consequence, current environmental law does not focus on the Earth and its system as a whole.[91] In addition, there is the complexity of the Earth systems and their interactions, as well as the various spatial and time scales that are used to describe Earth systems. Basic legal notions such as legal certainty and the rule of law require clear and understandable rules that can be complied with and enforced when necessary. Regulating an utterly complex planetary system in simple rules that comply with such notions as rule of law and legal certainty is at best extremely difficult. That probably is the main reason why environmental law took, and basically still takes, a sectoral approach (dealing with environmental problems individually) using command-and-control or financial instruments to steer concrete behaviour of firms and consumers.[92] Planetary boundaries and their interactions, however, 'are

---

[90] Exceptions are Kotzé, 'Rethinking Global Environmental Law and Governance in the Anthropocene' (n 3) at 121; NA Robinson, 'Beyond Sustainability: Environmental Management for the Anthropocene Epoch' (2012) 12(3) *Journal of Public Affairs* 181; D Vidas and others, 'International Law for the Anthropocene? Shifting Perspectives in Regulation of the Oceans, Environment and Genetic Resources' (2015) 9(1) *Anthropocene* 1.

[91] Vidas and others, 'International Law for the Anthropocene?' (n 90) at 3.

[92] M Lee, *EU Environmental Law, Governance and Decision-Making*, 2nd edn (Oxford, Hart Publishing, 2014) 81–107.

notoriously difficult (if not impossible) to pin down through a simple top-down governance approach such as an overarching global agreement'.[93]

So far, literature has not come up with concrete proposals for redrafted environmental rules that focus on protecting the Earth system. Most authors take the concept of sustainable development as a starting point for future environmental law. The foregoing discussion detailing the genesis of sustainable development in the relatively stable and harmonious Holocene shows that, in theory, the concept does require a long-term future-oriented holistic approach that is needed and that is currently lacking. Its focus on future generations and on the integration of environmental considerations into all relevant decision-making processes, particularly those aimed at socio-economic development, should enable humans to remain within the planetary boundaries. The problem is 'only', as has been widely noted, that despite the progress made, for the most part we continued on 'business as usual' growth patterns.[94] Robinson uses powerful language to describe what happened to the concept of sustainable development in this respect:

> [w]hen 'sustainable development' is invoked to support the proposition that humanity can grow its way out of Earth's escalating problems, or to legitimizing existing 'business as usual' practices, the concept promotes 'the great acceleration' [of industrial development]. Employed thus, it contains the seeds of its own destruction.[95]

Most authors do not advocate to drop the concept of sustainable development altogether but propose to reimagine it, to make it stronger. Kotzé argues for the adoption of 'strong sustainability in the Anthropocene', requiring an orientation towards a much more ecocentric ethic.[96] It has also been proposed to integrate planetary boundaries insights into international policymaking, and more specifically, into the recently proclaimed Sustainable Development Goals.[97] In fact, Sachs has recently shown how the nine planetary boundaries determine what exactly sustainable development means. It is within these boundaries that humanity has to remain in order to achieve economic development, social inclusion and environmental sustainability.[98]

Most authors do, however, acknowledge that a reoriented or reimagined focus of environmental law on sustainable development is not an easy fix. Knight, for example, argues that a planetary boundary view on sustainability means:

> that we cannot be sure that any one way of managing a resource, such as water flow in a river, is inherently 'better' than any other way. For example, although rates of groundwater

---

[93] V Galaz, *Global Environmental Governance, Technology and Politics. The Anthropocene Gap* (Cheltenham, Edward Elgar, 2015) 129.

[94] Robinson, 'Beyond Sustainability' (n 90) at 181.

[95] ibid, 183.

[96] Kotzé (n 3) at 152.

[97] Galaz, *Global Environmental Governance, Technology and Politics* (n 93) at 138; JD Sachs, 'From Millennium Development Goals to Sustainable Development Goals' (2012) 379 *The Lancet* 9832, 2117.

[98] JD Sachs, *The Age of Sustainable Development* (New York, Columbia University Press, 2015) 181.

depletion can be calculated with some precision, calculating the rate at which extraction can take place 'sustainably' is more difficult because there are multiple variables involved which have different spatial and temporal contexts. (...) In addition, anthropogenic intervention in the workings of different Earth Systems, and the feedbacks between and within these systems and with human activity, show that not all systems work in the same way, and that some systems are inherently more sensitive to be affected by human pressure and/or climate change in the Anthropocene epoch than others. Although this provides the justification for why sustainable management of Earth resources is needed, it also shows why 'sustainable management' is flawed in practice.[99]

Wishing for such concrete guidelines for decision-making around a complex governance object such as the environment is not compliant with the nature of principles of law. Principles are not legal rules: principles have to be taken into account and can lead in various directions, whereas rules usually require a clear outcome.[100] In its 'soft' guise, it requires decision-makers to integrate environmental considerations in their decisions, and in the 'stronger' version, to remain within the planetary boundaries, but the principle does not say exactly how this has to be done. It is generally accepted, as was shown in section II, that the concept of sustainable development is closely linked to other more concrete principles of environmental law, such as the integration principle and the precautionary principle. These and other principles of environmental law remain important in the Anthropocene. It is likely that the precautionary principle will gain importance in the Anthropocene, as the complexity, uncertainty and unexpected 'surprises' associated with an Earth Systems approach and with a focus on planetary boundaries, require decision-makers to be much more aware of their limitations and, thus, exercise precaution.[101]

The cooperation principle is another existing principle of environmental law that will have to gain importance in the Anthropocene. Together with the principle of sovereignty (see below), this is arguably currently the most basic principle of international environmental law, as it is reflected in virtually all environmental treaties and it is well established in international environmental case law.[102] Robinson shows that although cooperation nicely links to basic patterns of human-to-human relations and to human evolution, the principle currently lacks focus: cooperation to what end?[103] In the Holocene, states worked together in order to

---

[99] Knight, 'Anthropocene Futures' (n 86) at 514.

[100] Verschuuren, 'The Growing Significance of the Principle of Sustainable Development as a Legal Norm' (n 4).

[101] What this means has been thoroughly examined by Trouwborst: States have to take a course of action that (1) is timely; (2) is tailored to the circumstances of the case at hand; (3) does not replace one risk with another of equal or greater size; (4) is regularly reviewed and maintained as long as necessary to prevent the harm in question; and (5) in case of doubt regarding the aptness of different measures, errs on the side of environmental protection; A Trouwborst, *Precautionary Rights and Duties of States* (Leiden, Brill, 2006) 293.

[102] Sands and others, *Principles of International Environmental Law* (n 7) at 204.

[103] Robinson (n 90) at 191.

address local or regional linear environmental problems, such as pollution of transboundary rivers. In the Anthropocene, cooperation needs to be directed to preserving the Earth System, or, as Robinson puts it: to maximise our human capacity for resilience.[104] States should discard their relentless focus on geographical boundaries and economic and social self-interest.

Perhaps new principles have to be developed as well; a 'resilience principle' for example. Resilience is a recurring theme in Anthropocene literature. Kotzé argues that 'resilience thinking' should be part of the reimagined sustainability principle, as the concept of resilience offers guidance to decision-making in times of change and uncertainty: 'resilience thinking copes with constant change and thus rejects status-quo-based thinking; it allows for values to dictate decision; it allows for self-organisation; and it is sensitive to adaptive capacity and flexibility'.[105] Robinson takes this even further by suggesting the adoption of the resilience principle as a new legal principle as follows: '[s]tates shall conserve and enhance the characteristics of resilience within all systems under their jurisdiction or control'.[106] Vidas and others also centrally position the concept of resilience in the legal debate on the Anthropocene, although in a different way. For them, recognising the importance of resilience protects existing rules and institutions of international environmental law and governance against initiatives that weaken their ability to mitigate long-term environmental problems.[107]

B. Addressing Fragmentation

To argue that current international environmental instruments do not take a planetary approach at all and have been drafted by states that only focus on their self-interest would be incorrect. It is remarkable that the first explicit use of sustainable development in a legal document takes exactly such a planetary approach. A 1975 United Nations Environment Programme (UNEP) decision states: '[e]nvironmental management implies sustainable development of all countries, aimed at meeting basic human needs *without transgressing the outer limits set to man's endeavours by the biosphere*'.[108] The document innovatively refers to planetary boundaries; a reference one does not frequently encounter in environmental law. The only other clear example is the UNFCCC and the associated Paris Agreement. The UNFCCC sets as its 'ultimate objective' to achieve stabilisation of greenhouse gas concentrations in the atmosphere at a level that would prevent dangerous anthropogenic interference with the climate system.[109] The Paris Agreement adds

---

[104] ibid.
[105] Kotzé (n 3) at 154.
[106] Robinson (n 90) at 192.
[107] Vidas and others (n 90) at 8.
[108] UNEP Governing Council Decision 20(III) of 2 May 1975. Own emphasis.
[109] UNFCCC, Art 2.

a specific threshold: '[h]olding the increase in the global average temperature to well below 2 °C above pre-industrial levels and to pursue efforts to limit the temperature increase to 1.5 °C above pre-industrial levels'.[110] Despite the focus on sustainable development, certainly since 1992, environmental law, generally, is aimed at addressing local and regional environmental problems and is highly fragmented.[111] In addition, or perhaps partly because of fragmentation, international environmental law has not been very effective.[112] This does not mean, however, that we have to forget about the local level altogether. In order to achieve planetary goals set at the international level, all other levels of governance, *especially* including the local level, have to set and implement concrete legal requirements.[113]

The CBD preamble refers to 'the importance of biological diversity for evolution and for maintaining life sustaining systems of the biosphere' and affirms that 'the conservation of biological diversity is a common concern of humankind'. The definition of biodiversity encompasses the variability among living organisms from all sources, as well as the ecological complexes of which they are part.[114] Such language aptly connects to the necessary planetary approach, although similar language is not used throughout the remainder of the CBD's provisions. On the contrary; the objective of the Convention does not explicitly focus on the planet as a whole ('the conservation of biological diversity, the sustainable use of its components and the fair and equitable sharing of the benefits arising out of the utilisation of genetic resources'),[115] nor does the rather anthropocentric nature of some of the definitions (use of biological resources that have a value for humanity).[116] Such formulations encourage humans to cross planetary boundaries, rather than respect them.

Unfortunately, the above examples of international environmental law aimed at the planet as a whole are rare exceptions to generally fragmented legal and governance systems. Galaz, in his thought-provoking book on the Anthropocene, correctly observes that current international environmental governance is

---

[110] Paris Agreement, Art 2(1)(a).

[111] Vidas and others (n 90) at 7.

[112] An assessment of the effectiveness of 5 biodiversity-related conventions, eg, showed that none of these can be considered effective; K Baakman, *Testing Times. The Effectiveness of Five International Biodiversity-Related Conventions* (Oosterwijk, Wolf Legal Publishing, 2011). Similar studies into other areas of international environmental law give similar results or were inconclusive; eg: P Sand (ed), *The Effectiveness of International Environmental Agreements. A Survey of Existing Legal Instruments* (Cambridge, Cambridge University Press, 1992); O Young (ed), *The Effectiveness of International Environmental Regimes: Causal Connections and Behavioral Mechanisms* (Cambridge, MA, MIT Press, 1999); E Miles and others, *Environmental Regime Effectiveness: Confronting Theory with Evidence* (Cambridge, MA, MIT Press, 2002). It should be noted that different definitions of effectiveness are used; see Baakman (n 112) 44–46.

[113] LJ Kotzé, 'Fragmentation Revisited in the Context of Global Environmental Law and Governance' (2014) 131 *South African Law Journal* 548.

[114] CBD, Art 2.

[115] CBD, Art 1.

[116] CBD, Art 2.

characterised by severe institutional fragmentation, and has 'failed to make sense of human-environmental-technological system linkages'.[117] He adds:

> [r]egulation attempts are 'bottom-up' in the sense that they are driven by individual nations (…) with weak (if any) international steering. Clear patterns of stronger poly-centric coordination at the international level, are evidently absent which results in serious mismatches between the scale, speed and scope of the issue, and existing governance attempts.[118]

Such fragmentation is a logical consequence of taking the principle of sovereignty as the foundation of international environmental law:

> states have, in accordance with the Charter of the United Nations and the principles of international law, the sovereign right to exploit their own resources pursuant to their own environmental policies, and the responsibility to ensure that activities within their jurisdiction or control do not cause damage to the environment of other States or of areas beyond the limits of national jurisdiction.[119]

This principle favours a bottom-up approach, where individual states have the freedom to develop their own policies, and the duty to prevent harm to other states. Only when such harm occurs or may occur, do they become active and negotiate a bi- or multilateral agreement with other state(s) to avert the harm. As a consequence, international environmental law is ad hoc and fragmented.[120] The emergence of the principle of common-but-differentiated responsibilities has added to the fragmentation of international environmental law, as different groups of countries advocate different legal rules and policies for developed, and developing states, and also for emerging economies and least developed states.[121] In addition, stakeholders such as non-governmental organisations (NGOs) and businesses are intimately involved in international decision-making and some even have the capacity and are engaged with creating law-like norms relating to specific regulatory sectors such as the banking industry.[122] All of the foregoing considerations have made it extremely difficult to conclude environment-related agreements; let alone an agreement which advocates respect for the planet and its boundaries.

When looking at international environmental law in greater detail, four manifestations of fragmentation can be observed:

Fragmentation of the environmental governance level (vertical fragmentation): Similar environmental problems are simultaneously dealt with at various levels

---

[117] Galaz (n 93) at 128.

[118] ibid.

[119] As originally set out in Principle 21 of the Declaration of the United Nations Conference on the Human Environment, Stockholm, 16 June 1972, UN Doc A/CONF. 48/14/REV. 1 (1972), and subsequently laid down in many environmental treaties and recognised by international courts and tribunals; see extensively Sands and others (n 7) at 191.

[120] Vidas and others (n 90) at 7.

[121] ibid.

[122] See eg the equator principles adopted by a number of financial institutions around the world, www.equator-principles.com.

of governance through different international, regional and local instruments. There is, for instance, the UN Convention on the Law of the Non-navigational Uses of International Watercourses,[123] a global convention introducing the river basin approach to international rivers and the UNECE Convention on International Watercourses and Transboundary Lakes,[124] that more or less does the same, but then only for Europe. An amendment to the latter convention came into force in 2013,[125] allowing states outside of the UNECE region to accede, as a consequence of which there now exist two global instruments on transboundary rivers. Other examples of fragmentation of the environmental governance level can be seen with respect to various issues where the EU legal instruments compete with international instruments, usually with the EU setting stricter standards than those that follow from international law (for example shipments of waste, trade in endangered species, climate change and marine protection).[126] Such inevitable regulatory competition has its advantages as it may lead to more effective norms, but it also bears the risk of losing sight of the global scale of the problem it is tackling.

Fragmentation within a governance level (horizontal fragmentation): Fragmentation is also evident within a specific governance level. Biodiversity conservation, for instance, is regulated in an international context in the CBD, the Wetlands Convention,[127] the Convention on Migratory Species[128] and the European Wildlife Convention.[129] Within all of these international legal frameworks, considerable attention is being focused on the impact of climate change on biodiversity, a topic which is also addressed by the UNFCCC.[130] This not only leads to a fragmented approach, it is also a waste of time and resources to reinvent the wheel.

Fragmented instruments: In environmental law, usually, a mix of legal instruments is applied, and these are sometimes complemented by non-legal instruments. In EU climate law, for example, a wide range of instruments is used to mitigate the emission of greenhouse gasses, using both command-and-control type instruments and financial instruments, as well as soft-law instruments.[131]

---

[123] Convention on the Law of the Non-navigational Uses of International Watercourses, New York 21 May 1997, 36 ILM 700, entered into force 17 August 2014.

[124] Convention on the Protection and Use of Transboundary Watercourses and International Lakes, Helsinki 17 March 1992, 31 ILM 1312, entered into force 6 October 1996.

[125] Decision III/1 of 28 November 2003, Distr. Gen. ECE/MP.WAT/14 (12 January 2004).

[126] Jans and Vedder, *European Environmental Law after Lisbon* (n 46) at 492, 518, 431 and 417 respectively.

[127] Convention on Wetlands of International Importance Especially as Waterfowl Habitat, Ramsar 2 February 1971, 996 UNTS 245, entered into force 21 December 1975.

[128] Convention on the conservation of Migratory Species of Wild Animals, Bonn 23 June 1979, 10 ILM 15, entered into force 1 November 1983.

[129] Convention on the Conservation of European Wildlife and Natural Habitats, Bern 19 September 1979, ETS No. 104, entered into force 1 June 1982.

[130] A Trouwborst, 'Climate Change Adaptation and Biodiversity Law' in J Verschuuren (ed), *Research Handbook on Climate Change Adaptation Law* (Cheltenham, Edward Elgar, 2013) 308–11.

[131] For an overview of the impressive array of instruments used in the EU, see E Woerdman, M Roggenkamp, M Holwerda (eds), *Essential EU Climate Law* (Cheltenham, Edward Elgar, 2015).

In addition, international instruments, such as the Kyoto Protocol's CDM, directly operate within this package of EU instruments. Again, this type of fragmentation is not necessarily undesirable to the extent that as it is believed that an instrument mix is the best way to change behaviour,[132] but regulators have to make sure that the combined effect of all of the individual instruments achieves preservation of the planetary boundaries.

Fragmented standard-setting: NGOs and corporate actors increasingly set their own international rules with regard to global environmental issues, especially on those topics that involve trade (for example, trade in tropical timber or other biodiversity resources from developing countries such as palm oil or soya). In so doing, they fill the gap that is left by states that are unable to set international public law standards by providing their own (mostly self-regulatory) standards instead.[133]

On the one hand, fragmentation of environmental law and governance is problematic and should be addressed. On the other hand, it also offers a way forward because what is needed in the Anthropocene is to move away from the current dominant approach of tackling incremental linear environmental stresses, to a polycentric approach based on a thorough understanding of the interplay between networks, institutions and Earth system complexity, and acknowledging tipping point changes, cascade effects and surprise.[134] Incremental change no longer suffices to bring about societal change at the level and with the speed needed to mitigate and adapt to Earth systems transformation.[135] Kotzé has argued that we have to move beyond the state:

> environmental law and governance will have to become more multi-levelled, multi-actored and normatively plural, where states and their governments are only some of the role players and where the focus is shifting to the important contribution of non-state actors that operate on different levels and in other non-coercive ways.[136]

At the same time, a more centralised and powerful global environmental governance organisation is needed to guarantee a coordinated and effective approach at the global scale, tailored to the Earth systems at stake. This would then, according to Kotzé, have to lead to

> norms made by state and non-state actors with the explicit and implicit purpose of influencing human behaviour towards a holistically conceived global environment. There, rules would aim to change human behaviour in the global arena and the effect of human behaviour on the entire global environment, which is holistically construed

---

[132] N Gunningham, P Grabowsky, *Smart Regulation. Designing Environmental Policy* (Oxford, Oxford University Press, 1998).

[133] See extensively PhM Paiement, *Voluntary Sustainability Standards: Regulating and Coordinating in Transnational Law* (Tilburg, Tilburg University, 2015).

[134] Galaz (n 93) at 126.

[135] F Biermann and others, 'Navigating the Anthropocene: Improving Earth System Governance' (2012) 335 *Science* 1306.

[136] Kotzé (n 3) at 145.

to be an intransigent, interconnected and interacting whole, or a multilinear, multi-loop interactive feedback system.[137]

Environmental law from such a perspective should then provide the rules for an integrated governance system that focuses on Earth systems collectively in terms of the planetary boundaries, rather than on individual environmental problems.

What does this mean for the concept of sustainable development and the principles of environmental law; the focus of this chapter? Biermann and others have made a number of proposals to achieve institutional change and effective sustainability governance within the next 10 years.[138] The more normative proposals are closely linked to the concept of sustainability and the way the principle has been fleshed out in international law as discussed above. Achieving sustainable development at the global level remains the ultimate aim of international law.[139] One of the ways to achieve this aim is through the integration principle: 'environmental goals must be mainstreamed into global trade, investment, and finance regimes so that the activities of global economic institutions do not undermine environmental treaties because of poor coherence'.[140]

Besides the concept of sustainable development and the principle of integration, other principles could also facilitate a holistic Earth systems approach. The precautionary principle, for example, with its focus on uncertainty and risk, is perfectly geared towards taking into account in decisions and actions the wider interrelationships and feedback mechanisms that impact the Earth system. It seems, therefore, that the current concept of sustainable development and the principles of environmental law do not stand in the way of the necessary combat against fragmentation. On the contrary, when we take these principles seriously, they require us to adopt a holistic Earth Systems governance approach.

C. Enhancing Earth?

Technological innovation plays a major role in the Anthropocene debate. Emerging technologies, such as nanotechnology, smart technologies (smart grids for example), synthetic biology, solar panel roads that fuel electric cars and various forms of climate engineering (for instance those leading to negative global carbon emissions) may be of great importance when we seek to keep our development aspirations within the planetary boundaries. Such technological development may help us not only to mitigate adverse effects of human behaviour, but also to

---

[137] ibid, 146.
[138] Bierman and others, 'Navigating the Anthropocene' (n 135). See also in more detail F Biermann, 'The Anthropocene: A Governance Perspective' (2014) 1(1) *The Anthropocene Review* 57–61, referring to similar proposals by a range of international bodies and institutions, and F Biermann, *Earth System Governance. World Politics in the Anthropocene* (Cambridge, MIT Press, 2014).
[139] Bierman and others (n 135) at 1306.
[140] ibid, 1307.

improve resilience through enhancement of the environment.[141] The notion of the Anthropocene opens up an important new debate: since we now recognise that humans are able to interfere with basic Earth systems, are we obliged to use this capability to make sure that we remain within the planetary boundaries? As Somsen puts it:

> [t]he crucial ... question is whether states may have duties not just to preserve, protect and improve the environment but at some point may be mandated to 'enhance' the environment in those cases when mere 'improvement' will no longer do. If such a duty were to exist or arise, it is submitted, conventional environmental law will no longer do and a Law of Mammoth would be called for.[142]

According to Somsen, environmental enhancement is an intentional technological intervention in the environment in pursuit of human interests, needs or rights which take place outside the confines of agreed environmental baselines, examples of which are climate engineering or de-extinction projects.[143] Humankind must take control over the technological powers it yields if human catastrophe is to be avoided. We may have to engage in systematic and possibly large-scale intentional interventions in Earth systems in order to avert catastrophes such as those caused by climate change.[144]

This is a thought-provoking idea. If we were to take the limits imposed by planetary boundaries and Earth system integrity seriously, then drastic restoration or enhancement of the environment may indeed be needed. This task goes well beyond the aspirations of run-of-the-mill environmental law, and even significantly beyond the aspirations of environmental law principles.[145] According to Somsen, conventional principles of environmental law are designed to guide us in our pursuit of retrospective ecological conservation and improvement imperatives.[146] Technology-driven environmental enhancement policies, however, are prospective in nature and may clash with ecological values. The precautionary principle may very well have to be accompanied by a 'proactionary principle'.[147]

It is too early in the debate to propose firm conclusions, but my preliminary position would be that the enhancement principle may perhaps become a new principle of environmental law, closely related to the resilience principle as discussed above. Considering that some of the planetary boundaries have already been crossed while others are about to be crossed, drastic restoration and enhancement probably are inevitable, with all the risks involved in the deployment of such

---

[141] See also section III.A above.

[142] H Somsen, 'Towards a Law of the Mammoth? Climate Engineering in Contemporary Environmental Law' (2016) 7(1) *European Journal of Risk Regulation* 109.

[143] ibid.

[144] H Somsen, 'From Improvement towards Enhancement: A Regenesis of Environmental Law at the Dawn of the Anthropocene' in R Brownsword, K Young and E Scotford (eds), Oxford Handbook on the Law and Regulation of Technology (Oxford, Oxford University Press, 2016).

[145] ibid.

[146] ibid.

[147] ibid.

large-scale innovations. Such risks require the precautionary principle to be taken seriously in the decision-making process on the development and deployment of environmental enhancement technologies. As a counterpoint, however, given the power of Earth's natural forces, one might wonder whether we are really capable of managing these powers in the first place.

IV. Conclusion

In this chapter I attempted to answer the question: in the Anthropocene, what is or could the role of the concept of sustainable development and the associated principles of environmental law be? In order to answer this question, I first assessed the current impact of the principles of environmental law, relying on legal texts and case law, and then discussed what is needed for the future by relying on the Earth systems governance metaphor and Anthropocene governance literature. Three basic conclusions emerge:

First, although a growing impact of the concept of sustainable development and the principles of environmental law is visible (including the no harm principle, the cooperation principle, the integration principle and the precautionary principle), their role remains weak. They do not fundamentally determine the direction and content of all policies and laws and they do not seem able at the moment to prevent humanity crossing the nine planetary boundaries.

Secondly, these existing principles, in theory, can steer governance alongside the evolving Earth systems approach by specifically focusing on remaining within the planetary boundaries. The concept of sustainable development, as the overarching lead-'principle' is exceptionally well geared towards a holistic, planetary approach. The cooperation principle requires all actors, including non-state actors, to work together with the aim to preserving the Earth system. Cottier and others have argued that such a new, global focus of cooperation warrants the adoption of a new principle: the principle of common concern.[148] This principle

> seeks to address collective action problems and compensate for lack of appropriate global institutions by expounding enhanced obligations of States to cooperate, but also the obligation to take action at home and the right to address climate change mitigation even by measures having extraterritorial effect.[149]

The precautionary principle is important because the complexity, uncertainty and element of surprise associated with an Earth system approach and with a focus on planetary boundaries, require decision-makers to be much more aware of humanity's limitations and, thus, exercise precaution. The integration principle, which

---

[148] T Cottier, P Aerni, B Karapinar, S Matteotti, J de Sépibus, A Shingal, 'The Principle of Common Concern and Climate Change' (2014) 52 *Archiv des Völkerrechts* 293.
[149] ibid, 323.

is closely linked to, and to some extent forms part of the concept of sustainable development, requires the integration of environmental considerations into all relevant decision-making processes, particularly those aimed at socio-economic development, thus enabling humans to remain within the planetary boundaries. How we should make sure that these principles do indeed steer governance into such a direction is a topic more suited for future research. It is safe, however, at this point to argue that radically stronger normative and legal force with respect to the principles is needed, safeguarded by all legal institutions at all levels of governance across the planet. It seems that this requires a strong institution at the international level. As well, although actions are needed across all levels of governance, international law will definitely need to play an important role. After all, we are dealing with planetary processes. It will be impossible at the local level to assess what the impact of a certain local decision will be on the globe, as this also depends on what all other decision-makers around the world at all governance levels decide as well. The Paris Agreement's global stocktaking mechanism is a good example of what such a global assessment instrument might look like, as this instrument aims 'to assess the collective progress towards achieving the purpose of [the] Agreement and its long-term goals'.[150] Such an instrument, however, is only useful when countries can be forced to further reduce impacts, should the global assessment show that a certain planetary boundary is crossed. Such competence, however, is lacking in the Paris Agreement.

Thirdly, new principles that determine future law and governance may be needed as well, especially considering the fact that we have already crossed some of the planetary boundaries. These are the principles of resilience and enhancement. The very notion of the Anthropocene shows us that humans are capable of enhancing the Earth's environment with the aim to safely remain within the planetary boundaries. Technological innovations may help us to achieve this, but are also associated with risk and uncertainty, showing (again) the relevance of the precautionary principle.

---

[150] Paris Agreement, Art 14.

2

Reimagining International Environmental Law in the Anthropocene

TIM STEPHENS[*]

I. Introduction

The Anthropocene has become the dominant term for the current geological epoch.[1] Adopting the Anthropocene ('the human era') in place of the conventional stratigraphic label, the Holocene ('entirely recent'), recognises that *homo sapiens* is now the principal agent of global environmental change. This new geological terminology casts no judgement on the desirability, or otherwise, of this new state of affairs,[2] but it does invite profound normative questions. Among these is what purpose international environmental law should serve in the Anthropocene?

International environmental law emerged in the 1970s to address worsening transboundary environmental problems, such as the serious air pollution and accompanying acid rain in Europe and North America. Extrapolating from the experience of national environmental regulation, which by this time was well developed, it was thought that regional and international environmental

---

[*] Professor of International Law and Australian Research Council Future Fellow, University of Sydney Law School, University of Sydney, Australia.

[1] Although yet to be adopted formally by the International Commission on Stratigraphy as a geological unit in the International Geologic Time Scale (see http://quaternary.stratigraphy.org/workinggroups/anthropocene/) it is now the prevailing term for the present time interval in geological history. Ruddiman suggests that the Anthropocene began when deforestation increased CO_2 levels around 8000 years ago (WF Ruddiman, 'The Atmospheric Greenhouse Era Began Thousands of Years Ago' (2003) 61 *Climate Change* 261, 293), however this has been challenged by Hamilton and Grinevald who argue that the era began with the advent of the nuclear age, and contend that the search for antecedents to the Anthropocene concept has the tendency to deflate its significance as a recent, dangerous and 'radical rupture' (C Hamilton and J Grinevald, 'Was the Anthropocene Anticipated?' (2015) 2 *The Anthropocene Review* 59).

[2] This is the logical distinction between 'is' and 'ought' made famous by Hume, who argued that it is not possible to deduce moral conclusions from non-moral premises: D Hume, *Treatise of Human Nature*, LA Selby-Bigge, ed (Oxford, Clarendon, 1978).

problems were similar to local environmental threats, and called for the same kinds of technocratic interventions, albeit at a larger scale. There was limited, if any, appreciation that humankind was not only affecting regions but had begun to transform Earth systems in their entirety.

The Anthropocene undermines the instrumentalist assumption that environmental changes are discrete 'problems' that can be 'fixed' by targeted interventions. Such a view is, in part, a hallmark of Enlightenment humanism[3] that regards human and natural domains as separate.[4] As humanity is now transforming the planet's biophysical systems, and imperilling their functioning, the Anthropocene entails the collapse of the human/nature distinction. It is therefore a post-natural epoch, a 'New Earth' in which human and natural forces are intermixed and inseparable,[5] with the Earth now 'an interdependent integrated social-ecological system'.[6]

Scholars of environmental politics are increasingly considering the implications of this New Earth,[7] and are sketching principles and institutions of 'Earth systems governance' that can maintain 'the long-term stability of geobiophysical systems'.[8] Earth systems governance literature has been strongly influenced by the work of Earth systems scientists who have sought to map out nine 'Planetary Boundaries' that define the 'safe operating space for global societal development'.[9] However, with some exceptions,[10] most accounts of international environmental law have yet to come to grips with the immense consequences that the Anthropocene poses for global environmental governance.[11] This chapter, which is part of a larger project,[12] proposes modifications to key environmental regimes to meet the imperatives of Earth systems governance, and it offers some reflections on how international environmental law will need more fundamental reimagining if it is to maintain its role and relevance in the Anthropocene.

---

[3] Pope Francis in the celebrated encyclical *Laudato Si'* describes this as '[m]odern anthropocentrism' which 'priz[es] technical thought over reality': *Encyclical Letter Laudato Si' of Pope Francis on Care for the Common Home: Australian Edition* (Strathfield, St Pauls Publications, 2015) 115.

[4] C Hamilton, 'Theories of Climate Change' (2012) 47 *Theories of Climate Change* 721.

[5] C Hamilton, 'Human Destiny in the Anthropocene' in C Hamilton, C Bonneuil and F Gemenne (eds), *The Anthropocene and the Global Environmental Crisis* (Milton Park, Routledge, 2015) 32.

[6] F Biermann, *Earth System Governance: World Politics in the Anthropocene* (Cambridge MA, MIT Press, 2014) 16.

[7] See eg S Nicholson and S Jinnah (eds), *New Earth Politics: Essays from the Anthropocene* (Cambridge, MA, MIT Press, 2016).

[8] Biermann, *Earth System Governance* (n 6) at 30. See also www.earthsystemgovernance.org/about.

[9] W Steffen and others, 'Planetary Boundaries: Guiding Human Development on a Changing Planet' (2015) 347(6223) *Science* 736.

[10] Notably RE Kim and Klaus Bosselmann, 'International Environmental Law in the Anthropocene: Towards a Purposive System of Multilateral Environmental Agreements' (2013) 2 *Transnational Environmental Law* 285; and K Bosselmann, *Earth Governance: Trusteeship of the Global Commons* (Cheltenham, Edward Elgar, 2015).

[11] See eg the fine text by Dupuy and Vinuales that does not mention or address the Anthropocene: P-M Dupuy and JE Viñuales, *International Environmental Law* (Cambridge, Cambridge University Press, 2015).

[12] The author is undertaking a 4-year Future Fellowship research project funded by the Australian Research Council examining the implications of the Anthropocene for international law.

II. Earth Systems and Planetary Boundaries

The planetary boundaries framework has been proposed and subsequently reviewed and updated by Earth systems scientists in an effort to identify the key global environmental systems essential for maintaining the integrity of the planet as a self-regulating system.[13] The framework 'identifies levels of anthropogenic perturbations below which the risk of destabilization of the earth system is likely to remain low'.[14] In other words, it seeks to ascertain a 'safe operating space' for humanity. Nine processes which are integral to Earth-system functioning, but which are being substantially modified by human actions, form the basis of the planetary boundaries approach. These are climate change, novel entities, upper-atmosphere ozone depletion, atmospheric aerosols, ocean acidification, biogeochemical flows, freshwater use, land-system change and biosphere integrity (see Figure 2.1).

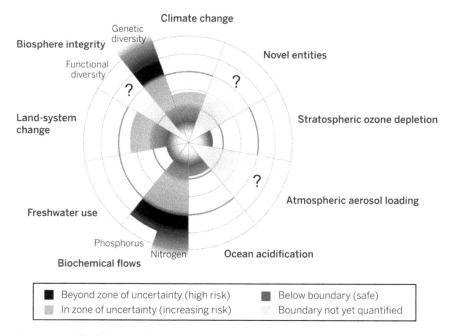

Figure 2.1: The 'Planetary Boundaries'

Source: W Steffen and others, 'Planetary Boundaries: Guiding Human Development on a Changing Planet' (2015) 347(6223) *Science* 736

[13] Steffen and others, 'Planetary Boundaries' (n 9) at 736.
[14] ibid.

There is some uncertainty with respect to the position of the boundaries for several of these Earth systems, but for others there is a good level of agreement on their locations, and the extent to which human activities are near to, or have crossed safe limits. In relation to biodiversity, climate change and global biogeochemical cycles (eg of nitrogen) the evidence is clear that humanity is overshooting planetary limits. Just as the new stratigraphy of the Anthropocene is descriptive, not normative, likewise the planetary boundaries framework does not specify policy pathways to remain within each of the nine planetary boundaries. It leaves those matters for governments, individually and collectively, to negotiate and implement as questions of global environmental policy and law. However, as humanity approaches and overshoots planetary boundaries, there will be fewer policy responses available to keep within a safe operating space. Some options to avoid overshooting the boundaries will disappear altogether (as some changes will be irreversible on human timescales) while remaining policy choices may have undesirable side-effects (as is the case with many geoengineering technologies).[15]

III. International Environmental Law and Planetary Boundaries

Kim and Bosselmann argue that respect for planetary boundaries should be the central purpose of international environmental law in the Anthropocene.[16] In an implicit appeal to natural law concepts, they contend 'respecting planetary boundaries is a dictate of reason' and that this should be recognised as the *Grundnorm* of international environmental law.[17] Kim and Bosselmann note that, as presently configured, this basic norm is absent from international environmental law. Although international environmental law does contain a core set of principles that are candidates as constitutional norms (such as sustainable development) these are too generic to provide the clear goals necessarily to avoid planetary crisis. This is a problem not only at the scale of international environmental law as a whole, but is also a feature of many individual environmental regimes, including those most relevant for guiding human development within key planetary boundaries.[18] The following discussion maps the nine planetary boundaries

---

[15] C Hamilton, *Earth Masters: The Dawn of the Age of Climate Engineering* (New Haven, Yale University Press, 2013); KN Scott, 'International Law in the Anthropocene: Responding to the Geoengineering Challenge' (2013) 34 *Michigan Journal of International Law* 309.

[16] Kim and Bosselmann, 'International Environmental Law in the Anthropocene' (n 10).

[17] ibid, 290.

[18] Not all, however. eg the ambitious and clear objective of the 1973 International Convention for the Prevention of Pollution from Ships, as Modified by the Protocol of 1978 Relating Thereto (MARPOL) is 'the complete elimination of intentional pollution of the marine environment by oil and other harmful substances and the minimization of accidental discharge of such substances' (Preamble, 4th Recital).

on to the relevant body (or bodies) of international environmental law and considers the extent to which environmental regimes have internalised goals consistent with the planetary boundaries.

A. Climate Change

Climate change and biosphere integrity are two planetary boundaries given special recognition as 'core' boundaries because of their central importance to the Earth system. Human-induced climate change is already well beyond the zone of safety, with atmospheric concentrations of CO_{2e} now around 450 parts per million (ppm), substantially above the 350 ppm widely considered to be a safe boundary.[19]

The climate regime provides an example of how regime effectiveness can be tied to the presence or otherwise of a clearly defined regime objective. The 1992 UN Framework Convention on Climate Change (UNFCCC) established an overarching legal framework for avoiding 'dangerous anthropogenic interference with the climate system',[20] but did not define what dangerous climate change is (for instance by reference to a temperature limit). Nor did the UNFCCC include global or national emissions targets or timetables to achieve its objective.

This latter deficiency was addressed, to some extent, by the 1997 Kyoto Protocol under which 37 industrialised states and the European Community (Annex I parties) agreed to reduce greenhouse gas emissions by an average of a mere 5 per cent below 1990 levels. In 2012, the Kyoto Protocol was amended by the Doha Amendments, by which Annex I parties agreed to take on further emission cuts (18 per cent below 1990 levels by 2020) in a second commitment period from 2013 to 2020. But not only were these new commitments also insufficient to curb dangerous climate change, the Doha Amendments have not entered into force.[21] Given the persistent weaknesses in the climate regime over several decades, other regimes have been examined to see if they might provide a way forward, although none provide anything more than marginal responses to the problem.[22]

The inherent weaknesses in the UNFCCC and the Kyoto Protocol are a product of their historical context, including the level of scientific knowledge at the time of their negotiation,[23] the strong resistance by some states to any emissions

---

[19] J Hansen and others, 'Ice Melt, Sea Level Rise and Superstorms: Evidence from Paleoclimate Data, Climate Modelling, and Modern Observations that 2°C Global Warming Could be Dangerous' (2016) 16 *Atmospheric Chemistry and Physics* 3761.

[20] UNFCCC, Art 2.

[21] They have attracted only 65 ratifications—significantly short of the 144 required to enter into force: http://unfccc.int/kyoto_protocol/doha_amendment/items/7362.php.

[22] A Boyle and NS Ghaleigh, 'Climate Change and International Law Beyond the UNFCCC' in CP Carlarne, KR Gray and R Tarasofsky (eds), *The Oxford Handbook of International Climate Change Law* (Oxford, Oxford University Press, 2016) 26.

[23] S Weart, 'The Development of the Concept of Dangerous Anthropogenic Climate Change' in JS Dryzek, RB Norgaard and D Schlosberg (eds), *The Oxford Handbook of Climate Change and Society* (Oxford, Oxford University Press, 2011) 67.

curbs, the power of organised denial groups and vested interests and the deep disagreement between developed and developing states over responsibility for the problem.[24] Kyoto's limited embrace, only over industrialised states, meant that its ultimate redundancy was written in its constitution. Although developed states are responsible for the majority of historical emissions, developing countries (particularly China and India) are responsible for over 60 per cent of current emissions and these must be brought under control to remain within the planetary boundary.[25] The 2009 Copenhagen Accord, though non-binding, went some way towards addressing the lack of a control variable and the North/South division, by adopting a clear temperature goal (to hold the temperature increase to below 2°C) and by calling on major developing countries to implement mitigation actions.

There are, finally, indications that the climate regime is undergoing a transformation in which its normative goals are being calibrated to match the scientific consensus on the need for decarbonisation of the global economy by mid-century. The Paris Agreement on Climate Change, which entered into force in November 2016, seeks to address a number of the failings of both the UNFCCC and the Kyoto Protocol. The purpose of the Paris Agreement, specified in Article 2(1), is to enhance the implementation of the UNFCCC and to 'strengthen the global response to the threat of climate change, in the context of sustainable development and efforts to eradicate poverty' by: (1) holding the increase in global average temperature to well below 2°C and to pursue efforts to limit the increase to 1.5°C; (2) increasing the ability to adapt to climate change; and (3) making finance flows from North to South consistent with low greenhouse gas emissions and climate-resilient development. This headline objective is elaborated in additional provisions that specify more detailed goals:

— the collective aim to reach global peaking of emissions 'as soon as possible' and to undertake rapid reductions thereafter 'in accordance with best available science' (Article 4(1)); and
— the collective aim to achieve a balance between anthropogenic emissions and removals in the second-half of the century (Article 4(2));

In addition to filling the 'objective gap' in UNFCCC, the Paris Agreement also addresses the 'emissions gap' in Kyoto in both its greater ambition, and in extending its reach to developing states:

— all parties are required to 'prepare, communicate and maintain successive nationally determined contributions that it intends to achieve'.[26] Parties are also required to 'pursue domestic mitigation measures, with the aim of achieving the objectives of such contributions';[27]

---

[24] O Young, 'Improving the Performance of the Climate Regime' in Dryzek, Norgaard and Schlosberg (eds), *The Oxford Handbook of Climate Change and Society* (n 23) at 625, 627–28.

[25] Center for Global Development, http://www.cgdev.org/media/developing-countries-are-responsible-63-percent-current-carbon-emissions.

[26] Paris Agreement, Art 4.2.

[27] ibid.

— Nationally Determined Contributions (NDCs) are to be updated on a five-yearly cycle and are subject to internationally administered accounting, reporting and transparency requirements. NDCs are to represent 'ambitious efforts' with 'a progression over time' that are taken 'with the view to achieving the purpose' of the Paris Agreement.[28]

— the commitment that each successive NDC of a party 'will represent a progression beyond the Party's then current [NDC] and reflect its highest possible ambition' (Article 4(3));

— an obligation on developed country parties to 'continue taking the lead by undertaking economy-wide absolute emission reduction targets' (Article 4(4)); and

— the establishment of a 'global stocktake' procedure, to commence in 2023 and continue every five years thereafter, which will assess collective progress towards achieving the purpose of the Paris Agreement (Article 14).

The climate regime now has the core of an effective response, but there are several elements that require further development. First, the NDCs to date are insufficient to keep emissions within the global carbon budget[29] that provides a reasonable chance of avoiding 1.5°C or 2°C temperature rise.[30] Current emissions growth places the planet on a trajectory of 4°C or more degrees well before 2100, a temperature rise likely to be beyond the limits of adaptation by human civilisation.[31] Secondly, the Paris Agreement does not attempt a systematic or equitable distribution of the carbon budget among individual nations. This is undoubtedly the most challenging aspect of international climate negotiations. Thirdly, the Paris Agreement is mostly silent on policy approaches for cutting emissions. It does not prescribe policies (such as a global carbon price) that are assumptions in modelled scenarios for staying under 1.5°C or 2°C.[32]

B. Novel Entities

Novel entities are defined under the planetary boundaries approach as 'new substances, new forms of existing substances, and modified life forms that have the potential for unwanted geophysical and/or biological effects'.[33] It is estimated that

---

[28] ibid, Art 3.

[29] GP Peters, 'The "Best Available Science" to Inform 1.5C Policy Choices' (2016) 6 *Nature Climate Change* 649; M Meinshausen and others, 'Greenhouse-gas Emission Targets for Limiting Global Warming to 2C' (2009) 458 *Nature* 1158.

[30] UNFCC Secretariat, *Synthesis Report on the Aggregate Effect of the Intended Nationally Determined Contributions*, 30 October 2015, UN Doc FCCC/CP/2015/7.

[31] R Garnaut, 'Compounding Social and Economic Impacts: The Limits to Adaptation' in P Christoff (ed), *Four Degrees of Global Warming: Australia in a Hot World* (Milton Park, Routledge, 2014) 141.

[32] Peters, 'The "Best Available Science"' (n 29) at 3.

[33] Steffen and others (n 9) at 736.

there are more than 100,000 chemical substances used in global commerce.[34] In addition to novel chemical compounds, there is an increasing number of artificial, genetically modified organisms (GMOs) that carry uncertain consequences for environmental systems.

Novel chemical substances and modified life forms have attracted attention under the planetary boundaries perspective because of their capacity for persistent effects, their movement across scales, and their possible impacts on Earth systems. One well-known example of the threat that novel chemicals can pose is chlorofluorocarbons (CFCs), the non-toxic carbon, chlorine and fluorine compounds which have had destructive effects on the stratospheric ozone layer.

There has been some scientific investigation of chemicals that by themselves, or in interaction with others, constitute threats to planetary boundaries.[35] Likewise, there is a growing body of science on the potential risks (and benefits) arising from the use of GMOs, which are defined by the 2000 Cartagena Protocol on Biosafety to the Convention on Biological Diversity as 'any living organism that possesses a novel combination of genetic material obtained through the use of modern biotechnology'.[36] At this stage there is insufficient knowledge of the global extent of chemical pollution or novel organisms in order to define a *general* planetary boundary with any certainty, although a boundary has been adopted for CFCs in relation to stratospheric ozone depletion (see section III.C below).[37]

As a product of 1970s concerns over the environmental impacts of industry, international environmental law has had a longstanding focus on the prevention of chemical pollution from industrial processes and accidents where these have transboundary impacts.[38] More recently, there have been global regulatory efforts to control the production, use and international trade in chemicals, including novel chemical substances. The two main regimes are the 1998 Rotterdam Convention on the Prior Informed Consent Procedure for Certain Hazardous Chemicals and Pesticides in International Trade (PIC Convention) and the 2001 Stockholm Persistent Organic Pollutants Convention (POPs Convention). Related to these regimes is the 1989 Basel Convention on the Control of Transboundary Movements of Hazardous Wastes and Their Disposal (which seeks to reduce the generation of hazardous waste, improve the management of hazardous wastes and restrict the transboundary movements of hazardous waste), and the recently adopted (but not yet in force) 2013 Minamata Convention on Mercury, which

---

[34] ibid, 744. 'Green chemistry' has emerged in response to this challenge, and which is guided by a set of core principles, including the need for new industrial chemicals to degrade after use. However it has not made serious inroads into planetary challenge posed by novel chemical substances. See United States Environmental Protection Agency, 'Basics of Green Chemistry', www.epa.gov/greenchemistry/basics-green-chemistry#definition.

[35] M MacLeod and others, 'Identifying Chemicals that are Planetary Boundary Threats' (2014) 48 *Environmental Science and Technology* 11057.

[36] Cartagena Protocol, Art 3(g).

[37] Steffen and others (n 9) at 744.

[38] See eg 1992 UN Economic Commission for Europe (UNECE) Convention on the Transboundary Effects of Industrial Accidents.

aims to protect human health and the environment from mercury and sets out various measures to achieve this goal (including limitations on the mining and trade of mercury).

The core feature of the PIC Convention is a system of prior informed consent and notification for the shipments of dangerous chemicals listed in Annex III to the Convention (on which there are 47 chemicals, 33 of which are pesticides (such as DDT)).[39] The POPs Convention has a broader objective than the PIC Convention, in restricting, prohibiting or eliminating the production and use, import and export, of the POPs listed in the three Annexes to the Convention.[40] Under the POPs Convention there are 12 chemicals the use and production of which must be eliminated (Annex A) or severely restricted (Annex B). These chemicals are known as the 'initial twelve' or 'dirty dozen' and overlap with the PIC Convention lists.

The PIC and POPs Conventions have successfully restricted the production and movement of some hazardous chemicals. However, they apply to a relatively small number of the most dangerous substances, and neither regime has incorporated a planetary boundaries approach which fully takes into account the global impacts of chemicals (including the interactions of multiple chemicals). Moreover, both regimes operate ponderously, as seen in the delays associated with decisions on additional chemicals proposed for listing. As a consequence, they have had limited effectiveness in controlling the development of novel substances within planetary boundaries.

C. Stratospheric Ozone Depletion

The thin layer of ozone (O_3) in the lower stratosphere performs a vital Earth system function in absorbing almost all of the ultraviolet radiation emitted by the Sun that would otherwise reach the Earth's surface and damage living organisms. Ozone layer concentration is usually measured by reference to the Dobson unit (DU), and under the planetary boundaries approach 275 DU is set as the boundary (a threshold that is breached over Antarctic each austral spring).[41] The ozone layer is now recovering following successful global action taken to reduce the production and consumption of a number of ozone-depleting substances.[42]

This outcome has been achieved as a consequence of the 1985 Convention for the Protection of the Ozone Layer and the 1987 Montreal Protocol on Substances that Deplete the Ozone Layer. Structurally, there are similarities between the climate and ozone regimes (and substantive overlaps as well,

---

[39] See www.pic.int/theconvention/chemicals/annexiiichemicals/tabid/1132/language/en-us/default.aspx.

[40] N Eckley, 'Traveling Toxics: The Science, Policy, and Management of Persistent Organic Pollutants' (2001) 43 *Environment* 24.

[41] Steffen and others (n 9) at 742.

[42] ibid.

as many ozone-depleting substances are potent greenhouse gases). Both have adopted the approach of a general framework convention, coupled with more specific implementing agreements. However, unlike the climate regime, the ozone regime acquired an effective implementing agreement very rapidly after the foundational convention was adopted.

Other features of the ozone regime mark a sharp separation from the climate treaties, at least prior to the Paris Agreement. The Montreal Protocol has a clear objective—the complete elimination of substances that deplete the ozone layer.[43] It does not expressly incorporate the planetary boundary that has been identified in the scientific literature as a safe concentration of stratospheric ozone. However, in practice, the objective of the regime, its specific control measures and production limits, and above all its adjustment procedure which allows the regime to respond to new scientific advice, means that it has been calibrated to the control variable and has accelerated the phasing out of ozone-depleting chemicals.

Also key to the ozone regime's success has been its evolution towards what Biermann has described as an 'egalitarian' approach in which industrialised states assumed the financial responsibility for ensuring that developing states (including rapidly developing states on the cusp of wide-scale production and use of ozone-depleting substances) were compensated for the phase out.[44]

D. Atmospheric Aerosol Loading

Aerosols are particulate matters, including black carbon (soot), which have localised impacts on human health and also have regional and global-scale impacts because of their effectiveness in absorbing solar energy. They are implicated in the phenomenon of 'global dimming' which has partially masked the effects of climate change, and also affected regional ocean-atmosphere circulation. For instance, excessive aerosol loading holds the potential for influencing the south Asian monsoon and resulting in drier conditions.[45] Steffen and others indicate that it is not yet possible to quantify a global-level boundary for aerosol loading.[46] However, it is possible to specify a regional boundary for south Asia. Taking a precautionary approach, the south Asia regional boundary for aerosol loading is suggested by Steffen and others to lie around 0.25 aerosol optical depth (AOD) (a measure of the amount of sunlight prevented from reaching the ground from airborne particles).[47] Current measures place annual average AOD at around 0.3, which is within the zone of uncertainty.[48]

---

[43] Preamble, 6th Recital.
[44] Biermann (n 6) at 169.
[45] Steffen and others (n 9) at 743.
[46] ibid, 736.
[47] ibid, 743.
[48] ibid.

There is no global treaty regime regulating atmospheric aerosol loading. There are several regional regimes of varying sophistication that currently have, or are acquiring, emission reduction targets for fine particulate matter. The best known and most detailed regional regime is the 1979 Geneva Convention on Long-Range Transboundary Air Pollution (Air Pollution Convention), which was initially designed to address acid rain in the northern hemisphere. The Air Pollution Convention has evolved significantly since 1979 through eight protocols that have extended the pollutants to which it applies (from sulphur to nitrous oxides, ammonia and volatile organic compounds), and introduced and tightened country-specific emissions targets. The 1999 Gothenburg Protocol to Abate Acidification, Eutrophication and Ground-level Ozone to the Air Pollution Convention was central in this process, and in 2012 was substantially amended to include the world's first binding emission limit targets for aerosols. The amendments, which impose limit values for the emissions of particulate matter, have responded to scientific guidance on the local and region-wide impacts of this pollutant. The revised Gothenburg Protocol is yet to enter into force, but provides a template for addressing the aerosol planetary boundary.

E. Ocean Acidification

Ocean acidification and climate change are closely linked planetary transformations with both phenomena primarily caused by emissions of CO_2 from human activities. Ocean acidification refers to the decline in oceanic pH, as CO_2 is drawn into the oceans from the atmosphere and reacts with water to form carbonic acid.[49] It is one of several major chemical changes underway in the oceans in the Anthropocene, including changes in salinity, reduced oxygen availability and an increase in concentrations of CO_2 (hypercapnia).[50]

If CO_2 emissions are not reduced, then the likely transformation of the geochemistry of the world's oceans will be unprecedented in at least the last 300 million years.[51] Among the most severe changes are to carbonate chemistry, as ocean acidification is reducing the concentrations of calcium carbonate required by many marine organisms (including corals). The planetary boundary suggested by Steffen and others for ocean acidification is 80 per cent of the pre-Anthropocene average annual global aragonite concentrations.[52] Currently concentrations sit at around 84 per cent, and the ocean acidification planetary boundary is therefore close to being transgressed.

---

[49] J-P Gattuso and L Hansson, 'Ocean Acidification: Background and History' in J-P Gattuso and L Hansson (eds), *Ocean Acidification* (Oxford, Oxford University Press, 2011) 1.

[50] BI McNeil & TP Sasse, 'Future Ocean Hypercapnia Driven by Anthropogenic Amplification of the Natural CO2 Cycle' (2016) 529 *Nature* 383.

[51] B Hönisch and others, 'The Geological Record of Ocean Acidification' (2012) 335 *Science* 1058, 1062.

[52] Steffen and others (n 9) at 740.

Ocean acidification is a classic example of the tendency for 'regime drift' and inaction without clarity on the applicable regime(s) or the adoption of clear science-based regulatory objective.[53] By regime drift is meant the tendency for some environmental treaties to 'coast' without attention to changing environmental conditions. Proposals for 'ecological reflexity' in environmental treaties have been made to address this weakness.[54] Ocean acidification sits in an international regulatory limbo, potentially governable by multiple oceans and atmospheric regimes, yet in practice addressed by none. Given the climate-oceans nexus and the key role of CO_2 to both processes, it is likely that the UNFCCC will be the primary vehicle for staying within the acidification boundary. However, while the UNFCCC has acquired increasingly clear goals in terms of temperature objectives, it is yet to incorporate any metrics for healthy ocean chemistry. The Paris Agreement refers to the oceans only once, in the preamble, and does not include a pH guardrail to match the 1.5°C/2°C global temperature limits. This appears to be an example of narrow regime-framing and diplomatic fatigue, with governments already overwhelmed with climate issues and not disposed to adding further topics to an already crowded and contentious negotiating agenda. As such, at least for the time being, the temperature limit in the Paris Agreement also serves as a proxy for the acidification boundary.

This state of affairs, in which the oceans governance regime defers to the climate regime on perhaps the most important question of marine environmental protection, and the climate regime in turn delivers no effective response, is clearly unsatisfactory. One potential way forward is for a group of concerned states to pursue the specification of an ocean acidification planetary boundary outside the UNFCCC. This approach, in which efforts are made in one regime to force change in another has been labelled 'strategic inconsistency'[55] by Raustiala and Victor. Such an outcome could conceivably be achieved through the treaty on biodiversity in oceans beyond national jurisdiction, which is currently under negotiation as a new implementing agreement under the 1982 United Nations Convention on the Law of the Sea (UNCLOS). Other fora could also be utilised, including the 1992 Convention on Biological Diversity which has previously adopted oceans-related moratoria (eg a moratorium on ocean fertilisation, except for scientific research)[56] and environmental targets (eg for the expansion of marine protected areas).[57]

---

[53] See further T Stephens, 'Ocean Acidification' in R Rayfuse (ed), *Research Handbook on International Marine Environmental Law* (Cheltenham, Edward Elgar, 2015) 431.

[54] See generally JS Dryzek and J Pickering, 'Deliberation as a Catalyst for Reflexive Environmental Governance' (2017) 131 *Ecological Economics* 353.

[55] K Raustiala and DG Victor, 'The Regime Complex for Plant Genetic Resources' (2004) *International Organization* 277.

[56] COP IX/16, UN Doc UNEP/CBD/COP/DEC/IX/16 (2008).

[57] COP X/2, UN Doc UNEP/CBD/COP/DEC/X/2 (2010), Aichi Biodiversity Target 11.

F. Biogeochemical Flows

This planetary boundary is concerned with the biogeochemical cycles of major chemicals through the biosphere, lithosphere, atmosphere and hydrosphere. Originally, the main focus for the boundary was nitrogen and phosphorus; key ingredients in fertilisers the production of which has increased immensely over the last century.[58] However, the planetary boundary now includes biogeochemical flows generally (with the exception of carbon which is addressed in the climate and acidification boundaries).[59] This means that sub-boundaries will need to be identified in respect of each relevant element.

At this stage the focus remains on nitrogen and phosphorus, and Steffen and others propose global and national boundaries by reference to the sustained flow of these elements into the oceans at levels that would prevent a large-scale ocean anoxia (low-oxygen levels) and widespread eutrophication of freshwater systems (eg excessive nutrients in rivers).[60] The boundaries are clearly being transgressed, but only in a few agricultural regions where there are very high application rates of nitrogen and phosphorus. Steffen and others suggest that a redistribution of nitrogen and phosphorus application rates globally would assist in reducing the transgression of the boundary.

Biogeochemical flows are almost entirely unregulated by international law (with the exception of carbon, and then only imperfectly). Nutrient loading in some shared international watercourses has been a focus of some conventions relating to international rivers and lakes. And UNCLOS provides a framework for the regulation of the pollution of the oceans from land-based sources of nitrogen and phosphorous and other substances. However, unlike vessel-source pollution from oil and other substances, land-based pollution is not regulated by global-scale, legally binding instruments. The non-binding 1995 Washington Declaration on Protection of the Marine Environment from Land-Based Activities is the closest there is to such a regime.

The Washington Declaration established the Global Programme of Action (GPA), an intergovernmental mechanism that seeks to reduce marine environmental damage as a result of land-based activities. The GPA is a non-binding plan of action to address major types of land-based marine pollution, including sewage, persistent organic pollutants, radioactive substances, heavy metals, oil, nutrients, sediments and litter. The recommended approaches and policies in relation to nutrients are of most direct relevance to nitrogen and phosphorus, and the GPA acknowledges that enhanced mobilisation of nutrients 'result in changes in species diversity, excessive algal growth, dissolved oxygen reductions and associated

---

[58] N Gruber and JN Galloway, 'An Earth-System Perspective of the Global Nitrogen Cycle' (2008) 451 *Nature* 293.

[59] Steffen and others (n 9) at 742.

[60] ibid.

fish kills and, it is suspected, the increased prevalence or frequency of toxic algal blooms'.[61] However the objectives and targets for reducing nutrient inputs are so general as to have little meaningful content, and certainly fall significantly short of an incorporation of a planetary boundary together with defined and legally binding targets for reducing the input of major pollutants.

G. Freshwater Use

One signature of the Anthropocene has been the substantial alteration of waterways to supply human uses including agriculture, industry, consumption, transportation and the reduction of flood risks. This has fragmented waterways, and altered the flux of sediments and nutrients between the land and the oceans. It has also involved ever-increasing consumption of freshwater. And it is this latter metric that is used in the planetary boundary approach. Freshwater use is assessed to be within the defined planetary boundary, with global consumption being around 2600 km^3 per annum of the available 4000 km^3.[62] As water use increases to meet the needs of a growing global population, and as availability decreases as a consequence of climate change, this boundary may be transgressed.

There is no global treaty that addresses access to, and conservation of, freshwater. Freshwater resources are instead considered matters for individual states to manage as they see fit. The only exception is with respect to watercourses shared by two or more states, for which there exist a collection of global, regional and bilateral treaties. The global regime is the 1997 United Nations Convention on the Law of the Non-Navigational Uses of International Watercourses which requires the equitable utilisation of shared rivers and lakes, and the protection of riverine environments. However, it does not seek to protect global freshwater resources as a global commons resource in a manner akin to the UNFCCC as regards the atmosphere, or UNCLOS as regards the oceans.[63]

H. Land-System Change

Another obvious feature of the Anthropocene has been significant change in land use, with forests and other terrestrial biomes transformed into cropland and pasture. Land-use change carries with it a number of impacts on other planetary boundaries, as the loss of forest cover contributes to global and regional climate impacts through direct emissions, and by changes in evapotranspiration (the movement of water from the soil and plants to the atmosphere).

The planetary boundary for land-system change focuses on the global area of forest cover, as the three forest biome types (tropical, temperate and boreal) are

---

[61] GPA, para 128.
[62] Steffen and others (n 9) at 741.
[63] T Stephens, 'Reimaging International Water Law' (2011) 71 *Maryland Law Review Endnotes* 20.

considered more important than other terrestrial biomes in the land-atmosphere interchange.[64] The global planetary boundary for forest cover is 75 per cent of original cover, with individual boundaries for the three biomes (tropical: 85 per cent; temperate: 50 per cent; boreal: 85 per cent).[65] The current extent of global forest cover is substantially less than this, at 62 per cent of original forest cover, and therefore this boundary is currently being transgressed.[66]

Protecting forested areas has proven to be one of the most controversial and intractable challenges for international environmental law. There has been unsatisfactory progress in restraining land-use change, especially in controlling deforestation in developing states such as Brazil and Indonesia. Given the importance of forests for the climate system, forest protection has emerged as a key issue in climate negotiations. The Paris Agreement recognises the need for greater forest protection, stipulating that parties should take action to conserve forests as sinks and reservoirs of greenhouse gases.[67] A key method by which this can occur is through schemes for 'reducing emissions from deforestation and forest degradation', known as 'REDD+', a scheme under which forests are conserved in exchange for payments (including through carbon markets).[68]

A range of legitimate questions surround REDD+ and whether it can deliver significant abatement of emissions over time. Some states are seeking to offset rising emissions from industry against falling emissions from land-use change, yet there are questions as to the 'additionality' and permanency of emissions reductions from forest protection. Nonetheless, so far as the land-system planetary boundary is concerned, it can potentially play a constructive role. And it may prove to be more effective than existing global instruments relating to forest protection, such as the 2007 Non-Legally Binding Instrument on All Types of Forest (Forests Instrument). That instrument does include four objectives which, if achieved, would assist in staying within the land-system change planetary boundary, but they are overly general to be used as measures of regime effectiveness.[69] The Paris Agreement and Forests Instrument are bolstered by the Strategic Plan for Biodiversity 2011–2020, adopted in 2010 by the Conference of the Parties to the 1992 Convention on Biological Diversity. The Strategic Plan incorporates the Aichi Biodiversity Targets, which specifically addresses forests in Target 5 (to halve, at least, and where feasible bring close to zero, the rate of loss of all natural habitats, including forests).The achievement of that target would make a significant contribution to staying within the planetary boundary for land-use change.

---

[64] Steffen and others (n 9) at 743.
[65] ibid, 741.
[66] ibid.
[67] Art 5(1).
[68] See generally C Voigt (ed), *Research Handbook on REDD+ and International Law* (Cheltenham, Edward Elgar, 2016).
[69] These objectives are (1) to reverse the loss of forest cover worldwide; (2) enhance forest-based economic, social and environmental benefits; (3) increase significantly the area of protected and sustainably managed forests; and (4) reverse the decline in overseas aid for sustainable forest management.

I. Biosphere Integrity

The biosphere is 'the totality of all ecosystems (terrestrial, freshwater, and marine) on Earth and their biota'.[70] Along with climate change, biosphere integrity is situated atop the hierarchical of planetary boundaries because it interacts with the whole Earth system, is regulated by, and itself regulates, other Earth systems, and the transgression of the boundary clearly involves the shifting of the Earth to a new state.[71] There are two components of this boundary: genetic diversity (the genetic variety that provides the capacity for life to continue to persist and evolve) and functional diversity (the functional diversity and importance of the organisms in an ecosystem). Given knowledge gaps, only interim thresholds have been set for each of these two variables. In the case of genetic diversity it is set at less than 10 extinctions for million species-years (ie less than 10 species lost every million years). This is being exceeded by several orders of magnitude, with between 100 and 1000 extinctions per million species-years.[72] As a result of human activities Earth is currently experiencing its sixth extinction event (also known as the Anthropocene extinction).[73] A 'biodiversity intactness index' of 90 per cent has been adopted as the interim boundary for functional diversity. Only one region, Southern Africa, has been assessed for performance against this index, and it is estimated that functional diversity stands at 84 per cent, again in breach of the boundary.[74]

At the international level there has been acute awareness of the biodiversity crisis, and a number of efforts made to adopt and implement targets and policies to reduce the rate of extinction both of species per se, and also functionally important species. There are a suite of treaty regimes that have a bearing on the problem, including the 1992 Convention on Biological Diversity (CBD), the 1973 Convention on International Trade in Endangered Species of Flora and Fauna and the 1971 Ramsar Convention on Wetlands of International Importance. A new instrument for the protection of high seas biodiversity is currently under negotiation.[75] The CBD defines biological diversity to mean 'the variability among living organisms from all sources including, inter alia, terrestrial, marine and other aquatic ecosystems and the ecological complexes of which they are part; this includes diversity within species, between species and of ecosystems',[76] and has three main

---

[70] Steffen and others (n 9) at 744.

[71] ibid.

[72] ibid, 740.

[73] G Ceballos and others, 'Accelerated Modern Human–induced Species Losses: Entering the Sixth Mass Extinction' (2015) 1 *Science Advances* 1; M L McCallum, 'Vertebrate Biodiversity Loss Points to a Sixth Mass Extinction' (2015) 24 *Biodiversity and Conservation* 2497.

[74] Steffen and others (n 9) at 740.

[75] See generally E Druel and KM Gjerde, 'Sustaining Marine Life Beyond Boundaries: Options for an Implementing Agreement for Marine Biodiversity Beyond National Jurisdiction under the United Nations Convention on the Law of the Sea' (2014) 49 *Marine Policy* 90.

[76] CBD, Art 2, definition of 'biological diversity'.

objectives: conserving biological diversity; the sustainable use biodiversity; and the fair and equitable sharing of the benefits from genetic resources.[77]

A significant feature in the evolution of the CBD regime has been the adoption of strategic plans that have included defined targets for addressing biodiversity loss. In 2002 the parties agreed to achieve by 2010 a significant reduction of the rate of biodiversity loss at global, regional and national levels.[78] COP Decision VI/26 noted, bleakly, that '[t]he rate of biodiversity loss is increasing at an unprecedented rate, threatening the very existence of life as it is currently understood'. In 2010, CBD COP10 adopted a revised and updated Strategic Plan for Biodiversity 2011–2020 which included, as an annexure, the 'Aichi Biodiversity Targets'. This was a far more comprehensive target-setting exercise, and was tethered as 'integral elements' in the Millennium Development Goals, particularly Goal 7 on enduring environmental sustainability. The vision at the centre of the Strategic Plan is 'living in harmony with nature', and the plan includes 20 headline targets for 2015 or 2020. Several of these are clear and precise and map well onto the planetary boundaries for biosphere integrity. For instance, Target 5 calls for the rate of loss of all natural habitats, including forests, to be at least halved and where feasible brought close to zero by 2020. Target 6 calls for all fisheries to be managed sustainably by 2020. Target 11 specifies that by 2010 at least 17 per cent of land areas and 10 per cent of marine areas are to be conserved in protected areas.

The CBD target-setting exercises provides insights into how goals can focus conservation efforts, but also illustrates the obvious point that target-setting by itself is not sufficient to observe planetary limits and must be implemented through effective policies and governance strategies. REDD+ is an example of such a policy which is directed at reducing greenhouse gas emissions but also carries biodiversity conservation 'co-benefits', not least because the focus of REDD+, tropical forests, are well-known 'hotspots' of biological diversity.[79] The Strategic Plan itself also includes three targets to enhance implementation, which includes Target 17 which calls for all parties by 2016 to have developed and adopted a national biodiversity strategy and action plan.

IV. A Reimagined International Environmental Law for the Anthropocene

International environmental law is the textual embodiment of the international institutions that have been developed to address global environmental challenges.[80]

---

[77] CBD, Art 1.
[78] COP 6, Decision VI/26.
[79] N Myers and others, 'Biodiversity Hotspots for Conservation Priorities' (2000) 403 *Nature* 853.
[80] K O'Neill, 'Institutional Politics and Reform' in S Nicholson and S Jinnah (eds), *New Earth Politics: Essays from the Anthropocene* (Cambridge MA, MIT Press, 2016) 157, 159.

It comprises a mixture of 'hard', legally binding, rules that are implemented and enforced, along with an array of 'soft', non-binding or general standards that play a role in shaping discourses of global environmental protection. Institutionalist and constructivist accounts have shown that while international environmental law is reflective of state power relations it can also have a significant influence on the interests of states and their behaviour.[81] Since it first emerged in the 1970s, international environmental law has undergone very significant evolution. There has been considerable institutional experimentation, with new types and forms of environmental treaties adopted, and new institutions created and utilised. Of particular importance has been the use of framework conventions, successive implementing protocols, and the adoption of decisions by conferences and meetings of the parties to environmental treaties to update regimes, and to set goals and standards of varying levels of specificity. This has equipped international environmental law with norms, processes and mechanisms of sophistication and agility that would have been inconceivable only decades ago. However, as has been seen in this chapter, most environmental regimes are not (yet) remotely up to the task of maintaining Earth's main biogeophysical systems.

At the opening of this chapter it was asked what purpose international environmental law should serve in the Anthropocene. International environmental law is facing a challenge both to its practical effectiveness and, more fundamentally, to its rationale. In the human era many of the objects of traditional concern for international environmental law are being so radically disfigured or expunged that some environmental regimes are losing their power, significance and purpose. The Anthropocene threatens to wash away the relevance and influence of the discipline, with international environmental law becoming an international law curio, devoted to preserving a natural world that no longer exists, in a manner akin to the haunting inconsequence of the League of Nations as the world marched to war in 1939. What, for instance, is the purpose of the 1972 World Heritage Convention if many of the cultural and natural properties it seeks to protect are destroyed by climate change?[82]

Despite its 'international' moniker, much of international environmental law is bound to defined places, spaces, habitats, ecosystems, species and objects. Turning again to the 1972 World Heritage Convention as an example, that regime is built on the premise that listed properties are best protected by conservation on site. Historically this made sense, with the Convention agreed at a time when the main threats to world heritage were localised. World Heritage shares much in common with the 'hotspots' approach to biodiversity conservation that focuses on protecting biodiversity in a relatively small number of the Earth's richest locations for biodiversity, rather than global species diversity generally. Mittermeier and others argue that '[t]he biodiversity crisis could be compared with burning down the

---

[81] ibid.
[82] See UNESCO, UCS and UNEP, *World Heritage and Tourism in a Changing Climate* (Nairobi, UNEP, 2016).

world's libraries without knowing the titles of 90% of the books or the content of most of the pages of the known books'.[83] They propose the hotspots approach as a necessary triage—not everything can be saved, so efforts must be rationalised and directed to those habitats and species that can be salvaged. Scaled-down and highly focused conservation strategies have obvious appeal given resource constraints; however, major questions surround their longer-term efficacy if larger environmental challenges are unaddressed.

In the Anthropocene, a focus on conservation *in situ* appears starry-eyed and antiquated, a throwback to the national parks movement which Purdy has described as 'the signal achievement of Romantic environmentalism'.[84] Localised conservation is clearly ineffective in the face of *ex situ* transformations to global environmental systems. In the Anthropocene, international environmental law cannot pretend to conserve all of the objects that have traditionally attracted its attention; the habitats, ecosystems, species, aesthetic wonders and natural and cultural heritage that are being (or will be) lost. If it is to retain its relevance, it is inevitable that international environmental law must lift and broaden its gaze, from localised environments to global environmental systems. In short, it has to alter the way in which it describes and structures the perception of the interrelated natural and human worlds. Rather than a set of discrete and spatially confined external objects to be managed, it must instead view the environment as an integrated Earth system upon which humanity depends. In actuality, this is not a notion that is entirely radical or foreign to international environmental law. As the International Court of Justice observed in the *Nuclear Weapons Advisory Opinion*, 'the environment is not an abstraction but represents the living space, the quality of life and the very health of human beings, including generations unborn'.[85] Nonetheless, despite this sentiment, expressed in the context of an assessment of the nuclear weapons technology that above all else epitomises the Anthropocene,[86] in practical terms international environmental law has yet to undergo the transformation that is required to maintain its relevance this century and beyond.

It has been argued in this chapter that one essential transformation required is to incorporate regime goals based upon the planetary boundaries framework, or similar efforts to identify the safe limits of human activities. The planetary boundaries provide scientific direction and rationale that has been absent from many environmental regimes. They provide a focus and fulcrum for epistemic communities to identify, articulate and institutionalise ecological ideas more effectively.[87] They also provide a basis for adaptive governance so that

---

[83] RA Mittermeier and others, *Hotspots Revisited* (Mexico, CEMEX, 2004) 19.

[84] J Purdy, *After Nature: A Politics for the Anthropocene* (Cambridge MA, Harvard University Press, 2015) 231.

[85] *Legality of the Threat or Use of Nuclear Weapons* [1996] ICJ Rep 226, [29].

[86] Hamilton and Grinevald, 'Was the Anthropocene Anticipated?' (n 1).

[87] See generally P Haas, 'Epistemic Communities' in D Bodansky, J Brunnée and E Hey (eds), *The Oxford Handbook of International Environmental Law* (Oxford, Oxford University Press, 2008) 792.

environmental regimes can evolve over time to respond to risk and uncertainty. A lesson of environmental treaty negotiations is that scientific and policy ideas that acquire currency in epistemic communities and in public discourse can strongly influence discussions at the negotiating table. For instance, the climate negotiations have been increasingly influenced by ideas originating outside the UNFCCC process, including scientific notions (eg the 1.5°C/2°C 'safe' temperature limits, carbon net neutrality and carbon budgets); and policy ideas ('contraction and convergence' of emissions, and commitments to phase out the use of fossil fuels). This illustrates the power of environmental discourses that construct and condition the ways in which environmental issues are perceived and the policy and regulatory responses that should be deployed.[88]

The planetary boundaries are highly policy relevant and are able to feed directly into the process of target-setting, which is a core technique of national environmental regulation (eg, water and air quality standards) that can be used at planetary and regional scales. Target-setting can provide not merely a rhetorical aspiration, but can transform expectations and state behaviour. Above all, targets crystallise regime goals that allow regime performance to be assessed. As Young explains, an insight of regime theory is the importance of 'articula[ting] common goals in forms that are easy to grasp and straightforward to use in assessing regime performance'.[89] Young provides the examples of phase-out timetables for ozone-depleting substances, the designation of Antarctica as a zone where militarisation and mining are prohibited, and water quality regulations for international rivers. Even when not set in hard law, a target or ecological limit provides a focus and leverage point for civil society (and active and concerned states) to apply pressure upon the international community to live up to promises made, and to transform non-binding commitments into legal rules.

Environmental regimes such as the climate and oceans treaties have been described by Kim and Mackey as 'complex adaptive systems'[90] which have the potential for significant evolution over time. However, there are a number of factors militating against the pace and scale of evolution required to meet the challenges of the Anthropocene. First, there is significant path-dependency. As Stevenson and Dryzek put it, '[i]nstitutions tend to have a life of their own, what is sometimes called path dependency, irrespective of the preferences and desires of those who labor within them'.[91] Path dependency describes an institutional conservatism or inertia, a by-product of the intrinsically slow and cumbrous diplomatic process, and also of the assumption that environmental issues can be addressed through

---

[88] JS Dryzek, *The Politics of the Earth: Environmental Discourses*, 2nd edn (Oxford, Oxford University Press, 2005) 10.

[89] Young, 'Improving the Performance of the Climate Regime' (n 24) at 627

[90] RE Kim and B Mackay, 'International Environmental Law as a Complex Adaptive System' (2014) 14 *International Environmental Agreements* 14.

[91] H Stevenson and JS Dryzek, *Democratizing Global Climate Governance* (Cambridge, Cambridge University Press, 2014) 210.

incremental improvements and reforms, rather than via a legal *gestalt* shift that would match the scale and pace of the planetary rupture that the Anthropocene involves.

Secondly, there is significant fragmentation and 'siloing' of regimes, as seen most obviously with the carbon-cycle challenge which, while implicating multiple Earth systems, is left for resolution in one, suboptimal, regime. For instance, the UNFCCC deals only with the atmospheric impacts of carbon emissions, and does not directly or expressly address the related problem of ocean acidification, while marine environmental protection regimes have deferred to the UNFCCC. This is a clear example of regime deference or abdication, and while serving an objective of regime harmony and comity, undermines overall regime effectiveness (Bosselmann and Kim refer to this as 'problem shifting').

Several antidotes have been suggested to these twin problems. Biermann and others have criticised the incremental approach to international environmental law since the 1972 Stockholm Conference, and called for a new 'constitutional' or 'charter' moment' akin to the transformation of international law and the creation of the United Nations following the Second World War.[92] As a metaphor, this 'charter' moment is a helpful analogue for the fundamental shift required in global environmental governance from an atomised, sectoral, approach to a systemic response that addresses environmental spheres in their entirety. However, Stevenson and Dryzek note that such a constitutional moment has not yet arrived for climate governance.[93] And while rapidly worsening global environmental conditions might prompt such a radical awakening and constitutional transformation, this would come too late as irreversible change would already have been set in motion.

So we must look elsewhere for institutional change, and an alternative to fundamental reform from the centre is a transformation driven by forces at the periphery. Rather than deference and abdication, there is a role for environmental regimes to engage in 'strategic inconsistency'[94] to disrupt the status quo and drive normative transformation.[95] This could be effected in the first instance through soft-law instruments which have lower political cost, and would involve only policy and not legal inconsistency and could serve as a rallying cry for civil society groups and other non-state actors. As has been noted, biodiversity targets have been adopted by the parties to the CBD, and because biosphere integrity is recognised as a core boundary with linkages with all other boundaries, the CBD may also be utilised as vehicle for other planetary boundary goal-setting. It could, for instance, specify an ocean acidification guardrail by reference to ocean pH, or

---

[92] F Biermann and others, 'Transforming Governance and Institutions for Global Sustainability: Key Insights from the Earth System Governance Project' (2012) 4 *Current Opinion in Environmental Sustainability* 51. For detailed discussion on this point, see L Kotzé, *Global Environmental Constitutionalism in the Anthropocene* (Oxford, Hart, 2016).

[93] Stevenson and Dryzek, *Democratizing Global Climate Governance* (n 91) at 212.

[94] Raustiala and Victor, 'The Regime Complex' (n 55).

[95] Stevenson and Dryzek, *Democratizing Global Climate Governance* (n 91) at 213.

carbonate concentration, consistent with its biodiversity targets. Another possibility is for a United Nations General Assembly resolution on planetary boundaries that is modelled on the Millennium Development Goals,[96] and the more recent 2030 Agenda for Sustainable Development.[97] The 2030 Agenda does make some progress towards this end. For instance, Goal 14.3 is to '[m]inimize and address the impacts of ocean acidification, including through enhanced scientific cooperation at all levels'. The advantage of a General Assembly resolution is that it can span multiple regimes and also carries global authority and legitimacy that individual regimes may not possess.

While important, there are limits to what can be achieved through target-setting. As Ginsberg notes in relation to biodiversity conservation, '[a]lthough priority-setting exercises help us focus limited financial and human resources, they tell us nothing about how to achieve conservation; at best they tell us what to save first but not how to save it'.[98] In other words, target-setting exercises are inherently teleological. They address environmental *ends* (what to save), but not the critical question of *means* (how to save it). A case in point is the climate regime, which has evolved from recognising the problem in abstract terms (in the UNFCCC) to internalising the planetary boundary as a regime objective (in the Paris Agreement), but which has yet to progress to detailed policy prescriptions, including the division of the carbon budget among nations and comprehensive rules and institutions for reducing emissions (eg carbon trading, moratoria on fossil fuel extraction etc).

Target-setting by reference to boundaries is therefore not sufficient; it must also be coupled with a new set of environmental norms. In the Anthropocene a key challenge is what content these will have and what overarching narrative they will subscribe to. A central tension in the process of reimagining and reconfiguring international environmental law in the Anthropocene is between competing conceptions as to the purpose of global environmental governance. Hamilton describes this as a contest of ideology between Soterians (named after the Greek god of safety and salvation) and the Stores Prometheans (named after the Greek god who gave humanity technology).[99] International environmental law has many aspects which are inherently Soterian, as seen in its preservationist and conservationist impulse, and its prevention and precautionary principles. Yet in the Anthropocene, humanity has already assumed a large degree of Promethean mastery over global environmental systems, albeit unintentionally. 'Eco-modernists'[100] celebrate

---

[96] UNGA Res A/RES/55/2 (2000).
[97] UNGA Res A/RES/70/1 (2015).
[98] J Ginsberg, 'Global Conservation Priorities' (1999) 13 *Conservation Biology* 5.
[99] Hamilton, *Earth Masters* (n 15) at 18.
[100] C Hamilton, 'The Theodicy of the "Good Anthropocene"' (2015) 7 *Environmental Humanities* 233.

the Anthropocene as the epitome of human control of the global environment, and advance grand geoengineering proposals in service of a Panglossian belief that humanity can enjoy a 'good Anthropocene'.[101] But it is a logical fallacy that because humanity has assumed a position of 'domination' over the environment that it must therefore have within its grasp the capacity to superintend the Earth's biophysical systems now and in the future. The mastery is only imagined, given that the disruption being wrought upon Earth's systems is likely to be beyond that which can be truly controlled. As Hansen and others put it, '[t]here is a possibility, a real danger, that we will hand young people and future generations a climate system that is practically out of their control'.[102]

International environmental law must therefore achieve a delicate (and quite conceivably impossible) balance in the Anthropocene. It must become more pragmatic, less focused on the local and more oriented towards protecting globally integrated environmental systems in order to sustain human civilisation. Yet at the same time it must not succumb to a technocratic temptation towards 'quick fixes'. The potential for geoengineering is attractive to governments because it provides an excuse for inaction, allowing business as usual to continue without hard choices being made to preserve environmental systems until such time that global technological intervention is unavoidable. It is apparently of no moment that such schemes are likely to be ineffective, or to carry such serious side-effects as to create more problems than they solve. It is the ultimate moral hazard. This is a dilemma for international environmental law in an age which is one of constant crises. As Purdy puts, it, '[c]limate change is the exemplary permanent crisis for an age of many permanent crises'.[103] International environmental lawmaking has many exemplified aspects of the 'crisis-model' of lawmaking,[104] with many regimes fashioned in the immediate aftermath of disasters. But over time a more preventative and anticipatory approach has been taken, motivated by a precautionary ethic. Looking forward, it is possible that international environmental law will come full circle to embrace a crisis approach again, yet this time on a much larger, indeed global, scale. In so doing a central conundrum will be how to maintain international environmental law's ethical and principled core that serves principles of fairness and justice,[105] and not to embrace a 'survivalist' ethic which discards fundamental values in service to wholly instrumentalist and utilitarian objectives.

---

[101] See 'The Ecomodernist Manifesto', available at: www.ecomodernism.org/manifesto.

[102] Hansen and others, 'Ice Melt, Sea Level Rise and Superstorms' (n 19).

[103] Purdy, *After Nature* (n 84) at 255.

[104] See T Stephens, 'Disasters, International Environmental Law and the Anthropocene' in S Breau and KLH Samuel (eds), *Research Handbook on Disasters and International Law* (Cheltenham, Edward Elgar, 2016) 153.

[105] See generally P Lawrence, *Justice for Future Generations: Climate Change and International Law* (Cheltenham, Edward Elgar, 2014).

V. Conclusion

It can be said that the Anthropocene has brought an end to the history of international environmental law as we have known it because it is now manifest that the natural and human spheres are inseparable. Climate change (and other global environmental transformations) have entailed the collapse of the humanist bifurcation of natural history and human history.[106] International environmental law can therefore no longer be concerned with preserving an external and insensate environment, for there is no such entity. In the Anthropocene, social scientists must become geophysicists, and geophysicists must become social scientists.[107] As such, the Anthropocene brings with it the potential for the enhanced role and relevance of global environmental norms given that they are now indispensable for maintaining the fundamental conditions of human dignity. In the Anthropocene, international environmental law could take equal footing with the highest order area of international law: the body of norms concerned with maintaining international peace and security. However, the Anthropocene also threatens to strip away much of the recognisable content of international environmental law as the common environmental goods that it protects are destroyed, and as pressure mounts to respond reflexively to disaster by turning to Earth system engineering. A reimagined international environmental law for the Anthropocene may remain faithful to its precautionary and preservationist core, or else, as planetary crises unfold, it may become a purely utilitarian normative order concerned only with protecting humanity from an increasingly hostile and hazardous Earth.[108] Which path is taken hinges on the success of the project to reimagine international environmental law.[109]

---

[106] D Chakrabarty, 'The Climate of History: Four Theses' (2009) 35 *Critical Inquiry* 197, 201.
[107] Hamilton, 'Human Destiny in the Anthropocene' (n 5) at 35.
[108] ibid, 40.
[109] Biermann (n 6) at 205.

3

Doing Time—The Temporalities of Environmental Law

BENJAMIN J RICHARDSON

I. Time and Environmental Change

A disturbing way to visualise the Anthropocene is Google Earth's time-lapsed, bird's-eye panoramas. Launched in 2013 by the United States Geological Survey and NASA, Google displays vivid satellite pictures of Earth for each year since 1984.[1] Users of the 'Earth Engine' can zoom into any corner of the planet to watch a time-lapsed sequence of images over about the past 30 years. Taken from Landsat satellites, they evoke a stunning historical vista of permutations in the Earth's landscape over a mere few decades—a fleeting moment in nature's timescales. One time-lapse series shows Dubai ballooning from a desert village into a metropolis complete with artificial islands; another tracks the carcinogenic-like sprawl around Las Vegas; while a further sequence depicts the ravenous deforestation of the Amazon.

The time-lapse imagery helps one to appreciate how a growing humanity and its insatiable demand for environmental resources is literally altering the face of the planet. Its shockingly rapid changes revealed through these time panoramas could not be so easily gleaned from the vantage of the present or a single image of the past. It is the compilation of numerous images, over time, and on a large spatial scale, that cumulative decline manifests: lakes and rivers that desiccate to satiate thirsty farms, the retreat of glaciers in a warming climate, and the paving of ever more terrain for roads and buildings. If we could stretch these timescales over longer periods to capture other trends, we would be even more alarmed. Depletions of marine fisheries in recent decades are worrying but disastrous when contemplated over the last century.[2] Throughout human history, the scale, intensity

---

[1] See http://earthengine.google.org/#intro. Users can also view the images on the *Time Magazine* website: http://world.time.com/timelapse.

[2] JB Jackson and others, 'Historical Overfishing and the Recent Collapse of Coastal Ecosystems' (2001) 293 *Science* 629.

and frequency of anthropogenic permeations on the biosphere have grown exponentially, spurred by technological advances (of which some ironically were introduced to improve our well-being), rising material consumption and the sheer numbers of humans. One can only dread how these changes will likely intensify in the coming decades as emerging economies such as China and Brazil ramp up their development.

The Anthropocene can be interpreted in a variety of ways, and this chapter argues that it is insightful to view it as related to a failure to align human affairs with Earth's timescales. Although many philosophical and sociological understandings of time exist, the most useful for this context is time as an intellectual framework to measure *change*, and thereby to sequence and compare events or actions.[3] As a way to identify change, time thus enables associations to be drawn between present environmental conditions with their former state and how they might alter in the future. The lack of symmetry between human and natural timescales, caused by factors such as economic and technological changes, is widening as human cultural evolution dramatically accelerates our trajectory away from nature's temporal rhythms. Natural resources are depleted more quickly than they can regenerate, past ecological damage remains unrepaired and future environmental changes are not adequately guarded against—the result of which is that natural systems lose their capacity to change and evolve according to their normal trajectory.

Environmental law exacerbates this temporal misalignment that characterises the Anthropocene. It codifies social understandings of environmental change, including mastery of natural processes,[4] and provides directions on how to respond to ecological disturbances. The law can be too temporally one-dimensional, and indeed quite static, lacking the adaptive flexibility to adjust to new circumstances and unwilling to acknowledge past losses. Mired in an overly contemporaneous time frame preoccupied with the present, environmental law has struggled to recognise the frequently slow and temporally dispersed harms inflicted on nature. Insidious threats such as climate change, which gradually unleash mayhem rather than spectacularly erupting to jolt our complacency, are perpetuated with minimal (if any) legal sanctions.[5] And past environmental losses, of which many continue to reverberate, are largely unaccounted for and ignored: for instance, the enormous depletion of biodiversity and abundance is rarely acknowledged in

---

[3] See eg PJ Corfield, *Time and the Shape of History* (New Haven, CT, Yale University Press, 2007); LN Oaklander and Q Smith (eds), *The New Theory of Time* (New Haven, CT, Yale University Press, 1994); J Brough and L Embree (eds), *The Many Faces of Time* (Dordrecht, Kluwer Academic, 2000); PK McInerney, *Time and Experience* (Philadelphia, Temple University Press, 1991).

[4] A Grear and E Grant, 'Introduction: Thought, Law, Rights and Action in an Age of Environmental Crisis—In Search of Better Future Histories' in A Grear and E Grant (eds), *Thought, Law, Rights and Action in an Age of Environmental Crisis* (Cheltenham, Edward Elgar Publishing, 2015) 1.

[5] BH Thompson Jr, 'The Trouble with Time: Influencing the Conservation Choices of Future Generations' (2004) 44 *Natural Resources Journal* 601.

the law as a loss that needs to be restored.[6] The temporally-stilted approach is also reflected in how regulatory controls, such as environmental assessment and licensing, are typically front-loaded at the initial approval phase for new development. Rarely is governance recalibrated, such as through relicensing and indeed, environmental regulation often 'grandfathers' existing developments, shielding them from change over time. On the other hand, when it comes to enabling economic development, the legal system responds much more quickly despite the heightened environmental risks. Many governments have introduced fast-track legislation to expedite approval of prestige development projects, while conversely the need for an emergency response to the Anthropocene faces insouciance from most states.[7] The acceleration of economic life is usurping environmental decision-making and compromising the due diligence needed to avert unfavourable environmental changes.[8]

The utility of time as a lens to understand the Anthropocene and how law deals with it has yet to be widely recognised because the literature dwells on the subject's spatial dimensions. The celebrated motto of the modern environmental movement—'Think Globally, Act Locally'—epitomises the dominance of spatial thinking among environmentalists. Land tenure, jurisdiction and liability standards hinge heavily on spatial concepts, as does preoccupation with the sheer physicality of ecological problems.[9] The emphasis on space in the doctrinal and theoretical development of environmental law dovetails with the wider fascination about it in legal scholarship. From physical places to socially and politically constructed spaces, 'space' has become a privileged framework for enquiry about the exercise of legal power and the structure of legal relationships.[10]

This conclusion is not to imply that scholars of environmental law ignore 'time', but that their analysis of it has been incomplete. Historical developments fascinate some researchers who investigate the evolution of environmental law and

---

[6] BJ Richardson and L Butterly, 'Lost in Time: The Missing Temporality of Environmental Law' (2016) February, *Australian Environment Review* 18.

[7] eg Greece (Acceleration and Transparency of Implementation of Strategic Investments or Fast Track Law, 2010), South Africa (Infrastructure Development Act 2014), state of Gujarat in India (Gujarat Infrastructure Development Act 1999) and the state of Tasmania in Australia (Pulp Mill Assessment Act 2007).

[8] One of many examples is initiatives in Australia to facilitate mining developments such as controversial coal seam gas projects: SJ Tasker, 'AGL Gets Go-Ahead to Start Fracking at Gloucester Project' *The Australian* (7 August 2014).

[9] eg J Holder and C Harrison (eds), *Law and Geography: Current Legal Issues*, vol 5 (Oxford, Oxford University Press, 2003); R Verchick, 'Critical Space Theory: Keeping Local Geography in American and European Environmental Law' (1999) 73(3) *Tulane Law Review* 739; D Grinlinton and P Taylor, *Property Rights and Sustainability* (Leiden, Brill, 2011); C Rootes (ed), *Acting Locally: Local Environmental Mobilizations and Campaigns* (London, Routledge, 2008).

[10] M Valverde, '"Time Thickens, Takes on Flesh": Spatiotemporal Dynamics in Law' in I Braverman and others (eds), *The Expanding Spaces of Law* (California, Stanford University Press, 2015) 53, 57 (discussing D Delaney, *The Spatial, the Legal and the Pragmatics of World-Making: Nomospheric Investigations* (London, Verso, 2010)); A Philippopoulos-Mihalopoulos, *Spatial Justice: Body, Lawscape, Atmosphere* (Abingdon, Routledge, 2015).

legislative milestones.[11] Others, taking a more normative orientation, investigate the future directions of environmental regulation and policy. The philosophy of sustainable development and associated concepts including intergenerational equity have generated a plethora of writings that both critique existing applications and chart new directions to avoid climate change, mass species extinctions and other apocalyptic scenarios.[12] None of these scholarly endeavours, however, provides a complete picture of the appropriate temporal morphology of environmental law. The uni-directional future gaze of sustainability overlooks the need to restore past ecological damage and because of uncertainty about changing environmental conditions it may also be necessary to adjust regulations to take account of new scientific information or evolving social values. The Anthropocene is not simply a manifestation of the dangerously accelerated tempo of *homo sapiens* and the articulation of new forms of 'social time' (eg in the economy) misaligned to Earth's temporalities, but also reflects the failure of the legal system to seriously address the adverse ecological changes. The law lacks the temporal breadth to appreciate the sheer magnitude of unfolding ecological change in such a short time frame, and the law naively assumes that the prevailing social and economic order can continue to flourish under the 'sustainability' banner without addressing past losses or adjusting urgently to changing future circumstances.

This chapter therefore addresses these lacunae. Rather than focusing on any specific jurisdictions or case studies, this brief analysis takes a broad-brush, conceptual approach with occasional examples of legal precedents and practices. Section II examines the deficiencies in how legislation that promotes sustainable development deals with the adaptation over time to a changing future. Section III considers how environmental law deals with the past, focusing on the differences between restoration of discrete environmental impacts such as a former mine and restoration of ecosystems and landscapes on a larger scale. The chapter concludes with re-emphasis on the need for a holistic perspective of the temporal dimensions of environmental law in order to cope with the global socio-ecological crisis of the Anthropocene. Overall, this chapter is about identifying problems and challenges rather than outlining specific solutions to the temporalities of environmental law.

---

[11] eg ZJB Plater, 'From the Beginning, a Fundamental Shift of Paradigms: A Theory and Short History of Environmental Law' (1994) 27(3) *Loyola of Los Angeles Law Review* 981; P Sand, *The History and Origin of International Environmental Law* (Cheltenham, Edward Elgar, 2015); WH Rodgers Jr, 'The Most Creative Moments in the History of Environmental Law: "The Whats"' (2000) *University of Illinois Law Review* 1.

[12] eg BJ Richardson and S Wood (eds), *Environmental Law for Sustainability* (Oxford, Hart Publishing, 2006); J Cameron and J Abouchar, 'The Precautionary Principle: A Fundamental Principle of Law and Policy for the Protection of the Global Environment' (1991) 14 *Boston College International and Comparative Law Review* 1; J Owley and KH Hirokawa (eds), *Rethinking Sustainability to Meet the Climate Change Challenge* (Washington DC, Environmental Law Institute, 2015).

II. Governing the Future

A. Valuing the Future

Under the philosophy of sustainable development, modern environmental law has acquired a seemingly progressive approach to time. As the aim is to avoid leaving burdensome environmental legacies for posterity, sustainable development implies that societal decisions should reflect time frames that match nature's temporal scales, such as those applicable to ecological succession, the capacity of species to adapt to their surroundings and the resilience of the environment to handle disturbances without adverse or irreparable consequences. Because these time frames often extend beyond the lifetime of any individual or involve environmental changes that are not perceptible to individuals during their lives, law acquired a special role in inculcating awareness of the future in economic, social and political institutions. Environmental law promises that the governance of human activity will be freed from the expedient preoccupation with the present and the dead weight of legal tradition. Unshackled from slavish accommodation of the myopic needs of the present generation, modern environmental law introduced a fresh, long-term outlook that would ensure the enduring well-being of nature and future generations.[13] With this embrace of the future, environmental law would also presumably loosen its hitherto dominant spatial orientation.

Of all the principles associated with legal enunciations of sustainable development, intergenerational equity evokes most strongly the importance of the future.[14] Unlike other contexts for the application of equity, intergenerational justice focuses on distributional issues that are temporal rather than based on class, geography or other spatial contexts. The principle has been enshrined in international environmental agreements, such as the 1992 Rio Declaration on Environment and Development,[15] and the 1992 United Nations Framework Convention on Climate Change.[16] Yet, intergenerational equity has gained only limited legislative recognition in most countries, one notable exception being Australia where the principle is acknowledged in many foundational federal and state laws albeit without much guidance on its implementations.[17] Courts have also occasionally considered the principle, such as in the Philippines case of *Minors Oposa*

---

[13] MC Cordonier Segger and A Khalfan, *Sustainable Development Law: Principles, Practices, and Prospects* (Oxford, Oxford University Press, 2005).

[14] E Brown Weiss, *In Fairness to Future Generations: International Law, Common Patrimony, and Intergenerational Equity* (New York, Transnational Publishers, 1989).

[15] 31 ILM 874 (1992), Principle 3.

[16] 31 ILM 849 (1992), Art 3(1)).

[17] eg Protection of the Environment Administration Act 1991 (NSW) s 6(2)(b); National Environment Protection Council Act 1995 (SA) sch 1, s 3.5.2; Environment Protection Act 1970 (VIC) s 1D.

v Factoran,[18] which largely turned on rights under the Philippines Constitution. The paucity of domestic legislative and judicial application of intergenerational equity reflects the difficulty of working out what justice between generations requires in specific instances. The legal system is well infused with notions of justice and fairness between contemporaries, but lacks tools to adjudicate equity between different generations separated by many years.[19] Edith Brown Weiss, a leading theorist on this subject, proposes trust law structures for this purpose.[20]

The confusion over intergenerational justice evokes a wider challenge to determine the appropriate time frame for a wide range of environmental decisions and how to deal with changes over time. Not only are rival ethical and economic criteria available, the appropriate time frame sometimes also depends on the specific environmental issue and threat: what is appropriate for protecting biodiversity may differ from that suitable for limiting climate change. A short time frame can cause one to downplay risks and threats to the environment because they might not be discernable except over long periods, while a long time frame may lead to unreliable predictions and wasted resources in trying to protect the environment. Alternatively, open-ended commitments without any quantified time interval, such as an obligation to manage for the 'long term' or 'foreseeable future', may give decision-makers too much latitude. It gives flexibility to adapt to new circumstances but with the downside that the lack of clarity may impede public confidence, enable unscrupulous government decisions and create opportunities for corporate mischief. Generally speaking, environmental legislation speaks vaguely of taking into account 'long term' issues,[21] but occasionally specifies time intervals that rarely extend beyond mid-century. One example is England's Climate Change Act 2008 that commits to 'contributing to sustainable development' and sets 2050 as the deadline for the government to ensure that the country's carbon emissions drop to levels at least 80 per cent lower than their state in 1990.[22]

Legislating time frames for action can elevate social awareness about the need to tackle the Anthropocene, although without necessarily improving legal accountability. For relatively distant targets such as 2050, it is difficult to hold any current decision-maker legally responsible because achievement of a target depends on the effect of the aggregation of numerous actions over many years. Instead, we must rely precariously on regulators having high levels of ethical commitment and good faith. Accountability is even more elusive with open-ended commitments to act for the long term or to safeguard the interests of posterity. Because environmental law is largely process oriented with considerable discretionary criteria,

---

[18] *Minors Oposa v Secretary of the Department of Environmental and Natural Resources* (1993) reprinted 33 ILM 173 (1994).
[19] J Thompson, *Intergenerational Justice* (London, Routledge, 2009) 3.
[20] Brown Weiss, *In Fairness to Future Generations* (n 14).
[21] eg Comprehensive Environmental Response and Compensation Liability Act 1980 27 42 USC s 9621(b)(1).
[22] Climate Change Act 2008, ss 1 and 13.

decision-makers have scope to deviate from targets to address more expedient considerations. The common reliance of cost-benefit analysis to evaluate the long- and near-term merits of a decision, such as construction of a dam or adopting a new regulation, is hugely controversial and can lead to the future being discounted heavily relative to near-term benefits.[23] In sum, inculcating a future orientation in environmental law remains a work-in-progress.

B. Managing Change

Because acting for the long term involves considerable uncertainty and risks in an Anthropocene that takes humanity into an uncharted future, environmental governance (and the juridical foundation it is based on) must be able to change to correct mistakes or to respond to new or fluctuating circumstances. In other words, the temporal challenge is not simply to value the future, but to respond to a *changing* future. This is a daunting challenge because environmental regula- tion tends, perhaps understandably, to resist change owing to the economic and social costs of 'redoing' its decisions. Adaptive governance, a term apparently first coined by Dietz and others in 2003, is increasingly advocated by academics and practitioners for coordinating and adjusting resource management in the face of the complexity and uncertainty accompanying rapid ecological change.[24] Adap- tive governance dovetails with broader theoretical enquiries into improving the resilience of human and natural systems to cope with adverse change.[25] Governing for these purposes requires expanding the role of law and other governance insti- tutions from not just limiting adverse change in the belief that the status quo can be maintained indefinitely, but also enhancing social and natural systems' capacity to adapt to further change.[26]

Environmental law has yet to adequately embody this adaptive agenda. Legisla- tion commonly 'grandfathers' existing resource uses and polluters from transi- tions to new environmental standards.[27] Grandfathering commonly features in pollution control, land-use planning and resource access governance, and it may involve beneficiaries receiving either a grace period before the new rules apply or indefinite exemption so long as the beneficiary does not change its activity.

---

[23] DA Farber and PA Hemmersbaugh, 'The Shadow of the Future: Discount Rates, Later Genera- tions, and the Environment' (1993) 46 *Vanderbilt Law Review* 267, 280–81; D Driesen, 'Is Cost-Benefit Analysis Neutral?' (2006) 77 *University of Colorado Law Review* 335.

[24] T Dietz, E Ostrom and PC Stern, 'The Struggle to Govern the Commons' (2003) 302 *Science* 1907.

[25] eg C Folke, 'Resilience: The Emergence of a Perspective for Social Ecological Systems Analyses' (2006) 16 *Global Environmental Change* 253; CS Holling, 'Understanding the Complexity of Economic, Ecological, and Social Systems' (2001) 4 *Ecosystems* 390.

[26] LH Gunderson and SS Light, 'Adaptive Management and Adaptive Governance in the Everglades Ecosystem' (2006) 39 *Policy Sciences* 323.

[27] J Remey Nash and RL Revesz, *Grandfathering and Environmental Regulation: The Law and Eco- nomics of New Source Review* New York School of Law, Working Paper No 07-03, 2007.

The main rationale of such concessions is to avoid the seeming injustice of coercing a person to incur costs in adjusting to a new regulation after having made investments to conform to a prior standard. Grandfather clauses, however, introduce temporal inertia in environmental governance, holding back reform. Research suggests new regulations with grandfather concessions retard investment in cleaner factories and keep inefficient, polluting plants operating longer than they otherwise would.[28] The grandfather privileges under the European Community's Emission Trading Scheme,[29] for example, greatly reduced incentives for industry to abate their carbon emissions.[30]

Another barrier to adaptive governance is the limited scope for relicensing. Regulation tends to be front-loaded with most of the effort expended when a development project or activity is first proposed. The regulatory system invests heavily in the initial due diligence, environmental assessments, cost-benefit analysis studies and public consultations that inform licensing and other types of regulatory decisions. Once approved, regulators give limited attention to what ensues, such as follow-up monitoring or adjusting licences in light of new information. Even ensuring compliance with approval conditions may not occur. The scope for reopening an approval decision is quite limited and usually confined to operational details rather than allowable use such as a mine or factory. To illustrate, New Zealand's Resource Management Act 1991 allows municipal authorities to review the conditions of resource consents in several contexts, including to address new adverse environmental effects.[31] However, the relevant authority must inter alia have regard to 'whether the activity will continue to be viable after the change' and, in the case of a review of a discharge permit or coastal permit, to have regard to 'the financial implications for the applicant of including that condition'.[32] In practice, such reviews are uncommon, averaging about 1 per cent of resource consents in a two-year survey period according to one study.[33]

For sustainable development, relicensing allows for the recalibration of a development with better information than existed when the original licence was granted. Environmental issues and risks may be better understood, and advances in scientific knowledge may have identified new environmental impacts previously overlooked in initial project assessments and approvals. Community judgements can also be based on evidence rather than projections and speculation. Further, social values may have shifted and, with time, a community might demand higher

---

[28] ibid, 28–30.
[29] European Community, Directive 2003/87/EC of the European Parliament and of the Council of 13 October 2003 establishing a scheme for greenhouse gas emission allowance trading within the Community and amending Council Directive 96/61/EC [2003] OJ L 275.
[30] A Endres and C Ohl, 'Kyoto, Europe? An Economic Evaluation of the European Emission Trading Directive' (2005) 19 *European Journal of Law and Economics* 17, 28.
[31] Resource Management Act 1991, s 128.
[32] ibid, s 131.
[33] R van Voorhuysen and M Cameron, 'Resource Consent Durations and Reviews' (2000) 2(9) *Resource Management Journal* 8, 10.

or different environmental standards. An activity once judged as environmentally acceptable might one day no longer be viewed so positively: coal mining, for instance, is becoming stigmatised as climate-conscious people shun dirty fossil fuels, as evident in the fossil fuels divestment campaign.[34] Another benefit of relicensing is that if operators know that their development will eventually need to be relicensed, they will presumably give greater attention to regulatory compliance and community relations.

In practice, relicensing or other regulatory changes occur only in limited circumstances and are not routinely built into development approval processes, except sometimes in regard to technical and operational matters rather than allowable land use.[35] Another trigger for relicensing is where the licensee itself requests a variation, such as to enable a change in operations, expansion or use of a new technology.[36] Another context is as a consequence of a statutory offence.[37] In addition, periodic renewal of licences may enable new regulations to be introduced. Licence renewal intervals vary dramatically, depending on the jurisdiction and subject matter. Routine pollution emission licences might be subject to renewal proceedings every five years. The principal barrier to environmental relicensing or renewals is pressure on authorities to ensure predictability and stability for business operations, especially where financial investors are involved. Further, major infrastructure developments may also not be capable, in a practical sense, of being redesigned or operated differently to accommodate a shift in licensing requirements. In their analysis of major water projects in North America, Cosens and others observed that '[o]nce major investment occurs in water infrastructure, it is highly resistant to change. There is strong incentive to shore up rather than alter infrastructure once built'.[38] Finally, the law itself has a degree of temporal inertia or 'path dependency', in which governance choices tend to be framed or limited by the status quo or choices previously made.[39]

The key challenge with relicensing and other forms of recalibration is to find an effective balance between a regulatory system that is lithe and responsive to change

---

[34] J Ayling and N Gunningham, 'Non-state Governance and Climate Policy: The Divestment Movement' (2015) *Climate Policy* 1.

[35] Some of the most extensive literature relates to hydro-power development relicensing: see eg SC Richardson, 'The Changing Political Landscape of Hydropower Project Relicensing' (2000) 25 *William and Mary Environmental Law and Policy Review* 499; CR Sensiba, 'Who's in Charge Here? The Shrinking Role of the Federal Energy Regulatory Commission in Hydropower Relicensing' (1999) 70 *University of Colorado Law Review* 60. See also JF Quichocho, 'License Renewal for the Dow Chemical TRIGA Research Reactor' (2012) 77(140) *Federal Register* 42771.

[36] eg Protection of the Environment Operations Act 1997 (NSW), s 58.

[37] ibid, s 79(4); Environment Protection Act 1993 (SA), s 5.

[38] B Cosens, L Gunderson and B Chaffin, 'The Adaptive Water Governance Project: Assessing Law, Resilience and Governance in Regional Socio-Ecological Water Systems Facing a Changing Climate' (2014) 51 *Idaho Law Review* 1.

[39] TC Boas, 'Conceptualizing Continuity and Change: The Composite-Standard Model of Path Dependence' (2007) 19(1) *Journal of Theoretical Politics* 33; EA Kirk, AD Reeves and K Blackstock, 'Path Dependency and the Implementation of Environmental Regulation' (2007) 25 *Environment and Planning C: Government and Policy* 250.

and contingencies, but without introducing too much uncertainty and unmanageable complexity into that system.[40] The prospect of frequent and costly changes to the environmental rules might deter economic investment and be politically unpalatable for any government to tolerate. One way to achieve that balance might be a system of staged development approvals, in which new activities are subject to a series of approval processes in which satisfactory performance at one stage entitles the operator to move to the next. Another option is to build licence renewals and re-evaluations more transparently into the initial regulatory decisions so that developers can factor such contingencies into their business models and operational plans.

Apart from shifts in official regulation, the regulatees themselves may initiate changes to their environmental policies and practices. The movement for corporate social responsibility (CSR) has intensified globally in recent decades as business enterprises voluntarily take steps to improve their environmental performance such as by adhering to industry codes of conduct, issuing sustainability reports or adopting in-house environmental management systems. Companies may undertake such commitments for a host of reasons including business advantages, improved relationships with stakeholders, peer pressure, or to stave off unwelcome regulation.[41] Corporate initiative can contribute to the responsive, adaptive qualities of environmental governance in a manner that responsive regulation and reflexive law theories suggests is efficient, as the participatory and incentive-based approaches to CSR governance are hypothesised as more likely to achieve positive results at a lower cost than coercive, top-down regulation.[42] But CSR is not necessarily an absolute alternative to official regulation, as corporate initiatives may be introduced in partnership with government regulators such as through negotiated agreements or fiscal incentives provided by the state. The theory of regulatory spaces is useful for understanding such hybrid public–private governance regimes.[43] Reliance on such hybrid governance is particularly useful to counteract the risk that CSR is camouflage for perfunctory or unscrupulous behaviour, otherwise known as 'greenwashing'.[44] In sum, therefore, while official

---

[40] Such an approach would also better accommodate the complex needs of Earth systems governance models: eg H Stevenson and JS Dryzek. *Democratizing Global Climate Governance* (Cambridge, Cambridge University Press, 2014) 4.

[41] JL Campbell, 'Why Would Corporations Behave in Socially Responsible Ways: An Institutional Theory of Corporate Social Responsibility' (2007) 32 *Academy of Management Review* 946; J Makower, *Beyond the Bottom Line: Putting Social Responsibility to Work for your Business and the World* (New York, Touchstone, 1995); ME Porter and MR Kramer, 'Strategy and Society: The Link between Competitive Advantage and Corporate Social Responsibility' (2006) 84(12) *Harvard Business Review* 76.

[42] I Ayres and J Braithwaite, *Responsive Regulation: Transcending the Deregulation Debate* (Oxford, Oxford University Press, 1992). G Teubner, L Farmer and D Murphy (eds), *Environmental Law and Ecological Responsibility: The Concept and Practice of Ecological Self-Organisation* (Chichester, John Wiley and Sons, 1994).

[43] L Hancher and M Moran, 'Regulatory Spaces' in L Hancher and M Moran (eds), *Capitalism, Culture and Economic Regulation* (Oxford, Clarendon Press, 1989) 278.

[44] H Glasbeek, 'The Corporate Social Responsibility Movement: The Latest in Maginot Lines to Save Capitalism' (1988) 11 *Dalhousie Law Journal* 363.

environmental regulation may sometimes seem static and unresponsive to change, by taking a wider view of environmental governance we can recognise that influential actors such as corporations that are causing Anthropocene-like conditions, themselves may sometimes be in the vanguard of innovative change.

III. Governing the Past and its Restoration

A. The Importance of the Past

A second major temporal shortcoming of environmental law relates to how, and the extent to which, it addresses the past. The Anthropocene is not a recent phenomenon of human history, with its origins traced back several millennia.[45] No doubt, people are often fascinated by natural history, as reflected in the increasing protection of wild and ancestral environments in national parks as well as the memorialisation of nature's relics in lavish museums. Environmental history is also not only a major scientific research endeavour but a popular reading as evident in bestsellers by John McNeil, Tim Flannery and Jared Diamond, and numerous television documentaries on similar subjects.[46] But this interest in nature's past as a source of recreational pleasure or intellectual curiosity rarely translates into restoring the massive past damage inflicted by humankind. At stake is not just the inconvenience and huge cost of restoration; there is also a disturbing degree of temporal amnesia in society in which past losses are deftly ignored or forgotten, or just assumed to be part of a 'natural' landscape since time immemorial.

Disregarding past losses hinders sustainable development because current natural conditions may be too degraded 'to sustain'. Lands may need to be replanted with trees, fish stocks replenished to their former riches and landscapes cleansed of contaminants. An appreciation of history can help curb the scourge of 'shifting' environmental baselines by revealing nature's former riches and opening possibilities to restore them as far as biologically feasible. Restoration can then recapture more complex and robust prior ecological conditions that enable sustainability to be more meaningful. To accept restoration as the necessary twin of sustainability, environmental law must be oriented not only prospectively but also *retrospectively*.

Restoration of damaged environments needs legal backing for a variety of reasons. While eco-restoration projects are sometimes undertaken voluntarily, such as Gondwana Link and Arid Recovery (both in Australia),[47] many people are

---

[45] YN Harari, *Sapiens: A Brief History of Humankind* (New York, Vintage Books, 2014).
[46] T Flannery, *The Eternal Frontier: An Ecological History of North America and Its Peoples* (New York, Grove Press, 2002); J McNeill, *Something New Under the Sun* (New York, WW Norton and Company, 2001); J Diamond, *Collapse: How Societies Choose to Fail or Succeed* (New York, Viking, 2005).
[47] BJ Richardson, 'Reclaiming Nature: Eco-restoration of Liminal Spaces' (2016) 2(1) *Australian Journal of Environmental Law* 1.

unwilling to act voluntarily when the costs of restoration are individual but the benefits are collective. Where restoration requires complex coordination of activities across diverse tenures and many resource users, law is also necessary. In areas controlled by governments, such as national parks, legal duties can help to create political expectations that can influence executive government action as well as enable oversight and enforcement of such obligations by courts.

Recognition in the law of the foregoing issues has tended to be confined to *environmental* restoration rather than *ecological* restoration ('eco-restoration'). The former is of limited spatial and temporal scope, such as rehabilitation of an abandoned mine, while the latter ambitiously seeks systemic improvements to entire ecosystems and landscapes. Environmental rehabilitation of an old mine, as discussed in the next section, can improve the aesthetics or functionality of the targeted site, but eco-restoration re-establishes the 'health, integrity and sustainability' of an entire ecosystem.[48] A failure to appreciate this difference can be confusing, waste resources and lead to unsatisfactory outcomes. Rehabilitation of a former mine may involve replanting an exotic plant because that species can best stabilise the soil and provide adequate ground cover; but that plant may be inappropriate where eco-restoration is sought because it does not provide habitat for native birds or insects.

The following sections examine the variety of approaches to environmental restoration in the law before canvassing some emerging initiatives for the more ambitious variety of eco-restoration. The aim is to highlight the spatial and temporal limitations of most examples of restoration law, and illustrate the few examples of a better approach that environmental law needs to expand in order to respond to the Anthropocene.

B. Environmental Restoration Law

Environmental restoration is not the subject of tailor-made legislation but rather is tackled in an ad hoc manner through miscellaneous regulations. Legal mandates and procedures for environmental restoration are most commonly found in the following six contexts:

1. Regulations governing natural resource users that require rehabilitation of exploited sites such as a former mine or forest coupe.
2. Remediation obligations on owners of brownfield sites contaminated with pollution.
3. Conservation law programs for the recovery of endangered species.
4. Development regulations that allow biodiversity offsets or other environmental offsets to restore degraded areas elsewhere as compensation for new losses caused by the development.

---

[48] International Science & Policy Working Group, *The SER International Primer on Ecological Restoration* (Society for Ecological Restoration, 2004).

5. Law enforcement sanctions that require persons who have unlawfully damaged an environmental place to restore it.
6. General statutory obligations on public agencies, such as conservation agencies that manage national parks, to undertake environmental restoration.

The first listed example commonly involves obligations to remove waste, revegetate and improve site appearances. These requirements may be included in licence conditions for resource developments, especially mining projects, as occurs with South Africa's Mineral and Petroleum Resources Development Act 2002 for instance.[49] The second legal context is remediation of contaminated land, a task usually assigned by authorities to current landowners even if the damage arose under previous occupants. England's Environment Act 1995 and America's American Superfund legislation of 1980 contain representative provisions for restoration of 'brownfield' property.[50] Site remediation can provide important local benefits, especially for public health, but they do not restore ecosystems as such.

Enabling the recovery of endangered species is a third application of restoration law. The United States pioneered endangered species legislation, with the federal Endangered Species Act of 1973 providing a mandate to restore wildlife populations.[51] Recovery programs may be undertaken *in situ* or *ex situ*; the former is more likely to offer collateral environmental benefits such as improved habitat for targeted species as well as associated plants and animals. Some recovery programs aim not to restore biodiversity per se, but rather to rebuild stock numbers for harvesting, as with fisheries management.[52] Recovery programs capture some of the wider ecological context of an endangered creature (eg removing a specific threatening process such as an invasive competitor species), but are not in themselves a mechanism for comprehensive eco-restoration. Furthermore, endangered species laws have tended to be unsuccessful if measured by the number of imperilled species that have recovered to the point where they are safely removed from statutory lists.[53]

Perpetrators of environmental damage may also be obliged to repair the damage as part of a statutory sanction.[54] An example is in Australia's Great Barrier Reef Marine Park Act 1975 (Cth), whose only mechanism for obliging restoration is in response to offences that damage the reef.[55] Similarly, the Wildlife and Natural Environment (Scotland) Act 2011 provides for a restoration order against any

---

[49] s 5(c); see also National Environmental Management Act 2002, s 24G(3).

[50] Environment Act 1995, pt 11A; Comprehensive Environmental Response, Compensation and Liability Act 1980, Public Law 96–510.

[51] 16 US Code, s 1532(3).

[52] eg Fisheries Management Act 1994 (NSW).

[53] L Jacobson, 'Only 1 Percent of Endangered Species List have been Taken Off List, Says Cynthia Lummis' *Politifact* (3 September 2013) www.politifact.com.

[54] See generally ML Larsson (ed), *The Law of Environmental Damage: Liability and Reparation* (The Hague, Martinus Nijhoff Publishers, 1999).

[55] s 61A.

person who unlawfully damaged the environment. The limitation of such provisions is that they do not empower authorities to initiate or require restoration when no offence has occurred, which is a problem given that much damage ensues from legally *authorised* activities such as farms and mines. The Great Barrier Reef itself is damaged by farm run-off and invasive species, having lost about 50 per cent of its coral since 1985 despite the reef having a World Heritage protection status.[56]

Environmental offsets have become another increasingly common context for restoration. Offsets are environmental improvements to counterbalance the residual impacts of a new activity that cannot be mitigated at the development site. An offset may be required as a condition of development approval. Environmental offsets began as informal experiments by regulators seeking creative ways to allow economic developments that otherwise would be environmentally unacceptable. They are increasingly enshrined in special legislation, such as Queensland's Environmental Offsets Act 2014, which tallies nearly 80 pages. Offsets are controversial because of potentially unacceptable trade-offs and difficulties in measuring equivalences in ecological values.[57] There may also be a significant temporal gap between the impacting development and the offsetting gains, and uncertainty whether the gains, such as a replanted forest, will ever accrue. Ensuring retention of an offset in perpetuity, a common condition of offsets approved for mining projects, is also a legal challenge.[58]

The last legal context for environmental restoration is in the broad statutory functions of public agencies that manage or supervise use of natural resources. Such legislation may offer broad plenary powers for restorative interventions, although their often vague, aspirational tone creates room for agencies to do nothing. South Africa's lodestar National Environmental Management Act 1988 includes 'remedying' environmental damage among its core principles to which decision-makers must give 'consideration'.[59] The official objects of South Australia's Environmental Protection Act 1993 include that 'proper weight should be given ... to ... *restoration* and enhancement' and 'to ensure that all reasonable and practicable measures are taken to ... *restore* ... the environment'.[60] But without performance criteria or statutory definition of these terms in these examples, it is unclear how one could determine whether 'proper weight' or 'consideration' has

---

[56] J Eilperin, 'Great Barrier Reef has Lost Half its Corals Since 1985, New Study Says' *Washington Post* (1 October 2012).

[57] P Gibbons and D Lindenmayer, 'Offsets for Land Clearing: No Net Loss or the Tail Wagging the Dog?' (2007) 8(1) *Ecological Management and Restoration* 26.

[58] eg as seen in the conditions in *Ironstone Community Action Group Inc v NSW Minister for Planning and Duralie Coal Pty Ltd* [2011] NSWLEC 195.

[59] s 2(4). See L Kotze and W du Plessis, 'Absolving Historical Polluters from Liability through restrictive judicial interpretation: Some Thoughts on Bareki No v. Gencor Ltd 2007' (2007) 18(1) *Stellenbosch Law Review* 161.

[60] s 10(1)(a)(ii) and 10(1)(b) (my emphasis). The Act contains numerous other references to 'rehabilitation'.

been given. And the assumption that the environment can be 'enhanced' (without further specification of how, when or where) touches on an assumed human optimism to master nature, a stance indelibly tied up in the sociological context of the Anthropocene. A further problem is the presence in legislation of undefined and inconsistent terminology, such as 'remediate', 'repair', 'rehabilitate' or 'restore'.

In sum, the law of environmental restoration is a fragmented hodgepodge, targeting specific issues and impacts, but often at the discretion of governing agencies, and without performance targets and without linkage of restoration interventions to the broader agenda of promoting sustainable development. Rehabilitation of mining sites or recovery of individual species are certainly useful outcomes, but they are insufficient to make much of a dent in slowing the Anthropocene. The continuing decline in ecological conditions in most countries suggests that current restoration efforts are failing to keep up with the intensity of those socio-ecological pressures that are now becoming increasingly vivid and urgent in the Anthropocene.

C. Ecological Restoration Law

Ecological restoration aims to restore ecological structure, complexity, diversity and integrity, as well as to enhance ecological functions such as clean water and fertile soil.[61] Such ambition requires governance systems to manage interventions across expansive land and seascapes, and taking into account many ecological variables including species composition, habitat requirements, historic environmental conditions and possible future changes. The importance of restoring ecosystems to a more viable, healthy state, as against repairing specific sites, has been advocated most strongly by the global 'rewilding' movement. It began with collaboration between American environmentalists David Foreman and Michael Soulé in the 1980s when they established the wildlands project to foster scientific and strategic support for enlarged networks of wilderness regions.[62] Rewilding has garnered popularity lately as high-prolife environmentalists such as George Monbiot have lauded its virtues.[63] Rewilding emphasises re-establishment of keystone species, such as top carnivores, large-scale re-afforestation and other land and seascape improvements, and in some cases removal of inappropriate human infrastructure such as dams and roads.[64] Harvard biologist Edward O Wilson has

---

[61] D Hughes, 'Land Conservation and Restoration: Moving to the Landscape Level' (2002–03) 115 *Vanderbilt Environmental Law Journal* 21; K Suding and others, 'Conservation: Committing to Ecological Restoration' (2015) 348(6235) *Science* 638.

[62] C Sandom and others, 'Rewilding' in D MacDonald and K Wills (eds), *Key Topics in Conservation Biology II* (Chichester, John Wiley & Sons, 2013) 430, 431.

[63] G Monbiot, *Feral. Searching for Enchantment on the Frontiers of Rewilding* (London, Penguin, 2013).

[64] D Foreman, 'The Wildlands Project and the Rewilding of North America' (1998) 76 *Denver University Law Review* 535; M Blumm and A Erickson, 'Dam Removal in the Pacific Northwest: Lessons for the Nation' (2012) 42(4) *Environmental Law* 1043, 1047.

led calls for setting aside 'half of Earth' for nature, as an overall target for rewilding[65] an aspiration that speaks directly to the challenges of the Anthropocene though in the near term it is impractical given the enormous social and economic dislocation. However, rewilding does not necessarily imply re-creation of absolute 'wilderness': the emphasis is making nature 'wild' again in the sense of allowing nature's ecological process to self-direct and self-sustain without human control beyond the initial restorative aid.

Eco-restoration of this genre is challenging. It does not respect the traditional political or legal boundaries of government responsibilities and requires a combination of instruments such as regulations, incentives and agreements. Socially, eco-restoration is also challenging because restoring large areas usually requires the cooperation of many people, such as landowners, nongovernmental organisations, local communities, farmers and businesses. Restoration will be unwelcome by such stakeholders if it creates inequitable hardships. The financial cost of eco-restoration may also be huge, given the size of some projects, sometimes covering thousands of square kilometres of damaged terrain. In an era where governments are shedding responsibilities and cutting budgets, these costs have to be borne increasingly by the private sector and local communities. Eco-restoration thus needs innovative financial mechanisms and civil societal support to gather resources and incentivise action.

Only a few jurisdictions such as the United States have introduced legislation for eco-restoration. One example is the Collaborative Landscape Restoration Program (CLRP), enacted by the US Congress in 2009 under the Omnibus Public Land Management Act.[66] Its statutory objectives are to 'encourage the collaborative, science-based ecosystem restoration of priority forest landscapes' through mechanisms that encourage 'sustainability', facilitate 'the reduction of wildfire management costs', improve 'watershed health' and use 'forest restoration byproducts' to 'offset treatment costs while benefitting local rural economies and improving forest health'.[67] Administered by the federal Department of Agriculture, CLRP eco-restoration projects that are approved by the national panel may receive financing from the CFLR Fund. Approved projects will restore at least 50,000 acres, foster collaboration with local stakeholders and provide local economic and social benefits. The eligible lands for restoration primarily comprise government owned lands, but may include adjacent private properties.

Significantly, the CFLR legislation defines the environmental baseline that funded projects will seek to restore, namely: 'restoration of, the structure and composition of old growth stands according to the pre-fire suppression old growth

[65] JB Mackinnon, *The Once and Future World: Nature As It Was, As It Is, As It Could Be* (Random House Canada, 2013); EO Wilson Biodiversity Foundation, 'E.O. Wilson on Saving Half the Earth' http://eowilsonfoundation.org/e-o-wilson-on-saving-half-the-earth.

[66] Pub L. 111-11; see http://www.fs.fed.us/restoration/CFLRP/index.shtml.

[67] s 4001.

conditions characteristic of the forest type'.[68] The legislation prescribes restoration outcomes that include to 'improve fish and wildlife habitat', 'maintain or improve water quality and watershed function' and 'prevent, remediate, or control invasions of exotic species'.[69] An example of a CFLR initiative is the Selway-Middle Fork Clearwater Project in Idaho, which is restoring 600,000 hectares through decommissioning roads, replacing culverts to restore fish passage, reducing fuel loads in forests and eliminating invasive plants. The project also aims to address the region's chronic unemployment by generating new opportunities for local biomass energy facilities.

Restoration of Florida's Everglades is an example of a state-level restoration initiative. Undertaken pursuant to the Everglades Forever Act 1994[70] and administered by the Florida Department of Environmental Protection and the South Florida Water Management District, the restoration projects aims to improve the Everglades' water quality by reducing phosphorus levels in the ecosystem, restoring water flows in the Everglades, and reducing invasive exotic species of plants and animals. Other goals include water resource development and supply, increased public access and increased protection of land through conservation easements. The Comprehensive Everglades Restoration Plan—the principal policy framework—comprises about 60 civil works projects being implemented over 30 years at an estimated cost of US $7.8 billion.[71] The Everglades Forever Act appears to have been successful, as measured by improving water quality standards (eg from reduced farm and urban run-off), improved stormwater treatment areas and improved habitat conditions for wildlife (eg increase in wading bird pairs).[72]

In the European Community (EC) the Habitats Directive[73] is the foremost legal instrument for promotion of eco-restoration. The directive aims 'to maintain or *restore*, at favourable conservation status, natural habitats and species of wild fauna and flora of Community interest'.[74] The accompanying European Biodiversity Strategy sets the following target for EC member states: '[b]y 2020, ecosystems and their services are maintained and enhanced by establishing green infrastructure and *restoring at least 15 % of degraded ecosystems*'.[75] The Habitats Directive is particularly important given Europe's long history of environmental transformation, but the directive yields no guidance on the historic benchmark for

---

[68] s 4003(c)(D).

[69] s 4003(c)(3).

[70] Fla Stat s 373.4592 (1994).

[71] W Perry, 'Elements of South Florida's Comprehensive Everglades Restoration Plan' (2004) 13(3) *Ecotoxicology* 185.

[72] National Research Council, *Progress Toward Restoring the Everglades: The Fourth Biennial Review, 2012* (Washington DC, National Academies Press, 2012).

[73] European Community, Directive 92/43/EEC of 21 May 1992 on the conservation of natural habitats and of wild fauna and flora [1992] OJ L 206.

[74] Art 2(2). My emphasis.

[75] European Commission, *Our Life Insurance, Our Natural Capital: An EU Biodiversity Strategy to 2020*, Communication from the Commission to the European Parliament, the Council, the Economic and Social Committee and the Committee of the Regions, Com/2011/0244 Final (my emphasis).

re-establishing lost or degraded ecosystems. In some cases eco-restoration projects are being initiated and governed by the private sector alone. Scotland's ancient Caledonian forest has been undergoing restoration since 1989 by a community group called Trees for Life (TfL).[76] The region was once a vast temperate rainforest, but after centuries of clearance, by 1600 AD, the forest was reduced to about 1.5 per cent of its original extent in scattered pockets unsuitable for farming. The TfL's vision is to create a contiguous stretch of forest of some 230,000 hectares, and so far it has planted about 1.5 million trees through volunteered labour.[77] In addition to the re-vegetation, the TFL project is associated with plans to re-introduce extirpated wildlife such as beaver, fish and butterflies. Remarkably, TfL relies largely on persuasion and goodwill with landowners to achieve its goals.

Some of the world's best eco-restoration is happening in New Zealand under the auspices of the Department of Conservation and its community partners who are aggressively combating pests and restoring habitat to save many of the country's endemic, endangered birds.[78] The commitment reflects the avowed importance of eco-restoration in New Zealand legislation. The statutory functions of the New Zealand Game Bird Habitat Trust Board, which administers the Wildlife Act 1953, include several references to restoration, such as: 'to identify and evaluate areas of New Zealand worthy of protection, *restoration* … primarily as game bird habitat and secondarily as habitat for other wildlife' and 'to negotiate, where appropriate, the protection, *restoration* … of game bird habitat with landowners'.[79] The Waitakere Ranges Heritage Area Act 2008 describes the heritage features of the designated heritage area, located near the city of Auckland, as including to 'provide opportunities for ecological *restoration*',[80] and the specified statutory goals for the region include to 'protect, *restore*, and enhance the area and its heritage feature', and 'to maintain the quality and diversity of landscapes in the area by … *restoring* and enhancing degraded landscapes'.[81]

While many ecological restoration projects are underway worldwide, both state-regulated and community-initiated, some may not be making much difference to mitigating the Anthropocene. A global study that reviewed 621 wetland restoration schemes, found that many had failed to meet expected results or match the character of equivalent natural systems, even after many decades.[82] A 2009 meta-survey of 240 studies of ecological recovery in aquatic and terrestrial systems, both passively and actively restored, found that 35 per cent achieved complete recovery

---

[76] See http://treesforlife.org.uk.

[77] A Watson Featherstone, 'The Wild Heart of the Highlands' (1997) 18 *ECOS* 48, 49.

[78] D Butler, T Lindsay and J Hunt, *Paradise Saved* (New Zealand, Random House, 2014).

[79] s 44D(b)–(c) (my emphasis).

[80] s 7(2)(a)(v) (my emphasis).

[81] s 8(g)(ii) (my emphasis).

[82] D Moreno-Mateoos and others, 'Structural and Functional Loss in Restored Wetland Ecosystems' (2012) 10(1) *PLoS Biology* e1001247.

while the remaining studies documented either moderate to limited recovery (35 per cent) or no recovery (30 per cent).[83] But the research also shows that ecological recovery is more likely when there is active restoration rather than no action.[84] The reasons for the success or failure of restoration projects are still being researched,[85] but the law has been identified as one key variable.[86] The quality of environmental law is deficient because of its lack of clarity on restoration standards, insufficient funding mechanisms and limited monitoring of post-restoration work and scope to adaptively adjust implemented approaches. The overall legal architecture must be effective, in terms of clear definitions, goals and workable tools, that communities are empowered as key partners, and that mandates to undertake restoration are not diluted and limited to the lesser forms of *environmental* restoration where the more ambitious approach is necessary.

IV. Conclusions

The pace of ecological degradation around the world continues to exceed the pace at which we can repair it. Global warming, species extinctions and acidifying oceans are among the barrage of grim news encountered daily. Such visions of destruction and decay increasingly substantiate concerns about the Anthropocene. As such, a strategy of sustainable development to maintain rather than enhance ecosystems may often leave ecosystems and biodiversity vulnerable to further decline. Unless human numbers and consumption dramatically fall in the near future, we have no alternative but to invest in the restoration and enhancement of nature.

Unfortunately, eco-restoration remains the poor cousin of sustainable development in the realm of law. Environmental law has a lopsided temporality, framed around a 'present future' outlook in which the priority is governing contemporary activities that pose future risks such as climate change. Sustainability, environmental law's temporal ballast, reinforces this bias through its attention to avoiding risks, mitigating impending damage and other prospective actions. Environmental law must reflect a deeper sense of nature's history, and the massive injuries inflicted on it by our ancestors and ourselves, in order to begin restoring the planet to its former riches.

---

[83] HP Jones and OJ Schmitz, 'Rapid Recovery of Damaged Ecosystems' (2009) 4(5) *PLoS One* e5653.

[84] JM Rey Benayas and others, 'Enhancement of Biodiversity and Ecosystem Services by Ecological Restoration: A Meta-Analysis' (2009) 325 *Science* 1121.

[85] L Wortle, JM Hero and M Howes, 'Evaluating Ecological Restoration Success: A Review of the Literature' (2013) 21(5) *Restoration Ecology* 537.

[86] BJ Richardson and T Lefroy, 'Restoration Dialogues: Improving the Governance of Ecological Restoration' (2016) 24(5) *Restoration Ecology* 668.

In addition to restoring past ecological damage, environmental law must become more temporally nimble, so as to respond to changing environmental conditions, new threats and shifting social demands. The Anthropocene conjures up imagery of dramatic environmental change that must be reckoned with urgently. The Earth is not static, and even a restored environment will require further monitoring and stewardship in years to come. Environmental law needs to jettison the prevailing static model of governance that assumes that new developments are subject to a one-off approval process and existing developments and uses are grandfathered and thus insulated from new and more robust environmental standards. The CSR movement has to some extent filled these lacunae by spurring companies to voluntarily change their environmental policies and practices regardless of the status of official regulations, but CSR carries governance risks that require vigilance by states and civil society organisations.

Both of these challenges of the Anthropocene, healing the past and adapting to change, are crucial dimensions of the temporal morphology of environmental law that must be priorities for the next generation of law reform.

Part 2

Radical Ontologies and Epistemologies for the Anthropocene

4

'Anthropocene, Capitalocene, Chthulucene': Re-encountering Environmental Law and its 'Subject' with Haraway and New Materialism

ANNA GREAR

I. Introduction

This chapter flirts with Donna Haraway's framing of 'Anthropocene, Capitalocene, Chthulucene'[1] in order to reflect upon environmental law and its assumed 'subject'. The chapter uses the threefold 'cene' iteration of its title to develop a progressively deepening critique of the assumptions underlying environmental law and its subject, read—in significant part here—as the *Anthropos* of the Anthropocene trope. The chapter then moves on to reflect on new materialist provocations concerning the possibility of a new materialist environmental legal imaginary.

II. Haraway's Framing: Three Stories

For Haraway, the Anthropocene, Capitalocene, Chthulucene are three framings of the contemporary epoch: 'three stories that are too big, and also not big enough'.[2] The 'Anthropocene', as Haraway notes, is the current proposal put forward for naming the current epoch,[3] though, as Haraway rightly argues, the epoch might better be named the 'Capitalocene'. The Chthulucene, Haraway's third (and countervailing) figuration, is inspired by altogether different energies and ways

---

[1] See 'Anthropocene, Capitolocene, Chthulucene: Staying with the Trouble', a lecture given by Donna Haraway at University of California, Santa Cruz on 5 September 2014, available at https://vimeo.com/97663518.
[2] Haraway, 'Anthropocene, Capitolocene, Chthulucene' (n 1) at 00:18.
[3] PJ Crutzen, 'Geology of Mankind' (2002) 23 *Nature* 415.

of seeing and being—and could, she argues, produce 'something—just maybe—*more liveable*'.[4]

Haraway inaugurates her analysis by pointing to the intellectual revolution underway in the natural sciences—a revolution characterised by the convergence of two powerful understandings. The first understanding is that 'individualism, methodological individualism and human exceptionalism' are now 'literally unthinkable' for the most pioneering work conducted across the disciplines. The second is the insistence in the biological sciences that the 'tissues of being anything at all' are ineluctably caught up in a *multi-species becoming*—the long overdue recognition 'that those who *are* have been in relationality all the way down'.[5] How is it then, Haraway asks, that despite these two seismic shifts in intellectual and cultural understanding, the 'Anthropocene' is the name 'seriously proposed' as the name for the present epoch? Why is the naming of the age thus dominated by 'the figure of the "Anthropos"'—the very figure whose individualism, methodological individualism and exceptionalism are now rendered so unthinkable?

A. Anthropocene: The Hierarchies of Anthropos

Haraway sets out in response to her own question both to 'justify' and to 'trouble' the human centrality figured by the terminology of the Anthropocene.[6] It is important to trouble this human centrality—and to trouble it, in part, for its failure to reflect the exclusions of the *Anthropos* itself. Crutzen's famous 2002 popularisation of Stoermer's original Anthropocene terminology[7] presents 'mankind' (Crutzen's word) as a Promethean species agent whose impacts operate at global scales and lock the planetary future onto a trajectory for which '[t]he impact of current human activities is projected to last over very long periods'.[8] Crutzen reasons that

> [c]onsidering these and many other major and still growing impacts of human activities on earth and atmosphere, and at all, including global scales, it is thus more than appropriate to emphasise the central role of mankind in geology and ecology by using the term 'Anthropocene' for the current geological epoch.[9]

Crutzen's account now represents the mainstream view on the Anthropocene's emergence, and it is an account, arguably, that exposes the distinctively Eurocentric origins of the new geological era characterised by 'large-scale human modification

---

[4] Haraway (n 1) at 01:05.

[5] ibid, 02:20.

[6] ibid, 03.23.

[7] Crutzen, 'Geology of Mankind' (n 3) at 415. As Haraway notes, the term was originally coined by Eugene Stoermer to drive at anthropogenic causes of water acidification and shifts in the nature of life on earth: Haraway (n 1) at 08.27.

[8] Crutzen (n 3); ibid.

[9] PJ Crutzen, 'The Anthropocene' in E Ehlers and T Krafft, *Earth System Science in the Anthropocene* (Berlin and Heidelberg, Springer, 2006) 13–18, 16.

of the Earth System, primarily in the form of climate change, the most salient and perilous transgression of Holocene parameters'.[10] Perhaps the naming of the 'Anthropocene' can be read as an admission, one marked by a problematic Eurocentric hubris; for *Anthropos* is an *intrinsically* Eurocentric, individualist and exceptionalist figuration.[11] Indeed, I have argued elsewhere that the terminology of the 'Anthropocene', circling as it does around the *Anthropos*, reflects the historically persistent centrality of a particular kind of 'human' rather than a species conception.[12]

The 'Anthropocene' discourse—for all its universalistic talk of 'humankind' and of the collective action of humanity the *species agent*—signals a planetary crisis triggered by logics of action reflecting the prioritisation of a far smaller category of humankind than 'humanity' as a whole. It thus remains critically important to ask what exactly the 'Anthropos' of the 'Anthropocene' includes and excludes. What privileges and violations are masked or performed by such terminology? The mainstream deployment of Anthropocene terminology attaches to a mainstream account of Anthropocene origins, which while contested, remains dominant—and relentlessly Eurocentric—criticised for being 'an effort to expand (rather homogenized) European historical experiences, frameworks and chronologies onto the rest of the world … and [for hiding] a disturbing extension of colonial discourse into a postcolonial world'.[13]

There is an important sense, then, in which the terminology of the 'Anthropocene' simply *extends* the logics of Eurocentric human exceptionalism and methodological individualism—the self-same logics that gave rise to the Anthropocene crisis itself. Crutzen traces the Anthropocene's emergence to markers in data 'retrieved from glacial ice cores' betraying a notable intensification of greenhouse gases (especially CO_2, CH_4 and N_2O) dated from the eighteenth century. 'Such a starting date', he observes, 'coincides with James Watt's invention of the steam engine in 1782'.[14] Accordingly, Crutzen installs the ultimate icon of European rational and technical mastery—the steam engine—at the heart of the 'standard Anthropocene narrative'.[15] Indeed, as Malm and Hornborg note, the steam engine is 'often referred to [within mainstream Eurocentric Anthropocene discourse] as the *one artifact* that unlocked the potentials of fossil fuel energy and

---

[10] A Malm and A Hornborg, 'The Geology of Mankind? A Critique of the Anthropocene Narrative' (2014) 1(1) *The Anthropocene Review* 62–69, 63. It is worth noting, of course, that while climate change can be read as the most 'salient and perilous' transgression of Holocene parameters, planetary boundary theory identifies a set of 9 Holocene parameters; see J Rockström and others, 'Planetary Boundaries: Exploring the Safe Operating Space for Humanity' (2009) 14(2) *Ecology and Society* 32 available at: www.ecologyandsociety.org/vol14/iss2/art32/.

[11] A Grear, 'Deconstructing Anthropos: A Critical Legal Reflection on "Anthropocentric" Law and Anthropocene "Humanity"' (2015) 26(3) *Law and Critique* 225-49.

[12] ibid.

[13] KD Morrison, 'Provincializing the Anthropocene' (2015) 673 *Seminar* 75, 75–76.

[14] Crutzen, 'The Anthropocene' (n 9) at 16.

[15] Malm and Hornborg, 'The Geology of Mankind?' (n 10) at 63.

thereby catapulted the human species to full spectrum dominance'.[16] Yet while steam-driven industrialisation is at the heart of the dominant account, and despite the narrow class of European males at the heart of such industrial expansion, for Crutzen (and others) the Anthropocene *also* constructs a forward-facing sense of *species-responsibility* to act in the face of its looming global climate crisis.[17] This claim could be seen as a call for the genesis of an eco-responsible Anthropocene environmental subject—and certainly such a call for responsibility is important. Yet, there is good reason to be wary of the implicit universalism folded into such a call (and its related potential Anthropocene ethic) and imported, by implication, into the dominant Eurocentric account of Anthropocene inauguration—for such universalism—as critical theoretical approaches to law suggest—is typically highly particularistic in real terms.

It is accordingly important to pause, at this point, to draw explicit attention to the narrowness of the *Anthropos*. Indeed, Haraway argues that the best figuration for *Anthropos* is 'fossil-making man burning fossils'.[18] 'Fossil-making man burning fossils' is scarcely representative of all humanity—*even now*. Let us therefore examine the implicit universality of Anthropocene 'humanity'—whether implied by the *species* language of 'mankind' as originator of the epoch or reflected in 'humanity's' responsibility in the face of the looming climate crisis (arguably the Anthropocene's most deadly marker).

Critical theorists of all kinds tend to be suspicious, as was just implied, in all disciplinary traditions, of universalising assumptions. Yet even critical theorists can be attracted to the allure of an Anthropocene universal as an important idea responding to the need for an Anthropocene ethic. Chakrabarty, one of the few critical theorists directly to engage the Anthropocene and its implications, suggests that the 'crisis of climate change appeals to our sense of human universals while challenging at the same time our capacity for historical understanding'.[19]

Historical understanding is challenged, Chakrabarty argues, because climate scientists have 'unwittingly destroying the artificial but time-honored distinction between natural and human histories' and because 'the human being has become something much larger than the simple biological agent that he or she always has been. Humans now wield a geological force'[20] as a collectivity. In response to this collective force of human species-impact, Chakrabarty poses two questions to the idea of the Anthropocene human universal. First, he asks whether it is fair to include the 'poor of the world', whose carbon footprint is small, in the notion of responsibility for the genesis of the Anthropocene.[21] And secondly, he asks whether the climate crisis presents a role for a universal human species agent. Chakrabarty's first question directs a powerful critical anxiety towards Crutzen's

---

[16] ibid. Emphasis added.
[17] Crutzen (n 3).
[18] Haraway (n 1) at 10.02.
[19] D Chakrabarty, 'The Climate of History: Four Theses' (2009) 35 *Critical Inquiry* 197–222, 201.
[20] ibid, 206.
[21] ibid, 217.

easy-sounding assertion of future-facing Anthropocene species responsibility: Can a generalised notion of Anthropocene species responsibility (facing back-wards, and by implication, forwards also) be so easily accepted? Or should there be a more carefully calibrated attentiveness to unevenness?[22] Chakrabarty's first question in a sense also sets up the answer to his second question. Chakrabarty is well aware of historical patterns of oppression, of global unevenness, but for him, climate change—*unlike* the crisis of capitalism—necessitates embracing a 'nega-tive universal' because climate precarity co-situates us all in so far as there is no escape for the privileged. The climate crisis, Chakrabarty asserts, presents a role for a universal human species agent, because, he reasons, '[u]nlike in the crises of capitalism, there are *no lifeboats here for the rich and the privileged* (witness the drought in Australia or recent fires in the wealthy neighborhoods of California)'.[23]

Accordingly, while Chakrabarty clearly affirms the familiar critical hermeneutic of suspicion directed at the production of a universal 'humanity', suggesting—rightly—that it remains 'an effective critical tool in dealing with national and global formations of domination',[24] he nevertheless argues that in the face of the climate crisis, the utility of this approach breaks down. This is because 'inchoate figures of us all and other imaginings of humanity invariably haunt our sense of the current crisis'—and, because the longstanding wall between natural and human history is breached by the emergence of the Anthropocene, 'we appear to have become one at the level of the species'.[25] This, then, is a new universal born of the 'emergent, new universal history of humans that flashes up in the moment of danger that is climate change'.[26] It is, Chakrabarty insists,

> a question of a human collectivity, an us, pointing to a figure of the universal that escapes our capacity to experience the world. It is more like a universal that arises from a shared sense of a catastrophe. It calls for a global approach to politics without the myth of a global identity, for, unlike a Hegelian universal, it cannot subsume particularities. We may provisionally call it a 'negative universal history'.[27]

This is not universalism as usual. Particularities are not subsumed. Yet, despite Chakrabarty's important critical rejection of the 'the myth of a global identity', a critical question persists: 'Is it not risky to accept the construction of a negative formation of humanity as a category that stretches to all human beings, *all other differences notwithstanding*?'[28] And is it not equally risky, we might add, to construct a future-facing Anthropocene ethic addressing a human *species* responsibility *all other differences notwithstanding*?

---

[22] On the centrality of unevenness to the global order, see R Radhakrishnan, *Theory in an Uneven World* (Oxford, Blackwell, 2003).

[23] Chakrabarty, 'The Climate of History' (n 19) at 221. Emphasis added.

[24] ibid, 221.

[25] ibid.

[26] ibid.

[27] ibid, 222.

[28] R Braidotti, *The Posthuman* (Cambridge, Polity, 2013) 88. Emphasis original.

Focusing directly on Chakrabarty's pivotal assertion that there are 'no lifeboats here for the rich and privileged', Malm and Hornborg point out that this assertion

> blatantly overlooks the realities of differentiated vulnerability on all scales of human society: witness Katrina in black and white neighborhoods of New Orleans, or Sandy in Haiti and Manhattan, or sea level rise in Bangladesh and the Netherlands, or practically any other impact, direct or indirect, of climate change. For the foreseeable future—indeed, as long as there are human societies on Earth—there *will* be lifeboats for the rich and privileged. If climate change represents a form of apocalypse, it is not universal, but uneven and combined: *the species is as much an abstraction at the end of the line as at the source.*[29]

The hermeneutics of suspicion, it turns out, cannot be so easily laid aside. And, relatedly, we can add that *Anthropos* cannot be assumed to represent 'us all' in 'our' 'moment of danger'. There may indeed be a growing sense of catastrophe concerning the future of humanity as a species on earth, but that sense of catastrophe is not monolithic or evenly felt. Impending (and actual) climate catastrophe for some is most emphatically not what it is for others. Even the sense of catastrophe may not yet (if ever) be meaningfully *shared*. If anything, the Anthropocene present is marked by a rapidly expanding set of (all too often juridically mediated) divisions: the rift between the richest and the rest; the multiplication of zones of exclusion and marginalisation; deepening entanglements of oppression between marginalised humans, non-human animals and ecosystems at the hands of the neoliberal order; corporate land grabs forcing communities in the Global South off their lands in order to securitise the Global North; profoundly uneven distributions of vulnerability and resilience; and the intensifying eco-governmentality (and 'neoliberalisation of nature') enacted by international environmental law and governance structures.

It seems implausible that the Anthropocene signals the emergence of a new universal—even a negative one—at least *not yet*—and despite the urgent need—as Haraway puts it—'to be less parochial'.[30] Parochiality—particularly when it comes to questions of distributive and environmental justice—seems if anything to intensify in response to climate-driven mass migrations, which are met by border-protective impulses and a generalised fear of 'the other'. The recently erected fences and barbed wire in Europe eloquently endorse Malm and Hornborg's critique of Chakrabarty's assertion that there are no lifeboats here for the rich and privileged. The parochial grabbing of lifeboats, and the desperate consignment of refugees and migrants to distinctly leaky boats, if anything, seems virulent of late. Thus, while climate pressures certainly point to a broadening awareness of

---

[29] Here the authors cite A Malm, 'Sea Wall Politics: Uneven and Combined Protection of the Nile Delta Coastline in the Face of Sea Level Rise' (2013) 39 *Critical Sociology* 803–32; A Malm and S Esmailian, 'Ways in and out of Vulnerability to Climate Change: Abandoning the Mubarak Project in the Northern Nile Delta Egypt' (2012) 45 *Antipode* 474–92. Emphasis added.

[30] Haraway (n 1) at 6.36.

catastrophe—and perhaps, given the evidence of emergent post-capitalist modes of social organisation, might signal a more inclusive and empathic sense of 'the human' in the making—the patterns of *Anthropos* and the patterns of privilege persist and 'the species [remains] as much an abstraction at the end of the line as at the source'.[31]

These patterns, I suggest, point directly towards the 'Capitalocene', which is, Haraway suggests, a more accurate term for the present epoch than the 'Anthropocene'.

B. Capitalocene: Entanglements of Law, Coloniality and Environmentality

If the Anthropocene is to have its full significance for environmental law, it must surely implicate the need to reflect upon the global juridical order. After all, as Haraway points out, the Anthropocene is intrinsically connected to the scale of the 'global', including in the policy imagination of bodies such as the Intergovernmental Panel on Climate Change. Yet the global—as Haraway also points out (and as longstanding critiques of universalism converge to insist)—is *also highly specific* in terms of its historical and material origins and development.[32] This specificity yet again raises the question of the identity of the *Anthropos*. If we were to use any single term to capture the trajectories leading to the current crisis and to the threatened mass extinction of species in the age of *Anthropos*, Haraway suggests, then that term should be 'Capitalocene'.[33]

The 'Capitalocene' is a term that resonates deeply with critical legal accounts of the current international juridical order and its origins in European colonial predation.[34] Such critical accounts converge powerfully with Haraway's description of the Capitalocene as a set of processes characterised by 'primitive accumulations and extractions, organisations of labour and productions of technology of particular kinds for the extraction and maldistribution of profit'.[35]

Malm and Hornborg's critical account of the 'Anthropocene' *also* strongly connects with critical accounts of the origins of the contemporary international legal order. Malm and Hornborg rightly argue that industrialisation—the origins of the Anthropocene on the dominant account—was fundamentally capitalist in ambition and motivation—and inseparable from European (especially British) colonialism. The authors point out that the origins of the Anthropocene lie in an expansion of British appropriative power exercised through the deployment of

---

[31] Malm and Hornborg (n 10).
[32] Haraway (n 1) at 14.02.
[33] ibid, 16.35.
[34] A Anghie, *Imperialism, Sovereignty and the Making of International Law* (Cambridge, Cambridge University Press, 2005).
[35] Haraway (n 1) at 16.51.

steam-power as a weapon by 'an infinitesimal fraction of the population of *Homo sapiens* in the early 19th century':

> A scrutiny of the transition to fossil fuels in 19th-century Britain … reveals the extent to which the historical origins of anthropogenic climate change were predicated on highly inequitable global processes from the start. The rationale for investing in steam technology at this time was geared to the opportunities provided by the constellation of a largely depopulated New World, Afro-American slavery, the exploitation of British labour in factories and mines, and the global demand for inexpensive cotton cloth. Steam-engines were not adopted by some natural-born deputies of the human species: by the nature of the social order of things, they could only be installed by the owners of the means of production. A tiny minority even in Britain, this class of people comprised an infinitesimal fraction of the population of *Homo sapiens* in the early 19th century. Indeed, a clique of white British men literally pointed steam-power as a weapon—on sea and land, boats and rails—against the best part of humankind, from the Niger delta to the Yangzi delta, the Levant to Latin America. Capitalists in a small corner of the Western world invested in steam, laying the foundation stone for the fossil economy.[36]

While Haraway dates the origin of the Capitalocene in trade relations existing before the Industrial Revolution, capitalism's long dependency upon a fossil fuel economy[37] and the convergent nature of capitalist impulses in the genesis of the fossil fuel-dependent international legal order explain precisely why the global juridical structures now in place 'lock in' the dependency of the global economic system on fossil fuels[38]—and why the international legal order is dominated by *Anthropos* as 'fossil-making man burning fossils'.

Anghie, in *Imperialism, Sovereignty and the Making of International Law*,[39] notes the combination of colonial suppression of 'Third World' peoples and the ambitions of Northern states for 'natural resources' to feed their increasingly industrialised social order as being key determinants of nineteenth-century Northern colonial and imperial expansionism.[40] He argues that the 'importance of raw materials to the global economy was always well understood by the more powerful States',[41] and that 'imperial expansion was powerfully motivated by the desire of colonial states to exploit the resources of non-European territories'.[42] In this highly uneven process, 'Western trading and mining companies' acquired 'extraordinarily favourable' terms in the then nascent system of colonial state relations, achieving such terms by a combination of direct force and legal sleight of hand in the form

---

[36] Malm and Hornborg (n 10) at 63–64.

[37] M Koch, *Capitalism and Climate Change: Theoretical Discussion, Historical Development and Policy Responses* (Basingstoke, Palgrave Macmillan, 2012). See also P Newell and M Paterson, *Climate Capitalism: Global Warming and the Transformation of the Global Economy* (Cambridge, Cambridge University Press, 2010).

[38] J Dangerman and HJ Schellnhuber, 'Energy Systems Transformation' (2013) PNAS E549-E558, available at www.pnas.org/cgi/doi/10.1073/pnas.1219791110.

[39] Anghie, *Imperialism, Sovereignty and the Making of International Law* (n 34).

[40] ibid, 211.

[41] ibid 212.

[42] ibid 211.

of 'agreements, which possessing a legal form, were hardly comprehensible to the natives who were ostensibly signatories to them'.[43] The very foundational purpose of international law was deeply capitalistic and predatory. As Simons puts it,

> [t]he underlying purpose of international law that was developed in the context of the colonial and post-colonial eras was precisely the promotion and protection of economic interests of the North. Thus, as newly independent states emerged from colonial rule as sovereign entities and attempted to assert their sovereignty and establish control over their natural resources, Northern states responded using legal doctrines such as state succession, acquired rights, contracts and consent to protect the interests of their corporate nationals in these states and to resist the attempts by these new sovereign actors to establish a new international economic order which included their own sovereignty over their natural resources.[44]

These dynamics are centrally important to understanding the climate crisis itself as a *crisis of human hierarchy*.[45] Woven into this crisis of hierarchy—and inseparable from the rationalistic orders of valuation placed upon the human species— are the ecocidal implications of European rationalism and capitalism[46] and the colonial practices and laws enacting those impulses.[47] International law, capitalism and colonialism are all interwoven with Eurocentric (and now Global North) impulses and logics of action fully discernible in the Anthropocene crisis. There is, therefore, great force in Haraway's contention that the Anthropocene is better understood as the Capitalocene. The Anthropocene-Capitalocene is an epoch— after all—of eco-violation reflecting well-practised, patterned and predictable global and globalising distributions of intra-species and inter-species injustice.[48] So foundational to the Anthropocene-Capitalocene are such injustices that the current ecological crisis cannot really be understood without them.[49]

---

[43] ibid.

[44] P Simons, 'International Law's Invisible Hand and the Future of Corporate Accountability for Violations of Human Rights' (2013) 3(1) *Journal of Human Rights and the Environment* 5–43, 21.

[45] A Grear, '"Towards Climate Justice"? A Critical Reflection on Legal Subjectivity and Climate Injustice: Warning Signals, Patterned Hierarchies, Directions for Future Law and Policy' (2014) Special Edition *Journal of Human Rights and the Environment* 103–33.

[46] C Merchant, *The Death of Nature: Women, Ecology and the Scientific Revolution* (New York, Harper Collins 1980); A Geisinger, 'Sustainable Development and the Domination of Nature: Spreading the Seed of the Western Ideology of Nature' (1999) 27 *Boston College Environmental Affairs Law Review* 43, 52–58.

[47] C Gonzalez, 'Bridging the North-South Divide: International Environmental Law in the Anthropocene' (2015) 32 *Pace Environmental Law Review* 407–34.

[48] See eg A Collard and J Contrucci, *The Rape of the Wild: Man's Violence against Animals and the Earth* (Bloomington, Indiana University Press, 1988); DA Nibert, *Animal Rights, Human Rights: Entanglements of Oppression and Liberation* (Oxford, Rowman and Littlefield, 2002); DA Nibert, *Animal Oppression and Human Violence: Domesecration, Capitalism, and Global Conflict* (New York, Columbia University Press, 2013).

[49] This is a central concern for Malm and Hornborg (n 10). See also the work of Bookchin, for whose social ecology account *intra*-species practices of domination were causally decisive for practices of ecological destruction; M Bookchin, *The Ecology of Freedom: The Emergence and Dissolution of Hierarchy* (Oakland, AK Press, 2005).

The 'subject' at the centre of the Anthropocene trope thus ineluctably reflects hierarchies foundational to European rationalism.[50] *Anthropos* is in a very real sense, the quintessential European (and then 'Western') rational subject—and, accordingly, also law's archetypical subject. Unsurprisingly, then, the subject-object relationalities of *Anthropos* are fully visible in environmental law: the (legal) subject provides the 'centre' (the very site of mastery, panoptic in its knowledge)[51] set against 'nature' or 'environment' as the backdrop or context for the rational subject's agency.[52]

The rationality of *Anthropos* is thus the self-same rationality that defines the subject-object relations undergirding the methodological individualism and human exceptionalism that Haraway rightly calls out as insupportable. Such rationality, it must be recalled, belongs only to the masculinist Eurocentric trope— all other human beings remain complexly immersed—to varying and shifting degrees—in the relative irrationality of embodiment, the primitive, the feminised, the animal, the natural—in all that needs civilising and/or ordering.[53]

This rationality was fully operative in coloniality and in the 'civilising mission' of early European expansionism. A range of critical accounts of the colonial foundations of the international legal order thus thoroughly support Haraway's contention that the current epoch is best captured by the terminology of the Capitalocene. And while Haraway argues that the Capitalocene predates the height of European colonial expansionism (in earlier trade relations), there can be no doubt that the Capitalocene reaches its apotheosis in the drives and ambitions of capitalism as an imperialistic ideology.[54] The figuration of the Capitalocene thus drives directly at the history and the present of the radical unevenness characterising the contemporary neoliberal juridical order and its antecedent periods of primitive capitalist accumulation.[55]

Turning now to an explicit consideration of environmental law, it could be argued that environmental law can be read as a *reaction to* the eco-destructiveness of the Anthropocene-Capitalocene, and to the ecological fallout of the imperatives driving it. However, even if that argument drives at a degree of reality, it

---

[50] Grear, 'Deconstructing Anthropos' (n 11).

[51] HY Yung, 'Merleau-Ponty's Transversal Geophilosophy and Sinic Aesthetics of Nature' in SL Cataldi and WS Hamrick, *Merleau-Ponty and Environmental Philosophy: Dwelling on the Landscapes of Thought* (New York, State University of New York Press 2007) 235–57, 239.

[52] As Weber puts it, since Descartes 'the sciences, whether natural, social or economic, try to grasp the world as if it were a dead, mechanical process that could be understood through statistical or cybernetic analyses … [as a] dead *res extensa*': A Weber, *Enlivenment: Towards a Fundamental Shift in the Concepts of Culture and Politics* (Berlin, Heinrich Böll Foundation, 2012) 14.

[53] See, for a fascinating example, M Dekha, 'Intersectionality and Post-humanist Visions of Equality' (2008) 23 *Wisconsin Journal of Law, Gender and Society* 249–67.

[54] EM Woods, *Empire of Capital* (London, Verso, 2005).

[55] See eg WH Ricketts Curtler, *The Enclosure and Redistribution of our Land* (Clarendon, Oxford, 1920); L Westra, 'Environmental Rights and Human Rights: The Final Enclosure Movement' in R Brownsword (ed), *Global Governance and the Quest for Justice: Volume IV: Human Rights* (Oxford, Hart Publishing, 2004) 107–19.

is abundantly clear that environmental law is *also* entirely continuous with the assumptions at work in the Anthropocene-Capitalocene.

Reflecting first upon the environmental legal subject, it seems that environmental law's central rational subject is indeed none other than *Anthropos*. The environmental legal subject, if anything, presents a site at which relatively disembodied subject-object relations emerge with particular clarity: This subject stands emphatically at the assumed onto-epistemic 'centre' beyond which its 'others'—*especially* 'nature' as 'the environment'—range along a spectrum of objectifications. Environmental law's quintessential subject is the pivot around which 'the environment' revolves.[56] This masterful subject is the very subject assumed by the rationalistic, hierarchical scales of value decisive to the expansion of European capitalist ambition across the globe.[57] And even in these more eco-conscious times—even in the light of an Anthropocene awakening to the dark side of capitalism's 'progress'—marginalised, colonialised 'others' are still rendered susceptible to acts and forms of domination legitimated by Global North assumptions of rationalistic superiority and mastery enacted from 'the centre'.[58] If anything, the centre-periphery trajectories implicit in the Anthropocene-Capitalocene are more intense: the forms of eco-governmentality operationalised in contemporary environmental law—legitimated by the concern of 'the centre' with the 'global' management of the planet in the name of various forms of 'security' (Global North (food-water-energy) security)—are widely accused of being intensifying spasms of neocolonial domination.[59] For example, Luke, drawing on Foucault's brilliant analysis of the production of biopolitical subjects and on the implications of Foucault's analysis for the fate of 'the environment', argues that contemporary environmentalism (which includes environmental law and governance) enacts forms of eco-knowledge and geopower reflecting a distinctively neoliberal 'environmentality'.[60]

The subject-object relations of the Anthropocene-Capitalocene are fully visible in Luke's analysis. First, there is the binary cut between *Anthropos* and 'nature' thoroughly implicit in Luke's reflection upon how 'nature' became 'environment' as the result of 'eco-diction'—the discursive iteration through which 'nature' was made to 'speak' as 'environment'.[61] This process, placed by Luke between the 1960s

---

[56] A Philippopoulos-Mihalopoulos, 'Towards a Critical Environmental Law' in A Philippopoulos-Mihalopous (ed), *Law and Ecology: New Environmental Foundations* (Abingdon, Routledge, 2011) 18–38, 22: the word derives from '*en*' (in) and '*virer*' ('to turn')—'This implies an inside that stands erect and an outside that surrounds us, the dervish-like outside that whirls like frilly skirt around a stable pivot … not only stable, fixed and unyielding but significantly "central"'.

[57] G Huggan and H Tiffin, 'Green Postcolonialism' (2007) 9(1) *Interventions: International Journal of Postcolonial Studies* 1–11.

[58] See ibid; and Gonzalez, 'Bridging the North-South Divide' (n 47).

[59] Geisinger, 'Sustainable Development and the Domination of Nature' (n 46).

[60] TW Luke, 'On Environmentality: Geo-Power and Eco-Knowledge in the Discourses of Contemporary Environmentalism' (1995) 31 *Cultural Critique* 57–81.

[61] ibid, 59.

and the 1990s, produced a terminology that remains underdetermined, because even expert discourse on 'the environment', Luke argues, presents no clear definition of what 'the environment' actually is—other than something so all-embracing as to lack definitional precision.[62] Luke turns, in a search for clarity, to a genealogical analysis of the word 'environment', tracing it back to its historical linguistic roots.

> In its original sense, which is borrowed by English from Old French, an environment is an action resulting from, or the state of being produced by a verb: 'to environ'. And environ-ing as a verb is, in fact, a type of strategic action. To environ is to encircle, encompass, envelop, or enclose … to environ a site or a subject is to beset, beleaguer, or besiege that place or person. An environment, as either the means of such activity or the product of these actions, now might be read in a more suggestive manner. It is the encirclement, circumscription, or beleaguerment of places and persons in a strategic disciplinary policing of space.[63]

This analysis, Luke continues, aptly exposes the nature of environmentalised places as 'sites of supervision'—'environments can be disassembled, recombined and subjected to the disciplinary designs of expert management … redirected to fulfil the ends of other … scripts': 'Environing', Luke argues, 'engenders "environmentality", which embeds instrumental rationalities in the policing of ecological spaces'.[64] In short, Luke's analysis reflects the governmentality of Anthropocene-Capitalocene subject-object relations, with their long provenance in the Cartesian foundations of the modern worldview. In a sense, what Luke describes is precisely a logic of rational agency carving 'nature' up (always set against the subject's panoptic mastery) into 'environment'—the dicing and slicing of the living order into eco-enclosures. Needless to say, environmental law's classifications, lists, definitions and so forth are legible as precisely such discursive-juridical (and material) enclosures.

   And unsurprisingly, such environmentality reflects predictable Capitalocene trajectories ordering the entrenched concatenation of colonialisms, appropriations and maldistributions of profit and—increasingly—the commodification and financialisation of 'nature' itself—so thoroughly associated with neoliberalism. 'The environment' is an increasingly policed space for impulses of financial accumulation, expressing logics of (capitalistic, Global North-favouring) market-based development discourse as a rationalisation for neoliberal governmentality.[65]

---

[62] ibid.
[63] ibid, 64.
[64] ibid, 65.
[65] P McMichael, 'The Land Grab and Corporate Food Regime Restructuring' (2012) 39(3–4) *The Journal of Peasant Studies* 681–701; C Corson and KI MacDonald, 'Enclosing the Global Commons: the Convention on Biological Diversity and Green Grabbing' (2012) 39(2) *The Journal of Peasant Studies* 263–83.

As Luke puts it, as 'new mediations of development and growth were constructed after 1945, the geo-power/eco-knowledge nexus of environmentalization came to comfortably supplement the high technology, capital intensive development strategies that have since been implemented'.[66]

The scripts now driving such acts of environing are profoundly neoliberal—and complexly continuous with earlier colonising impulses lying at the dark heart of the Anthropocene-Capitalocene. The resource managerialism at the heart of contemporary responses to environmental challenges is operationalised by dense networks of corporate-managerial-administrative regulatory regimes facilitating a spectacular (if historically familiar) range of 'land grabs' and dispossessions in the name of 'environmental protection'. Whether in the Convention on Biological Diversity (the CBD), or in practices around food and biofuels production, there is an extensive, planetary land grab underway, driven by the 'rational planning of the planet for Northern security'.[67] This falls out into the extensive and intensive 'environing' of the Global South—fully visible in predatory patterns of dispossession and domination that reflect the histories of enclosure, land grab and violence long associated with capitalism and its voracious, colonising dynamics.

Accordingly, the subject assumed by environmental law—the meta-agency expressed through environmental legal rationality—is, in the final analysis, *Anthropos* as 'fossil-making' man re-birthing himself: *Anthropoos* re-presented as eco-trope rationalising forms of geopower and eco-knowledge in the name of 'ecological sustainability', the 'global commons', 'food security' and other forms of future-facing 'justifications' deployed in service of the Capitalocene. Indeed, the burning of fossils is now *facilitated* by market mechanisms enabling carbon leakage and unjust distributions of responsibility.[68] Meanwhile, the eco-market mandates the commodification of biodiversity and generates new speculative forms of deadly commodities trading on species extinction, food crisis, water shortage and the like.

The subject of environmental law in the Capitalocene increasingly enacts iteratively deepening forms of neoliberal eco-governmentality—and—as Luke argues, 'to the degree that modern subjectivity is a two-sided power/knowledge relation, scientific-professional declarations … essentially describe a new mode of environmentalized subjectivity'.[69]

What hope and what forms of environmental law and perhaps even insurgent eco-subjectivity might the trope of the Chthulucene offer?

---

[66] Luke, 'On Environmentality' (n 60) at 67.
[67] McMichael, 'The Land Grab and Corporate Food Regime Restructuring' (n 65) at 685, citing W Sachs (ed), *Global Ecology* (London, Zed Press, 1993) 20.
[68] See eg R Aichele and G Felbermayr, 'Kyoto and Carbon Leakage: An Empirical Analysis of the Carbon Content of Bilateral Trade' (2015) 97 *The Review of Economics and Statistics* 104–55.
[69] Luke (n 60) at 75.

C. Chthulucene—Materiality's Semiosis and the Future of Environmental Legal Subjectivity

At the heart of the questions just posed lies a central challenge: can environmental law exceed the centripetal impulse of neoliberal governmentality? Can environmental law respond to alternative modes of knowing and coordination? Can environmental law respect multiple forms of sharing the world?

Such sharing would need to recognise the companion status of all species and systems entangled in the dance of life itself—to reflect, in short, the grounding, complex energies of the Chthulucene.

Let us reflect first upon Haraway's framing of the Chthulucene. Haraway emphasises two main thoughts: first, she points to the way in which biology is shattering the myth of human exceptionalism and individualism, arguing that '[w]e are all lichens now. We have never been individuals. From anatomical, physiological, evolutionary, developmental, philosophic, economic—I don't care what perspective—we are all lichens now'.[70] Haraway emphasises, also, the tentacularity associated with the Chthulucene. Chthulu is famously the lead character in a famous short story, *The Call of Chthulu*, published in 1926, a creation of HP Lovecraft[71]—but this is not what Haraway references. While the name Chthulu is likely drawn from the word 'chthonic', meaning 'subterranean' with its invocations of the underworld, and while Chthulu is part-octopus, part-man, part-dragon with a tentacled head—an image reflected by Haraway's deployment of similar images of facial tentacularity on slides drawn from science fiction, Haraway insists that she is not naming her epoch after the Lovecraft's 'misogynist racial-nightmare monster Cthulhu'

> but rather after the diverse earth-wide tentacular powers and forces and collected things with names like Naga, Gaia, Tangaroa... and many many more. 'My' Chthulucene, even burdened with its problematic Greek-ish tendrils, entangles myriad temporalities and spatialities and myriad intra-active entities-in-assemblages—including the more-than-human, other-than-human, inhuman, and human-as-humus.[72]

Tentacularity, I suggest, has distinctive epistemological implications that will be explored below. For now, however, we will turn our attention back to the significance of the claim that 'we are all lichens now' and to Haraway's distinctively new materialist entanglement of spatialities, temporalities and lively assemblages.

Haraway's language draws on a phrase from Scott Gilbert, who (with Sapp and Tauber) proposes the necessity for a symbiotic view of life, insisting that 'we have

---

[70] Haraway (n 1) at 22.33.

[71] HP Lovecraft, 'The Call of Cthulhu' in ST Joshi (ed), *The Dunwhich Horror and Others* (Sauk City, WI, Arkham House, 1984) [1928]: Of Chthulu, Lovecraft writes, '[i]t represented a monster of vaguely anthropoid outline, but with an octopus-like head whose face was a mass of feelers, a scaly, rubbery-looking body, prodigious claws on hind and fore feet, and long, narrow wings behind'.

[72] D Haraway, 'Anthropocene, Capitalocene, Plantationocene, Chthulucene: Making Kin' (2015) 6 *Environmental Humanities* 159–65, 160.

never been individuals'.[73] Gilbert and others begin by noting the way in which individualism, which emerged 'with the appearance of the independent citizen' (a quintessentially Eurocentric construction reflecting the ontology of *Anthropos*) shaped biological assumptions concerning the existence of individual animals, plants and the like, before such individualist assumptions gave way to systems as complements to individuals in the second half of the nineteenth century with the emergence of ecology.[74] With the emergence of ecology, the rigidly binary Cartesian separation between (disembodied, rational) humanity and *the rest* begins to fray, although it is clear from the phrasing used by Gilbert and others that the individual continued, even with the emergence of new system-facing conceptions, to be regarded as an ontologically significant referent. Gilbert and others note, however, that new technologies problematise the status of individuality (and, necessarily therefore, individualism). Hence, new technologies already in existence

> dramatically transform our conceptions ... [and] have not only revealed a microbial world of complex and intermingled relationships—not only among microbes, but also between microscopic and macroscopic life. These discoveries have profoundly challenged the generally accepted view of 'individuals'. Symbiosis is becoming a core principle of contemporary biology, and it is replacing an essentialist conception of 'individuality' with a conception congruent with the larger systems approach now pushing the life sciences in diverse directions. These findings lead us into directions that transcend the self/non-self, subject-object dichotomies that have characterized Western thought.[75]

Turning then to Haraway's insistence that we are all lichens, it is clear that she is pointing to a biological reality capable, if we embrace it, of fundamentally transforming the boundaries of the thinkable. Lichens have been defined as 'symbiotic associations between two (or sometimes more) entirely different types of micro-organism'.[76] Importantly, though, unlike the many other examples of symbiosis common in the living order, 'lichens are unique because they look and behave quite differently from their component organisms. So lichens are regarded as organisms in their own right'.[77] Gilbert, Sapp and Tauber argue that all 'animals are symbiotic complexes of many species living together'.[78] This includes humans. 'We' are lichen now, and increasingly recognising ourselves as such, because new technologies enable a fuller appreciation of the symbiotic generativity of life. In a symbiotic view, the 'all' of the 'we' is profoundly interspecies—(or intra-species if we count 'earthlings' in an all embracing way)—a lively entanglement of beings and systems that are never individual in the traditional Western sense. Haraway's Chthulucene

---

[73] S Gilbert, J Sapp and AI Tauber, 'A Symbiotic View of Life: We Have Never Been Individuals' (2012) 87(4) *The Quarterly Review of Biology* 326–41.

[74] ibid, 326.

[75] ibid, 326 (original citations omitted).

[76] J Deacon, 'The Microbial World: Lichens' (Institute of Cell and Molecular Biology, The University of Edinburgh) available at: http://archive.bio.ed.ac.uk/jdeacon/microbes/lichen.htm.

[77] ibid.

[78] Gilbert and others, 'A Symbiotic View of Life' (n 73) at 326–27.

is a world relational 'all the way down'—and framing the Chthulucene as an epoch is an invitation to celebrate the porous hybridities, the tangles and knots and dynamic materialities of the world at multiple scales.

The interwoven becomings and symbiotic complexes at the heart of this invitation are particularly well reflected by New Materialism as a broad contemporary school of thought. Just as the biological sciences incontrovertibly reveal the radical continuities between complex lively relationalities at all scales, from the microscopic to the macroscopic, so New Materialist accounts point to the assemblages between multiple factors that operate at multiple scales. New Materialists also point towards the lively meaning-making capacities of materiality itself—to materiality's semiosis.

Embracing and responding to the ethical implications of materiality seems fundamentally urgent if environmental law is to become responsive to the implications and promise of the Chthulucene. Indeed, as Coole and Frost argue in the opening sentences of their book, *New Materialisms: Ontology, Agency and Politics*,[79] 'foregrounding material factors and reconfiguring our very understanding of matter are prerequisites for any plausible account of co-existence and its conditions in the 21st century'.[80]

Indeed, foregrounding material factors and reconfiguring our very understanding of matter will *necessarily* transform law's fundamental construct of 'the environment' because what is at stake is precisely

> nothing less than a challenge to some of the most basic assumptions that have underpinned the modern world, including its normative sense of the human and its beliefs about human agency, but also regarding its material practices such as the ways we labor on, exploit and interact with nature.[81]

Environmental law's existing ontology is profoundly at stake in New Materialist insights that go to the very heart of the question of what matter *is* and, relatedly, to the question of what the *ethical implications of matter are*. If matter has escaped its imposed (imagined) inertia—if matter begins to evade categorisations, to over-spill linear conceptions of causality, to generate meanings—then matter necessarily challenges the previous *taken for granted* of environmental law. Cartesian subject-object relations are thus thoroughly challenged by an understanding of matter as 'materialization [,] a complex, pluralistic, relatively open process' in which 'humans [are] thoroughly immersed within materiality's productive contingencies'.[82] And since matter has its own lively agencies, 'the conventional sense that agents are exclusively humans who possess cognitive abilities, intentionality and freedom to make autonomous decisions and the corollary presumption that

---

[79] D Coole and S Frost (eds), *New Materialisms: Ontology, Agency and Politics* (Durham, Duke University Press, 2010).
[80] ibid, 2.
[81] ibid, 4.
[82] ibid, 7.

humans have the right or ability to master nature' is entirely disrupted.[83] Taken seriously, such disruption strikes at the very heart of the anthropocentric assumptions underlying the eco-governmentality expressed in the environmental legal priorities of the Capitalocene.

Such lively complexity, taken seriously, has further implications. Key among these are its implications for the environmental legal subject. The individualistic, exceptionalist human agent 'acting on' or 'governing' 'the environment' becomes an intellectually unsustainable idea. Matter's lively, self-emergent properties and the sense in which 'we are all lichens now' folds human flesh and the generation of human meaning into a much wider field of materio-semiotic energies. The decentred subject is presented with a demand for epistemic humility, repositioned as just one partner in a 'spatial and temporal web of interspecies dependencies'.[84] Environmental epistemology thus becomes fully and radically *ecological* in the richest sense.[85] And environmental subjects are themselves *ecologies*[86]—and seen as such, in place of the panoptic subject radically separated from 'the environment' it 'acts upon'.

What then, might such realisations indicate in practical terms? First, there is a need to foreground materiality and its significance. The way in which New Materialist thought transversally dissolves the material/cultural dualism so long assumed by Cartesianism and its conceptual descendants necessarily broadens and deepens the focus of theoretical vision. As Coole and Frost suggest, New Materialist frames of analysis draw together the effects of macro-structural projects such as the international economy, 'well-honed micro-powers of governmentality' and the sheer materiality of existence as corporeal beings inhabiting 'a world of natural and artificial objects' and having biological needs.[87] Environmental legal thought, likewise, could embrace the 'elements' interacting at various different levels ('micro, meso and macro'), and respond to the fact that dynamics are multi-directional rather than moving in the traditionally conceived top-down ways assumed by environmental law and governance structures *or* by uni-directional bottom-up responses. Interrelationalities should be seen as rhizomatic rather than arboreal.

For the environmental legal subject, New Materialist thought necessarily means that the focus moves away from 'individual bodies, subjects, experiences or sensations' towards 'assemblages of human and non-human, animate and inanimate, material and abstract, and the affective flows within these assemblages'.[88] Indeed, it makes sense—as Barad has argued—to eschew the notion of a stable subject-object split entirely.

---

[83] ibid, 10.

[84] D Haraway, *When Species Meet* (Minnesota, University of Minnesota Press, 2008) 11.

[85] L Code, *Ecological Thinking: The Politics of Epistemic Location* (Oxford, Oxford University Press, 2006).

[86] Again, see Haraway, *When Species Meet* (n 84) at 3–4.

[87] Coole and Frost, *New Materialisms* (n 79) at 27.

[88] ibid, 406.

This shift will be profoundly challenging for an environmental law that continues to assume its broadly Cartesian ontology of the subject. That said, law is not a stranger to shifts of meaning—and environmental law is closer than many forms of law to the materiality of the world and potentially responsive to materiality as an ethical matter. Law is in any case, adaptive. Law both attempts to 'capture', 'fix' and 'stabilise' meanings and referents for coordinative/control purposes—but law also destabilises meanings, not least through legal argument, interpretive variance and the semiotic shifts operationalised by appeal processes. It is not impossible to believe that environmental law's particular focus on material relations could, if pursued into Chthulucene realities, hold out hope for environmental law as a conduit of more liveable futures.

And while the destabilisation of fixed subject-object relations presents a particularly profound challenge to law's assumption of the construct of the rational juridical individual, it is just possible to imagine the environmental legal subject as a contingent position relevant to a particular context or purpose. And if environmental law can face up to the fact that such choices represent a contingent 'fixing' of an underlying complexity, then perhaps environmental law, within parameters responsive to its own nature, including its institutional dynamics, can become more radically responsive to the materiality it seeks to engage with.

Relatedly, the de-centering of the environmental legal subject has distinctive epistemological implications. If the subject becomes a contingent identification, not a fixed a priori designation of an exceptionalist status, then the subject's knowledge, likewise, is de-centred. The dethroning of the epistemology of mastery (the dissolution of the 'eye in the sky') necessarily brings the *politics of epistemic location*[89] centre-frame for environmental law and legal process. De-centering epistemic power challenges the panoptic 'knowing centre' at the heart of intensifying levels of eco-governmentality and the neoliberalisation of nature under the imperatives of the Capitalocene. Environmental law and environmental legal enquiry are invited by such foundational shifts to become overtly reflexive, alert to premature closure and to the overly rigid fixing of boundaries drawn for theoretical, operational or doctrinal purposes.

Environmental law is also invited by such insights to broaden its epistemic 'receptor sites', and to embrace a form of epistemic tentacularity. If environmental law and methodologies were to 'begin in the middle'[90] rather than 'at the centre', and if environmental epistemology were to abandon the panoptic for a tentacular exploration of materiality, then the entire epistemic focus of environmental law could include previously unconsidered constituencies of meaning-making. Tentacularity (and the partial knowing that such an epistemic approach might even *celebrate*) points towards a fully 'ecological epistemology'.[91] An ecological

---

[89] Code, *Ecological Thinking* (n 85).
[90] Philippopoulos-Mihalopoulos, 'Towards a Critical Environmental Law' (n 56).
[91] This is the project of Code (n 85).

epistemology, in the words of Lorraine Code, 'emerges from and addresses so many interwoven and sometimes contradictory issues ... that its implications require multifaceted chartings'.[92] Importantly, such an epistemology is character-ised, first and foremost, by responsible epistemic practices particularly sensitive to local, situated diversities and

> proposes a way of engaging—if not all at once—with the implications of patterns, places and the interconnections of lives and events in and across the human and nonhuman world ... in projects of inquiry ... where epistemic and ethical-political concerns are reciprocally informative'.[93]

A tentacular epistemology would, I suggest, necessarily feel its way along particu-lar, situated puzzles and questions, inviting a mode of knowing that was know-ingly incomplete and open to perceptual ambiguity in a way that invites epistemic relationality—of all kinds, including interspecies relationalities—into epistemic enquiry. And examples of legal epistemic strategies along (and/or analogous to) such lines of approach already exist.

Pieraccini, for example, explores materio-semiotic inter-species encounters between sheep and humans on upland commons in the United Kingdom: There, it is the bodily habits and repetitions, practices, movements, modes of stopping and of dwelling of sheep that are used to guide property relations and to suggest new ways of seeing property as being, in the words of Pieraccini, the 'contingent product of humans and non-human animals'.[94] There is a kind of ecological epis-temology at work in such partnerships of knowing. There is a kind of tentacularity in the way that the community feels its way along, guided by animal movements and habits in a dance with the slower movement of landscape—a most lichen-like 'mutual and dynamic crafting of people and environments'.[95] Such an ecologi-cal epistemology would exceed environmental law's traditional epistemic mono-culturalism to allow (and *by allowing*) non-human intelligences and agencies their place in the formation of legal and normative relations.

An environmental law responsive to the Chthulucene might just be able to cast aside the eco-destructive assumptions and ideological closures of the Anthropocene-Capitalocene. The newly de-centred environmental subject would no longer stand at the 'centre' of a world rendered oppressively fungible and commodified. Then, perhaps, environmental law might, by responding to the energies of the Chthulucene, become an important mode of coordinating 'something—just maybe—*more liveable*'.[96]

---

[92] ibid 4.
[93] ibid.
[94] M Pieraccini, 'Property Pluralism and the Partial Reflexivity of Conservation Law: The Case of Upland Commons in England and Wales' (2012) 3 *Journal of Human Rights and the Environment* 273–87, 273.
[95] ibid, 280.
[96] Haraway (n 1) at 01:05.

5

Critical Environmental Law and the Double Register of the Anthropocene: A Biopolitical Reading

VITO DE LUCIA

I. Introduction

We live in times marked by uncertainties and contestations. The deep and pervasive influence of humankind on all planetary processes and ecosystems has been taken to indicate a new geological epoch, aptly called the Anthropocene—the 'age of man'. The Anthropocene, however, while the ultimate consequence of modernity and of its categories, signals simultaneously a crisis. Nature is either dead or has entered a post-natural state.[1] Science has arguably entered a post-normal state where a plurality of knowledges co-exist and make competing claims to truth. Environmental law, closely intertwined with epistemological, axiological and material problematics, is itself an increasingly complex and contested field of law and its traditional reference categories no longer offer critical purchase. Against this background, this chapter will try to offer a biopolitical reading of environmental law, with a view to further advancing the project of what has been tentatively called critical environmental law.[2] Critical environmental law aims at making visible the slippages that intervene at the margins of the intersection between law and ecology. In my own articulation of critical environmental law I utilise a genealogical method of inquiry, in order to problematise linear histories. Genealogy is in fact aimed at the reconstruction of the contingencies and contestations (what Foucault, following Nietzsche, calls respectively descent[3]

---

[1] See eg B McKibben, *The End of Nature* (New York, Random House, 1989); and J Purdy, *After Nature: A Politics for the Anthropocene* (Cambridge, MA Harvard University Press, 2015).

[2] For a first discussion of a 'critical' environmental law, see the edited volume A Philippopoulos-Mihalopoulos (ed), *Law and Ecology: New Environmental Foundations* (London, Routledge Glasshouse Book, 2011).

[3] M Foucault, 'Nietzsche, Genealogy, History' in DF Bouchard (ed), *Language, Counter-Memory, Practice: Selected Essays and Interviews* (Ithaca, New York, Cornell University Press, 1977) 80–83.

and emergence)[4] constituting the complex history of phenomena, concepts and, importantly, law. A genealogical approach, moreover, and importantly, leads to a methodology that is inevitably pluralist and perspectival,[5] insofar as every concept is capable of having 'many antagonistic senses that depend on the perspective of the forces that try to dominate it'.[6] As such, critical environmental law radically problematises analyses that understand environmental law as a legal-technical mechanism that applies 'the science of ecology',[7] or as inevitably moving from anthropocentric to ecocentric forms. Within this methodological context, biopolitics offers a particularly suited framework for disarticulating the binaries and the linearities traversing environmental law (and environmental legal scholarship) in the Anthropocene. Indeed genealogy and biopolitics are highly complementary, in that biopolitics is at bottom genealogical.[8]

In this chapter, I specifically explore critical environmental law through the lens of biopolitics. In part II, I discuss the crisis of three key referents of modernity: knowledge, nature and law. In part III, I present two registers of engagement with the challenges of the Anthropocene. In parts IV and V, I will first present biopolitics as a theoretical and methodological device, and then use that analysis to read and problematise environmental law.

II. Knowledge, Nature and Law in the Anthropocene

A. The Anthropocene in Brief

The human influence on Earth has arguably acquired the character of a distinct geological force.[9] A proposal is under discussion to introduce a new formal geological epoch, namely the Anthropocene (the current epoch being the Holocene),[10]

---

[4] ibid, 83–86.

[5] C Douzinas and A Geary, *Critical Jurisprudence. The Political Philosophy of Justice* (Oxford and Portland, Oregon, Hart Publishing, 2005) esp 49ff.

[6] ibid, 49

[7] ibid, 2; see also C Voigt, 'The Principle of Sustainable Development. Integration and Ecological Integrity' in C Voigt (ed), *Rule of Law for Nature: New Dimensions and Ideas in Environmental Law* (Cambridge, Cambridge University Press, 2013), which, similarly, maintains that 'science has the answers', and that law is tasked with implementing those answers; at 153.

[8] Thus eg T Lemke, *Biopolitics. An Advanced Introduction* (New York, New York University Press, 2011) ch 9, 177ff. Drawing on Lemke, I have also combined genealogy and biopolitics in my PhD thesis: V De Lucia, *The Ecosystem Approach in International Environmental Law. A Biopolitical Critique*, PhD Thesis (Faculty of Law, UiT, Arctic University of Norway, 2016).

[9] J Zalasiewicz, M Williams, W Steffen and P. Crutzen, 'The New World of the Anthropocene' (2010) 44(7) *Environmental Science and Technology* 2228.

[10] A proposal to formalise the Anthropocene as a new geological unit within the Geological Time Scale is under development by the 'Anthropocene' working group of the Subcommission on Quaternary Stratigraphy, with the view of presenting it for consideration to the International Commission on Stratigraphy (the largest scientific organisation within the International Union of Geological Sciences), available at: http://quaternary.stratigraphy.org/workinggroups/anthropocene/.

whose distinctiveness is precisely the dominant role humanity has achieved over Earth and its systems.[11] Already in 1873, the growing influence of humanity on the natural world prompted Italian geologist Antonio Stoppani to speak of an 'anthropozoic era'.[12] Much more recently, Paul Crutzen, in a now famous essay published in *Nature* and entitled 'The Geology of Mankind', mainstreamed the term Anthropocene.[13] More specifically, the Anthropocene denotes the particular depth, pervasiveness and permanence of humankind's impact on Earth and all of its ecosystems.

Even pending its formal recognition as a new geological epoch however, the Anthropocene has already become an important conceptual framework whose currency and purchase has 'rapidly escalated'.[14] To be sure, in a very short time, the Anthropocene has given rise to at least three dedicated academic journals.[15] The Anthropocene raises new and crucial questions related to the identification of

> the non-negotiable planetary preconditions that humanity needs to respect in order to avoid the risk of deleterious or even catastrophic environmental change at continental to global scales.[16]

While the exact periodisation of the Anthropocene is not entirely clear (nor, perhaps, of crucial significance), it can be argued that there is significant overlap between modernity and at least an important intensification of the effects of the Anthropocene, and that the key conjunction between the two is arguably represented by the rise of capitalism.[17] In this respect, and perhaps paradoxically, the very modern categories that underpin the Anthropocene, faced with the socio-ecological consequences of their 'success', are in a state of crisis. The Anthropocene then signals simultaneously a deep socio-ecological crisis (whose details need not be rehearsed here)[18] and a deep cultural crisis.

B. The Crisis of the Categories of Modernity

As anticipated, at least three key referent categories of modernity—knowledge, nature and law—are today visibly in a state of crisis. The modern concept

---

[11] S Lewis and M Maslin, 'Defining the Anthropocene' (2015) 519 *Nature* 171.

[12] P Crutzen, 'Geology of Mankind' (2002) 415 *Nature* 23.

[13] ibid, 23.

[14] Lewis and Maslin (n 11) at 171.

[15] Such as *Anthropocence*, published by Elsevir, www.journals.elsevier.com/anthropocene/; *The Anthropocene Review*, published by Sage, http://anr.sagepub.com/; *Elementa: Science of the Anthropocene*, published by BioOne, www.elementascience.org.

[16] J Rockström and others, 'Planetary Boundaries: Exploring the Safe Operating Space for Humanity' (2009) 14 (2/32) *Ecology and Society* 2.

[17] On the 'interpenetration' of modernity and capitalism, see eg B De Sousa Santos, *Toward a New Common Sense. Law, Science and Politics in a Paradigmatic Transition* (New York, London, Routledge, 1995).

[18] eg the United Nations Environment Programme's (UNEP) 5th Global Environmental Outlook Report emphatically articulates how: '[t]he scale, spread and rate of change of global drivers are without precedent. Burgeoning populations and growing economies are pushing environmental systems to

of knowledge, modelled on Newtonian physics premised on universal and predictable natural laws, and articulated as an 'epistemology of mastery',[19] has been upset and rendered unstable by biological and ecological models of knowledge that are increasingly described as postmodern[20] or post-normal.[21] Knowledge in the Anthropocene is characterised by epistemological pluralism[22] and by an inevitable entanglement with values,[23] while a central role is assumed by uncertainty and complexity.[24] From this (postmodern) vantage, science can no longer offer predictions, but rather plausible scenarios,[25] while ignorance acquires a crucial epistemic role.[26] Moreover, in the context of 'truth pluralism'[27]—that is of competing claims to truth which cannot be adjudicated objectively—science is fully revealed to be 'normative science'.[28]

Nature, in turn, has been repeatedly declared dead;[29] or has been exposed for being a crucial political category aimed at excluding certain voices (mostly non-human) rather than describing reality objectively;[30] or has been problematised from a pluralist perspective, which would rather speak of a plurality of *natures*,

---

destabilizing limits', UNEP, *The Fifth Global Environment Outlook*, GEO-5, Environment for the Future We Want (DEW/1417/NA, 2012) 4.

[19] That is as a mode of knowledge that is ordained at the mastery, or domination, of the natural world. See esp W Leiss, *The Domination of Nature* (Montreal and Quebec, McGill-Queens University Press, 1994).

[20] T Allen, C Zellmer and C Wuennenberg, 'The Loss of Narrative'; and K deLaplante, 'Is Ecosystem Management a Postmodern Science?', both in in K Cuddington and B Beisner (eds), *Ecological Paradigms Lost: Routes of Theory Change* (Burlington, Mass, Elsevier Academic Press, 2005).

[21] deLaplante, ibid; DeLaplante specifically discusses Ravetz and Funcowitz's framework of post-normal science in relation to the ecosystem approach.

[22] S Gutwirth and E Naim-Gesbert, 'Science et droit de l'environnement: réflexions pour le cadre conceptual du pluralism de vérités' (1995) 34 *Revue interdisciplinaire d'études juridiques* 33; M Sagoff, 'The Plaza and the Pendulum: Two Concepts of Ecological Science' (2003) 18(4) *Biology and Philosophy* 529; deLaplante, 'Is Ecosystem Management a Postmodern Science'; M Tallacchini, 'A Legal Framework from Ecology' (2000) 9(8) *Biodiversity And Conservation* 1085; K Shrader-Frechette, 'Methodological Rules for Four Classes of Scientific Uncertainty' in J Lemons (ed), *Scientific Uncertainty and Environmental Problem Solving* (Oxford, Blackwell Science, 1996).

[23] Tallacchini, 'A Legal Framework from Ecology' (n 22); Shrader-Frechette, 'Methodological Rules for Four Classes of Scientific Uncertainty' (n 22).

[24] Tallacchini (n 22).

[25] Climate science is a perfect case in point, where each prediction of the IPCC is framed by and nuanced with specific boundaries of uncertainty and so-called 'confidence' values and offers scenarios, rather than predictions; see eg C Field and others (eds), *Climate Change 2014: Impacts, Adaptation and Vulnerability, Part A: Global and Sectoral Aspects. Contribution of Working Group II to the Fifth Assessment Report of the Intergovernmental Panel on Climate Change* (Cambridge, United Kingdom and New York, Cambridge University Press, 2014).

[26] Thus eg Tallacchini (n 22).

[27] Gutwirth and Naim-Gesbert (n 22).

[28] ibid, 61: 'Le pluralisme de vérités montre bien que ce rôle absolu, extra-politique, extra-juridique et indiscutable accordé à la science et ses verities est inacceptable'. See also, on normative science, R Lackey, 'Appropriate Use of Ecosystem Health and Normative Science in Ecological Policy' in D Rapport and others, *Managing for Healthy Ecosystems* (Boca Raton, FL: CRC Press, 2002).

[29] McKibben, *The End of Nature* (n 1).

[30] B Latour, 'An Attempt at a "Compositionist Manifesto"' (2010) 41 *New Literary History* 471.

(whether the result of plural cultural interpretations of nature or of ontological diversities) that refract it in a multiplicity of *worlds*, each with its own particular ontological articulation, both human and non-human.[31]

Law, particularly in its modern rational and sovereign articulation (whether in the natural law or positivist inflection), is also in a state of crisis. Historically, law, hand in hand with science, has arguably had the role of taming and 'othering' nature, through the operation of what has been termed the 'scientifico-legal complex',[32] which was developed largely under the influence of the prevailing Cartesian ontology.[33] In this sense law has been a central enabling element of the Anthropocene, by binding together science and the political epistemology of nature in an authoritative and operative framework. Yet, as Anna Grear suggests, law has 'failed thus far to respond [to the challenges of the Anthropocene] in any way that really counts'.[34] Environmental law, whose special relevance derives from being the specific legal response to the unfolding socio-ecological crises, has proved ultimately inadequate, largely owing to its reproduction of the ontological and epistemological commitments of legal modernity.[35] Yet environmental law is located at an epistemological crossroads (and that is perhaps what makes its inadequacy overlaid with tragic self-awareness). On the one hand, environmental law's organising logic responds to the central categories of modernity; on the other, environmental law can no longer rely on those categories, that is, on uniform and stable truths, on a stable concept of nature, and on a positivist concept of law. Entangled in an unresolvable series of ontological, epistemological and axiological conflicts, environmental law itself thus becomes postmodern,[36] 'hot',[37] and complexly contested.[38] Environmental law is thus affected by a 'deep contradiction',[39] a contradiction that perpetuates and even extends, rather than resolves the pervasiveness and intensity of environmental problems:[40] self-reflexively aware of how

---

[31] See eg M Cadena, 'Indigenous Cosmopolitics in the Andes: Conceptual Reflections beyond "Politics"' (2010) 25(2) *Cultural Anthropology* 334 and E Vivieros de Castro, 'Perspectival Anthropology and the Method of Controlled Equivocation' (2004) 2(1) *Tipiti: Journal of the Society for the Anthropology of Lowland South America* 3.

[32] J Holder, 'New Age: Rediscovering Natural Law' (2000) 53(1) *Current Legal Problems* 151, 165.

[33] Characterised by a powerful set of binaries reflecting a fundamental dualism.

[34] A Grear, 'Towards a New Horizon: in Search of a Renewing SocioJuridical Imaginary' (2013) 3(5) *Oñati Socio-Legal Series* 966, 970.

[35] Thus eg ibid; M M'Gonigle and L Takeda, 'The Liberal Limits of Environmental Law: A Green Legal Critique' (2013) 30(3) *Pace Environmental Law Review* 1005.

[36] N De Sadeleer, *Environmental Principles: From Political Slogans to Legal Rules* (Oxford, Oxford University Press, 2002).

[37] Environmental Law is considered '"hot law" insofar as it deals with "hot situations" in which the agreed frames, legal and otherwise, for how we understand and act in the world are in a constant state of flux and contestation'; E Fisher, 'Environmental Law as "Hot" Law' (2013) 25(3) *Journal of Environmental Law* 347, 347–48.

[38] V De Lucia, 'Competing Narratives and Complex Genealogies: The Ecosystem Approach in International Environmental Law' (2015) 27(1) *Journal of Environmental Law* 91.

[39] M'Gonigle and Takeda, 'The Liberal Limits of Environmental Law' (n 35) at 1005.

[40] ibid, 1005.

the 'environmental problematic' can only be addressed by a change in paradigm, *'environmental law itself does not address this problematic; it operates within it'*.[41] Its crisis, in other words, is inevitably inscribed in its very core.

In summary, all three categories—knowledge, nature and law—have played a crucial role towards the conceptual articulation and material concretisation of the Anthropocene. But while the Anthropocene has emerged and intensified largely thanks to these three key categories, it has also determined their destabilisation, to the extent that the Anthropocene has revealed the limits of normal Newtonian science, while nature as a stable political epistemology and law as a sovereign form, have also shown all their limitations and are in a state of crisis.

III. The Double Register of the Anthropocene

The Anthropocene has prompted very different registers of intellectual engagement with its challenges. Conservation ethics is no longer clear-cut, and is rather a hotly contested field of discursivity, stretched between two internal articulations that are struggling for the 'soul' of conservation biology as a discipline. Simultaneously, and in parallel fashion, two main registers are emerging as competing orientations in relation to environmental law and policy. In fact, some invoke the Anthropocene as evidence of the end of nature, and suggest (in what will turn out to be a *biopolitical* argument, as will be made clear in the next part), that the entire world needs to be inserted into a matrix of human control in order to be protected, or indeed enhanced.[42] I will call this particular register 'interventionist'. A second register, which I will call 'radical', suggests rather that '[i]n the climate-pressed Anthropocene epoch, nothing could be more urgent than fresh engagements with the fractious relationships between "humanity", law and the living order'.[43] What is required thus is a 'complete rethink' of law.[44] What these two modes of engagement with the questions raised by the Anthropocene share, however, is the acknowledgement of the critical ecological juncture that the onset of the Anthropocene (both in its geological and more immediately

---

[41] ibid, 1019–20.

[42] See eg D Botkin, *Discordant Harmonies: A New Ecology for the Twenty-first Century*, 1st edn (Oxford, Oxford University Press, 1990); M Marvier, 'New Conservation is True Conservation' (2013) 28(1) *Conservation Biology* 1–3; M Marvier and P Kareiva, 'The Evidence and Values Underlying "New Conservation"' (2014) 29(3) *Trends in Ecology and Evolution* 131–32; P Kareiva, M Marvier and R Lalasz, 'Conservation in the Anthropocene Beyond Solitude and Fragility' (2012) *The Breakthrough Journal*.

[43] A Grear and E Grant (ed), *Thought, Law, Action and Rights in the Age of Environmental Crisis* (Cheltenham, Edward Elgar, 2015); see www.e-elgar.com/shop/thought-law-rights-and-action-in-the-age-of-environmental-crisis.

[44] L Kotzé, 'Human Rights and the Environment in the Anthropocene' (2014) 1(3) *The Anthropocene Review* 252, 252.

material dimension, and in its discursive articulations) marks. I will discuss both in turn, and then, before moving on to develop my biopolitical argument, canvass the ways in which both can be located in a biopolitical 'zone of irreducible indistinction'.[45] I start the analysis by outlining the heart of the debate that underpins both the interventionist and the radical register.

A. The Heart of the Dilemma: Conservation Ethics at a Crossroad

An internal struggle is affecting conservation biology, the branch of biology behind the development of the concept of biodiversity and a significant, even decisive, scientific and normative influence on environmental law and policy. This struggle, characterised by some commentators as a 'battle for the soul of conservation science',[46] is primarily linked to the ethics of conservation, as especially captured by the question: *why* should we conserve nature? The binary anthropocentrism/ecocentricsm is a key boundary in this debate. Yet the *methods* and *tools* of conservation are also a key element. To defuse the increasingly hot debate, a call for unity appeared in *Nature* in November 2014.[47] The comment takes up the 'age-old conflict around [the] seemingly simple question [...] of why [...] we conserve nature'.[48] The authors of the comment—and 238 additional signatories—propose

> a unified and diverse conservation ethic; one that recognizes and accepts all values of nature, from intrinsic to instrumental, and welcomes all philosophies justifying nature protection and restoration, from ethical to economic, and from aesthetic to utilitarian.[49]

This, in many ways, is a recognition of the epistemological plurality that characterises ecology as a postmodern science. Yet there are two main competing approaches to conservation. One is attuned to the tradition of protected areas and ecological integrity, strongly advocating that nature should be conserved for its 'intrinsic value' (rather than merely for instrumental purposes) and finds its most prominent representative in Michael Soulé, one of the scientists behind the concept of biodiversity.[50] The other approach, which finds leading advocates in Peter Kareiva and Michelle Marvier, acknowledges the end of nature in the Anthropocene and therefore favours a pragmatic embrace of artificial nature and human

---

[45] G Agamben, *Homo Sacer. Sovereign Power and Bare Life* (Stanford, Stanford University Press, 1998) 12.

[46] K Kloor, 'The Battle for the Soul of Conservation Science' (2015) XXXI(2) *Issues in Science and Technology* available at: http://issues.org/31-2/kloor/.

[47] H Tallis and J Lubchenco, 'A Call for Inclusive Conservation' (2014) 515 *Nature* 27.

[48] ibid, 27.

[49] ibid, 27.

[50] See eg M. Soulè, *Conservation Biology: The Science of Scarcity and Diversity* (Sunderland, MA, Sinauer Associates Inc, 1986), or more recently, a book where Soulè defends the idea of nature conservation against what he calls 'postmodern deconstruction'; M Soulé and G Lease (eds), *Reinventing Nature? Responses to Postmodern Deconstruction* (Washington, DC, Island Press, 1995).

management in order to conserve a nature beneficial to humans through what is called 'new conservation'.[51]

While traditional conservation ethics, born of the national parks movement, reproduces a certain separation between humanity and nature through the crucial policy tool of protected areas, Kareiva and other new conservationists shift perspective, and envision a '[f]orward-looking conservation' that 'protects natural habitats where people live and extract resources', and that 'works with corporations to find mixes of economic and conservation activities that blend development with a concern for nature'.[52] Their argument hinges on two primary reasons. First, protected areas, the primary tool of traditional conservation, are insufficient and under siege.[53] Secondly, linking nature conservation and human benefits (ie ecosystem services) allows to prioritise conserving areas that deliver important benefits to human communities (especially poor ones) which 'is imperative for conservation effectiveness'.[54] In this respect, Marvier and Kareiva urge conservation to become pluralist, ie to adopt a larger toolbox, rather than rely only on protected areas. Yet in response, Soulé argues that such an approach would only hasten 'ecological collapse globally, eradicating thousands of kinds of plants and animals'.[55] Soulé's perspective, which underlies much environmental scholarship and much of the environmental movement, underpins also the legal notion of protected areas. However, and here we encounter one of the contradictions affecting environmental law, this turns arguably environmental law into a mechanism 'designed to keep chaos [...] at arm's length',[56] separating 'the sacred [from] the abject'.[57] In this light, environmental law's protection and preservation of 'the more 'majestic' aspects of Nature' rely upon acts of partition and classification of vulnerable areas worthy of protection, 'islands of wildness' which are 'conceivable only on the basis of an [otherwise] ongoing and generalized

---

[51] See eg M. Marvier, 'New Conservation is True Conservation' (2013) 28(1) *Conservation Biology* 1; M Marvier and P Kareiva, 'The Evidence and Values Underlying "New Conservation"' (2014) 29(3) *Trends in Ecology and Evolution* 131.

[52] Kareiva and Marvier, quoted in Kloor, 'The Battle for the Soul of Conservation Science' (n 46).

[53] Marvier and Kareiva, 'The Evidence and Values Underlying "New Conservation"' (n 51) at 131.

[54] Marvier, 'New Conservation is True Conservation' (n 51) at 1.

[55] Soulé, as quoted in Kloor (n 46). Soulé, Kareiva and Marvier have been prominently debating conservation in the past few years; see eg M Soulé, 'The New Conservation' (2013) 27(5) *Conservation Biology* 895; Marvier (n 51); Marvier and Kareiva (n 51); and P Karieva, 'New Conservation: Setting the Record Straight and Finding Common Ground' (2014) 28(3) *Conservation Biology* 634.

[56] M Hasley, 'Majesty and Monstrosity: Deleuze and the Defence of Nature' in Philippopoulos-Mihalopoulos (ed), *Law and Ecology* (n 2) at 218–19.

[57] ibid, 219. In a similar fashion, Lee Godden emphasises how modernity constructs nature as other, and in doing so allows only one of two alternative views: either as an object of control—through property rights—or as 'wilderness to be preserved apart from human society'; L Godden, *Nature as Other: The Legal Ordering of the Natural World*, PhD Thesis (Queensland, Faculty of Law, Griffith University, 2000) 2. See also S Chaplin, 'Fictions of Origin: Law, Abjection, Difference' (2005) 16(2) *Law and Critique* 161, which describes law as a 'dividing line that serves to exclude filth', that is, to separate the filth of industrial modernity from the purity that protected areas are supposed to guarantee and protect, through law; ibid, 165–66.

ecological violence'.[58] This maintains the discourse within a dialectic between the monstrous and the majestic, the abject and the sacred,[59] the filth and the pure,[60] which traditionally traverses and shapes environmental law throughout.[61]

This section has outlined the debate that animates and translates in the two registers of engagement with the Anthropocene alluded to. The next two sections will briefly describe each in turn.

B. The Interventionist Register

The interventionist register starts from two basic premises. First, current conservation policies do not work. Second, the distinction between natural and artificial no longer has any meaning. The conclusion is that, rather than protect enclaves of pristine nature (which is from the interventionist perspective an illusion), we should impose a comprehensive system of management and control on the entire planet in order to ensure its conservation, and even its enhancement.[62] In the face of it, the argument is apparently sensible. The conclusions that are drawn from the premises are, however, problematic, as I will show below.

At the forefront of this orientation, one finds Daniel Botkin (one of the main minds behind the so-called New Ecology) and more recently,[63] Peter Kareiva, Chief Scientist of the Nature Conservancy, and charismatic figure of the conservation biology community (see above).[64] The interventionists' central argument is that the rapid decline in all planetary health indicators suggests that traditional conservation does not work.[65] Moreover, we live in a post-natural world, and conservation 'cannot promise a return to pristine, prehuman landscapes', because humans have 'already profoundly transformed the planet'.[66] What conservation can promise, on the other hand, is

> a new vision of a planet in which nature—forests, wetlands, diverse species, and other ancient ecosystems—exists amid a wide variety of modern, human landscapes. For this to happen, conservationists will have to jettison their idealized notions of nature, parks,

---

[58] Hasley, 'Majesty and Monstrosity' (n 56) at 219; Kotzé, 'Human Rights and the Environment in the Anthropocene' (n 44) at 124.

[59] Hasley (n 56).

[60] S Chaplin, 'Fictions of Origin: Law, Abjection, Difference' (2005) 16(2) *Law and Critique* 161, 165–66.

[61] Hasley (n 56).

[62] See eg Botkin, *Discordant Harmonies* (n 42); Marvier (n 51) 1–3; Marvier and Kareiva (n 51) at 131–32.

[63] Botkin is a prominent figure in the 1990s, and especially within the North American context. See eg the debate that ensued in relation to ecosystem management and to Botkin's work in the pages of the *Pace Journal of Environmental Law* between Bruce Pardy and JB Ruhl.

[64] See eg Kareiva, Marvier and Lalasz, 'Conservation in the Anthropocene' (n 42).

[65] ibid.

[66] ibid. Similarly Botkin (n 42).

and wilderness—ideas that have never been supported by good conservation science—and forge a more optimistic, human-friendly vision.[67]

This message hinges on the conviction that parks and protected areas alone do not and cannot halt the degradation of natural ecosystems, and that other approaches are necessary that aim at conserving *all* nature, letting go of the illusion of a pristine nature that requires a legal demarcation of inaccessibility in order to remain pristine. Indeed, in the Anthropocene, nature 'will be a nature that we make; the question is the degree to which this molding will be intentional or unintentional, desirable or undesirable [to humans]'.[68]

If worldviews and conservation paradigms are changing in light of the Anthropocene, where does that leave law? More pertinently, what is the direction of change for environmental law? Botkin himself complained in the mid-1990s that despite the ecological revolution 'our laws and policies are still based on outmoded [ecological] concepts',[69] though he was not the only one that explored the significance of the 'new ecology' for environmental law.[70] He argued for a change in paradigm in environmental law,[71] one no longer based on what he called the 'myth' of the balance of nature, but rather a new paradigm, embracing the chaotic 'discordant harmonies' traversing natural processes.[72] As already anticipated, the problematic, and even troubling, aspect of the interventionist approach, from the perspective of the present writer, is the conclusions that are drawn, as we shall see.

C. The Radical Register

The Anthropocene however, informs also an increasing number of radical scholarly reflections and ethico-political projects. Critical scholars argue that the Anthropocene requires, not an intensification of human interventions, but a radical, paradigmatic shift in human theoretical endeavours.[73] Louis Kotzé argues in this respect that 'the arrival of the Anthropocene is possibly set to require a *complete rethink*' of the framework of human rights in relation to the

---

[67] Karieva, Marvier and Lalasz (n 42).

[68] Botkin (n 42) 193. Emphasis mine.

[69] D Botkin, *Adjusting Law to Nature's Discordant Harmonies* (1996) 7 *Duke Environmental Law and Policy Forum* 25.

[70] See in this respect esp D Tarlock, 'The Nonequilibrium Paradigm in Ecology and the Partial Unraveling of Environmental Law' (1994) 27 *Loyola LA Law Review* 1009; and J Wiener, 'Law and the New Ecology: Evolution, Categories and Consequences: Review Essay' (1995) 22(2) *Ecology Law Quarterly* 325

[71] ibid.

[72] Botkin (n 42).

[73] See, among an increasing scholarship, the papers presented at 'The Thousand Names of Gaia: From the Anthropocene to the Age of the Earth' conference (Rio de Janeiro, 15–19 September 2014) available at: https://thethousandnamesofgaia.wordpress.com/the-conferences-texts/. See also eg Kotzé (n 44); D Vidas, 'The Anthropocene and the International Law of the Sea' (2011) 369 *Philosophical Transactions of the Royal Society A* 909–25.

environmental regulatory domain.[74] Similarly, a recent collection edited by Anna Grear and Evadne Grant, and titled *Thought, Law, Rights and Action in the Age of Environmental Crisis*, emphasises the urgency of this task by underlining how '[i]n the climate-pressed Anthropocene epoch, nothing could be more urgent than fresh engagements with the fractious relationships between 'humanity', law and the living order'.[75] More specifically, one of the contributions to that collection articulates very clearly one of the pathways through which this urgent need to think law beyond the Anthropocene (that is, beyond legal modernity) may emerge: 'today', suggests Pieraccini, '[t]he task for legal scholars is [to] produce a new language' so as to disentangle law and legal strategies 'from the constraints imposed by the tradition of [modernity]'.[76]

Arguably, the particular environmental legal scholarship approaching the challenges of the Anthropocene via the radical register, regardless of theoretical or methodological inclinations, increasingly finds a common unifying premise in the recognition that the unfolding socio-ecological crises are a consequence of the anthropocentric foundation of modernity.[77] Law, in turn, understood as a 'significant description of the way a society perceives itself and projects its image to the world',[78] is part of the problem: 'the legal order reflect[s] a harmful and outdated anthropocentric worldview',[79] one which ought to be replaced by ecocentrism.[80] Yet ecocentrism remains silent as regards the ways to address the crisis of the categories of modernity discussed above. Indeed, it arguably presumes their existence in order to function as a conceptual framework.[81] But as it has been convincingly shown, multiple ethical positions can be derived from the science of ecology through a series of 'alchemic' arguments,[82] in ways that further confirm the postmodern and contested character of knowledge in the Anthropocene.

---

[74] Kotzé (n 44) at 252, emphasis mine.

[75] Grear and Grant, *Thought, Law, Action and Rights in the Age of Environmental Crisis* (n 43).

[76] M Pieraccini, 'Reflections on the Relationship between Environmental Regulation, Human Rights and beyond—with Heidegger' in Grear and Grant (n 43) at 95.

[77] See eg K. Bosselmann, 'Losing the Forest for the Trees: Environmental Reductionism in the Law' (2010) 2(8) *Sustainability* 2424; R Kim, and K Bosselmann, 'International Environmental Law in the Anthropocene: Towards a Purposive System of Multilateral Environmental Agreements' (2013) 2(2) *Transnational Environmental Law* 285; C Cullinan, *Wild Law: A Manifesto for Earth Justice* (South Africa, Siber Ink, 2002); P Burdon, *Earth Jurisprudence: Private Property and the Environment* (New York, Glasshouse/Routledge, 2014).

[78] P Burdon, 'Wild Law: The Philosophy of Earth Jurisprudence' (2010) 35(2) *Alternative Law Journal* 58, 58.

[79] P Burdon, *Earth Jurisprudence: Private Property and Earth Community*, PhD Thesis (Adelaide Law School, the University of Adelaide, 2011) 131.

[80] P Taylor, *An Ecological Approach to International Law: Responding to the Challenges of Climate Change* (Abingdon, Routledge, 2008) 32.

[81] See esp, in this respect, the normative implications that Earth jurisprudence draws from reference to ecology as a science, and esp Cullinan, *Wild Law* (n 77); Burdon, *Earth Jurisprudence* (n 77).

[82] K deLaplante, 'Environmental Alchemy: How to Turn Ecological Science into Ecological Philosophy' (2004) 26(4) *Environmental Ethics* 361.

D. Two Registers, a Common Envelope?

So, on the one hand, a radical register of engagement with the challenges of the Anthropocene promotes an ecocentric approach set to radically rethink the relation between humanity and nature. Paradoxically, however, this register emphasises the need to consider nature as a subject, largely assuming an unproblematic and unproblematised idea of nature, and it seems to uphold the modern fence between humanity and nature—epistemologically, and, crucially, practically, through concepts such as ecological integrity[83]—and the continued emphasis on protected areas. On the other hand, we have a new conservation attuned to a postmodern, 'Anthropocenic' view of nature, and hence apparently more responsive to the need to re-interrogate crucial categories of modernity. Yet, while purportedly moving beyond the anthropocentric/ecocentric binary, it is also still in line with the modern trajectories of mastery and domination, especially when understood, as we shall see later in this chapter, in a biopolitical key.

The differences between the two registers are thus suddenly not as clear-cut as one might have imagined, giving further credibility to the project of critical environmental law, insofar as the latter intends precisely to show the slippages, the incongruences, the contradictions and the complexities that traverse the field of environmental law (and of environmental scholarship). What space is left for critique then, and for a critical environmental law more specifically? The answer lies, I will argue, in a biopolitical reading of environmental law. But what is biopolitics? And how does biopolitics help find a novel critical space that is able to explore the challenges of the Anthropocene without being entangled in either one of the two registers, without being folded within the same envelope? The next sections will explore these questions.

IV. Biopolitics

The claim made in this chapter, as mentioned, is that biopolitics offers a theoretical and methodological framework better capable of capturing the slippages, incongruences, contradictions and complexities affecting environmental law. It is now time to explore what biopolitics entails. By way of the shortest summary, biopolitics is a mode of government rationality that regulates populations through subsuming life under the care of power.[84] For our purposes, biopolitics is more

---

[83] Which at least in the articulation promoted by key environmental legal scholars entail a distinction between pristine areas and areas subject to human impacts; see eg L Westra and others, 'Ecological Integrity and the Aims of the Global Integrity Project' in D Pimentel, L Westra and RF Noss (eds), *Ecological Integrity: Integrating Environment, Conservation and Health* (Washington, DC, Island Press, 2000).

[84] Biopolitics, particularly in the Foucauldian articulation, is 1 of 2 poles of biopower (the other being anathomopolitics), whereby power disciplines bodies and regulates populations; see eg M. Foucault, *The History of Sexuality. Volume I: an Introduction* (New York, Pantheon Books, 1978).

specifically a mode of governing nature with the objective of achieving 'overall states of equilibration or regularity' in relation to its bio-ecological processes.[85] A key methodological benefit of reading environmental law through biopolitics is that from a biopolitical perspective, nature is no longer simply an object of exploitation, but becomes subjected to a series of positive interventions that aim at its optimisation, and at the enhancement of its productive forces.[86] In a biopolitical context, importantly, law proceeds not from a sovereign will, but from a technical norm and from scientific regimes of knowledge.

Yet the dilemma of biopolitics lies in the continuous and perhaps inevitable transformation of the positive care for nature into its subjugation. Combining ecological knowledge with legal principles and institutions, biopolitics facilitates particular forms of management and interventions that, in order to optimise and regularise natural processes, 'enframe'[87] nature in a grid of multiple systems of surveillance and control that, while trying to protect it, ultimately degrade it.

But biopolitics has another methodological advantage. Environmental law is most often assessed in terms of which view of nature it reflects: anthropocentric or ecocentric.[88] This assessment renders operative a set of binary equivalences that largely categorise anthropocentric law as bad and ecocentric law as good.[89] However, this binary grid is not capable, I claim, of capturing the genealogical complexities and contestations that traverse environmental law in the Anthropocene, complexities that require to appreciate *simultaneously* both negative and positive elements,[90] but without falling into one of two camps, the apologist or the utopian.[91] Relatedly, from the perspective of biopolitics there is no possibility of passing judgement from outside. Indeed the biopolitical declension of power penetrates and enfolds life so that there remains no outside.[92] Biopolitics, moreover, represents arguably the broad horizon of sense within which the entire tradition

---

[85] M Foucault, *Society Must be Defended. Lectures at the Collège de France 1975–1976* (London, Penguin Books, 2004) 246.

[86] T Lemke, *Biopolitics. An Advanced Introduction* (New York, New York University Press, 2011) 68; see also more generally M Hardt, and A Negri, *Empire. The New World Order* (Cambridge, MA, Harvard University Press, 2000).

[87] The Heideggerian concept of 'enframing' indicates a 'mode of revealing the world which sets it out before [human beings] in a mode of instrumentality and utility that Heidegger famously called "standing-reserve"'; C Wolfe, *Before the Law: Humans and Other Animals in a Biopolitical Frame*, (Chicago, IL, University of Chicago Press, 2013) 3–4. Here biopolitics and anthropocentrism clearly intersect and, indeed, overlap.

[88] D, Wilkinson, 'Using Environmental Ethics to Create Ecological Law' in J Holder and D McGillivray (eds), *Locality and Identity: Environmental Issues in Law and Society* (Ashgate and Dartmouth, Dartmouth Pub Co, 1999); Cullinan (n 77); Burdon, *Earth Jurisprudence* (n 77).

[89] For some exceptions, in relation to the so-called 'weak anthropocentrism', see B Norton, 'Environmental Ethics and Weak Anthropocentrism' (1984) 6(2) *Environmental Ethics* 131.

[90] I have argued at length for the disarticulation of this binary grid in my PhD, esp ch 10; De Lucia, *The Ecosystem Approach in International Environmental Law* (n 8).

[91] See on this dialectic M. Koskenniemi, *From Apology to Utopia. The Structure of International Legal Argument. Reissue with a new epilogue* (Cambridge, Cambridge University Press, 2005).

[92] Hart and Negri, *Empire* (n 86).

of modernity can be organised.[93] To be sure, biopower—or biopolitics—is *only one* vantage or perspective through which modernity can be understood;[94] yet it arguably represents a crucial horizon of sense that finds its most decisive intensification precisely today (in ways that will be explained later), and in relation not only to human populations, but in relation to life in the broadest sense, inclusive of all ecosystem processes and living organisms that are constructed in both science and law as biodiversity.[95] In this sense, and considering the significant overlap of the Anthropocene and modernity, the Anthropocene is biopolitical.

Expanding the concept of biopolitics to encompass the natural environment can be approached from two analytically distinct, but materially inextricable and complementary, perspectives. One entails the expansion of the care for the human population through the inclusion, within the purview of the practices of regularisation enacted through a biopolitical *dispositif*,[96] of all those environmental processes which affect the well-being and the productivity of human populations. The environment can thus be considered to always already within the scope of biopolitics. Indeed, as Rutherford observes, 'the definition and administration of populations simultaneously requires the constitution and management of the environment in which those populations exist and upon which they depend'.[97] This perspective roughly corresponds to anthropocentric environmental law.

A second perspective, however, is more directly focused on natural entities and populations, and on the direct protection, regularisation and enhancement of *their* life. While still perhaps ultimately linked to the well-being of human populations (and at any rate always inevitably emerging from a human *perspective*) the primary focus is on the protection of the structure, function, health and integrity of ecosystems, and can be read, at least to an extent, together with the recognition of the intrinsic value of nature. This second perspective, in other words, can be characterised as ecocentric. However, even this ecological re-calibration of law and politics can be understood ambivalently not only as a critique of the prevalent, increasing instrumental control of the natural world, but as a new set of normalising strategies *extending* the scope of biopolitical technologies of power to the entire world.[98]

---

[93] R Esposito, *Bíos: Biopolitics and Philosophy* (Minneapolis, University of Minnesota Press, 2008).

[94] As Esposito himself, a leading advocate of the intrinsic biopolitical foundation of modernity, recognises; ibid.

[95] On the 'construction' of biodiversity, and its political genealogy, see eg A Kotsakis, *The Biological Diversity Complex: A History of Environmental Government*, PhD Thesis (London School of Economics, 2011) esp chs 2 and 3; D Erasga, 'Biopolitics: Biodiversity as Discourse of Claims' in D Erasga (ed), *Sociological Landscape—Theories, Realities and Trends* (Rijeka, Intech, 2012); A Vadrot, *The Politics of Knowledge and International Biodiversity* (London: Routledge, 2014).

[96] That is, that set of governmental apparatuses, including law, that constitute the institutional architecture and operational mechanics of the particular biopolitical regime.

[97] P Rutherford, 'The Entry of Life into History'; and E Darier, 'Foucault and the Environment: An Introduction' in E Darier (ed), *Discourses of the Environment* (London, Blackwell Publishers, 1999) 45.

[98] E Darier, 'Foucault and the Environment: An Introduction' (n 97) at 23.

Another important element relates to the co-implicated relation between power and knowledge,[99] and to the role of ecology. In this respect, the expansion of biopolitical regimes to the natural environment is historically contingent on the development of the sciences of biology and, especially, ecology. Ecology in particular has a double (and ambiguous) epistemic role,[100] and its conceptual framework is in fact easily mobilised in defence of highly incompatible projects.[101] In this respect, I have framed elsewhere ecology in terms of a 'framework of ambiguity', to emphasise the genealogical complexities underlying its key concepts.[102]

The ambivalence or ambiguity of ecology hinges on the fact that, while ecology has helped problematise the relation between the social and the natural world, and its Cartesian separation, thus casting doubt on the self-image of the modern subject, it has simultaneously 'provided the political technology for new forms of regulatory intervention in the management of the population and resources'.[103] These new forms of intervention combine in ways that make possible a novel *ecological* governmental rationality that can be applied to the regulatory management of nature; what Rutherford calls 'ecological governmentality',[104] and others have called 'ecopolitics'[105] or 'ecopower'.[106] In this respect, ecology (in both its scientific and ethical declension) is able to underpin both registers of interpretation of the Anthropocene. Ecology, both Botkin and Cullinan claim, underpins and lends credibility to *their* project.[107]

Ecology (and in particular its relational ontology and its plural epistemology) is thus simultaneously mobilised in support of a radical project of rethink of law and of its categories, and of a 'bio-economic model' of nature that provides 'the "analytic tools" needed to "intensively farm" the Earth's resources'.[108] It is at this point that we can begin reading environmental law biopolitically.

---

[99] See eg M Foucault, *Discipline and Punish. The Birth of the Prison*, 2nd edn (London, Vintage Books, 1995) esp 27–28.

[100] D Worster, *Nature's Economy: The Roots of Ecology*, 2nd edn (Cambridge, Cambridge University Press, 1994); W Sachs, *Global Ecology. A New Arena of Political Conflict* (London, ZED Books, 1993); Darier (n 97).

[101] For examples of how this plays out specifically with regards to the ecosystem approach, see esp A Bell, 'Non Human Nature and the Ecosystem Approach. The Limits of Anthropocentrism in Great Lakes Management' (2004) 20(3) *Alternatives Journal* 20; and De Lucia, 'Competing Narratives and Complex Genealogies' (n 38).

[102] De Lucia (n 38).

[103] P Rutherford, *The Problem of Nature in Contemporary Social Theory*, PhD Thesis (The Australian National University, 2000) 4.

[104] ibid, 4.

[105] Darier (n 97) at 23.

[106] P Lascoumes, *L'éco-pouvoir Environnements et Politiques* (Paris, La Découverte, 1994).

[107] See respectively Botkin (n 42) and Cullinan (n 77).

[108] P Rutherford, 'The Entry of Life into History' in Darier, *Discourses of the Environment* (n 97) at 53. See also D Worster, 'The Vulnerable Earth: Towards a Planetary History' (1987) 11(2) *Environmental Review*87; and Worster, *Nature's Economy* (n 100), on which Rutherford draws.

V. Reading Environmental Law Biopolitically

The 'intensive farming' just referred to, while enabled by ecology, is enacted and legitimated through law. In fact, if ecological science's ambivalent role is here made very explicit, for our purposes the centrally relevant element is the equally ambiguous, if not outright and thoroughly complicit, role of environmental law, a role linked primarily to the ways in which environmental law institutionalises knowledge in particular politico-juridical regimes. Environmental law thus legitimises the biopolitical interventions necessary to optimise life and its productivity through the authoritative discourse of (the rule of) law. If ecology, as Rutherford argues, can be understood as the 'rationale behind a new, and increasingly influential, form of political economy',[109] then environmental law becomes crucial in facilitating and providing the legal framework necessary to that new mode of biocapitalism concerned with the construction and maintenance of ecological regimes of accumulation.[110]

The effects of this postmodern scientifico-legal complex[111] thus a enable panopticism that subsumes life/nature under a comprehensive 'modality of intervention'.[112] And indeed international environmental law and policy facilitate intense and comprehensive monitoring programs such as the International Biological Program,[113] the Global Census of Marine Life[114] or the Global Taxonomy Initiative.[115] The very notion of biodiversity contains this biopolitical panopticism in its birthmark, even as it moves ambivalently across the demarcation line that apparently separates interventionists and radicals.

What I wish to underline here is particularly the fact that both the concept of biological diversity and conservation biology (the branch of science that articulated the notion of biodiversity and its normative inflection)[116] can be understood biopolitically.[117] The tactics of conservation biology are concretised in a series of prescriptions and interventions aimed at 'the defence of life', regardless of whether conservation takes an anthropocentric or ecocentric ethical approach.[118] For

---

[109] Rutherford, *The Problem of Nature in Contemporary Social Theory* (n 103) at 134.

[110] M Paterson, 'Legitimation and Accumulation in Climate Change Governance' (2010) 15 *New Political Economy* 345.

[111] Holder, 'New Age: Rediscovering Natural Law' (n 32).

[112] Rutherford (n 103) at 140.

[113] Aimed at 'understanding the biological basis of productivity and human welfare'; ibid, 135.

[114] 'A 10-year international effort undertaken in to assess the diversity (how many different kinds), distribution (where they live), and abundance (how many) of marine life [that] produced the most comprehensive inventory of known marine life ever compiled and cataloged' www.coml.org/about-census.

[115] Aimed at removing the so-called 'taxonomic impediment', ie the lack of taxonomic knowledge, allegedly a key to the conservation of biological diversity, www.cbd.int/gti/default.shtml.

[116] Kotsakis, *The Biological Diversity Complex* (n 95); Erasga, 'Biopolitics' (n 95).

[117] C Biermann and B Mansfield, 'Biodiversity, Purity, and Death: Conservation Biology as Biopolitics' (2014) 32(2) *Environment and Planning D: Society and Space* 252.

[118] ibid, 257.

example, the global biodiversity census proposed by famous conservation biologist Edward Wilson with the goal of protecting biodiversity from the ongoing
extinction crisis, can be understood as a form of 'panopticism' which, through its
processes of 'identification, collection of specimens, and subsequent research [...]
neatly packages' non-human nature into a set of designations which, in turn,
simultaneously facilitate 'conservation *and* commodification'.[119] These types of
programs are arguably necessary in order to protect natural ecosystems, and yet
they also subsume nature within a grid of control that subdues them while trying
to conserve and sustainably optimise them. Youatt argues in this respect that from
the biopolitical perspective embodied in practices such as the global biodiversity
census, 'nonhumans are regulated and rationalised in matrices of knowledge and
science, through which they are readied as productive resources for capitalism and
mined as repositories of genetic information'.[120]

This biopolitical project of panopticist surveillance, and the related aporia that
constantly and incessantly transforms the care for life into its destruction, are in
fact inscribed in the very birthmark of sustainable development—a key concept
in environmental law. The Report of the World Commission on Environment and
Development, envisioned a 'planetary management' enacted through the establishment of surveillance mechanisms aimed at monitoring 'the vital signs of the
planet' so as to 'aid humans in protecting its health'.[121] Indeed, the discourse of
ecosystem (or ecological) health has become central (despite its ambiguities)[122] in
the context of environmental law (along with the intertwined discourse of integrity; indeed the two are considered by some 'inseparable').[123] Environmental law
in this respect, facilitates 'an extension of "biopolitics" [...] to all life-forms',[124]
and can be ultimately understood as a 'normalizing strategy' attempting 'to extend
control ("management") to the entire planet'.[125]

A key example to further support the argument outlined in this chapter is
offered by the ecosystem approach, as it captures the slippages that traverse and
complicate both the interventionist and the radical register. In the most general
terms (and regardless of the complexities involved),[126] the ecosystem approach

[119] R Youatt, 'Counting Species: Biopower and the Global Biodiversity Census' (2008) 17(3) *Environmental Values* 393.

[120] ibid, 394.

[121] WCED, *Our Common Future: Report of the World Commission on Environment and Development*,
4 August 1987, UN Doc A/42/427, 1987, para 56.

[122] See esp Lackey, 'Appropriate Use of Ecosystem Health and Normative Science in Ecological
Policy' (n 28); E Hearnshaw, R Cullen and K Hughey, 'Ecosystem Health Demystified: an Ecological
Concept Determined by Economic Means' (Conference paper presented at the Economics and Environment Network Workshop, Australian National University, Canberra, 4–6 May 2005); De Lucia
(n 38).

[123] R Siron and others, 'Ecosystem-Based Management in the Arctic Ocean: A Multi-Level Spatial
Approach' (2008) 61 *Arctic* 86, 87.

[124] Rutherford 1993, quoted in Darier (n 97) at 23.

[125] Sachs, *Global Ecology* (n 100), quoted in Darier (n 97) at 23.

[126] See eg De Lucia (n 38).

can be characterised as a legal and governance 'strategy for the integrated management of land, water and living resources'.[127] The ecosystem approach, built
on the concept of ecosystem (that is, the 'dynamic complex of plant, animal
and micro-organism communities and their non-living environment interacting as a functional unit')[128] promotes integration, challenging the traditionally
fragmentary approach of environmental law, and promoting a transversal ecosystem perspective cutting across fragmented jurisdictional, political and social
boundaries and domains. The ecosystem approach transplants, importantly, a
number of central ecological principles into law, and some argue that it is the
clearest evidence of a shift from an outdated anthropocentric legal framework,
to an ecocentric one attuned to ecology as both a science and as a new ethico-
philosophical paradigm.[129] The ecosystem approach seems to move past both
'classic' and 'modern' articulations of environmental law[130] and towards an 'ecological' form or mode of law that, incorporating an ecocentric ethics, signals the
shift to a new phase of its development, a phase which, as has been noted, is 'little
short of a paradigm shift'.[131] The ecosystem approach may then offer an answer to
calls for an urgent and complete rethink of law in the Anthropocene.

Yet the ecosystem approach, I argue, embodies *precisely* the biopolitical aporia
investing environmental law, and illustrates how the two registers discussed above
are easily enveloped within the same biopolitical horizon. By way of example,[132]
first, while the ecosystem approach embraces the need for protecting both the
ecological integrity and the ecological health of ecosystems, such a goal requires
a comprehensive system of ecosystem monitoring/surveillance in order to be
achieved, and is furthermore inscribed within the broader systemic goal of sustainable development. Secondly, the ecosystem approach also promotes an ecological geography (ie a geography of conservation based on ecosystem boundaries
rather than political jurisdictions) and yet simultaneously enables the subjection
of nature to a transnational management through global and regional programs
that extracts sovereignty from states and redistributes it across a range of global
institutions and legal regimes. Thirdly, while recognising that humans are inevitably immersed in nature, the ecosystem approach simultaneously makes possible
the organisation of nature as a productive resource through the framework of
ecosystem services, leading to that enframing that the ecosystem approach, in its
more holistic and ecocentric inflection, apparently leaves behind. The ecosystem

---

[127] COP Decision V/6 'Ecosystem Approach' adopted by the Conference of the Parties to the
Convention of Biological Diversity at its Fifth meeting, Nairobi, 15–26 May 2000, UNEP/COP/5/23.

[128] Art 2 of the Convention on Biological Diversity, 1760 UNTS 79.

[129] See eg already E Grumbine, 'What is Ecosystem Management?' (1994) 8(1) *Conservation Biology*
27, but also, more recently, R Brooks, R Jones and R Virginia, *Law and Ecology: The Rise of the Ecosystem
Regime* (Aldershot, Ashgate, 2002).

[130] This distinction in 'phases' of environmental law is Jane Holder's, Holder (n 32).

[131] ibid, 167.

[132] The full argument is developed in my PhD; De Lucia (n 8). Some of these contradictions are
discussed also in De Lucia (n 38).

approach, in other words, can be located precisely at that juncture where, through a multiplicity of slippages, incongruences and contradictions the interventionist and the radical register intersect and overlap.

From the preceding it should have become apparent how there is a 'zone of irreducible indistinction'[133] where the two discourses of the Anthropocene meet and become entangled. Both an ecocentric approach to conservation and a methodological programme of surveillance and intervention to protect nature follow from the same logic and remain entangled despite their apparently opposite project. This is precisely the aporetic logic of biopolitics, a logic that has no outside. A space for critique, then, can only be found inside biopolitics, in the midst of the complexities and contestations involved.

VI. Conclusions

As this chapter has attempted to show, critique in the Anthropocene can no longer rely on the key referents of modernity. In the Anthropocene, knowledge is plural and uncertain, nature no longer beyond contestation, and values in continuous conflict. Yet those key referents remain implicitly operative in both anthropocentrism and ecocentrism. In the Anthropocene, however, they are no longer sufficient, and rather counter-productively perpetuate binary polarisations that prevent to find a truly novel space and language for critique.

Environmental law, I have argued, cannot be neatly aligned with any one project, as no project is fully coherent or free from slippages, incongruences, contradictions or genealogical complexities. Environmental law needs to be recognised then as a complex biopolitical field. This recognition of the biopolitical character of environmental law, and of the totalising reach of biopower (of which biopolitics is a specific declension), allows instead to articulate a critique that cuts across that zone of indistinction where biopolitics neutralises ecocentric critiques by continuously reproducing an aporetic logic that transforms every attempt at protecting nature into its opposite.

A biopolitical reading has furthermore the key advantage of allowing reading environmental law *simultaneously* negatively and positively, to the extent that life, situated at the 'moving margins' of intersection and tension between biology and history,[134] knowledge and nature, ecology ethics and law, is both enhanced and subjugated by power in the same gesture.[135] The key question in the Anthropocene is then not to identify a static truth external to the current state of affairs—that

---

[133] Agamben, *Homo Sacer* (n 45).
[134] Esposito, *Bíos* (n 93) at 31.
[135] ibid, 37.

is, a transcendent utopia[136]—in order to enact a righteous closure, but to explore a dynamic process of critique from within, in order to enable responsive and responsible participation to the juridical field of discursivity where environmental law is constantly made and remade, on the part of the critical legal scholar or practitioner. Critical environmental law, through biopolitics, in other words, does not level a critique from outside, but articulates its critique inside *and* against the current biopolitical paradigm. In the Anthropocene, critique needs to divaricate the incongruences and contradictions of environmental law; needs to embrace and leverage its complexities, and to exploit its slippages. Through the language of biopolitics (critical environmental) legal scholars will be able to disentangle law and legal strategies, thought and practice, 'from the constraints imposed by the tradition of' modernity,[137] embedded in the language of anthropocentrism and ecocentrism. By rupturing the biopolitical envelope, critical environmental law opens space for a critical new legal language for the Anthropocene.

---

[136] Utopias are 'unreal places' where a society can imagine itself in 'a perfected form'; M Foucault, 'Of Other Spaces: Utopias and Heterotopias' in N Leach (ed), *Rethinking Architecture: A Reader in Cultural Theory* (New York, Routledge, 1997) 332.

[137] Pieraccini (n 43).

6

Critical Environmental Law in the Anthropocene

ANDREAS PHILIPPOPOULOS-MIHALOPOULOS

I. Introduction

The amount of text produced on the Anthropocene[1] across the disciplines is rapidly generating a digital (and occasionally paper) imprint worthy of the geological imprint of its subject matter. One might even be tempted to talk of an 'Anthropocene-turn': as with the spatial turn,[2] of which the Anthropocene is a close bedfellow, a new grammar is inaugurated, a different theoretical perspective is tried out, and an updated methodology ensues. The Anthropocene has managed to provide for all these new steps, influencing an unexpectedly large and broad variety of disciplines. Environmental law has not been left out of this wave,[3] since, more than any other branch of law, it is directly involved in some of the fossilising and anthropogenic processes in the core of the Anthropocene. But so far, most attempts to deal with the Anthropocene from an environmental point of view have been partial,[4] or even worse, espousing of the ubiquitous neoliberal 'green' economic agenda, entrusting the future of the planet to more technology, stronger ('but cleaner') industry, aggressive geoengineering, and other market-oriented mechanisms which sadly confirm Swyngedouw's characterisation of the Anthropocene as the 'opiate of the masses'.[5]

---

[1] PJ Crutzen and E Stoermer, 'The Anthropocene' (2000) 41 *IGBP Newsletter* 17.

[2] B Warf and S Arias (eds), *The Spatial Turn: Interdisciplinary Perspectives* (New York, Routledge, 2009).

[3] See eg C Gonzalez, 'Bridging the North-South Divide: International Environmental Law in the Anthropocene' (2015) 32 *Pace Environmental Law Review* 407; D Houston, 'Crisis Is Where We Live: Environmental Justice for the Anthropocene' (2013) 10(3) *Globalizations* 439; see also N Robinson, 'Fundamental Principles of Law for the Anthropocene?' (2014) 44 *Environmental Policy and Law* 1–2, 13, whose work on principles for the Anthropocene is based on strong ethical considerations.

[4] Exceptions of course abound. See indicatively, A Grear, 'Deconstructing *Anthropos*: A Critical Legal Reflection on "Anthropocentric" Law and Anthropocene "Humanity"' (2015) 26(3) *Law and Critique* 225; S Adelman, 'Climate Justice, Loss and Damage and Compensation for Small Island Developing States' (2016) 7(1) *Journal of Human Rights and the Environment* 32.

[5] E Swyngedouw, 'The Non-political Politics of Climate Change' (2011) 12(1) *Acme* 1.

What is needed instead, is a return to the basics of the discipline of environmental law, and a reconsideration of some of its major tenets. Grammar, perspective and methodology of the Anthropocene, therefore, are the three focal points of this text. Briefly, grammar refers to the need for a new, anthropocenic vocabulary that will deal with the challenges of the Anthropocene and its introduction in social sciences and humanities in a way suitable to the disciplines but also faithful to the origin of the term. The theoretical perspective, on the other hand, refers to the way current thinking changes or at least is affected by the Anthropocene—indeed, how current thinking is turning in order to accommodate the needs of the new epoch. Finally, methodology refers to the way the Anthropocene changes the way we seek knowledge and the epistemological presuppositions of the limits of such knowledge. I will examine the first two in the context of environmental law, and will suggest an anthropocenic methodology in the form of what I have initiated elsewhere by the name *Critical Environmental Law*,[6] namely a way of looking into the law that takes into consideration the various developments in other disciplines and on the planet as a whole.

Rather unsurprisingly, the law has been lagging behind in terms of riding the Anthropocene wagon. This is partly because the law is always characterised by a slower, more ponderous temporality, typically operating later than politics and certainly much later than most humanities and social sciences. The reasons for this are multiple, but perhaps the most obvious ones are the fact that law often operates as the final arbiter on events in which several other institutions have already been involved, such as politics, media, science and so on. Things *end up* in law, and for that reason, law carries the weight of confirming societal expectations. These expectations refer to the assumption that the circumstances will carry on being the way they have been so far, and that they can be relied upon not to change arbitrarily.[7] This rather conservative aspect of the law is coupled to a more proactive and future-tending aspect, and the second main reason for which law is characterised by a slower temporality: the law is expected to bind the future. Every act and decision (if one wishes to look at the law narrowly), every legal spatialisation and expansion (geopolitical law), every legal gesture and movement (embodied law), and indeed every piece of legal research, bears the responsibility of capturing the future. This is simply because every piece of the legal system, to a smaller or greater extent, at the same time *constructs* the law and *binds* social expectations on how the law will be in the future.

Environmental law is no exception to this, although its slow temporality might be a greater disappointment because of the different expectations we have of it.[8]

---

[6] A Philippopoulos-Mihalopoulos, 'Towards a Critical Environmental Law' in A Philippopoulos-Mihalopoulos (ed), *Law and Ecology: New Environmental Foundations* (London, Routledge, 2011).

[7] N Luhmann, *Law as a Social System*, trans K Ziegert (Oxford, Oxford University Press, 2004).

[8] See eg Elizabeth Fisher's ruminations on the particularities of environmental law as 'hot law' responding to 'hot' problems that lack an adequate knowledge base and involve a plurality of parameters and agents; E Fisher, 'Environmental Law as "Hot" Law' (2013) 25(3) *Journal of Environmental Law* 347.

In view of the urgency of environmental issues and the relatively uncrystallised nature of the particular branch of law, the expectations would be that environmental law would act faster and without the laboriousness that characterises the rest of the legal areas. These expectations are bound to be disappointed, since environmental law remains part of the legal machine that needs to reduce real facts into legal facts, while at the same time inserting itself into existing administrative legal mechanisms. Current environmental law, therefore, is as fast or as slow as the rest of the legal system, with occasional bouts of acceleration if the particular case, story or concept has been taken up by the media, politics, the economy or other spheres of social life.

It would now seem, however, that the law has found its match. Geology is notoriously slow and so far has operated outside the speed demands of other disciplines. Its method relies on the construction of a continuity that spans vast durations before and indeed following human presence.[9] Humans are often considered a brief interval in an otherwise multiscalar process that is concerned with what withstands time and therefore remains in time and space. But even geology is changing: with the emergence of the Anthropocene, lithostratigraphy is being complemented by biostratigraphy (namely, not just non-anthropogenic rocks but also urban environments created by humans). The focus is more zoomed in and as a consequence, the epistemic velocity speeds up. This, in combination to the fervour with which the Anthropocene as a new geological epoch has been embraced by various disciplines, has propelled the discipline of geology to an accelerated mode—so much that, as Bruno Latour puts it,

> we find geologists flabbergasted by the quick pace of human history; a pace that forces them to try lodging a 'golden spike' in a span of two hundred or even of sixty years (depending on whether you prefer a short or very short temporal boundary demarcating the emergence of Anthropocene).[10]

The term has provided us with a sizeable amount of interdisciplinary work by geology scholars that aim to converse with other disciplines in ways never occurring before. Although the discipline itself has stalled for a characteristically long time on its decision whether there is enough scientific evidence to accept the term,[11] the Anthropocene has managed to mobilise an extraordinary inter- and even supra-disciplinary surge of interest—a great indication of which is also this

---

[9] See eg 'Landscape modification will only persist as long as human land management persists; there will be a lag time, *probably of a few centuries...* After this, sedimentary processes will revert to approximately natural'; J Zalasiewicz and others, 'Stratigraphy of the Anthropocene' (2011) 369 *Philosophical Transactions of the Royal Society A* 1036, 1047, added emphasis.

[10] B Latour, *Facing Gaia: Six Lectures on the Political Theology of Nature* (the Gifford Lectures on Natural Religion, Edinburgh, 18–28 February 2013) 77, www.giffordlectures.org/lecturers/bruno-latour.

[11] See however the report of the Anthropocene Working Group of 29 August 2016, to the International Geological Congress, subsequently to be considered by the International Commission on Stratigraphy for their final decision, on how the Anthropocene is stratigraphically verifiable, making the Anthropocene an official geological epoch.

very volume. We are all united in the search for our position with regards to the Anthropocene—or at least this is what it would seem. And why not? It is rare to witness and be offered the opportunity to cogitate on the change of a geological epoch, and the law must not abstain from it.

In what follows, I embrace this responsibility of thinking of the new geological epoch which has been entirely instigated by us humans. I will suggest some new terms to deal with the Anthropocene from an environmental legal point of view, such as continuum/rupture, human/non-human/inhuman, as well as geologic immersion and planetary withdrawal. These are merely the tools in order to start constructing a theoretical perspective faithful to the Anthropocene and its demands, which takes place in section III of this text. To conclude, I offer four theses in the form of suggestions on how Critical Environmental Law needs to adapt in order to integrate the Anthropocenic grammar and perspective.

II. Anthropocenic Grammar

In the opening pages of his book *Ecological Thought*, Timothy Morton writes: 'one of the things that modern society has damaged, along with ecosystems and species and the global climate, is thinking'.[12] The kind of thinking Morton refers to, has been long forgotten in the name of problem-solving and solution-oriented practices. This does not mean that problem-solving precludes thinking. On the contrary, it demands a thinking that is specific, unidirectional and targeted. By definition, it needs to bracket issues that are not immediately relevant and assume a temporality that targets the present and the immediate future. This mode of thinking is applied in most environmental legal production processes.[13] The Anthropocene, however, opens up a different temporality and depth of thinking. It requires a focus that zooms out rather than in, observing humanity and its shenanigans from a distance. It requires a counter-intuitive pause and an opening up to include previously considered irrelevant issues, planetary futures and inhuman bodies, as I show below. It demands a supra-disciplinarity, some work on which must take place within the confines of every individual discipline (every discipline has the responsibility to start thinking of other disciplines) and also in unison as a collective emergence.

The challenge for environmental law is considerable. It must expand beyond the increasing epistemic closure that always demands a return to the law and its habitual mechanisms, and consider other disciplines in both its theoretical and applied manifestation. Indeed, the latter is the lesser of the two problems: in

---

[12] T Morton, *Ecological Thought* (Cambridge, MA, Harvard University Press, 2010) 4.
[13] F Capra and U Mattei, *The Ecology of Law: Toward a Legal System in Tune with Nature and Community* (Berrett-Koehler, 2015).

any environmental legal statute or court decision there is an inherent interdisciplinarity that needs to bring together epistemic advances from science, ecology, politics and economy, to name a few. But this interdisciplinarity is instrumentalised and as such, does not reach beyond the law and its needs. The various disciplines become translated into law for the demands of the particular problem, with its pre-determined, mostly short-term temporality. This remains the case despite some of the more visionary legal concepts, such as the principle of intergenerational equity that urges towards a slightly ampler but ultimately still limited temporality, especially when compared to the Anthropocenic temporality. So, the main challenges for environmental law are: *adopt an interdisciplinary approach that escapes the narrow instrumentalism of decision-making, and extend this on a supra-disciplinary horizon of long-term futurity*.

Similarly to what has been called the grammars of climate change,[14] which refer to the questions of who speaks and how one speaks for pressing environmental issues, the need for a grammar of the Anthropocene is pressing and invites the re-emergence of a supra-disciplinary thinking of the kind in which the Renaissance excelled. While a Renaissance breadth of knowledge would now be impossible owing to the depth of specialised knowledge, an epistemic propensity towards supra-disciplinarity is the main grammatical invitation of the Anthropocene. In a way, this challenge is superior to the one augured by sustainable development— another mobilising concept that transcended disciplines. Indeed, very few concepts have managed to mobilise the various disciplines so fiercely and with such an effect on current thinking as the Anthropocene hypothesis. Let me, therefore, point to some of the new grammatical structures that are proposed with the Anthropocene.

First, the Anthropocene changes the way we understand the connection between humanity and the rest of the planet. It demands a fine, somewhat paradoxical, balance. On the one hand, an understanding that, not only do humans depend on the planet (which is in the basis of many anthropocentric theories where nature is protected as resource); not even that nature is central to humanity (in the way ecocentrism and Earth jurisprudence has it)[15]; but that there is such a continuity between them and the rest of the planet that any distinction is often arbitrary and on the basis of partial interests. On the other hand, the Anthropocene invites a return of *Anthropos* as a new political and legal body that embraces the scientific developments of posthumanism, and yet asserts that humans are *not* the same as other material and immaterial bodies that populate the planet.[16]

---

[14] C Barnett, P Cloke, N Clarke and A Malpass, *Globalizing Responsibility: The Political Rationalities of Ethical Consumption* (London, Blackwell, 2011).

[15] What I suggest is different from ecocentrism in that, emphatically, here there is no centre yet there is difference. See my work on this in 'Actors or spectators? Vulnerability and Critical Environmental Law' in A Grear and E Grant (eds), *Thought, Law, Rights and Action in the Age of Environmental Crisis* (Cheltenham, Edward Elgar, 2015).

[16] A Grear, 'Deconstructing *Anthropos*: A Critical Legal Reflection on "Anthropocentric" Law and Anthropocene "Humanity"' (2015) 26(3) *Law and Critique* 225–49.

The oft-rehearsed deep-ecology notions of oneness in terms of human and non-human bodies points to a need for an ecological flatness that does not offer any criteria of distinction, and therefore cannot differentiate between the various bodies. It is important, therefore, to retain difference and even perhaps human priority. As Kathryn Yussof puts it, 'this priority is isomorphic and is not something that should be flattened out in relation to other life/minerals (as some argumentation in the posthumanities inadvertently does)'.[17] The other end of the spectrum is, however, a human exceptionalism, the kind of which we often witness and practise, whether consciously or unconsciously. This is especially the case in law, which in its majority is characterised by anthropocentric values. Paradoxically, this needs to be managed as an anthropocenic asset in terms of retaining human responsibility. Yussof again:

> [i]t is a case of negotiating human exceptionalism rather than trying to do away with it all together, because that elision negates the power and responsibility that comes with what is inherited as a consequence of our humanism (the ontological debt).[18]

In other words, the Anthropocene is inviting us to consider the connection between *the indistinguishability between bodies* on the one hand, and the de facto emergence of *different bodies* on the other. The indistinguishability between bodies refers to the way bodies are always assembled in collectivities with other bodies, to the point that the limits of a (human but also any other) body become actually and epistemically fuzzy. Bodies, in other words, constitute a *continuum*. I have elsewhere defined the continuum as the surface that cuts across animate and inanimate objects, bodies, discourses and so on.[19] This continuum is not equivalent to a flat ontology, nor to the vastness of the plane of immanence ('the "holding together" of heterogeneous elements').[20] It draws on Moira Gatens' description as 'a plane of experimentation, a mapping of extensive relations and intensive capacities that are mobile and dynamic',[21] in that it emphasises experimental and therefore unpredictable mobility of both material (extensive) and immaterial (intensive) bodies. It also draws on Jane Bennett's

> ontological field without any unequivocal demarcations between human, animal, vegetable or mineral. All forces and flows (materialities) are or can become lively, affective, and signaling … portions congeal into bodies, but not in a way that makes any one type the privileged site of agency.[22]

---

[17] K Yussof, 'Geologic Subjects: Nonhuman Origins, Geomorphic Aesthetics and the Art of Becoming Inhuman' (2015) 22(3) *Cultural Geographies* 383, 399.

[18] ibid, 399–400.

[19] A Philippopoulos-Mihalopoulos, *Spatial Justice: Lawscape Body Atmosphere* (London, Routledge, 2015).

[20] G Deleuze and F Guattari, *A Thousand Plateaus: Capitalism and Schizophrenia*, B Massumi trans (London, Athlone Press, 1988) 323; G Deleuze and F Guattari, *What is Philosophy?*, H Tomlinson and G Burchell trans (New York, Columbia University Press, 1994) 141.

[21] M Gatens, 'Through a Spinozist Lens: Ethology, Difference, Power' in P Patton (ed), *Deleuze: A Critical Reader* (Oxford, Blackwell, 1996) 165.

[22] J Bennett, *Vibrant Matter: A Political Ecology of Things* (Durham, Duke University Press, 2010) 117.

Indeed, the continuum I am suggesting here is acentral and multi-agentic, constituted of affective excess and of bodies melting into each other's contours. But it is not flat, like much of current ontologies, new materialisms and some ecological thinking seem to suggest. It is instead a *manifold*, full of fissures and planes, heavily politicised by historical and geographical processes. It is also a *tilted*, power-structured surface, on which bodies move, rest and position themselves, affecting the tilt while being affected by it. Stronger bodies affect the continuum in radical ways, making it tilt according to their positions: the global North is stronger than the South; a corporation is often stronger than a single individual; a collective is sometimes stronger than a developer; a tsunami is nearly always stronger than the holiday-makers, and global warming is stronger than all of us.

The concept of indistinguishability refers to the commonality of all bodies as 'inhabitants' of the continuum. But so far, the anthropocentric continuum reserved a special place for the human, indeed for Man. Think of the idea of 'man' as propagated in the Enlightenment: a white male of ideal corporeal proportions, gifted with reason, common sense, knowledge, potential, ready to conquer the world.[23] But we know now, after the extensive discussion on the posthuman, that the human has never been what we thought. The human is always mediated (by its body, by the space around it and by the space that the human body generates, by other bodies, whether human, natural, artificial and so on). This is intimately connected to the fact that a body cannot be a neatly defined entity. The body does not have an outline. If they were a painting, bodies would be Venetian dashes of colour without drawn linear boundaries, staging through their expansive leaking a radical withdrawal from the Florentine canon of humanist containment. Deleuze writes: 'the edge of the forest is a limit. Does this mean that the forest is defined by its outline?…We can't even specify the precise moment at which there is no more forest'.[24] All bodies are leaking. By 'all bodies' I mean human and non-human. While in traditional environmental thinking, whenever included, non-human bodies have been either resource, context or the negative of the dialectics of humanity, here I follow the schools of thought largely identified as new materialisms, non-representational theory, speculative realism and object-oriented ontologies,[25] themselves generally drawing from a Spinozan/Deleuzian understanding of the body. Thus, for Deleuze, 'a body can be anything: it can be an animal, a body of sounds, a mind or idea; it can be a linguistic corpus, a social body, a collectivity'.[26] All bodies are *assemblages*, namely aggregations of human and non-human bodies that are contingent upon the conditions of

---

[23] See A Grear, 'Challenging Corporate "Humanity": Legal Disembodiment, Embodiment and Human Rights' (2007) 7(3) *Human Rights Law Review* 511.

[24] G Deleuze, 'Cours Vincennes: Sur Spinoza' in L Lambert, *The Funambulist Pamphlets 01: Spinoza* (New York, Punctum Books, 2013) 74.

[25] See eg D Coole and S Frost, *New Materialisms: Ontology, Agency and Politics* (Durham, Duke University Press, 2010); Bennett, *Vibrant Matter* (n 22).

[26] G Deleuze, *Spinoza: Practical Philosophy*, R Hurley trans (San Francisco, City Light Books, 1988) 127.

their emergence and which do not presuppose the centrality, and certainly not the exclusive presence, of the human. What is more, assemblages are both actual, namely space and matter, and virtual, namely potential, but still real. Actual and virtual are not found in a dialectical opposition; nor does the actual determine the virtual.[27] Rather, there is no ontological distinction between the two, and if anything, the actual is determined through its folding with the virtual. In this sense, current weakness or at least lack of strength is always affected by the virtual potential of its evolution into a much stronger body. Postcolonial environmental legal studies amply show both how the various positions of the bodies (North/South, urban poor versus urban elite and so on) are artificially maintained in positions of subjugation due to capitalist interests; and how these positions can and do change, usually according to a neoliberal economic machine that encourages growth at the expense of environmental protection.[28]

So, if all bodies are assemblages and if no body has a definitive contour, how do bodies differentiate themselves from each other? How do singularities emerge from the continuum? These singularities emerge through *ruptures*. Ruptures interrupt the continuum, cutting the links between bodies and allowing differences/individualities/subjectivities and eventually singularities to emerge. In thinking of the continuum, I have been inevitably influenced by Foucaultian biopolitics because its sovereignty is diffused and embodied in each participating body. It differs from the biopolitical, however, because it is characterised by the persistent erection of boundaries in the form of ruptures without predetermined ethical value. Ruptures can be both positive differences that encourage identity, as well as exclusions or hierarchies that discourage specific kinds of identity; they can be conflicts (necessary or engineered) as well as Deleuzian folds, namely co-emerging assemblages, and therefore ontological differentiations and 'gatherings'; they can also be epistemological necessities: we *need* to differentiate, according to the foundational fantasy of distinction between self and environment, as Teresa Brennan writes.[29] Whatever they are, ruptures remain part of the continuum. Rather than annulling it, ruptures nourish the continuum, which can be thought of as a (continuous) series of ruptures. I have employed the term 'continuum' in different contexts, but it is consistently characterised by this one quality: it is always ruptured, indeed self-ruptured, through foldings and distinctions on its surface. Sometimes illusionary necessities and other times ontological facts, ruptures are the locus of singularity in the continuum. Ruptures constitute the continuum, to the point that one is left only with a continuity of ruptures.

According to Spinoza, bodies differentiate themselves on the basis of their differentiated velocities or pauses—it is all about how a body moves or rests.

---

[27] G Deleuze, *Cinema 1: The Movement-Image* (London, Athlone Press, 1986).

[28] See C Gonzalez, 'Bridging the North-South Divide: International Environmental Law in the Anthropocene' (2015) 32 *Pace Environmental Law Review* 407; S Humphreys and Y Otomo, 'Theorising International Environmental Law' in F Hoffmann and A Orford (eds) *The Oxford Handbook of International Legal Theory* (Oxford, Oxford University Press, 2014).

[29] T Brennan, *The Transmission of Affect* (Ithaca and London, Cornell University Press, 2004).

A human body will be faster than a chair will be faster than the plant will be faster than the fossil, and all of them will be slower than a typhoon. Rupture enables a difference in movement that results in a repeated difference. Yet, precisely because the continuum is a series of ruptures, ruptures do not rupture the continuum as such: they are all inscribed within. So, the continuum is crossed by lines that produce meaning, while continuously being ruptured by them. Lisa Blackman in her seminal work on the body,[30] has called this the problem of 'the one and the many', namely the ontological difficulty of being coherent yet multiple, in other words, self yet othering. Karen Barad has introduced the term 'agential separability' to signal the need for boundaries between bodies.[31] These boundaries are not placed as fixed constructions between subject and object, human and non-human, or indeed animate and inanimate. Rather, they emerge in order to produce meaning relative to the continuum on which the boundary appears. I understand this as a rupture that brings agency forth without flattening it to an all-connected ontology. It is significant that these boundaries are not conceptualised as either prior or immutable: they are drawn every time as part of the emergence of differentiated bodies—namely, the emergence of agency. The main challenge is how to avoid categorising either continuum or rupture as inferior, namely how to escape the trap of mapping them 'onto differentiations made between the civilized and the primitive, the superior and the inferior, the simple and the complex, and the impulsive and the environmental'.[32] Indeed, how *not* to make rupture and continuum a dialectic of opposites, namely a question of positive presence and negative absence, but a folding co-emergence.

This is also the challenge for the Anthropocene: to put it more concretely, how to manage the fact that humans are everywhere, affecting the geology and future history of the Earth even after our extinction, while at the same time being embedded in a continuum of indistinguishability. As the editors of *New Materialisms* Diana Coole and Samantha Frost write, we have moved away from an epoch where:

> agents are exclusively humans who possess the cognitive abilities, intentionality, and freedom to make autonomous decisions and the corollary presumption that humans have the right or ability to master nature. Instead, the human species is being relocated within a natural environment whose material forces themselves manifest certain agentic capacities and in which the domain of unintended or unanticipated effects is considerably broadened.[33]

For environmental law, this means that there can no longer be a boundary between a body and its environment. The main find of the Anthropocene is that our presence on the Earth necessarily *includes* our 'environment', whether

---

[30] L Blackman, *Immaterial Bodies* (London, Sage, 2012).
[31] K Barad, *Meeting the Universe Halfway: Quantum Physics and the Entanglement of Matter and Meaning* (Durham, Duke University Press, 2006) 175.
[32] Blackman, *Immaterial Bodies* (n 30) at 59.
[33] Coole and Frost, *New Materialisms* (n 25) at 10.

'natural' or otherwise. We are always in an assemblage with the planet. A body is an assemblage of various conditions and materialities. Eben Kirksey's multi-species families[34] is an example of such an assemblage containing human and animal bodies, discursive bodies of economics, politics and law, conservation agencies, wildlife experts, government agents and hobbyists, specific spatialities, affects from gentleness to aggression, and so on. The total sum of these connections constitutes a body that is internally ruptured in an infinity of modalities.[35]

The Anthropocene, therefore, invites us to think of a grammar of continuum and ruptures, of ruptured continuum and continuous ruptures. These are heuristic tools, indeed a vocabulary or at least a mode of thinking that allows disciplines such as environmental law to extend on the ways it is intimately connected to everything else by engaging with the indistinguishability of bodies, and also to accept the need for differentiation and draw it in a velocity and mode that serves its purpose. This enables the law to question the unchallenged perpetuation of such existing accepted assemblages as environment and economy, or sustainability and growth, and start experimenting with different assemblages that include the non-human in its ruptured polyvalence.

III. Anthropocenic Theoretical Perspective

Claire Colebrook writes:

> the anthropocene thought experiment also alters the modality of geological reading, not just to refer to the past as it is for us, but also to our present as it will be without us. We imagine a viewing or reading in the absence of viewers or readers, and we do this through images in the present that extinguish the dominance of the present.[36]

The perspective is changing radically. The Anthropocene demands an epistemological distance from the object of study, both spatially and temporally. In order to observe the effects of the human onto the Earth, we must *withdraw* from it: spatially to get an understanding of the way the crust of the Earth is altering due to our presence; temporally and into the future of a human extinction, 'in the absence of viewers or readers', where the planet returns to its slowness after that brief human interval.

These notions perhaps seem too large for environmental law. They open up existential gushes that have little to do with the day-to-day operations of, say,

---

[34] E Kirksey, 'Multispecies Families, Capitalism, and the Law' in I Braverman (ed), *Lively Legalities* (London, Routledge, 2016); see also J Lorrimer, 'Multinatural Geographies for the Anthropocene' (2012) 36(5) *Progress in Human Geography* 59.

[35] T Morton, *Hyperobjects: Philosophy and Ecology after the End of the World* (Minneapolis, University of Minnesota Press, 2013).

[36] C Colebrook, *Death of the PostHuman: Essays on Extinction*, vol 1 (Ann Arbor, Open Humanities Press, 2014) 30.

the laws on pollution. As Upendra Baxi writes, 'the question of urgency of global social policy is often considered vast enough to permit the luxury of ethical deliberation'.[37] But if the Anthropocene is to be heeded, this has to change. An environmental law open to the ruptured continuum must adopt a different, more ethically situated perspective to the one traditionally understood. The anthropocenic perspective I am suggesting here is the fold between, on the one hand, a withdrawal of the law from the object in hand, in order for a planetary jurisprudence to emerge; and, on the other, an immersion to the geological strata of law with an aim of understanding a mineralised jurisprudence.

I employ withdrawal here as a tool of resistance against an atmosphere of absolute inclusion in what Timothy Morton has named *hyperobjects*: objects characterised by viscosity, nonlocality, temporally undulating and constantly phasing. Morton's prime example of a hyperobject is global warming. As a hyperobject, global warming is characterised by an absence of distance between the implicated bodies: raindrops on our face is global warming, just as the act of flushing away our toilet waste thinking that it ends somewhere *away*. Its viscous nature means that there is no distance between here and away. Everything is within, assembling into the continuous space of the hyperobject yet at the same time withdrawing from it: global warming is not *here* either. 'The octopus of the hyperobject emits a cloud of ink as it withdraws from access. Yet this cloud of ink is a cloud of effects and affects'.[38] The affects and effects left behind are not causal, at least not in the sense of being merely the sign of the cause. Rather, they all constitute the hyperobject; but they are often cut into palatable pieces of locality and present: they all become little ruptures placed at a distance in order to be apprehended. 'It's never the case that those raindrops only fall on my head! They are always a manifestation of global warming!'[39] These ruptures are also part of the object, 'are simply the invisible presence of the hyperobject itself, which looms around us constantly'.[40] In their phasing, objects appear only partially, as indexical signs of their spatiotemporal distribution, and never in their entirety. Indeed, what is there to appear in global warming, if not the entire Earth, fractal and multiscalar, apprehended by different systems, such as politics, media, science, economics, ecology and so on, all putting between themselves and the hyperobject a desperately constructed distance of observation? How can it present itself, and to whom, if everyone is implicated in this hyperobjective implicate order of global warming? We are all in it, complicitly constituting its continuum.

The total inclusiveness of the hyperobject (which is not of course just climate change but also the Earth's environmental degradation as a whole) is an aspect of the continuum from which environmental law needs to withdraw and

---

[37] U Baxi, 'Towards a Climate Change Justice Theory?' (2016) 7 *Journal of Human Rights and the Environment* 7, 10.

[38] Morton, *Hyperobjects* (n 35) at 39.

[39] ibid, 48.

[40] ibid, 7.

resemiologise. The operations of the hyperobject need to be conceived *as a whole* in an integrated, planetary manner, however strong the gravitational attraction of the hyperobject might be. The Anthropocene offers just this possibility of withdrawal. Clare Colebrook writes:

> the positing of the anthropocene era relies on looking at our own world and imagining it as it will be when it has become the past...We can see, now, from changes in the earth's composition that there will be a discernible strata that—in a manner akin to our dating of the earth's already layered geological epochs—will be readable.[41]

The withdrawal is both spatial and temporal, planet-embracing and future-tending.

Environmental law needs to see the whole hyperobject (or at least attempt a construction) as a planetary problem, and elevate the planet on an agentic level. Only subsequently can environmental law define its own role accordingly. As Rory Rowan writes,

> whereas 'the global' suggests a relatively flat, anthropocentric conception of the Earth focused on the construction of social relations on the surface, 'the planetary', by contrast, points to a more complex, volumic, stratified understanding of an Earth constituted through dynamic geo-social entanglements. Accordingly, the Anthropocene creates opportunities to cast the planet itself as a key player in the drama of human politics rather than simply its stage.[42]

The role of environmental law in this is pivotal, as long as it starts thinking in terms of the *planet* rather than in the old geopolitical terms of globality (this does not only apply to international environmental law but also very much to regional and national manifestations). Such a shift would come about with a withdrawal from given legal mechanisms such as the standard balance of interests and legalistic issues of interest, harm and proof. Environmental law must perform a withdrawal from the very inclusivity of this hyperobject: if it carries on operating within it, environmental law falls victim to the devastating rhetoric of piecemeal action and generally accepted impossibility of actually doing anything radical enough that will halt environmental decline. In a way, environmental law needs to stop being so thoroughly *law* and begin becoming more *environmental*: to withdraw from itself and its own habitual legal mechanisms and to move to a different plane from where the issue of environmental degradation will appear as a whole, in its all-ingesting hyperobject presence. From there on, preventive action must be given priority over economic interests and lack of scientific proof, in accordance to a more idealised (but critically realistic, in view of the conditions) understanding of the precautionary principle; issues of intergenerational equity on a planetary scale that includes the future of human extinction must tangibly affect every legal decision and in course change the core of environmental law, from a generally rather

[41] Colebrook, *Death of the PostHuman* (n 36) at 26.
[42] R Rowan, 'Notes on Politics after the Anthropocene' in E Johnson and others (eds), Special Issue 'After the Anthropocene: Politics and Geographic Inquiry for a New Epoch' (2014) 38(3) *Progress in Human Geography* 439, 448.

conservative, piecemeal and overtly technical legal branch to the visionary, open and given to futurity way of legal thinking and acting that it could be.

On the other side of withdrawal lies immersion. It begins with the fact, suggested by Timothy Morton,[43] that we are witnessing the end of the biologically determined human subject and the inauguration of a distributed humanity operating as a *geological* agent. Humanity and its activities can no longer be understood as mere thought advances, or even corporeally embedded presences, but significantly as mineralised temporalities. Kathryn Yussof puts it clearly:

> [t]he Anthropocene can be seen as a remineralization that is prompting reflection of the future fossilization of humanity…This is largely a result of being able to 'take up' a bloated payload of geologic force, courtesy of fossil fuels. In this sense the Anthropocene represents a moment of acknowledgement of a geologic social body politic, but in which our discourses for the critique of power (ie biopolitics) are configured to a version of 'life' that does not take account of this geology.[44]

The Anthropocene presents us with a depth (of subjectivity, politics, law) that has so far been excluded, and in which we need to immerse ourselves: the geological depth and its effect on existing discussions on biopolitical control. What will happen to the law if it considers the mineralisation of the body? The law will be required to immerse itself deeper in the geology of the Anthropocene and, once again, reconsider its basic notions. Think, for example, of the understanding of private property as a fundamental human right. In the light of anthropocenic mineralisation, property becomes a planetary loan that has relied on the overexploitation (a 'bloated payload') of fossil fuels. Property becomes less secure, less exclusionary, much more permeable. It needs to accommodate the logic of geologic circularity, namely the eventual fossilisation of humanity, and indeed the vanity of it all. It moves increasingly towards a much more expanded understanding of commons.

Immersion entails an acknowledgement of chthuloid (namely, of the deep Earth) verticality and a serious engagement with the ethical consequences of such an acknowledgement. This is what Donna Haraway has called the *Chthulucene*, namely an epoch which gives priority to the constant assemblaging of human with other non-human materialities.[45] Haraway prefers this to the Anthropocene because it describes more accurately the constant implication of the human with other Earthly entities, rather than artificially detaching the human from the assemblage. As Kathryn Yussof puts it, 'considering the human within geologic time poses the problem of thinking an inhuman milieu, both before, after and internal

---

[43] T Morton, *The Ecological Thought* (Cambridge, MA, Harvard University Press 2010).

[44] K Yussof, 'Anthropogenesis: Origins and Endings in the Anthropocene' (2016) 33(2) *Theory, Culture & Society* 5.

[45] See 'Anthropocene, Capitalocene, Chthulucene: Staying with the Trouble', a lecture given by Donna Haraway at University of California, Santa Cruz on 5 September 2014, available at: https://vimeo.com/97663518.

to "us"".[46] The *inhuman*, namely the geological, becomes part of the human and expands it from within. What is more, the Anthropocene demands a *geophilosophical* situatedness of thought in relation to the Earth. Reza Negarestani writes:

> geophilosophy is a philosophy that grasps thought in relation to earth and territory…it is a philosophy that, perhaps unconsciously, grasps thought in relation to two traumas, one precipitated by the accretion of the earth and the other ensued by the determination of the territory. Whilst the former trauma lies in the consolidation of the earth as a planetary ark for terrestrial life against the cosmic backdrop, the latter is brought about by a combined geographic and demographic determination of a territory against the exteriority of the terrestrial plane and fluxes of populations of all kinds.[47]

These two traumas, distinctly anthropocentric and a direct effect of the Anthropocene, are also specifically legal. They both require an intervention that guarantees limits, while at the same time allocating responsibility. This is an anthropocentric legality that chops up the surface of the Earth in territorial modes that include other populations as resources (rather than allowing for multiple territories in terms of animal populations); and then delegates the whole Earth to the status of resource ('ark') for the human future. A geophilosophical position attempts to mend these traumas through the only way possible. Colebrook writes:

> the anthropocene thought experiment also alters the modality of geological reading, not just to refer to the past as it is for us, but also to our present as it will be without us. We imagine a viewing or reading in the absence of viewers or readers, and we do this through images in the present that extinguish the dominance of the present.[48]

Rethinking the basics would also include the very term 'Anthropocene' which will need to be ruptured too: not all can be equal in terms of their responsibility towards the overexploitation of resources. As Chakrabarty writes,[49] the Anthropocene risks becoming another totalising imposition (a hyperobject?) flattening historical and geographical injustices and presenting a total, unified humanity in terms of the share of systematic destruction of nature. In other words, 'how humanity is deployed as a method of erasure that obfuscates climate racism, social injustice in fossil fuels, and differentiated histories of responsibilities through homogenization in a "we" of the Anthropocene'.[50] The tilt in the continuum disrupts the happy flatness of some of the Anthropocenic rhetoric. We are not one humanity facing its responsibility before the Anthropocene. Rather, we are a continuum of ruptured shares, some more, some less (no one, however, with no share in the responsibility).

---

[46] Yussof, 'Geologic Subjects' (n 17) at 388.
[47] R Negarestani, 'Triebkrieg', unpublished manuscript, 5, cited in B Woodard, *On an Ungrounded Earth: Towards a New Geophilosophy* (New York, Punctum Books, 2013) 14.
[48] Colebrook (n 36) at 30.
[49] D Chakrabarty, 'The Climate of History: Four Theses' (2009) 35 *Critical Inquiry* 197.
[50] Yussof, 'Anthropogenesis' (n 44) at 6–7.

The continuum changes: rather than flat, it is now revealed to be manifold, full of fissures and deep ruptures. Environmental law in the Anthropocene is to cultivate 'a depth relation that is something like a charge in its fathoming of deep, underground spaces'.[51] Inhuman (geology) and non-human (biology) constitute the assemblage of what the human is in the epoch of the Anthropocene. In other words, the responsibility in the Anthropocene epoch is one of both withdrawal and immersion: withdraw from the present in order to read it as non-human future; withdraw from centrality while retaining omnipresence; withdraw from the given legal mechanisms in order to withdraw from the hyperobject. But also, immerse ourselves in the geophilosophical understanding of the human; immerse the law in a mineralisation that extends into a deep future; and immerse into the differentiated responsibility that humanity has in the face of anthropocenic environmental degradation.

IV. Anthropocenic Methodology: Critical Environmental Law

There is no question that the Anthropocene affects the way environmental legal research and thinking in general should take place. But the Anthropocene is not an isolated move. If it were, it would not have captured the collective imagination in the way it has. It is one more stage in the recent evolution towards a more embedded, material thinking about the human and the world at large. What has started with Catherine Merchant's *Death of Nature*[52] and carried on with Deep Ecology and post-ecologism,[53] has now found an outlet in arguably more supra-disciplinary ventures such as the spatial turn, the corporeal turn, the affective turn, and such philosophical currents of thought as posthumanism, new ontologies, new materialism and speculative realism. The Anthropocene is an addition to this long yet compact thinking evolution, and brings the need for an expansive thinking and acting, a differential understanding of space and time in terms of depth, a need for strategic withdrawal for hyper-inclusion, and a reconfiguration of human exceptionalism.

In what follows, I would like to offer four theses on Critical Environmental Law in order to show how they are affected by the Anthropocene. This is not a programmatic description of how things should be solved, but suggestions for a methodology of environmental law in the epoch of the Anthropocene, which demands a conceptualisation of environmental law that moves beyond the usual distinctions between anthropocentrism and ecocentrism; unproblematised

---

[51] Yussof, 'Geologic Subjects' (n 17) at 401.
[52] C Merchant, *The Death of Nature: Women, Ecology and the Scientific Revolution* (London, Wildwood House, 1980).
[53] I Blühdorn, *Post-ecologist Politics* (London, Routledge, 2000).

distinctions between environment and human; and standard methodologies of legal access to knowledge.

A. An Ontologised Environmental Law

'With the arrival of the Anthropocene, this division [between human/non-human or nature/culture] is de-ontologized; as such, the separation appears instead as an epistemological product mistakenly presumed as a given fact of being'.[54] The Anthropocene brings to the fore an ontology of continuous connection between bodies. In so doing, it instructs us to question the well-trodden paths of epistemology, and begin placing them in a wider context. Why is it that human rationality needed this rupture between human/non-human? Why this need to naturalise what should have remained transparent epistemological distinctions, arguably necessary to understand the world, but ultimately misleading and obscuring of the ontology of the continuum? Continuing in this vein, one would be forced to question that major distinction between epistemology and ontology:[55] can we afford to carry on allowing Eurocentric, Capitalocenic,[56] neoliberal, market-originating epistemological tools to determine what we take as ontological truths? Can such a distinction seriously be maintained in view of the fact that the Anthropocene also augurs the de-individualisation of the human in favour of a human collectivisation as a geological agent that affects the Earth,[57] and further a human fossilisation as a return to the Earth as the a priori agent? This ontological take would affect environmental law in two main ways: first, it would collapse the distinction of a mechanistic, slow, procedure-led environmental law on the one hand, and an urgent tool of rapid dealing of environmental degradation on the other, that would deal with the issues as a priority and on a planetary level where resources are not about economic capabilities of access but about geological finitudes. The method of accessing knowledge (epistemology) is responsible for the construction of such knowledge—thus, if environmental law follows a method of slow legal deliberation, it also generates a reality filled with unresolvable problems. Secondly, the ontological practice of the Anthropocene demands the collapse of traditional disciplinary boundaries, further fossilised by research councils, discipline-specific assessment exercises and sclerotic university structures that operate along obsolete disciplinary distinctions.

---

[54] E Turpin, 'Who Does the Earth Think It Is, Now?', in E Turpin (ed), *Architecture in the Anthropocene: Encounters Among Design, Deep Time, Science and Philosophy* (Ann Arbor, Open Humanities Press, 2013) 8.

[55] See R Brasier, 'Concepts and Objects' in L Bryant, N Srnicek and G Harman (eds), *The Speculative Turn: Continental Materialism and Realism* (Melbourne, re.press, 2011).

[56] Haraway, 'Anthropocene, Capitalocene' (n 45).

[57] T Morton, *Ecological Thought* (n 43).

B. A Material Environmental Law

Critical environmental law can no longer hide behind the usual legal logocentric panoply that insulates environmental law from materiality. We now know that, as Austin Sarat writes, 'the law is all over':[58] this is a call to claim law's spatial, corporeal, emotional, sensory presence that has been subsumed to the critique of discourse. More than other legal disciplines, environmental law is exposed to its own materiality: dealings with scientific thresholds, ecological catastrophes, urban poverty, sick bodies and polluted atmospheres. Above all, the Anthropocene shows that environmental law is already itself a body,[59] namely an assemblage of various materialities, spaces and disciplines. As a body, environmental law is both singular and part of the continuum: it affects and is affected by other bodies. Environmental law must be thought critically, as a multi-layered, planetary, fragmented discipline, characterised by horizontalities that follow the transboundary nature of pollution and verticalities that reach deep into the planet's space and time. There is no more room for such antiquated debates as anthropocentrism versus ecocentrism.[60] The Anthropocene has exposed the grand paradox of the absence of centre. To be a singularity amidst a plane of other singularities entails a radical *acentricity*, which is much more than a call for the inclusion of uncertainty in environmental law. Rather, it is an invitation to a praxis-oriented, spatially specific, material approach that considers every problem in its singularity.

C. A Mineralised Environmental Law

Environmental legal agency in the era of Critical Environmental Law cannot be limited to humans. The earlier posthuman understanding of the human as an assemblage is enough to cloud the agentic certainty. The Anthropocenic mineralisation of thought introduces an agentic tripartite: human (as assemblage, without contours), non-human (assemblages where the biological—animals and plants—but not the human prevails), inhuman (assemblages where the mineral prevails). Any carving of agency from the continuum requires a rupture, often artificial and arbitrary.[61] Critical environmental law, however, must move towards a closer reading of the Anthropocenic geological circularity (life has always originated in

---

[58] A Sarat, '"…The Law is All Over": Power, Resistance and the Legal Consciousness of the Welfare Poor' (1990) 2(2) *Yale Journal of Law and Humanities* 343.

[59] This is why, as D Houston 'Crisis Is Where We Live: Environmental Justice for the Anthropocene' (2013) 10(3) *Globalizations* 439, points out, we must not forget the existing environmental narratives of environmental activism but build on their successes and carry on with local action.

[60] See my take on this in 'Epistemologies of Doubt' in A Grear and L Kotzé (eds), *Research Handbook On Human Rights And The Environment* (Cheltenham, Edward Elgar, 2015).

[61] For agentic emergence in the law, see A Philippopoulos-Mihalopoulos, 'Lively Agency: Life and Law in the Anthropocene' in I Braverman, *Lively Legalities* (London, Routledge, 2016).

and will always return to minerals) and consider issues such as the recognition of legal agency of bodies such as mineral formations (such as fossil fuels) and even the planet as a whole.[62]

D. A Situated Environmental Law

Human exceptionalism must be managed in order to create the conditions for assuming responsibility, regardless of proof of causal link. There is no doubt that humans are only one participant in the environmental decline, but also, as the Anthropocene has taught us, they are always a participant, always situated within the ecological conditions of our planet. Strict liability for historical anthropocenic environmental degradation is consonant with assemblage-thinking, where all bodies are complicit with the degradation. However, the responsibility is not flat. Depending on where each body is situated in the assemblage, the responsibility changes. This is not about *proof* but about historical presence. It is clear that responsibility now becomes situational: it is the juridical responsibility of situating one's body within an assemblage. Responsibility needs to be thought of as extended, namely both material and unrestricted by the immediate or the local. Doreen Massey puts this as 'the Russian Dolls issue of care and responsibility: we always begin with the proximate, home, and then move outwards. But care diminishes as we move out'.[63] We might think we try to be 'responsible' about our presence in a locality, even a locality that 'thinks globally', as the motto goes. But the problem is much vaster. Timothy Morton writes: 'the problem goes beyond how to dispose of human-sized things, like the stuff that gets flushed down a toilet. What should we do about substances on whose inside we find ourselves?'[64] Critical environmental law is expected to situate itself at a distance from the hyperobject of environmental degradation and yet immerse itself in the geologic verticality of responsibility. This is the way to encourage that humans assume their responsibility in relation to their position in the planetary assemblage.

V. Conclusion

These theses are mere indications of how environmental law can remodel itself critically by taking into consideration some of the important challenges of the

---

[62] Especially the latter is connected to what A Neimanis, C Åsberg and J Hedréncall, 'Four Problems, Four Directions for Environmental Humanities: Toward Critical Posthumanities For the Anthropocene' (2015) 20(1) *Ethics & Environment* 67, call the problem of compartmentalisation of environmental questions.

[63] D Massey, 'Geographies of Responsibility' (2004) 86(1) *Geografiska Annaler, Series B, Human Geography, Special Issue: The Political Challenge of Relational Space* 5, 9.

[64] Morton (n 35) at 140.

Anthropocene. This is neither an easy, nor a unilateral task. Environmental law itself is part of an assemblage of material and immaterial bodies and to a large extent is bound by the general continuum around it. It can, however, organise itself politically and start withdrawing from the traditionally understood legal methodology. What is more, it bears a particular responsibility to do so—more than any other branch of law, environmental law needs to reflect critically on what is expected of it and how to achieve it. And when bodies move, the assemblage often moves along and the continuum's tilt might change a little.

7

Materiality and the Ontological Turn in the Anthropocene: Establishing a Dialogue between Law, Anthropology and Eco-Philosophy

SASKIA VERMEYLEN

I. Introduction: The Crisis of the Anthropocene

One of the earlier editorial pieces of the *Journal of Human Rights and the Environment* opened with the quote of the American anthropologist Margaret Mead '[w]e won't have a society if we destroy the environment'.[1] Unfortunately, if we look into the evidence of biophysical signs, the threat of environmental breakdown is imminent,[2] and humanity's survival might indeed be under threat. Our ecological footprint on Earth is at such a scale that we find ourselves in a geological epoch called the Anthropocene,[3] characterised as it is by human terraforming of the Earth.[4] Our biosphere is sick and behaves like an infected organism; every living organism in the biosphere is declining. The evidence is increasingly clear: in a scientific study commissioned by the United Nations in 2005, it was reported that humans are responsible for the extinction of 50,000–55,000 species each year.[5]

At the core of this environmental crisis lies the long held belief that humans consider themselves to be different from nature and nature is seen as a resource for

---

[1] K Morrow, 'Ontological Vulnerability: A Viable Alternative Lens through which to View Human/Environmental Relations' (2011) 2 *Journal of Human Rights and the Environment* 1, 1.

[2] A Grear, 'Multi level Governance for Sustainability: Reflections from a Fractures Discourse' (2010) 5 *Europe Institute Journal* 73, 88.

[3] See eg LJ Kotzé, 'Rethinking Global Environmental Law and Governance in the Anthropocene' (2014) 32 *Journal of Energy & Natural Resources Law* 121; LJ Kotzé, 'Human Rights and the Environment in the Anthropocene' (2014) *The Anthropocene Review* 1.

[4] E Fitz-Henry, 'Decolonising Personhood' in M Maloney and P Burdon (eds), *Wild Law—in Practice* (London, Routledge, 2014) 133–48.

[5] P Burdon, *Earth Jurisprudence and Earth Community* (Adelaide Law School, The University of Adelaide, 2011).

human use and consumption. From a regulatory perspective, an intricate system of property rights has provided the tools to appropriate and commodify nature and increasingly, nature's landscapes and environments get caught up in market-based solutions.[6] This market-based and corporate-sponsored approach towards the protection of the environment is rooted in an anthropocentric understanding of nature and is vehemently opposed in the more critical circles of the humanities and social sciences, often under the banner of the posthuman condition.[7]

It is no different for law, which itself is perceived as being deeply anthropocentric and rotating around the *Anthropos* (conceptualised as human/man),[8] and as reducing all other forms of life to objects.[9] The central position of the human subject in the juridical order as both agent and beneficiary has been profusely problematised in critical legal scholarship.[10] The natural world has been reduced to a 'subaltern'[11] object, a process that has characterised nature as an 'exploited proletariat'.[12] As we find ourselves in what has been perceived as a new geological epoch, a human-centric worldview may no longer be tenable. Life as we know it can no longer sustain itself and global environmental change has introduced a new urgency to critical legal thinking and demands that 'normal' certainties are inverted, or even dissolved.[13] Extreme weather, volcanic eruptions, earthquakes, pollution and flooding have come to symbolise the sensitivity of Gaia, but planet Earth is also materially affected and the idea of some critical thinkers that we only have one Earth,[14] forces us to think about the ecology of the Anthropocene.[15]

---

[6] S Sullivan, J Igoe and B Büscher, 'Introducing "Nature on the Move"—A Triptych' (2013) 6 *New Proposals: Journal of Marxism and Interdisciplinary Inquiry* 15, 15.

[7] Fitz-Henry, 'Decolonising Personhood' (n 4). Some of the scholarship on the posthuman condition Fitz-Henry refers to are (and this list is not exhaustive) eg J Bennett, *Vibrant Matter: A Political Ecology of Things* (Durham, NC, Duke University Press, 2010); T Morton, *The Ecological Thought* (Cambridge, MA, Harvard University Press, 2010)

[8] V Plumwood, *Feminism and the Mastery of Nature* (London, Routledge, 1993); C Merchant, *The Death of Nature: Women, Ecology, and the Scientific Revolution* (New York, HarperCollins Publishers, 1980).

[9] A Grear, 'Deconstructing *Anthropos*: A Critical Legal Reflection on "Anthropocentric" Law and Anthropocene Humanity' (2015) 26 *Law Critique* 225.

[10] See eg A Philippopoulos-Mihalopoulos (ed), *Law and Ecology: New Environmental Foundations* (Abingdon, Routledge, 2011); P Burdon (ed), *Exploring Wild Law: The Philosophy of Earth Jurisprudence* (Kent Town, Wakefield Press, 2011); C Cullinan, *Wild Law: Manifesto for Earth Justice* (Totnes, Chelsea Green Publishing, 2011).

[11] G Spivak, *Death of a Discipline* (New York, Columbia University Press, 2003).

[12] E Fitz-Henry, 'The Natural Contract: From Lévi-Strauss to the Ecuadorian Constitutional Court' (2012) 82 *Oceania* 264.

[13] T Morton, *Hyperobjects: Philosophy and Ecology after the End of the World* (Minneapolis, Minneapolis University Press, 2013).

[14] See eg B Latour, *A Cautious Prometheus: A Few Steps towards a Philosophy of Design (with Special Attention to Peter Sloterdijk)* (Keynote Lecture, Networks of Design meeting of the Design History Society, Falmouth, Cornwall, 3 September 2008) www.bruno-latour.fr/sites/default/files/112-DESIGN-CORNWALL-GB.pdf.

[15] MMJ Fischer, 'The Lightness of Existence and the Origami of "French" Anthropology: Latour, Descola, Viveiros de Castro, Maillasoux, and their so-called Ontological Turn' (2014) 4 *HAU: Journal of Ethnographic Theory* 331, 336.

In pursuit of such an endeavour, this chapter explores the challenges and opportunities of the Anthropocene for environmental law. Through a closer reading of anthropology and eco-philosophy, a new legal terrain is (re)discovered wherein the laws of nature dictate a new contract between living and non-living entities in the universe as an 'ultimate' attempt to save the Earth and all its living and non-living habitants. To this end, Part II below explores rights of nature from a historical perspective as a counter narrative to the commodification of nature. Parts III and IV discuss the material and ontological turn in anthropology respectively. Part V looks into representing alterity from an ontological perspective which is then further discussed in Part VI where anthropology is brought into conversation with law through a detailed reading of the work of the eco-philosopher Michel Serres. The final part of the chapter offers contemporary examples of rights of nature, which resemble some of the legal propositions that were discussed in the previous parts.

II. Counter Discourse

As a counter force to the principle of commodification and capitalisation of nature, Ecuadorian activists have lobbied and embraced a rights-based approach to nature.[16] In 2008, the Ecuadorian Constituent Assembly became the first juridical body in the world to legalise what Michel Serres called a 'natural contract';[17] a concept to which I return later in the chapter. With the assistance of the United States based Community Environmental Legal Defense Fund, representatives at the Assembly in July of 2008 rewrote their 1998 Constitution to include a landmark series of provisions delineating the rights of nature. While the world had to wait until 2008 to witness the constitutional materialisation of rights of nature, the French anthropologist Claude Lévi-Strauss already lobbied in 1976 in the French National Assembly for the recognition of the 'rights of the living'.[18]

Lévi-Strauss' vision was very much based around the idea that the centrality of the rights of people that were being debated in the Assembly had to be dismantled and displaced.[19] He argued that the concept of rights needed to encompass all living species. For Lévi-Strauss it was clear that humans had no right to wipe out whole ecosystems or species without charges that border on genocide. Yet, several

---

[16] Fitz-Henry 'The Natural Contract' (n 12).

[17] M Serres, *The Natural Contract*, E MacArthur & W Paulson trans (Ann Arbor, The University of Michigan Press, 1995 [1990]).

[18] Fitz-Henry (n 12). A lengthier version of this speech at the National Assembly (1985) can be found in the concluding chapter of C Lévi-Strauss, *The View from Afar* (Chicago, Chicago University Press, 1992) 282.

[19] Lévi-Strauss, *The View from Afar* (n 18).

years later we are still debating the viability of ecocide as a potential new crime in law.[20]

As an anthropologist immersed in local settings and other non-Western worldviews, Lévi-Strauss was particularly concerned about extending rights to all living species, including rocks and birds:

> The right to life and to the free development of the living species still represented on the earth, is the only rights that can be called inalienable—for the simple reason that the disappearance of any species leaves us with an irreparable void in the system of creation.[21]

Lévi-Strauss saw his intervention at the French National Assembly as the 'beginning of a new declaration of rights'.[22] One approach that has been widely advocated to embody to some extent the idea of the rights of nature, is a human right to a healthy environment.[23] Doubts are raised though if a human rights framework is sufficient to raise the principle of environmental protection to a higher level of ecological sustainability that recognises human obligations towards ecosystems and the environment as a foundational principle or *Grundnorm* of legal, political and social systems.[24] In the present worldview, the biosphere has no legal standing within human rights law and a non-negotiable ecological bottom line fails to materialise in what is essentially and to its core an anthropocentric human rights regime.[25] The issue of climate change has been trying to call us to attention and to move us into action, but as Anna Grear observes:

> While we wrestle with epistemological quandaries and doubts concerning the best state of our knowledge and debate the best way forward, we are faced with a planetary crisis. The evidence is mounting: a multitude of material and bio-physical signs point to the threat of impending environmental breakdown.[26]

According to Grear, responding to planetary ontic limits seems beyond the reach of human rights language, despite its wider and powerful achievements: '[t]he

---

[20] In 2010, the proposal to amend the Rome Statute to include an international crime of Ecocide was submitted by Polly Higgins to the International Law Commission (ILC). The ILC is the UN body 'mandated to promote the progressive development of international law and its codification'. The submission was published as chs 5 and 6 in P Higgins, *Eradicating Ecocide: Exploring the Corporate and Political Practices Destroying the Planet and Proposing the Laws to Eradicate Ecocide* (London, Shepheard-Walwyn (Publishers) Ltd, 2010).

[21] Lévi-Strauss (n 18) at 284.

[22] ibid, 284.

[23] A turning point for the relationship between human rights and environmental concerns came in 1972 with the introduction of a distinct human right to a healthy environment formulated first in Principle 1 of the 1972 Stockholm Declaration: '[m]an has the fundamental right to freedom, equality and adequate condition of life, in an environment of a quality that permits a life of dignity, well-being, and he bears a solemn responsibility to protect and improve the environment for present and future generations'.

[24] K Bosselmann, 'Environmental and Human Rights in Ethical Context' in A Grear and LJ Kotzé (eds), *Research Handbook on Human Rights and the Environment* (Cheltenham, Edward Elgar Publishing, 2015).

[25] Bosselmann, 'Environmental and Human Rights in Ethical Context' (n 24).

[26] A Grear, 'Multi Level Governance for Sustainability: Reflections from a Fractures Discourse' (2010) 5 *Europe Institute Journal* 73, 88.

anthropocentric limitations of the Western human rights tradition reinforces anthropocentrism as a form of grave ecological blindness'.[27] In practice, this means that environmental law needs to step up and provide adequate protection mechanisms for preserving nature and ecosystems. Unfortunately, environmental law has often been developed without taking into account the wider ethical context.[28] What is important within the context of the urgency of the Anthropocene is to embrace and think through the possibilities that could be developed if environmental law were to shift its focus to establish a more ethical and sustainable relationship between human cultures and non-human 'others'.[29] For present purposes, this means that environmental law should, among others, seek inspiration from other disciplinary theoretical debates about the relationship between culture and nature, by specifically reflecting upon the encounter between humans and non-humans and how this encounter has been theorised in anthropology and (environmental) continental philosophy and apply some of the thinking in these other disciplines to environmental law.

III. Materiality

A dialogue needs to be established amongst different cultures how we—as a collective of human species—engage with the environment. The most compelling discourse on this matter resides in indigenous peoples' cultures and their worldviews,[30] a proposition that I will return to later. The cultural and legal milieu of indigenous peoples' being and worldviews can provide novel cognitive insights into the materiality of the current environmental crisis and can become the conduit for taking the question of materiality to environmental law. A renewed focus on the material world offers a fresh look at what it means to be human and its relationship with the non-human world. The material world has for a long time been the central focus of actor-network theories in science and technology. Socio-cultural and philosophical anthropology have also experienced what has been labelled an ontological turn, with a renewed interest in the meaning of the material world. Explained in more detail later, the turn to ontology in anthropology is mainly associated with the work of Philippe Descola, Eduardo Viveiros de Castro and Bruno Latour.[31] Their scholarship has mainly been in reaction to their belief that the broad humanist linguistic turn in socio-cultural anthropology is ill-equipped to grapple with and confront the environmental and socio-ecological

---

[27] Grear, 'Multi level Governance for Sustainability' (n 26) at 88

[28] Bosselmann (n 24).

[29] A Pelizzon, 'Earth Laws, Rights of Nature and Legal Pluralism' in M Maloney and P Burdon (eds), *Wild Law—in Practice* (London, Routledge, 2014).

[30] Pelizzon, 'Earth Laws' (n 29) at 177.

[31] E Kohn, 'Anthropology of Ontologies' (2015) 44 *The Annual Review of Anthropology* 311.

problems in the Anthropocene. What defines the Anthropocene is the entanglement of human and non-human conditions and futures, raising ethical and political questions that can no longer be treated as exclusively human problems.[32]

Kohn defines ontological anthropology as 'a non-reductive ethnographic exploration of realities' that is not socially constructed. The ontological turn in anthropology is in response to current ecological, existential, ethical and political problems.[33] These problems force us to think about human life in a world where the future of the human being is in danger. Consequently we also need to consider the kind of life and future that is beyond the human being, as it were.[34] The ontological turn follows on from a previous correlational turn in philosophy which, according to Quentin Meillassoux, has limited philosophy to the study of human thought and kept philosophy away from studying the 'great outdoors'; the world beyond human representation.[35]

In the troubling times of the Anthropocene, however, Latour[36] calls us to attention when he compares the apocalyptic collapse of Gaia[37] to the apocalyptic futurism of the Paraguyan Ayereo.[38] Gaia is perceived as the immunological reaction of the Earth;[39] for Latour, Gaia has the power to summon us in the same way as gods used to do. As the Earth is placed in a 'state of exception',[40] it demands everyone to make decisions about life and death until a new political body emerges. Describing the condition of Gaia as a 'feverish form of palsy',[41] usefully summarises the need to acknowledge that the world is not just made up of signifying or discursive realities; there is something deeply material about the world.[42] Having been greatly entangled in discourses, or what Levi Bryant describes as the 'diacritical differences of the signifier', 'the real physical efficacy of fossil fuels, pollutants and automobiles'[43] has been overlooked. For too long, we have focused on the text instead of material factors; materiality has been lost and embedded in a socially

---

[32] ibid.

[33] ibid, 315.

[34] ibid.

[35] Q Meillassoux, *After Finitude: An Essay on the Necessity of Contingency*, R Brassier trans (London, Bloomsbury, 2012); G Harman, *Quentin Meillassoux: Philosophy in the Making* (Edinburgh, Edinburgh University Press, 2015).

[36] B Latour, An Inquiry into Modes of Existence: An Anthropology of the Modern (Cambridge MA, Harvard University Press, 2013) quoted in Fischer, 'The Lightness of Existence' (n 15).

[37] Gaia is one of the Greek primordial goddesses and the ancestral mother of all life. Gaia is also an ecological term coined by James Lovelock in 1979. As a theory Gaia denotes that the Earth itself is viewed as a living organism with self-regulatory capacities and functions.

[38] Fischer (n 15) at 336.

[39] ibid, 336.

[40] C Schmitt, *Political Theology* (Chicago, University of Chicago Press, 2005 [1922]) quoted in Fischer (n 15).

[41] B Latour, *Facing Gaia: Six Lectures on the Political Theology of Nature* (The Gifford Lectures, University of Edinburgh, 18–28 February 2013) www.bruno-latour.fr/node/487, quoted in Fischer (n 15) at 80.

[42] Fischer (n 15).

[43] L Bryant, *Onto-Cartography: An Ontology of Machines and Media* (Edinburgh, Edinburgh University Press, 2014) ix.

constructed understanding of cultural practices. As Bryant warns, reducing materialism to something that is cultural and discursive is not without analytical and political consequences. First, it makes physical agencies invisible; the power of 'things' or reality is reduced to an economic, linguistic or cultural representation. Acknowledging that reality can produce an effect beyond being a conduit for social relations has been labelled, at best, as a naïve approach.[44] Secondly, it has obscured our thinking and has paralysed our political actions to address climate change, among others: '[t]hinking climate change requires thinking ecologically and thinking ecologically requires us to think how we are both embedded in a broader natural world and how non-human things have power and efficacy of their own'.[45] Climate change forces us to think beyond symbolic representation since we are facing encounters with real materiality, with physicality. To this end it seems that a new vogue of an ontological turn is calling upon us.[46]

IV. Ontological Turn in Anthropology

Given that the entangled relationship between humans and non-humans is one of the most defining characteristics of the Anthropocene (Donna Haraway speaks of the Chthulucene),[47] anthropology may be the discipline par excellence that can inspire us how to study this relationship with non-humans, or the 'Other'.[48] In anthropology, thinking through and about difference is not done through our own (often Western) worldviews and perceptions; the other world (human and non-human) is experienced through the concepts and queries as understood by the 'Other'.[49] The great divide between nature and culture is not only questioned, but also transcended. To be sure, the recent ontological turn in anthropology has reinforced the importance of studying alterity.[50]

With this ontological paradigm shift, the question is no longer about understanding different cultures, or how people think about nature. As Kohn manages to capture eloquently in the title of his book, it is rather about understanding

---

[44] ibid.

[45] ibid, 4.

[46] ibid, 4.

[47] Donna Haraway rejects the term 'Anthropocene' as the focus is still too much on the Anthropos and human beings are not the only important actors. Therefore, Haraway proposes the term Chutulucene as human beings are part of the Earth and the other biotic and abiotic powers of this Earth are the main story. See further DJ Haraway, *Staying with the Trouble, Making Kin in the Chthulucene* (Durham, Duke University Press, 2016). See also JW Moore (ed), *Anthropocene or Capitalocene: Nature, History, and the Crisis of Capitalism* (Oakland, CA, PM Press, 2016).

[48] W Edelglass, J Hatley and C Diehm (eds), *Facing Nature: Levinas and Environmental Thought* (Pittsburgh, Duquesne University Press, 2012).

[49] L Bessire and D Bond, 'Ontological Anthropology and the Deferral of Critique' (2014) 41 *American Ethnologist* 440.

[50] Bessire and Bond, 'Ontological Anthropology' (n 49).

'how forests think'.[51] Human *exceptionism* is questioned and a posthuman anthropology is proposed in which a multispecies ethnography is pursued, exploring the perspectives of non-human life forms and non-life forms.[52] The postcolonial question that Spivak asked a few decades ago: '[c]an the Subaltern speak',[53] is now extended to '[c]an the mosquito think',[54] or '[d]o glaciers listen?'.[55]

Christopher Stone asked a related question in 1972 when he questioned in *Should Trees Have Standing*,[56] if natural objects such as lakes and forests, could get the status of legal persons.[57] But while an anthropological understanding transcends the distinction between nature and culture or human and tree, law seems to limit legal personality to human species as the natural is placed outside the border of personality. Properly reflecting on the limits of law, this means that despite Stone's efforts to argue the opposite, nature and the environment remain property, and not persons, or at least rights-bearing entities for the purpose of law.[58]

This is where multispecies ethnographies have an advantage as they can provide a conceptual and methodological toolkit to de-centre traditional approaches to human agency and politics; the centrality and hegemonic position of the *Anthropos* is challenged and human and non-human relationships can be represented through other (non-human) perspectives.[59] As Kohn writes, '[t]his reach beyond the human changes our understanding of foundational analytical concepts such as contexts but also others, such as representation, relation, self, ends, difference, similarity, life, the real, mind'.[60] With the ontological turn, socio-cultural anthropology has managed to move on from its humanistic and linguistic background steeped in social construction. This puts ontological anthropology in a privileged position to conceptualise an epoch characterised by entanglements of human and non-human worlds and futures.[61] Ontological anthropology provides

---

[51] E Kohn, *How Forests Think: Toward an Anthropology beyond the Human* (Berkeley, University of California Press, 2013) 7.

[52] Kohn, 'How Forest Think' (n 51).

[53] Spivak, 'Death of a Discipline' (n 11) at 24.

[54] T Mitchell, 'Can the Mosquito Speak?' in T Mitchell (ed), *In the Rule of Experts: Egypt, Techno-Politics, Modernity* (Berkeley, University of California Press, 2012) 19.

[55] J Cruikshank, *Do Glaciers Listen? Local Knowledge, Colonial Encounters, and Social Imagination* (Vancouver, University of British Columbia Press, 2005) 3. For more examples, see Y Orr, JS Lansing and MR Dove (2015) 'Environmental Anthropology: Systemic Perspectives' (2015) 44 *The Annual Review of Anthropology* 153.

[56] CD Stone, 'Should Trees Have Standing?—Toward Legal Rights for Natural Objects' (1972) 45 *Southern California Law Review* 450.

[57] CD Stone, 'Response to Commentators' (2012) 3 *Journal of Human Rights and the Environment* 3, 100, 100.

[58] N Naffine, 'Legal Personality and the Natural World: On the Persistence of the Human Measure of Value' (2012) 3 *Journal of Human and the Environment* 68, 69.

[59] See eg AL Tsing, *The Mushroom at the End of the World: On the Possibility of Life in Capitalist Ruins* (Princeton, NJ, Princeton University Press, 2015); DJ Haraway, *When Species Meet* (Minneapolis, University of Minnesota Press, 2008); R Braidotti, *The Posthuman* (Cambridge, Polity Press, 2013).

[60] Kohn (n 51) at 22–23.

[61] Kohn, 'Anthropology of Ontologies' (n 31) at 311–27.

insights into how to study and acknowledge a multiplicity of actual worlds.[62] A (somewhat disparate) collective of avant-garde post-humanist thinkers[63] passionately expose, *once and for all*, the irrelevance of the culture–nature divide; the outmoded Western cosmological binary is transcended with euphoric contemporary entanglements.[64]

The twentieth-century epistemological turn is now succeeded with a new ontological turn that addresses both perspectivism (through Descola's anthropology rooted in ethnology and Amazonian ethnography), and technology (through Latour's Science and Technology Studies and technographic development of French philosophers of emergence).[65] Descola's and Latour's theoretical endeavours (often labelled as philosophical anthropology) are in close dialogue with Viveiros de Castro.[66] Each of these three theoretical framing—'foundational perspectivism', 'beyond nature and culture' and 'modes of existence'—will be discussed further below.

A. Foundational 'Perspectivism'

When the work of the Brazilian anthropologist Eduardo Viveiros de Castro[67] was translated, the term ontology was introduced in the Anglo-Saxon anthropological canon.[68] Doyens in anthropology such as Marilyn Strathern,[69] Bruno Latour[70] and Roy Wagner,[71] clearly left their mark in Viveiro de Castro's work who advocated for a special kind of perspectivist cosmology of predation, cannibalism and reincarnation as a way to critique the distinction between nature and culture.[72] This type of cosmology is typical for Lowland Amazonia and inverts the Western or

---

[62] P Descola, 'Modes of Being and Forms of Predication' (2014) 4 *HAU: Journal of Ethnographic Theory* 271.

[63] John Kelly has given an overview of these thinkers and classified them as those who focus on (1) multispecies ethnographies; (2) experimental scientific realism in Science and Technology Studies and Actor-Network Theory; (3) ethnographies of indigenous cosmologies; and (4) phenomenologically inflicted accounts of dwelling and material vitality. For more details, see JD Kelly, 'The Ontological Turn: Where are we?' (2014) 4 *HAU: Journal of Ethnographic Theory* 537.

[64] Kelly, 'The Ontological Turn: Where are we?' (n 63) at 359.

[65] J Kelly, 'Introduction: The Ontological Turn in French Philosophical Anthropology' (2014) 4 *HAU: The Journal of Ethnographic Theory* 259.

[66] Kohn (n 31) at 311.

[67] E Viveiros de Castro, 'Cosmological Deixis and Amerindian Perpsectivism' (1998) 4 *Journal of the Royal Anthropological Institute* 469; E Viveiros de Castro, *Cannibal Metaphysics* (Minneapolis, Univocal, 2014).

[68] A Salmond, 'Transforming Translations (Part 2): Addressing Ontological Alterity' (2014) 4 *HAU: Journal of Ethnographic Theory* 155.

[69] M Strathern, *Kinship, Law and the Unexpected: Relatives Are always a Surprise* (Cambridge, Cambridge University Press, 2005).

[70] R Wagner, *The Invention of Culture* (Chicago, University of Chicago Press, 1975).

[71] B Latour, 'Perspectivism: Type or Bomb?' (2009) 25 *Anthropology Today* 1.

[72] Salmond, 'Transforming Translations (Part 2)' (n 68) at 165.

modern model of nature and culture: nature becomes the variable and culture is constant.[73]

Based on the many ethnographic observations and reflections in Amazonia, Viveiros de Castro develops an indigenous theory according to which, in very simple terms, the European claim that jaguars are not people is overturned because jaguars *are* people with their own communities and shamans. In essence, Amazonian perspectivism shows an alternative viewpoint of human and non-human entanglements.[74] Animals and people see themselves as people; the form of species is just merely a clothing or an 'envelope' hiding an internal human form.[75] Usually only trans-specific beings such as shamans, can see the internal form or spirit of the animal,[76] but in general terms animals are: 'an intentionality or subjectivity formally identical to human consciousness, materialisable, [...], in a human bodily schema concealed behind an animal mask'.[77] Perspectivism offers law another view on personhood which is no longer an 'absolute, diacritical property' of some (elitist and chosen) species, but to occupy a point of view or to have personhood depends on the context and is a question of degree. In some Amazonian contexts, animals may have more agency than some humans and are therefore perceived to have the characteristics of a human rather than an animal. This does not mean that non-human personhood is a given fact; whether or not a specific species can be a prosopomorphic agent capable of affecting humans is always open-ended, dependent as it is on context and personal experience.[78] The context though is defined in Amerindian terms and cannot be imported ready-made from our own perspective.[79] The relevance of perspectivism for environmental law is that it offers the opportunity to go beyond an anthropocentric understanding of law as perspectivism clearly shows that the distinction between nature and culture is a Western point of view not shared in other worldviews, such as the Amazonian ones.

B. Beyond Nature and Culture

Although the translation of the work of Viveiros de Castro has raised the awareness of an ontological turn in anthropology, Descola and his suspension of the

---

[73] Descola contests Viveiros de Castro's multinaturalism-monoculturalism and cosmology of predation by showing contrasts among different Amazonian groups. For further details, see Fischer (n 15) and Bessire and Bond (n 49) at 442.

[74] Although Viveiros de Castro has developed his theory on the reflections of Amazonian encounters, he also gives examples of other cultures' perspectivism and cosmological transformism in other scholars' ethnographic accounts. Viveiros de Castro, *Cosmological Pespectivism in Amazonia and Elsewhere* (Masterclass Series 1, Manchester, HAU Network of Ethnographic Theory, 2012) 49–53.

[75] Viveiros de Castro, *Cosmological Pespectivism in Amazonia and Elsewhere* (n 74) at 48.

[76] It is important to note that perspectivism usually involves only those species that perform a symbolic or practical role in Amazonian cultures, such as the great predator who are the main rivals of humans and the main prey for humans. A fundamental aspect of perspectival inversions is the relative and relational statuses of predator and prey; Viveiros de Castro (n 74) at 53–54.

[77] ibid, 48.

[78] ibid, 54.

[79] ibid, 54.

category 'nature' as the basis of an anthropological enquiry about difference, provided the initial groundwork for an ontological turn.[80] Lévi-Strauss' work, focusing on native thoughts and worldviews as having merit in their own right, has influenced Descola and others. His legacy is even more radical when he argues that when anthropologists attempt to think through the thoughts of the 'Others', ontological properties of the universe can be revealed.[81] Descola shares with Lévi-Strauss 'an emphasis on broad ethnological comparison and the formalist insistence that the apparently infinitely diverse ways in which people live in relation to others are the product of more finite ways of apprehending and constructing these relations'.[82] According to Descola, this means one can only understand others, human or non-human, through self-comparison. In practice this entails that there is only a certain form of ontological assumptions possible. If the 'Other' is understood in comparison to oneself, the 'Other' can be categorised according to their similar or dissimilar interiorities and dissimilar or similar exteriorities.[83] This leads to a categorisation of four possible worldviews, namely 'animism', 'naturalism', 'totemism' and 'analogism'.

Having similar interiorities and dissimilar exteriorities, is labelled by Descola as *animism*, which is perceived as an ideal type and can be found among many indigenous peoples in the Amazon and the boreal regions of North America. For the animist all beings are persons as their selfhood is comparable with that of human persons, and beings are differentiated by their exteriority. For example, for an animist, a shaman can become a jaguar when wearing canine teeth or other markers that make jaguars distinctive predatory beings. It is a psychic continuity that permits a movement across physical discontinuities.[84] Modern westerners distinguish themselves as *naturalists* as they assume dissimilar interiorities and similar externalities. What marks the difference is a unique interior. Nature is seen as an 'object' that is external to our subjective selves.[85] *Totemism* assumes that others have similar interiorities and similar exteriorities, and can be found amongst certain aboriginal societies in Australia. Distinctions between interiority and exteriority are broken down; what is important is the perception that humans and non-humans share the same world. The fourth worldview is labelled *analogism*, which is characterised by dissimilar interiorities and dissimilar exteriorities and historically was widely distributed in the Americas, Asia, Africa and Europe. Analogists distinguish themselves by creating local groupings among entities that do not seem to have a relation with each other in a quest to create order out of chaos.

Descola's categorisation has been criticised in anthropology,[86] but what can be distilled from his work is an awareness and acceptance that other, non-Western

---

[80] Kohn (n 31) at 317.
[81] ibid, 316.
[82] ibid, 317.
[83] ibid, 317.
[84] ibid.
[85] ibid.
[86] eg Sahlins has criticised Descola for creating a form of anthropomorphism. For more details, see M Sahlins, 'On the Ontological Scheme of Beyond Nature and Culture' (2014) 4 *HAU: Journal of Ethnographic Theory* 281.

metaphysics exist and need to be recognised at the very least. Descola's work can help law to think beyond the impermeable boundary and distinction that has been created between nature and culture. He dismantles not only the binary thinking around the headings of nature and culture, but his work also allows a deeper rejection of binary thinking between universal and particular, objective and subjective, physical and social, fact and value, immanence and transcendence, body and mind, animality and humanity, and many more.[87] All these binaries play an important role in law for creating boundaries and for excluding some humans and non-humans from the law.

C. Modes of Existence

Latour, in his writings on the Anthropocene, has potentially offered the most salient contribution to the ontological turn for law.[88] Latour forcefully argues that despite the Anthropocene putting humans centre stage and conceiving them as a force of nature, anthropology can no longer be just about humans. Drawing upon his earlier work on actor network theory (ANT), Latour argues that while ANT can contribute in making humans and non-human part of the same analytical framework, in order to value nature, other non-human voices should also be recognised. In other words, Latour pleads for the acceptance of 'other modes of existence' or ontologies.

Latour is particularly known for bringing nature into culture and culture into nature. His work has often been labelled as being part of the broad ontological turn, as it is linked to ANT and therefore perceived as a form of symmetrical anthropology. This means that we are dealing with a flat ontology which refuses to give priority to any one actor. The world consists of many different actors and agencies and none is more important than the other. ANT overcomes the mind–body dualism by assuming that everything is like minded, both in agency as matter.[89]

Studying encounters between humans and non-humans in science and technology studies, Latour has 'discovered' a sense of material worlds and social actions between humans and non-humans. According to Latour, any kind of knowledge, including legal knowledge, is not just abstract knowledge but is always part of society and its social fabrications and also has a material aspect.[90] Latour highlights the materiality of law through its engagement with space, archives, databases and forensic models.[91] For the purpose of law, the question remains: can law's

---

[87] P Descola, *Cosmological Perspectivism in Amazonia and Elsewhere* (Masterclass Series 1. Manchester, HAU Network of Ethnographic Theory, 2012) 45–46.

[88] See eg B Latour, *An Inquiry into Modes of Existence: An Anthropology of the Moderns* (Cambridge, MA, Harvard University Press, 2013).

[89] Kohn (n 31).

[90] Latour, 'An Enquiry into Modes of Existence' (n 88).

[91] A Pottage, 'The Materiality of What?' (2012) 39 *Journal of Law and Society* 168.

materiality also be extended to other forms of materiality such as pollution, flooding, earthquakes and climate change?

V. Knowledge and Experience in the Anthropocene

The ontological turn described above is not without its critics,[92] but instead of engaging with some of these critiques—valuable as they may be—it is more useful for present purposes to distil the main points that unite the ontologists and then to use these as a starting point for the wider dialogue concerning the relationship between law and anthropology. Anthropology, maybe more than any other discipline, must accept and confront the crisis that the concept of the Anthropocene is bringing on. As a discipline, it has to face the challenge that the *Anthropos* can no longer be the central focal point (a point that has been made by Anna Grear)[93] and has been replaced by ideas such as the post-subjective, the posthuman and the post-plural.[94] Anthropocentric thinking is no longer fashionable, so out of the *Anthropos'* ashes something new has to emerge. The attack on the *Anthropos* is a symbol of a wider critique against epistemology and the way knowledge is represented. The linguistic turn of the 1980s and 1990s has been criticised because culture is seen as 'a realm of discourse, meaning and value [...] conceived to hover over the material world but not to permeate it'.[95] To counter cultural relativism, ontologists emphasise alterity (otherness) and radical difference, and distinguish themselves from earlier attempts to treat difference as a function of diverse ways of knowing and representing reality.[96] Instead, they accept and promote a variety of 'truths' about being and how the world is made. Embracing these other ways of being is not only perceived as a means to rescue anthropology in a posthuman world, but it is also thought that the ontological turn could come to the rescue of the planet and its life forms.[97] To summarise, as the cosmos is in a desperate state, the *Anthropos* needs to be rethought and the ontological turn in anthropology offers the scope to think beyond the human, and revive a radical alterity. This is not just a task for anthropology, but also for law, which will have to think and act upon its own need for an ontological turn (see the discussion further below).

---

[92] See eg Sahlins, 'On the Ontological Scheme of Beyond Nature and Culture' (n 86).

[93] A Grear, 'Deconstructing *Anthropos*: A Critical Legal Reflection on "Anthropocentric" Law and Anthropocene "Humanity"' 2015(26) *Law and Critique* 225–49.

[94] CB Jensen, *Ontologies for Developing Things: Making Health Care Future through Technology* (Rotterdam, Sense Publishers, 2010) quoted in Salmond (n 68); M Holbraad, 'Response to Daniel Miller's Review of Thinking through Things' *Material Worlds* (blog), 4 March 2007, www.materialworldblog.com/2006/12/thinking-through-things/, quoted in Salmond (n 68).

[95] T Ingold, *The Perception of the Environment: Essays in Livelihood, Dwelling and Skill* (London, Routledge, 2000) 340, quoted in Salmond (n 68) at 162.

[96] Salmond (n 68).

[97] P Heywood, 'Anthropology and What There Is: Reflections on Ontology' (2012) 30 *Cambridge Anthropology* 143, 146, quoted in Salmond (n 68).

The ontological turn must be interpreted as a clear reaction to the linguistic turn in anthropology and has been part of a wider turn in philosophy. The linguistic, representational, or what Quentin Meillassoux[98] has labelled 'correlational turn' is often associated with the work of Immanuel Kant, who shifted the focus from substance of the world to 'those conditions under which the humans know or represent the world'.[99] The reality of phenomena is socially constructed and is the product of 'contingent, and conventional contexts, be they historical, social, cultural or linguistic. The circular, reciprocal, coconstitutive nature of these constructions makes them language-like, regardless of whether the items related are explicitly treated as linguistic'.[100] In other words, the ontological turn also seeks to create an alternative understanding of language and semiology. Human language is perceived to be a sign, which in the Saussurean tradition[101] is treated simultaneously as having no direct connection to the object it represents and the meaning of the sign is also pre-fixed by 'a set of codified relations it has to other such signs in the system of signs'.[102] The Saussurean approach towards language distinguishes between the signs and the world to which these signs refer to without giving any thought how these gaps can be connected. In sum, language in the Saussurean tradition has created a dualism between representation and the actual world. However, if human reality is represented as language and social construction, we are confronted with the difficulty to conceptualise and represent 'that which is outside of language or culture'.[103] What the ontological turn in anthropology is ultimately challenging is 'to reconfigure [its] relationship to language [and] the ethnographic study of how humans communicate with a host of nonhuman beings in a world that is itself communicative but not symbolic or linguistic'.[104]

Particularly, the work of the anthropologist Eduardo Kohn in the rainforest of Ecuador's Upper Amazon could provide us with insights into a series of different forms of communication that are representational but not language-like.[105] Kohn draws upon the work of the philosopher Charles Peirce[106] who, contrary to Saussure, has focused on the representation of what lies beyond the human, or in the words of Peirce, 'the outward clash'.[107] By focusing on the communicative processes between humans and non-humans outside the framework of *language* offers a new perspective on the relationship between the human and the non-human in

---

[98] Meillassoux, 'After Finitude' (n 35).

[99] Kohn (n 31) at 314.

[100] Kohn (n 31) at 314.

[101] F de Saussure, *Course in General Linguistics* (LaSalle, IL, Open Court, 1986 [1916]), quoted in Kohn (n 51).

[102] Kohn (n 31) at 314.

[103] ibid.

[104] ibid.

[105] ibid and Kohn (n 51).

[106] CS Peirce, 'Logic as Semiotic: The Theory of Signs' in J Buchler (ed), *Philosophical Writings of Peirce* (New York, Dover, 1955) quoted in Kohn (n 31).

[107] W Keane, 'Semiotics and the Social Analysis of Material Things' (2003) 23 *Language Communication* 409 in Kohn (n 31) at 315.

a post-humanist world. Shifting the focus on the relationship between language and non-language representations has given anthropology the tools to *ecologise*.[108] It has allowed for anthropology to show that focusing on language and its properties as ways to represent the world has troubled our understanding of difference, context and commensurability, or the relationality between humans and non-humans *tout court*.

Encounters with other kinds of being make us aware that seeing, representing, and perhaps even knowing and thinking, are not exclusively human affairs. Representation is thus more than just linguistic and symbolic; representation can go beyond language and, by extension, beyond the human. Non-human life forms can equally represent the world. Nevertheless, for us humans, this concept is difficult to comprehend, as social theory has a very long history of conflating representation with language.[109] A poignant issue that emerges from the ontological turn in anthropology for (environmental) law is then to ponder how the world beyond language can be accessed and represented in law.

VI. Law in the Anthropocene

By way of summary, the ontological turn in social and cultural theory shows that language plays an important role in representation and realisation of knowledge; but critically, it also obscures the world and prevents direct access to experience. This occurs against the backdrop of the Anthropocene, which calls for a renewed interest in how bodies sense environments and events, including 'activities which cannot be captured with words but have a material existence on and beyond the boundaries with language and knowledge'.[110]

Critical environmental law may be particularly receptive to an ontological turn.[111] Environmental law has been for too long dislodged from reality; a reality which is currently vividly explicated by the Anthropocene. As is widely accepted, (environmental) law is deeply entwined with anthropocentrism to the extent that it treats nature as objects. Although more recently nature, and particularly animals, may be treated as legal subjects, this subjectivity or legal personhood is still very different from that of humans and it is language that plays a crucial role in this distinction.[112] The language in which environmental law has to express

---

[108] Kohn (n 31) at 315.

[109] Kohn (n 31) and Kohn (n 51).

[110] I Tucker, 'Sense and the Limits of Knowledge: Bodily Connections in the Work of Serres' (2011) 28 *Theory, Culture & Society* 149.

[111] A Philippopoulos-Mihalopoulos, 'Epistemologies of Doubt' in Grear and Kotzé, 'Research Handbook on Human Rights and the Environment' (n 24) at 28.

[112] R Youatt, 'Interspecies Relations, International Relations: Rethinking Anthropocentric Politics' (2014) 43 *Millennium: Journal of International Studies* 207.

itself or communicate its intentionality needs a radical shift. A promising start has been made within the wider debate of critical environmental law. Andreas Philippopoulos-Mihalopoulos has proposed useful interventions, which resonate with my suggestions for a legal ontological turn. As he argues:

> [T]he task of a critical environmental law is to work along its connection with ecology, indeed within this open ecology of disciplinary and ontological fluidity, and construct a new language in order to communicate about this new home. The challenge is multiple, not least because this language can no longer be 'just' a language but rather a performance of wholehearted embracing of materiality. It is not coincidental that environmental law is the most readily available means to drag law outside its linguistic ivory tower and land it on the material, the social, the corporeal, the gendered, the spatial, the animal, the molecular.[113]

Acknowledging that environmental law is self-destructive as it exudes considerable violence against the environment (often expressed through its anthropocentric character), one of the main interpolations Philippopoulos-Mihalopoulos proposes for environmental law is to de-individualise the individual and to de-centre the human in an ecological field that goes beyond an anthropocentric and ecocentric dualism. He draws upon critical autopoeitic theory to rescue environmental law from its own paradox(es). He brings Luhman's theory of autopoeitic systems into conversation with post-ecological and posthuman understandings of law drawing upon, among others, Deleuzian and feminist thoughts, but also includes some reflections about new material and object-oriented ontologies. Whilst Philippopoulos-Mihalopoulos engages with Luhmann's autopoeitic theory,[114] I am particularly interested in the ontological turn in anthropology to create a better understanding about the role *alternative* semantics may play in bringing back materiality into the law. As Philippopoulos-Mihalopoulos argues, the non-recognition or exclusion of various non-human and non-linguistic positions in (environmental) law has contributed to the distinction between citizens and non-citizens, humans and subalterns, and the natural and artificial.[115] Ultimately, the rejection of posthuman and non-linguistic positions has a major impact upon law and lawmaking and leads to instances of injustice and environmental destruction. So far, (critical) environmental law has not reflected how anthropology and its interest in biosemiotics[116] or non-human linguistic signs can help in developing a

---

[113] A Philippopoulos-Mihalopoulos, 'Looking into the Space between Law and Ecology'. A Philippopoulos-Mihalopoulos (ed), *Law and Ecology New Environmental Foundations.* (Abingdon, Routledge, 2011) 3.
[114] A Philippopoulos-Mihalopoulos, 'Critical Autopoeisis and the Materiality of Law' (2014) 27 *International Journal of Semiotics Law* 389.
[115] ibid, 406.
[116] Barbieri defines biosemiotics as the synthesis of biology and semiotics, and its main purpose is to show that semiosis is a fundamental component of life, ie that signs and meaning exist in all living systems. For more details, see M Barbieri, 'A Short History of Biosemiotics' (2009) 2 *Biosemiotics* 221; J Hoffmeyer, *Signs of Meaning in the Universe*, BJ Haveland trans (Bloomington, IN, Indiana University Press, 1996); J Hoffmeyer, *Biosemiotics: An Examination into the Signs of Life and the Life of Signs*, J Hoffmeyer and D Favareau trans (Scranton, University of Scranton Press, 2008).

more inclusive form of environmental law that can regulate in a more ethical way the relationship between humans and non-humans.

What defines the Anthropocene is not so much the centrality of the *Anthropos* in creating a new epoch but, in the words of Latour, what makes the Anthropocene distinctive is that '[t]he Earth has become—has become again!—an active local, limited, sensitive, fragile, quaking, and easily tickles envelope'.[117] Typical for Latour, this raises the issue what kind of agency can be attributed to this new Earth. The question of agency takes us to the core of a classical legal distinction between subject and object. Whilst previously the Earth was a subject dictating its natural laws to humankind, in the Anthropocene the Earth has been reduced to an object; it is trembling and shaking because of human interventions. Humans are no longer left at the mercy of the trembling of the Earth, as we are now responsible for disturbing its autonomy.[118] Ultimately what defines the Anthropocene is that both Earth and humans have lost their status as subject, both have become objects and are forced together in their loss of being able to act autonomously; they are both doomed to share agency with other subjects that have lost their freedom to act. This also means that what previously was deemed impossible in the ontology of science to be both subject and object, the Anthropocene has blurred the boundaries between subjects and objects.[119]

As a consequence, dreams of human mastery over Earth have to be abandoned; a proposition that has repercussions for law and how law treats nature. The urgency of the Anthropocene no longer allows us to reduce nature and the Earth to our object; to share agency with the Earth means that we may have to question the presumption that we humans occupy an exceptional position in law because of our linguistic freedom. This is where the conversation between anthropology and law may contribute to a new understanding that humans no longer occupy a special place in law based on their linguistic skills. As Hoffmeyer argues:

> The needs of all living beings for expressing a degree of anticipatory capacity is seen as an evolutionary lever for the development of species with increased semiotic freedom. Human intentionality is not therefore unique in the world but must be understood as a peculiar and highly sophisticated instantiation of a general semiotics of nature. Biosemiotics offers a way to explicate intentionality naturalistically.[120]

As the Anthropocene is the epoch that subverts and mixes objects and subjects, the meaning of the world is no longer just an expression of language. The Anthropocene requires an ontological proposition to semiotics. The world, the Earth, the cosmos and the universe need to be understood in themselves and are not only a feature of representation through the language about the world, the Earth, the

---

[117] B Latour, 'Agency at the Time of the Anthropocene' (2014) 45 *New Literary History* 4.
[118] Serres, *The Natural Contract* (n 17).
[119] Latour, 'Agency at the Time of the Anthropocene' (n 117) at 3; Serres (n 17) at 86.
[120] J Hoffmeyer, 'The Natural History of Intentionality, A Biosemiotics Approach'. The Symbolic Species (2012) 6 *Biosemiotics* 97.

cosmos and the universe. They have meaning in their own sense; existence and meaning are synonymous and as long as all agents act, they have agency. Law, just like any other system, has captured, translated and morphed agency into speech. Yet, as Amazonian examples of communicative encounters have shown so aptly,[121] not everything in the world is a matter of discourse in the sense of a speech act. The possibility of discourse resides in every agent looking for its existence. As the Anthropocene shows us so dramatically, storytelling is no longer the prerogative of human language; being thrown in the world is by itself already a story that is fully articulated and active.[122]

The French eco-philosopher Michel Serres, whose work is dedicated 'to (re-)connect the modern subject to the universe and to (re-)discover his or her small place in the larger biotic community of life',[123] provides insights in how to capture the materiality of the human condition, and shows the opportunity that can be created for law when the distinction between objects and subjects is blurred. Serres explores 'what it means for a sentient being to be tossed into the chaos of existence with other particles of matter in a complex, interdependent, and inter-connected cosmic network'.[124] In his book, *The Five Senses: A Philosophy of Mingled Bodies,*[125] Serres returns to the role of the body which expresses 'the primary materiality of the human condition, through which we feel, touch, taste and see the world'.[126] Serres is critical of traditional empiricism since he believes it shades the senses and may have influenced how we have conceptualised knowledge.[127] Through the rich world of sense, experience can be produced and knowledge can no longer be reduced to individual bodies or language.[128] Senses allow getting closer to the experience of the everyday life, something that cannot be achieved

---

[121] What Kohn shows in his accounts of Amazonian encounters is that thinking is not circumscribed by language, the symbolic or the human. Reflecting upon a hunting expedition he witnessed, Kohn records in detail how monkeys fled high up in palm trees when a hunter failed to kill them. He describes subsequently how the hunter was first imitating the sound of a falling tree before he actually cut down the tree, but the monkey reacted already to the before-the-fact imitation, she took the imitation of a falling tree as a sign that could shake the monkey out of its security. According to Kohn the monkey perceived the sound of the shaking perch as a sign of danger, for Kohn the monkey's reaction to the moving perch was not a mechanical reaction of cause and effect. The monkey was able to connect the sign of the trembling perch as something dangerously different from the present sense of security: the branch could break off, a jaguar might be climbing up the tree, but something is going to happen and the monkey felt she had to do something about it; the sign of the shaking branch provided information to the monkey to make a connection between what was currently happening and what might potentially happen, the sound and the movement of the shaking branch gave the monkey information about an absent future and she reacted accordingly. For more details, see Kohn (n 51) at 27–71.

[122] Latour (n 117) at 14.

[123] Tucker, 'Sense and the Limits of Knowledge' (n 110) at 149.

[124] ibid, 150.

[125] M Serres, *The Five Senses: A Philosophy of Mingles Bodies*, M Sankey and P Cowley trans (London, Continuum, 2008).

[126] Tucker (n 110) at 156.

[127] ibid.

[128] ibid.

through language as the latter can only mediate knowledge and cannot provide direct access to experience.[129] In the poetic words of Serres:

> Since the beginning of our history, the global and the local world—from the glory of the heavens down to its smallest details and folds, furrows, marshy places and small pebbles—has slumbered beneath the waters of language, inaccessible and swallowed up like the great cathedral. No-one could go to the object without passing through it, just as no-one gathers seaweed, without, in some unimaginable space, getting his arm wet.[130]

Serres' oeuvre shows that the origin of language lies in the rhythms and calls of the natural world.[131] Through a deeply poetic engagement, he manages to capture the fragility and beauty of the Earth.[132] Serres' attempts to rethink the relationship between humanity and the rest of the universe through expressing the ontological principles that govern the universe and the existence of all living and non-living creatures is poignant, especially now that the Earth is facing one of its most epic challenges. Serres' biosemiotics also challenge and shape our understanding of the existence of the non-human world.[133] The field of biosemiotics shows that signification[134] is not limited to the human (of which Kohn's examples of Amazonian semiotic interactions between humans and non-humans are representative examples). Serres' narrative of the universe 'affords a way to revitalize the hitherto anthropocentric notion of narrative identity at a moment when solutions to the most important global questions must increasingly surpass the bounds of narrowly human and cultural worlds'.[135] In the Anthropocene, a desire awakens to understand the relationality through which individuals and bodies are produced; focus shifts from the meaning of words to the material existence of bodies. Bodies signify not only the material existence beyond language, but also encompass the relations and intricate networks between multiple material forms in the world.[136] Inspired by the theoretical underpinnings of the science and technology

---

[129] ibid.

[130] Serres, (n 125) at 342.

[131] C Watkin, 'Michel Serres' Great Story: From Biosemiotics to Econarratology' (2015) 44 *SubStance* 171.

[132] Tucker (n 110) at 413.

[133] Watkin, 'Michel Serres' Great Story' (n 131) at 171.

[134] As Kohn explains, linguistic representation (or signification) is based on signs that are systematically related to one another, and arbitrarily related to their objects of reference. But drawing upon the work of Charles Peirce, Kohn shows in his work that conventional signs which are usually human representational forms and whose properties make human language possible, are actually linked to other ways of representation such as iconic signs (these are signs that share a likeness with the things they represent) or are indexical (these are signs that are affected or correlate with the things they represent). It is these other symbolic modalities (iconic and indexical) that are shared with non-humans. So while human language may represent conventional signs, Kohn through his ethnographic encounters in the Amazon and drawing upon the work of Charles Peirce, shows that there are two other ways of signification (indexical and symbolic) that are permeating the living world and are shared between humans and non-humans. For more details, see Kohn (n 51).

[135] Watkin (n 131) at 171.

[136] Tucker (n 110) at 434.

movement, Serres seeks to re-empiricise social and cultural theory, but his turn to bodies and senses should not be understood as a return to a phenomenological embodied experience, as these are still limited to a signification and representation in which language plays a dominant force. In essence, senses must be freed from this meaning.

As argued throughout this chapter, the first step towards an ontological turn in (environmental) law is to experiment how to understand the non-human world. Crucial in this endeavour is for law to find a way to go beyond the old dichotomous thinking of nature versus culture. After all, it is such Cartesian thinking that has been held accountable for the current socio-ecological crisis. While Amazonian encounters between humans and non-humans may provide insights on how to achieve conversations between humans and non-humans, they are context specific and therefore will not travel easily to a Western context. This is not to say that the dialogue that was set up in this chapter between anthropology and law has been fruitless. On the contrary, it offered us a platform from which to start thinking that human language is not the only way to represent the world. This means that law is not just language; nature dictates laws through its natural processes. Biosemiosis may be precisely the tool that could (re)-acquaint the discourse of law with its materiality. As environmental law deals with pollution, climate change, flooding, drought and ecological disasters, it is automatically exposed to its own materiality; environmental law has a material presence.[137] Therefore law not only needs to deal with the continuum between humans and non-humans, it also needs to find its own materiality; or to put it differently, law needs to claim its own sensory presence.[138]

This is where Serres' narratology may become a useful 'instrument' to challenge and shape the way law understands the non-human world and the relationship between humans and non-humans. Serres has developed what he calls a *Grand Récit* (the Great Story) of the universe as a way to develop a new non-anthropocentric humanism.[139] For Serres, humanity derives its identity from its place in the universal narrative of the Great Story, and not from any biological or psychological specificity that highlights the difference between humans and non-humans. Next, Serres pulls the human further into the story that it shares with the rest of the universe. Serres identifies four moments in the Great Story that leads to the existence of human beings, but what is remarkable is that Serres tells the story through an inversed ordering, where each event is more ancient than the last. The first event takes us back millions of years when *homo sapiens* emerged on the planet. The second event is the emergence of life on Earth,

> from the first RNA (ribonucleic acid) with the capability to duplicate itself, through the three billion of years when bacteria were the dominant life-form, to the explosion of

---

[137] Philippopoulos-Mihalopoulos, 'Epistemologies of Doubt' (n 111) at 42.
[138] ibid, 404.
[139] Watkin (n 131) at 171.

multi-cellular organisms recorded in the Burgess shale and the huge proliferation of orders, families, genera and species.[140]

The third event travels back from biology to astrophysics and the formation of material bodies or matter in a young universe that was still expanding and cooling. The last and most distant event is 'the birth of the universe itself, the origins of the origins'.[141] What is the relevance of these stories in terms of discrediting the nature-culture divide and what can it tell us about the role of law in the Anthropocene?

Serres answers the first part of this question during an interview in the *Cahier de l'Herne*, when he argues that understanding humanity in the context of the Great Story, allows us to get a new sense of culture that can be traced back not only to Greek and Mesopotamian civilisations, but in fact 15 billion years ago. The Great Story also highlights that the universe can 'write' its own story through its physical presence and the rhythms of its natural processes. The story of the universe is much older than the act of writing, which was discovered some 4000 years ago. Critics or sceptics may argue that no matter how far you go back with the story, it still needs to be told by humans for humans, as a result of which the non-human simply gets ventriloquised. Serres, however, argues that this is incorrect because nature is recounted by nature; for Serres semiotics is natural as all life—and beyond—receives, processes, stores and emits information; there is no ontological difference between crystals, plants, animals and the order of the world. The world does not need to wait for the arrival of the human to tell its story; things can 'write autobiographically'.[142] For the logic of Serres' argument to work, the story of the rhythms and events of nature are not modelled on a human syntactic prose. Human storytelling is just an expression of a much broader phenomenon. For Serres, writing human stories is a metonym of the story like the world: 'I write like the light, like a crystal or like a stream'.[143]

The eco-narratives of Serres should not be perceived as metaphorical extensions of human storytelling. On the contrary, they embody a move from metaphor to metonymy. Human storytelling should not be used as a yardstick against which all other narratives are measured. For Serres, eco-narratives point out that narratives are not just for humans; nature seizes our claim of using language as an exclusivity to represent the world. This means that a narrative identity extends well beyond the *Anthropos*. Serres' Great Story also offers us valuable insights into the role of law and the institutional model that can govern in the Anthropocene. Even though the Anthropocene originated as a geological epoch of a new Earth period, it is above all an ethical and normative concept; it is an epoch that demands a new form of governance and law.[144]

---

[140] ibid, 173.
[141] ibid.
[142] Serres (n 17) at 39.
[143] Watkin (n 131) at 175.
[144] K Jens, 'The Enjoyment of Complexity: A New Political Anthropology for the Anthropocene?' in H Trischler (ed), 'Exploring the Future of the Age of Humans' (2013) 3 *RCC Perspectives* 41.

In his seminal work, *le Contrat Naturel*,[145] Serres, inspired by Jean-Jacques Rousseau's social contract, argues that the only way to save the planet and by extension our own species, requires a paradigm shift that ultimately redefines the relationship between human beings and the rest of the universe. In his distinctive style, Serres holds humans accountable for waging a war against the planet with an arsenal of homocentric logic, scientific discoveries and technological advances. One of the ethical imperatives that Serres develops is the parasite,[146] a trope he uses to remind us that 'a parasite with an insatiable appetite for consumption inevitably destroys its host, thereby preparing its own disappearance'.[147] Serres refers to another trope of mastery to prompt us that we should stop 'attempting to master every last material particle for the exclusive benefit of humanity'.[148] Instead, Serres proposes that we develop a partnership—a natural contract—with the universe as a way to emphasise that as a species we are interdependent.[149]

Serres argues that at the basis of our civilisation lies the social contract that we humans signed as a collective, and that allowed us to leave the state of nature before there was a state.[150] As Hobbes argued, humans are poor creatures and 'life of man' in its natural state was 'solitary, poor, nasty, brutish, and short'.[151] In the state of nature everyone was at war with everyone and in the quest for the good life and for fear of dying, humanity formed the state and signed a contract to protect its own self-interest.[152] The social contract had far-reaching implications for the relationship between humans and nature as we placed ourselves at the centre, as the masters of nature. In his own typical style, Serres uses stories and examples of pollution, possession, dirt and mastery as powerful tropes to make the point that humanity has placed itself at the centre of all things:

> Let's have lunch together: when the salad bowl is passed, all one of us has to spit in it and it's all his, since no one else will want any more if it. He will have polluted that domain and we will consider dirty that which, being clean only to him he now owns. No one else ventures again into the places devastated by whoever occupies them in this way. [...] A living species, ours, is succeeding in excluding all the others from its niche, which is now global: how could other species eat or live in that which we cover with filth? If the soiled world is in danger, it's the result of our exclusive appropriation of things.[153]

---

[145] Serres (n 17) at 35.

[146] Serres has devoted a whole book on the parasite: M Serres, *The Parasite*, LR Schehr trans (Minneapolis, University of Minnesota Press, 2007).

[147] K Moser, 'The Eco-philosophy of Michel Serres and J.M.G. Le Clézio: Launching a Battle Cry to Save the Imperiled Earth' (2014) 21 *Interdisciplinary Studies in Literature and Environment* 413.

[148] ibid, 416.

[149] ibid.

[150] Serres (n 17) at 34.

[151] T Hobbes, *Leviathan, or The Matter, Forme, & Power of a Commonwealth Ecclesiasticall and Civill* (London, Penguin, 1985 [1651]) in Jens, 'The Enjoyment of Complexity' (n 144) at 50–51.

[152] Jens (n 144) at 51.

[153] Serres (n 17) at 33.

The contract we signed that allowed us to leave the state of nature to form society was silent about the natural world; the pact that was signed neglected nature.[154] Natural law as perceived by the Enlightenment philosophers, was the law of reason and reason governs everyone; natural law was universal and followed human nature, which was reduced to either reason or history.[155] The natural law of reason nullified the natural law of nature.[156] Human reason conquered nature through a system of property rights; nature was possessed and pronounced as an object of the law. Initially only civilised *men* could be legal subjects, but progressively the definition of legal subjects has broadened and over time, women, indigenous peoples and other poor and marginalised groups were given the status of legal subject. The social contract became more of a completed project, but nature that gave us food, shelter, heat and water never became a legal subject. In the Anthropocene, nature writes back and (re)claims its legal status as subject. As humans have abused nature, nature threatens or has already taken away our food, shelter, heat and water.

Descartes' philosophy of bifurcation (nature versus culture) has left us now with the choice of either death or symbiosis. With a relentless passion, Serres urges us to master our mastery.[157] If our mastery is left unregulated, we will turn against ourselves:

> former parasites have to become symbionts; the excesses they committed against their hosts puts the parasites in mortal danger, for dead hosts can no longer feed or house them. When the epidemic ends, even the microbes disappear, for lack of carriers for their proliferation.[158]

The only way that we can prevent from destroying the Earth—and ourselves—is by signing a contract with nature.[159] Law is the institution that can limit a one-sided parasitic action.[160] In order to (re)-discover the Earth we have to taste, touch, feel, smell and hear a cosmos to which everything is linked.[161] For the universe as our host to become our symbiont, we need to be in tune again with the world, the

---

[154] ibid, 34.

[155] ibid, 35.

[156] It is beyond the scope of this chapter to give an in-depth analysis of natural law theory and the different schools of thinking within this tradition. However, it is useful to highlight the work of Henry Veatch and his contemporary reconstruction of Thomas Aquinas' theory and the Aristotelian tradition. Veatch argues that the ontological route provides insights and forms the basis for Aristotelian and Aquinan moral theory. Veatch sets out that an adequate foundation for moral theory is a viable ontology based on natural philosophy or an Aristotelian physics. Veatch is critical of the transcendental turn in legal philosophy and disagrees with the Finnis-Grisez argument that nature can never provide the support for ethics and morality. For more details about this debate, see AJ Lisska, *Aquinas's Theory of Natural Law: An Analytical Reconstruction* (Oxford, Clarendon Paperbacks, 1996).

[157] Serres (n 17) at 34.

[158] ibid, 34.

[159] ibid, Moser, 'The Eco-philosophy of Michel Serres and J.M.G. Le Clézio' (n 147).

[160] Serres (n 17) at 36.

[161] Moser (n 147) at 430.

worldly and the physical. We need to go back to nature.[162] But Serres poses the questions: '[w]hat language do the things of the world speak, that we might come to an understanding with them, contractually?'[163] The answer lies in the way Earth *speaks* to us, 'in terms of forces, bonds, and interactions, and that's enough to make a contract'.[164]

If nature is a subject and no longer an object, it can sign a legal contract, and the language of the contract is scripted in the rhythms of nature, the Earth. Serres gives the example of the floods of the Nile as a sign or rhythm of property law:

> EGYPT'S WAY. The first laws on Earth. Given normal weather, the Nile's floods submerged the borders of tillable fields in the alluvial valley fertilized by the great river. At the return of low water, royal officials called *harpedonaptai*, who were surveyors or geometers, measured anew the land mixed with mud and silt to redistribute or attribute its parts. Life got going again. Everyone went home to get back to work.[165]

Flood thus influences laws of property. Floods take away previous measurements of parcels; 'it takes the world back to disorder, to primal chaos, to time zero, right back to nature'.[166] Laws of nature make decisions and divide the fields, and while the legislator may dictate and apply the law, the origins lie in the force and rhythms of nature. The birth of law lies in nature; the redistribution is in the hands of the *harpedonaptai* who give birth to a new law that uses the technology of geometry to divide the land.[167]

VII. Conclusion

This chapter attempted to establish a dialogue with those disciplines that have embraced more fully than law has managed to do, the continuum between culture and nature, and consequently a return to the material world. A closer reading of the ontological turn in anthropology and a conversation with the eco-philosophy of Serres has shown us the need to urgently return to the laws of nature, albeit in a very different way than classical natural law, which considers nature our host and not our symbiont.

The Anthropocene and its material expression of climate change, environmental destruction and loss of biodiversity, to name a few, have made nature and the Earth a legal subject again. Nature is no longer just material for appropriation. While law has tried to limit the abusive parasitism of human beings through social contracts, the same action of a contractual obligation to curb parasitism has not yet been applied to the relationship between nature and humans. The sustained

---

[162] Serres (n 17) at 38.
[163] ibid, 39.
[164] ibid.
[165] ibid, 51.
[166] ibid.
[167] ibid, 52.

reason that has been used to justify politics and law as exclusive human activities still rests on the uniqueness of human language. The missing capacity for language imposes an objectivity to nature and deprives nature of any legal subjectivity. As nature lacks language, it cannot reason order through speech as a substitute for violence, and nature thus remains in a state of violence and excluded from political and legal life.

This chapter has shown that there are other ways of signification than just through language. Nature has its own way of complicated and unique ways of signification. Accepting non-linguistic representations as a form of signifying practice, opens up new possibilities for extending sovereignty beyond the state and the relationship with the human. As argued in this chapter, the Anthropocene is characterised by the blurring of boundaries between humans and non-humans, and between legal subjects and objects. The Anthropocene forces us to think more along the lines of a continuum, but this also has consequences for the concept of sovereignty. Sovereignty is no longer a political or legal concept that can only be attributed through language or human species. As Youatt shows:

> if we consider what sovereignty looks like from the perspective of other animals, we see that they encounter human polities on their own semiotic terms—a wolf-pack cannot recognise a nation-state as sovereign in a formal or declarative way, but it can recognise human markers of territoriality, make judgments about insiders and outsiders, and assess threats to its way of life on which it acts. …The politics of sovereignty takes place not only in human language, but also in other registers, involving semiotic markers of bodily gesture, visual and pheromonal signals, and complex forms of vocalisations.[168]

All this amounts to recognising that non-human life can be a legal subject, and around the world examples are emerging of explicitly granting rights for nature. Ecuador's Constitution is the most well-known example that acknowledges respect for the existence of *Pacha Mama* and providing it a right to restoration.[169] Bolivia recognises that nature has the right to continue its ecosystem processes without human alteration and protected from pollution.[170] In New Zealand, the Whanganui River has been granted legal personhood.[171] Despite the sense that we should celebrate that rights of nature are being recognised in constitutions

---

[168] Youatt, 'Interspecies Relations, International Relations' (n 112) at 220.

[169] Chapter 7 of the Ecuadorian Constitution 2008 on the Rights of Nature states in Art 71 that 'nature, or Pacha Mama, where life is reproduced and occurs, has the right to integral respect for its existence and for the maintenance and regeneration of its life cycles, structure, functions and evolutionary processes'. For more details, see the Ecuadorian Constitution, ch 7, Arts 71–74, which can be downloaded at: http://pdba.georgetown.edu/Constitutions/Ecuador/english08.html.

[170] Bolivia, Framework Act for the Rights of Mother Earth and Holistic Development to Live Well (2012) Bolivia, Ley Marco de la Madre Tierra y Desarrollo Integral para Vivir Bien 2012 (Bolivia) www.lexivox.org/norms/BO-L-N300.xhtml.

[171] In 2013, the Tūhoe people and the New Zealand government agreed upon the Te Uewera Act, giving the Te Urewera National Park 'all the rights, powers, duties, and liabilities of a legal person', www.legislation.govt.nz/act/public/2014/0051/latest/DLM6183601.html. Te Uewera Act 2014, Public Act 2014 No 51.

Similarly, the Maori people have successfully pursued similar results for the Whanganui River and its tributaries, under the Maori worldview 'I am the River and the River is me'. Under the Tutohu

and statutes, we also need to recognise with caution that the way nature has been brought into these legal framings is not without its own flaws. What made nature appear in the Ecuadorian Constitution, is not the recognition of nature as a political actor per se, but it involved a decade-long struggle between Chevron and indigenous peoples over environmental damage caused by oil spills.[172] It seems that for all their progressiveness, the above examples all suggest that the inclusion of non-human life forms in political and legal institutions still require human speech acts. The danger is that these so-called broad-minded forms of recognising rights of nature continue to reproduce anthropocentrism.

According to Latour, Serres' pacific project of a contract among parties may be inappropriate as the Anthropocene suggests that war may be more likely and imminent.[173] This suggests that we may have been too late with a natural contract. Ideals of deep ecology may have inspired Serres when he wrote *The Natural Contract* and we may have to wonder to what extent deep ecology as a concept can still save the planet. For Latour, we have entered another time where we need to think of protecting ourselves against one another and the revenge of Gaia. This may require a different legal code than civil law in the form of a contract; Latour even suggests that a penal code may be more appropriate. To be sure: '[i]n Serres' time we could still dream of making a natural contract with nature, but Gaia is another subject altogether- maybe also a different sovereign'.[174]

If Gaia has sovereign power, the Anthropocene also opens up the debate of environmental constitutionalism and legality, wherein states, international and domestic law, all have a duty to protect Gaia. When the Inter-American Court of Human Rights ruled in 2012 in the case *Sarayaka v Ecuador* that the state had an obligation towards the protection of indigenous dignity and rights, these rights were clearly linked to a right to property.[175] This ruling gives little hope that nature will ever become a legal subject; once more nature has been reduced to an object. Reading the court's ruling is a sombre experience in that respect. The law of the forest was not represented in the court case, let alone being recognised. Other ways of representing communication and non-linguistic signification has clearly not yet entered the legal domain. Yet, a closer conversation between law and anthropology may inject a much-needed understanding about what indigenous peoples' worldviews and ontologies may actually mean, including an appreciation of a wider implication that law may turn its attention to the importance of biosemiotics when studying the meaning and role of (environmental) law in the Anthropocene.

Whakatupua Treaty Agreement, the river is given legal status under the name Te Awa Tupua. Te Awa Tupua is recognised as 'an indivisible and living whole' and 'declared to be a legal person'. Te Awa Tupua (Whanganui River Claims Settlement) Bill, Government Bill 129—1, www.legislation.govt.nz/bill/government/2016/0129/latest/whole.html#DLM6830851. For more general details, see www.earthlawcenter.org/international-law/2016/8/new-zealand.

[172] Fitz-Henry (n 12) at 264.
[173] Latour (n117) at 6.
[174] ibid, 6.
[175] *Indigenous Peoples of Sarayaku v Ecuador*, Merit and Reparation Judgement, Inter-American Court of Human Rights (ser C) No 245, ¶151 (27 June 2012).

Part 3

Planetary Stewardship and Global Justice Reimagined

8

Global Environmental Governance in the Anthropocene: Setting and Achieving Global Goals

MARIA IVANOVA AND NATALIA ESCOBAR-PEMBERTHY[*]

I. Introduction

Humans have always been setting goals. Ambitious visions allow us to chart trajectories, articulate strategies and mobilise resources. They create global narratives that define national and local priorities and actions. We aimed to put a man on the moon, to create a common European market, to eradicate polio, malaria and other diseases, to halve poverty, to attain environmental sustainability. We have achieved many goals but many more remain elusive. In the epoch of the Anthropocene where humans have become a significant geological force,[1] the magnitude of the effects of human activities on the environment demands even more ambitious goals. Scientists note that we have crossed four of nine planetary boundaries: climate change, land system change, loss of biosphere integrity and altered biogeochemical cycles,[2] and that continuing transgression can be catastrophic.

In 2015, governments adopted the latest global goals—the Sustainable Development Goals and the climate goals. At the UN summit in September 2015, 195 governments agreed to 17 goals covering all aspects of sustainable development. At the 21st Conference of the Parties to the United Nations Framework Convention on Climate Change (UNFCCC) (COP21) in December that year, they committed to staying within less than 2 degrees Celsius of warming worldwide and to reach net zero emissions in the second half of the century. These goals are ambitious—articulating high expectations—and universal—committing all countries to their

---

[*] Support for this project is provided by Carnegie Corporation of New York, through the Andrew Carnegie Fellows Program, by the Federal Office of the Environment of Switzerland and by the University of Massachusetts Boston.

[1] PJ Crutzen, 'The "Anthropocene"' in E Ehlers and T Krafft (eds), *Earth System Science in the Anthropocene* (New York, Springer, 2006).

[2] J Rockström and others, 'Planetary Boundaries: Exploring the Safe Operating Space for Humanity' (2009) 14 *Ecology and Society*, www.ecologyandsociety.org/vol14/iss2/art32/.

implementation—and will frame policies for the next 15 to 30 years. While notable and noticeable on social media worldwide,[3] these goals are not new. They follow on previous commitments to enhance development and to operate within environmental limits. Combining them into one agenda, however, is an innovative effort that seeks to match the challenges of the Anthropocene epoch.

The vision for an international development agenda dates back to the end of the Second World War when governments saw development as a strategy to reduce poverty *and* to guarantee security and stability in the international system by providing for basic needs.[4] In the 1990s, the Organisation for Economic Cooperation and Development (OECD), identified poverty reduction as 'the central challenge' and proposed a global partnership around the goals that had been defined by United Nations summits and the increasing concerns around poverty, debt and the environmental consequences of globalisation and economic growth.[5] OECD member states then adopted a set of seven concrete, medium-term development goals—the International Development Goals (IDGs). After intensive deliberations among countries and international development organisations officials, the International Development Goals transformed into the eight Millennium Development Goals (MDGs) in 2001 incorporating the various policy areas articulated earlier, ranging from education and health to gender equality, environmental sustainability and foreign aid.[6]

Global environmental goals were articulated through global environmental conventions and global summits starting in the early 1970s. As early as 1971, for example, the threat to wetlands from increased development led to the Ramsar Convention on the Protection of Wetlands. The Convention on International Trade in Endangered Species was adopted two years later, in 1973, to regulate the hazards to animals and plants from increased trade. Subsequently, global environmental conventions on ozone-depleting substances, biodiversity, desertification, climate change, and chemicals and waste followed. They all articulated global goals for the particular issue area and created the governance mechanisms to support and review implementation. The Stockholm Conference of 1972, the Rio Earth Summit of 1992 and Rio+20 of 2012 outlined priorities and actions to attain them.

The new Sustainable Development Goals (SDGs) brought together the development imperative of the MDGs, the environmental ambitions of the global

---

[3] See the short video by a number of prominent individuals articulating the 17 sustainable development goals: 'We The People' for The Global Goals. www.youtube.com/watch?v=RpqVmvMCmp0

[4] M Duffield and N Waddell, 'Securing Humans in a Dangerous World' (2006) 43 *International Politics* 1; OECD, 'Development Partnerships in the New Global Context' (1995) www.oecd.org/dataoecd/31/61/2755357.pdf.

[5] B Boutros-Ghali, *An Agenda for Development 1995: with Related UN Documents* (United Nations, 1995); JH Michel, 'The Birth of the MDGs' (OECD, 2005) www.oecd.org/dac/thebirthofthemdgsdacnewssept-oct2005.htm.

[6] M Ivanova and N Escobar-Pemberthy, 'The Quest for Sustainable Development: The Power and Perils of Global Development Goals' in T Pogge, G Köhler and AD Cimadamore (eds), *Poverty & the Millennium Development Goals (MDGs): A Critical Assessment and a Look Forward* (London, CROP/Zed Books, 2016).

environmental conventions, and fundamental social goals. And as the world embarks on a trajectory of attaining the new set of global goals that integrates many of the existing development and environmental goals, it will be important to learn from the successes and challenges of past efforts. In this chapter, we look for lessons from the implementation of the MDGs and the global environmental conventions. We seek to learn from these governance mechanisms because, in the Anthropocene epoch, governance will be critical. The geological impact of human activities could only perhaps be counteracted with equally powerful impacts on human society through a range of governance instruments at all levels. Ultimately, the effectiveness of any goals and governance arrangements will hinge on implementation.

Overall, the MDGs sought to motivate action and improve the ability of countries to deliver on core development indicators. The use of concrete targets and indicators proved an effective instrument for focusing efforts, monitoring the evolution of different strategies, and prompting global political mobilisation around concrete targets for development.[7] Environmental conventions also set up different objectives, which even though considered general, offer guidelines on the purpose and implementation of each agreement. Surprisingly, there exists no systematic and comparative assessment of performance on the global environmental conventions. While parties submit reports to the convention secretariats at regular intervals, the data have not been systematised and made available in a comprehensive and comprehensible manner. Governments, convention secretariats and scholars have therefore not been able to determine the level of performance, its change over time, and compare it to other parties in an effort to learn and improve.

This chapter discusses global goals as a key governance instrument. We argue that decisions about global goals have two equally important dimensions: the articulation of goals and the implementation of these goals. To this end, we trace the historical evolution of existing goals and explain their implementation. We bring into the analysis empirical work on six global environmental conventions[8] we have initiated and carried out over several years, which for the first time assesses the performance of convention parties; and we point out the synergies between existing global goals and the sustainable development goals. Our analysis offers insights on the importance of monitoring, measuring and assessing progress in the achievement of global goals, also through law, in the Anthropocene epoch. Clearly, the

---

[7] F Bourguignon and others, *Millennium Development Goals at Midpoint: Where do we Stand and where do we Need to Go* (Mobilising European Research for Development Policies, 2008); A Haines and A Cassels, 'Can the Millennium Development Goals be Attained?' (2004) 329 *British Medical Journal* 394; R Manning, *Using Indicators to Encourage Development: Lessons from the Millennium Development Goals* (DIIS Reports/Danish Institute for International Studies, 2009); Michel, 'The Birth of the MDGs' (n 5).

[8] The 6 agreements included in this study are: In the Chemicals and Waste cluster: The Basel Convention on the Transboundary Movement of Hazardous Waste and the Stockholm Convention on Persistent Organic Pollutants; in the Biodiversity cluster: The Ramsar Convention on Wetlands, the Convention on International Trade in Endangered Species (CITES) and the African-Eurasian Waterbirds Agreement of the Convention on Migratory Species; and the World Heritage Convention.

Anthropocene demands both action and accountability. Contemporary problems are urgent and need to be addressed through action at all levels of governance. Accountability for the effects of such action can be attained through systematic monitoring and reflection on lessons learned. In this chapter, we seek to contribute to this effort.

II. Global Goals for the Anthropocene

In September 2015, after two years of public consultations, intergovernmental negotiations and stakeholder engagement, all UN member states adopted 17 sustainable development goals and 169 targets. These global goals are the core manifestation of the new 2030 development agenda, an effort to establish integrated sustainable development strategies across economic, social and environmental dimensions at all governance levels. Conceived as a new plan of action for *people, planet* and *prosperity*, this agenda also seeks to strengthen *peace* and freedom, and calls on all stakeholders to build a collaborative *partnership* for implementing the goals and targets.

The new global goals built on the existing foundation of the MDGs and environmental goals across the various conventions. They were conceived as universal and inclusive, applicable to 'all nations and peoples and for all segments of society'.[9] They explicitly recognise that development cannot be achieved without safeguarding the ability of the planet to maintain the conditions critical to human well-being,[10] and are therefore 'integrated and indivisible and balance the three dimensions of sustainable development: the economic, social and environmental'.[11] Through this integration, the global goals emphasise the connection between poverty eradication and environmental sustainability, efficient use of resources, and meaningful contribution from multiple stakeholders. They also include specific targets to create the necessary frameworks, policies and partnerships to ensure implementation. The targets reflect the fundamental connections among environment, economic well-being, and social development.

Each of the 17 goals incorporates a number of economic, social and environmental dimensions. The scope of the global goals also includes governance mechanisms, values and lifestyles, and equality. Cutting across all the other goals, Goal 17, on the means of implementation for global partnership, has the largest number

---

[9] UN General Assembly, *A/RES/70/1 Transforming our World: the 2030 Agenda for Sustainable Development* (UN, 2015) para 4.

[10] United Nations, 'Millennium Development Goals Report 2015' (UN, 2015) 10 www.un.org/millenniumgoals/2015_MDG_Report/pdf/MDG%202015%20rev%20(July%201).pdf.

[11] HLP-P2015, *A New Global Partnership: Eradicate Poverty and Transform Economies through Sustainable Development* (2013) 5.

of targets (19), and incorporates finance, technology, capacity-building, trade, institutional coherence, partnerships and data, monitoring and accountability (see Table 8.1).

Table 8.1: Integrating the Dimensions of Sustainable Development through Targets

Global Goals	Targets				
	Economic	Social	Environmental	Finance & Governance	Total
Goal 1: Poverty	2	2	1	2	7
Goal 2: Hunger	2	2	1	3	8
Goal 3: Healthy lives		8	1	4	13
Goal 4: Education	1	5	1	3	10
Goal 5: Gender equality		6		3	9
Goal 6: Water and Sanitation		2	4	2	8
Goal 7: Energy		1	2	2	5
Goal 8: Economic growth and employment	4	5	1	2	12
Goal 9: Infrastructure	3	1	1	3	8
Goal 10: Inequality	2	5		3	10
Goal 11: Cities	1	3	3	2	10
Goal 12: Consumption and Production	2	1	5	3	11
Goal 13: Climate change		1	2	2	5
Goal 14: Oceans	2	1	5	2	10
Goal 15: Terrestrial ecosystems/biodiversity	1	1	7	3	12
Goal 16: Peaceful societies		3		9	12
Goal 17: Means of implementation	Cross-cutting				19

As the analysis of the dimensions of the sustainable development goals illustrates, the political process around their articulation recaptured the spirit of integration and the political process around their implementation would need to do so as well. In the following parts, we explain the origins of global goals in the development and environmental fields as a governance tool, trace the trajectory of their implementation, and offer lessons for the 2030 sustainable development agenda, the core strategy for governance in the Anthropocene.

III. The Evolution of Global Goals

Outcomes of mega-conferences and/or global conventions, global goals have become a core governance mechanism. They strategically define objectives that boost the motivation of actors involved, provide a common yardstick for measuring progress, procedures for reporting and comparing advancement, and help identify ways to improve countries' capacity to undertake the necessary measures to achieve them.[12] Global goals have indeed become the cornerstone of an effective system of global governance, one that designs and executes policies with the objective of solving common problems.

A. Development Goals

The evolution of a common international development agenda dates back to the end of the Second World War. Governments began conceptualising a development mechanism to not only reduce poverty, but also to guarantee security and stability in the international system.[13] The expectation was that global development goals would contribute to peace, security and to the stability of the international system by providing for basic needs, the absence of which could cause conflict and instability.[14] These goals had profound effects in some parts of the world. Economic transformation such as the one brought by the Marshall Plan in Europe and the one in South Korea reflect the positive use of economic assistance as an instrument for development and a conflict-prevention mechanism. In other cases, development goals were instrumental for developing countries that attained independence from colonial rulers. For example, as part of the efforts of the Bretton Woods system in 1945, the International Bank for Reconstruction and Development (IBRD) focused on development assistance and poverty reduction through development goals.

Poverty reduction and subsequently poverty eradication emerged as 'the central challenge' and the global human development agenda focused on concerns around poverty, debt and the environmental consequences of globalisation and

---

[12] Ivanova and Escobar-Pemberthy, 'The Quest for Sustainable Development' (n 6).

[13] Duffield and Waddell, 'Securing Humans in a Dangerous World' (n 4); OECD, 'Development Partnerships in the New Global Context' (n 4).

[14] CROP, *Brief No 13: Mobilizing Critical Research for Preventing and Eradicating Poverty* (2013); ECE and others, *Building on the MDGs to Bring Sustainable Development to the post-2015 Development Agenda* (UN, 2012); A Evans and D Steven, *Sustainable Development Goals—a Useful Outcome from Rio+20* (New York, Center on International Cooperation, 2012); D Griggs and others, 'Policy: Sustainable Development Goals for People and Planet' (2013) 495 *Nature* 305; M Iguchi, S Hoiberg Olsen and I Miyazawa, *Current Outlook on the Sustainable Development Goals (SDGs): A Brief Analysis of Country Positions* (Tokyo, Tokyo Tech and the Institute for Global Environmental Strategies, 2012).

economic growth.[15] International aid became not only a way to reduce poverty but also a strategy to guarantee the stability of the international system. To this end, OECD member states, the primary international donors, developed a 'set of concrete, medium-term goals, all based on the recommendations of major United Nations conferences, to be pursued on the basis of agreed principles' and articulated specific strategies around the three dimensions of sustainable development with timelines for their attainment.[16]

In preparation for the 2000 UN Millennium Summit, the UN Secretary-General, the Secretary-General of the OECD, the Managing Director of the IMF and the President of the World Bank produced a joint report, 'A Better World for All', which presented a set of seven International Development Goals (IDGs) as a 'common framework to guide our policies and programmes and to assess effectiveness'.[17] Twenty indicators articulated the seven goals at a more granular level. Importantly, the IDGs sought to provide goals for all countries. Designed by the donor community, however, they were never completely accepted by those developing countries that were especially concerned with issues such as economic growth, development and increasing inequality.[18] Yet, the eight MDGs encompass the IDGs fully.

In April 2000, the UN Secretary-General called for a new international development agenda in the joint report with the other international organisations, 'We the Peoples: The Role of the United Nations in the 21st Century'.[19] The initial proposal was followed by the UN General Assembly's adoption of the Millennium Declaration as a new mandate for the definition, financing and implementation of international development as a global strategy.[20] This process led to the articulation and approval of the eight MDGs in 2001 as a global strategy to improve human development, incorporating concerns of both donor and aid recipient countries but creating a framework applicable exclusively to developing nations.[21] Ambitious, yet concrete, the MDGs offered a multidimensional perspective on poverty. They represented a set of global goals that incorporate different policy areas ranging

---

[15] Kl Dervis, 'Bridging the Gap: How the Millennium Development Goals are Uniting the Fight Against Global Poverty' (2005) 6 *Sustainable Development Law & Policy* 3; D Hulme, 'The Millennium Development Goals (MDGs): A Short History of the World's Biggest Promise' 100 Brooks World Poverty Institute Working Paper Series; J Zall Kusek, RC Rist and EM White, *How Will We Know the Millennium Development Goal Results When We See Them?* (2005) 11(1) *Evaluation* 7–26.

[16] Duffield and Waddell (n 4); OECD (n 4).

[17] IMF and others, *A Better World for All* (2000) 3.

[18] JH Michel, 'Shaping the 21st Century: The Contribution of Development Co-operation' in OECD (ed), *Sustainable Development: OECD Policy Approaches for the 21st Century* (OECD, 1998).

[19] UN Secretary General, *A/54/2000 We the Peoples: The Role of the United Nations in the 21st Century* (UN, 2000).

[20] S Fukuda-Parr and D Hulme, 'International Norm Dynamics and the "End of Poverty": Understanding the Millennium Development Goals' (2011) 17 *Global Governance* 17; IMF and others, *A Better World for All* (n 17); UNDP, *Human Development Report 2003—Millennium Development Goals: A Compact Among Nations to End Human Poverty* (UN, 2003).

[21] Fukuda-Parr and Hulme, 'International Norm Dynamics' (n 20).

from education and health to gender equality, environmental sustainability and foreign aid. These core areas, and the targets and indicators they include, were present in the original articulation of the IDGs. Financing, baselines for indicators and differing perspectives among developed and developing countries, however, remained contentious.[22]

Table 8.2: Evolution of Global Development Goals and their Content

International Development Goals (IDGs)	Millennium Development Goals (MDGs)	Sustainable Development Goals (SDGs)
Goal 1: Reducing extreme poverty: The proportion of people living in extreme poverty in developing countries should be reduced by at least one-half between 1990 and 2015. **Goal 2:** Universal primary education: There should be universal primary education in all countries by 2015. **Goal 3:** Gender equality: Progress towards gender equality and the empowerment of women should be demonstrated by eliminating gender disparity in primary and secondary education by 2005. **Goal 4:** Reducing infant and child mortality: The death rates for infants and children under the age of five years should be reduced in each developing country by two-thirds between 1990 and 2015.	**Goal 1:** Eradicate extreme poverty and hunger. **Goal 2:** Achieve universal primary education. **Goal 3:** Promote gender equality and empower women. **Goal 4:** Reduce child mortality. **Goal 5:** Improve maternal health. **Goal 6:** Combat HIV/AIDS, malaria and other diseases **Goal 7:** Ensure environmental sustainability. **Goal 8:** Develop a global partnership for development.	**Goal 1:** End poverty in all its forms everywhere. **Goal 2:** End hunger, achieve food security and improved nutrition and promote sustainable agriculture. **Goal 3:** Ensure healthy lives and promote well-being for all at all ages. **Goal 4:** Ensure inclusive and equitable quality education and promote lifelong learning opportunities for all. **Goal 5:** Achieve gender equality and empower all women and girls. **Goal 6:** Ensure availability and sustainable management of water and sanitation for all. **Goal 7:** Ensure access to affordable, reliable, sustainable and modern energy for all. **Goal 8:** Promote sustained, inclusive and sustainable economic growth, full and productive employment and decent work for all.

(continued)

---

[22] Hulme, The Millennium Development Goals' (n 15).

Table 8.2: (*Continued*)

International Development Goals (IDGs)	Millennium Development Goals (MDGs)	Sustainable Development Goals (SDGs)
Goal 5: Reducing maternal mortality: The rate of maternal mortality should be reduced by three-quarters between 1990 and 2015. **Goal 6:** Reproductive health: Access should be available through the primary health care system to reproductive health services for all individuals of appropriate ages, no later than 2015. **Goal 7:** Environment: There should be a current national strategy for sustainable development, in the process of implementation, in every country by 2005, so as to ensure that current trends in the loss of environmental resources are effectively reversed at both global and national levels by 2015.		**Goal 9:** Build resilient infrastructure, promote inclusive and sustainable industrialisation and foster innovation. **Goal 10:** Reduce inequality within and among countries. **Goal 11:** Make cities and human settlements inclusive, safe, resilient and sustainable. **Goal 12:** Ensure sustainable consumption and production patterns. **Goal 13:** Take urgent action to combat climate change and its impacts. **Goal 14:** Conserve and sustainably use the oceans, seas and marine resources for sustainable development. **Goal 15:** Protect, restore and promote sustainable use of terrestrial ecosystems, sustainably manage forests, combat desertification, and halt and reverse land degradation and halt biodiversity loss. **Goal 16:** Promote peaceful and inclusive societies for sustainable development, provide access to justice for all and build effective, accountable and inclusive institutions at all levels. **Goal 17:** Strengthen the means of implementation and revitalise the global partnership for sustainable development.

Importantly, while the MDGs included economic, social and environmental dimensions of sustainable development, they reflected these as independent factors, did not establish links among them, and did not recognise that attaining some of the targets is a prerequisite to progress in several of the goals.[23] In the case of environmental sustainability, for example, environmental degradation and natural resource management also affect poverty, health and development. The 21 targets established 'learning goals'; intermediary benchmarks that allowed for planning, monitoring and evaluation, and change of course, but they retained the silo approach rather than form an integrated agenda.

In addition, the MDGs had a clear time frame; governments committed to attaining them by 2015 and to rethink the goals after that date. In anticipation of the final date for the MDGs, in 2010, the High-level Plenary Meeting of the UN General Assembly on the MDGs requested the UN Secretary-General to initiate a process on the future of the development agenda after the 2015 deadline of the MDGs. Governments, international agencies, academics and NGOs established formal and informal dialogues to examine possibilities for enhancing the international development agenda after the MDGs, the so-called Post-2015 development agenda. To this end, UN Secretary-General Ban Ki-Moon created the System Task Team to serve as a consultation mechanism with stakeholders. It brought together more than 60 UN agencies and international organisations that provide 'analytical inputs, expertise and outreach'[24] to the definition of new stages in international efforts for development. The Division of Development Policy and Analysis within the UN Department of Economic and Social Affairs coordinated this global conversation.

At the same time, at the 2012 United Nations Conference on Sustainable Development—Rio+20—governments recognised the need to reaffirm sustainable development as the foundational principle for the global development agenda beyond 2015: '[a] realistic development agenda can no longer neglect the link among the economic, social and environmental dimensions of development', a number of UN agencies noted in a report. 'Long-term development will thus require integrated policy making, where social equity, economic growth and environmental protection are approached together'.[25] Departing from debates on the continuation of global goals,[26] the outcome of Rio+20 initiated an intergovernmental process to define a set of SDGs to contribute to the 'full implementation of the outcomes of all major summits in the economic, social, and environmental fields'[27] according to the three dimensions of sustainable development and the

---

[23] ECE and others, *Building on the MDGs to Bring Sustainable Development to the post-2015 Development Agenda* (n 14).

[24] United Nations, *A/RES/55/2 United Nations Millennium Declaration* (UN, 2000).

[25] ECE and others (n 14).

[26] S Fukuda-Parr, *Should Global Goal Setting Continue, and how, in the post-2015 Era?* (New York, UN Department of Economic and Social Affairs, 2012).

[27] ECE and others (n 14).

connections between them. These goals were expected to constitute an instrument for the international community to prioritise the issues required for improving socio-economic development and responsible environmental governance.

B. Environment Goals

Environmental goals explicitly emerged in the 1970s and, like development goals, have also been pursued largely in isolation. The explicit recognition of the magnitude of human impacts on the environment upon which life on Earth depends, emerged during the preparations for the 1972 UN Conference on the Human Environment (the Stockholm Conference), where governments noted that 'man has acquired the power to transform his environment in countless ways and on an unprecedented scale'.[28] They also recognised, however, that humans possess increasing capabilities to improve the state of the environment by creating the necessary conditions 'to defend and improve the human environment for present and future generations'.[29] Part of the creation of these conditions included the definition of a system of governance to promote international collective action to address multiple environmental threats, calling for 'cooperation among nations and action by international organizations'. The main outcome of this process was the creation of the first UN body 'to promote international cooperation in the field of the environment'—the UN Environment Programme (UNEP)—that for the past 45 years has been at the centre of the system of global environmental governance. Over time, scholars have debated the role, capacity and authority of UNEP and argued for a strong global environmental institution.[30] Governments initiated a reform process in 1997 in the run-up to the 2002 Johannesburg World Summit on Sustainable Development but could not mobilise sufficient support for significant change. They relaunched the initiative in 2006 and concluded in 2012, at the Rio Earth Summit, with a mandate to make UNEP's membership universal (creating a UN Environment Assembly), increase its funding through direct contributions from the UN regular budget and reconfirm its role as the leading global environmental institution.[31]

During the 1970s, a number of global conventions emerged as the core international legal instruments to regulate specific environmental issues. The advocacy

---

[28] United Nations, *A/CONF.48/14 Declaration of the United Nations Conference on the Human Environment (Stockholm Declaration)* (1972) para 1.

[29] ibid, para. 6.

[30] A Najam, 'The Case against GEO, WEO, or whatever-else-EO' in D Brack and J Hyarinen (eds), *Global Environmental Institutions: Perspectives on Reform* (Royal Institute of International Affairs, 2002); F Biermann and S Bauer, *A World Environment Irganization: Solution or Threat for Effective International Environmental Governance?* (Aldershot, Ashgate Publishing Ltd, 2005); M Ivanova, 'UNEP in Global Environmental Governance: Design, Leadership, Location' (2010) 10 *Global Environmental Politics* 30; M Ivanova, 'Institutional Design and UNEP Reform: Historical Insights on Form, Function and Financing' (2012) 88 *International Affairs* 565

[31] M Ivanova, 'The Contested Legacy of Rio+20' (2013) 12 *Global Environmental Politics* 1.

and mobilisation capacity of organisations such as the International Waterfowl and Wetlands Research Bureau (IWRB, now Wetlands International) and the International Union for the Conservation of Nature (IUCN) were particularly important. They motivated the drafting and signature of the Ramsar Convention in 1971 and CITES in 1973. In 1972, governments signed the World Heritage Convention, which explicitly recognises the interconnection between nature conservation and the preservation of culture. The Convention obliges parties 'to adopt a general policy which aims to give cultural and natural heritage a function on the life of the community'.[32]

As awareness about the interconnectedness of environmental and development issues increased, sustainable development emerged as the core concept that would define the international agenda. The 1987 Brundtland Report articulated the three dimensions of sustainable development—environment, development and social issues. It emphasised that ecological interactions do not respect 'individual ownership and political jurisdiction', and urged the creation of structured mechanisms of international cooperation.[33] In the 1990s, globalisation and the post-Cold War context brought key transformations to the global system of governance. The second of the three mega-conferences that have delineated the structure, institutions and global narrative of environmental governance, the 1992 UN Conference on Environment and Development, was held in Rio de Janeiro, Brazil. Known as the Rio Earth Summit, the conference acknowledged the increasing pace of globalisation and the geopolitical changes of the 1990s, and called for new approaches to social, economic and environmental challenges. 172 governments gathered in Rio and defined sustainable development as the central pillar of environmental governance.[34] They adopted an implementation plan, known as Agenda 21. This plan recognised the need to accelerate the implementation of existing international agreements, and to integrate the goals defined by the international community into specific national and local policies.[35] Agenda 21 also moved away from traditional state-based forms of governance, creating new mechanisms for the participation of non-governmental organisations and non-state stakeholders.[36]

The number of global environmental conventions also increased dramatically. Under the auspices of UNEP, governments drafted the 1987 Vienna Convention for the Protection of the Ozone Layer (later complemented by the Montreal Protocol

---

[32] UNESCO, Convention concerning the protection of the world cultural and natural heritage 1972, Art 5(a).

[33] World Commission on Environment and Development (WCED), 'Our Common Future—The Brundtland Report' www.un-documents.net/wced-ocf.htm.

[34] United Nations, *A/CONF.151/26 Rio Declaration on Environment and Development* (1992).

[35] UNCED, *Agenda 21* (1992).

[36] DA Sonnenfeld and APJ Mol, 'Globalization and the Transformation of Environmental Governance An Introduction' (2002) 45 *American Behavioral Scientist* 1318; United Nations, *A/CONF.151/26 Rio Declaration on Environment and Development*.

on substances that deplete the ozone layer), and the 1989 Basel Convention on the Transboundary Movement of Hazardous Wastes (Basel Convention) to address increasing concerns around the atmosphere, pollution and the effects of chemicals and wastes on human health and the environment. The 1992 Earth Summit led to the creation of three additional agreements: the Convention on Biological Diversity (1992) (CBD), the UN Framework Convention on Climate Change (1992) (UNFCCC) and the UN Convention to Combat Desertification (1994) (UNCCD). They were followed by the Stockholm Convention on Persistent Organic Pollutants (2001) and the Minamata Convention on Mercury (2013).

The new SDGs fully incorporate an environmental dimension both collectively and individually.[37] Besides specific environmental goals such as SDG13 Climate Action, SDG14 Life Below Water and SDG15 Life on Land, other goals and targets include critical environmental dimensions on topics such as clean water and sanitation (SDG6), clean energy (SDG7), sustainable cities (SDG11) and responsible consumption and production (SDG12). At the same time, some of the targets established, even though they are not part of environmental policies per se, contribute to the reduction and eradication of the harmful effects of development on the environment. This is the case for poverty eradication (SDG1), food security (SDG2), sanitation (SDG6), innovation (SDG9), institutions (SDG16) and partnerships (SDG17).

Environmental goals were developed over 40 years through multiple legal instruments and they clearly cover a broad range of issues. They cannot therefore be distilled into a concise set like the MDGs. In an effort to catalogue and analyse existing global environmental goals, UNEP published a summary of 90 goals drawn from the mega-conferences' declarations, from the environmental conventions and from other non-binding agreements. The report also notes that 'the aims and goals of these policy instruments have often fallen far short of their original ambition and intentions'.[38] One explanation could simply be that governments and stakeholders are not aware of the number and scale of the goals they have committed to over the years. UNEP's initiative therefore intended to offer coherent and harmonised guidelines for governments and other stakeholders to move forward with their environmental commitments. The analysis identified important gaps in data collection and measurement of progress. Despite the existence of indicators and targets, data is not necessarily available, which hinders monitoring and assessment of implementation. Governance responses need to support the setting of goals and metrics to support implementation, capacity building, resource mobilisation and the sharing of best practices.[39]

---

[37] UN General Assembly.
[38] UNEP, *Measuring Progress: Environmental Goals & Gaps* (2012).
[39] UNEP, *Global Environmental Outlook 5* (United Nations Environment Programme edn, UN, 2012).

IV. The Challenge of Implementation

Once policy goals have been established, the main issue is their implementation. The extensive set of goals established by the range of global goals brought the concepts of compliance and implementation to the fore. Compliance—and by association implementation—refer to the consequences that international agreements have on states' behaviour when they result in changes in foreign and domestic policies,[40] or when states do not change their policies and behave contrary to expectations, generating processes of non-compliance.[41] Implementation evaluates the extent of adoption of domestic regulations to facilitate compliance with the international commitments. The creation of conditions that facilitate and enable the fulfilment of the international agreement is critical to countries' ability to address the global problems that the conventions seek to resolve.[42]

The UN has consistently monitored the implementation of the development agenda within the MDGs framework. Every year it presented the UN Millennium Development Goals Report assessing the achievement of all targets and indicators, and identifying areas of progress throughout the year as well as main challenges to implementation. In 2005, five years into the MDGs process, the Millennium Project began raising awareness about implementation.[43] In 2010, the MDGs Summit recognised 'that without substantial international support, several of the Goals [were] likely to be missed by many developing countries by 2015'.[44] Such support remained scarce.[45]

While not all countries have attained all goals, substantial achievements have been made in reducing the poverty rate, improving access to safe water, increasing educational coverage and improving disease prevention and maternal health.[46]

---

[40] A Chayes and A Handler Chayes, 'On Compliance' (1993) 47 *International Organization* 175 RB Mitchell, 'Institutional Aspects of Implementation, Compliance, and Effectiveness' in U Luterbacher and DF Sprinz (eds), *International Relations and Global Climate Change* (Cambridge, MA, MIT Press, 2001) http://books.google.com/books?hl=en&lr=&id=BKSIXRsYnQoC&oi=fnd&pg=PR7&dq=international+relations+and+global+climate+change&ots=EVSG_9udV-&sig=kGJgnVh3bHAjkUjwu z6fGi1kYU4; OR Young, *Compliance and Public Authority: a Theory with International Applications* (Baltimore, Md, Johns Hopkins University Press, 1979).

[41] GW Downs, DM Rocke and PN Barsoom, 'Is the Good News about Compliance Good News about Cooperation?' (1996) 50 *International Organization* 379; BA Simmons, 'Compliance with International Agreements' (1998) 1 *Annual Review of Political Science* 75.

[42] HK Jacobson and E Brown-Weiss, 'Strengthening Compliance with International Environmental Accords: Preliminary Observations from Collaborative Project' (1995) 1 *Global Governance* 119.

[43] UN Millennium Project, *Investing in Development: A Practical Plan to Achieve the Millennium Development Goals* (Earthscan, 2005).

[44] UN General Assembly, *A/RES/65/1 Keeping the Promise: United to Achieve the Millennium Development Goals* (UN, 2010).

[45] T Pogge, G Köhler and AD Cimadamore, 'Poverty and the Millennium Development Goals: A Critical Look Forward' in Pogge, Köhler and Cimadamore (eds), *Poverty & the Millennium Development Goals (MDGs): A Critical Assessment and a Look Forward* (n 6).

[46] Open Working Group on Sustainable Development Goals, *Issues Brief—Conceptual Issues* (UN, 2013).

Extreme poverty has been reduced across all regions and the percentage of people living on less than $1.25 a day went from 47 per cent in 1990 to 14 per cent in 2015, meaning that 1 billion people no longer live in these conditions. The proportion of people with access to improved sources of drinking water increased from 76 per cent in 1990 to 91 per cent in 2015, achieving the target of halving the proportion of people without sustainable access to safe drinking water. Parity in primary education between girls and boys has also been achieved. In Southern Asia for example, the ratio of girls' enrolment grew from 74 for every 100 boys in 1990 to 103 in 2015.[47]

Progress on other goals like gender inequality, household and urban/rural inequalities, environmental change, hunger, unemployment and the persistence of conflicts as fundamental threats to human development has unfortunately been limited.[48] Gender inequality persists at the education, employment and government participation levels. Women and youth are still holding insecure and poorly remunerated positions and women earn 24 per cent less than men globally. Half of people living in rural areas lack adequate sanitation facilities. Environmental challenges like increasing global emissions, deforestation and overexploitation of natural resources persist largely unabated. 850 million people still live in extreme poverty and suffer from hunger, 160 million children suffer from malnutrition and the absolute number of people living in slums has increased from 689 million in 1990 to an estimated 880 million in 2015.[49] Clearly, inadequate capacity and structural constraints to enacting the necessary measures at the national level have hindered countries' abilities to enact the global goals, while these conditions create circumstances that generate conflict.

Evidence of low implementation in some of the goals raises questions about the conditions required for optimal implementation and about the future of the international development agenda. For example, the pressure of human activities and economic development on the environment has generated concerns about the extent of countries' progress in implementing global commitments. Environmental conventions provide an insightful example. International law scholars contend that the implementation of international environmental commitments is relatively high.[50] In practice however, measuring implementation is a difficult task. There is no systematic empirical assessment of the extent to which countries perform as convention parties and contribute, through domestic policies, to the achievement

---

[47] JD Sachs, 'The Challenge of Sustainable Development' (3rd Interdisciplinary PhD Workshop in Sustainable Development); United Nations, 'Millennium Development Goals Report 2015'.

[48] Manning, *Using Indicators to Encourage Development* (n 7); C Melamed and L Scott, *After 2015: Progress and Challenges for Development* (Overseas Development Institute, 2011) J Waage and others, 'The Millennium Development Goals: a Cross-sectoral Analysis and Principles for Goal Setting after 2015' (2010) 376 *The Lancet* 991.

[49] United Nations, 'Millennium Development Goals Report 2015'.

[50] Chayes and Chayes, 'On Compliance' (n 40); TE Crossen, 'Multilateral Environmental Agreements and the Compliance Continuum' Bepress Legal Series; Downs, Rocke and Barsoom, 'Is the Good News about Compliance Good News about Cooperation?' (n 41).

of global environmental and development goals. In general, if an environmental problem is resolved because of the change in state behaviour owing to the provisions in a specific regime, as with the recovery of the ozone layer because of the Montreal Protocol, it is clear that the regime has been successful. If however, the problem exacerbates, as in the case of climate change and biodiversity loss, it is more difficult to put the blame solely on the particular international agreement, as there are a number of intervening variables. Furthermore, state parties have consistently discussed—through the different meetings and institutional arrangements established by each convention—the need for better strategic frameworks to achieve the goals defined by each agreement, and the definition of multiple scientific, technical, legal, organisational and financial issues critical for countries to achieve their environmental commitments.

The lack of clarity on obligations and of specific standards to determine what constitutes 'good compliance', and the fact that the different sources of goals do not share a common definition for measurement standards, prevent the development of a systematic empirical assessment to evaluate implementation.[51] And even when efforts have focused on identifying and evaluating goals, experts have found that targets and data are lacking, and that gaps exist in the implementation of specific policies that address environmental challenges.[52] Monitoring, measuring and assessing progress then become critical as countries seek to implement the new sustainable development agenda and to avoid the crossing of planetary boundaries. As we move through the Anthropocene and realise how interconnected our actions are, implementation of *global* commitments will be critical. To this end, conceptual and practical lessons from previous sets of global goals are important to ensure that progress will be achieved.

V. Lessons from the MDGs and Global Environmental Conventions

Global goals are indispensable governance instruments and set the agenda and provide the main point of reference at the international level in the respective policy area. The MDGs aimed at improving the quality of life for the most vulnerable populations. They set out to galvanise attention, motivate political will and improve the ability of countries to deliver on core development priorities.[53] They have been largely successful in this respect despite the challenges in attaining

---

[51] Chayes and Chayes (n 40); Jacobson and Brown-Weiss, 'Strengthening Compliance with International Environmental Accords' (n 42).
[52] UNEP, *Measuring Progress: Environmental Goals & Gaps*.
[53] WCED, 'Our Common Future—The Brundtland Report' (n 33).

all the goals. The environmental conventions address specific concerns about the protection of benefits, such as biodiversity or cultural and natural heritage, or the elimination of harm, including the presence of chemicals and waste in the environment and the illegal traffic of wildlife. They set agendas, proscribe behaviour, prescribe actions, contribute to the socialisation of environmental issues, reduce uncertainty around regulation and generate domestic policy responses.[54] Member states have implemented many of the goals though the overall vision for environmental sustainability has remained elusive. In the Anthropocene epoch, a global vision for human and planetary well-being would be fundamental. Global goals and global conventions, piecemeal as they have been, are the legal instruments used to date to articulate and attempt to implement such a vision. Both sets of instruments offer important lessons and a springboard for the 'next steps' in global governance.[55]

A. Ambition, Vision, Integration

Perhaps the most important feature of any global goal is the level of ambition. Bold, visionary goals inspire and motivate action. And when multiple goals produce an integrative global vision, that action is more likely to resolve the multidimensional global problems. The MDGs were ambitious but their focus on traditional forms of development resulted in lack of recognition of interconnections and in a superficial treatment of the environmental and social dimensions. For example, MDG7 on achieving environmental sustainability was too broad as a goal and its targets (only on biodiversity, water and urbanisation) too limiting. In the social sphere, issues such as security, human rights and governance were neglected. In addition, the MDGs did not consider the differing initial conditions of countries in terms of international development and did not recognise special situations within countries where the goals were adopted.

Integration through synergy of existing mechanisms refers to the need for coordination among and within different issue areas. Global environmental conventions have launched synergy processes in the biodiversity cluster and in the chemicals and waste cluster. Convention secretariats therefore have initiated joint activities on common issues and policy goals as well as established joint operations

---

[54] J Brunée, 'Enforcement mechanisms in International Law and International Environmental Law' in U Beyerlin, P-T Stoll and R Wolfrum (eds), *Ensuring Compliance with Multilateral Environmental Agreements: A Dialogue between Practitioners and Academia* (Leiden/Boston, Martinus Nijhoff Publishers, 2006); PM Haas, RO Keohane and MA Levy, *Institutions for the Earth: Sources of Effective International Environmental Protection* (Cambridge, MA, MIT Press 1993); RB Mitchell, *International Politics and the Environment* (London/Thousand Oaks, CA/New Delhi/Singapore, Sage Publications Limited, 2010); A Steiner, LA Kimball and J Scanlon, 'Global Governance for the Environment and the Role of Multilateral Environmental Agreements in conservation' (2003) 37 *Oryx* 227.

[55] United Nations, 'Millennium Development Goals Report 2015'.

where appropriate.[56] The SDGs built on these examples and called for additional synergies between the conventions and the sustainable development agenda.[57]

B. Universality of Membership and Differentiation of Responsibility

Importantly, the MDGs were applicable only to developing countries. Consequently, they did not explicitly acknowledge the responsibility of developed countries to act and support developing countries in the achievement of the goals. They therefore offered a weak approach to addressing the issues of social justice, equality, vulnerability and exclusion. Most of the global environmental conventions, on the other hand, have universal or close to universal membership.[58] Responsibility for action, however, is 'common but differentiated' as enshrined in the 1992 Rio Declaration.[59] The principle of common but differentiated responsibilities recognises the responsibility of all states for the protection of the environment and acknowledges the differing national ability to prevent, reduce or control the threat as well as the various contributions to the environmental problems.

The UN Framework Convention on Climate Change articulated obligations for its parties based on this principle. Annex I countries (developed countries and countries with economies in transition) were obliged to take the lead in global efforts by limiting their emissions and by protecting and enhancing their greenhouse gas sinks and reservoirs.[60] Developing countries had no explicit obligations. As many began to industrialise rapidly, however, and became significant emitters of greenhouse gases, the asymmetry in obligations led to an unwillingness to act, especially in the United States, which noted that '[n]othing developed countries

---

[56] Basel Convention, *COP Decision BC VII/8 Cooperation and Coordination between the Basel, Rotterdam and Stockholm Conventions* (UNEP, 2006); Stockholm Convention, *COP Decision SC 4/34 Enhancing Cooperation and Coordination among the Basel, Rotterdam and Stockholm Conventions* (UNEP, 2006); Rotterdam Convention, *COP Decision RC 4/11 Enhancing Cooperation and Coordination among the Basel, Rotterdam and Stockholm Conventions* (FAO, 2008).

[57] UNEP, *Role of Multilateral Environmental Agreements (MEAs) in Achieving the Sustainable Development Goals* (UN, 2016).

[58] Membership to the global environmental conventions used in this study ranges from 169 countries in the case of the Ramsar Convention on Wetlands, to 191 for the World Heritage Convention. CITES has 181 state parties, while the Basel and Stockholm Conventions have 183 and 179 states parties respectively. The Rio Convention also had universal membership; the Convention on Biological Diversity has 196 parties, the UN Framework Convention on Climate Change, 197 and the UN Convention to Combat Desertification, 195.

[59] The Rio Declaration states: 'In view of the different contributions to global environmental degradation, States have common but differentiated responsibilities. The developed countries acknowledge the responsibility that they bear in the international pursuit of sustainable development in view of the pressures their societies place on the global environment and of the technologies and financial resources they command'.

[60] United Nations, *Framework Convention on Climate Change* (1992) Art 4.

do will matter if the large emerging economies are not held accountable for their rapidly growing emissions'.[61]

Environmental conventions have established specific mechanisms to address capacity building, and to provide technical and financial assistance to support developing countries in the process of implementation. Learning from these challenges, the new sustainable development agenda was designed to be applicable for all, taking into account different national conditions and priorities. The SDGs were therefore designed as 'universal goals and targets which involve the entire world, developed and developing countries alike. They are integrated and indivisible and balance the three dimensions of sustainable development'.[62] Such goals could provide the foundation for policymaking at a global level in the Anthropocene epoch.

C. National Ownership and Ability

Implementation of global goals is a function of effort and ability.[63] Effort is determined by motivation, and ability by resources. The MDGs motivated policy action and mobilised resources around several of the goals. In many countries, the MDGs also became the overarching development strategy and steered investment— through Official Development Assistance (ODA) or other funds—into sectors identified as important by the MDGs shaping risk and investment preferences. Environmental conventions also request, through different mechanisms, that states parties define national implementation plans, strategies and legislation that incorporate international agreements into domestic policies to guarantee ownership and implementation. Progress in national strategies has also required the support of donor countries and international funds. However, precious resources could be easily steered into areas that do not necessarily reflect national priorities. The process of developing the SDGs explicitly recognised national realities and capacities, noting that 'national ownership is key to achieving sustainable development' across all the processes from implementation, to follow-up, monitoring and review.[64]

---

[61] R Clémençon, 'The Two Sides of the Paris Climate Agreement Dismal Failure or Historic Breakthrough?' (2016) 25 *The Journal of Environment & Development* 3, 5.

[62] UN General Assembly, *A/RES/70/1 Transforming our World: the 2030 Agenda for Sustainable Development*.

[63] S Bernstein and others, *Coherent Governance, the UN and the SDGs* (United Nations University Institute for the Advanced Study of Sustainability, 2014); Open Working Group on Sustainable Development Goals, *Proposal of the Open Working Group on Sustainable Development Goals* (UN, 2014), Third World Network, *SDG Negotiations Reveal the Hard Fight for Means of Implementation* (2014).

[64] UN General Assembly, *A/RES/70/1 Transforming our World: the 2030 Agenda for Sustainable Development*.

D. Articulation and Concreteness

One of the main purposes of global goals is to set agendas and establish priorities that are to be implemented at the national level. Both the MDGs and environmental conventions aim at that. However, in the case of the conventions the concreteness of the obligations and objectives have been a concern and resulted in a twofold challenge for implementation: on the one hand, countries lack clarity in the definition of domestic measures coherent with their international commitments. On the other hand, conventions are forced to establish additional strategic frameworks and mechanisms that should also be implemented by countries, delaying the overall process of implementation and demanding additional resources for design, monitoring and review. In the Anthropocene, these challenges are critical because decisive work would be necessary for the provision, support and regulation of environmental goods and services.[65] Moreover, robust frameworks for policy and action will be necessary for countries to move forward with implementation.

E. Targets and Indicators

One of the core lessons from the MDGs is that the definition of adequate targets and indicators, measurement of progress, and support for implementation are critical elements to success.[66] Concrete measurement strategies and mechanisms provide governments and international organisations with the necessary data and science-based information to evaluate advancement and take corrective measures as required. Despite concerns about the extent to which metrics reflected the real speed of progress,[67] the use of concrete targets and indicators for the MDGs proved to be an effective instrument for focusing the efforts of numerous actors, monitoring the evolution of the different strategies, and prompting global political mobilisation around concrete targets for development.[68] Targets and indicators also helped to create a culture of monitoring and evaluation, which, despite the need for further improvement, brought to the international community more and better data about poverty, education, health, gender equality etc particularly in developing regions in Latin America and Asia. Indicators of education enrolment, disease incidence, access to safe water and gender empowerment, among others, are now carefully measured as part of states' commitment to the MDGs. Countries

---

[65] W Steffen and others, 'The Anthropocene: From Global Change to Planetary Stewardship' (2011) 40 *Ambio* 739

[66] Open Working Group on Sustainable Development Goals, *Programme of Work 2013-2014* (UN, 2013).

[67] Pogge, Köhler and Cimadamore, *Poverty & the Millennium Development Goals* (n 6).

[68] Bourguignon and others, *Millennium Development Goals at Midpoint* (n 7); Haines and Cassels, 'Can the Millennium Development Goals be Attained?' (n 7); Manning (n 7); Michel (n 5).

note, 'the monitoring of the MDGs taught us that data are an indispensable element of the development agenda'.[69] Unfortunately, environmental conventions have not been as comprehensive as the MDGs in the definition of specific targets and indicators to measure progress on implementation, and still need to make progress in a culture of monitoring and indicators.[70] Lessons from the MDGs can also be applied in these instruments of environmental governance.[71] The SDGs provide an opportunity for environmental conventions to identify measures of their actual contribution to the indicators and targets established by the sustainable development agenda. The successful implementation of the SDGs will also require that synergies between the SDGs and other forms of global governance be built to respond to the complex challenges in the Anthropocene.

F. Engagement

The MDGs were largely expert-driven and civil society and even policymakers had little influence. The environmental agenda, on the other hand, has always engaged civil society. The importance of political and social engagement was an important lesson for the SDGs process, which was purposefully designed as a political process with the goal to guarantee the commitment of governments, international organisations and stakeholders. An Open Working Group was therefore created, open to all governments and stakeholders,[72] with a twofold mandate: to articulate the scope and form of the SDGs and to provide the required mechanisms for full participation of stakeholders from civil society, the scientific community and agencies from the UN system. Although the composition of the group was political, government representatives were urged to engage experts, take into account lessons from the MDGs, and ensure that the new set of goals includes all three dimensions of sustainable development mainstreaming the environment at the core of the goals. An integrative approach would be fundamental in addressing the challenges in the Anthropocene and connecting sustainable development policy to science and knowledge will help establish baselines, design policies and measure

---

[69] CROP United Nations, 'Millennium Development Goals Report 2015'.

[70] US General Accounting Office, *GAO/RCED-92-43 International Agreements Are Not Well Monitored* (1992).

[71] M Ivanova and N Escobar-Pemberthy, 'The Environmental Dimension of Sustainable Development: What the SDGs Can Learn from Global Environmental Conventions' (2016 ACUNS Annual Meeting, New York, June 2016)

[72] On 22 January 2013, the UN General Assembly adopted decision 67/555 establishing the Open Working Group, which would comprise 30 representatives from the 5 UN regional groups, nominated by member states. Selecting 30 countries, however, proved more difficult than expected, as most member states requested to be engaged in the process. The final composition of the group therefore grew from 30 to 70 countries as several countries agreed to share seats, creating a constituency-based system of representation and breaking the usual political negotiating blocks (G77, European Union, etc.).

progress.[73] The new SDGs agenda incorporates the environmental dimension as a crosscutting issue. However, the Anthropocene requires that in practice decisions in different policy areas integrate an environmental dimension both individually and collectively.

G. Remaining Concerns

Attainment of global goals is determined by national effort and ability, but also by structural constraints and the political economy of development. Structural constraints and political economy are difficult for countries to influence and need to be taken into account when setting expectations about implementation and delivery.[74] The MDGs provided a structure to focus advocacy and spur motivation as well as to target investment and thereby improve ability.[75] They did not, however, address structural constraints and had no significant influence on the political economy dynamics in countries. Even when environmental conventions include some programs to improve countries' capacity, technology and institutional resources to implement global environmental goals, they do not address structural constraints either. The SDGs will face the same deep-seated challenges.

Importantly, the institutional framework to support the processes of implementation, monitoring and review remains fragmented and contentious. Ownership of the different MDGs by UN specialised agencies was unclear and the competition among agencies was not conducive to collaborative processes and outcomes. Environmental convention secretariats and other institutional arrangements are also central to the implementation of their goals. However, overlapping of efforts among different conventions and ownership and functional fragmentation at the national level are some of the obstacles in the achievement of the overall objectives of the agreements.

These institutional challenges persist for the SDGs. It is necessary to define clear roles for the main governing bodies of the UN—the General Assembly and the Economic and Social Council—and for other platforms working on sustainable development to integrate the SDGs into their operations. The challenges of the Anthropocene require institutional frameworks that protect the environment while meeting socio-economic objectives, including worldwide strategies that protect ecosystems from the negative effects of human activities.[76] During

---

[73] RS DeFries and others, 'Planetary Opportunities: a Social Contract for Global Change Science to Contribute to a Sustainable Future' (2012) 62 *BioScience* 603

[74] MF Montes, 'The MDGs vs. an Enabling Global Environment for Development: Issues for the post-2015 Development Agenda' in Pogge, Köhler and Cimadamore (n 6).

[75] United Nations, *A/67/L.48/Rev.1 Open Working Group of the General Assembly on Sustainable Development Goals* (UN, 2013).

[76] F Biermann, 'Greening the United Nations Charter: World Politics in the Anthropocene' (2012) 54 *Environment: Science and Policy for Sustainable Development* 6; F Biermann, 'The Anthropocene: A Governance Perspective' (2014) 1 *The Anthropocene Review* 57.

the SDGs negotiation process, developing countries also advocated strongly for a transparent and open assessment process, including the creation of a stakeholder review process or a monitoring system that guarantees effective implementation. The lack of accountability mechanisms still presents a significant shortcoming.

Ultimately, the SDGs were purposefully designed as 'integrated and indivisible, global in nature and universally applicable, taking into account different national realities, capacities and levels of development and respecting national policies and priorities'.[77] The SDGs communicate clearly to countries and stakeholders the meaning of sustainable development and the mechanisms to implement it. Obligations under the SDGs are for all countries, regardless of their level of development, as all states are accountable for the implementation of the outcome of the Rio+20 mandate. Contextualised specific indicators and the process of national reviews can be used to measure progress at the different levels, to complement the general approach of global goals.[78] The implementation of the new framework also requires transparency, participation and engagement from all groups.

VI. Conclusion

In the past four decades, environmental and development goals have been key instruments to set the international agenda and to advance governance and action to undertake the challenges of globalisation and human progress. As humanity moves into a new geological epoch—the Anthropocene—these challenges become more acute, making the success in achieving global goals critical to human security, environmental protection and sustainability. Both global development and environmental agendas have articulated specific expectations, and committed countries to the implementation of specific policies and targets to enhance development while promoting sustainability. However, the Anthropocene requires an integrative vision of the environmental, economic and social challenges and the interlinkages among them, in order to safeguard the environment *and* human security. By including an environmental dimension across the SDGs, the new goals mediate in the relationship between societies and environment, guaranteeing that challenges are tackled together and that none of the dimensions diminishes the importance of the other two.

---

[77] UN General Assembly, *A/RES/70/1 Transforming our World: the 2030 Agenda for Sustainable Development*.

[78] ECOSOC, *E/CN.3/2016/2 Report of the Inter-Agency and Expert Group on Sustainable Development Goal Indicators* (UN, 2015) UN General Assembly, *A/70/684 Critical Milestones towards Coherent, Efficient and Inclusive Follow-up and Review at the Global Level—Report of the Secretary-General* (UN, 2016) UNEP, *Measuring Progress: Environmental Goals & Gaps*.

The socio-ecological crisis of the Anthropocene requires coordinated action, monitoring, review and accountability at all levels of governance. As the SDGs become the new set of ambitious and universal global goals, it is important to reflect on the previous experiences of the MDGs and environmental conventions that have brought economic, social and environmental imperatives to the international agenda. Ambition, integration, monitoring, universality, engagement and ownership are critical factors to integrate the existing development and environmental goals. As a core governance mechanism in the Anthropocene, the SDGs could build on and even exceed previous efforts. Particularly important will be the creation of synergies among the existing environmental agreements and the SDGs. Furthermore, designing systematic and comparative assessments for the sustainable development targets and indicators, and the additional governance instruments that support them, is a prerequisite for the improvement of indicators and policies.

9

Global Environmental Constitutionalism in the Anthropocene

LOUIS J KOTZÉ[*]

I. Introduction

If ever there has been a clarion call for far-reaching regulatory interventions to halt, minimise and remediate ecological damage as a result of human actions and to adapt to Earth system changes, it is now. To do so we will have to change human behaviour by means of our social regulatory institutions. Usually crafted alongside a particular ethical framework, such regulatory institutions are a way of expressing responsibility towards human and non-human constituents and towards the Earth system, while simultaneously addressing vulnerability and socio-ecological insecurity. While its emergence has an obvious relationship with and implications for the natural sciences, the elaboration of the Anthropocene mindset and its imagery (reinforced by the empirical evidence of its emergence) are destabilising society's perceptions and expectations of the classic regulatory institutions that are situated in the humanities and that we usually employ to mediate the human-environment interface:

> The framing of world order by reference to a global crisis associated with a troublesome and highly dangerous transition from state-centric borders to globally allocated limits is a fundamental challenge that human society has never before faced on a global scale … the present crisis is mainly a product of anthropocene [sic] activities: carbon emissions, population growth, nuclear weapons and nuclear energy, resource depletion.[1]

Acting as an epistemological framework to think about socio-ecological security, the Anthropocene's imagery is evidence of both the scale and severity of

---

[*] This chapter is based on L Kotzé *Global Environmental Constitutionalism in the Anthropocene* (Oxford, Hart Publishing, 2016).
[1] R Falk, 'Can We Overcome the Global Crisis: Obstacles, Options, and Opportunities' (Keynote Address Delivered at the Tanner Conference on Global Crisis, University of Utah, 2012) www.global.ucsb.edu/climateproject/publications/pdf/Richard,%20Falk.%20Can%20We%20Overcome%20the%20Global%20Crisis.pdf.

human-driven ecological destruction, as well as an urgent reminder of Earth system limits, vulnerability and human fragility that are vividly expressed through fast-approaching planetary boundaries.[2] At the same time, the Anthropocene's imagery 'challenges us to think differently about many things';[3] it calls for restorative and less fatalistic approaches to the future; it challenges the idea of unbridled human development; and it highlights the urgency to start thinking about human responsibilities in relation to the global socio-ecological crisis.

Departing from the idea that constitutionalism, or a constitutionalised legal order is a form of good, apex law that could transform a society to its core for the better, I suggest in this chapter that the Anthropocene demands nothing less than the constitutionalisation of the global environmental law and governance order. While the idea of global constitutionalism is gaining increased traction in academic discourse, to date global constitutionalism has not yet been meaningfully situated in the *environmental* law and governance domain. With rare exceptions, environmental lawyers have been surprisingly reluctant to comprehensively explore the potential of the burgeoning global constitutionalism movement for their own globally relevant regulatory concern (ie the environment).[4] Conversely, there is reluctance among global constitutionalists to invite environmental conversations into their specialist discourse.[5] Reflecting on this lack of sustained and critical mutual engagement, Bosselmann points out that:

> we can think of the environment as a universal concern. Arguably, the environment is even more fundamental than human rights as it represents the natural conditions of all life including human beings. Both the protection of human rights and the protection of the environment are constitutionally relevant precisely because of their fundamental importance ... If we accept that the twenty-first century will be defined by its success or failure of protecting human rights and the environment, then global environmental constitutionalism, like global constitutionalism in general, becomes a matter of great urgency.[6]

The global constitutionalism discourse and the environmental law and governance fraternity are arguably poorer for not more deliberately creating common epistemological spaces to merge the increasingly pressing and overlapping themes of global constitutionalism and environmental protection. In this chapter I attempt to create such a common epistemological space to think about

---

[2] J Rockström and others, 'Planetary Boundaries: Exploring the Safe Operating Space for Humanity' (2009) 14(2) *Ecology and Society* 1.

[3] L Head, 'Contingencies of the Anthropocene: Lessons from the "Neolithic"' (2014) 1 *The Anthropocene Review* 113, 113.

[4] Some examples are L Kotzé, 'Arguing Global Environmental Constitutionalism' (2012) 1(1) *Transnational Environmental Law* 199–233; K Bosselmann, 'Global Environmental Constitutionalism: Mapping the Terrain' 2015 (21) *Widener Law Review* 171–85; L Kotzé, 'The Conceptual Contours of Global Environmental Constitutionalism' (2015) 21 *Widener Law Review* 187–200.

[5] Environmental concerns are dealt with to a limited extent in C Schwöbel, *Global Constitutionalism in International Legal Perspective* (Leiden, Brill Nijhoff, 2011).

[6] Bosselmann, 'Global Environmental Constitutionalism' (n 4) at 173.

global environmental constitutionalism and to propose a more systematic and comprehensive understanding of global environmental constitutionalism and its possible manifestations in the Anthropocene.

I do so first in part II by constructing a motivation in support of opening closed epistemic spaces in the constitutionalism discourse that could be more receptive to 'radical' ideas such as global constitutionalism and the Anthropocene. Part III maps the different tracks that pervade global constitutionalism debates with a view to providing a systemised division of the possible different approaches to global environmental constitutionalism. Part IV discusses in some detail how constitutionalism currently does, and could manifest in the global environmental constitutionalism paradigm. In doing so, a framework is constructed for envisioning global environmental constitutionalism in terms of its possible component parts, ie a global environmental constitution, global environmental rule of law, separation of global environmental powers, the global environmental judiciary, global environmental democracy, global environmental constitutional supremacy and, finally, global environmental rights.[7]

II. From Domestic to Global Constitutionalism

From a domestic perspective and generally speaking, constitutionalism embodies the notion of progress in that it is perceived to foster progressive social orderings that are characterised by the 'creation and maintenance of a dichotomy between right and wrong, good and evil';[8] thus seeking to provide a stable and legitimate framework for making possible interaction between a polity's citizens. Constitutionalism also evokes positive emotive properties that are associated with regime change, stability, order and protection against abuse of power; it signifies progression and progressiveness; and as part of its elevated relative juridical position, constitutionalism provides guarantees of individual freedoms, democracy, representation, rights and participation, among others. Anastaplo argues that '[i]n the background, if not even at the foundations, of any constitutional system are reflections upon the very notion of morality',[9] which galvanises the institutionalisation of prudence and that which we recognise as being 'good'. In this sense, constitutionalism transcends 'normal' politics and law, reaching deep into the moral fabric of a society that seeks to be good, as expressed through its constitutionalised political and legal order.

Perhaps because of constitutionalism's potential as an apex form of law and its aim to improve a legal and political order for the common good, in recent

---

[7] While there may be others, I specifically focus on these elements since they are generally regarded as the main components or elements of constitutionalism.

[8] G Galindo, 'Constitutionalism Forever' (2010) 21 *Finnish Yearbook of International Law* 137, 144.

[9] G Anastaplo, 'Constitutionalism and the Good: Explorations' (2003) 70 *Tennessee Law Review* 738, 738.

years several scholars have been searching for traces of constitutionalism in the global law and governance sphere beyond the state, as it were. Admittedly, because the idea of constitutionalism is inherently state-bound, tied as it is to state sovereignty, physical borders, a *demos* and a government, the global law and governance domain is an unlikely regulatory space to look for traces of constitutionalism. Our geographically limited and epistemologically constrained domestic focus on and experience of constitutionalism is a consequence of long-held conceptions of the state in the context of the axiomatic Westphalian paradigm, which has been reinvigorated as a result of a fragmented Europe after the Second World War, the emergence of newly decolonised states in Africa and South America, and the emergence of new liberal countries in the Eastern Bloc, among others.

Today, however, the prevailing insular and geographically limited perception of world order and associated understandings of constitutionalism are gradually being altered by the forces of globalisation; by significant advances in communication technology and social media that are connecting the world; by modes of travel that enable unprecedented physical global connectivity; by systems of free trade; by the creation of regional and international superstructures of governance such as the European Union; by dissolving state boundaries to create transfrontier conservation areas such as in Southern Africa; by the rise of non-state actors such as epistemic networks and non-governmental organisations including non-state, but law-like, rules in the global realm; by the emergence of treaty regimes and international norm-producing functional organisations such as the World Bank that enable inter-state cooperation in specific areas; the steady growth of multinational corporations that function in an intermeshed transnational setting; and by the emergence of global environmental problems such as climate change that are affecting everyone everywhere with scant regard to physical borders or to the sanctity of state sovereignty.[10] Because the state is increasingly unable to regulate these issues that transcend its borders and lie beyond the sphere of direct sovereign influence, there is a growing need for notions of constitutionalism to be applied beyond the nation state, thereby extending constitutionalism's relevance, application and currency to the global sphere.

While no direct transplantation of domestic constitutionalism to the global sphere is possible, at least not in any unqualified way, it is more likely that core constitutional ideas, norms and/or features could be more or less replicated in the global sphere:

> [I]t is quite possible to separate State and constitution and to transfer the notion of constitution into non-State contexts. The point is, that the concept of constitution changes its meaning when it is transferred and this change of meaning is reinforced by the current

---

[10] These non-traditional state entities have all become 'autonomous forms of social orderings which constitutes [sic] their own cognitive spaces on a global scale'; P Kjaer, *Constitutionalism in the Global Realm: A Sociological Approach* (New York, Routledge, 2014) 4.

structural changes of the international system: the disaggregation of the State on the one hand, and the process of sectoralization within international law.[11]

Because the totality of the state is not absolute any longer, the modernist idea that constitutionalism can and should only manifest in domestic, state-bound terms is gradually giving way to alternative understandings of constitutionalism's potential relevance and application that reaches beyond the state.[12] This realisation indicates that the terms 'constitution' and 'constitutionalism', while historically state-bound, cannot continue to operate only within the exclusive purview of the nation state; they should and in fact are now loosing up in ways that are going beyond the state:[13]

> an exclusive focus of constitutionalism on the Nation State cannot be maintained. It needs to give way to a graduated approach which views constitutionalism as a process, extending constitutional structures to fora and layers of governance other than nations.[14]

While this process is already occurring, the application of constitutionalism in the global sphere and discussions about its application can only be worthwhile if they are attuned to the particular idiosyncrasies of the global order.[15] Whereas domestic constitutionalism's is a familiar narrative, made up as it is by foundational concepts such as a clearly defined *demos, trias politica* and the rule of law that are not easily translatable beyond the conceptually comfortable imagery of the state, constitutionalism in the global sphere will instead demand an opening of discursive and analytical closures and different questions to be asked that may lead to counter-intuitive answers somehow relating to, but not always fully replicating, the domestic constitutionalism referent. A 'black and white' approach to global constitutionalism is therefore likely to fail.[16]

III. Five Approaches to Global Environmental Constitutionalism

There is little consensus about the meaning of global (environmental) constitutionalism. The complexity and controversy that permeate the global constitutionalism

---

[11] C Walter, 'International Law in a Process of Constitutionalization' in J Nijman and A Nollkaemper (eds), *New Perspectives on the Divide between National and International Law* (Oxford, Oxford University Press, 2007) 193–94.

[12] N Walker, 'Taking Constitutionalism Beyond the State' (2008) 56 *Political Studies* 519.

[13] A Peters, 'Compensatory Constitutionalism: The Function and Potential of Fundamental International Norms and Structures' (2006) 19 *Leiden Journal of International Law* 579, 581.

[14] T Cottier and M Hertig, 'Prospects of 21st Century Constitutionalism' (2003) 7(1) *Max Planck Yearbook of United Nations Law* 261, 264.

[15] N Tsagourias, 'Introduction—Constitutionalism: A Theoretical Roadmap' in N Tsagourias (ed), *Transnational Constitutionalism: International and European Models* (Cambridge, Cambridge University Press, 2007) 5–6.

[16] Cottier and Hertig, 'Prospects of 21st Century Constitutionalism' (n 14) at 287.

debate are immense, with the different approaches to global constitutionalism already having been identified and systemised by other commentators.[17]
A detailed replication here serves no purpose other than repetition. This part
instead seeks to briefly map the different tracks that pervade global constitutionalism debates with a view to providing a systemised classification of the different
manifestations and understandings of global constitutionalism in the environmental context.

A. The Internationalist Approach

The mainstream internationalist approach to global environmental constitutionalism focuses on the constitutionalisation of international environmental law and
its institutions, including on aspects related to the existence or emergence of an
international environmental organisation, a global environmental constitution,
and a hierarchy of environmental norms such as environmental rights.[18] The
chapter returns to the issue of a global environmental constitution, environmental rights and *jus cogens* norms below. Whether a global environmental authority
exists or should exist has been and continues to be a contentious issue in the literature and in global environmental diplomacy. While the most obvious candidate
for such an authority is the United Nations Environment Programme (UNEP),
the majority view today remains that UNEP is not a powerful international environmental organisation in the true sense of the word, and that it is unlikely that
global environmental diplomacy will lead to the creation of such a powerful institution in the short or medium term.[19]

According to Biermann, 'upgrading' UNEP to full-fledged United Nations
organisation status could result in increased financial and human resources, competencies and a broadened legal mandate; provide a venue for the integration
and joint administration of the myriad convention secretariats, thus addressing
fragmentation concerns; provide innovative use of financial mechanisms, such as
revenues from emissions trading regimes; and offer awareness raising, technology
transfer and the provision of environmental expertise to international, regional
and domestic governance bodies.[20] Such an upgrade seems critically necessary to
augment global environmental governance in the Anthropocene. While there are

---

[17] See, among others, Schwöbel, *Global Constitutionalism in International Legal Perspective* (n 5).
[18] Bosselmann (n 4); D Bodansky, 'Is There an International Environmental Constitution?' (2009)
(16) (2) *Indiana Journal of Global Legal Studies* 565–84, 567; F Biermann, 'Reforming Global Environmental Governance: From UNEP towards a World Environmental Organization' in L Swart and
E Perry (eds), *Global Environmental Governance: Perspectives on the Current Debate* (Centre for UN
Reform Education, 2007) 103–23.
[19] F Biermann and S Bauer (eds), *A World Environment Organization: Solution or Threat for Effective
International Environmental Governance?* (Aldershot, Ashgate, 2005).
[20] Biermann, 'Reforming Global Environmental Governance (n 18) at 104.

minor initiatives afoot to contemplate the establishment of a world environmental organisation,[21] if the current lack of political will to establish such an organisation is anything to go by, the guiding and coordinating functions of UNEP are more likely to be gradually strengthened and supplemented in the short and medium term, possibly through the High-Level Political Forum on Sustainable Development that replaced the Commission on Sustainable Development and/or the recently established United Nations Environment Assembly.

B. The Regionalist Approach

Regional environmental governance is now a fully recognised manifestation or aspect of global environmental governance. It has emerged as a response from regionally grouped states to shared environmental problems and as a means to exert greater influence as a regional collective in global environmental diplomacy, lawmaking and governance. To this end, regional environmental governance is especially desirable under circumstances:

> when the global seems to fail (or, at least, is not an appropriate level to deal with collective action problems) and states simply cannot solve their own environmental problems through unilateral action or where scaling up has the potential to deliver more effective outcomes, then the 'goldilocks principle' kicks in; regionalism becomes attractive as it is neither 'too hot' nor 'too cold' but 'just right'.[22]

Other benefits include that regional environmental governance has the potential to provide for enhanced commonalities to address a particular environmental challenge; greater familiarity with key actors; the ability to tailor mitigating and adaptation actions to a smaller global constituency; and the ability to focus on ecologically defined regions such as river basins, rather than political-administrative entities.[23]

The regionalist approach to global environmental constitutionalism seeks constitutionalism in broader regional environmental governance orders, especially with respect to their normative and institutional environmental aspects, such as in the European Union, the African Union and the Association of Southeast Asian Nations. The European Union, currently more than any other regional governance organisation, exudes several global environmental constitutional characteristics.[24]

---

[21] See www.un-ngls.org/IMG/pdf/ReformingInternationalEnvironmentalGovernance-mtg_report. pdf.

[22] L Elliot and S Breslin, 'Researching Comparative Regional Environmental Governance Causes, Cases and Consequences' in L Elliot and S Breslin (eds), *Comparative Environmental Regionalism* (New York, Routledge, 2011) 4.

[23] J Balsiger and S VanDeveer, 'Navigating Regional Environmental Governance' (2012) 12(3) *Global Environmental Politics* 1–17, 3.

[24] See M Maduro, 'How Constitutional can the European Union be? The Tension between Intergovernmentalism and Constitutionalism in the European Union' in J Weiler and C Eisgruber (eds), *Altneuland: The EU Constitution in a Contextual Perspective* Jean Monnet Working Paper 5/04, available at: www.jeanmonnetprogram.org/archive/papers/04/040501-18.pdf.

It is an influential environmental governance actor internally with respect to its member states and externally vis-à-vis the rest of the world, with several considerations collectively playing at the idea of the Union becoming, or being, a regional constitutional federation (*Verfassungsverbund*) that also focuses on environmental regulation.[25] First, the 28 member states of the Union could increasingly be seen acting as a unified, if still imperfect, collective, reminiscent of the idea of an 'international community' that acts collectively on behalf of its members and in their environment-related interests.[26] Second, formally the Union derives its environmental governance mandate from what could be considered its constituting instruments. Article 4(2) of the Treaty on the Functioning of the European Union provides that the Union shall share competence with member states, inter alia, in the areas of the environment and energy. Article 3 of the Treaty on European Union declares that the Union 'shall work for the sustainable development of Europe based on … a high level of protection and improvement of the quality of the environment'. This suggests that environmental protection and achieving sustainable development have been laid down 'constitutionally' in a formal sense as two of the main goals of the European Union. There is also a significant degree of distribution of powers evident between the member states and the Union as a result of the principles of proportionality and subsidiarity.[27] Based on the foregoing, a unified and more or less uniform environmental normative framework is continuously created through environmental regulations and directives according to which member states are required to align their domestic legal systems.[28] Third, in terms of substantive higher-order environmental norms, none of the European Union's constituting treaties provide for an explicit environmental right or any other explicit form of higher-order environmental norm. Based on the imperative that human rights protection is a primary aim of the Union,[29] environmental rights protection is rather to be found in several rights-related instruments. The European Convention for the Protection of Human Rights and Fundamental Freedoms of 1950 does not provide for an explicit environmental right,[30] but environmental entitlements are nevertheless raised and protected through the assertion of other incidental rights.[31] The European Court of Human Rights is very active in protecting environmental interests such as through the Convention's right to privacy (Article 8), as can be seen from its rich jurisprudence on human

----

[25] I Pernice, 'Multilevel Constitutionalism in the European Union' (2002) 27 *European Law Review* 511.

[26] See B Simma and A Paulus, 'The 'International Community' Facing the Challenge of Globalization' (1998) 9 *European Journal of International Law* 266–77, 268.

[27] See TEU, Art 5.

[28] TFEU, Art 288.

[29] TEU, Art 6.

[30] Available at: at: www.coe.int/t/dghl/standardsetting/hrpolicy/Publications/Manual_Env_2012_nocover_Eng.pdf.

[31] O Pedersen, 'European Environmental Human Rights and Environmental Rights: A Long Time Coming?' (2008) (21) *The Georgetown International Environmental Law Review* 73–111.

rights in the environmental context.[32] The more recently adopted Charter of Fundamental Rights of the European Union of 2000, includes under its section on solidarity rights an environmental provision which states '[a] high level of environmental protection and the improvement of the quality of the environment must be integrated into the policies of the Union and ensured in accordance with the principle of sustainable development'.[33] This provision, which has become binding on all Union member states since 2009 along with all the other provisions of the Charter,[34] although relatively weak and devoid of the classic rights-jargon, 'may become a benchmark for judicial review by the EU Court of Justice of legislative and executive EU acts as well as national measures implementing EU environmental obligations'.[35] Also, the United Nations Economic Commission for Europe (UNECE) Convention on Access to Information, Public Participation in Decision-making and Access to Justice in Environmental Matters (Aarhus Convention) 1998 provides an environmental right, although this right is non-justiciable.[36] In doing so, the Convention significantly strengthens the force of substantive regional environmental constitutionalism by allowing communications to be brought before its Compliance Committee by one or more members of the public concerning any party's compliance with the Convention.[37]

The foregoing suggests that the European Union exudes various environmental constitutionalism characteristics that allow it collectively as a regional organisation, and its member states individually, to steer environmental regulatory outcomes in a regional setting. But this is not the case with all regional governance regimes. Other regional organisations such as the African Union still have a long way to go before they achieve any meaningful, coherent or influential measure of regional global environmental constitutionalism.[38] It will arguably be these comparatively poorer regions and countries with least adaptive capacity, that are most likely to be affected by global environmental change in the Anthropocene. While it

---

[32] See for a summary of environment related cases the summary in the European Court of Human Rights: www.echr.coe.int/Documents/FS_Environment_ENG.pdf.

[33] Art 37.

[34] The Charter has been incorporated as a binding legal text in the Lisbon Treaty of 2007 and as a result it has become binding on all European Union member states since 2009.

[35] J Verschuuren, 'Contribution of the Case Law of the European Court of Human Rights to Sustainable Development in Europe' in W Scholtz and J Verschuuren (eds), *Regional Environmental Law: Transnational Comparative Lessons in Pursuit of Sustainable Development* (Cheltenham, Edward Elgar, 2015) 363–84.

[36] See generally S Kravchenko, 'The Aarhus Convention and Innovations in Compliance with Multilateral Environmental Agreements' (2007) 18(1) *Colorado Journal of International Environmental Law and Policy* 1–50.

[37] United Nations Economic Commission for Europe www.unece.org/env/pp/pubcom.html.

[38] While the African Union has developed an impressive array of regional agreements pursuant to the goal of sustainable development, national implementation of these instruments in general is a problem, since effective regional, sub-regional and domestic compliance and enforcement mechanisms are often lacking or are ignored completely; L Kotzé and W Scholtz, 'Environmental Law-Africa, Sub-Saharan' in K Bosselmann, D Fogel and JB Ruhl (eds), *The Berkshire Encyclopaedia of Sustainability, Vol 3: The Law and Politics of Sustainability* (Great Barrington, Berkshire Publishers, 2010) 179–87.

is unrealistic and probably undesirable to suggest that the European model should be replicated elsewhere to the letter, the obvious regulatory advantages that global environmental constitutionalism hold out in the European context could serve regions such as Africa well as examples in their efforts to augment environmental protection in the wake of the Anthropocene's socio-ecological crisis.

C. The International Environmental Regulatory Regime Approach

The international regulatory regime approach to global constitutionalism traces constitutionalism in increasingly autonomous clustered regimes of international law that are organised around a broadly defined regime such as global trade or the environment. The focus of this approach could also be more specific in that it looks for constitutionalism in narrower regimes that are components or building blocks of the more encompassing general environmental or global trade regimes. Examples in the environmental context are the biodiversity and climate change regimes. Usually, these regulatory regimes are either made up of a cluster of treaties and their concomitant institutions, or they could revolve around a full-fledged and more powerful international organisation such as the World Trade Organization, its norms and institutional apparatus.

While the World Trade Organization has international legal personality, which means that it has the capacity to perform international legal acts, no international environmental institution has a similar degree of international legal personality or independence.[39] UNEP comes closest to such a construction, even though it is not nearly comparable to other United Nations organisations in terms of its capacity and authority to create and enforce international environmental law and adjudicate environmental disputes. Thus, the international regulatory regime approach to global environmental constitutionalism in a broad sense will probably only take deliberate shape when a more influential international environmental organisation with international legal personality is considered (see above).

Traces of global environmental constitutionalism could arguably be found more clearly in the narrower international regulatory regime approach. As an intergovernmental body, despite its lack of United Nations organisation status, UNEP plays an important role in initiating and supporting global environmental governance among states inter se and among states and other international organisations.[40] To its credit, various multilateral environmental agreements and entire environmental treaty regimes, have been developed under the coordinating

---

[39] See on the juridical and political details in relation to international organisations generally, including aspects related to their international legal personality, J Klabbers and Å Wallendahl (eds), *Research Handbook on the Law of International Organizations* (Cheltenham, Edward Elgar, 2011).

[40] M Drumbl, 'Actors and Law-making in International Environmental Law' in M Fitzmaurice, D Ong and P Merkouris (eds), *Research Handbook on International Environmental Law* (Cheltenham, Edward Elgar, 2010) 7–8.

leadership of UNEP.[41] It is within the aggregated collection of this burgeoning body of agreements that one finds narrowly clustered normative and institutional constructions such as the ocean governance, climate change and biodiversity regimes that could have global environmental constitutionalism characteristics. While the successes and failures of multilateral environmental agreements are debatable and often debated, there is evidence that '[i]ssue specific regimes have achieved a relatively high level of performance in a wide range of dimensions'.[42]

With the possible exception of the ocean governance regime with its International Maritime Organization (that only partly deals with environmental matters), none of these narrowly clustered issue-specific regimes revolve around a strong centralised international organisation that in terms of their status and power are equivalent to United Nations organisations. Taking the biodiversity regime as an example, several multilateral environmental agreements perform basic formal constitutive functions by establishing institutions, specifying the rules that guide and constrain these institutions, and entrench these rules through amendment procedures. These include the Ramsar Convention on Wetlands 1971; the Bonn Convention on Migratory Species 1979; and the Convention on Biological Diversity 1992. In addition to regular Conferences of the Parties, these instruments and their protocols constitute and regulate various treaty institutions such as Standing Committees, Advisory Committees, Scientific Councils, Working Groups and Convention Secretariats, which in turn are responsible for implementing treaty provisions and for monitoring compliance and creating new and amending existing treaty provisions, among many other governance functions.[43] To this end, it is possible to observe a degree of formal global environmental constitutionalism that is embedded in these regimes, notably to the extent that their 'constitutional' treaties and protocols comprehensively constitute them, provide their governance institutions and associated governance procedures, and other formally constitutive provisions that make them work, as it were.

It is also possible to observe substantive constitutional aspects in these treaty regimes in the sense that they constrain behaviour, limit free will, and counter arbitrary actions, however minimal this may be. To this end, treaties are able to constrain state behaviour, not only through formal global constitutional institutions and processes, but also through setting substantive limitations on what states can and cannot do. Of course the constraints that these treaties impose are not comparable to the normative force, authority and ethical/moral urgency of typical higher-order constitutional instruments such as rights or *jus cogens* norms (see the discussion at section IV.F). States could also admittedly be more inclined to ignore or breach treaty provisions than they would be in the case of rights or

---

[41] N Kanie, 'Governance with Multilateral Environmental Agreements: A Healthy or Ill-equipped Fragmentation?' in Swart and Perry (n 18) at 68.

[42] ibid, 73.

[43] A Wiersema, 'The New International Law-makers? Conferences of the Parties to Multilateral Environmental Agreements' (2009) 31 *Michigan Journal of International Law* 232–87.

jus cogens norms. It is therefore probably more appropriate to speak in this instance of a softer form of substantive global environmental constitutionalism, or constitutionalism with a little "'c'" rather than a big "C"';[44] but it is a minimal incarnation of substantive global environmental constitutionalism nevertheless.

D. Global Civil Society Environmental Constitutionalism

Famously abstract, amorphous and indeterminate, the civil society approach to global constitutionalism focuses on the emergence of pockets of non-state 'law' or 'civil constitutions' as a result of informal normative processes and (often self-regulatory) instruments and structures emanating from non-state entities such as non-governmental organisations.[45] These global civil society actors usually share common characteristics in that they are organisations with an institutional presence and structure; they function separately from the state and thus exercise private instead of public authority; they usually operate on a non-profit basis; and they are self-governing to the extent that they control their own affairs alongside (or sometimes in the absence of) more formal state regulation.[46] In terms of these generic characteristics, it is not entirely impossible to think of global civil society in global constitutional terms especially insofar as they are constituted entities with their own internal rules, have the ability to make softer forms of regulatory norms, and have the ability to exert some regulatory influence in global regulatory spaces beyond the state; however minimal this may be in practice.[47]

The environment clearly has also become a proper concern of global civil society actors and it is gradually appealing to social movement energies and energetic global solidarities. Acting outside of the formal government setting, environmental non-governmental organisations 'affirm values that are universally recognized but politically manipulated in their own interest by political agencies'.[48] Aiming to 'undo evil or to do good',[49] non-governmental environmental organisations are popular and enjoy broad-based public support; their activities focus on practical and current matters, specific cases and concrete expressions of human solidarity.

---

[44] Bodansky, 'Is There an International Environmental Constitution?' (n 18) at 578.

[45] G Teubner, 'Societal Constitutionalism: Alternatives to State-Centred Constitutional Theory?' in C Joerges, I-J Sand and G Teubner (eds), *Transnational Governance and Constitutionalism* (Oxford, Hart, 2004) 3–28.

[46] L Salamon and H Anheier, 'Civil Society in Comparative Perspective' in L Salamon and others (eds), *Global Civil Society Dimensions of the Nonprofit Sector* (Baltimore, The Johns Hopkins Center for Civil Society Studies, 1999) 3–4.

[47] H Breitmeier and V Rittberger, *Environmental NGOs in an Emerging Global Civil Society* (Tübinger Arbeitspapiere zur Internationalen Politik und Friedensforschung, 1998) available at: https://bibliographie.uni-tuebingen.de/xmlui/bitstream/handle/10900/47202/pdf/tap32.pdf?sequence=1&isAllowed=y.

[48] M Castells, 'The New Public Sphere: Global Civil Society, Communication Networks, and Global Governance' (2008) 616 *The ANNALS of the American Academy of Political and Social Science* 78–93, 84.

[49] ibid, 85.

While global non-state actors remain unable to participate fully in global environmental lawmaking and diplomacy as a result of them lacking international legal personality, these actors increasingly influence the outcomes of the more formal global juridical processes, thereby indirectly contributing to the development of global environmental constitutional norms and structures beyond the state.[50] Through deliberate and broad-based civil society participation in global environmental governance and lawmaking, it is possible to influence indirectly the content and design of global environmental norms; to change the ideational context of an issue and enhance the sensitivity of society for new problem-solving approaches;[51] and to expand and enrich whatever notions of global democracy may be at play in the global regulatory domain which, in turn, could increase the legitimacy and effectiveness of global environmental law and governance (see also the discussion below).

E. Transnational Comparative Environmental Constitutionalism

Transnational comparative constitutionalism has to do with the emergence of environmental norms around the globe.[52] 'Transnational' or 'global' describes both a space and a process, which entail finding constitutional elements in domestic, international and regional regimes from around the world and then comparing them with a view to comparative interpretation that often leads to law reform. Arguably more than any of the previous four approaches discussed above, transnational comparative environmental constitutionalism is emerging as a result of globalisation.[53] The transnational comparative approach predominantly traces an emerging global constitutional dialogue that is mostly carried by domestic courts, legislatures and scholars who, through processes consisting of cross-jurisdictional learning, comparative interpretation and legal transplantation, are increasingly developing a more uniform (if not absolutely identical) normative approach to specific elements of global environmental constitutionalism, such as approaches to environmental rights. While there are many others,[54] one example is the 1976 Portuguese Constitution's formulation of a 'right to a healthy and ecologically balanced human living environment' that is now found in 21 other constitutions around the world. Another is the Supreme Court of India's decisions on

---

[50] The number of non-governmental environmental organisations at global United Nations conferences has steadily increased, notably since the Stockholm Conference on the Human Environment in 1972. See www.un-documents.net/aconf48-14r1.pdf, 43.

[51] Breitmeier and Rittberger, *Environmental NGOs in an Emerging Global Civil Society* (n 47).

[52] See eg K Kersch, 'The New Legal Transnationalism, the Globalized Judiciary, and the Rule of Law' 2005(4) *Washington University Global Studies Law Review* 345–87.

[53] M Howlett and S Joshi-Koop, 'Transnational Learning, Policy Analytical Capacity, and Environmental Policy Convergence: Survey Results from Canada' (2011) 21 *Global Environmental Change* 85–92.

[54] See J May and E Daly, *Global Environmental Constitutionalism* (Cambridge, Cambridge University Press, 2015).

environmental rights that have significantly influenced other courts in Bangladesh, Pakistan, Sri Lanka, Uganda and Kenya.[55]

IV. Seven Elements of Global Environmental Constitutionalism

The remainder of this chapter identifies how seven elements of environmental constitutionalism currently manifest in the global regulatory domain within the context of the various approaches to global environmental constitutionalism outlined above. The various elements of global environmental constitutionalism discussed here cannot offer a final typology and topography of global environmental constitutionalism. The utility of finding and describing these elements rather lies therein that they could be used as a framework to inform an evaluation that determines in broad terms the emergence of global environmental constitutionalism.

A. A Global Environmental Constitution

In one of the first publications that focused on global environmental constitutionalism, Bodansky asked: '[i]s there an International Environmental Constitution?'[56] He concluded that there is not. Others have indicated that '[t]he prospect of a global environmental constitution may not be realistic for many years to come'.[57] One reason for the absence of a global environmental constitution, and doubt as to its immediate emergence, is related to the absence of a strong, centralised international environmental organisation; a consideration that was canvassed above. These two issues are intimately related and it is likely that conversations and reform efforts in this respect will only gain more deliberate traction once sufficient political will is mustered to overcome the prevailing political reticence that is hampering the creation of such an organisation and an accompanying constitution. To this end, the unprecedented socio-ecological decline globally, as evidenced by the Anthropocene, should in theory serve as sufficient motivation for states and global civil society actors to embark on paradigm-shifting reforms of global environmental law, governance and its institutions. While the recent Paris Climate Agreement in 2015 has been criticised for being too weak,[58] it is an indication,

---

[55] D Boyd, *The Environmental Rights Revolution: A Global Study of Constitutions, Human Rights, and the Environment* (Vancouver, UBC Press, 2012) 108.

[56] Bodansky (n 18).

[57] Bosselmann (n 4) at 182.

[58] Centre for Research on Globalization 'The COP21 Climate Summit: The Ambitions and Flaws of the Paris Agreement. Outcome of Deception and Bullying', www.globalresearch.ca/the-cop21-climate-summit-the-ambitions-and-flaws-of-the-paris-agreement-outcome-of-deception-and-bullying/5495512.

however slight, that global environmental governance actors might eventually be willing to forgo some unhindered economic expansion in favour of reforms that support growth within limits.

If a remote possibility does exist for the eventual creation of a global environmental constitution, how could it look? One example that might serve as a blueprint for a global environmental constitution is the ecocentric-oriented Earth Charter. Currently the Charter neither has the required level of state-backed support and universal state-endorsement to render it sufficiently influential at the high strategic political level, nor does it collectively represent shared ecological values that all states endorse in order for it to gain widespread support. But in a possible new geological epoch that signifies socio-ecological upheaval affecting all life on Earth, there is a chance that global civil society driven initiatives such as the Earth Charter might be taken up by more formal United Nations political and lawmaking processes. After all, one of the most influential global human rights instruments that has managed to instigate paradigm-shifting changes in the global order, the Universal Declaration of Human Rights of 1948, was developed as a response to shared global civil society and state-led human rights concerns in the aftermath of World War II.

Similar to the type of language used in the Declaration, the Earth Charter is fashioned around four foundational themes that are reflective of typical constitutional language including: respect and care for the community of life; ecological integrity; social and economic justice; and democracy, non-violence and peace.[59] The Charter also contains both formal and substantive constitutional aspects alongside which a global environmental constitution could be fashioned. While there is no clear division, the substantive aspects are broadly outlined in the first three themes that entrench commitments towards the Earth, ecological processes and the community of life, including aspects of inter-species justice and justice between humans. Part four, while it does not establish a responsible institution for global environmental governance, provides formal constitutional aspects including the need to strengthen democratic institutions at all levels, and to provide transparency and accountability in governance, inclusive participation in decision-making and access to justice.

In line with what has already been proposed above, and while initiatives such as the Earth Charter gain increased traction as potential key elements of global environmental constitutionalism, it would be necessary to utilise, expand and significantly improve multilateral environmental agreements, and their institutions. Another option could be to create and/or strengthen regional environmental governance regimes, their founding treaties, normative environmental frameworks, and their governance institutions, including their adjudicating bodies. It would be crucial that the constituting treaties of these regional governance bodies and their subsequent environmental instruments, including those related to higher-order

---

[59] See the text of the Charter at http://earthcharter.org/discover/the-earth-charter/.

norms such as rights, are revised to more comprehensively cater for environmental concerns. Where they do not exist yet, they must be established. These
reforms, which should also include initiatives for inter-regional alignment, should
run concurrently with efforts to reform global environmental treaties and their
regimes and they could contribute to creating regional pockets of constitutionally
more coherent and effective environmental governance in a formal and substantive sense.

B. Global Environmental Rule of Law

In his famous list of essential elements of legality (or in this context the rule of
law), Fuller determined that the law must be general and publicly promulgated,
clear, not demand something impossible, prospective in effect (as opposed to
being retrospective), understandable, consistent and constant by applying equally
to all cases, non-contradictory, and relatively stable and congruent.[60] A contemporary vision of the rule of law is that it provides certainty in a legal order, it
prevents the entrenchment of power, and it plays a more-than-symbolic role in
the constitutional state in that it offers a normative justification and foundation
for the entrenchment of procedural and substantive mechanisms to prescribe and
proscribe power. Whereas the formal/procedural aspects of the rule of law provide
for and determine those elements that are necessary to establish and maintain a
governance order on the basis of positive law, the material/substantive aspects of
the rule of law bind those that exercise governance power to substantive standards. The formal aspects have several objectives: legality, functional delimitation
of governance competencies, and clear allocation of powers. The primary objectives of the material aspects are to ensure limited government, justice and morality
through, among others, rights protection, judicial oversight, as well as the general
principles of justice.[61]

Measured against this core meaning of the rule of law, the existence of the global
environmental rule of law could depend on, among others: the extent to which
it could be said that (a) global environmental authority(ies) exist; the extent to
which the entire collection of global laws regulating the human environment
interface is available, clear and effective and able to ensure adequate compliance
and enforcement; the extent to which state and non-state actor accountability with
respect to environmentally damaging acts is ensured through checks and balances
such as strengthened judicial control and citizen suits; and the extent to which the
law is able to protect higher-order rights-based environmental guarantees.[62]

---

[60] L Fuller, *The Morality of Law* (New Haven, CT, Yale University Press, 1964) 33–94.

[61] B Enzmann, *Der Demokratische Verfassungsstaat: Entstehung, Elemente, Herausforderungen*
(Wiesbaden, Springer, 2014) 43–163.

[62] Garver proposes an alternative view of 'ecological rule of law', which combines the notion of
ecological law with the notion of the rule of law. Ecological law emphasises ecological integrity and the

In a global setting, the formal aspects of environmental rule of law could be regulated by constitution-like instruments in the global environmental governance sphere containing provisions that seek to provide for and determine the constitutive/formal elements that are necessary to establish and maintain the global environmental governance order; in other words, those provisions that enable and carry global environmental governance. These formal provisions focus on both the powers of environmental governance entities such as treaty secretariats themselves, and on the institutional arrangements that facilitate the involvement of states in each treaty's governance effort. Although it would have been far easier to determine these in terms of a hitherto non-existent single international environmental organisation and its constitution, such formal aspects are currently evident to some extent in the disaggregated collection of multilateral environmental agreements that create environmental governance institutions, regulate their internal functions and guide the actions of states parties, and consequently the manner in which states regulate those residing in their jurisdictions, including individuals and corporations (see the discussion above).

Substantive global environmental rule of law aspects would aim to achieve some measure of limitation on all entities that exercise power in the global environmental governance domain including states, treaty bodies and international organisations; separation of these powers; checks, balances and judicial oversight; processes and institutions to advance democratic participation and legitimacy; and the provision and protection of rights-based guarantees. To date, as with the formal aspects of the global environmental rule of law, the global environmental law and governance order lacks a single all-encompassing instrument through which these goals could collectively be achieved. While treaties do set out some limitations on the free will of states and sanctions for non-compliance, these provisions are not absolute or sufficiently comprehensive, and on their own, treaties would not be solely up to the task of determining and enforcing higher-order normative obligations. The substantive aspects of the global environmental rule of law, such as rights and *jus cogens* norms exist to some extent, but they are scattered across the global regulatory landscape, as we will see below.

C. Separation of Global Environmental Governance Powers

The separation of powers doctrine entails that the authority to govern should be divided among different government powers ie the executive, the legislature and the judiciary.[63] Related to the formal aspects of the rule of law, this doctrine

---

need for the law to ensure such integrity by making clear that global ecological limits constrain the economic and social spheres; G Garver, 'The Rule of Ecological Law: The Legal Complement to Degrowth Economics' (2013) 5 *Sustainability* 316–37.

[63] C Fombad, 'The Separation of Powers and Constitutionalism in Africa: the Case of Botswana' 2005 (25) *Boston College Third World Law Journal* 301–42.

essentially seeks to counter centralisation and abuse of authority, to promote accountability, and to enhance governance efficiency. Separation of powers is hardly ever determined through a single explicit provision in a constitution. It usually emerges from the collective formal constitutional provisions that establish these powers and that determine and delimit their authority.[64]

Globally, it is far more difficult to determine a measure of separation of powers than it is in the domestic sphere: there is no unitary global government based on a unified constituted power with a clearly defined judiciary, executive and legislature that derive their powers from a single constituent power or instrument. Such a separation of global powers can only be vaguely detected in the United Nations and European Union's constitutional architecture. Considering, however, that domestic understandings of constitutionalism should be applied globally in a nuanced way, a close connection between three distinct separate global powers arguably need not exist, as long as the separation of powers doctrine more or less fulfils its objectives. Globally this could entail: preventing the concentration of power in any single state, group of states, an international governance organisation or a treaty body; creating accountability by requiring (a) limited global government(s) to justify decisions and actions and to act responsibly towards the international community; and increasing global governance efficiency where some global governance institutions are better placed to perform certain governance functions than others.

Measured against these broad characteristics of the separation of powers doctrine how could the separation of powers doctrine be understood in the global environmental governance domain? There are at least two possible scenarios. The first is the most evident, but for reasons outlined above still the most unlikely scenario, where a global environmental government, or a global government with a distinct environmental arm, is created. Such a construction would create an opportunity to establish three distinct nodes revolving around executive, legislative and judicial functions that need not be entirely separated, but that allows for some form of convergence, within the confines of constitutionalism more generally, where this is necessary and permissible to ensure optimal global environmental governance of a complex and integrated Earth system in a balanced manner.

The second, and more likely option, is fashioned around O'Donoghue's proposition, namely to think about the separation of existing global environmental powers in geographical terms.[65] In terms of this description, vertical separation of global environmental powers would result in a clear distinction being drawn between local, federal (provincial or state), national, regional (such as the European Union) and international (the United Nations) centres of power. Because it includes the national sphere of powers and that sphere's unique horizontal division of powers as well, by necessary implication, geographical division of powers

---

[64] See generally R Masterman, *The Separation of Powers in the Contemporary Constitution: Judicial Competence and Independence in the United Kingdom* (Cambridge, Cambridge University Press, 2011).

[65] A O'Donoghue, *Constitutionalism in Global Constitutionalisation* (Cambridge, Cambridge University Press, 2014) 34–35.

would include the traditional horizontal division of powers within a state, while including the national horizontal division of powers within the regional and international 'territorial centres'.[66] At the same time, the geographical separation of powers would include whatever minimal form of separation of powers is evident in the United Nations and European Union context as well. Such a construction might provide the means to limit the concentration of environmental governance powers at any single geographical level by divesting each sphere of some power through the multi-levelled geographical arrangement.

D. The Global Environmental Judiciary

Many domestic courts around the world have been active in adjudicating environmental disputes, interpreting environmental laws, and more generally, upholding the dictates of environmental constitutionalism by, for example, restricting state activities that could harm the environment.[67] While these are usually courts with general jurisdiction, there are examples of specialised domestic environmental courts such as the Australian New South Wales Land and Environment Court.[68] Apart from developing domestic environmental jurisprudence, these courts also contribute, through processes of trans-jurisdictional comparison, to the steady growth of transnational comparative environmental constitutionalism, as was shown above. In doing so, some latent degree of uniformity is developing globally with respect to the interpretation, application and development of environmental law, including constitutional aspects such as environmental rights.[69]

While not nearly comparable to the efforts of domestic courts, regional courts and adjudicating bodies have also in recent years increasingly engaged with environmental concerns, including the enforcement and development of substantive higher-order rights-based norms. Even though the European Convention on Human Rights of 1950 does not entrench an explicit environmental right, the European Court of Human Rights has been remarkably active in protecting environmental and related concerns through a range of other rights enshrined in the Convention.[70] In doing so, the Court is intensifying the development of higher-order

---

[66] ibid, 35.

[67] See for a comprehensive discussion, May and Daly, *Global Environmental Constitutionalism* (n 54).

[68] See B Preston, 'Benefits of Judicial Specialization in Environmental Law: The Land and Environment Court of New South Wales as a Case Study' (2012) 29 *Pace Environmental Law Review* 396–440.

[69] This is not to suggest, however, that some unqualified uniformity is emerging as it would be unrealistic to expect courts all over the world to become entirely uniform in their approaches to interpretation and the subsequent development of law; T Stephens, 'Multiple International Courts and the "Fragmentation" of International Environmental Law' (2006) 25 *Australian Year Book of International Law* 227–71, 231.

[70] These cases are too numerous to list here. See for a comprehensive overview, European Court of Human Rights, www.echr.coe.int/Documents/FS_Environment_ENG.pdf; and for a comprehensive discussion, J Jans and H Vedder, *European Environmental Law after Lisbon* 4th edn (Groningen, Europa Publishing, 2012).

rights-based norms and it provides checks and balances on power within the emerging European constitutional ecological federation, while it contributes to strengthening global environmental constitutionalism at the regional level. The Court of Justice of the European Union is the judicial institution of the Union. As a more general judicial forum, it focuses on disputes related to the legality of European Union measures and ensures the uniform interpretation and application of European Union law. In the environmental domain, the Court busies itself with the interpretation and application of Union environmental law, notably actions for failure to fulfil binding legal obligations.[71] As was mentioned above, the Court is likely to become an active role player in interpreting, protecting and enforcing the environment-related rights-based provisions in the Charter of Fundamental Rights of the European Union of 2000.

While the International Court of Justice (ICJ) serves as the pre-eminent international judicial forum, it is not an international environmental court. An opportunity for it to fulfil this role presented itself with the creation of the Court's Special Chamber for Environmental Matters in 1993. While it was periodically reconstituted since its creation, it was unfortunately dismantled in 2006 and by that time had not adjudicated any environmental dispute. At least the fact that a judicial institution such as the ICJ contemplated the establishment of a specialised chamber was then, and today remains significant, especially to the extent that it indicates some state recognition of the political importance of the environment in international politics, law and governance.[72] The failure of the Chamber is not to suggest, however, that the ICJ has not dealt with environmental disputes between states, or that it does not remain crucially important as an institution in this respect. The complex body of ICJ environmental jurisprudence is too burgeoning to discuss here and others have extensively done such an analysis.[73] What is clear is that the ICJ has significantly contributed to developing international environmental law through its judgments,[74] advisory opinions,[75] and more creatively, through separate and dissenting opinions by some of its judges (notably those of Judge Weeramantry).[76]

---

[71] See for a detailed exposition of the Court's decisions on nature and biodiversity, European Commission, http://ec.europa.eu/environment/nature/info/pubs/docs/others/ecj_rulings_en.pdf.

[72] P Sands, 'International Environmental Litigation and its Future' (1999) 32 *University of Richmond Law Review* 1619–41, 1626.

[73] See among the many publications, T Stephens, *International Courts and Environmental Protection* (Cambridge, Cambridge University Press, 2009).

[74] Including eg *Corfu Channel (United Kingdom of Great Britain and Northern Ireland v Albania)* 1949; *Nuclear Tests Case (New Zealand v France)* 1974; *Gabčíkovo-Nagymaros Project (Hungary v Slovakia)* 1997; *Certain Phosphate Lands in Nauru (Nauru v Australia)* 1992; *Pulp Mills on the River Uruguay (Argentina v Uruguay)* 2006.

[75] eg *Advisory Opinion on the Legality of the Threat or Use of Nuclear Weapons* 1996.

[76] D French, 'The Heroic Undertaking? The Separate and Dissenting Opinions of Judge Weeramantry during his Time on the Bench of the International Court of Justice' (2006) 11 *Asian Yearbook of International Law* 35–68.

Acting complementary to domestic criminal systems, the International Criminal Court is not part of the United Nations system, but a treaty-based regime that aims to 'help end impunity for the perpetrators of the most serious crimes of concern to the international community'.[77] It focuses specifically on adjudicating 'the most serious crimes of concern to the international community as a whole', including genocide, crimes against humanity, war crimes and acts of aggression.[78] It is unclear from this wording whether, and none of its past judgments suggest, that environmental crimes could be included within its jurisdictional reach.[79] If they could be included, an important avenue will be created to ensure greater accountability where states, for example, commit acts of aggression that have an environmental impact or dimension.

Stephens indicates that internationally, 'environmental dispute settlement is increasingly dominated by issue-specific, judicial bodies called upon to determine essentially environmental disputes, often essentially by default'.[80] There are various bodies of this nature such as the World Trade Organization and its General Agreement on Tariffs and Trade Panels, the International Tribunal on the Law of the Sea, the Permanent Court of Arbitration and the International Centre for the Settlement of Investment Disputes that are contributing to the normative development of international environmental law. While the jurisprudence of these institutions is too vast to deal with here, it has since become clear that despite their divergent focus areas, they have 'established an embryonic framework within which issues of international environmental law could be raised in the context of international litigation'.[81] The judgments of these judicial bodies do not necessarily contribute to develop higher-order environmental constitutional norms; they are far more effective in integrating environmental considerations with various globalised processes such as trade, and to some extent, they restrict the free will of states to engage in activities that may cause environmental harm.

What emerges from the foregoing discussion is that 'there is no established international environmental jurisdiction, much as there is no global environmental organisation,'[82] and global environmental dispute settlement remains a fragmented affair. This insight is particularly important for global environmental constitutionalism: clearly there are multiple judicial fora at various geographical levels available to enforce environmental law, to assert higher-order rights-based claims, and to integrate environmental considerations into the multifarious rubric

---

[77] International Criminal Court, www.icc-cpi.int/en_menus/icc/about%20the%20court/Pages/about%20the%20court.aspx.

[78] The Rome Statute of the International Criminal Court 1998, Art 5.

[79] See further T Smith, 'Creating a Framework for the Prosecution of Environmental Crimes in International Criminal Law' in W Schabas, Y McDermott and N Hayes (eds), *The Ashgate Research Companion to International Criminal Law* (Aldershot, Ashgate, 2013) 45 ff.

[80] Stephens, 'Multiple International Courts and the "Fragmentation" of International Environmental Law' (n 69) at 233.

[81] P Sands, 'International Environmental Litigation and its Future' (n 72) at 1625.

[82] Stephens (n 69) at 234.

of concerns that domestic, regional and international law seeks to address. These judicial institutions simultaneously act to enforce the rule of law and in particular, accountability by keeping the actions of (mostly) states in check. Considering the many diverse dimensions and interrelated complexity of global environmental concerns, it is unlikely and probably even undesirable that one global court that has jurisdiction over all environmental disputes beyond the borders of states will or should ever exist. While there are concerns about the fragmented global environmental judiciary[83] (understood as including the panoply of the institutions discussed above), the current set-up provides the means for global judicial bodies to extend their influence into numerous global governance spaces at various geographical levels where environmental concerns might arise. In time it will be necessary, however, to create judicial bodies where they do not exist or strengthen existing ones; expand the jurisdictions of these bodies; and create specialised environmental units within each to deal with highly technical and specialised environmental issues. The Anthropocene after all requires a greater measure of scientific and technical specialisation to deal with the comprehensive range of Earth system changes that it evinces.

E. Global Environmental Democracy

Democracy serves as an enabler of constitutionalism, as an expression of the majority will of people and as a necessary condition for the establishment and legitimacy of a constitutional state to the extent that democratic processes are required to constitute a structured polity.[84] Democracy in the global context is more difficult to discern than at the domestic level because of the absence of a single global government and a constituent power, and it takes on a more nuanced meaning in the global governance sphere. Departing from an enlarged notion of an 'international community' consisting of states and non-state actors, an aggregated global constituent power should ideally be enabled to drive participative, representative, inclusive and transparent modes of global environmental governance in the spaces where states and their citizens, international organisations as global representatives of states, and global civil society actors operate.[85] The potentially potent link between democracy and what we seek to achieve through constitutionalism in the environmental law and governance domain is evident:

> Most scholarship envisions environmental politics as the pursuit of already fixed interests. That approach ignores the power of political communities to change both their values and their interests through the self-interpreting activity of democratic politics.

---

[83] ibid.

[84] See eg M Loughlin, 'Rights, Democracy, and Law' in T Campbell, KD Ewing and A Tomkins (eds), *Sceptical Essays on Human Rights* (Oxford, Oxford University Press, 2001).

[85] F Biermann and A Gupta, 'Accountability and Legitimacy in Earth System Governance: A Research Framework' (2011) 70 *Ecological Economics* 1856–64, 1856.

In that politics, new forms of normative identity—who we take ourselves to be and what matters most to us—arise from reciprocal efforts at persuasion, arguments about the meaning of shared ideas and commitments. *Nature*, like *liberty* and *equality*, is a centerpiece of public language[86]

How can the actors in global environmental governance contribute, through a more sustained and influential 'public language' that is carried by processes of democratic deliberation, to change prevailing and deep-seated values and interests related to nature? First, in the state-dominant domain, measures should be put in place to more equally represent all countries and regional groupings in environmental law and governance. Global environmental governance remains a matter of unequal partners and the global climate change negotiation arena is an example of an instance where states and regional organisations are disproportionally represented as a result of capacity concerns and hegemonic struggles.[87] Anthropocene events are particularly evident in the Global South, and the Anthropocene's socio-ecological crisis is set to affect these countries the most. There is accordingly now, more than ever before, sufficient justification and motivation to level the global environmental political playing field by affording all states, including their global representatives, equal recognition and power in the processes and structures that determine global human-environment relations.

Secondly, in a transnational sense, it is likely that the many actors in global governance will themselves be more democratic and inclined to observe the minimum dictates of democracy and constitutionalism in the global regulatory realm when these actors hail from domestic constitutional democracies. Acting as an ideological orientation for states in the global domain, the extent to which the citizens of a state are thus able to constitute, interact with and legitimise a constituted domestic power, including the aspects of that power responsible for domestic environmental governance, may have a meaningful persuasive bottom-up impact on how states act in and through global environmental governance. Efforts to transform non-democratic states and to strengthen domestic democratic regimes where they fall short, could thus indirectly contribute to the expansion of global environmental democracy in post-state spaces.

Thirdly, while it is not the only one,[88] a binding instrument that comes closest to comprehensively regulating and improving the participation, transparency and

---

[86] J Purdy, 'The Politics of Nature: Climate Change, Environmental Law, and Democracy' (2010) 119 *Yale Law Journal* 1125–209, 1125.

[87] ClimDev-Africa 'Africa's Journey in the Global Climate Negotiations' www.climdev-africa. org/sites/default/files/DocumentAttachments/Africa%E2%80%99s%20Journey%20in%20the%20 Global%20Climate%20Negotiations,%20SPM%20-%20EN_0.pdf.

[88] The procedural aspects of global environmental governance currently exist in a much more comprehensive and complex global regulatory regime consisting of soft-law instruments and regional and global treaties. See for a detailed discussion J Razzaque, 'Human Right to a Clean Environment: Procedural Rights' in Fitzmaurice, Ong and Merkouris (eds), *Research Handbook on International Environmental Law* (n 40) at 284–300.

accountability aspects of global environmental democracy is the Convention on Access to Information, Public Participation in Decision-Making and Access to Justice in Environmental Matters 1998 (Aarhus Convention). The significant potential of the Aarhus Convention to enhance global environmental democracy lies, among others, in the effectiveness of its Compliance Committee and the fact that it is open for ratification to all members of the United Nations.[89] The Convention provides extensive measures and remedies to promote access to environmental information, public participation and access to justice in environmental matters. Through the expansion of binding multilateral agreements such as the Aarhus Convention, and the encouragement of non-member states to sign up to these agreements, a greater measure of accountable and democratic global environmental governance could possibly take root in future.

Fourthly, outside of the more formal state-driven global law and governance arena, global civil society is able to assert themselves as observers during global conferences and to cooperate more closely with states to achieve global governance objectives (see above). Multi-actor transnational networks are also increasingly created that contribute to realising some of the goals of global environmental governance in a bottom-up way. In relation to multinational corporations, the United Nations Global Compact provides a platform that engages corporations, governments and other stakeholders to collectively work towards sustainability goals.[90] Gradually expanding non-governmental organisations and global epistemic communities, such as the Global Network for the Study of Human Rights and the Environment, encouragingly evince more deliberate and possibly influential collective civil society energies that could influence and legitimise the predominantly state-driven global environmental governance agenda.

F. Global Environmental Constitutional Supremacy

The idea of constitutional supremacy assumes that there is no higher juridical norm in a state than the constitution and its provisions.[91] This creates a normative and institutional hierarchy in terms of which all laws, decisions and acts of government are subject to the constitution and in terms of which these laws, decisions and acts could be declared unconstitutional and invalid. In domestic constitutions, such norms are usually encapsulated within rights and it is mainly the judiciary that will play a key role in upholding and protecting constitutional

---

[89] See generally E Hey, 'The Interaction between Human Rights and the Environment in the European Aarhus "Space"' in A Grear and LJ Kotzé (eds), *Research Handbook on Human Rights and the Environment* (Cheltenham, Edward Elgar, 2015) 353–76.

[90] B Richardson, *Socially Responsible Investment Law: Regulating the Unseen Polluters* (Oxford, Oxford University Press, 2008).

[91] J Limbach, 'The Concept of the Supremacy of the Constitution' (2001) 64(1) *Modern Law Review* 1–10.

supremacy. Constitutional supremacy is best understood in the global sphere by determining whether a normative hierarchy exists in terms of which higher-order non-derogable norms supersede other norms and which bind states to the extent that their free sovereign will is limited.[92] In the absence of a global constitution that would have made this determination fairly straightforward, such norms are most likely to be found as human rights that are contained in regional and international human rights instruments, in *jus cogens* norms and customary international law with *erga omnes* obligations.[93]

Focusing for present purposes on *jus cogens* norms, the rules of international law generally accepted as having *jus cogens* status include, among others: the prohibition of the threat or use of force against the territorial integrity or political independence of any state; the prohibition of genocide; the prohibition of torture; crimes against humanity; the prohibition of slavery and slave trade; the prohibition of piracy; the prohibition of racial discrimination and apartheid; and the prohibition of hostilities or force directed at a civilian population. It remains unclear if explicit environment-related *jus cogens* norms exist and/or if future peremptory norms could emerge in international environmental law.[94] There is, for example, no norm that prohibits severe and widespread pollution; or a norm that prohibits states from transgressing a minimum threshold of sustainability; or a norm that prohibits states from changing the climate through greenhouse gas emissions. Various scholars have confirmed this view. According to Birnie, Boyle and Redgwell:

> What cannot be supposed is that environmental rules have any inherent priority over others save in the exceptional case of *ius cogens* norms ... No such norms of international environmental law have yet been convincingly identified, nor is there an obvious case for treating them in this way.[95]

To date no international court or tribunal has explicitly identified any norm that has, or that could in future gain, peremptory status in the environmental domain; nor has any international court or tribunal invoked Articles 53 and 64 of the Vienna Convention on the Law of Treaties (VCLT) in practice to settle an environment-related treaty dispute. The closest that the ICJ came in doing so was in its *Gabčikovo-Nagymaros* judgment where it accepted by implication Slovakia's contention that none of the norms on which Hungary relied was of a peremptory nature.[96]

If we accept that a global hierarchy of constitutional-like environmental norms could be useful in restricting the free will of states in their actions that impact the

---

[92] E de Wet and J Vidmar (eds), *Hierarchy in International Law: the Place of Human Rights* (Oxford, Oxford University Press, 2012).

[93] E de Wet, 'The International Constitutional Order' (2006) 55(1) *International and Comparative Law Quarterly* 51–76.

[94] See for a detailed discussion, L Kotzé, 'Constitutional Conversations in the Anthropocene: in Search of *Jus Cogens* Norms' 2015 (46) *Netherlands Yearbook of International Law* 241–71.

[95] P Birnie, A Boyle and C Redgwell, *International Law and the Environment* 3rd edn (Oxford, Oxford University Press, 2009) 109–10.

[96] *Gabčikovo-Nagymaros*, ICJ Reports 1997, 59, [97].

environment, we need to ask if it is possible for environmental *jus cogens* norms to develop over time? The gradual Anthropocene-induced epistemological shift is redirecting our attention away from territorially limited and individual state-bound environmental concerns to a more globally collective conception of Earth system changes, their impacts on the international community of states, and the collective responsibility of states in this respect. The ICJ in the *Nuclear Weapons* Advisory Opinion, has made tentative steps to more directly connect *jus cogens*, *erga omnes* obligations and the common heritage of mankind in the context of a globalised community of states that should be seeking collective responses to shared environmental problems. The Court noted that we are witnessing:

> the gradual substitution of an international law of co-operation for the traditional law of co-existence, the emergence of the concept of 'international community' and its some-times successful attempts at subjectivization. A token of all these developments is the place which international law now accords to concepts such as obligations *erga omnes*, rules of *jus cogens*, or the common heritage of mankind. The resolutely positivist, vol-untarist approach of international law still current at the beginning of the [twentieth] century has been replaced by an objective conception of international law, a law more readily seeking to reflect a collective juridical conscience and respond to the social neces-sities of states organised as a community.[97]

At a practical level and in light of the epistemological freedom that such pro-nouncements provide, Article 53 of the VCLT offers states an opportunity to determine themselves what are peremptory norms and what are not.[98] In practice, this would occur through a process that first identifies a norm as customary inter-national law and then an agreement on whether derogation is permitted from that customary norm or not.

Considering the deep controversy that surrounds the burgeoning debate on which international environmental law norms have or have not attained custom-ary law status,[99] this discussion focuses for present purposes on the one rule that has unequivocally been recognised as customary environmental law, namely the no harm rule (or *sic utere tuo ut alienum non laedas*) that imposes a negative obli-gation on states (as *jus cogens* norms typically do) not to cause environmental harm to another state. The rule was first recognised by an international court in the *Trail Smelter* arbitration, which settled an environmental utilisation conflict between Canada and the United States.[100] The ICJ has subsequently endorsed the

---

[97] *Legality of the Threat or Use of Nuclear Weapons (Advisory Opinion)* ICJ Reports (1996) 268, 270–71 (per President Bedjaoui).

[98] E de Wet, '*Jus Cogens* and Obligations *Erga Omnes*' in D Shelton (ed), *The Oxford Handbook on International Human Rights Law* (Oxford, Oxford University Press, 2015) 542.

[99] U Beyerlin and T Marauhn, *International Environmental Law* (Oxford, Hart Publishing, 2011) 47–84.

[100] *Trail Smelter Arbitration* (1949) 3 RIAA 1903.

concept in its *Nuclear Weapons* Advisory Opinion, and specifically emphasised the *erga omnes* obligations that flow from it:

> The existence of the general obligation of States to ensure that activities within their juris-diction and control respect the environment of other States or of areas beyond national control is now part of the corpus of international law relating to the environment.[101]

Today the no harm principle

> has been so widely accepted in international treaty practice, numerous declarations of international organisations, the codification work of the ILC [International Law Commission], and in the jurisprudence of the ICJ that it can be considered to be a customary substantive rule at the universal level.[102]

It should thus satisfy the VCLT peremptory requirement of being 'a norm accepted and recognized by the international community of States as a whole' (the first stage of acceptance).[103] Whether it has attained the status of a norm 'from which no derogation is permitted'[104] (the second stage of acceptance) is, however, debatable. It is still unlikely that states have universally accepted any 'strong ethical [ecological] underpinning'[105] that should be associated with the no harm principle. Yet, because of its customary status, the fact that it applies at an inter-state level to environmental resources within state territories as well as to the global environmental commons, and that it imposes negative obligations, suggest that at least theoretically, it has the potential to become a peremptory norm in future. In the light of the Anthropocene and various implicit ethical obligations to desist from causing irreversible ecological harm, there is increasing motivation auguring support for universal recognition of the no harm rule's potential strong ethical underpinning that is necessary for enhanced global ecological care.

G. Global Environmental Rights

Rights are also part of the international normative hierarchy's set of apex norms. Domestically, the transnationalisation of global environmental rights presents rich opportunities for the cross-fertilisation of legal ideas and best practices and it has the potential to influence the creation of common global legal rules on environmental rights that are at least based on the same ideas and influences, if not exactly on the same content. Regionally, in addition to environmental rights provisions

---

[101] *Legality of the Threat or Use of Nuclear Weapons (Advisory Opinion)* ICJ Reports (1996) 268, [29].
[102] Beyerlin and Marauhn, *International Environmental Law* (n 99) at 44.
[103] VCLT, Art 53.
[104] ibid.
[105] J Vidmar, 'Norm Conflicts and Hierarchy in International Law: Towards a Vertical International Legal System?' in de Wet and Vidmar (eds), *Hierarchy in International Law: the Place of Human Rights* (n 92) at 26.

in the European Union instruments, the African Charter on Human and People's Rights and the American Convention on Human Rights' San Salvador Protocol, Article 3(2) of the Asian Human Rights Charter of 1998 provides for the right to a 'clean and healthy environment'.[106] The Arab Charter on Human Rights 2004 also includes a right to a healthy environment as part of the right to an adequate standard of living that ensures well-being and a decent life.[107] It was also shown that the Aarhus Convention declares a non-justiciable environmental right and it provides a whole set of procedural guarantees to facilitate inclusive and participative environmental governance.

These domestic and regional initiatives, and their relatively active judicial oversight bodies, are set to be bolstered by the increasingly vocal and influential global civil society movements that champion environment-related rights protection. Often working from their domestic jurisdictions and increasingly beyond these, such as in the case of the International Rights of Nature Tribunal, it is especially global civil society actors that contribute to cementing, strengthening and further expanding environment-related rights at the global level through their core functions.[108]

To date, however, there is neither a universally applicable global treaty that explicitly provides for an environmental right,[109] nor has such a right been accepted into the corpus of customary international law.[110] As an ultimate expression of constitutionalism, and specifically with the view to providing greater global ecological care that is premised on strong sustainability, it will be crucial to commence with discussions about eventually creating such a right, either in a future global environmental constitution or as an element of an existing or new global human rights instrument. Considering the Anthropocene's demands for current regulatory institutions and higher-order norms to become more ecocentric, part of this discussion must also reflect on the orientation of this right. The Ecuadorean Constitution provides an example of constitutional rights of nature, while the ecocentric Earth Charter also provides a generic framework for such a discussion.[111]

The Bolivian government has recently proposed to the United Nations an ecocentric rights reformulation in terms of the Universal Declaration of Rights of

---

[106] Available at: http://www.refworld.org/pdfid/452678304.pdf.

[107] Art 38. Notably, neither the Asian Human Rights Charter nor the Arab Charter on Human Rights has enforcement mechanisms.

[108] B Gemmill and A Bamidele-Izu, 'The Role of NGOs and Civil Society in Global Environmental Governance' in D Esty and M Ivanova (eds), *Global Environmental Governance: Options and Opportunities* (Yale, Yale Centre for Environmental Law and Policy, 2002) 77–100.

[109] See generally S Turner, *A Global Environmental Right* (Abingdon, Routledge, 2013).

[110] At most, environmental entitlements are inferred indirectly from the provisions of other human-focused but environment-related rights treaties; see D Shelton, 'Human Rights and the Environment: Substantive Rights' in Fitzmaurice, Ong and Merkouris (n 40) at 266–67.

[111] L Kotzé and P Villavicencio Calzadilla, 'Somewhere between Rhetoric and Reality: Environmental Constitutionalism and the Rights of Nature in Ecuador' *Transnational Environmental Law* (to appear 2017).

Mother Earth of 2010.[112] The Declaration recognises that the Earth is a living entity and as a result 'Mother Earth' could lay claim to the full range of fundamental rights normally attributed to humans including, among others: the right to life and to exist; the right to be respected; the right to regenerate its bio-capacity and to continue her vital cycles and processes free from human disruptions; the right to maintain her identity and integrity as a distinct, self-regulating and interrelated being; the right to water as a source of life; the right to clean air; the right to integral health; the right to be free from contamination, pollution and toxic or radioactive waste; the right to not have her genetic structure modified or disrupted in a manner that threatens her integrity or vital and healthy functioning; and the right to full and prompt restoration.[113] Considering the legal fraternity's continued apprehension about such an ecological formulation and its possible legal and governance implications, as well as the prevailing strong political resistance to such a drastic proposal, it is understandably unlikely that it will gain any credence soon. Yet, the fact that the debate has been initiated in the global political arena, suggests that it could make it less difficult in future to negotiate for a global environmental right that is at once also more ecocentric in its orientation. In sum, an ecological reorientation of rights evinces the potential that human rights have in the Anthropocene to refocus exclusive attention away from serving human needs, to an approach that instead seeks to ensure care for human well-being, while simultaneously respecting the limits of Earth's life supporting systems and the well-being of other species. At the very least it is one, among other attempts, to give 'ethico-juridical significance to the material situations of countless human beings, non-human animals and living ecosystems placed in unprecedented danger by the irresponsible pursuit of profit and by its associated ecological legacies'.[114]

V. Conclusion

Global environmental constitutionalism is a comparatively radical juridical intervention to address a critical global regulatory problem: the socio-ecological crisis of the Anthropocene. Understandably, while it is much easier to situate constitutionalism in the domestic environmental law and governance sphere, it is far more difficult to do so with respect to global environmental law and governance. We need to accept that:

> The barriers to facilitating such global rethinking remain immense and must be challenged both individually and collectively by those who wish to reform the existing order

---

[112] http://therightsofnature.org/bolivia-experience/.

[113] Art 2 of the Declaration. See World People's Conference on Climate Change and the Rights of Mother Earth, *Proposed Universal Declaration of the Rights of Mother Earth*, available at: http://pwccc. wordpress.com/programa/.

[114] A Grear, 'Human Bodies in Material Space: Lived Realities, Eco-crisis and the Search for Transformation' (2013) 4(2) *Journal of Human Rights and the Environment* 111–15, 111.

... the barriers we need to identify and dismantle are ones created by ideologies and modes of reasoning that funnel thinking and keep us from acting on these common sensibilities.[115]

The ideas that were canvassed in this chapter sought to prise open some of the epistemological closures that continue to shut out more radical thinking in the constitutional and global environmental law and governance domains. While the analysis emphasised the positive contribution that environmental constitutionalism could make to improve global environmental law and governance, it also fully accepts that the mere incorporation of environmental concerns into a global constitutional framework, or conversely, the consitutionalisation of the global environmental law and governance framework, is only part of many strategies that would be necessary to counter Anthropocene exigencies. While environmental constitutionalism cannot therefore be the panacea for all the Anthropocene's regulatory challenges, as a value-laden manifestation of law carrying with it substantial normative force, the promise of 'new beginnings' and the potential to change polities to the core, there is an argument to be made out in support of thinking about global environmental law and governance reforms in constitutional terms, and to identify and further develop environmental constitutionalism elements in the global regulatory space beyond the state.

---

[115] S Jasanoff, 'A World of Experts: Science and Global Environmental Constitutionalism' (2013) 40(4) *Boston College Environmental Affairs Law Review* 439–52, 443–44.

10

Global Justice in the Anthropocene

CARMEN G GONZALEZ[*]

I. Introduction

Scientists believe the world has entered a new geological epoch in which human economic activity is the primary driver of global environmental change. Known as the Anthropocene, this epoch is characterised by human domination and disruption of Earth system processes essential to the planet's self-regulating capacity.[1] Climate change, deforestation, species extinction and other ecological transformations have exceeded safe biophysical thresholds, rendering the planet increasingly dangerous, unpredictable, unstable and incompatible with human flourishing.[2]

The environmental crises of the Anthropocene are deeply connected to economic policies that have enabled the world's most affluent populations to consume a disproportionate share of the planet's resources while relegating vast swathes of humanity to abject poverty.[3] 20 per cent of the world's population consumes roughly 80 per cent of the planet's resources[4] and owns approximately 95 per cent

---

[*] Professor of Law, Seattle University School of Law. This chapter has been adapted from CG Gonzalez, 'Bridging the North-South Divide in the Anthropocene' (2015) 32 *Pace Environmental Law Review* 407.
[1] See PJ Crutzen, 'Geology Of Mankind—The Anthropocene' (2002) 415 *Nature* 23.
[2] See generally W Steffen and others, 'Planetary Boundaries: Guiding Human Development on a Changing Planet' (2015) 347 *Science* 1259855.
[3] See C Bonneuil and J-B Fressoz, *The Shock of the Anthropocene* (London, Verso, 2015) 242–52 (describing the massive extraction by Western industrial countries of the mineral and renewable resources of the Third World to fuel the post-1945 period of rapid economic growth known as the 'Great Acceleration'); Oxfam, 'An Economy for the 1%: How Privilege and Power in the Economy Drive Extreme Inequality and How This Can Be Stopped' (January 2016), www.oxfam.org/en/research/economy-1 (discussing the economic policies of the past 4 decades that have exacerbated economic inequality between and within nations and allowed basic human needs to go unmet).
[4] See WE Rees and L Westra, 'When Consumption Does Violence: Can There Be Sustainability and Environmental Justice in a Resource-Limited World?' in J Agyeman, RD Bullard and B Evans (eds), *Just Sustainabilities: Development in an Unequal World* (Cambridge, MA, MIT Press, 2003) 110–12; World Bank, *2002 World Development Indicators* (2008) 4, http://data.worldbank.org/sites/default/files/wdi08.pdf.

of the planet's wealth.[5] In 2015, just 62 individuals possessed the same wealth as the planet's poorest 3.6 billion.[6] As inequality grows and the environment deteriorates, billions of people struggle to satisfy basic human needs. Nearly 750 million people are unable to obtain clean drinking water, and 2.5 billion lack access to sanitation.[7] Approximately 800 million people suffer from chronic undernourishment because they lack the resources to grow or purchase sufficient food to satisfy their dietary energy needs.[8] Another 2.8 billion people lack modern energy for cooking, heating, lighting, transportation or basic mechanical power.[9]

International environmental law has generally failed to halt or reverse the rapid deterioration of the planet's life support systems.[10] Conflicts between affluent and poor countries (the North-South divide) grounded in colonial and postcolonial political and economic relations have frequently paralysed international lawmaking, resulting in deadlocks in environmental treaty negotiations and agreements marred by ambiguity, lack of ambition and inadequate compliance and enforcement mechanisms.[11] Although more than 700 multilateral agreements have been adopted since 1857, the rate of anthropogenic environmental change continues to accelerate.[12] In almost every area of environmental concern, North-South negotiations have featured a deep and growing chasm between the call by some Northern states for collective action to protect the environment and the South's demand for social and economic justice.[13]

Of course, the North-South divide is not the only obstacle to international environmental cooperation. Conflicts between powerful Southern countries (such as China and India) and more ecologically vulnerable nations (such as the small island states) have also compromised international environmental negotiations,

---

[5] See D Hardoon, 'Wealth: Having It All And Wanting More' (Oxfam International, 2016) 2 www.oxfam.org/en/research/wealth-having-it-all-and-wanting-more.

[6] See Oxfam (n 3) at 2.

[7] See World Health Organization (WHO)/United Nations Children's Fund (UNICEF), *Progress on Drinking Water and Sanitation* (WHO/UNICEF 2014) www.who.int/water_sanitation_health/publications/2014/jmp-report/en/.

[8] See United Nations Food and Agriculture Organization (FAO), *The State of Food Insecurity in the World (SOFI) 2015: Meeting the 2015 International Hunger Targets: Taking Stock of Uneven Progress* (FAO, 2015) 4, www.fao.org/publications/card/en/c/c2cda20d-ebeb-4467-8a94-038087fe0f6e/.

[9] See International Energy Agency (IEA), *World Energy Outlook 2012* (Organization for Economic Co-operation and Development (OECD) 2012) www.iea.org/publications/freepublications/publication/WEO2012_free.pdf.

[10] See JC Carlson, G Palmer and B Weston, *International Environmental Law and World Order: A Problem-Oriented Coursebook* (St Paul, Minnesota, West Academic Press, 2012) 293.

[11] See generally S Atapattu and CG Gonzalez, 'The North-South Divide in International Environmental Law: Framing the Issues' in S Alam, S Atapattu, CG Gonzalez and J Razzaque (eds), *International Environmental Law and the Global South* (Cambridge, Cambridge University Press, 2015) 1–20.

[12] RE Kim and K Bosselmann, 'International Environmental Law in the Anthropocene: Towards a Purposive System of Multilateral Environmental Agreements' (2013) 2 *Transnational Environmental Law* 285, 285–86.

[13] U Natarajan and K Khoday, 'Locating Nature: Making and Unmaking International Law' (2014) 27 *Leiden Journal of International Law* 573, 579.

most notably in the case of climate change.[14] In addition, the United States and the European Union have clashed over climate policy and over the regulation of toxic chemicals and genetically modified organisms.[15]

In order to bridge the North-South divide and respond to the ecological crises of the Anthropocene, international environmental law must be normatively grounded in respect for nature and in the quest for social, economic and environmental justice within as well as between countries. It must also challenge the dominant growth-oriented economic paradigm rather than merely mitigating its excesses.

This chapter proceeds in four parts. Part II examines the ways in which international law has historically engaged with nature and with the peoples of the global South in order to identify the policies and practices that subordinate the South and degrade the planet's ecosystems. Part III analyses the role of international economic law in perpetuating unsustainable and inequitable patterns of production and consumption. Part IV argues that sustainable development, a central orientation for international environmental law and politics, has failed to contest the dominant, growth-oriented economic paradigm at the core of the ecological and socio-economic crisis. Part V discusses the way forward.

II. The Colonial and Postcolonial Origins of the Anthropocene

The origins of the Anthropocene are contested. Some scholars argue that the Anthropocene began when humans first engaged in large-scale agricultural production that transformed the planet's landscapes and emitted sufficient greenhouse gases to influence the planet's climatic trajectory.[16] Others identify the Industrial Revolution and the post-World War II decades of rapid economic growth as the first and second stages of the Anthropocene.[17] Regardless of the outcome of these debates, the Anthropocene did not materialise fully formed during

---

[14] See generally S Happaerts and H Bruyninckx, 'Rising Powers in Global Climate Governance: Negotiating in the New World Order' (2013) Working Paper No 124 Leuven Centre for Global Governance Studies.

[15] DE Adelman, 'A Cautiously Optimistic Appraisal of Trends In Toxics Regulation' (2010) 32 *Washington University Journal of Law and Policy* 377; J Brunnee, 'Europe, The United States, and the Global Climate Regime: All Together Now?' (2008) 24 *Journal of Land Use & Environmental Law* 1; CG Gonzalez, 'Genetically Modified Organisms and Justice: The International Environmental Justice Implications of Biotechnology' (2007) 19 *Georgetown International Environmental Law Review* 583.

[16] See generally WF Ruddiman, 'The Anthropogenic Greenhouse Era Began Thousands of Years Ago' (2003) 61 *Climatic Change* 261; WF Ruddiman, 'How Did Humans First Alter Global Climate?' (2005) 292 *Scientific American* 46.

[17] See Bonneuil and Fressoz, *The Shock of the Anthropocene* (n 3) 50–51.

any particular historic moment, but emerged gradually 'from a long historical process of economic exploitation of human beings and the world, going back to the sixteenth century and making industrialization possible'.[18]

The Industrial Revolution was fuelled by colonialism, which provided the natural resources to feed European workers and machines and the markets for European industrial output.[19] The colonial encounter devastated the indigenous civilisations of Asia, Africa and the Americas, and enabled Europeans to appropriate and exploit their lands, labour and natural resources through slavery, conquest, and indentured servitude.[20] Colonialism converted self-reliant subsistence economies into outposts of Europe that exported agricultural products, minerals, and timber, and imported manufactured goods for the benefits of a few people at the expense of many.[21] Mining, logging and cash-crop production destroyed forests, dispossessed local communities, and dramatically altered the ecosystems of the colonised territories.[22] The transatlantic slave trade generated the revenues for industrial development by commodifying human beings, and produced a legacy of social and economic exclusion that lingers to the present day.[23]

International law justified the colonial enterprise by constructing native populations as racially and culturally inferior and by asserting a moral duty to 'civilise' them though compulsory assimilation to European ways.[24] Influenced by Enlightenment scholars and philosophers, international law decreed the domination of nature and the development of industry as the key obligations of civilised states.[25] Societies that lived in harmony with nature were pronounced 'uncivilised' and in need of 'modernisation' and 'development'.[26]

Colonialism universalised European notions of nature as a commodity for human exploitation while creating a global economy that systematically subordinated the global South. Even after political independence, postcolonial states in Asia, Africa and Latin America were integrated into the Northern-dominated world economy as exporters of primary commodities and importers of manufactured

---

[18] ibid, 228–29.

[19] ibid, 231–35.

[20] See C Ponting, *A Green History of the World* (New York, Sinclair-Stevenson, 1991) 130–36.

[21] See ibid, 194–212.

[22] See K Miles, 'International Investment Law: Origins, Imperialism and Conceptualizing the Environment' (2010) 21 *Colorado Journal of International Environmental Law and Policy* 1, 21–22.

[23] See HMcD Beckles, *Britain's Black Debt: Reparations for Caribbean Slavery and Native Genocide*, (Kingston, Jamaica, University of the West Indies, 2013) 82–108; Bonneuil and Fressoz (n 3) 230–32 (arguing that the transatlantic slave trade sparked the Industrial Revolution); F Brennan and J Packer (eds), *Colonialism, Slavery, Reparations and Trade: Remedying the Past?* (Abingdon, Routledge, 2012) (explaining the ongoing impacts of the slave trade and arguing for reparations).

[24] See generally A Anghie, *Imperialism, Sovereignty and the Making of International Law* (Cambridge, Cambridge University Press, 2005).

[25] See A Geisinger, 'Sustainable Development and the Domination of Nature: Spreading the Seed of the Western Ideology of Nature' (1999) 27 *Boston College Environmental Affairs Law Review* 43, 52–58; Natarajan and Koday, 'Locating Nature' (n 13) 586–87.

[26] See V Argyrou, *The Logic of Environmentalism: Anthropology, Ecology, and Postcoloniality* (Oxford/ New York, Berghahn Books, 2005) 7–26.

products.[27] Because the terms of trade consistently favoured manufactured goods over primary products, the nations of the global South were required to export increasing amounts of their output in order to acquire the same amount of manufactured goods.[28] Efforts to boost national earnings by increasing the production of minerals, timber and agricultural products generally glutted global markets with primary commodities and depressed prices, thereby reducing Southern export earnings, exacerbating Southern poverty and reinforcing the North-South economic divide.[29]

The North's control over a large part of the world's resources from the colonial era to the present fuelled the North's industrial development and enabled the North to maintain levels of consumption far beyond the limits of its own natural resource base.[30] As historian Clive Ponting observes, '[m]uch of the price of that achievement was paid by the population of the Third World in the form of exploitation, poverty, and human suffering'.[31]

The South's economic dependency on export production enabled the North to exploit Southern resources at prices that did not reflect the social and environmental costs of production.[32] Far from producing prosperity, export-led development strategies depleted the South's natural resources, harmed human health and reinforced social and economic inequality by imposing disparate environmental burdens on the communities targeted for petroleum extraction, mining and other forms of resource exploitation.[33] Much of the environmental degradation in the global South has been caused by export-oriented production to satisfy the needs and desires of Northern consumers, rather than local consumption.[34]

III. International Economic Law and the North-South Divide

The legal architecture of contemporary globalisation was developed in the aftermath of the Second World War when much of the global South remained under colonial rule. International economic law exacerbated the North-South divide and sparked the post-1945 period of unprecedented neoliberal economic

---

[27] See Ponting, *A Green History of the World* (n 20) at 213–14.

[28] See JM Cypher, *The Process of Economic Development* (Abingdon, Routledge, 2014) 198–212.

[29] See Ponting (n 20) at 223.

[30] See ibid.

[31] ibid.

[32] See J Martinez-Alier, *The Environmentalism of the Poor: A Study of Ecological Conflicts and Valuation* (Cheltenham, Edward Elgar Publishing, 2003) 214.

[33] RM Bratspies, 'Assuming Away the Problem? The Vexing Relationship Between International Trade and Environmental Protection' in CM Bailliet (ed), *Non-State Actors, Soft Law, And Protective Regimes: From the Margins* (Cambridge, Cambridge University Press, 2012) 228–30, 239–40.

[34] See Rees and Westra, 'When Consumption Does Violence' (n 4) at 110.

growth and environmental devastation known as the Great Acceleration.[35] This section discusses the ways that both investment law and trade law exacerbated the North-South divide and contributed to the Great Acceleration.

Modern investment law inherited from the colonial era an instrumentalist view of the environment as an object for Northern exploitation, with no corresponding duty to protect the health of local ecosystems, enhance the well-being of local communities, or advance the goals and interests of the host state.[36] Thus, contemporary bilateral investment treaties (BITs) and regional investment agreements seek to provide foreign investors with unfettered access to natural resources by restricting the ability of host states to adopt health and safety, environmental, labour and human rights standards.[37] If these social and environmental standards impair the economic value of the investment, they may be challenged as indirect expropriations or breaches of fair and equitable treatment standards.[38] Designed to maintain a stable legal and business environment for foreign investors, these one-sided agreements generally impose no human rights and environmental obligations on foreign investors and provide no mechanism for holding corporations accountable for the harms to human health and the environment that their activities cause in the host state.[39] Indeed, as one scholar has noted, investment law may actually impede climate change adaptation in the global South by requiring states to compensate foreign investors when measures enacted to address changing and unstable environmental conditions (such as water shortages produced by drought) depress the value of the foreign investment.[40]

While international investment law provided the global North with the raw materials from the global South that fed the Great Acceleration, the 1947 General Agreement on Tariffs of Trade (1947 GATT) facilitated the global trade flows that supplied markets for the North's petroleum-intensive manufactured goods and agricultural products.[41] The 1947 GATT disproportionately benefited the global North by requiring all nations to reduce tariffs on manufactured goods (produced primarily by Northern industries) while allowing the North to maintain agricultural subsidies and import barriers that disfavoured Southern agricultural producers.[42] When cheap oil and generous government subsidies produced a glut

---

[35] See Bonneuil and Fressoz (n 3) at 242–52. Some scholars have argued that the Great Acceleration should be regarded as the beginning of the Anthropocene. See generally W Steffen and others, 'The Trajectory of the Anthropocene: The Great Acceleration' *The Anthropocene Review* published online 16 January 2015 [DOI: 10.1177/2053019614564785].

[36] See Miles, 'International Investment Law' (n 22) at 23–24.

[37] See ibid, 40–44.

[38] See ibid, 40.

[39] See ibid, 44.

[40] See S Baker, 'Climate Change and International Economic Law' (2016) 43 *Ecology Law Quarterly* 53, 93.

[41] See Bonneuil and Fressoz (n 3) at 244.

[42] See CG Gonzalez, 'Trade Liberalization, Food Security and the Environment: The Neoliberal Threat to Sustainable Rural Development' (2004) 14 *Transnational Law & Contemporary Problems* 419, 456–57.

of agricultural products in Northern markets, Northern agribusiness sold the surplus food in the global South at prices far below the local cost of production, undermining the livelihoods of small farmers and provoking an exodus to urban slums.[43]

In the decades following World War II, a coalition of Southern states (known as the Group of 77) attempted to reform the international economic system through a series of resolutions at the United Nations General Assembly, where the South held a numerical majority.[44] The Group of 77 sought to achieve a more equitable international economic order by advancing the doctrine of permanent sovereignty over natural resources and the right to nationalise the Northern companies exploiting the South's natural resources.[45] They mobilised to achieve a New International Economic Order (NIEO) that would enhance Southern participation in global governance, provide debt relief, secure preferential access to Northern markets and stabilise export prices for primary commodities.[46] The Group of 77 also attempted to mitigate the economic legacy of colonialism and promote economic prosperity through differential treatment in international economic law (special and differential treatment) and international environmental law (common but differentiated responsibility).[47]

The debt crisis of the 1980s marked the demise of the NIEO and the ascendancy of the free market economic model known as the Washington Consensus.[48] In exchange for debt repayment assistance, the International Monetary Fund (IMF) and the World Bank imposed on heavily indebted Southern nations a series of neoliberal economic reforms that included trade liberalisation, deregulation, privatisation, elimination of social safety nets and the intensification of export production to service the foreign debt.[49]

The export-led economic policies mandated by the IMF and the World Bank exacerbated poverty and inequality; reinforced the South's environmentally and economically disadvantageous dependence on the export of primary commodities; and enabled Northern transnational corporations to dominate many of the newly

[43] See Bonneuil and Fressoz (n 3) 244; CG Gonzalez, 'Food Justice: An Environmental Justice Critique of the Global Food System' in Alam, Atapattu, Gonzalez and Razzaque (eds), *International Environmental Law and the Global South* (n 11) at 408.

[44] See L Rajamani, *Differential Treatment in International Environmental Law* (Oxford, Oxford University Press, 2006) 17–18.

[45] See RE Gordon and JH Sylvester, 'Deconstructing Development' (2004) 22 *Wisconsin International Law Journal* 1, 53–56.

[46] See Rajamani, *Differential Treatment in International Environmental Law* (n 44) at 17–18; Gordon and Sylvester, 'Deconstructing Development' (n 45) at 56–68; R Gordon, 'The Dawn of a New, New International Economic Order?' (2009) 72 *Law and Contemporary Problems* 131, 142–45.

[47] See C Gonzalez, 'Environmental Justice and International Environmental Law' in S Alam, MJH Bhuiyan, TMR Chowdhury and EJ Techera (eds), *Routledge Handbook of International Environmental Law* (London/New York, Routledge, 2013) 87–92.

[48] See Gordon, 'The Dawn of a New, New International Economic Order?' (n 46) at 145–50.

[49] See ibid; Gonzalez, 'Environmental Justice and International Environmental Law' (n 47) at 82.

privatised economic sectors.[50] Trade liberalisation destroyed rural livelihoods in the global South by placing small farmers in direct competition with highly sub-sidised Northern agribusiness.[51] The elimination of social safety nets exacerbated the misery of the poor, and resulted in food riots (known as 'IMF riots') in many Southern countries.[52] Under pressure to repay the foreign debt, Southern coun-tries 'mined' natural resources to maximise export earnings rather than managing them in a sustainable manner.[53] Desperate for foreign investment, impoverished Southern nations became magnets for polluting industry and dumping grounds for hazardous wastes from the global North.[54]

The World Trade Organization (WTO) Agreements that succeeded the 1947 GATT failed to dismantle the import barriers of greatest concern to the global South (particularly in the areas of agriculture, clothing and textiles) while impos-ing new and onerous obligations in the areas of intellectual property, invest-ment and services.[55] They also required Southern countries to curtail the import barriers that protected nascent Southern industries from more technologically advanced Northern competitors, and restricted the right of Southern countries to deploy tariffs and subsidies to strategically promote dynamic new industries (a practice known as industrial policy).[56] Economic history reveals that the United States, Germany, Japan, the United Kingdom, Taiwan and South Korea achieved economic prosperity through protectionism (including industrial policy).[57] By depriving Southern nations of the tools used by the global North and by cer-tain middle-income Southern states to diversify and industrialise their econo-mies while imposing new requirements to protect the rights of foreign investors and intellectual property holders, international economic law has institutional-ised Southern poverty.[58] Indeed, the North's unsustainable model of economic

---

[50] See ibid, 82.

[51] See Gonzalez, 'Trade Liberalization, Food Security and the Environment' (n 42) at 466–67.

[52] See ibid, 465–66.

[53] See Bratspies, 'Assuming Away the Problem?' (n 33) at 239.

[54] See generally DN Pellow, *Resisting Global Toxics: Transnational Movements for Environmental Jus-tice* (Cambridge, MA, MIT Press, 2007).

[55] See FJ Garcia, 'Beyond Special and Differential Treatment' (2004) 27 *Boston College International and Comparative Law Review* 291, 297–98.

[56] See Yong-Shik Lee, *Reclaiming Development in the World Trading System* (Cambridge, Cambridge University Press, 2006) 41–42.

[57] See generally Ha-Joon Chang, *Bad Samaritans: The Myth of Free Trade and the Secret History of Capitalism* (New York, Bloomsbury Publishing, 2008); Ha-Joon Chang, *Kicking Away the Ladder: Development Strategy in Historical Perspective* (London, Anthem Press, 2002); AH Amsden, *Escape from Empire: The Developing World's Journey through Heaven and Hell* (Cambridge, MA, MIT Press, 2009); ES Reinert, *How Rich Countries Got Rich…and Why Poor Countries Stay Poor* (London, PublicAffairs, 2008); AH Amsden, *The Rise of 'the Rest': Challenges to the West from Late-Industrializing Economies* (Oxford, Oxford University Press, 2003).

[58] See Gonzalez (n 47) at 92–94. Countries that disregarded the Washington Consensus and adopted state-led industrialisation as a more reliable path out of poverty nevertheless pillaged the environment. For example, China ignored the policy prescriptions of the Washington Consensus and used tariffs, import quotas, technology transfer requirements, local content requirements and aggressive indus-trial policy to achieve economic prosperity. China's defiance of neoliberal orthodoxy and embrace of

development was made possible by under-consumption of the global South.[59] The Great Acceleration was based on the importation of the South's raw materials and the over-exploitation of the world's ecosystems to assimilate the North's prodigious emissions of pollutants and greenhouse gases.[60]

IV. Sustainable Development: Part of the Solution or Part of the Problem?

The root cause of the contemporary socio-ecological crisis is an international economic order premised on unlimited economic growth that impoverishes the global South and facilitates the over-consumption of the planet's resources by its more affluent inhabitants. This economic order reinforces the colonial notion that all societies must evolve through particular stages until they achieve the apex of civilisation represented by the global North.[61] It casts development as the 'ubiquitous goal of all states and peoples',[62] and equates development with rising material consumption.[63] Pioneered by Europe and the United States, this economic model has now been exported to the global South, and imposes ever-increasing demands on the world's finite natural resources and waste sinks.[64]

The unbridled pursuit of economic growth has brought the planet's ecosystems to the brink of collapse. The 2005 United Nations Millennium Ecosystem Assessment Synthesis Report concluded that human economic activity during the previous 50 years produced more severe degradation of the planet's ecosystems than in any prior period in human history.[65] A decade later, an influential study published

state-led development (known as the 'Beijing Consensus') has been touted as a model for the global South after decades of failed neoliberal economic reforms. However, China is now facing an environmental crisis of breath-taking proportions while contributing significantly to global environmental problems, including climate change, transboundary air pollution and the illegal timber trade. See CG Gonzalez, 'China in Latin America: Law, Economics, and Sustainable Development' (2010) 40 *Environmental Law Reporter News & Analysis* 10171, 10174–76.

[59] See Bonneuil and Fressoz (n 3) at 249–50; C Flavin and G Gardner, 'China, India and the New World Order' in The Worldwatch Institute, *State of the World 2006: Special Focus: China and India* (New York, WW Norton & Co, 2006) 16–18 (explaining that the Global North, along with China and India, is currently utilising 75% of the planet's biocapacity, making it impossible for other countries to pursue economic growth without provoking global environmental catastrophe).

[60] See Bonneuil and Fressoz (n 3) at 249–50.

[61] See G Rist, *The History of Development: From Western Origins to Global Faith* (London, Zed Books, 1997) 238; Natarajan and Khoday (n 13) at 588–89.

[62] See Natarajan and Khoday (n 13) at 588.

[63] See JG Speth, *The Bridge at the Edge of the World: Capitalism, the Environment, and Crossing from Crisis to Sustainability* (New Haven, CT, Yale University Press, 2009) 46–51.

[64] See Gonzalez, 'China in Latin America' (n 58) at 10176, 10181.

[65] See United Nations Millennium Ecosystem Assessment, *Synthesis Report: Ecosystems and Human Well-Being: General Synthesis* (Island Press/World Resources Institute, 2005) 1–24, www.millenniumassessment.org/en/Synthesis.html.

in the journal *Science* explained that the global economy has already transgressed four of the nine planetary boundaries essential to the planet's ability to maintain an environment hospitable to human and non-human life.[66]

The global North, with only 18 per cent of the world's population, is responsible for approximately 74 per cent of the extraordinary post World War II economic expansion.[67] While the North reaps the material benefits of the Great Acceleration, the environmental consequences are borne disproportionately by Southern countries, by nature, and by the planet's most vulnerable human beings, including indigenous peoples, racial and ethnic minorities, and the poor.[68] Having industrialised by appropriating the South's natural resources and by using more than its fair share of the global commons for waste disposal, the North's per capita ecological footprint continues to significantly outstrip that of the South.[69] Scholars and activists have argued that the global North owes an ecological debt[70] to the countries and peoples of the global South for 'resource plundering, unfair trade, environmental damage and the free occupation of environmental space to deposit waste'.[71] Indeed, this ecological debt is at the heart of many North-South conflicts in international environmental law.

International environmental law has failed to challenge the fallacy of unlimited economic growth. Although its meaning is highly contested, sustainable development is widely recognised as one of the guiding principles of contemporary international environmental law, and it was designed to restrict unbridled, environmentally destructive economic activity.[72] The World Commission on Environment and Development (the Brundtland Commission) defined sustainable development as 'development that meets the needs of the present without compromising the ability of future generations to meet their own needs'.[73] While this definition attempted to reconcile economic development and environmental protection, it did not explicitly challenge the growth-oriented development paradigm.[74] Indeed, the Brundtland Commission boldly asserted that '[g]rowth has no set limits in terms of population or resource use beyond which

---

[66] See Steffen and others (n 2). Climate change, species extinction, deforestation and the run-off of phosphorus and nitrogen into regional watersheds and oceans have exceeded the safe biophysical thresholds known as planetary boundaries, thereby creating a dangerous and unstable environment.

[67] See United Nations Millennium Ecosystem Assessment (n 65) at 11.

[68] See Rees and Westra (n 4) at 100–03.

[69] See ibid, 109–12.

[70] See K Mickelson, 'Leading Towards a Level Playing Field, Repaying Ecological Debt, or Making Environmental Space: Three Stories about International Environmental Cooperation' (2005) 43 *Osgoode Hall Law Journal* 138, 150–54; D McLaren, 'Environmental Space, Equity and the Ecological Debt' in Agyeman, Bullard and Evans (eds), *Just Sustainabilities: Development in an Unequal World* (n 4) 30–32.

[71] E Paredis and others, *The Concept of Ecological Debt: Its Meaning and Applicability in International Policy* (Ghent, Academia Scientific, 2008) 7.

[72] See generally NJ Schrijver, *The Evolution of Sustainable Development in International Law: Inception, Meaning and Status* (Leiden, Brill, 2008).

[73] See World Commission on Environment and Development (WCED), *Our Common Future* (Oxford, Oxford University Press, 1987) 8.

[74] See Rist, *The History of Development* (n 61) at 193; W Sachs, 'Environment' in W Sachs (ed), *The Development Dictionary: A Guide to Knowledge as Power* (New York, Zed Books, 2010) 29.

lies ecological disaster'.[75] Instead of encouraging the global North to reduce its ecological footprint in order to increase the living standards of the poor without exceeding biophysical limits, the Brundtland Commission extolled the benefits of international trade as the engine of economic growth and the solution to poverty and inequality.[76] As Gilbert Rist observes:

> The main contradiction, then, in the Report of the Brundtland Commission is that the growth policy supposed to reduce poverty and stabilize the ecosystem hardly differs at all *from the policy which historically opened the gulf between rich and poor and placed the environment in danger.*[77]

Far from questioning the dominant development model that subordinated the global South and sparked a socio-ecological crisis of epic proportions, sustainable development 'naturalizes and obfuscates the process whereby some people systematically under-develop others'.[78]

Although the impossibility of unlimited economic growth has become increasingly evident, international environmental law has failed to mount a frontal assault on the global economic order or to attack its fundamental assumptions. Environmental treaties repeat the mantra that the poor need economic development without acknowledging ecological limits or the fact that the dominant economic model has increased North-South inequality and widened the gap between the rich and the poor in all nations.[79] Global environmental degradation has been constructed as an externality to be mitigated and internalised through multilateral environmental agreements,[80] thereby treating the symptoms of the disease rather than addressing its underlying causes. Instead of confronting head-on an economic model based on the unrestrained extraction, trade and consumption of natural resources, international environmental law has left intact the contemporary global economic (dis)order that enriches the affluent, exacerbates the plight of the poor and accelerates Earth system destruction. Clearly then, international environmental law is a field in crisis because the problems it currently confronts are deeply embedded in the existing economic order and cannot be adequately addressed by tinkering on the margins.

V. The Way Forward

Environmental justice provides a compelling moral framework for the reconceptualisation of international environmental law. The primary cause of global

---

[75] WCED, *Our Common Future* (n 73) at 45.
[76] See ibid, 50–51, 89.
[77] Rist (n 61) at 186. Emphasis in original.
[78] Natarajan and Khoday (n 13) at 589.
[79] See ibid, 589–90.
[80] See C Carlarne, 'Delinking International Environmental Law and Climate Change' (2014) 4 *Michigan Journal of Environmental & Administrative Law* 1, 15–16.

environmental degradation is the over-consumption of the planet's finite resources by global elites located primarily in the global North. International economic law has facilitated this over-consumption, with the complicity of international environmental law. While global elites reap the benefits of unsustainable economic activity, the South and the planet's most vulnerable communities bear a disproportionate share of the resulting pollution and resource depletion.[81] In response to this inequity, transnational environmental justice movements have emerged in both the North and the South, including grassroots social movements for climate justice, food justice, energy justice and water justice.[82] Emphasising intra-generational justice, many of these movements have framed their demands for environmental justice in the language of human rights.[83] Human rights tribunals have concluded that failure to protect the environment can violate a variety of human rights, including the rights to life, health, property, privacy, the collective rights of indigenous peoples to their ancestral lands and resources and the right to a healthy environment.[84]

Environmental justice movements have also articulated a more robust conception of environmental justice that includes intergenerational justice (the rights of future generations)[85] and the rights of nature.[86] For example, the principles of environmental justice developed by the delegates to the 1991 First National People of Color Environmental Leadership Summit held in Washington, DC, recognise both intergenerational justice and the rights of nature.[87] Principle 1 'affirms the sacredness of Mother Earth, ecological unity and the interdependence of all species, and the right to be free from ecological destruction'.[88] Principle 3 'mandates the right to ethical, balanced and responsible uses of land and renewable resources in the interest of a sustainable planet for humans and other living things'.[89] Principle 17

> requires that we, as individuals, make personal and consumer choices to consume as little of Mother Earth's resources and to produce as little waste as possible; and make the conscious decision to challenge and reprioritize our lifestyles to ensure the health of the natural world for present and future generations.[90]

---

[81] Gonzalez (n 47) at 78–84.

[82] See J Martinez-Alier and others, 'Between Activism and Science: Grassroots Concepts for Sustainability Coined by Environmental Justice Organizations' (2014) 21 *Journal of Political Ecology* 19, 27–42.

[83] See J Agyeman and others, 'Joined-up Thinking: Bringing Together Sustainability, Environmental Justice and Equity' in Agyeman, Bullard and Evans (n 4) at 10–12.

[84] See generally DK Anton and DL Shelton, *Environmental Protection and Human Rights* (Cambridge, Cambridge University Press, 2011).

[85] See generally E Brown Weiss, *In Fairness to Future Generations: International Law, Common Patrimony, and Intergenerational Equity* (Dobbs Ferry NY, Transnational Publishers, 1989).

[86] See generally R Nash, *The Rights of Nature* (Madison, WI, University of Wisconsin Press, 1989).

[87] See First People of Color Environmental Leadership Summit, 'Principles of Environmental Justice' (24–27 October 1991) www.ejnet.org/ej/principles.html.

[88] ibid, Principle 1.

[89] ibid, Principle 3.

[90] ibid, Principle 17.

In order to operationalise these principles, some scholars have proposed specific criteria for equitably allocating the planet's resources between humans and other living creatures.[91]

Finally, environmental justice has important North-South dimensions.[92] North-South environmental inequities manifest themselves in the form of distributive, procedural, corrective and social injustice.[93] The North-South divide is grounded in *distributive injustice* because the North reaped the economic benefits of natural resource exploitation with no concern for environmental, social and economic consequences. Northern excesses have produced potentially irreversible environmental harm that will constrain the economic development options of present and future generations, particularly in the global South.[94] North-South relations are characterised by *procedural injustice* because the North dominates decision-making in the World Bank, the IMF, the WTO and multilateral environmental treaty negotiations. The views of Southern countries are frequently marginalised.[95] North-South relations are marred by *corrective injustice* because Southern nations (such as the small island developing states facing the imminent uninhabitability of their territories due to climate change) have generally been unable to obtain compensation for the North's prodigious contribution to global environmental degradation or cessation of the offending conduct.[96] Finally, North-South environmental conflicts are reflective of *social injustice* 'because they are inextricably intertwined with colonial and postcolonial economic policies that impoverished the global South and facilitated the North's appropriation of its natural resources'.[97]

With this normative framework in mind, this section provides a very preliminary sketch of potential paths forward. Because it is impossible to re-invent international environmental law in a few short paragraphs, this section provides an illustrative rather than exhaustive list of possible alternatives to the status quo.

A. The Rights of Nature and Future Generations

Many scholars have recognised that the root of the socio-ecological crisis is the universalisation of a Northern economic model that separates humans from nature

---

[91] See J Riechmann, 'Tres principios básicos de la justicia ambiental' (2003) 21 *Revista Internacional de Filosofía Política* 103, 107–08, 112–15.

[92] See generally R Anand, *International Environmental Justice: a North-South Dimension* (Aldershot, Ashgate Publishing, 2004).

[93] See Gonzalez (n 47) at 78–80.

[94] See ibid, 79; Flavin and Gardner, 'China, India and the New World Order' (n 59) at 16–18.

[95] See Gonzalez (n 47) at 79.

[96] See eg M Burkett, 'Climate Reparations' (2009) 10 *Melbourne Journal of International Law* 509.

[97] Gonzalez (n 47) at 79.

and promotes the domination of nature to satisfy human desires.[98] Ironically, the legal systems of many of the peoples of the global South who were deemed 'uncivilised' and in need of 'modernisation' and 'development' recognise the interdependence of humans and the environment and the rights of future generations.[99] For example, indigenous legal systems generally regard human beings as part of the Earth (and not superior life forms), and have devised ethical and legal rules to facilitate each group's adaptation to its distinct ecological niche and to protect the ecological systems upon which human and non-human life depend.[100] Instead of attempting to 'civilise' and 'develop' the peoples of the South in accordance with Northern preferences and priorities, it would perhaps be better to focus on transforming the practices and beliefs emanating from the North that have triggered the contemporary socio-ecological crisis.

Where might we seek inspiration for alternatives to the dominant economic paradigm? Judge Christopher Weeramantry, in his separate Opinion in the *Gabčíkovo-Nagymaros* case,[101] argues that international law should draw upon the wisdom of the world's diverse civilisations to enrich and clarify the evolving principles of contemporary international law:

> In the context of environmental wisdom generally, there is much to be derived from ancient civilizations and traditional legal systems in Asia, the Middle East, Africa, Europe, the Americas, the Pacific, and Australia—in fact the whole world. This is a rich source which modern environmental law has left largely untapped.[102]

Judge Weeramantry offers specific examples of civilisations that managed to survive and thrive in harmony with the environment, and discusses the philosophies, legal traditions and technologies that made these accomplishments possible:[103]

> There were principles ingrained in these civilizations as well as embodied in their *legal systems*, for legal systems include not merely written legal systems but traditional legal systems as well, which modern researchers have shown to be no less legal systems than their written cousins, and in some respects even more sophisticated and finely tuned than the latter.[104]

Among the principles of traditional legal systems that can be incorporated into contemporary environmental law are the trusteeship rather than ownership of natural resources, the principle of intergenerational rights and the rights of the

---

[98] See BH Weston and D Bollier, *Green Governance: Ecological Survival, Human Rights, and the Law of the Commons* (Cambridge, Cambridge University Press, 2014) 49, 78; Geisinger, Sustainable Development and the Domination of Nature' (n 25) at 44–46.

[99] See eg R Tsosie, 'Tribal Development Policy in an Era of Self-Determination: The Role of Ethics, Economics, and Traditional Ecological Knowledge' (1996) 21 *Vermont Law Review* 225, 276–300.

[100] ibid; VF Cordova, *How It Is: The Native American Philosophy of V.F. Cordova*, K Dean Moore and others eds (Tucson, University of Arizona Press, 2007).

[101] See *Gabčíkovo-Nagymaros Project (Hungary v Slovakia)* 1997 ICJ 7 (Separate Opinion of. Judge Weeramantry) [97].

[102] ibid, [98].

[103] See ibid, [98]–[106].

[104] ibid, [109]. Emphasis in original.

nature. For example, in 2008, Ecuador became the first country to adopt a national constitution recognising the rights of nature based on the principle of *sumac kawsay*, the Kichwa idea of living in harmony with nature (known in Spanish as *el buen vivir*, or living well).[105] In 2012, New Zealand accorded legal personhood to its longest navigable river, the Whanganui, as an important step towards resolving the historic grievances of Maori peoples.[106] That same year, Bolivia adopted the Framework Law of Mother Earth and Integral Development for Living Well, which acknowledged the rights of nature.[107] In addition, several constitutions, including those of Bolivia, Ecuador, Kenya and South Africa, have recognised the rights of future generations.[108]

Contrary to popular misconception, the South is not indifferent to global environmental problems. Rather, Southern countries are deeply suspicious of the North's tendency to 'reform' the South without assuming responsibility for the policies, practices and ideologies emanating from the North that impoverished the South and created the present socio-ecological crisis. For example, in a speech delivered at the 1972 Stockholm Conference on the Human Environment, Indian prime minister Indira Gandhi recognised that human beings are part of nature and dependent on nature, criticised mainstream understandings of development as growth and emphasised the need for North-South cooperation to protect the environment and address the plight of the planet's most vulnerable human beings.[109] Decades later, in response to the Rio+20 outcomes, Southern states and non-governmental organisations called for new approaches to environment and development, condemned efforts to merely 'green' the neoliberal economic model and called for local solutions to contemporary economic and environmental crises rather than models and solutions imported from the North.[110] Reimagining some of the foundations of international environmental law such as rights and intergenerational reach of environmental protection through the histories and traditions of other civilisations might enable us to develop alternative philosophies and

---

[105] M Becker, 'Correa, Indigenous Movements, and the Writing of a New Constitution in Ecuador' (2011) 38 *Latin American Perspectives* 47, 50; P Burdon, 'Jurisprudence of Thomas Berry' (2011) 15 *Worldview* 151, 164; J Pinto, '"Right for Nature" in Ecuador: The Mediated Social Construction of Human/Nature Dualisms' in A Latta and H Wittman (eds), *Environment and Citizenship in Latin America: Natures, Subjects and Struggles* (Amsterdam Berghahn Books, 2012) 227, 236–37.

[106] See 'New Zealand's Whanganui River Gets Personhood Status' *Environment News Service* (13 September 2012) available at: http://ens-newswire.com/2012/09/13/new-zealands-whanganui-river-gets-personhood-status/.

[107] See Ley Marco de La Madre Tierra y Desarrollo Integral Para Vivir Bien (Framework Law of Mother Earth and Integral Development For Living Well), Ley No 300, Gaceta Oficial del Estado Plurinacional de Bolivia, Edición No 0431 (15 October 2012).

[108] See UN Secretary-General, *Intergenerational Solidarity and the Needs of Future Generations*, 26, UN Doc A/68/x (5 August 2013) available at: http://sd.iisd.org/news/unsg-issues-report-on-intergenerational-solidarity/.

[109] See K Mickelson, 'The Stockholm Conference and the Creation of the South-North Divide in International Environmental Law and Policy' in Alam, Atapattu, Gonzalez and Razzaque (n 11) at 116–17.

[110] ibid, 128–29.

economic relations that will scale back the North's consumption of the planet's resources for the benefit of subordinated states and peoples, future generations and the other living creatures with whom we share the planet.

B. Minding the Justice Gap—Taking Intra-Generational Equity Seriously

Climate change and other ecological disasters will intensify the suffering of the millions of people in the global South who lack adequate access to environmental necessities, such as clean water, food and modern energy. However, this environmental injustice remains largely outside the purview of international environmental law. Instead, food, water and energy are regulated through a patchwork of legal instruments and private arrangements, many of which fall in the economic law field.[111]

International environmental law can bridge the North-South divide and promote environmental justice by developing creative solutions to seemingly intractable problems that simultaneously benefit marginalised states and peoples, curb environmental degradation and forge a new path to sustainability. For example, despite their minimal greenhouse gas emissions, the world's poorest countries will be disproportionately affected by climate change as a consequence of their vulnerable geographic locations, agriculture-based economies and limited resources for adaptation and disaster response.[112] The 2.8 billion people who lack access to energy to meet their needs for cooking, heating, sanitation, lighting, transportation or basic mechanical power (the energy poor), will be disparately burdened by death, disease and dislocation as a consequence of the droughts, floods, rising sea levels and more frequent and severe storms caused by climate change.[113]

The climate change regime presents the global North with an opportunity to repay the ecological debt, foster environmental justice and promote the transition to clean energy by financing the provision of renewable energy to the energy poor. The preamble to the United Nations Framework Convention on Climate Change (UNFCCC) explicitly recognises that increasing energy consumption in the global South is necessary to eradicate poverty.[114] Similarly, the Paris

---

[111] See Natarajan and Khoday (n 13) at 592. For an analysis of some of the food, water and energy justice issues confronting the international community, see the chapters by Carmen G Gonzalez, Jackie Dugard & Elisabeth Koek, and Lakshman Guruswamy in Alam, Atapattu, Gonzalez and Razzaque (n 11) at 401–34, 469–90, 529–49. For a discussion of the human rights, environmental and economic dimensions of access to food, see CG Gonzalez, 'International Economic Law and the Right to Food' in NCS Lambek, P Claeys, A Wong and L Brilmayer (eds), *Rethinking Food Systems: Structural Challenges, New Strategies and the Law* (New York, Springer, 2014) 165–93.

[112] See Anand, *International Environmental Justice* (n 92) 35–41.

[113] See F Birol, 'Achieving Energy for All Will Not Cost the Earth' in A Halff, J Rozhon and BK Sovacool (eds), *Energy Poverty: Global Challenges and Local Solutions* (Oxford, Oxford University Press 2014) 14.

[114] See United Nations Framework Convention on Climate Change (UNFCCC). Concluded at Rio de Janeiro, 9 May 1992. Entered into force, 21 March 1994. 1771 UNTS 107, preamble.

Agreement negotiated at the December 2015 UNFCCC Conference of the Parties acknowledges 'the need to promote universal access to sustainable energy in developing countries, in particular in Africa, through the enhanced deployment of renewable energy'.[115] Although the Paris Agreement does not operationalise this commitment or allocate funding to fulfil this objective, one important vehicle for incorporating energy access into the climate change regime is the Green Climate Fund developed at the UNFCCC Conference of the Parties in December 2009 in Copenhagen.[116]

While a detailed discussion of the Green Climate Fund is beyond the scope of this chapter, it is important to emphasise the benefits of incorporating energy access into climate change mitigation and adaptation projects. First, the reliance by the energy poor on biomass (such as wood and dried animal dung) for cooking poses significant risks to human health.[117] The smoke released by inefficient and inadequately ventilated cooking facilities produces four million premature deaths each year (primarily among women and children) due to a variety of ailments caused by exposure to indoor air pollution.[118]

Secondly, the black carbon released by the combustion of biomass is the second most significant contributor to climate change after carbon dioxide. Black carbon, when it is released into the air, exacerbates climate change by absorbing solar radiation more effectively than other greenhouse gases, such as methane and tropospheric ozone.[119]

Thirdly, the burning of biomass for energy contributes to deforestation. Deforestation destroys valuable carbon sinks, accelerates soil erosion and deprives local communities of essential ecosystem services, including flood control, drought resistance, regulation of rainfall, habitat for biodiversity and enhancement of water quality.[120]

Finally, reducing black carbon emissions is quite inexpensive relative to other greenhouse gases, and the benefits are potentially enormous.[121] While carbon dioxide can reside in the atmosphere for 50 to 200 years, black carbon dissipates in

---

[115] United Nations Framework Convention on Climate Change, Paris Agreement, FCCC/CP/2015/L.9, 12 December 2015, preamble.

[116] See M Hiller, A Zahner, K Harvey and A Meyer, 'Green Climate Fund, Sustainable Development Goals, and Energy Access' in L Guruswamy (ed), *International Energy and Poverty: The Emerging Contours* (London, Routledge, 2016) 192–203.

[117] See IEA, *World Energy Outlook 2012* (n 9) at 51.

[118] See World Health Organization (WHO), 'Household Air Pollution and Health' (WHO, 1 February 2016) www.who.int/mediacentre/factsheets/fs292/en/.

[119] V Ramanathan and G Carmichael, 'Global and Regional Climate Changes due to Black Carbon' (2008) 1 *Nature Geoscience* 221, 222; TC Bond and others, 'Bounding the Role of Black Carbon in the Climate System: A Scientific Assessment' (2013) 118 *Journal of Geophysical Research: Atmospheres* 5380, 5381.

[120] See generally N Meyers, 'The World's Forests and Their Ecosystem Services' in G Daily (ed), *Nature's Services: Societal Dependence on Natural Ecosystems* (Washington DC, Island Press, 1997).

[121] See L Guruswamy, 'Energy Justice and Sustainable Development' (2010) 21 *Colorado Journal of International Environmental Law and Policy* 231, 238.

as little as one week if existing emissions cease.[122] Thus, providing efficient sources of energy to the energy poor will mitigate climate change more effectively than merely targeting carbon dioxide emissions.[123]

In short, reducing black carbon emissions by addressing energy poverty represents a win-win proposition that bridges the North-South divide and enhances the well-being of the energy poor while avoiding environmental 'tipping points' by producing immediate emissions reductions. Although providing modern electrical energy to the energy poor would be an expensive decades-long undertaking, numerous appropriate sustainable energy technologies (ASETs) are presently available, including decentralised electricity generating systems based on solar, wind and local biodiesel; efficient cook-stoves; and solar thermal heating.[124]

Decentralised renewable energy-based systems can provide the energy poor with electrical power without binding them to existing fossil-fuel based energy systems that are expensive, polluting and vulnerable to capture by transnational corporations and kleptocratic national elites. ASETs thereby promote democracy, self-determination and local control in addition to mitigating climate change and accelerating the global South's transition to sustainable energy. By producing an immediate decline in a very potent but short-lived greenhouse gas (black carbon), ASETs also provide a short reprieve from climate catastrophe and an opportunity to develop long-term solutions to climate change and energy poverty.

The fragmentation of international law has created regulatory gaps in areas of acute environmental, economic and social concern, such as food, water and energy. In order to meet the challenges of the Anthropocene, international environmental law must break out its narrow silo and foster long-term solutions to global environmental problems that advance the interests of socially and economically powerless groups while hastening the transition to more sustainable patterns of production, consumption and living. Food, energy and water—the basic necessities of life—should be central rather than peripheral to the mission of international environmental law.

C. Challenging the Global Economic Order

International law's longstanding commitment to commerce is linked, in complex ways, with its inability to address environmental degradation. From the colonial era to the present, international law and institutions have facilitated the free flow of goods, services and capital across national borders without taking into account the impact on local ecosystems and livelihoods.[125]

---

[122] See ibid, 246.
[123] See ibid.
[124] L Guruswamy, 'Energy Poverty' (2011) 36 *Annual Review of Environment and Resources* 139, 144.
[125] See Bratspies (n 33) at 228.

The early authors of international law regarded commerce as a 'consensual act of reciprocal mutual beneficial exchange' that would build peace and friendship among the world's scattered peoples.[126] This idealised view of commerce bore little relationship to the coercive practices of the colonisers, slave-traders and settlers of the colonial era, and assumed an abundant and inexhaustible supply of natural resources.[127]

Despite growing awareness that human economic activity is exceeding biophysical limits, contemporary advocates of trade liberalisation have adopted an equally sanguine theory of the relationship between international trade and environmental protection.[128] Known as the Environmental Kuznets Curve (EKC) hypothesis, this theory posits an inverted-U relationship between per capita income (on the x-axis) and environmental degradation (on the y-axis), with environmental quality improving as per capita income rises.[129] While pollution initially increases as income grows, environmental quality supposedly improves at higher income levels.[130]

The EKC hypothesis has, however, been challenged on empirical grounds. Empirical studies have not found a consistent inverted-U relationship between per capita income and environmental degradation,[131] and some economists have rejected the hypothesis altogether.[132] Indeed, greenhouse gas emissions, loss of biodiversity, depletion of fisheries, waste production and overall ecological footprint generally increase with rising wealth.[133] Export-driven resource extraction can also produce irreversible environmental harm (such as species extinction), and imposes enormous burdens on vulnerable communities, who bear the environmental costs of mining, logging and petroleum extraction while reaping few of the benefits.[134]

---

[126] See I Porras, 'Appropriating Nature: Commerce, Property, and the Commodification of Nature in the Law of Nations' (2014) 27 *Leiden Journal of International Law* 641.

[127] See ibid.

[128] See Bratspies (n 33) at 231–32.

[129] See generally GM Grossman and AB Krueger, 'Economic Growth and the Environment' (1995) 110 *The Quarterly Journal of Economics* 353; G M Grossman and AB Krueger, 'Environmental Impact of a North American Free Trade Agreement' in P Garber (ed), *The Mexico-U.S. Free Trade Agreement* (Cambridge, MA, MIT Press, 1993) 13–56. The theoretical relationship between environmental degradation and per capita income is referred to as the Environmental Kuznets Curve (EKC) hypothesis because it parallels the inverted-U relationship between income inequality and per capita income put forward by economist Simon Kuznets. See Swee Chua, 'Economic Growth, Liberalization, and the Environment: A Review of the Economic Evidence' (1999) 24 *Annual Review of Energy and the Environment* 391, 395; S Kuznets, 'Economic Growth and Income Inequality' (1955) 46 *The American Economic Review* 1, 1–28.

[130] See Grossman and Krueger, 'Economic Growth and the Environment' (n 129) at 366–69; Chua, 'Economic Growth, Liberalization, and the Environment' (n 129) at 395.

[131] Chua (n 129) at 395–96.

[132] See generally DI Stern, 'The Rise and Fall of the Environmental Kuznets Curve' (2004) 32 *World Development* 1419.

[133] See generally EB Barbier, 'Introduction to the Environmental Kuznets Curve Special Issue' (1997) 2 *Environment and Development Economics* 369; K Arrow and others, 'Economic Growth, Carrying Capacity, and the Environment' (1995) 268 *Science* 520.

[134] See Bratspies (n 33) 238–40.

Nevertheless, this quasi-religious belief in the benefits of liberalised trade has produced an international economic order that generally ignores the environmental and social consequences of production and implicitly encourages environmental subsidies. Global markets determine what level of environmental degradation and social dislocation Southern exporters will have to bear regardless of local preferences.[135] Bilateral investment treaties shield foreign investors from efforts by Southern countries to impose social and environmental standards.[136] Sophisticated corporate investors evade the social, financial and environmental risks of their activities by operating through multiple subsidiaries and a complex web of contracts.[137] The separation between consumption and production obscures the environmental and social impacts of the production process and encourages consumers to purchase the lowest cost goods regardless of their impact on exhaustible natural resources.[138] Moreover, the global economic order transfers wealth from the South to the North by encouraging the sale of commodities at prices that do not reflect the social and environmental costs of production.[139]

Regrettably, Northern efforts to address the negative environmental impacts of liberalised trade have often exacerbated the North-South divide. The United States' decision to restrict the importation of products that did not meet its environmental requirements resulted in a series of high-profile trade disputes in the 1990s, including the *Tuna/Dophin*, *Shrimp/Turtle* and *US-Gasoline* cases.[140] In all three cases, Southern countries challenged the United States restrictions as GATT/WTO violations, and argued that they constituted a 'neocolonial stick, a protectionist barrier designed to keep their economies down'.[141] While the GATT/WTO resolved all three cases in favour of the Southern complainants, the WTO Appellate Body subsequently shifted its approach and recognised the legitimacy of unilateral trade restrictions to protect the environment.[142]

The North's use of trade-restrictive environmental measures inflamed North-South tensions because these restrictions enabled Northern countries to dictate how the South would use its natural resources without providing technical or financial assistance to resource-poor Southern producers and without taking responsibility for the far greater environmental harm wrought by the North's consumption-driven lifestyle.[143] Instead of addressing the systemic nature of

---

[135] See ibid, 248–49.

[136] See Miles (n 22) at 37–44.

[137] See generally SH Baker, 'Unmasking Project Finance: Risk Mitigation, Risk Inducement, and an Invitation to Development Disaster?' (2010) 6 *Texas Journal of Oil, Gas, and Energy Law* 273.

[138] See CG Gonzalez, 'Beyond Eco-Imperialism: An Environmental Justice Critique of Free Trade' (2001) 78 *Denver University Law Review* 979, 1003–04.

[139] See Martinez-Alier, *The Environmentalism of the Poor* (n 32) at 214.

[140] See M Wu and J Salzman, 'The Next Generation of Trade and Environment Conflicts: The Rise of Green Industrial Policy' (2014) 108 *Northwestern University Law Review* 401, 408–11.

[141] ibid, 409.

[142] See ibid, 409–13 (describing the evolution of the GATT/WTO jurisprudence on trade-restrictive environmental measures).

[143] See Gonzalez, 'Beyond Eco-Imperialism' (n 138) at 1004–09.

trade-induced environmental degradation and seeking to scale back its over-consumption of the planet's resources, the North imposed the cost of compliance with a series of ad hoc environmental requirements on the South. In so doing, the North perpetuated the narrative that casts Northern countries as 'leaders in advancing the global environmental protection, at times resorting to tariffs and trade restrictions on imports to encourage developing countries seen as unwilling to do their share'.[144] This narrative is hypocritical given the North's historic and ongoing over-exploitation of the South's resources. It also reproduces the 'civilising mission'—this time in environmental garb—and undermines North-South environmental cooperation.

While an analysis of specific proposals to reform international economic law is beyond the scope of this chapter,[145] the reorientation of the world economy towards more just and sustainable practices will require an unprecedented level of North-South collaboration. De-mythologising the narratives about the unequivocal benefits of commerce and about the North's 'civilising mission' is an essential first step to bridge the North-South divide and to dismantling the legal regimes that perpetuate this divide. International environmental law does not exist in a vacuum. In order to develop effective solutions to the socio-ecological crises of the Anthropocene, it is essential to harmonise the disparate stands of international law (including environmental, economic and human rights law) in order to promote the rights of nature, and the rights of present and future generations. International economic law systematically accelerates environmental degradation, subordinates the global South and consigns environmental issues to the peripheries of legal discourse and policymaking, while international environmental has not managed to successfully keep humanity from crossing planetary boundaries and reaching critical tipping points. Without a fundamental restructuring of international economic and environmental law, a just and sustainable planet in the Anthropocene epoch is impossible.

VI. Conclusion

The Anthropocene presents both promise and peril. The growing recognition that human beings have altered the planet's biophysical and biochemical processes in ways that threaten human and non-human life challenges the ontological separation between humans and nature central to international law and many

---

[144] Wu and Salzman, 'The Next Generation of Trade and Environment Conflicts' (n 140) at 413.

[145] For discussion of specific reforms to the global economic order, see eg H Mann, 'Reconceptualizing International Investment Law: Its Role in Sustainable Development' (2013) 17 *Lewis & Clark Law Review* 521; CG Gonzalez, 'An Environmental Justice Critique of Comparative Advantage: Indigenous Peoples, Trade Policy, and the Mexican Neoliberal Economic Reforms' (2011) 32 *University of Pennsylvania Journal of International Law* 723.

other disciplines.[146] As one observer points out, we find ourselves 'in the position of the Catholic cleric confronting the Copernican theories that supplanted geocentrism'.[147] This unique moment in human history calls for critical engagement with international law and its different strands in order to develop effective tools that address our responsibility to nature, to one another, and to future generations.

This chapter has provided an overview of the origins of the Anthropocene in colonial and postcolonial economic law and policy and the failure of international (environmental) law to remedy its social, economic and environmental consequences. The objective is to provoke further discussion and analysis about new approaches to international environmental and economic law that will promote environmental justice in an era of growing economic inequality and looming ecological collapse.

---

[146] See Bonneuil and Fressoz (n 3) at 6–14, 250–87.
[147] Cordova, *How It Is* (n 100) at 218.

11

The Imperative of Ecological Integrity: Conceptualising a Fundamental Legal Norm for a New 'World System' in the Anthropocene

KLAUS BOSSELMANN

I. Introduction

This chapter aims to show the importance of ecological integrity as an objective or fundamental norm of law and governance for the Anthropocene. While effective environmental law will be a key part of staying within planetary boundaries, all areas of law are affected by the imagery of the Anthropocene, including commercial law, taxation regimes, constitutions and traditional legal concepts such as property, human rights and state sovereignty.

In the Anthropocene, it is time for the message of environmental law to become clear and urgent: the opposite of strong sustainability and ecological integrity is collapse.[1] Moreover, true, strong sustainability, has radical implications for the West, implying social organisation at a far lower level of complexity and consumption. The chapter therefore starts with the simple thesis that if ecological integrity does not become accepted as a fundamental norm of the legal system in the Anthropocene, the default choice is collapse.[2] But how can ecological integrity as a fundamental norm be conceptualised and what does it entail in concrete terms? If such a norm is not adopted, what does collapse mean in concrete terms? These questions are becoming increasingly pressing in the Anthropocene, and are worth exploring here.

---

[1] This dichotomy is explicitly expressed in works such as, R Costanza, LJ Graumlich and W Steffen (eds), *Sustainability or Collapse? An Integrated History and Future of People on Earth* (Cambridge, MIT Press, Cambridge, 2007).

[2] The term 'ecological integrity' is used in conjunction with 'sustainability', owing to the overuse and watering down of the latter term. On the definition of 'strong sustainability', see K Bosselmann, *The Principle of Sustainability*, 2nd edn (Abingdon, Routledge, 2017).

II. Jurisprudential Conceptualisations of Ecological Integrity

As a central hypothesis, it is suggested that ecological integrity must attain the same fundamental normative status in law as human rights, the abolition of slavery, the rights of women and the rule of law. Jurisprudentially, can ecological integrity be conceptualised as a *Grundnorm*, or 'fundamental norm'?[3] After a consideration of Kelsen, Kant and Alexy, it is explained that a traditional natural law approach provides the most robust foundation from which the normative bindingness of ecological integrity could be asserted.

A. *Grundnorm* Theories

i. Kelsen

Kelsen's *Pure Theory of Law* is the jurisprudential position with which the term *Grundnorm* (or 'basic norm') is commonly associated. In Kelsen's theory, the status and meaning of *Grundnorm* is not a conceptually simple matter.[4] The key point about Kelsen's position is that the basic norm has no ethical or political function; it only has an epistemological function.[5] For Kelsen, who emphasised the separation of law and morality, the normativity of 'ecological integrity' (in the sense of *you should act in accordance with ecological integrity*) can be understood as a *moral* basic norm (there can be a variety of basic norms in a system of moral norms), and not as a *legal Grundnorm*. There can only be one legal *Grundnorm* that provides unity to the legal system. The basic norm of a legal system addresses the question of legal validity in terms of authorisation, and is not a question of

---

[3] See, eg, K Bosselmann, 'A Normative Approach to Environmental Governance: Sustainability at the Apex of Environmental Law' in D Fisher (ed), *Research Handbook on Fundamental Concepts of Environmental Law* (Cheltenham, Edward Elgar, 2016), 30–70; P Bridgewater, R Kim and K Bosselmann, 'Ecological Integrity—A Relevant Concept for Environmental Law in the Anthropocene?' (2016) 25(1) *Yearbook of International Environmental Law* 61–78; K Bosselmann 'The Rule of Law in the Anthropocene' in P Martin, Paul and others (eds), *In Search of Environmental Justice* (Cheltenham, Edward Elgar, 2015) 44–61; K Bosselmann, 'The Rule of Law Grounded in the Earth: Ecological Integrity as a Grundnorm' in L Westra and M Vilela (eds), *The Earth Charter, Ecological Integrity and Social Movements* (Abingdon, Routledge, 2014) 3–11.

[4] eg Douglas Fisher, in *Legal Reasoning in Environmental Law* (Cheltenham, Edward Elgar, 2013), seems to use the term '*grundnorm*' in different senses. It appears he is building on Kelsen (who is cited). It is stated that: 'An example of a *grundnorm* is a constitution' (at 7), and later that a 'Constitution may include a range of *grundnorms*'. Also, it is later noted that 'Sustainability, represents a principle of justice fundamental to civilized nations, similarly to the principles of freedom and equality. In this way, sustainability emerges as a fundamental principle or *grundnorm* of the system' (at 59). Thus '*Grundnorm*' can be conceptualised in Kelsen's narrow sense, or in the broader sense of an 'important norm'. The following attempts to further refine this discussion conceptually.

[5] H Kelsen, *Pure Theory of Law*, trans M Knight (Berkeley, UCLA Press, 1967) 218.

content.[6] Kelsen observes that a constitution may contain substantive limits to lawmaking, but for Kelsen, a constitution *itself* is not a *Grundnorm*.[7] The *Grundnorm* is a hypothetical construct about a constitution, functioning to give an order of legal norms validity.

A *Grundnorm can* provide a foundation for the legal bindingness of ecological integrity, provided proper constitutional processes are followed. Or, a *Grundnorm* may change.[8] For example, there may be a revolution as a result of which an older constitution is displaced, and a new 'sustainable constitution' put in place by revolutionary forces (with substantive limits to lawmaking in terms of ecological integrity). If the new constitution becomes efficacious to the requisite degree, the new *Grundnorm* of society would then be: 'the sustainable constitution is to be obeyed'. However, environmental law can find more robust normative reasoning in other jurisprudential concepts. In Kelsen's terms, 'ecological integrity' cannot be a (legal) *Grundnorm*.

ii. Kant

Kant formulated the idea of a 'basic norm' (though he did not use this specific term) as a source of the validity of positive law in his 1797 work, *The Metaphysics of Morals* (commencing with a treatise on the philosophy of law).[9] In contrast to Kelsen, who thinks that the basic norm is simply an epistemological premise, for Kant the basic norm is a natural law, recognised by means of reason. For Kant, a legal system can consist entirely of positive law, but must be 'preceded by a natural law that establishe[s] the legislator's authority…to bind others simply by his arbitrary action'.[10]

In contrast to classical natural law, which looks to the content of positive law in terms of reason and justice, in Kant's attenuated version of natural law—the natural law basic norm—reason *dictates* that people leave a state of nature and move into a civil or legal state of affairs, 'subjecting oneself to a publicly lawful, external coercion'.[11] Most relevant (from the point of our enquiry) is that it is problematic to assert that respect for ecological integrity could somehow be included (as a 'dictate of reason') in Kant's natural law basic norm. This is because substantial content, such as natural rights, are not secured—it is exclusively oriented to legal certainty and peace.[12] Moreover, Kant excludes any right to resist unjust laws,

---

[6] ibid, 217.

[7] ibid, 223.

[8] See JW Harris, 'When and why does the Grundnorm Change?' (1971) 29(1) *Cambridge Law Journal* 103.

[9] U Bindreiter, *Why Grundnorm? A Treatise on the Implications of Kelsen's Doctrine* (The Hague, Kluwer, 2002) 15.

[10] R Alexy, *The Argument from Injustice*, trans SL Paulson and BL Paulson (Oxford, Clarendon Press, 2002) 116, fn 202, citing Kant *Metaphysical Elements of Justice* (pt 1 of *Metaphysics of Morals*).

[11] Alexy, *The Argument from Injustice* (n 10) at 118, fn 206, citing Kant, *Metaphysical Elements of Justice*.

[12] ibid, 118.

asserting that the moral requirement of obedience to positive law is 'absolute'.[13] While doubts have been raised about the coherence of Kant's legal theory,[14] the fundamental importance of ecological integrity can, perhaps, be conceptualised more fully in traditional natural law terms.

iii. Alexy

Alexy argues for the need to redefine the legal *Grundnorm* to include 'content'.[15] He reinterprets Kelsen's basic norm as making a claim to substantive justice with respect to the content of the laws it purports to authorise. The basic norm 'may include moral elements that take the argument of injustice into consideration. ... [the basic norm] needs grounding'.[16] One critique of a *Grundnorm* with content is that an approach such as Alexy's could lead to a muddling of concepts. Vinx argues that Kelsen's emphasis on the positivity of law should be maintained. Rather than deriving from a crude moral relativism (of which critics have accused Kelsen), Vinx cites a deeper motivation for Kelsen's 'separation' thesis. The 'normativity' we can attribute to a 'legally valid' norm, is different from assessments of substantive justice of its content. This is a unique type of legal normativity Vinx calls 'legal legitimacy'.[17] While Vinx's ideas about 'legal legitimacy' are not directly relevant for present purposes, the point about maintaining conceptual clarity is valid. The addition of substantive content (though minimal, such as a Radbruch-type rule about injustice) brings us away from Kelsen and closer to traditional concepts of natural law.

B. Fundamental Norm of Natural Law

Writing in 1994 of New Zealand's newly introduced Resource Management Act 1991, Harris commented 'the statute has started the environmental rule-maker and decision-maker on the only path into the future that can be taken by a rational human community'.[18] Without specifically making reference to the jurisprudential tradition of 'natural law', a connection was made between the use of reason and the provision of legal protection to safeguard the environment, which sustains the existence of the community.

---

[13] *Kant: Political Writings*, H Reiss ed and HB Nisbet trans, 2nd edn (1991) 81 cited by J Waldron 'Kant's Legal Positivism' (1996) 109(7) *Harvard Law Review* 1535, fn 34.

[14] Alexy (n 10) at 120.

[15] L Vinx, *Hans Kelsen's Pure Theory of Law: Legacy and Legitimacy* (Oxford, Oxford University Pres, 2007) 58 cites R Alexy, *Begriff und Geltung des Rechts* (Alder, Freiburg, 1994) 154–97 (English trans: *The Argument from Injustice*).

[16] Alexy (n 10) at 147.

[17] Vinx, *Hans Kelsen's Pure Theory of Law: Legacy and Legitimacy* (n 15) at 58–59.

[18] BV Harris, 'Sustainable Management as an Express Purpose of Environmental Legislation: The New Zealand Attempt' (1993) 8 *Otago Law Review* 51.

Finnis provides a contemporary account of natural law. He explains, 'the prin-cipal concern of a theory of natural law is to explore the requirements of practical reasonableness in relation to the good of human beings'.[19] He lists seven 'basic goods', as equally important components of human flourishing—life, knowledge, play, aesthetic experience, sociability (friendship), practical reasonableness and 'religion'.[20] Protection of the life-supporting capacity of the natural environment most obviously relates to the first 'good' on the list, ie 'life'. Finnis observes that all societies in some sense are concerned with 'life' (in the sense of survival). Thus, the argument for the fundamental importance of ecological integrity in natural law terms is fairly straightforward—it is reasonable that humanity not destroy itself.

Practical reasonableness refers to 'bringing intelligence to bear on problems, choosing one's actions'.[21] One of the nine requirements of practical reasonableness is that the good of one's community be advanced. One's view of what reason and natural law requires will vary, depending on who one's 'community' is perceived to be, and the time horizon within which the good of one's community is viewed. The *Earth Charter's* emphasis on respect for the 'community of life' is perhaps one of the broadest, non-anthropocentric articulations of community.[22] If one takes a *long-term* view of the good of one's community, owing to the borderless nature of many environmental challenges, it becomes apparent that laws which facilitate breaches of the limits of global ecological integrity do indeed put the good of one's community at risk. As such, these laws may ultimately be assessed as contrary to reason (and thus contrary to natural law).

Classical natural law holds that positive law can be derived from natural law by deduction or determination (*determinatsio*). Though the importance of ecologi-cal integrity has not been explicitly to the fore of the natural law tradition in the law of nations throughout history, it can arguably be arrived at through rational deduction. Alternatively, through determination, reason ascertains law as being appropriate for its historical context. In doing so, the congruence of positive law with reason will be within a specific range of parameters. In our present era, with the global ecological crisis so vividly explicated by the Anthropocene, laws that violate ecological integrity are unlikely to be within the reasonable range of deter-mination, and can therefore said to be in tension with natural law.

In light of the discussion above, it becomes apparent that the terms *Grundnorm* and basic norm, owing to their association with Kelsen, are probably best left con-ceptually unmodified.[23] Rather than saying that ecological integrity must become

---

[19] J Finnis, *Natural Law and Natural Rights*, 2nd edn (Oxford, Oxford University Press, 2011) 351.

[20] ibid, 86.

[21] ibid, 87.

[22] K Bosselmann and R Engel, 'Introduction' in K Bosselmann and R Engel (eds), *The Earth Charter: A framework for global governance*, (Amsterdam, KIT Publ, 2010), 10–15.

[23] *Bindreiter, Why Grundnorm?* (n 9) at 44: "'aus dem Grund" (in German), a phrase rooted in the idea of a firm point of departure (a basis). Grund changed meaning. Beginning 16th century *grund* (meaning foundation) was used in the sense of "essential or necessary assumption". In the field of philosophy, *grund* stood for "ultimate principle" and was used in this sense by Kant. However, *grund*

a *Grundnorm* (though in a sense distinct from Kelsen), a different term may better promote conceptual clarity. 'Grounding norm', or 'foundational norm' are possibilities in English. However, it is suggested that ecological integrity is best termed (in English) a 'fundamental norm' of natural law. On 'norms' of natural law, discernable by reason and universally applicable, Finnis explains:

> Any sound theory or philosophy of law will need to attend to two broad kinds of principle, norm and standard: those applicable by persons of practical reasonableness only because of they are standards chosen or otherwise factually established by past choices of their community, and those that are applicable whether or not so chosen or ratified. [T]he latter ... has been decisive for our vocabulary, making its way through Aristotle, the Stoics, Cicero, St Paul, Gaius and Aquinas and their successors down to the United Nations Charter and today.[24]

C. A Fundamental Norm in International Law

It has been observed that in some form or another, 'global sustainability must become a foundation of society. It can and must be part of the bedrock of nation states'.[25] If ecological integrity is properly understood as a fundamental norm of natural law as was argued above, in international law it should (eventually) emerge as a peremptory norm, or *jus cogens*. The Draft Convention on State Responsibility, Article 19(3), ILC, proposed that breach of sustainable resource management qualify as a 'crime by a state' towards the international community. That is, 'sustainable resource management' was proposed to be defined as a peremptory norm, whose infringement would constitute a 'serious breach of an international obligation of essential importance'. This *jus cogens* proposal was, unsurprisingly, rejected by a considerable number of states.[26] However, in the Anthropocene it is possible to image the recognition by the community of nations of the deep ethical and legal significance of ecological integrity (and strong sustainability). Attaining such status, a 'breach' may come to be seen as worthy of moral and legal condemnation, perhaps as much so as current peremptory norms of genocide, torture, the execution of juvenile offenders and slavery.

Take slavery as a point of comparison. Slavery was defined in Roman law as 'an institution according to the law of nations whereby one person falls under

---

(foundation) changed meaning in the causal direction too. A grund, that to which a thing was owing its existence. (to found, create; give reasons for something)....Grund stood for "ultimate principle" and was used in this sense by Kant. However, Grund (*foundational*), changed meaning in the causal direction: a grund was that to which a thing was owing its existence'.

[24] J Finnis, 'What is the Philosophy of Law?' (2012) 1 *Rivista di Filosofia del Diritto* 67.

[25] SE Gaines, 'Reimagining Environmental Law for the 21st Century' (2014) 44 *Environmental Law Reporter* 10188, 10213.

[26] P Orebech, *The Role of Customary Law in Sustainable Development* (Cambridge, Cambridge University Press, 2005) 389.

the property rights of another, contrary to nature'.[27] Though slavery was legal in Rome, attempts to justify it starting with Aristotle, generally focused on supposedly inferior qualities of some ethnic group, rather than the institution itself (which was known to be unjustifiable in terms of natural law).[28] It may come to be seen that living in violation of ecological integrity, too, becomes broadly understood as 'contrary to nature' in two senses: contrary to the physical 'laws of nature' *and* contrary to natural law as determined by reason. Ophuls, in *Plato's Revenge*, uses a reinterpretation of natural law, looking to the physical 'laws of nature' to provide legal constraints.[29] Finnis, on the other hand, contrasts 'laws of nature' (as in the laws of the sciences) and 'natural law'.[30]

D. Recognition through Ecological Thinking and Jurisprudence

Dennis Meadows points out that 'the world is a complex, interconnected, finite, ecological-social-psychological-economic system'.[31] In light of such a holistic perspective, Gaines rightly emphasises the importance of an interdisciplinary approach to environmental legal research. It is here proposed that a holistic approach would see environmental lawyers reconceptualise their starting point as 'sustainability thinkers'. Rather than a specialist, niche discipline, thinking must go beyond a narrow approach of considering systems of 'natural resources' (and their ecological integrity or lack thereof).[32] The challenge of 'sustainability thinking' is to take on the 'world' (as defined below) in all its complexity.

As a point of departure, it is important to recognise that jurisprudential characterisations of ecological integrity can only do so much. In achieving ecological integrity, changing consciousness is still the bottom line. Indeed, emphasising the need for a community 'ethos' of sustainability, Gaines has said that '[t]he world does not need new ideas or new principles'.[33] Rather, he stresses the importance of

---

[27] Florentius in Justinian's Institutes (1.5.4.1).

[28] D Graeber, *Debt: The First 5,000 Years* (New York, Melville House, 2011) ch 7, fn 2.

[29] W Ophuls, *Plato's Revenge: Politics in the Age of Ecology* (Cambridge MA, MIT Press, 2011).

[30] Finnis, *Natural Law and Natural Rights* (n 19).

[31] Gaines, 'Reimagining Environmental Law for the 21st Century' (n 25) at 10205. Such a holistic definition of the 'world' as a system is more useful for sustainability thinking than merely a focus on the 'earth' and its systems (in the sense of biophysical processes). As an illustrative aside, the continuing dominance of Descartian dualism can be seen in comments by the 'busy lawyer', who fondly mentions his well-meaning but hopelessly utopian environmental law colleagues attending conferences, 'off to save the earth'. No matter of concern to him, though, as if the 'busy lawyer', the rational subject, can continue to exist independently of the Earth. A Descartian mentality persists, even though Heidegger provided a thorough critique of the 'rational subject' and put forward his own more holistic concept of the human being as a 'Being-in-the-world'. See M Heidegger, *Being and Time*, J Maccquarrie trans (Oxford, Basil Blackwell, 1962, original 1927) 78.

[32] This is not a blanket condemnation of the whole discipline, which has done much creative work probing the philosophical foundations of the environmental crisis. Rather, it is a call to make holistic 'sustainability thinking' a more explicit ethos of the discipline.

[33] Gaines (n 25) at 10211.

education in fostering a 'sufficiently enlightened society', and particularly the need for 'ecological awareness'.[34] While this is true, perhaps it is necessary to go further than ecology. As noted above, environmental law could usefully engage with more holistic thinking and an interdisciplinary approach. As such, an approach to raising public awareness would constructively approach ecological challenges holistically. Part of doing so would include conveying the interrelated nature of energy, economic and environmental challenges.[35] Lack of political will or community ethos is surely at least in part due to lack of awareness (particularly in relation to energy). So an understanding of these interrelated issues is arguably necessary before there can be any political will to achieve comprehensive solutions through law. Though there may be other practical obstacles, it is conceivable that a largely aware public will at least be ready to think about taking steps appropriate to a rational human community.

At this point it is worth pausing to consider the current prospects for the actual recognition, acceptance and implementation collectively by states of ecological integrity as a norm of fundamental importance. Doing so, states would be able to comprehensively and sustainably reshape all areas of law and policy. This is the preferable way to deal with the Anthropocene's global socio-ecological crisis. However, as will become apparent, there is a growing sense of frustration with the limitations of the state-centric system. Nevertheless, global governance to maintain global ecological integrity is an objective for which environmental law scholarship must continue to argue strenuously. At the same time, in the Anthropocene, it appears to be time to start considering the implications and challenges for law and governance of the possibility that states will opt to continue with 'business as usual' practices.

One alternative to a business as usual approach which could instil ecological integrity as a foundational norm, is ecological economics; an economic model which effectively works out the implications of a fundamental norm of ecological integrity for economic activity within truly sustainable limits.[36] After an elegant explanation of ecological economics, contrasting it with the current

---

[34] ibid, 10204.

[35] An example of a resource which provides an accessible introduction to such an integrated perspective is C Martenson *The Crash Course: The Unsustainable Future of our Economy, Energy and Environment* (Hoboken, New Jersey, John Wiley & Sons, Inc, 2011). Rees (discussed below) expresses hope that the internet might enable a cascade of data to give rise to a 'global consciousness' of the importance of ecological integrity. 'Data' in the form of short, attractive videos (some of which may 'go viral', with millions of viewers) is one avenue which environmental law could productively explore in 'educating the public'. The basic components of the problem of environmental law are conveyed in Chris Martenson's series of videos, 'The Crash Course', widely available online. As another example, a video lecture of Dr Albert Bartlett, provocatively titled 'The Most Important Video You'll Ever See' (and conveying the substance of his article *Arithmetic, Population and Energy*) has at time of writing over 5 million 'hits'. He memorably says: 'the greatest shortcoming of the human race is our inability to understand the exponential function'. A grasp of the exponential function is surely essential in considering the relationship between ecological integrity and economic growth.

[36] H Daly, *Beyond Growth* (Boston, Beacon Press, 1996).

dominant model of economic growth Rees observes: '[t]here is, of course, almost no possibility that the global community will opt voluntarily for anything like the sustainable steady-state-with-equity described above'.[37] What prompts such pessimism? Rees takes history as a guide, though holding out hope that this time it is different.[38] He offers a glimmer of hope, pointing to modern communication technology and the power of the internet, which may yet enable a cascade of data, giving rise to global consciousness around the modern global ecological predicament. At a critical tipping point, public opinion may force effective political responses within nations and international agencies.[39]

Similarly, Engel notes 'no previous complex human society of significant size has ever achieved sustainability'.[40] The literature on reasons for past societal collapse is ample, including interesting developments in complexity theory.[41] As Engel points out, one key difference is that, in contrast to previous localised collapses, the stakes are so much higher when trying to secure *global* ecological integrity. Gaines, discussing the complexity and scale of environmental challenges, observes that global conservation efforts

> will require drastic changes in current behaviors of most of the world's [nearly 7,5] billion people, but also mean that decisions about the coordination of those efforts will require international cooperation of a scope and intensity that has no precedent in human history. [and that] Such cooperation is conceivable[42]

Legal analysis, then, cannot assume that the required cooperation between all sectors of society including governments is assured. Indeed, some sustainability thinkers have shifted emphasis in their calls for action. In 1972, with the original *Limits to Growth*, Dennis Meadows and his team called for changes to modes of activity that respected planetary limits. He now believes it is too late to achieve 'sustainable development', and rather calls for raising resilience of systems to attempt to mitigate the worst effects of collapses in resources and energy availability.[43]

In sum, in the Anthropocene, various forms of 'collapse' (the antithesis of sustainability, as it were) are challenges which communities, nations and regions will possibly have to face. Given the more than de minimis likelihood of such events,

---

[37] WE Rees, 'Confronting Collapse: Human Cognition and the Challenge for Economics' in L Westra, P Taylor and A Michelot (eds), *Confronting Ecological and Economic Collapse* (Abingdon, Routledge, 2013), 310.

[38] Rees, 'Confronting Collapse' (n 37) at 310.

[39] ibid, 311: 'If history is any guide, rather than adopt a steady-state strategy, the world community is likely to further entrench the growth-bound, competitive, every-nation-for-itself status quo'.

[40] JR Engel, 'Beyond Collapse: Claiming the Holistic Integrity of Planet Earth in Westra, Taylor and Michelot *Confronting Ecological and Economic Collapse* (n 37) at 240.

[41] See generally J Tainter, *The Collapse of Complex Societies* (Cambridge, Cambridge University Press, 1990); J Diamond *Collapse: How Societies Choose to Fail or Succeed* (New York, Penguin, 2005). Interesting work on Complexity Theory is also being done by Prof Geoffrey West. See 'Cities, Scaling and Sustainability' www.santafe.edu.

[42] Gaines (n 25) at 10201.

[43] D Meadows, Speech to Smithsonian Institution Washington, DC (29 February 2012).

it is worth at least considering the possible implications for law and governance. As such, the implications of the fundamental norm of ecological integrity will be considered below from two different angles: first, the implications of ecological integrity as part of pre-collapse reform efforts through the conventional state-centric approach; and, secondly, the possible role such a fundamental norm could play in law and governance of communities ignoring the limits to growth and experiencing some form of collapse.

Before exploring what ecological integrity as a fundamental norm entails in concrete terms, a metaphor may prove useful. The idea of 'universal acid' provides a memorable metaphor from which a range of issues can be viewed. Writing about the impact of the ideas of Charles Darwin, as formulated in *On the Origin of Species by Natural Selection* (1859), psychologist Daniel Dennett comments:

> Did you ever hear of a universal acid? This fantasy used to amuse me and some of my schoolboy friends... Universal acid is a liquid so corrosive it will eat through anything. The problem is: what do you keep it in? It dissolves glass bottles and stainless-steel canisters as readily as paper bags. What would happen if you somehow came upon or created a dollop of universal acid? Would the whole planet eventually be destroyed? What would it leave in its wake? After everything had been transformed by its encounter with universal acid, what would the world look like? Little did I realize that in a few years I would encounter an idea—Darwin's idea—bearing an unmistakable likeness to universal acid: it eats through just about every traditional concept, and leaves in its wake a revolutionized world-view, with most of the old landmarks still recognizable, but transformed in fundamental ways.[44]

The acceptance of ecological integrity as a fundamental norm will need to have the impact of a 'universal acid'. As Steffan Westerlund has argued, sustainability must take the entire legal system into account: 'each and every legal principle has to be reassessed from this perspective'.[45] While this is correct, a universal acid cannot be contained within the legal system alone. The Anthropocene, as a time of instability and disruption, also provides the opportunity to fundamentally re-evaluate broader norms of the status quo.

III. Analysing the 'World-System'

The following discussion is an attempt to clarify the *problem* of ecological integrity. How might we get ecological thinking more firmly embedded in social and economic systems? How might ecological integrity function as a fundamental norm?[46] What are the powerful interests and barriers arranged against a fundamental norm of ecological integrity which might impede its effective realisation

---

[44] D Dennett, *Darwin's Dangerous Idea* (New York, Touchstone, 1996) 63.
[45] Gaines (n 25) at 10192.
[46] ibid.

in law?[47] Attempting to consider such questions, this section builds on Meadows' holistic definition of the world as a 'complex, interconnected, finite, ecological-social-psychological-economic system'. It will consider the world in the Anthropocene as a complex 'ecological-energy-financial-commercial-political-social system'.[48] Each component can be viewed in terms of the sustainability-collapse dichotomy, while the concept of integrity will be used as a universal acid, as described above. Because we are considering the Anthropocene, it is worth taking a look at the bigger picture. Doing so provides the opportunity to critically assess the integrity of each aspect, and to reimagine possibilities in terms of a different ethic or ethos. Such *lex ferenda* ideas may be perceived by the status quo as radical and implausible. Nevertheless, in the twilight of idols, one must philosophise with a hammer.[49]

The rationale for the following holistic approach is the notion that ecological integrity is partly a reflection of the integrity of societies inhabiting the ecological space. With a healthy, vibrant society, it is suspected that chances are higher we will see healthy vibrant nature. On the other hand, with a society lacking in integrity, loss of ecological integrity is not surprising. Can we expect to achieve ecological integrity if we have a financial system and financial culture that lacks integrity? And, what is commercial integrity? What might implications for ecological integrity be of a commercial system involving personal economic relations of trust and mutual aid, in contrast to a depersonalised system emphasising self-interest (as expressed in classic economics)? Moreover, to what extent do practical difficulties arise in achieving global *ecological* integrity without global *political* integrity? Finally, how important is the social integrity of a community in the Anthropocene (and its social resilience, as an aspect of integrity)? As Rockstrom, Steffen and colleagues observe, how well a community might manage in the face of environmental shocks of the Anthropocene will be determined by its social-ecological resilience.[50]

The aim here is to explore the interrelationships of systems at the conceptual level. In doing so, it is useful to keep the terms 'integrity' and 'collapse', but leave them open to their various resonances. 'Integrity' thus signifies wholeness, soundness, completeness, resilience, health and naturalness. 'Ecological integrity' is a scientifically measurable aspect of the overarching concept of strong sustainability. It is a useful term, because it provides not only the scientifically measurable aspect of ecological systems, but also moral resonances, such as something or someone one can rely on, and the idea of honesty, for example. 'Collapse', in

---

[47] L Godden, 'Book Review: The Principle of Sustainability' (2009) 47(4) *Osgoode Hall Law Journal* 807.

[48] A framework adapted from D Orlov, *The Five Stages of Collapse* (Canada, New Society Publishers, 2013).

[49] F Nietzsche, *Twilight of the Idols, or, How to Philosophize with a Hammer* (1889).

[50] J Rockstrom and others, 'Planetary Boundaries: Exploring the Safe Operating Space for Humanity' (2009) 14(2) *Ecology and Society* 32.

contrast, is considered the opposite of ecological integrity and strong sustainability. 'Collapse' is defined by Joseph Tainter as a significant, relatively quick reduction in complexity.[51] It is a loss of integrity beyond a system's threshold of resilience from which it can recover. Collapse has occurred when integrity has eroded beyond a certain (often unhealthy) extent.

Collapse is not always necessarily a bad thing. It depends on what it is that collapses, and where one is situated in relation to the collapse. For example, a collapse in house prices, while bad for property investors, may not be a bad thing for a young couple wishing to buy a house to live in. However, the worst effects of some collapses are worth considering and trying to avert. For example, the collapse of safety systems in a nuclear power-plant would be important to avoid. So, too, would a collapse in the resilience of planetary life supporting systems.

'Collapse' in the everyday sense has connotations of rapidity. A house of cards collapses quickly, as does a building. However, many collapses of systems, in relation to an individual human lifetime, are 'slow collapses'. Thus, the collapse of an empire can take many centuries. It is worth recognising that collapse has often been part of the flow of history. Sometimes it has been judiciously avoided. However, often collapses of systems have proven difficult to manage. It is worth considering why, and the implications for ecological integrity.

The following analysis looks at various spheres of social organisation such as responses to environmental change, energy supply, financial organisation, commercial transactions and the political system. For each sphere, we will consider the current status quo, which leads to the default position in the absence of a norm of integrity: collapse. The possibilities for reform of law and governance pre-collapse will then be explored. That is, what might enhanced integrity in this aspect of the world-system look like? Finally, consideration will be given to the implications for law and governance in a post-collapse scenario. This is no utopian (or dystopian) blueprint, merely an attempt to prompt a holistic conversation and think in a concrete way what ecological integrity might entail.

A. Ecological Integrity

The twentieth century saw exponential increases in fossil fuel use (especially oil), global population and levels of debt (money loaned into existence by banks). These three exponentials are surely interrelated. A plausible interpretation is that energy was driving economic growth, with the larger economy sustaining a larger population and increase in debt (based on future hopes for growth).[52] Growth in human population, energy use and economic consumption has put increasing stress on ecosystems, as has been well documented.[53]

---

[51] Tainter, *The Collapse of Complex Societies* (n 41), 4.
[52] Orlov, *The Five Stages of Collapse* (n 48) at 27.
[53] See R Heinberg, *Peak Everything: Waking up to the Century of Declines* (Canada, New Society Publishers, 2007).

No disaster or accident is required in order for environmental collapse to unfold—just more business as usual practices. Meadows holds that the actual form of any environmental collapse will be too complex for any model to predict. 'Collapse will not be driven by a single, identifiable cause simultaneously acting in all countries', he observes; '[i]t will come through a self-reinforcing complex of issues'—including climate change, resource constraints and socio-economic inequality.[54]

The planetary boundary framework has suggested 'the need for novel and adaptive governance approaches at global, regional, and local scales'.[55] An institution for trusteeship of the global commons is one example for global governance.[56] A novel framework for national governance has been proposed by Woolley.[57] As Gaines has observed, 'the ideas are there'. Or, as the Millennium Ecosystem Assessment concluded: '[t]he warning signs are there for all to see. The future lies in our hands'.[58] It is now a question of whether societies and governments are able to undertake the required changes quickly enough.

One governance issue in the Anthropocene is that of 'climate refugees', and other displaced populations due to changes in habitat. Shifts in large numbers of populations will present challenges. For example, New Zealand (currently with a population of around 4 million people) might choose to implement a comprehensive transition to a steady-state economy based on a stable population and calculated standard of living.[59] Under pressure to receive climate refugees, will New Zealand take them all, or refuse to compromise its plans for ecological integrity? New Zealand will probably have to absorb some refugees from island nations like Kiribati (or Palau), which are in the process of becoming ocean shoal nations. But consider nations irrigated by rivers that are fed by rapidly disappearing glaciers, like Vietnam, Laos, Cambodia, Thailand, Pakistan and Bangladesh. Owing to climate change, it is conceivable that these nations might experience decades of floods as the glaciers rapidly melt, followed by the challenges of drought. In such circumstances, the territories of these nations may only support a far smaller population than at present, creating a substantial refugee crisis. It has been proposed that ecological integrity be recognised as a fundamental norm. However, it is unlikely that ecological integrity will prevail in such pressing circumstances, and unlikely that it should ethically. It is a norm which will have to be balanced against other norms, such as human rights.

---

[54] M Mukerjee, 'Apocalypse Soon: Has Civilization Passed the Environmental Point of No Return?' (23 May 2012) scientificamerican.com.

[55] Rockstrom and others, 'Planetary Boundaries' (n 50).

[56] See K Bosselmann, *Earth Governance* (Cheltenham, Edward Elgar, 2015).

[57] See O Woolley, *Ecological Governance: Reappraising Law's Role in Protecting Ecosystem Functionality* (Cambridge, Cambridge University Press, 2014).

[58] Millennium Ecosystem Assessment, *Living Beyond Our Means* (2006).

[59] As envisioned in J Adams and others, *Strong Sustainability for New Zealand: Principles and Scenarios* (Nakedize, 2009).

Though seemingly distant, global ecological collapse is no longer an impossibility in the Anthropocene. The process may take many more centuries. Or, multiple planetary thresholds may be crossed relatively quickly, resulting in more rapid ecological decline; the data is not yet clear.[60] The requisite extent of ecological collapse to be termed 'global' would have to be extensive (though not necessarily complete). It is always possible to imagine various scenarios, ultimately at the end of which we are left without a home, having rendered Earth uninhabitable. But such a scenario is avoidable, while it is worth remembering that ultimately, the opposite of global ecological integrity and sustainability is global ecological collapse which must be avoided at all cost.

B. Energy Integrity

The twentieth century has been an age of energy abundance (especially for the developed world). Anthropogenic climate change has been one consequence. In the Anthropocene, in addition to dealing with challenges of human impacts on the atmosphere and ecological systems, the era is likely to be characterised by increasing energy scarcity. This is due to a depletion of fossil fuels (particularly those with high 'net energy', understood as the energy returned on energy invested in extraction). Historically, economic activity has boomed when concentrated, easily produced sources of energy were discovered. The progression went from wood to coal, to oil and gas, and in some cases nuclear energy. Now, most of the easy, cheap, plentiful reservoirs of these fossil fuels have been depleted; what remains are those resources that are difficult, risky and expensive to extract.[61] Of particular relevance here is the issue of 'peak oil', which has been explained by a number of authors.[62]

Locally, a significant decline in a country's access to energy, such that the term 'energy collapse' of energy availability is appropriate, would have significant impacts on economic activity. Lower quality sources of coal may also be turned to by nations experiencing energy scarcity, which will entail further adverse effects for climate change. Reduction in availability of conventional oil has already prompted a use of unconventional oil, such as tar sands (which has extensive adverse effects on ecological integrity). Globally, an overall reduction in availability of quality sources of fossil fuels has the potential to lead to geopolitical tensions. (Nations with oil have been contested spaces in the best of times.)

Some countries, such as Russia, still have high levels of energy integrity and resilience. Others, which are totally dependent on energy imports, have much lower levels of resilience. Efforts to increase energy resilience, for example, through intensive investment in renewable technologies, are being pursued with differing levels of urgency. The challenge for nations will be to enable a relatively smooth

---

[60] See Rockstrom and others (n 50).
[61] Orlov (n 48) at 27.
[62] See R Heinberg, *The End of Growth* (New Society Publishers, 2011).

transition from high fossil fuel dependence to economic activity with cleaner, less centralised and more resilient energy systems.

A permanent decrease in access to high levels of fossil fuel energy will mean that economies will have to reconfigure into a more local, simpler mode of economic activity. This will have a monumental impact on systems of food production, transportation and trade, among others. It will also have implications for what we envision as suitable levels of governance.

C. Financial Integrity

What is the relationship between current financial arrangements and ecological integrity? Most financial systems and the cultures they are based on are short term-ist and they often lack integrity. However, here we attempt to go beyond issues such as irresponsible behaviour in investments (which is the proper target of regulation), to a consideration of the very fabric of the financial system itself. Max Weber said that the essence of capitalism was never to settle down, but to engage in endless expansion. This is at least in part because of the nature of money. Global finance is based on fiat currencies loaned into existence by banks at interest.[63] The universally revered 'magic of compound interest' results in exponential growth.[64] As a mathematical function, this can be characterised as debt raised to the power of time.[65] With a positive interest rate, as time passes, the debt needs to grow faster. Unfortunately, exponential growth eventually outpaces every physical process, resulting in collapse.[66] Interest-bearing debt is a driver of perpetual economic growth.[67] It is only viable in an expanding economy. If economic growth stops (say, owing to planetary boundaries being crossed or because of energy constraints) debt will become a problem.[68] Interestingly, the connection between expansion and debt is not new. In Ancient Mesopotamia (where the practice of loaning money at interest was first invented), debt amnesties were instituted to avoid threats of social breakdown. In contrast, Ancient Greek cities facing debt crises (after Solon) turned to policies of expansion.[69]

As an illustration of the exponential function in early British case law take *Thornborow v Whitacre* (1705).[70] In the words of Baker:[71]

> Thornborow met farmer Whitacre and said to him: 'Let us strike a bargain: If I pay you a £5 note down now, will you give me two rye corns next Monday, four on Monday week,

---

[63] See D Kent, *Healthy Money, Healthy Planet* (Craig Potton, Nelson, NZ, 2005).
[64] See Albert Bartlett, above.
[65] Orlov (n 48) at 22.
[66] ibid.
[67] See B Lietaer, *The Future of Money* (Random House, 2001).
[68] Orlov (n 48) 22.
[69] Graeber, *Debt* (n 28).
[70] *Thornborow v Whitacre* (1705) 2 Ld Raym 1164, 92 ER 270 (KB).
[71] JF Baker, *A Treatise on the Law of Sales of Goods, Wares and Merchandise As Affected By the Statute of Frauds.* (London, Forgotten Books, 2013) (Original work published 1887) 318–19.

eight on Monday fortnight, and so on, doubling it every Monday for a year?' Farmer Whitacre not stopping to estimate the result of such a bargain, and thinking the money easily earned, with avidity accepted the offer, and the bargain was made. But when the too hasty Whitacre came to calculate how much rye he should have to deliver, he found that it came to more than was grown in a year in all England.

The Court noted that 'the contract was a foolish one'. Reading the case today, we are perhaps amused by the hapless farmer Whitacre; yet modern economies are locked in to the same kind of exponential function.

Gibbon's *Decline and Fall* illustrates that collapses of empires can take many centuries. Similarly, the Earth has a threshold of resilience, meaning that trends in the erosion of global ecological integrity are gradual.[72] In contrast, history shows that financial collapses can occur rather rapidly. A financial collapse could be triggered by a shock in the real world (such as energy or resource constraints), but could also be triggered by a psychological phenomenon such as a rapid loss of confidence. There is also the possibility of an unexpected event (which Taleb calls a 'black swan').[73] In a financial collapse, faith in business as usual approaches is lost. The future is no longer assumed to resemble the past in any way that allows risk to be assessed and financial assets to be guaranteed. Financial institutions become insolvent, savings are wiped out and access to capital is lost.[74]

Margrit Kennedy argues for monetary reform, proposing interest and inflation free money.[75] There are various other proposals for monetary reform, at national levels and local levels.[76] However, large-scale reform seems unlikely, owing to the power of banks and financial institutions. Ecological economics provides an alternative to the model of infinite economic model growth described above.[77] Heinberg explains:

> a sustainable society's economy will necessarily be steady-state, not requiring constant growth. It will be based on the use of renewable resources harvested at a rate slower than that of natural replenishment; and on the use of non-renewable resources at declining rates, with metals and minerals recycled and reused wherever possible. Human population will have to achieve a level that can be supported by resources used in this way[78]

While conceivable, many believe it unlikely that states will voluntarily adopt an alternative economic paradigm.[79]

A financial collapse could entail a reduction in economic complexity. Thus, rather than by choice, something like a steady-state economy may be determined

---

[72] Rockstrom and others note that this can 'lull us into a false sense of security'.
[73] NN Taleb, *The Black Swan: The Impact of the Highly Improbable* (New York, Random House, 2007).
[74] Orlov (n 48) at 17.
[75] M Kennedy, *Interest and Inflation Free Money* (Lansing MI, Seva International, 1995).
[76] See M Shuman, *Local Dollars, Local Sense* (Vermont, Chelsea Green, 2012).
[77] Rees (n 37).
[78] Heinberg, *The End of Growth* (n 62) at 281.
[79] Rees (n 37).

by default. Such a reversion to simpler, stable and more sustainable activity will only work on a smaller scale. After a community experiences a financial collapse, it will become apparent that money is just a set of human arrangements. Money has always been a matter of political contention.[80] For example, Ancient Greek city states would issue their own currencies, as a mark of independence. In the Anthropocene, local currencies may have more of a chance to increase in importance, as outlined in Michael Shuman's *Local Dollars, Local Sense.* Lawyers may play a role here, for example, in developing legal frameworks for local government means of exchange.

A community may assume that money is a *conditio sine qua non* for its existence and well-being. But, after a financial collapse, communities may wish to reevaluate that assumption. Many thriving communities have little or no money (as will be illustrated in 'Commercial Integrity', below). When we use money, we cede power to those who create money (by creating debt) and who destroy money (by cancelling debt).[81] It depersonalises economic relations, so that people, animals and ecosystems become numbers. Money has been used since its earliest examples as a tool of wealth extraction.[82] However, life without abject reliance on global or even national finance, is possible and maybe even desirable. It has happened before and it can happen again.

D. Commercial Integrity

Let us now consider, what the relationship is between commercial integrity and ecological integrity. Are these spheres related, and if so, how? What might commercial integrity mean? Gaines has rightly expressed concern about 'depersonalized economic relationships'.[83] Does this perhaps point us to an alternative conception of commercial relations, more congruent with the achievement of ecological integrity? Most people in 'developed' economies are dependent for survival on strangers halfway across the world who provide most of their material needs. There is a high level of dependence on financialised, commercialised, impersonal systems. Global supply chains are long and distant. In an environment where most of one's needs are addressed by readily available, standardised product-service offerings, actual human relationships become a luxury reserved for sex and fun.[84] People live in communities, but they do not need each other for the essentials of life. Rather, impersonal trade currently occupies the dominant position in commercial relations between people.[85]

---

[80] Graeber (n 28).
[81] Orlov (n 48) at 51.
[82] ibid.
[83] Gaines (n 25) at 10208.
[84] D Orlov, *Reinventing Collapse* (Canada, New Society Publishers, 2011) 165.
[85] ibid, 99.

It is possible that a financial collapse (that is, in the abstract realm of modern finance) could lead to a disruption of actual commercial activity. This may be minor, or more severe. In a commercial collapse, faith that 'the market shall provide' is lost. Money is devalued and/or becomes scarce. Commodities are hoarded, import and retail chains break down and widespread shortages of survival necessities become the norm.

Ecological economics (discussed above) provides a model which would enhance both resilience of commercial systems and ecological integrity. As one example, global commerce moves masses of freight, much of which could not be considered essential in terms of Maslow's hierarchy of needs. Efforts can be made to reduce long, energy-hungry supply chains, by relocalising food production. Governance policies could conceivably reverse, to an extent at least, the move to large industrial agribusinesses (which are addicted to fossil fuels and artificial inputs), and revert to smaller-scale family farming. There is no reason why food production should be relegated to the area of technology. People grew and gathered food with little or no technology for many thousands of years.[86] FH King's fascinating 1911 book, *Farmers of Forty Centuries; Or, Permanent Agriculture in China, Korea, and Japan*, explains how these regions sustained enormous populations for millennia on tiny amounts of land, without mechanisation, pesticides or chemical fertilisers. Instead, they relied on sophisticated crop rotation, interplanting and ecological relationships among farm plants, animals and people. With such a model, for most of its history China maintained the highest standard of living in the world—even England only really overtook it in the 1820s, well past the time of the Industrial Revolution.[87] The example of Ancient China shows that while there may be dismay at the current lack of environmental consensus between states, a large, hierarchical state *can* be ecologically sustainable (at least, when based on sophisticated governance and organic farming). As JM Greer observes,

> while Utopia is not an option, societies that are humane, cultured and sustainable are quite another matter. There have been plenty of them in the past; there can be many more in the future.[88]

An example of one model of commerce more congruent with ecological sustainability is the so-called 'gift economy'. Depersonalised modern commerce is a commercial model markedly different from other historical modes of economic activity. It is a curious point that in traditional societies, trade and theft formed a continuum.[89] These societies had 'gift economies'.[90] The norm in many traditional societies can be conceptualised by a relationships pyramid (like the

---

[86] ibid, 33.
[87] Graeber (n 28).
[88] JM Greer, *The Ecotechnic Future* (Gabriola Island, BC: New Society, 2009).
[89] Orlov, *Reinventing Collapse* (n 84) at 88. The links can also be seen in Adam Smith's term 'truck and barter', where the 'truck' is related to the word 'trick' (Graeber).
[90] M Mauss, *The Gift* (1950, I Cunnison trans 1954).

food pyramid).[91] Fitting in the bottom of the pyramid, most economic relations occurred between immediate and extended family and one's tribe or community in the form of gift. In the middle layer of the pyramid would be situated friends and allies, with (still personal) economic acts in the form of barter and tribute (less frequently than gifts). Finally, in the smallest, top triangle would be placed strangers, with whom one occasionally engaged in (impersonal) trade. In modern commerce, therefore, we have flipped the 'gift economy' upside down, with trade predominating and with gifts used mainly for ceremonial uses.

Of course, it is not suggested that reversion to a traditional 'gift economy' would be a viable option in the Anthropocene. However, the anthropological record shows it has been present for long stretches of human prehistory and appears to have been ecologically sustainable. Perhaps it can throw the current system into sharper relief, prompting reflection on how to increase commercial resilience and integrity. For example, steps may be taken to rehumanise economic relations, by dealing with people you actually know, and dealing with them face to face; avoiding use of money and documents, while emphasising trust, integrity and verbal agreements.[92] Commercial resilience (and thus integrity) could be enhanced by giving preference to family, relations (even distant ones), then old friends and neighbours, then new friends and neighbours; while doing one's best to minimise dealings with distant strangers, including representatives of corporations.[93] The transition from a framework where services are rendered by strangers to one where needs are served by friends and acquaintances will bring more and more activities back into the home: the kitchen, the basement workshop, the back yard and the home office.[94] Governance structures which promote, or at least permit such developments, will allow an increase in commercial resilience (and therefore, commercial integrity). Furthermore, commercial dealings based on trust will foster a different ethos in the community.

It is possible that in the Anthropocene, with a reduction in opportunities for individualistic economic activity, the family could re-emerge as a fundamentally important economic unit. The 'family as an economic unit' is a successful human cultural universal: a family is usually three generations (at a minimum), living together, pooling resources and allocating them in the best interests of the whole. This, in turn, could strengthen communities, because a strong community is made up of strong families.[95] A community, in its truest sense, is one in which people know each other and are willing to help each other. This may lead to increased prospects for alternative, autonomous governance. An autonomous community is a band of such families capable of self-governance.[96]

---

[91] Orlov (n 84) at 85–86.
[92] ibid, 99.
[93] ibid, 99.
[94] ibid, 165.
[95] ibid, 39.
[96] ibid, 42.

Another model of commerce emerges from historical research (of court cases) done by Craig Muldrew.[97] This has revealed that, in smaller towns in sixteenth and seventeenth-century England, ordinary people such as the local butcher or baker would put things on 'tab'. In a typical village, the only people likely to pay in cash were passing travellers. Everyone was thus both creditor and debtor, with accounts settled around every six months. These English villagers seem to have seen no contradiction between older systems of mutual aid and 'the market'. On the one hand, they believed strongly in the collective stewardship of fields, streams and forests, and the need to help neighbours in difficulty. On the other hand, markets, too, were entirely founded on mutual trust.

In such a context, credit did not denote interest-bearing bank-debt (as it largely does for us today). The word credit comes from the same root as the words creed or credibility, referring to one's trustworthiness.[98] This can perhaps provide a starting point to imagine a rehumanised commercial context. Commercial integrity would increasingly be based on one's own integrity, in the moral sense of one's honesty, keeping one's word and faithfully fulfilling one's obligations. This is a stark contrast to Adam Smith's vision of rational economic actors motivated by self-interest.[99] In such a market economy, individuals are motivated by greed and fear. The pernicious nature of this kind of market is illustrated by the common view that friends and family shouldn't have business dealings with each other.[100] Such commercial relations may even be considered corrosive to the human spirit. If, in the Anthropocene, a community experiences commercial collapse in the form of seriously disrupted access to global supply chains, in addition to difficulties in making a transition, a new ethic of commercial autonomy and integrity may be a possibility. The community may revert from a Darwinian or Hobbesian 'war of all against all' to a Kropotkin-like ethic of community cooperation.[101]

E. Political Integrity

Governments are good at some things: protecting national borders, building infrastructure and providing primary education and basic health care. But, in the current situation, states seem to be having great difficulty in agreeing about

---

[97] C Muldrew, *The Economy of Obligation: The Culture of Credit and Social Relations in Early Modern England* (New York, Palgrave, 1998).

[98] Graeber (n 28).

[99] There is a curious link between commercial integrity and prohibitions of lending money at interest. Legalisation of interest began to change things by the 1580s, with interest-bearing loans common between villagers. This had a social impact, with 'credit' becoming unlatched from real relations of trust between individuals. (Interestingly, 'self-interest' is formed using '*interesse*', the Roman word for 'interest'). The *psychology of debt* is a factor to consider in relation to achieving ecological integrity. For the debtor, the world is reduced to potential merchandise and human relations become a matter of cost-benefit calculation (Graeber).

[100] Orlov (n 84) at 92.

[101] P Kropotkin, *Mutual Aid: A Factor in Evolution* (London, William Heinemann, 1902).

the fundamental importance of sustainability and ecological integrity (including implementing it through meaningful change). What can be holding states back? To take just one issue, ie that of defence from the perspective of the realist school of political philosophy. That is, a nation with an economy within the bounds of ecological integrity (a steady-state economy) would have difficulty securing its well-stewarded resources against a more powerful aggressor with a resource-hungry industrial-military growth economy.[102] Ancient China was noted above as a sustainable state, based on organic farming. China's arrangements were unable to compete with the industrialised West, leading to its 'century of shame'. Pre-Meiji Japan also discovered, in the nineteenth century, that the options were either to maintain its low impact agrarian economy and be overrun by Western industrial-military powers, or to rapidly industrialise and earn a place—by defeating Russia in 1904–05—at the conference table of nations. It is clear that before the Industrial Revolution states were not inherently incapable of sustainability. The state system after the Industrial Revolution with industrial military technology might have changed things. Consider, for example, the level of complexity proper to the current world military powers (such as China and the United States), if they were to transition their economies to maintain ecological integrity. It emerges, therefore, that political integrity is a practical issue which is worth considering in relation to the achievement of global ecological integrity.

States will remain the primary form of political organisation for the foreseeable future.[103] However, this is an attempt to think through the Anthropocene in terms of the big picture. (Heidegger, in 1966, said he thought it might take 300 years to think through the fundamental thrust of our present age.)[104] Perhaps later in the Anthropocene, the nation state will be viewed as an ephemeral form of political organisation. From an anthropological point of view, anarchic systems of governance have been the norm in human societies for most of human existence.[105] If states continue with the current model over the longer term, the various possibilities of ecological, energy, financial and commercial collapse may lead to a drastic reduction in political integrity. When this loss of integrity goes beyond a certain threshold point, the term political collapse becomes apt.

In the Anthropocene, the following extreme scenario could be imagined. A southern European nation finally decides that its farce with debts has gone on long enough. Its unorthodox economic measures cause catastrophic loss of confidence in the tools of globalised finance, leading to a global financial crisis. This causes problems in commerce, because cargos cannot be financed. With global supply chain disruption, a nation's business activity is drastically curtailed. This

---

[102] Of course, at the dawn of the 21st century, military technology has progressed to levels of lethality far beyond the capabilities of the somewhat quaint and archaic term, *industrial* military.

[103] Rees (n 37) at 309.

[104] M Heidegger, 'Nur noch ein Gott kann uns retten' (May 1976) 30 *Der Spiegel* 193–219. Trans by W Richardson as 'Only a God Can Save Us' in *Heidegger: The Man and the Thinker*, T Sheehan ed (1981) 45–67.

[105] Graeber (n 28).

impacts tax revenues, which reduces the state's ability to govern and control some areas, particularly in areas distant from main centres. In a scenario of political collapse, faith that the government will take care of you is lost. For example, as official attempts to mitigate widespread loss of access to commercial sources of survival necessities fail to make a difference, the political establishment loses legitimacy and relevance. Political collapse could be relatively swift (like a financial collapse), or it could be a much slower process, with legitimacy and control over areas gradually eroding over the long term.

The conventional solution to the environmental crisis is to hope that our politicians will eventually come through in response to a dramatic shift in the consciousness of the people. The dream of a global economy, globally governed to remain within global ecological limits, would (if achieved) be preferable. It is looking increasingly likely, however, that reality will prove less tidy. Doubts have been expressed about states voluntarily and collectively agreeing to transition to a model which respects planetary boundaries. However, at present there is not an easily detectable, broad shift in consciousness nationally or globally. If such a shift happens, possibly emerging from grassroots democracy, reform may be possible.

Others perceive insurmountable obstacles at the present time.[106] There are still calls for change. But, one gets the sense that hopes for such calls for change are different from when they were made in the 1970s. Frustrated with official structures, some try to act for change outside these institutions. Of politicians, they may adhere to Solzhenitsyn's maxim of '[d]on't trust them, don't fear them, don't ask anything of them'.

The degrowth movement has rediscovered anarchy's charms. Anarchy can be defined as of hierarchy (from the Greek '*an*', not/without and '*archos*', ruler).[107] With this concept, different forms and levels of governance can be viewed to fall somewhere on a continuum of anarchy to hierarchy. The degrowth movement has doubts about large-scale representative democracy, suspecting true democracy to only function in a smaller *polis* or community.[108] The concept of autonomy is an important notion in the movement. Autonomy derives *auto* (self) and *nomos* (custom, law). A community seeking autonomy will attempt to become free from contingent global mechanisms.[109]

It has been suggested that the city state, or smaller political communities, may be more sustainable in scale and a better form of political organisation to achieve ecological integrity than larger-scale nation states.[110] The city state has been one of the most successful political constructs in human history. The Ancient Greek

---

[106] See eg PD Burdon, 'The Project of Earth Democracy' in Westra, Taylor and Michelot (n 37) at 252: 'the capitalist class will never willingly surrender power'.

[107] Orlov (n 84) at 133.

[108] G Garver, 'Moving Forward with Planetary Boundaries and Degrowth' in Westra, Taylor and Michelot (n 37).

[109] N Candiago, 'The Virtuous Cycle of Degrowth and Ecological Debt: A New Paradigm for Public International Law?' in Westra, Taylor and Michelot (n 37) at 223.

[110] Ophuls, *Plato's Revenge* (n 29).

polis and the free cities of medieval Europe were conducive to sophisticated culture and learning.[111] Yet, proposals advocating the city state have been criticised by Sanford, who disavows the idea as elitist.[112] This is a valid concern. However, as will be outlined, lower level scales of governance may become the default choice, in some places, in the Anthropocene. It is also worth noting that many current nation states have elitist elements that undermine social coherence and trust. For example, it is not an unheard of sentiment that justice systems in some states tend in practice to work in favour of the educated, the corporations and the rich, and take unfair advantage of the uneducated, the private citizen and the poor.

Burdon is attracted to successful models of the Paris commune and Israeli Kibbutzim.[113] However, he recognises the issue of scale, with small communities being unequipped to deal with large-scale problems such as climate change. Like Burdon, Garver notes the problem of interdependencies (pollution having no borders), and sees the European principle of subsidiarity as a way to reconcile the local and transnational.[114] Along with the issue of scale is the practical issue that the current political arrangement is unlikely voluntarily to devolve into such small communities, or even to an artisanal set of intensely local polities, along the lines of the prosperous city states of medieval Europe.

In the Anthropocene, ecological challenges will probably result in stress for affected communities. In challenging times, there is the danger of people starting to think about strong leadership. During the difficult times of the Roman republic, dictatorship was seen as a good form of governance in a bad situation. Similarly, even 'sustainability thinkers' may at times feel a sense of frustration with the slow progress democracy is making in relation to pressing environmental challenges.[115] However, history shows that dictatorships can be problematic. Particularly, in attempting to achieve ecological integrity and sustainability, without a broad change in community ethos through education (among others), any reforms will themselves be unsustainable. Therefore, any erosions of democracy must be rejected. Rather, the importance of education (stressed above) re-emerges. Thomas Jefferson reminds us: 'I know of no safe repository of the ultimate power of society but people. And if we think them not enlightened enough, the remedy is not to take the power from them, but to inform them by education'.[116]

Ideas about local autonomy and anarchist thought about governance could not compete in the West in the twentieth century. Under 'New Deal' arrangements,

---

[111] It is noted, however, that Athens was still built on slave labour and—as Thucydides describes—eventually had their own little 'empire', with many conniving great plans to dominate the whole Mediterranean.

[112] Gaines (n 25) at 10205.

[113] Burdon, 'The Project of Earth Democracy' (n 106) at 248.

[114] ibid.

[115] Burdon (n 106) at 246, mentions (but rejects) the idea of a benevolent totalitarian regime. For a detailed discussion, see ME Zimmerman, 'Rethinking the Heidegger-Deep Ecology Relationship' (1993) 15 *Environmental Ethics* 195.

[116] Thomas Jefferson to William C. Jarvis, 1820. Memorial Edition 15, 279.

the working class gained the right to unionise, strike and bargain collectively. Public education, government pensions and health care were provided. This was all in exchange for submitting to the hierarchical control system of an industrial state.[117] Now, for various reasons, the industrial experiment is looking increasingly unattractive, and ideas about local autonomy are re-emerging in sustainability thinking.

In a situation of political collapse, when the centralised state no longer governs, people will have to revert to various forms of anarchic, autonomous self-governance. If the state loses coercive power, it can remain defunct as a ceremonial vestige.[118] In its stead will come a myriad of tiny polities, with smaller-scale economies. Those groups that have sufficient social cohesion, direct access to natural resources, and enough cultural wealth (especially in the form of face-to-face relationships and oral traditions), would manage to reconfigure in the absence of modern finance, commerce and the state. While imaginable in some countries, obviously there are significant challenges which might arise in such a scenario in other contexts.[119] Sustainable governance voluntarily chosen by the state would make for a smoother transition. But, in the Anthropocene, it is conceivable that a country (outside or even within the West) may experience loss of political integrity to some extent. The Anthropocene as a geological epoch, is by definition a very long time frame. What will future governance look like in 300 years? If this question were asked by John Locke and Constantine, the latter would probably be more surprised than the former by the actual shape of governance 300 years after his time. While 'anarchic' forms of governance seem implausible now, they may well gain more prominence during the Anthropocene. So, the challenge in the Anthropocene may be, in Hegelian terms, to progress from the thesis of anarchic governance in human prehistory, through the antithesis of the modern nation state, and achieve a synthesis that is able to incorporate true local autonomy and deal with transnational pollution and ecological destruction arising from modern technology.

IV. Conclusion: Shaping the 'New Story'

Under the prevailing story of economic growth, people will continue to live unsustainably, until they can no longer do so.[120] It is likely there will be various

---

[117] Orlov (n 84) at 126.

[118] ibid, 162.

[119] eg in a state with nuclear power-plants, it is obviously desirable that the government maintains the ability to manage them. All of them have to be supplied with sufficient energy for many decades, or they will be in danger of melting down like Fukushima. Perhaps in the Anthropocene it is time to challenge the assumption that all nations with nuclear power will—for the time frame required—be intact enough to manage them and handle any nuclear emergency.

[120] See J Randers, *2052: A Global Forecast for the Next Forty Years* (Vermont, Chelsea Green, 2012).

successful efforts for 'change' (stemming from business, technology and sub-cultures). But, ultimately, within the old story, smart business or smart technology will not be enough to stay within the safe operating space for humanity that planetary boundaries require. The narratives that shape our lives, attitudes and behaviours urgently need changing. In the Anthropocene, it is possible that people will increasingly find the old story of growth uncompelling. In such a scenario, ecological law can perhaps play a part in shaping a new story. The narrative will, of course, also be influenced by the experiences of our children and grandchildren, to whom we have bequeathed a planet very different to the one enjoyed by humanity during the Holocene. It is conceivable that, through such experience, the next few generations will fully embrace (as a crucial and self-evident norm of natural law) the fundamental importance of ecological integrity. The scenarios of the world-system sketched in this chapter are just that, sketches, but they may be sufficient to illustrate how foundational ecological integrity will have to be for living success-fully in the Anthropocene.

Part 4

Possible Futures in Critical 'Spaces'

12

Of Human Responsibility: Considering the Human/Environment Relationship and Ecosystems in the Anthropocene

KAREN MORROW

I. Introduction

Whilst there is widespread agreement in scientific and academic circles, and increasingly in the more radical reaches of a whole range of social and political spheres, that the existential challenges posed by the Anthropocene require nothing less than a wholesale refashioning of the human/environment paradigm; how this might be achieved remains, at best, highly debatable. The exploitative archetype of mastery over nature is deeply ingrained within our species' psyche and praxis, and it has, on balance, served us well for most of our evolutionary development. Where human behaviour has imposed costs on the natural world, the latter has, broadly speaking, long proved remarkably resilient in absorbing much of the impact of our excesses. Nonetheless, all indications are that this will not be the case in perpetuity and that, as we transgress an increasing number of crucial planetary boundaries, our habitual ways of thinking and behaviours represent an existential threat to at least our own species, if not the biosphere as a whole. Our increasing (if still woefully incomplete) knowledge of how planetary systems function and the significance of the impacts of human activities upon them could, if acted upon swiftly, and with a thorough-going commitment that recognises the true position of humans within the biosphere and the consequent imperative to curb our own over-indulgence, represent our best chance to continue to flourish as a species in a viable global context. Achieving such a fundamental alteration in our ontological perspective would arguably represent a seismic shift in human affairs on a par with the Enlightenment. In the past we have enjoyed the luxury of experiencing such change as gradual evolution, but current conditions require our next perspectival shift to be achieved with an unprecedented degree of urgency.

This chapter considers one area in which we might trial our ability to adopt reasoned behavioural change that short-circuits norms that have ultimately become counter-productive: our relationship to ecosystems. This is the area where the human/nature nexus and the implications of its current malignant pathology are arguably at their most immediate. A plethora of potential routes have been identified in order to recraft the terms of this aspect of our interconnection with nature in a more sustainable fashion. This chapter will look specifically at the voguish but vexed concept of ecosystems services, arguing that, as currently envisaged, rather than representing innovation, it pursues the paradigm of mastery to its logical and damning conclusion. The chapter will briefly consider the pros and cons of applying selected rights-based approaches (representative of an important strand in current thinking in this area) in the context of ecosystems services as correctives to this course. The rights approaches considered include: (likely prevailing) individual property rights; collective human rights; and 'rights for nature' archetypes. The chapter will conclude by considering the idea that, while rights discourse has something to offer in this context, where human attitudes and behaviour are in play, absent the crucial counter-point of an ethic of human responsibility, it cannot offer more than a partial solution to the conundrum of how to fashion a sustainable version of the human/environment bond.

II. The Paradigm of Mastery and its Consequences

The current prevailing paradigm shaping the human/nature relationship, while it has until quite recently, served (or at least appeared) to promote human flourishing, has now reached the point where it must be regarded as inherently unsustainable. In recognising the shift to the Anthropocene epoch, we are coming to understand that our cosmology, the dominant[1] epistemology founded upon it, and resulting global praxis, has set us on a trajectory that is changing the face of the biosphere to the point that it poses multiple, potentially existential, threats to our species,[2] and is reshaping the nature of life itself.[3] Critique of this state of affairs is ubiquitous; here though, discussion will draw on ecofeminist scholarship,

---

[1] While there are numerous (indigenous/religious) worldviews that situate humanity as part of nature, rather than as its master, these currently represent counter-hegemonic perspectives, rather than accepted orthodoxy; see eg JA Grim, *Indigenous Traditions and Ecology: the Interbeing of Cosmology and Community* (Cambridge MA, Harvard University Press, 2001).

[2] See the work of the Stockholm Resilience Centre on planetary boundaries, which focuses on those areas of the biosphere that most directly support human life, and which are subject to varying degrees of threat, notably W Steffen and others, 'Planetary Boundaries: Guiding Human Development on a Changing Planet' (2015) 347 (6223) *Science* 736 DOI: 10.1126/science.1259855.

[3] See A Weisman, *The World Without Us* (London, Virgin Books, 2008) which suggests that, absent humanity, life on Earth would continue, though potentially in radically different fashion.

and in particular the germinal work of Val Plumwood on what she terms the 'paradigm of mastery'.[4] Central to Plumwood's analysis for present purposes is the application of the prevailing post-Enlightenment Western philosophical conception of dualism[5] to delineate, differentiate and distinguish, between (human) culture and nature. In this context, she points to the centrality of 'denied dependency'[6] in the human/nature relationship. In sum, the approach separates the realm of the human/master and reason from environment/nature, whereby:

> To be defined as 'nature' ... is to be defined as a *terra nullius*, a resource empty of its own purposes or meanings, and hence available to be annexed for the purposes of those supposedly identified with reason or intellect[7]

Law has been profoundly implicated in this annexation of nature to human purposes. As Stone observes, natural objects:

> have traditionally been regarded by the common law, and even by all but the most recent legislation, as objects for man to conquer and master and use ... and even where natural objects are conserved this is done 'for us'.[8]

The paradigm of mastery is characterised by Plumwood as invoking a 'multiple, complex cultural identity of the master formed in the context of class, race species and gender domination';[9] and for present purposes it essentially casts the environment/nature as inherently inferior and a means to privileged humanity's ends, rendering it ripe for what is assumed to be self-evidently justified and thus largely unquestioned exploitation. Interestingly, psychology refers to the 'mastery perception' as a motivation for active attempts to govern one's environment,[10] but—worryingly in the context of ecological crisis—points to the fact that if control goals are not attained, disengagement results (in order to conserve physical and—in humans—emotional resources).[11] We can now understand the pursuit of the paradigm of mastery as a form of malignant pathology, the adverse consequences of which for the environment, are amply evidenced in resource depletion, pollution, ecosystem and ultimately even biospheric disruption, and all too apparent.[12] Less discussed, and little investigated but arguably no less important, are the consequences of enjoying the ultimately illusory position of mastery for humanity as a species: treating nature as a mere means to human ends has led us to develop an ultimately erroneous sense of god-like superiority.

---

[4] V Plumwood, *Feminism and the Mastery of Nature* (London, Routledge, 1993).

[5] ibid, ch 2.

[6] ibid, 41.

[7] ibid, 4.

[8] CD Stone, 'Should Trees Have Standing?—Towards Legal Rights for Natural Objects' (1972) 45 *Southern California Law Review* 450, 463.

[9] Plumwood, *Feminism and the Mastery of Nature* (n 4) at 5.

[10] J Heckhausen, 'Evolutionary Perspectives on Human Motivation' (2000) 43(6) *The American Behavioral Scientist* 1015, 1023.

[11] ibid, 1024.

[12] Steffen and others, 'Planetary Boundaries' (n 2).

As we enter the Anthropocene, the moral and physical toxicity of this is becoming increasingly evident.

Our now rapidly emerging scientific understanding of the complexities of the functioning of the biosphere and of the existence of systemic planetary boundaries mean that we no longer have any excuse for viewing the paradigm of mastery as anything more than an illusion founded on self-serving delusion. As Plumwood points out, we are well aware that the biosphere is no mere 'background part of our field of action or subjectivity',[13] and ecology has (re)introduced us to the profound knowledge that that we are intimately enmeshed in nature, rather than separate from, or in any way above it. While these are things that on one level we know, we have yet to truly grasp their import[14] and express this centrally in the way that we conduct ourselves vis-à-vis the environment. Rather, we have made comparatively minor adjustments to some of our more egregiously damaging activities under the auspices of environmental law, but these have not altered the fundamental underlying paradigm of mastery. Dis/replacing the paradigm will be challenging, for as Plumwood convincingly argues, ending the systemic bifurcation of dualism and according value to the other, cannot be addressed by mere merger or even reversal of current approaches[15]—something much more ambitious is required, entailing: 'recognition of a complex, interacting pattern of both continuity *and* difference'.[16]

When applied to the human/nature relationship, this observation enables us to garner important insights: in terms of continuity, it acknowledges that humans are undoubtedly part of nature, and indeed intimately and entirely enmeshed within it; at the same time, in terms of difference, humans are distinct from the rest of nature in our ability to manipulate natural systems on a variety of scales from local to, now, planetary. In some ways, locally, and in the short term, humanity has been able to sway nature for our own ends (though not entirely and with unintended consequences and externalities); it is, however, now becoming clear with the advent of the Anthropocene, that the cumulative spatial and temporal impacts of human activity pose such substantial threats that we urgently need to rethink our place in the biosphere. This brings us to the central question: what would it require to motivate the shift that this would need to engage in the dynamics and characterisation of the human/nature relationship? Human history has shown that societal (and legal) responses to moral/ethical arguments for altering key aspects of human behaviour are comparatively slow to develop, partial in their

---

[13] V Plumwooegd: 'Ecological Ethics from Rights to Recognition: Multiple Spheres of Justice for Humans, Animals and Nature' in N Low (ed), *Global Ethics and Environment* (Abingdon, Routledge, 1999) 197.

[14] See eg DA Hantula, 'Evolutionary Psychology and Consumption' (2003) 20(9) *Psychology & Marketing* 757 and G Marshall, *Don't Even Think About It: Why Our Brains Are Wired to Ignore Climate Change* (New York, Bloomsbury, 2014).

[15] Plumwood (n 4) at 59–64.

[16] ibid, 67.

draw, and ultimately require legal compulsion for their realisation.[17] When we do respond to such imperatives, as Delgado puts it:

> we are almost inevitably drawn to doomed, moderate approaches ... when society needs more sweeping, ambitious ones. We resist precisely the medicine that could save us. We turn to strong solutions only when it is either too late, or when our thinking has advanced so far that the solutions seem commonplace and tame.[18]

This is clearly applicable to the current context, wherein it may be argued that, in the past, we could allow ourselves the luxury of shifting perspectives through societal evolution, rather than revolution: in the Anthropocene, in a world of relatively rapid human-induced change, tipping points and interconnected and systemic threats, this can no longer be the case. Swift change requires a rapid response. So, if we cannot fashion an effective morally prompted new relationship between environmental ethics, law and societal practice, desirable in principle as this may be,[19] can practical considerations—and scientific evidence furnished by ecology (itself the subject of rapid and radical development)[20]—supply the deficit?

In this context, as Folke and others observe:

> The old way of thinking implicitly assumes a stable and infinitely resilient environment, a global steady state. The new perspective recognizes that resilience can be and has been eroded and that the self-repairing capacity of ecosystems should no longer be taken for granted.[21]

One potential response to this knowledge would be (the admittedly hugely challenging) development of 'ecological thinking':

> perhaps the first subject-matter that transcends or shatters discourse boundaries and strains both imagination and human powers when selecting between conceptual frameworks[22]

Kaldis questions whether the 'disciplinary borrowing' that commonly features in emerging ecological thinking discourse is 'merely unfortunate? Or is it, rather, logically inescapable?', seeing it as an inevitable route to social constructionism

---

[17] See eg discussion of developments in gender equality and abolishing slavery; Stone, 'Should Trees Have Standing?' (n 8).

[18] R Delgado, 'Our Better Natures: A revisionist View of Joseph Sax's Public Trust Theory of Environmental Protection, and Some Dark Thoughts on the Possibility of Law Reform' (1991) 44(6) *Vanderbilt Law Review* 1209, 1212.

[19] J Purdy, 'Our Place in the World: A New Relationship for Environmental Ethics and Law' (2013) 62(4) *Duke Law Journal* 857.

[20] Discussed in LA Vivanco, 'Green Encounters: Shaping and Contesting Environmentalism in Rural Costa Rica' (Oxford, Berghahn Books, 2006) notably at 54 ff.

[21] C Folke, S Carpenter, B Walker, M Scheffer, T Elmqvist, L Gunderson and CS Holling, 'Regime Shifts, Resilience, and Biodiversity in Ecosystem Management' 35 (2004) *Annual Review of Ecology, Evolution, and Systematics* 557, 558.

[22] B Kaldis, 'Could the Environment Acquire its Own Discourse?' (2003) 16(3) *History of Human Sciences* 73.

and anthropocentrism.[23] I would argue, in common with eco-pragmatists,[24] that given the pan-dimensional issues involved, disciplinary borrowing is inevitable—but that it is also desirable, though requiring careful handing in order to avoid the mere absorption of ecological insights into current discourse, rather than their application prompting a transformation therein. One consequence of the need to develop ecological thinking is that emerging scientific discourse at the very frontiers of the human/environment interface is increasingly being brought to the fore in informing discussion of the hard choices that we face. The influential work of the Stockholm Resilience Centre (SRC) on planetary boundaries is prominent in this regard.[25] Of particular interest in the current context is the holistic, systemic and biosphere-based approach being adopted by the SRC—the Earth System perspective—to evaluating the impacts of human activity on the environment. As befitting the science of the Anthropocene, human activity is viewed as an integral part of the Earth System, which is defined as:

> the integrated biophysical and socioeconomic processes and interactions (cycles) among the atmosphere, hydrosphere, cryosphere, biosphere, geosphere, and anthroposphere (human enterprise) in both spatial—from local to global—and temporal scales, which determine the environmental state of the planet within its current position in the universe. Thus, humans and their activities are fully part of the Earth System, interacting with other components.[26]

When applied to the nine planetary boundaries identified by the SRC, namely: the stratospheric ozone layer; biodiversity; chemicals dispersion; climate change; ocean acidification; freshwater consumption and the global hydrological cycle; land system change; nitrogen and phosphorus inputs into the biosphere and oceans; and atmospheric aerosol loadings, it is clear that the planetary system is operating under an unprecedented slew of multidimensional, interactive and anthropogenic, pressures. It is clear that, if these pressures are being made manifest at the planetary/biospheric level, they are also being experienced in the ecosystems which comprise much of it.

III. The Human/Nature Relationship and Ecosystems

Individual ecosystems represent the most immediate manifestation of the human/environment nexus and therefore provide an excellent glimpse into the state,

---

[23] ibid, 74.

[24] See eg DA Farber, *Ecopragmatism* (Chicago, University of Chicago Press, 1999), examining the interface between economics, science and environmental regulation.

[25] Heir apparent to the more rudimentary modelling approaches pioneered by the Club of Rome—DH Meadows, DL Meadows, J Randers, WW Behrens III, *The Limits to Growth* (New York Universe Books, 1972).

[26] J Rockström and others, Planetary Boundaries: Exploring the Safe Operating Space for Humanity (2009) 14(2) *Ecology and Society* 32, www.ecologyandsociety.org/vol14/iss2/art32/ and Steffen and others (n 2).

character and viability of the human/environment relationship. They are of course also hugely significant in their own right in the current, seemingly unending, cycle of environmental degradation.[27] Ecosystems may be defined as: 'the complex of a community of organisms and its environment functioning as an ecological unit'.[28] Our modern understanding of ecosystems, as indicated above, encapsulates humanity within this 'community of organisms'. It also acknowledges that 'regime shifts in ecosystems are, to a large extent, driven by human actions'.[29] Managing the human/ecosystem interface (more accurately expressed than the usual description of managing ecosystems) has therefore come to be a pressing issue and is focused on a range of human activities ranging from: 'top-down' (encompassing the products of deliberate action); to 'bottom up' (encompassing inadvertent impacts of human activity); and 'altering disturbance regimes'.[30]

Whilst current discussion of the specific human/ecosystem interface is dominated by Ecosystem Services Approaches (ESAs) which we will consider shortly, these are located in the broader ecology-driven approach that emerged in the conception of Ecosystem Based Management (EBM) of terrestrial environments in the 1960s. EBM may be defined as: 'comprehensive and integrative management decisions and actions in relation to ecosystem dynamics and the provision of interconnected ecosystem services, or human benefits'.[31] The concept of EBM with its strong management bent,[32] despite its nomenclature, constitutionally tends to the prioritisation of human interests. The conception of ESAs as an element of EBM, which further enhances certain human priorities in this context, emerged in scientific literature in the 1980s, rising to prominence by the late 1990s. The United Nations' Millennium Ecosystem Assessment[33] (MEA) brought the concept to global prominence. It identified four categories of 'ecosystem services', namely: provisioning; regulating; cultural; and supporting. The signifying language of 'service' is crucial—as the: 'words we use to describe things are also the way we value them';[34] in this case value being explicitly based on the delivery of human well-being. The spectrum of services involved represents the complex and challenging mix of quantitative and qualitative elements that need somehow to be effectively combined in order to meet the multidimensional demands of EBM.

---

[27] See eg Millennium Ecosystem Assessment (MEA), *Ecosystems and Human Wellbeing—Synthesis Report* (2005) available at: www.millenniumassessment.org/documents/document.356.aspx.pdf.

[28] www.merriam-webster.com/dictionary/ecosystem.

[29] Folke and others, 'Regime Shifts, Resilience, and Biodiversity in Ecosystem Management' (n 21) at 573.

[30] ibid.

[31] C White, C Costello, BE Kendall and C J Brown, 'The Value of Coordinated Management of Interacting Ecosystem Services' (2012) 15(6) *Ecology Letters* 509, 509.

[32] See Kaldis, 'Could the Environment Acquire its Own Discourse?' (n 22) at 85 on the orientation of management approaches.

[33] MEA, *Ecosystems and Human Wellbeing—Synthesis Report* (n 27).

[34] P Evans, 'Reclaiming the Language' in Caught by the River, *On Nature: Unexpected Ramblings on the British Countryside* (London, HarperCollins, 2011) 107.

The attraction of ESAs from a management perspective, as described by Constanza and others, lies in the recognition that:

> Sustaining and enhancing human well-being requires a balance of all our assets—individual people, society, the built economy, and ecosystems. The reframing of the way we look at 'nature' is essential to solving the problem of how to build a sustainable and desirable future for humanity.[35]

That said, while ESAs ostensibly function as a tool within EBM, the manner in which they are deployed in practice and the degree of prominence accorded to them vis-à-vis other components of EBM is of central importance. At a superficial level the conceptual origins of the concept of 'ecosystem services' in a science-driven model of EBM[36] appear to be at least partially ecocentric—invoking the concept of the ecosystem, of which humanity is a part, as the framing for protection. In real terms, however, currently ESAs are driven by economics rather than science.[37] The explicit harnessing of ESAs to economics, in effect stressing 'services' above 'ecosystems' is a deliberate policy choice, reflecting dominant social mores. Nowhere is this bent more clearly exemplified than in the six reports on 'The Economics of Ecosystems and Biodiversity' (TEEB).[38] These brought consideration of the valuation of ecosystems into the mainstream in international affairs, and formed a central plank of the wider 'green economy' initiative in the run up to the UNCSD (Rio+20) in 2012. Despite a somewhat lukewarm reception for the concept of the green economy in general at the conference,[39] the ESA strand of the initiative seems to have a sustained momentum of its own.[40]

While the TEEB initiative was hosted by the United Nations Environment Programme (UNEP), it was initiated by the G8+5 as a part of the antidote to the burgeoning global economic crisis. To this end, it aspired to tackle the 'economic invisibility' of most ecosystem services and 'mainstream' the environment into financial services by incorporating the 'values of nature' into societal decision-making

---

[35] R Constanza and others, 'Changes in the Global Value of Ecosystem Services' (2014) 26 *Global Environmental Change* 152, 153.

[36] JMcP Dick, RI Smith and E M Scott, 'Ecosystem Services and Associated Concepts' (2011) 22 *Environmetrics* 598.

[37] ibid.

[38] For the sake of practicality, discussion here will focus specifically on the synthesis report drawn from these: *The Economics of Ecosystems and Biodiversity: Mainstreaming the Economics of Nature: A Synthesis of the Approach, Conclusions and Recommendations of TEEB* (TEEB Synthesis) (2010), available at: www.teebweb.org, which provides an overview of the work as a whole.

[39] Discussed in K Morrow, 'Rio +20, the Green Economy and Re-orienting Sustainable Development' (2012) 14(4) *Environmental Law Review* 279.

[40] Rio +20 Outcome Document, A/RES/66/288, *The Future We Want*, available at: www.un.org/ga/search/view_doc.asp?symbol=A/RES/66/288&Lang=E, para 91. UNGA RES 70/1. *Transforming our world: the 2030 Agenda for Sustainable Development* (The Sustainable Development Goals) available at: www.un.org/en/ga/search/view_doc.asp?symbol=A/RES/70/1, makes frequent reference to ecosystems, referring to ecosystem services in Goal 15.1, indicating the continuing currency of the concept, committing to: 'By 2020, ensure the conservation, restoration and sustainable use of terrestrial and inland freshwater ecosystems and their services'.

processes at all levels.[41] This ostensibly acknowledged the centrality of ecosystem health to a viable economy. Furthermore, in positing a more economically grounded approach to environmental protection, it sought to:

> provide a bridge between the multi-disciplinary science of biodiversity and the arena of international and national policy as well as local government and business practices.[42]

Furthermore, the TEEB characterised the established relationship between humanity and nature as one of 'self-destructiveness'[43] and presented attributing monetary value to ecosystem services not as a motivating factor implicated in this state of affairs; but rather as a potent corrective to it. To this end, the TEEB stated that:

> Valuation can act as a powerful form of feedback, a tool for self-reflection, which helps us rethink our relation to the natural environment and alerts us to the consequences of our choices and behaviour on distant places and people.[44]

The TEEB further envisaged:

> the introduction of mechanisms that *incorporate the values* of ecosystems into decision making *through incentives and price signals*. ... It needs to come along with *reinforcing rights* over natural resources and liability for environmental damage.[45]

Thus the TEEB advocated the adoption of ESAs, which it defined as evaluating; 'flows of value to human societies as a result of the state and quantity of natural capital'.[46] Taken in context, it is clear then that, despite its 'ecosystem' nomenclature, what was being advocated by ESAs here was not only (like EBM) fundamentally anthropocentric, but also primarily economic in approach.[47] This has appeal, notably in seeking to address market failures, specifically: the fact that pricing of ecosystem services had tended to be confined to use values (eg provisioning services) with non-use values (eg cultural services) rarely being considered in monetary terms. More ambitiously, it also seeks to encapsulate indirect use values (regulating services) which are only beginning to be assigned economic value, though they in fact make the most significant contribution to human well-being.[48] There are, however, significant problems attached to the TEEB's conception of ESAs, not least those related to valuation. In principle, pricing ecosystem services arguably further commodifies or objectifies the natural world, reinforcing the paradigm of mastery. Furthermore, focusing narrowly on economics reinforces the dominance of market-based ideologies and ultimately represents a damagingly

---

[41] TEEB Synthesis (n 38) at 3.
[42] ibid, 4.
[43] ibid, 12.
[44] ibid.
[45] ibid. Emphasis in the original.
[46] ibid, 7.
[47] NY Turgut, 'The Influence of Ecology on Environmental Law: Challenges to the Concept of Traditional Law' (2008) 10 *Environmental Law Review* 112.
[48] TEEB Synthesis (n 38) at 7–8.

reductionist attempt at the quantification of qualitative considerations.[49] Even if these objections are overlooked as idealistic/ideological, and we accept the assertion that engaging with the market is necessary in order to protect ecosystems, the practical problem of ascribing appropriate monetary value to ecosystem services remains. In order for ESAs to improve upon current approaches, they would need to attain a degree of accuracy in valuing the services in question—otherwise they will simply serve to add spurious legitimacy to erroneous assumptions. At a minimum this would require them to be founded on a thorough, science-based, understanding of ecosystems coupled with due consideration of human systemic impacts on and interactions with them. The difficulties of capturing value in this context are exacerbated by the fact that our baseline knowledge of ecosystems generally,[50] let alone ecosystem services, is poor, with our limited understanding of ecosystem function and maintenance, critical thresholds, uncertainty and precaution, all raising serious concerns. Additionally, arguments for the valorisation of ESAs would be considerably more convincing if our well-established attribution of economic value to the considerably more straightforward category of environmental goods was such as to ensure their sustainable use. In fact, experience has shown that: 'admitting the traditional economic valuation methods almost always undervalues biological diversity'.[51] Furthermore, expanding the role of the market in such contexts only provides protection to the environment 'unless degrading it becomes more profitable'.[52] In light of this, sending out inaccurate price signals on ESAs would have potentially disastrous consequences, yet proponents argue for their potential draw income from 'wildlands' through giving the invisible hand of the market a 'green thumb'.[53]

Such issues notwithstanding, the TEEB asserts that the process of pricing ESAs: 'should be uncontroversial for many ecosystem services, especially at the local scale'[54] yet at the same time it acknowledges that the process presents enormous challenges.[55] Bennett engages with the latter noting that, while our knowledge base is developing:

> despite extensive work on ecosystem services in recent decades, our understanding of their ecological foundation, their impacts on human well-being, and our knowledge about how to govern their benefits remains (sic) insufficient.[56]

---

[49] M Sagoff, 'On the Value of Natural Ecosystems: The Catskills Parable' (2002) 21 *Politics and the Life Sciences* 19–25.

[50] GC Daily and others, 'The Value of Nature and the Nature of Value' (2000) 289(5478) *Science* 395.

[51] SB Banerjee, 'Who Sustains Whose Development? Sustainable Development and the Reinvention of Nature' (2003) 24(1) *Organization Studies* 143, 156.

[52] ibid, 153.

[53] EO Wilson, *The Diversity of Life* (Cambridge, MA, Harvard University Press, 1992) 271.

[54] TEEB Synthesis (n 38) at 25.

[55] ibid, 12.

[56] EM Bennett and others, 'Linking Biodiversity, Ecosystem Services, and Human Well-being: Three Challenges for Designing Research for Sustainability' (2015) 14 *Current Opinion in Environmental Sustainability* 76, 77.

Our fragmented knowledge base was initially largely confined to conceptual consideration of interactions between hard science (incomplete in itself) and economics, which, while challenging in itself, in no way reflected the full complexity of the issues involved. Latterly, the social sciences[57] and empirical studies[58] are beginning to play a more prominent role in this regard, countering the established dominance of scientific and economic information sets. While on one level this is all to the good, it is also the case that, as the range of inputs increases, the challenges posed by cross-disciplinary dialogue become, if anything, more vivid.[59]

In the end, the TEEB, despite employing a slew of expertise in its deliberations, ended up merely paying lip-service to the plurality of disciplines in play, opting for a mainstream economic approach, reliant on the popular but highly problematic (demand-led, hypothetical) concept of 'willingness to pay'[60] as the basis for valuation. This reductionist stance misses the point, for, as Stone observes, the: 'environmental "values" of which we are now speaking are by definition over and above those that the market is prepared to bid for: they are priceless'.[61]

The approach to valuation of ESAs advocated by the TEEB is at best implausible and at worst woefully inadequate, sidestepping the real challenge that we face which is, as Adelman puts it: 'to develop a notion of sustainability within rather than against nature'.[62] Instead ESAs as currently construed arguably represent a retrograde step as, not only are they anthropogenic in focus, they in fact even narrow the range of human concerns addressed by foregrounding economic considerations at the expense of other relevant factors. The only viable—if undoubtedly socially and economically painful approach—would be to build our economic system on respect for ecological limits as a constraining foundation for this aspect and all other aspects of human endeavour. So, can ESAs deliver this? As currently envisaged that answer has to be no: in reality what they offer is a further manifestation of 'business as usual' though this has obvious if superficial attractions, not least in the creation or augmentation of existing property rights[63] and associated facilitation of payment, offset, trade and substitution in environmental credits. ESAs are already, despite their flaws, being embraced with some enthusiasm by

[57] DK Loomis, SK Paterson, 'Human Dimensions Indicators of Coastal Ecosystem Services: A Hierarchical Perspective' (2014) 44 *Ecological Indicators* 44, 63.

[58] See eg HW Schroeder, 'Place Experience, Gestalt, and the Human-Nature Relationship' (2007) 27 *Journal of Environmental Psychology* (2007) 293.

[59] See eg Loomis and Paterson, 'Human Dimensions Indicators of Coastal Ecosystem Services' (n 57); and Bennett and others, 'Linking Biodiversity, Ecosystem Services, and Human Well-being' (n 56).

[60] TEEB Synthesis (n 38) at 4.

[61] Stone (n 8) at 476.

[62] S Adelman, 'Rio+20: Sustainable Injustice in a Time of Crisis' (2013) 4(1) *Journal of Human Rights and the Environment* 6, 10.

[63] See, with regard to the EUETS, *Armstrong DLW GmbH v Winnington Networks Ltd* [2012] EWHC 10 (Ch) in which the Court considered the legal status of an emissions trading allowance (EUA). Both parties regarded the EUA as property ([40]), a view with which the Court concurred ([50]).

international institutions, governments, the business community and to some degree in popular culture.[64]

IV. Is it Possible to Reorient ESAs? A Preliminary Exploration of Rights-based Approaches

A. Property Rights, ESAs and PES

Proponents of ESAs, such as Constanza and others, are at pains to stress that their valuation is not about ownership/privatisation, but rather:

> their value in monetary units is an estimate of their benefits to society expressed in units that communicate with a broad audience. This can help raise awareness of the importance of ecosystem services to society and serve as a powerful and essential communication tool to inform better, more balanced decisions[65]

Nonetheless, once we place an economic value on something, it inevitably becomes the subject of property rights that are owned and traded; this inevitably and significantly alters the dynamics of the relationships clustered around it. The TEEB for example, in alluding to 'reinforcing rights over natural resources',[66] clearly envisaged an extension of property rights in this context—facilitated by the fact that many ESAs are located on land and that payments for ecosystem services (PES) will be tied to the existing legal rights that manifest in this regard. Thus ESAs, rather than adopting ecological thinking and developing conceptions of the environment as 'provider of basic (human) needs',[67] can be viewed as further extending the conception of the environment as property, with damaging environmental and social consequences.[68]

Individual property rights arising in the context of PES would naturally raise concerns akin to those raised by of property rights in land and the environment more generally in that, while an individual property owner/occupier may be disposed to protect the environment,[69] there is no obligation on them to do so.[70] There are, however, already models in place that partially engage with the need to attenuate individual property rights in the name of the broader public interest

---

[64] See eg considering the broader issue of natural capital, within which ESAs are located, MC O'Connor, 'Can you Put a Price on Nature? A Californian Nonprofit Thinks it Can' *Guardian* (13 March 2016).

[65] Constanza and others, 'Changes in the Global Value of Ecosystem Services' (n 35) at 157.

[66] TEEB (n 38) at 12.

[67] DR Bell, 'Liberal Environmental Citizenship' (2005) 14(2) *Environmental Politics* 179, 180.

[68] See eg G Monbiot, 'Putting a Price on the Rivers and Rain Diminishes us all' *Guardian* (6 August 2012).

[69] As eg NGOs running preserves—discussed in Vivanco, 'Green Encounters' (n 20).

[70] Discussed at length in Stone (n 8).

in the environment. Some are primarily negative in their approach, employing various forms of coercive control—for example, requiring the grant of state permission in order to lawfully develop land; or rendering certain activities unlawful (such as the use of fertiliser in areas vulnerable to nitrate pollution) in the name of environmental protection. Such regimes are often contentious and generate considerable potential for legal challenge. PES on the other hand offers a species of positive incentivisation, which like certain nature conservation initiatives, pays landowners/occupiers to act, or refrain from acting, for the benefit of the environment, albeit in the narrower context of species or habitat protection. However, this type of approach too has proven contentious, not least in generating property rights based litigation.[71] In any case, it is arguable that, where PES are concerned, individual property rights would need to undergo considerable adaptation and may only play a role within broader arrangements countenancing the public interest in order to be applied effectively to the governance of ESAs.[72]

Additionally, where PES are concerned, reasoning by extension from the approach adopted to the similarly artificial market-based construct of tradeable emissions permits,[73] they could be construed as intangible property. In the alternative, PES could be treated as akin to an environmental licence/permit—which may be more apposite as they are conditional upon mandated behaviours being observed; they would also constitute property on this view.[74] There are important commonalities between tradeable emissions permits and environmental licences in that they offer individual benefit to their owners, chiefly in allowing them to operate lawfully, albeit against a backdrop of realising regulatory priorities in the public interest (and in the former case profiting from efficiency in so doing); PES are not quite analogous, in that they incentivise certain actions/refraining therefrom by landowners/occupiers in the public interest, but this alone would not preclude like treatment being accorded to them.

B. Other Human Rights, Rights for Nature and ESAs

In terms of accommodating the broader public interest in ESAs, both the compulsive and incentivist approaches referred to above are strongly statist in their orientation and essentially bipartite in nature, focusing on the relationship between the state as regulator/incentive provider and landowners/occupiers; the statist focus is ameliorated only to the extent that the strategies employed effectively incorporate public participation. Delivering meaningful public participation would be

---

[71] See K Morrow, 'European Habitat Conservation Activities and Individual Property Rights: Law and the Meaning of LIFE' (2009) 17 *Italian American Law Digest* 301.

[72] See RA Barnes, The Capacity of Property Rights to Accommodate Social-Ecological Resilience' (2013) 18(1) *Ecology and Society* 6.

[73] See *Armstrong DLW GmbH v Winnington Networks Ltd* (n 63).

[74] See *In re Celtic Extraction Ltd* [2001] Ch 475, in which the Court found that a waste management licence fell within the definition of 'property' under s 436 of the Insolvency Act 1986.

particularly demanding in respect of ESAs and PES, given that many ecosystem services provide for complex, indivisible, social and/or collective goods, rather than the 'things' (provisioning services partially excepted) that form the traditional province of private property. This renders the extension of property rights in their traditional form into this emerging arena inherently problematic, largely because the collective benefits in question extend well beyond individual landowners to neighbouring communities, regions and even (in some cases) the globe, and are highly unsuitable subjects for individuation.

Furthermore, when private property rights have been extended into new realms in the past, as for example with the introduction of individual ownership regimes to land previously held in common through enclosure,[75] and under colonialism, this has proved highly problematic.[76] Such developments saw the introduction of individual property into spheres that had previously accommodated collective resource-holding regimes and the associated concentration of economic benefit in the hands of a privileged, wealthy, minority at the expense of excluded, poor, minorities.[77] These developments commodified[78] and corporatised[79] land as a resource, generating conflict and adverse social and environmental impacts. In the context of the former, Richards points out that:

> Perhaps the most typical conflict … is that over the exploitation of a natural resource that has become valuable and marketable. … Issues of stability, tradition, and nostalgia are pitted against the excitement of new wealth and productivity in internecine elite conflict.[80]

In respect of the environmental problems that have arisen in this context, Rangarajan observes that: '[t]he twin themes of the decline of older patterns of land-use and the degradation of ecosystems are interwoven'.[81] It seems reasonable to infer that, as PES commodify collective ecosystem services which are themselves attached to land, they have the potential to generate similar social and environmental conflicts.

Likewise, there are also potential parallels to be drawn between the introduction of PES and the creation of both government[82] and non-governmental organisation (NGO) owned habitat and species preserves for study/ecotourism,[83] in employing (now largely discredited)[84] 'fortress conservation', effectively commodifying

---

[75] Monbiot, 'Putting a Price on the Rivers and Rain Diminishes us all' (n 68).

[76] JF Richards, 'Toward a Global System of Property Rights in Land' in E Burke III and K Pomeranz (eds), *The Environment in World History* (Berkeley, University of California, 2009).

[77] See eg International Institute for Environment and Development, 'Markets and Payments for Environmental Services', available at: www.iied.org/markets-payments-for-environmental-services.

[78] Richards, 'Toward a Global System of Property Rights in Land' (n 76) at 58.

[79] ibid, 71.

[80] ibid, 73.

[81] M Rangarajan, 'Environmental Histories of India: Of States, Landscapes, and Ecologies' in Burke and Pomeranz (eds,), *The Environment in World History* (n 76) at 238.

[82] See J Roberts, *Environmental Policy*, 2nd edn (Abingdon, Routledge, 2011) 79–80.

[83] See Vivanco (n 20).

[84] ibid, 55–56.

aspects of ecosystems: appropriating control of them; deriving income from them; and excluding local/indigenous communities from benefits and resources to which they traditionally had access. In all of these cases, the traditional human element of the ecosystems in question is effectively stripped out and replaced with a modern one, which can pay for the privilege.

In recent times precisely such closures have been important in promoting the use of human rights claims based on broadly environmental grounds—a development that has, at least in part, been the product of the failure of environmental law to adequately address the pressure points posed by the impacts of environmental degradation on people.[85] This has been an essentially pragmatic course of action, but it has proved complex and piecemeal and it is not an unalloyed success. Nonetheless, it is now an established part of the international legal landscape,[86] and it may have some application to tempering the adverse impacts of ESAs on the interests of human communities and by extension (at least in some cases) on the natural world. At the very least, in potentially extending the range of relevant considerations beyond the purely economic, importing certain classes of human rights-based argument can serve to open up the issues up to fuller consideration.

A potential corrective to an individual property rights focus in ESAs, and one that more accurately reflects the broader role and value of ecosystem services, could be achieved by employing rights claims in order to give legal cognisance to the fact that many of them—in particular those falling into the regulating, supporting and cultural categories are, wholly or in part, collective and indivisible in nature. Thus safeguarding the interests of the people who benefit from these ecosystem services, but do not own the host land, would require a novel form of engagement with human rights, eschewing the solely individualistic focus that dominates current human rights law in favour of a more collective slant. This type of approach found expression in the soft-law United Nations Declaration on the Rights of Indigenous Peoples[87] (UNDRIP) which (although it does not specifically refer to ecosystems) not only recognises the conception of collective rights in respect of the environment,[88] but also that these are founded upon a very different conception of the relationship between humanity and the environment than that which prevails in current thought. The former is evident in the Declaration's

---

[85] P Simons: 'Selectivity in Law-making: Regulating Extraterritorial Environmental Harm and Human Rights Violations by Transnational Extractive Corporations' in A Grear and L Kotze (eds), *Research Handbook on Human Rights and the Environment* (Cheltenham, Edward Elgar, 2015) points out that international environmental law instruments tend to be particularly lacking in terms of compliance mechanisms in comparison to international human rights law regimes; at 486.

[86] K Conca, 'Environmental Governance After Johannesburg: From Stalled Legalization to Environmental Human Rights' (2005) 1 *Journal of International Law and International Relations* 122, 133.

[87] United Nations General Assembly (2007) Resolution 61/295 'Declaration on the Rights of Indigenous Peoples (UNDRIP), available at: www.un.org/esa/socdev/unpfii/documents/DRIPS_en.pdf.

[88] M Barelli, 'The Role of Soft Law in the International Legal System: the Case of the United Nations Declaration on the Rights of Indigenous Peoples' (2009) 58(4) *International and Comparative Law Quarterly* 957.

acknowledgement of the right of indigenous peoples, as collective entities, to the: 'conservation and protection of the environment and the productive capac- ity of their lands or territories and resources' and consequent invocation of state obligations in this regard.[89] The latter finds partial expression in the preambular provision which recognises that: 'respect for indigenous knowledge, cultures and traditional practices contributes to sustainable and equitable development and proper management of the environment' and in the body text in relation to pro- tection for indigenous:

> cultural heritage, traditional knowledge and traditional cultural expressions, as well as the manifestations of their sciences, technologies and cultures, including human and genetic resources, seeds, medicines, knowledge of the properties of fauna and flora [etc.]'

and intellectual property therein;[90] coupled with rights to determine resource development/use within their lands or territories; and associated rights of redress for interference (including express reference to environmental impacts) with them.[91] These provisions are sufficiently broadly drafted to accommodate all classes of eco- system services and, read together, they arguably combine to situate our understand- ing of those services in a more realistic social and environmental fashion than an individualistic, property-rights style model can ever do. Nonetheless, on one level it is possible to argue that the UNDRIP approach is still essentially anthropocentric in its rights-based approach to humans and nature; this interpretation is not however borne out when considered against the background of indigenous cosmologies, as expressed for instance in the 2000 Earth Charter,[92] and latterly, more specifically, in the 2010 Universal Declaration of the Rights of Mother Earth (UDRME),[93] the preamble of which states that: 'we are all part of Mother Earth, an indivisible, liv- ing community of interrelated and interdependent beings with a common destiny'. This view, founded on a common feature of many indigenous cosmologies, cru- cially belies the paradigm of mastery, breaking down artificial distinctions between humanity and nature. This type of approach has also played a key role in pioneering theoretical work, both philosophical[94] and jurisprudential, challenging the way in which we regard the relationship between humanity and the environment. In the latter category, Stone famously made the case for changing the way law treats the natural world by extending rights claims to it, arguing that:

> the notion of something having a 'right' … brings into the legal system a flexibility and open-endedness that no series of specifically stated legal rules … can capture. Part of

---

[89] UNDRIP (n 87) Art 29.

[90] ibid, Art 31.

[91] ibid, Art 32.

[92] See http://earthcharter.org/invent/images/uploads/echarter_english.pdf.

[93] The Universal Declaration of the Rights of Mother Earth (UDRME), available at: http://therightsofnature.org/universal-declaration/.

[94] See eg the pioneering A Leopold, *A Sand County Almanac* (Oxford, Oxford University Press, 1968) and, more recently, C Cullinan, *Wild Law: A Manifesto for Earth Jurisprudence*, 2nd edn (White River Junction, Vermont, Chelsea Green Publishing Co, 2011).

the reason is that 'right[s]' ... have meaning—vague but forceful—in the ordinary language and the force of these meanings, inevitably infused with our thought, becomes part of the context against which the 'legal language' of our contemporary 'legal rules' is interpreted.[95]

The extension of legal rights to nature could provide a further counterbalance to naked human economic interest in the conception of ecosystem services. This type of approach was argued for in the Global Scenario Group's[96] Great Transition Report, which sought to promote a 'rights revolution' in defence of the biosphere by invoking the 'inviolable rights of people and nature' through developing a 'natural communities and ecosystems' based approach towards rights for nature.[97] The idea of rights for nature continues to be very much a live issue for debate and activism in the international arena,[98] expressed for example in the Rights of Mother Earth Treaty (part of the Peoples Sustainability Treaties (PSTs) initiative begun in the run up to the UNCSD in 2012)[99] which begins by recognising the: 'inherent rights of 'Mother Earth and all ecosystems and species of which she is composed';[100] and in the ongoing work of the International Rights of Nature Tribunal[101] (itself rooted in the UDRME).

C. The Limits to Rights: The Question of Responsibility

Even were we to develop a more nuanced, less individualistically focused conception of rights in respect of ecosystem services and to extend rights coverage to nature itself, it is arguable that this would still be insufficient in and of itself to fully address the issues raised by ESAs. The less prominent, but emergent question of human responsibility may offer an interesting complementary avenue which could be pursued to this end. Whilst the notion of legally embodying individual human responsibilities tends to have fairly limited reach in the current,

[95] Stone (n 8) at 488.
[96] The Global Scenario Group (GSG) presents itself as an international, independent, interdisciplinary group that focuses on sustainability, available at: www.gsg.org/gsgintro.html.
[97] P Raskin, T Banuri, G Gallopin, P Gutman, A Hammond, R Kates and R Swart, 'Great Transition: The Promise and Lure of the Times Ahead' (Global Scenario Group, Stockholm Environment Institute, 2002) 59. The report, which represented the culmination of the GSG's activities, was the product of a global initiative, drawing on the work of hundreds of scholars and activists.
[98] There is also considerable state activity in this regard in some states, not least Bolivia and Ecuador, which has been the subject of considerable scholarly interest, and critique; see eg J Jaria i Manzano, 'The Rights of Nature in Ecuador: An Opportunity to Reflect on Society, Law and Environment' in RV Percival, J Lin and W Piermattei (eds), *Global Environmental Law at a Crossroads* (Cheltenham, IUCN Academy/Edward Elgar, 2014).
[99] K Morrow, 'Peoples Sustainability Treaties at Rio+20: Giving Voice to the Other' in P Burdon and M Maloney (eds), *Wild Law—In Practice* (Abingdon, Routledge Glasshouse, 2014).
[100] Peoples Sustainability Treaties (2012), available at: https://sustainabilitytreaties.org/.
[101] http://therightsofnature.org/rights-of-nature-tribunal-paris/.

state-oriented human rights canon,[102] it occasionally becomes a live issue even in mainstream human rights debate.[103] Employing the notion of responsibility in an environmental context tends to be viewed rather more enthusiastically, rooting the notion in both moral and practical terms:

> we, the most powerful species on earth, have the capability to destroy, create, modify and otherwise affect the ecosystems of the planet, their life forms and our own future.[104]

Invoking individual and collective human responsibility towards the environment would place a limit on the pursuit of rights, responding to the unique position of humans as ecosystem actors in respect of other humans and other life forms. Such an approach is not without precedent; for example, the moral and ethical need to exercise ecological responsibility *qua* future generations of humans (though not in terms of nature in its own right) featured in the 1997 United Nations Educational, Scientific and Cultural Organization (UNESCO) Declaration on the Responsibilities of the Present Generations Towards Future Generations.[105] Article 4 of this document, on the 'Preservation of life on Earth', states that:

> Each generation inheriting the Earth temporarily should take care to use natural resources reasonably and ensure that life is not prejudiced by harmful modifications of the ecosystems and that scientific and technological progress in all fields does not harm life on Earth.

The idea of human responsibility tends to be more prominently endorsed by environmental activists than their human rights counterparts and it has re-emerged in Article 3 of the UDRME, which delineates broad-ranging and detailed obligations applicable to all human beings to: 'respect, protect, conserve and where necessary, restore the integrity, of the vital ecological cycles, processes and balances of Mother Earth'.[106] PSTs too considered this issue, notably in the Charter of Universal Responsibilities (CUR),[107] which advocated an expansion of human rights-based approaches that recognised the 'interdependences' between 'humankind and the biosphere'[108] and an 'awareness of our shared responsibilities to the planet' as a 'condition for the survival and progress of humankind'.[109] These days

---

[102] See eg the International Council on Human Rights Policy, 'Taking Duties Seriously: Individual Duties in International Human Rights Law—A Commentary' (1999) available at: www.ichrp.org/files/reports/10/103_report_en.pdf.

[103] Notably in a civil society context, see the 1997 Inter Action Council, A Universal Declaration of Human Responsibilities, http://interactioncouncil.org/universal-declaration-human-responsibilities.

[104] ST Trudgill, Barriers to a Better Environment: What Stops us Solving Environmental Problems? (London, Belhaven Press, 1990) 13.

[105] Available at: http://portal.unesco.org/en/ev.php-URL_ID=13178&URL_DO=DO_TOPIC&URL_SECTION=201.html.

[106] UDRME (n 93) Art 2(f).

[107] Available at: https://docs.google.com/viewer?url=http%3A%2F%2Fsustainabilitytreaties.files.wordpress.com%2F2012%2F05%2Fpeoples-sustainability-treaty-on-a-charter-of-universal-responsibility-draft-for-rio20.pdf.

[108] ibid, Principle 1.

[109] ibid, Principle 5.

we can ill-afford to scoff at such thinking as mere idealism—instead, in light of the enmeshed environmental crises we face and the potential existential threats that they pose, it should be viewed an expression of realism.

Were ESAs to be engaged with through a sustainability lens, then their environmental importance would be the prime consideration, the base line against which their social and economic importance would be assessed and invoking broader rights talk in this regard could help to achieve the reorientation necessary to render them ecologically literate and effective.

V. Conclusion

All things have their time, and the shift from the newly, if still informally, recognised Anthropocene to what may be termed the biocene may well be inevitable; such a transition, instituted by damaging the ecosystem services that promote human flourishing and breaching Earth system tipping points, is likely to occur in less than the blink of an eye in comparison to that between other epochs. The role of humanity in the epoch to come remains to be seen, for while life will continue to flourish, albeit perhaps in very different ways, humanity may not. As Emily Dickinson puts it:

> How much can come
>
> And much can go,
>
> And yet abide the World![110]

For now, our destiny is (at least partly) in our own hands. The continued flourishing of humanity will, however, require nothing less than a new ecological enlightenment. This cannot take the form of an anti-anthropocentric model—in light of humanity's distinctive position within the biosphere this would be at best implausible (if not impossible)[111]—but must rather entail the adoption of a new worldview. This must be ecologically contextualised and fully understand what it means to be human; embedded in the environment, but also in a unique position to shape and influence it—and see us act accordingly.

---

[110] From E Dickinson, 'There came a Wind like a Bugle' in A Oswald (ed), *The Thunder Mutters: 101 Poems for the Planet* (London, Faber and Faber, 2005), 24.
[111] Kaldis (n 22) at 87.

13

The Corporation and the Anthropocene

SALLY WHEELER

I. Introduction

The corporation, with its own heritage of anthropomorphic descriptions,[1] is one of the key creations of the Anthropocene epoch—although the precise dating of the start of the Anthropocene might be a matter for discussion,[2] there can be no doubt that the corporate form has been in existence across even the suggested longest reaches of the period. So successful has the corporation been, particularly in the years from 1850 or so onwards, as an accumulator of property and a distributor of wealth, that for some commentators the descriptor of the current epoch should be 'Capitalocene'[3] rather than Anthropocene.[4] Corporate capital expenditure decisions and global supply chains, designed in boardrooms to satisfy the capital return ambitions of investors, dominate global production, dictate global consumption and presently shape the future of the biosphere through their use of resources and their impact on the environment.[5] Corporations are, in terms of their ability to impact on lives and local environments, the dominant institution in global society and yet have the ability to be a transient presence across geographical locations.[6] In general terms states have been, if not happy, then certainly

---

[1] L Johnson, 'Law and Legal Theory in the History of Corporate Responsibility: Corporate Personhood' (2012) 35 *Seattle University Law Review* 1135–64.

[2] For a succinct discussion of historical timelines and dates, see J Zalasiewicz, M Williams, W Steffen and P Crutzen, 'The New World of the Anthropocene' (2010) 44 *Environmental Science and Technology* 2228–31; and J Oak Taylor, *The Sky of Our Manufacture* (Charlottesville, University of Virginia Press, 2016) 193–200.

[3] D Haraway, 'Anthropocene, Capitalocene, Plantationocene, Chthulucene: Making Kin' (2015) 6 *Environmental Humanities* 159–65. See the discussion at n 6 for the origin of the term *Capitalocene*.

[4] G Di Chiro, 'Environmental Justice and the Anthropocene Meme' in J Meyer and others (eds), *The Oxford Handbook of Environmental Political Theory* (Oxford, Oxford University Press, 2016) 362–81.

[5] P Crutzen and C Schwägerl, 'Living in the Anthropocene: Towards a New Global Ethos' (2011) *Yale Environment* 360 available at: http://e360.yale.edu/feature/living_in_the_anthropocene_toward_a_new_global_ethos/2363

[6] T Gladwin, 'The Global Environmental Crisis and Management Education' (1993) 3 *Total Quality Environmental Management* 109–14.

complicit, in conceding power in these areas to the neoliberal market economy for a variety of reasons depending on their stage of development,[7] the nature of their statehood,[8] and geopolitical security. The Global Financial Crisis, ironically, resulted in even greater divestment by developed states, pursuing policies of austerity, of services provided for citizens to the private sector thus entrenching and extending corporate influence still further in states such as the United Kingdom where the greatest opportunity for some sort of curtailment of corporate aggrandisement had been present.[9]

Part II of this chapter examines the connections between globalisation, the corporate form and the degradation of the Earth's ecological systems. Following ideas from environmental justice[10] and environmental history,[11] it looks at how the intersection of these three phenomena has produced huge inequalities across geographical regions and within individual societies. For reasons of space and contrast it offers a stereotypical account of capitalist endeavour and the corporate form that underpins it. Consequently, it does not attempt to capture some of the nuances that can be identified around the fringes of corporate behaviour such as philanthrocapitalism,[12] or conscious capitalism.[13] Part III of the chapter looks at a possible brake on corporate behaviour in the form of corporate social responsibility and at a philosophically grounded alternative distributive mechanism in the form of stakeholding that has been suggested as a way of making the corporate form more responsive to a wider range of interests, including non-human ones. Both of these approaches are ultimately rejected in favour of a new ethical model to underpin corporate activities that is explored in the final section of the chapter. This model is based on the work of Emmanuel Levinas. The ecological time bomb that is the Anthropocene has corporate activity at its centre,[14] and whilst corporate

---

[7] J Rigg and K Oven, 'Building Liberal Resilience? A Critical Review from Developing Rural Asia' (2015) 32 *Global Environmental Change* 175–86 offers a detailed review of the linkage between policies of market liberalisation and economic growth.

[8] The idea of 'limited' statehood articulated by Risse is particularly useful in the context of environmental degradation, corporations and states. Limited statehood, Risse argues, describes states which lack full domestic sovereignty (ie are unable to make and/or enforce laws) either in relation to territorial spaces, sectors of the population or, most importantly in this context, specific policy areas; see T Risse, 'Governance in Areas of Limited Statehood' in T Risse (ed), *Governance Without A State* (New York, Columbia University Press, 2011) 1–37.

[9] D Cowan and S Wheeler, 'The Reach of Human Rights' in T Xu and J Allain (eds), *Property and Human Rights in a Global Context* (Oxford, Hart Publishing, 2016) 197–221.

[10] J Carmin and J Agyeman (eds), *Environmental Inequalities Beyond Borders* (Cambridge, MA, MIT, 2011).

[11] R Nixon, *Slow Violence and the Environmentalism of the Poor* (Cambridge, Harvard University Press, 2013).

[12] L McGoey, 'Philanthrocapitalism and its Critics' (2012) 40 *Poetics* 185–99.

[13] N Farrell, '"Conscience Capitalism" and the Neoliberalisation of the Non-Profit Sector' (2015) 20 *New Political Economy* 254–72

[14] This has echoes of the point made by Ellis and Trachtenberg that the Anthropocene has a moral core; it is not about evolving science and technology or about judging the consequences of humanity dominating nature but about dealing with 'human responsibility' for global environmental changes; see M Ellis and Z Trachtenberg, 'Which Anthropocene is it to be? Beyond Geology to a Moral and Public Discourse' (2013) 2 *Earth's Future* 122–25, 123.

ethics in the form of Kantian or Aristotelian inspired ethics have become familiar discourses to those working in business ethics, neither of them has managed to lay out a way forward that moves beyond a broad calculation of rationally defined self-interest set out in a codification of the 'ethical'. This chapter suggests that Levinasian ethics can do this.

II. Situating Corporate Behaviour

The consequences of human activities, perhaps most acutely explicated by global warming, are reshaping the natural environment. In geophysical terms this means that extreme weather conditions,[15] desertification and rising sea levels[16] are all occurring so regularly and quickly[17] there is the potential for the Earth to become a very different living space,[18] 'practically a different planet'[19] if climate change continues at even a substantially reduced pace.[20] In the context of the Paris climate negotiations in 2015,[21] commentators have cast doubt on the ability of global actors to hold temperature rises to no more than 2 degrees Celsius;[22] while predicting potentially devastating consequences[23] for island nations and those heavily dependent on subsistence agriculture. In terms of human action there has been population growth in the last three centuries from 6 billion inhabitants to a projected 10 billion by the end of the 21st century; more nitrogen-based fertiliser is used than can be absorbed naturally by the terrestrial ecosystem and more than 50 per cent of accessible freshwater is used by humans.[24] Land grabbing by transnational corporations (TNCs) for large-scale biofuel production or by financially

---

[15] These will affect high population areas as well as isolated islands; see K Emanuel, 'Increasing Destructiveness of Tropical Cyclones over the Past 30 years' (2005) 436 *Nature* 686–88.

[16] J Barnett and W Adger, 'Climate Dangers and Atoll Countries' (2003) 61 *Climate Change* 321–327.

[17] Muller estimates that in recent decades the number of people affected by weather-related disasters has quadrupled; see B Muller, *Equity in Climate Change* (Oxford, Oxford Institute for Energy Studies, 2002) 4.

[18] A McMichael, 'Globalization, Climate Change and Human Health' (2013) 368 *New England Journal of Medicine* 1335–43.

[19] See T Flannery, *The Weather Makers: How Man is Changing the Climate and What It Means for Life on Earth* (New York, Atlantic Press, 2005) where he suggests that continuing emissions could lead to a collapse of civilisation.

[20] M Meinshaussen and others, 'Greenhouse-gas Emission Targets for Limiting Global Warming to 2°C' (2009) 458 *Nature* 1158.

[21] 2015 United Nations Climate Change Conference held in Paris from 20 November to 12 December 2015.

[22] The idea of restricting climate change to a 2 degree rise above pre-Industrial Revolution levels was contained in the Copenhagen Accord in 2009 and was agreed to in the 2010 Cancun Agreement.

[23] A Pfeiffer, R Millar, C Hepburn and E Beinhocker, 'The "2 C Capital Stock" for Electricity Generation: Committed Cumulative Carbon Emissions from the Electricity Generation Sector and the Transition to a Green Economy' (2016) 179 *Applied Energy* 1395–408, http://dx.doi.org/10.1016/j.apenergy.2016.02.093.

[24] P Crutzen, 'Geology of Mankind' (2002) 415 *Nature* 23.

wealthy but resource poor states for their domestic food security, often occurs in some of the poorest and least developed regions of the world—Africa and Eurasia for example—with the result that indigenous populations are forced, at best, into using global food markets rather than relying on their own locally produced food. They suffer food insecurity so that privileged others in more developed countries do not.[25] At worst, these indigenous populations become migrants in search of other spaces to cultivate. Land-use change on this scale often involves deforestation, soil erosion, pressure on water resources and the redesignation of fertile food producing land to fuel producing land.[26]

The painful effects of the Anthropocene are not borne equally by the world's inhabitants; ecological disasters caused by climate change, resource extraction, inappropriately placed production facilities, or by rapid change of land use, tend to occur where the most impoverished live.[27] The poorest nations on Earth contribute less than 1 per cent of the carbon emissions that drive climate change[28] and those who rely on subsistence agriculture have less resilience to withstand and adapt to changing weather patterns, for example. This inequity is part of the double exposure that some populations have to the negative impacts of both environmental change and the processes of globalisation.[29] For example, the Arctic Region is resource rich and resources extracted from there are used both as components in product manufacture and to power the very same manufacturing process. The inhabitants of the Arctic region suffer the negative impacts of resource extraction *and* the negative impacts of global environmental change on their fragile relationship with nature.[30]

The Anthropocene clearly is made up of a 'constellation' of events that play out in different ways for different groups as a result of complex political and social power structures.[31] These structures transcend the power and borders of individual states. They are assemblages of bilateral investment treaties, development assistance and actors such as finance organisations, non-governmental

---

[25] P McMichael, 'The Land Grab and Corporate Food Regime Restructuring' (2012) 39 *Journal of Peasant Studies* 681–701.

[26] As S Borras and J Franco, 'Global Land Grabbing and Trajectories of Agrarian Change: A Preliminary Analysis' (2012) 12 *Journal of Agrarian Change* 34–59 point out there are also potentially crucial long-term and life-changing effects in property relations and in the social and political processes involved in land-use change. As yet, we know rather less about these than we do about the obvious environmental effects.

[27] S Barca, 'Telling the Right Story: Environmental Violence and Liberation Narratives' (2014) 20 *Environment and History* 535–46.

[28] W Steffen, A Persson, L Deutsch and others, 'The Anthropocene: from Global Change to Planetary Stewardship' (2011) 40 *Ambio* 739–61.

[29] R Leichenko and K O'Brien, *Environmental Change and Globalization: Double Exposures* (Oxford, Oxford University Press, 2008) and K O'Brien and R Leichenko, 'Winners and Losers in the Context of Global Change' (2003) 93 *Annals American Geographers* 89–103.

[30] L Ogden and others, 'Assemblages, Resilience, and Earth Stewardship in the Anthropocene' (2013) 11 *Frontiers Ecology and the Environment* 341–47.

[31] A Hoffman and P Jennings, 'Institutional Theory and the Natural Environment: Research in (and on) the Anthropocene' (2015) 28 *Organization and Environment* 8–31, 19.

organisations (NGOs) and, most significantly, large corporations. Earth itself has an important role in these assemblages—it is not a passive observer—resource location for exploitation and life support is key to these assemblages. Poorer states are pulled into these assemblages through the exploitation and export of natural resources and/or through being able to supply almost unlimited low-cost labour.[32] For them the possibility of development and growth hangs on this, but it is also the case that states with this typology are most vulnerable to the vagaries of global market movements and have populations that are least able to withstand either economic or natural shocks. The result is increasing inequality and vulnerability. It is the corporation's place at the front and centre of these assemblages as the vehicle for accumulation that makes the label 'Capitalocene' so attractive.

As I argue below, it is the basic form and shape of the corporation as it emerged as a capital generating vehicle in the years post the Industrial Revolution that makes it ideally suited to capturing the gains of the 'Capitalocene', holding them closely and perhaps later distributing some of them as dividends but across a very narrow field of privileged beneficiaries. Whilst the label 'Capitalocene' captures the idea that what has driven global climate change is not a single event underwritten by humanity in general, but a series of interventions over at least the last two centuries[33] that has transformed nature into capital, in effect, at a much higher cost for some than others,[34] it does risk disguising the reality of the Anthropocene. This reality is that the effects of the Anthropocene will be felt by all, albeit unevenly. Thus '*Anthropos*', emphasising the totality of the crisis, should be the underpinning idea rather than what might be seen as a focus on a limited capital accruing or benefiting class.[35]

The external governance context of corporate activity in relation to climate change is about its amelioration. This takes place in a framework created by intergovernmental agreements (for example the Paris Climate Agreement of 2015 in which 186 states submitted emission reduction promises and the United Nations Framework Conventions on Climate Change) and interpreted by nation states (for example the UK Climate Change Act 2008, South Africa's National Climate Change Response White Paper 2011) into national level policies.[36] Some corporations devise adaptions to their business models, partly in response to the saliencies

---

[32] A Tsing, *The Mushroom at the End of the World: On the Possibility of Life in Capitalist Ruins* (Princeton New Jersey, Princeton University Press, 2016).

[33] K Rigby, *Dancing with Disaster: Environmental Histories, Narratives, and Ethics for Perilous Times* (Charlottesville, University of Virginia Press, 2015).

[34] S Barca, 'Energy, Property, and the Industrial Revolution Narrative' (2011) 70 *Ecological Economics* 1309–15.

[35] R Rowan, 'Notes on Politics after the Anthropocene' (2014) 38 *Progress in Human Geography* 447–50; and A Grear, 'Deconstructing Anthropos: A Critical Legal Reflection on 'Anthropocentric' Law and Anthropocene "Humanity"' (2015) 26 *Law and Critique* 225, 237f.

[36] The database of national level legislation on climate change maintained by the Grantham Research Institute at the LSE contains over 800 pieces of legislation. See also *2015 Global Climate Change Legislation Study* www.lse.ac.uk/GranthamInstitute/publication/2015-global-climate-legislation-study/.

of these policies,[37] although many do not as they do not see climate change as an important short-term risk.[38] Climate change offers a different level of risk to different business sectors and the corporations within them.[39] Energy-intensive industries are likely to face greater regulation certainly at the supranational level and possibly more financial risks in relation to stranded assets.[40] This point is expanded upon below in the discussion of investor priorities in marshalling financial gain. Some corporations have organisational structures that allow them to be more innovative in their mitigation of climate change risk through product development or process modification, for example.[41]

The broad picture of regulatory response at national level (obviously the specifics of individual national regimes differ) is a combination of government-made market-based controls of environmental pollution[42]—corporations can trade carbon by purchasing emission credits and engage in offsetting emissions[43] by contributing to foresting,[44] for example—and to a lesser extent taxation regimes that create funds for reinvestment in smart technology, renewable energy and so on. The role of the corporate sector in influencing policy choice and shape cannot be overestimated.[45] The response to climate change is, then, one that from the regulatory perspective exists at a number of different levels, but from the corporate perspective is a series of national prescriptions with individual corporations and the emissions they produce being portable across nation states.[46]

The current structure of the corporate form is characterised by limited liability for shareholders—thus separating risk and liability incurred by corporate managers from the corporate perspective from the potential loss of personal

---

[37] *Climate Change Action and Profitability* (2014) CPD North America www.cdp.net/CDPResults/CDP-SP500-leaders-report-2014.pdf.

[38] According to PwC's 19th Annual Global CEO Survey of January 2016 climate change was ranked alongside unemployment and access to affordable capital as the risks of least threat to growth in the near future. Over-regulation was seen as the most significant threat; see www.pwc.com/gx/en/ceo-agenda/ceosurvey/2016.html.

[39] F Kapfudzaruwa, 'Corporate Response to Climate Change in Areas of Limited Statehood: An Outline of the Organizational Configurations in Kenya and South Africa' in T Börzel and R Hamann (eds), *Business and Climate Governance* (Basingstoke, Palgrave MacMillan, 2013) 31–54.

[40] See the speech of Mark Carney, Governor of the Bank of England, to Lloyds of London on the financial risks to investors of stranded assets, 29 September 2015. www.bankofengland.co.uk/publications/Pages/speeches/2015/844.aspx.

[41] A Kolk and J Pinkse, 'Business Responses to Climate Change: Identifying Emergent Strategies' (2005) 47 *California Management Review* 6–20; and W Stubbs and C Cocklin, 'Conceptualizing a "Sustainability Business Model"' (2008) 21 *Organization and Environment* 103–27.

[42] AD Ellerman and others, *Markets for Clean Air: The U.S. Acid Rain Program* (Cambridge, Cambridge University Press, 2010) 253f.

[43] H Lovell and D Liverman, 'Understanding Carbon Offset Technologies' (2010) 15 *New Political Economy* 255.

[44] R Bayon and others, *Voluntary Carbon Markets* (London, Earthscan, 2007); on carbon sinks, see M Gutiérrez, 'Making Markets Out of Thin Air: A Case of Capital Involution' (2011) 43 *Antipode* 639.

[45] J Meckling, *Carbon Coalitions: Business, Climate Politics, and the Rise of Emissions Trading* (Cambridge Mass, MIT, 2011).

[46] J Aragón-Correa and others, 'The Natural Environmental Strategies of International Firms: Old Controversies and New Evidence on Performance and Disclosure' (2016) 30 *Academy of Management Perspectives* 24–39.

wealth for shareholders. As Adam Smith commented, limited liability encourages many people to become investors 'who would.......[not] hazard their fortunes in any [unlimited] copartnery'.[47] Limited liability became available in England[48] in 1855[49] through legislative intervention[50] and subsequent judicial amelioration of the ultra vires doctrine[51] allowed corporations to expand their business endeavours almost without limit. What began as a derogation of authority from the sovereign, and later the state,[52] to pursue particular and limited purposes usually for public gain, became, as it remains today, a right[53] to accumulate and insulate wealth for private gain, tightly held.[54] Limited liability was accompanied by the rise of the rentier investor.[55] The emergence of a market for company stock[56] as opposed to lower yield government bonds created the opportunity for relatively risk-free capital growth across a portfolio of shareholdings. The tradability of shares reduced the need for these investors to engage themselves in the management of the corporation; they ceased to be *owner-managers* and instead employed professional managers to act on their behalf.

From the early years of the twentieth century onwards, corporations have been increasingly characterised by this separation of ownership and control, with 'ownership' resting with shareholders[57] and day-to-day control residing with managers. Large institutional investors such as insurance funds, pension funds and investment funds[58] dominate the ownership of shares in listed companies across the world. In these circumstances corporate managers are in place to maximise

---

[47] A Smith, *An Inquiry into the Nature and Causes of the Wealth of Nations* Book V.i.e.18 (1776) (Oxford, Clarendon edn) 741.

[48] For an account of this development in the US, see J Chausovsky, 'State Regulation of Corporations in the Late Nineteenth Century: a Critique of the New Jersey Thesis' (2007) 21 *Studies in American Political Development* 30–65.

[49] See M Djelic and J Bothello, 'Limited Liability and its Moral Hazard Implications: the Systemic Inscription of Instability in Contemporary Capitalism' (2013) 42 *Theory and Society* 589–615 at 599f for a historically orientated discussion of limited liability.

[50] Limited Liability Act 1855.

[51] *Attorney General v Great Eastern Railway Company* (1880) 5 AC 473.

[52] M Horwitz, 'Santa Clara Revisited: The Development of Corporate Theory' (1985) 88 *West Virginia Law Review* 173–224.

[53] Incorporation became available as a right upon completion of the relevant formalities as a result of the Joint Stock Companies Act 1856.

[54] C Perrow, *Organising America: Wealth, Power and the Origins of Corporate Capitalism* (Princeton New Jersey, Princeton University Press, 2002).

[55] P Ireland, 'Limited Liability, Shareholder Rights and the Problem of Corporate Irresponsibility' (2010) 34 *Cambridge Journal of Economics* 837–56.

[56] P Ireland, I Grigg-Spall and D Kelly, 'The Conceptual Foundations of Modern Company Law' (1987) 14 *Journal of Legal Studies* 149.

[57] The legal nature of the shareholder's interest in the corporation is shrouded in conceptual confusion, much of which is brilliantly dissected by Paddy Ireland in 'Company Law and the Myth of Shareholder Ownership' (1999) 62 *Modern Law Review* 32–57. Ownership is used in the text above in a purely colloquial sense to indicate control of major corporate constitutional issues such as board membership.

[58] For detailed numerical information on the growth of institutional investment, see S Çelik and M Isaksson, 'Institutional Investors and Ownership Engagement' (2013) 9 *OECD Journal: Financial Market Trends* 93–114.

shareholder value and as such are agents of shareholders, in an economic[59] sense, if clearly not a legal sense,[60] where the duty is a holistic one to promote the success of the corporation.[61] Other interest groups and stakeholders connected to the corporation, such as those affected by environmentally damaging corporate operations are considered, through the descriptive force of the agency paradigm,[62] to be external to the nexus between shareholders and managers.

What this rather telescopic account of the corporate structure reveals is that the issue is not whether corporations can or will adapt their business models to prevent irreversible environmental damage, but more about the terms on which this question can be asked. The rationale for the corporation is as a vehicle for increasing the capital of shareholders, or providing a return on that capital through the often exclusive and rapacious use of natural resources. The structure of the corporate form in terms of its purpose and its relationships is incompatible with the world's fragile environmental ecosystem. There are circumstances where corporations see first mover advantage in adopting 'clean technology' in production; there can be a competitive advantage achieved by say aggressive marketing or by persuading the appropriate regulator to require less financially secure competitors to also adopt that technology and so raise their product prices. State support for the green economy might be considered as an opportunity for growth if subsidies are made available to support particular strategies. However, this does not lead to corporations adopting all available strategies of environmental protection, but rather simply to them taking available short-term gains.[63]

The shareholdings of many institutional investors are managed on their behalf by financial intermediaries. These intermediaries focus on capital enhancement and return at the expense of commitment to, or oversight of, any individual corporation. Shares are commodities in and of themselves, traded within short-time horizons. There can be no suggestion that the majority of corporate investors have anything approaching a long-term nurturing interest in the corporation in which they hold shares. The Brundtland Report definition of sustainable development as development 'that meets the needs of the present without compromising the ability of future generations to meet their needs'[64] is not capable of being satisfied within the present model of the corporation. Leaving to one

---

[59] J Veldman and H Wilmott, 'What is the Corporation and Why Does it Matter' (2013) 16 M@n@gement 605–20.

[60] Automatic Self-Cleansing Filter v Cuninghame [1906] 2 Ch 34; and C Daily, D Dalton and A Cannella, 'Corporate Governance: Decades of Dialogue and Data' (2003) 28 Academy of Management Review 371–82.

[61] 'Success' of the corporation is the formula found in the relevant UK legislation; Companies Act 2006 s 172. In other common law jurisdictions, the duty is expressed as 'best interests' of the corporation.

[62] J Veldman and H Willmott, 'The Cultural Grammar of Governance: The UK Code of Corporate Governance, Reflexivity, and the Limits of Soft Regulation' (2016) 69 Human Relations 581–603.

[63] V Jankovic and A Bowman, 'After the Green Gold Rush: the Construction of Climate Change as a Market Transition' (2014) 43 Economy and Society 233–59.

[64] Our Common Future (the Bruntdland Report) from the World Commission on Environment and Development (Oxford, Oxford University Press, 1987).

side socially responsible investment (SRI) which has an increasing but still small market share,[65] there is no evidence[66] to suggest that institutional investors, informed by disclosures of carbon consumption through reporting mechanisms such as the Global Reporting Initiative or the Carbon Disclosure Project,[67] use, or will in the future use, their influence to promote climate change mitigation strategies or production process adaptions. The horizon for investment return when the principal-agent nexus of investor and manager defines the corporation, is far too short term for this to occur.[68]

III. Adapting the Model of the Corporation

This section examines two mechanisms—corporate social responsibility (CSR), and stakeholding—that have gained some traction[69] as possible ways in which the shareholder focus of the principal-agent corporation has been, or can be, diluted to make it more amenable to recognising and supporting a wider range of interests. The widespread emergence of CSR policies at the level of individual firms and codes of conduct and best practice at industry sector level, broadly defined as the adoption of voluntary initiatives often in the form of social investment and service provision for groups outside the shareholder distribution paradigm,[70] can be seen as a response offered by capital owners to those who raise concerns about corporate global dominance and the way in which it has achieved that global dominance.

A. Corporate Social Responsibility

The mining industry which sees CSR as its effort to balance 'the imperative to protect the environment with the ever present need to make a profit',[71] provides one of

---

[65] The complexities of SRI such as whether investment screens are applied on a sectoral basis or a transversal basis are teased out in G Capelle-Blancard and S Monjon, 'The Performance of Socially Responsible Funds: Does the Screening Process Matter?' (2014) 20 *European Financial Management* 494–520.

[66] In fact, there is evidence of the exact converse; see P Griffin and others, 'Science and the Stock Market: Investors' Recognition of Unburnable Carbon' (2015) 52 *Energy Economics* 1–12. The authors map the effect that a heavily publicised paper in *Nature* on corporate holdings of unburnable carbon had on market movements. They report a very small short-term stock price drop with no lasting effect.

[67] P Pattberg, 'How Climate Change Became a Business Risk: Analyzing Nonstate Agency in Global Climate Politics' (2012) 30 *Environment and Planning C* 613–26.

[68] A Harmes, 'The Limits of Carbon Disclosure: Theorizing the Business Case for Investor Environmentalism' (2011) 11 *Global Environmental Politics* 98–119.

[69] C Dolan and D Rajak, 'Ethnographies of Corporate Ethicizing' (2011) 60 *Focaal* 3–8.

[70] For a detailed history of the evolution of CSR and its definitional constructs, see A Carroll, 'Corporate Social Responsibility' (1999) 38 *Business and Society* 268–95; and W Frederick *Corporation Be Good!* (Indianapolis, Dog Ear Publishing, 2006).

[71] H Jenkins, 'Corporate Social Responsibility and the Mining Industry: conflicts and constructs' (2004) 11 *Corporate Social Responsibility and Environmental Management* 23–34.

the best examples of an industry level body—the International Council on Mining and Metals (ICMM) and its predecessor the International Council on Metals and the Environment (ICME)—that has produced a suite of policies and standards for enhancing CSR practice amongst its members.[72] The 'social responsibility' part of CSR is a co-option of the language of the critics of corporate profit as that profit is currently acquired and enjoyed.[73] This, when added to the potential of CSR policies and activities to allow corporations to supply private governance interventions[74] in these areas by acting pre-emptively ahead of possible supranational or state intervention or NGO pressure,[75] perhaps explains the enthusiasm of the ICMM to provide industry level leadership in this area.[76]

The choice of focus, design and longevity of corporate social responsibility interventions rests with corporate managers. There is no necessity that CSR policies address areas of serious environmental harm or irreparable environmental damage that corporate activity is responsible for. This leads to the cherry-picking of issues[77] that might be easy and cheap to address or have traction with target audiences. Initiatives selected in this way will fulfil the CSR brief of social assistance above the level required by regulation, but will nevertheless offer considerable benefit to the corporation. In CSR terms this is seen as assisting the bottom line and in the current model of the corporation a CSR policy that could not be justified in this way might leave managers in breach of their fiduciary duty to shareholders.[78] The absence of any link between actual damage and harms and CSR policy means that CSR is at best a reputational tool and not an amelioration or restorative strategy.

The activities of Coca Cola in Rajasthan, India provide an illustration of this. Rajasthan in the north west of India is a state known for water scarcity and its economic dependence on agriculture. The Coca Cola production facilities located there are thought to be responsible for over-drawing subterranean ground water,[79]

---

[72] R Goodland, 'Responsible Mining: The Key to Profitable Resource Development' (2012) 4 *Sustainability* 2099–126.

[73] S Kirsch, 'Sustainable Mining' (2010) 34 *Dialectical Anthropology* 87–93; and P Benson and S Kirsch, 'Corporate Oxymorons' (2010) 34 *Dialectical Anthropology* 45–48.

[74] There is a very long back-story to the pressures, both governmental and non-governmental on the mining industry and its responses. For a full account, see H Dashwood, *The Rise of Global Corporate Social Responsibility* (Cambridge, Cambridge University Press, 2012).

[75] O, Young 'Governance for Sustainable Development in a World of Rising Interdependencies' in M Delmas and O Young (eds), *Governance for the Environment* Cambridge, Cambridge University Press, 2009) 12–40.

[76] S Prakash Sethi, 'The Effectiveness of Industry-Based Codes in Serving Public Interest: the Case of the International Council on Mining and Minerals' (2005) 14 *Transnational Corporations* 55–100.

[77] ISO 26000 on corporate responsibility is a guidance standard rather than the more usual certification standard. It too reflects cherry-picking when referring to the 'organization's responsibility to identify which issues are relevant and significant …through its own considerations and through dialogue with stakeholders' (at vi) www.iso.org/iso/home/standards/iso26000.htm.

[78] P Benson, *Tobacco Capitalism: Growers, Migrant Workers, and the Changing Face of a Global Industry* (Princeton New Jersey, Princeton University Press, 2011) 57f.

[79] Over-drawing ground water requires other users such as local farmers to dig deeper wells and purchase more powerful pumps. The milk yield from cattle declines because of the lack of water and local conflicts occur at the few wells that remain operational.

causing widespread water shortages and polluting the remaining water and soil with toxic industrial waste.[80] Leaving aside the issue that location of production facilities in an area like Rajasthan is not socially responsible because of the local water and agriculture situation, Coca Cola's CSR policy[81] refers to the provision of schools in India and a project of female empowerment. Both of these are commendable interventions in themselves, but neither of them restore ground water levels[82] or deal with the problem of polluted soil. The affected local population and the generations to come are unlikely to think that these CSR initiatives were a suitable restorative or compensatory strategy.

Corporate managers use CSR as a form of chiaroscuro;[83] certain activities are pushed forward for scrutiny, awards even, while others remain firmly in the shade.[84] This might be seen within the corporate sector as efficient and effective management of business and reputational risk. Zadek has identified a three-stage development model for CSR which he maps against the changing landscape of societal expectations of corporations. His linear three generations move from CSR as corporate philanthropy that is unconnected with business operations, to CSR that is integrated into a longer-term business strategy, recognising that promotion of ideas like cause-related marketing and socially responsible investment will lead to 'win-win' scenarios and finally to a form of CSR that tries to interrogate the largest global challenges around environmental degradation, poverty and social and economic exclusion.[85] Other commentators employ similar developmental models for CSR.[86] All these models describe how corporations make strategic business decisions to achieve particular market reputations in the context of changing social pressures.[87] There are exceptions to this, of course, but for the

---

[80] K Ravi Raman, 'Corporate Social Responsibility, Local Livelihood and Human Rights: The Case of *Coca Cola* in India' in K Ravi Ramen and R Lipschutz (eds), *Corporate Social Responsibility* (Basingstoke, Palgrave Macmillan, 2010) 182–200.

[81] www.coca-colaindia.com/sustainability/.

[82] Coca Cola has been able to reduce its water consumption by switching to plastic bottles from reusable glass bottles that required washing. However, this brings new disposal problems. Claims by Coca Cola that it recharged 15 times its water consumption through the use of rain water harvesting technology were rejected as lacking merit by an independent assessment; see A Karnani and S Ross, 'Corporate Social Responsibility Does Not Avert the Tragedy of the Commons—Case Study: Coca-Cola India' (2012) Ross School of Business Working Paper No 1173

[83] N Jackson and P Carter, 'Organizational Chiaroscuro: Throwing Light on the Concept of Corporate Governance' (1995) 48 *Human Relations* 875.

[84] J Conley and C Williams, 'Engage, Embed and Embellish: Theory versus Practice in the Corporate Social Responsibility Movement' (2005–06) 31 *Journal of Corporation Law* 1–38.

[85] S Zadek, *The Civil Corporation* (London, Earthscan, 2001) and 'The Path to Corporate Responsibility' (2004) *Harvard Business Review* (December).

[86] Stage models of CSR development pre-date Zadek; see P Sethi, 'Dimensions of Corporate Social Performance: An Analytical Framework' (1975) 75 *California Management Review* 58–64. For a more modern example, see A Warhurst, 'Past, Present and Future Corporate Responsibility: Achievements and Aspirations' in C Crouch and C Maclean (eds), *The Responsible Corporation in Global Economy* (Oxford, Oxford University Press, 2011) 55–85.

[87] B Holzer, *Moralizing the Corporation* (Cheltenham, Edward Elgar, 2010) 94–96.

most environmentally damaging industries, especially mining,[88] CSR could not be anything other than reputation management; it is not possible to mine in a sustainable way or to return the environment to its previous state.

B. Stakeholding

Stakeholding in its corporate rather than its wider political[89] context encourages managers to use relationships within and outside the corporation to connect business to broader ethical values in the pursuit of creating better value for all stakeholders.[90] Deciding exactly which relationships are included in stakeholding is a matter of some contention, as explained below, however even at the narrowest construction stakeholding goes beyond shareholding and includes others such as employees. Proponents of stakeholder theory assert that it is about addressing 'morals and values' as 'a central feature of managing organizations'.[91] At this normative level, stakeholding is not about a description of interests,[92] but rather about the legitimacy of interests other than those of shareholders within the corporate endeavour. Identification of interests as 'legitimate' or not is a point of some importance for the natural environment, and it is returned to below. Stakeholder management demands more than the pursuit of wealth maximisation for shareholders.[93] Not unlike the majority of ethical discussions within modernity, stakeholding relies on Kantian imperatives with its strapline expressed as 'no stakeholder should be used as a means to an ends'.[94]

There is little suggestion within stakeholder theory that the interests of the stakeholder to be considered are solely or even predominantly financial. To this extent it is not about a wider socialisation of the corporation's assets in a

---

[88] The critique of CSR in mining from the academy belongs to anthropologists. 2 particularly vibrant accounts come from Dinah Rajak's work on South Africa, *In Good Company: An Anatomy of Corporate Social Responsibility* (Stanford, Stanford University Press, 2011) and Marina Welker's work on Indonesia, *Enacting the Corporation* (Berkeley, University of Calif Press 2014).

[89] From around 1996 onwards the idea of a stakeholder society expressed as reciprocity and responsibility between state and citizen underpinned the political philosophy of the UK Labour Party, then in opposition. For an account of the extent to which it informed subsequent Labour policy when in government, see R Prabhaker, 'Whatever Happened to Stakeholding' (2004) 82 *Public Administration* 567–84.

[90] RE Freeman, *Strategic Management: a Stakeholder Approach* (Boston, Pitman, 1984)

[91] R Phillips, RE Freeman and Andrew Wicks, 'What Stakeholder Theory is Not' (2003) 13 *Business Ethics Quarterly* 479–502, 481.

[92] J Lozano, 'Towards the Relational Corporation: from Managing Stakeholder Relationships to Building Stakeholder Relationships (waiting for Copernicus)' (2005) 15 *Corporate Governance* 60–77.

[93] T Donaldson and L Preston, 'The Stakeholder Theory of the Corporation: Concepts, Evidence, and Implications' (1995) 20 *Academy of Management Review* 65–91.

[94] W Evan and RE Freeman, 'A Stakeholder Theory of the Modern Corporation: Kantian Capitalism' in T Beauchamp and N Bowie (eds), *Ethical Theory and Business* (Englewood Cliffs, Prentice Hall, 1993) 97–106. There are other normative foundations such as property rights and feminist ethics (see RE Freeman and others, *Stakeholder Theory* (Cambridge, Cambridge University Press, 2010) 213–22 for a comprehensive list) but a Kantian starting point is the most widely used.

political sense, but about achieving an ideal of economic justice through the stakeholders' participation in fair decision-making[95] (in a procedural and process sense)[96] about resource allocation. There are suggestions that stakeholders' involvement increases value creation opportunities for the corporation and that stakeholders are more likely to accept outcomes if they perceive the process of reaching those allocative decisions as a fair process.[97] In the event of conflict arising between divergent stakeholder interests—both *intra* stakeholder group and *inter* stakeholder group—it is the role of the manager to create ways in which value is added to each interest, presumably in line with its legitimate expectations.[98] There is no specification offered by the theory as to how interests should be weighted, balanced or assessed by managers when they are making everyday decisions.[99] What holds stakeholding theory back from this is a refusal to set out in advance what the interest of each stakeholder might be.[100] The absence of a distributive methodology gives stakeholding something in common with the position under Levinasian ethics set out below in section IV of this chapter. However, a major difference between them is the view of stakeholder theory that stakeholder interests are derived from the corporation and so consequently subsumed into it.

There appear to be two views of who or what is a stakeholder in relation to the corporation in functional terms. Leaving aside labels such as 'primary and secondary' stakeholder[101] and 'normative and derivative' stakeholder,[102] stakeholders are seen either as claimants or as influencers.[103] 'Claimant' enjoys a narrow definition and identifies those who have a claim, right or interest as stakeholders. 'Influencer' is a wider definition pulling in those who can affect or be affected by the corporation as stakeholders.[104] Across these two definitions there could

---

[95] This explains in part the link between ideas of stakeholding and employee participation either in the full sense of co-determination or in particular areas like executive compensation; see J Williamson, C Driver and P Kenway, *Beyond Shareholder Value* (London, TUC, 2014).

[96] H Spitzek and E Hansen, 'Stakeholder Governance: How Stakeholders Influence Corporate Decision Making' (2010) 10 *Corporate Governance* 378–91.

[97] B Parmar and others, 'Stakeholder Theory: State of the Art' (2010) 4 *Academy of Management Annals* 403–45.

[98] J Harrison, D Bosse and R Phillips, 'Managing for Stakeholders, Stakeholder Utility Functions and Competitive Advantage' (2010) 31 *Strategic Management Journal* 58–74.

[99] This opens stakeholding up as a theoretical proposition set in opposition to shareholder primacy to a range of criticisms; see A Keay, 'Stakeholder Theory in Corporate Law: Has it Got What it Takes' (2010) 9 *Richmond Journal of Global Law & Business* 249, 277–90.

[100] S Reynolds, F Schultz and D Hekman, 'Stakeholder Theory and Managerial Decision-Making: Constraints and Implications of Balancing Stakeholder Interests' (2006) 64 *Journal of Business Ethics* 285–301.

[101] M Clarkson, 'A Stakeholder Framework for Analyzing and Evaluating Corporate Social Performance' (1995) 20 *Academy of Management Review* 92–117.

[102] R Phillips, *Stakeholder Theory and Organization Ethics* (San Francisco, Berrett-Koehler, 2003).

[103] J Kaler, 'Morality and Strategy in Stakeholder Identification' (2002) 39 *Journal of Business Ethics* 91–99.

[104] See Freeman, *Strategic Management* (n 90) at 46. Freeman famously included terrorists in his 'influencer' definition (at 53) which sent many commentators scurrying for a less controversial identifier such as legitimacy.

be numerous potential stakeholders; any contact with the corporation, well beyond the statuses of shareholder, employees, suppliers and customers, could see inclusion as a stakeholder.[105] Stakeholding also appears to focus on the inclusion of other groups in the economic goals of the corporation by means of the corporation radiating its tentacles outwards.

The position of the natural world within stakeholding illustrates the focus that stakeholding places on economic actors. Commentators differ on whether the environment can be considered as a stakeholder. For some the inclusion of the environment as a stakeholder of the corporation dilutes the concept of stakeholding,[106] since that means there are no boundaries to be drawn between inclusion and exclusion; the environment is everywhere and lacks needs that corporate managers could presumably address. For others,[107] it is this omni-presence that dictates that the environment must be considered as a stakeholder. Wherever the environment is placed—inside or outside the stakeholding matrix—it is being consigned it to the category *other*; it is not an economic interest with a voice like the other economic interests,[108] and if it acts as a back-drop to all stakeholder activity is a peripheral background presence. Stakehold-ing may have merit as an alternative distribution model for the gains of the corporation. It may even address how those gains are made, but it does so only in the context of the existing economic model of the corporation. Stakeholding cannot make the claim for the natural environment to stand as a prior consid-eration before corporate activity. This claim can only be made by Levinasian ethics.

IV. A Levinasian Approach to the Corporation

Stakeholding and CSR are mechanisms that originate from within the corpora-tion, albeit in rather different ways. They are not mechanisms that allow for a priori consideration of interests, and yet the environment is something so funda-mental to human life, let alone capital accumulation, it surely demands this. The purpose of deploying stakeholder narratives and designing CSR policies is to nor-malise the way in which the corporate form accumulates and distributes its gains in relation to those who are considered to have 'an impact upon the perception of

---

[105] Y Fassin, 'Stakeholder Management, Reciprocity and Stakeholder Responsibility' (2012) 109 *Journal of Business Ethics* 83–96.

[106] R Phillips and J Reichart, 'The Environment as a Stakeholder? A Fairness-Based Approach' (2000) 23 *Journal of Business Ethics* 185–97, E Orts and A Strudler, 'The Ethical and Environmental Limits of Stakeholder Theory' (2002) 12 *Business Ethics Quarterly* 215–33; and M Laine, 'The Nature of Nature as a Stakeholder' (2010) 96 *Journal of Business Ethics* 73–78.

[107] C Driscoll and M Starik, 'The Primordial Stakeholder: Advancing the Conceptual Consideration of Stakeholder Status for the Natural Environment' (2004) 49 *Journal of Business Ethics* 55–73.

[108] M Starik 'Should Trees have Managerial Standing? Towards Stakeholder Status for Non-Human Nature' (1995) 14 *Journal of Business Ethics* 207–17.

the corporate body'.[109] As a counterpoint to these narratives, this section draws on the work of Levinas to suggest an ethics for the corporation that admits of interests and a responsibility for the fate of those interests prior to the corporation, rather than focusing on interests that are acknowledged by the corporation only to soften or legitimise its activities.

Baxi comments on the 'enormous exegetical labours' and 'the dense intertextuality' of Levinas' work.[110] These observations are well made. Levinas has a large canon of work largely made available through translation. Much of his early work in particular is framed as an oppositionary discourse to Heidegger.[111] Levinas is concerned with positioning ethics as first philosophy over being and knowledge.[112] On a practical level he uses terminology (often inconsistently) that is unfamiliar to those not deeply immersed in continental philosophy.[113] Nevertheless his work provides a deeper foundation to ideas of ethics and recognition in relation to the corporation than many of the alternatives,[114] including the two explored in this chapter even if Levinas has, as yet, less traction in the field of corporate ethics.[115] A Levinasian account of ethics is an account of an immediate responsibility for the [O]ther[116] where that responsibility is infinite, non-reciprocal and cannot be refused or ignored.[117] The encounter we have with the other is structured through the idea of the face of the other. Levinas uses the face as a concept not to point to a particular other in an empirical sense, but rather to explain that no image can represent alterity or otherness. The image of the face is a plastic image and when

---

[109] J Roberts, 'The Manufacture of Corporate Social Responsibility: Constructing Corporate Sensibility' (2003) 10 *Organization* 249–65, 261.

[110] U Baxi, 'Judging Emmanuel Levinas? Some Reflections on Reading *Levinas, Law, Politics*' (2009) 72 *Modern Law Review* 116–29, 116.

[111] C Jones, 'As if Business Ethics Were Possible, "Within Such Limits"....' (2003) 10 *Organization* 223; and E Levinas, *Entre Nous Thinking-of-the-Other* (New York, Columbia University Press 2000) 116.

[112] E Levinas, 'Ethics as First Philosophy' in S Hand (ed), *The Levinas Reader* (Oxford, Blackwell 1989) 75–87.

[113] The best short secondary account of Levinasian Ethics is provided by C Jones, M Parker and R Ten Bos, *For Business Ethics* (Abingdon, Routledge 2005) 73–79.

[114] Aristotelian ethics, a Rawlsian inspired social contract theory and feminist ethics are all present within the canon of business ethics scholarship; see generally M Painter-Morland and R Ten Bos (eds), *Business Ethics and Continental Philosophy* (Cambridge, Cambridge University Press, 2011).

[115] This is surprising given that considerable space is devoted to the issue of ethics in the economy by Levinas in *Totality and Infinity* (Pittsburgh, Duquesne University Press, 1969). See also D Aasland, 'On the Ethics behind "Business Ethics"' (2004) 53 *Journal of Business Ethics* 3–8; and E Karamali, 'Has the Guest Arrived Yet? Emmanuel Levinas, a Stranger in Business Ethics' (2007) 16 *Business Ethics: A European Review* 313–21.

[116] French language has two forms for 'other'; *autre* and *autrui*. Levinas uses *Autrui* in his later works to refer to 'the rest' in general terms but to the concretised 'other' of radical difference. Levinas' use of *Autrui* in this way has an intellectual hinterland of its own; see S Moyn, *Origins of the Other* (Ithica, Cornell University Press, 2005) 164–94. The use of upper case 'A' by Levinas is not consistent across his writings or even within his writings, thus in translated quotes from his work capitalisation of 'O' follows Levinas' original work; see A Peperzak, S Critchley and R Bernasconi (eds), *Emmanuel Levinas: Basic Philosophical Writings* (Bloomington, Indiana University Press, 1996) xiv–xv.

[117] E Levinas, *Ethics and Infinity—Conversations with Philippe Nemo* (Pittsburgh, Duquesne University Press, 1985) 96, 98–99.

the plastic is removed, what is left is ethics.[118] The face is a face of vulnerability that demands a response from us.

Responsibility is to the other in the current context or situation that the other is in now, even to the point of substitution of ourselves for the other.[119] The appeal to context is an appeal to recognise the uniqueness of the other and so not to reduce the other to positions in categories that reflect our own experiences.[120] The charge of uniqueness and singularity go to the heart of the intellectual difficulties around the 'face'; language, the other pillar of Levinasian ethics, is required to explain singularity through the face, but once it has been explained, it then loses its singularity.[121] It is an anti-essentialist position[122] and in this anti-essentialist position there is a challenge to the intellectual basis of stakeholding in the corporate context. Stakeholding is dependent on an essentialist reduction—the construction of individuals into broad categories such as shareholder or employee, for example. The same challenge can be made to discourses of climate change. The identification and presentation of island populations as vulnerable climate refugees obscures the difference of individuals; their preferences, their ambitions and their personal resilience.[123] Our understanding of the other's position should come not from our rational judgement, but from our experience. This stands in sharp contrast to most other moral philosophies where the production of ethics comes from individual moral deliberation around values and behaviours.

For Levinas the capacity to be human is founded upon the recognition of responsibility for the other.[124] The other needs to do nothing to trigger this responsibility; it is their existence that provides the call to action. This raises the issue of whether an ethics that is so overtly orientated towards the human can be applied to the corporation.[125] Can a corporation be open to an ethics which speaks of subjectivity and responsibility based on encounter and social relations? There is a huge spectrum of opinion, supported by copious amounts of literature, on the 'materiality' of the corporate form, ranging from the overtly anthropomorphic reading of it to the starkly inhuman approach of the nexus of contracts construct.[126] One way of moving outside these debates is to use the idea

---

[118] Levinas, *Totality and Infinity* (n 115) at 50, 75, 177.

[119] Levinas, *Entre Nous Thinking-of-the-Other* (n 111) at 63.

[120] Levinas (n 115) at 43.

[121] D Perpich, 'Figurative Language and the "Face" in Levinas' Philosophy' (2005) 38 *Philosophy and Rhetoric* 103–21.

[122] E Levinas, *Alterity and Transcendence* (New York, Columbia University Press 1999) 90.

[123] C Farbotko and H Lazrus, 'The First Climate Refugees? Contesting Global Narratives of Climate Change in Tuvalu' (2012) 22 *Global Environmental Change* 382–90.

[124] H Jodalen and A Vetlesen (eds), *Closeness: An Ethics* (Oslo, Scandinavian University Press 1997).

[125] D Bevan and H Corvellec, 'The Impossibility of Corporate Ethics: for a Levinasian Approach to Managerial Ethics' (2007) 16 *Business Ethics: A European Review* 208–19 take the position that Levinasian Ethics can have no relationship with the corporation whereas Roberts ('The Manufacture of Corporate Social Responsibility' (n 109)) does not identify this as an issue.

[126] For a summary of the positions taken on this, see G Faldetta, 'A Relational Approach to Responsibility in Organizations: The Logic of Gift and Levinasian Ethics for a "Corporeal Responsibility"' (2015) *Culture and Organization* DOI: 10.1080/14759551.2015.1122600, 2–4.

of corporate or organisational 'culture'[127] as the underpinning descriptor for the corporation thus allowing us to think about the corporation, its employees and its artefacts, as one unit that has beliefs, operating principles and relationships with other actors.

Beyond resolving the question of whether the corporation can bear responsibility in the Levinasian sense of the word, there is a further question as to whether the environment (or non-human actors more generally, such as animals), can be the object of an ethical responsibility drawn from Levinas. There are certainly passages within Levinas' work that would suggest that the 'face' has to be a human face,[128] but there are others where he can be read as being more supportive of the moral standing of non-human others.[129] Several possibilities present themselves as ways of presenting an ethical relationship between human experience and the environment. One is to accept Levinas as offering an entirely anthropocentric ethics and see concern for ecosystem damage and the ravages of climate change as a concern for those who are presently and those who will be in the future affected by it.[130] Levinas' appeal to responsibility is based upon the vulnerability and suffering of the other; the potential for both of these to occur is increased by individual acts that cause environmental harm and damage in the ways that part II of this chapter set out.[131] Alternatively we can see the emotions that the other's claim makes on us being triggered not just by other human beings, but also by animals and nature more broadly.[132] Reading Levinas as going beyond human existence in this way has a certain symmetry with the position adopted above in

---

[127] Schein explains organisational culture as a pyramid. At the cornerstone of the pyramid are shared but unexpressed assumptions and beliefs that form the beating heart of the corporation. These are the governing assumptions of those who work at the corporation and as such structure their actions as individuals and the actions of the corporation; see E Schein, *Organizational Culture and Leadership* (San Francisco, Jossey Bass, 1985).

[128] See eg Levinas (n 115) at 66, 74–75; and E Levinas, *Difficult Freedom* (Baltimore, John Hopkins University Press 1990) 26. Much of the commentary around the anthropocentric of Levinas' work comes from those who are concerned expressly with animals; see eg M Calarco, *Zoographies: The Question of the Animal from Heidegger to Derrida* (New York, Columbia University Press, 2008). For a broader account of the issues with the environment, see E Casey 'Mapping the Earth Otherwise' in A Hooke and W Fuchs (eds), *Encounters with Alphonso Lingis* (Lanham, Lexington Books 2003) 147–62 and the essays contained in W Edelglass, J Hatley and C Diehm (eds), *Facing Nature* (Pittsburgh, Duquesne University Press, 2012).

[129] J Llewelyn, 'Am I Obsessed by Bobby' in R Bernasconi and S Critchley (eds), *Re-reading Levinas* (Bloomington, Indiana University Press, 1991) 234 and *The Middle Voice of Ecological Conscience* (Basingstoke, Macmillan, 1991).

[130] Similar debates between ecocentrism and anthropocentric ethics exist in environmental ethics; see A Thompson, 'Anthropocentrism: Humanity as Peril or Promise' in S Gardiner and A Thompson (eds), *The Oxford Handbook of Environmental Ethics* (Oxford, Oxford University Press, forthcoming).

[131] For a discussion of this point and for a rejection of the 'collective action' argument in relation to environmental damage, see W Edelglass, 'Rethinking Responsibility in an Age of Anthropogenic Climate Catastrophe' in W Edelglass, J Hatley and C Diehm (eds), *Facing Nature* (Pittsburgh, Duquesne University Press, 2012) 209–28.

[132] C Diehm, 'Alterity, Value, Autonomy' in Edelglass and others, *Facing Nature* (n 131) at 11–24.

relation to the corporation and has the advantage of seeing 'nature' as an entity in its own right.[133]

Corporate ethics, from a Levinasian standpoint, stands outside the self-interest of the corporation. It is not the only ethical discourse that suggests this—virtue ethics can certainly also be read that way[134]—but Levinasian ethics makes the claim more strongly, precisely because it places ethics above ideas of community-designed and evaluated morality. The corporation in a Levinasian reading of it is an actor charged with much more than an economic accountability to selected interests, and more than a social responsibility of its own design. It does not determine to whom and how it is accountable because its responsibility and obligation to others is always and already there.[135] Drawing on Levinas, a corporation and its managers are responsible for both intended and unintended consequences of their actions as an ethical rather than an economic calculation.[136]

Responsibility for the other, according to Levinas, cannot be reduced to a series of ethically normative propositions like those found in corporate codes of conduct, pledges of sustainable operations and other similar corporate pronouncements.[137] Even if we look benignly upon such devices as going beyond merely securing corporate reputation, for Levinas a good conscience under-pinned by good will is not sufficient. It is not for a corporation to attempt to determine the extent of its responsibility. This raises the question of how using Levinasian ethics can change the relationship between the environment and the corporation,[138] although it should be noted that stakeholding does not offer any normative guidance either on the structuring of relationships and this is rarely advanced as a fatal critique of its viability. The answer is that every norm and principle of behaviour is contestable through media such as context, culture and history. What cannot be contested or dismissed as being outside a particular code's remit, for example, is the demand that the other makes at the moment that it makes it.[139] In these circumstances a corporation cannot hide behind the demands of its shareholders for investment return or disclaim the actions of

---

[133] A third alternative offered by Perpich is to see the environment captured as part of what Levinas terms 'politics'; see D Perpich, *The Ethics of Emmanuel Levinas* (Stanford, Stanford University Press, 2008) 168–72 and 'Scarce Resources' in Edelglass and others (n 131) at 76.

[134] S Wheeler, *Corporations and the Third Way* (Oxford, Hart Publishing, 2002).

[135] N Macintosh, T Shearer and A Riccaboni, 'A Levinasian Ethics Critique of the Role of Management and Control Systems by Large Global Corporations: The General Electric/NuovoPignone Example' (2009) 20 *Critical Perspectives on Accounting* 751–61.

[136] M Lewis and J Farnsworth, 'Financialisation and the Ethical Moment: Levinas and the Encounter with Business Practice' (2007) 2 *Society and Business Review* 179–92.

[137] E Levinas, *Otherwise than Being or Beyond Essence* (Pittsburgh, Duquesne University Press, 1998) 120.

[138] This is an important issue for scholars of Levinas—if Levinas does not support the use of specific norms then it cannot follow that Levinas' idea of responsibility has no practical impact for this would be to deny his foray into the ethical; see R Bernasconi, 'What is the Question to Which "Substitution" is the Answer' in S Critchley and R Bernasconi (eds), *The Cambridge Companion to Levinas* (Cambridge, Cambridge University Press, 2002) 234–51, 250.

[139] Perpich, *The Ethics of Emmanuel Levinas* (n 133) at 146–49.

individual employees as not its own. The environment is a face that is always in view and cannot be dismissed as beyond consideration. The demand of the environment in an era of rapid environmental degradation, such as the Anthropocene suggests, and huge corporate expansion, must be heard. It is heard through a mixture of dialogue, corporate disclosure and corporate learning.[140]

V. Conclusion

This chapter has mapped the rise of the corporate form as the dominant mode of accumulation within the Anthropocene. It takes the position that while the corporation in its present form has produced great wealth for some, others are not only excluded from its wealth, but also suffer a range of harms because of the effects of its activities on the Earth's systems. Stakeholding and CSR have considerable support as mechanisms that operate to modify corporate behaviour. However, both are mechanisms that emerge from inside the corporation as subject to corporate designs and desires in their construction. An alternative to this is an ethics that begins when Levinas suggests that ethics should begin—the moment that the face comes into view. It is an alternative that requires corporations and their managers to ask of themselves not 'how can sufficient be done' but 'how can more be done'.

---

[140] B Arya and J Salk, 'Cross-Sector Alliance Learning and Effectiveness of Voluntary Codes of Corporate Responsibility' (2006) 16 *Business Ethics Quarterly* 211–34.

14

Judging the Anthropocene: Transformative Adjudication in the Anthropocene Epoch

LYNDA COLLINS

Judicial intervention is necessary if the [other branches of government] continue to deplete and mismanage natural resources into a state of bankruptcy [--a] situation that threatens human life, welfare and, ultimately, civilization itself.[1]

I. Introduction

The newly proposed geological epoch, known by many in the scientific community as the Anthropocene, is unprecedented in the history of Planet Earth.[2] Unlike past epochs, marked by natural shifts in climate or the organic rise and fall of key species, the Anthropocene is characterised by profound anthropogenic disruptions in the biosphere.[3] Put simply, humans have now eroded natural systems on a global scale and to an extent that threatens the present and future well-being of people, plants, animals and ecosystems. But science and history also teach us that there is hope; the same human ingenuity that created this unprecedented problem can be mobilised to solve it.[4] In many cases, technological solutions exist to meet the daunting environmental challenges of our time.[5] If we collectively commit to mitigate, reverse and prevent environmental harms,

---

[1] MC Wood, 'Advancing the Sovereign Trust of Government to Safeguard the Environment for Present and Future Generations (Part II): Instilling a Fiduciary Obligation in Governance' (2009) 39 *Environmental Law* 91, 117.

[2] See generally J Davies, *The Birth of the Anthropocene* (Oakland, CA, University of California Press, 2016); CN Waters and others, 'The Anthropocene is Functionally and Stratigraphically Distinct from the Holocene' (2016) 36:6269 *Science* 10.1126.

[3] See International Commission on Stratigraphy, 'International Chronostratigraphic Chart' www.stratigraphy.org/index.php/ics-chart-timescale.

[4] See DR Boyd, *The Optimistic Environmentalist* (Toronto, ECW Press, 2015).

[5] See eg G Dauncey, *The Climate Challenge: 101 Solutions to Global Warming* (Gabriola, BC, New Society Publishers, 2009).

a sustainable future is possible. This process will arguably require broad-based engagement by nearly every sector and community on Earth, but some actors enjoy a unique power to catalyse the necessary shift away from environmentally destructive modes of living and towards long-term sustainability.[6] This chapter will analyse the role of the judiciary in this critical collective project.

As the arbiters of justice in the Anthropocene, judges have the potential to radically transform environmental governance in the public interest or, alternatively, to be mere spectators in the ongoing process of environmental degradation.[7] In many countries, the bulk of environmental litigation concerns the scope and content of environmental statutes, constraining judges within the boundaries of existing legislation, which is largely concerned with facilitating, or at best mitigating, industrial activity. Frequently, judges in such cases defer to the ostensible expertise of government decision-makers, resulting in what Wood refers to as an 'administrative tyranny' in environmental law.[8] This concentration of environmental power in the hands of government officials is presumptively neutral, but has unfortunately failed utterly in the project of environmental protection. A robust body of scholarship demonstrates that statutory environmental law has yet to produce sustainable environmental protection, even in well-resourced nations.[9] Indeed, environmental legislation as currently structured is arguably directly implicated in the global socio-ecological crisis that characterises the Anthropocene.[10] Until legislators embrace transformative and effective environmental governance, judges will need to locate radical environmental law outside the bounds of statute.

This chapter will assess four potential arenas for transformative environmental adjudication in the Anthropocene: civil actions for damages; the public trust doctrine; constitutional environmental rights; and indigenous environmental law. Though doctrinally diverse, these four areas of law collectively create a substantial judicial space for progressive environmental adjudication. Judges ruling on matters falling into one of these four areas have the power to make, interpret and enforce law that actually achieves our collective goal of environmental protection and sustainability. Without usurping the role of elected legislators or fuelling any counter-majoritarian dilemma, judges can fulfil their own critical role as environmental stewards through progressive adjudication in these key areas.

---

[6] See LJ Kotzé, 'Rethinking Global Environmental Law and Governance in the Anthropocene' (2014) 32(2) *Journal of Energy & Natural Resources Law* 121.

[7] For an excellent comparative survey of existing judicial roles in environmental governance, see LJ Kotzé and AR Paterson (eds), *The Role of the Judiciary in Environmental Governance: Comparative Perspectives* (Alphen aan den Rijn, Kluwer Law International, 2009).

[8] MC Wood, 'Advancing the Sovereign Trust of Government to Safeguard the Environment for Present and Future Generations (Part I)' (2009) 39 *Environmental Law* 43, 61.

[9] See eg C Collins, *Toxic Loopholes: Failures and Future Prospects for Environmental Law* (Cambridge, Cambridge University Press, 2010); DR Boyd, *Unnatural Law: Rethinking Canadian Environmental Law and Policy* (Vancouver, University of British Columbia Press, 2003); RF Kennedy, Jr, *Crimes Against Nature* (New York, HarperCollins, 2004); JG Speth, *The Bridge at the Edge of the World: Capitalism, the Environment, and Crossing from Crisis to Sustainability* (New Haven, CT, Yale University Press 2008).

[10] See Boyd, *Unnatural Law* (n 9); Speth, *The Bridge at the Edge of the World* (n 9).

II. Context: The Failure of Administrative Environmental Law

While there is no question that the regulatory environmental state has done much to reduce pollution, it is equally clear that governmental approaches to environmental law have failed to secure a sustainable future. Indeed, the complex infrastructure of environmental laws and regulations that originated primarily in the United States (US) and has been exported all over the world, has presided over this unprecedented period of socio-ecological crisis. An in-depth analysis of the reasons for this 'colossal failure'[11] is beyond the scope of this chapter, but a few key factors deserve mention. The voluminous scholarship on point reveals that environmental regulatory agencies in governments around the world are enormously complex, technocratic, isolated from each other and from ecological realities, jurisdictionally constrained, inaccessible to the non-expert public, and vulnerable to political and economic pressures that have no respect for non-negotiable environmental imperatives.[12] Environmental statutes are characterised by the pervasive presence of discretion and this discretion is habitually exercised in favour of business-as-usual as opposed to environmental protection.[13] Indeed, Wood contends that '[t]he modern environmental administrative state is geared almost entirely to the legalization of natural resource damage… [T]he majority of agencies spend nearly all of their resources to permit, rather than prohibit, environmental destruction'.[14] As a result, radical environmental law must extend beyond the realm of statutory regulation. The judiciary has the power to articulate and enforce trans-legislative, overarching principles of law that supplement, expand or even invalidate legislative provisions where necessary to achieve sustainability in the Anthropocene.

III. The Unique Role of Judges in Global Environmental Sustainability

Judges have a unique capacity to protect ecosystems (including human and non-human health) through the development, interpretation and enforcement of environmental law principles within case law, legislation and constitutions. At the 2002 Global Judges Symposium, a gathering of senior judges from around the

---

[11] Wood, 'Advancing the Sovereign Trust (Part I)' (n 8) at 43.
[12] ibid, 55–60; Boyd (n 9).
[13] Wood (n 8).
[14] Wood (n 8) at 55.

world developed The Johannesburg Principles on the Role of Law and Sustainable Development, recognising

> that the Judiciary, well informed of the rapidly expanding boundaries of environmental law and aware of its role and responsibilities in promoting the implementation, development and enforcement of laws, regulations and international agreements relating to sustainable development, plays a critical role in the enhancement of the public interest in a healthy and secure environment.[15]

More recently, the Rio +20 Declaration on Justice, Governance and Law for Environmental Sustainability recognised that '[e]nvironmental law is essential for the protection of natural resources and ecosystems and reflects our best hope for the future of our planet' and further:

> Environmental sustainability can only be achieved in the context of fair, effective and transparent national governance arrangements and rule of law, predicated on: [inter alia] accessible, fair, impartial, timely and responsive dispute resolution mechanisms, including developing specialized expertise in environmental adjudication, and innovative environmental procedures and remedies

In the years before and since these significant declarations, courts around the world have struggled to identify and effectuate an appropriate judicial role in environmental regulation. In some instances, courts have made great advances in protecting the environment through progressive interpretations of relevant law.

In India, for example, the Supreme Court ordered the City of Delhi to convert its huge fleet of diesel buses to compressed natural gas to ameliorate air quality and reduce pollution-related mortality and morbidity.[16] In Argentina and the Philippines, courts imposed detailed, ongoing and ambitious remedies resulting in massive remediation efforts that cleaned up two of the most polluted watersheds in those nations.[17] In June of 2015, a Dutch court ordered the state to reduce greenhouse gas emissions by a minimum of 25 per cent by 2020, based on Dutch constitutional and tort duties owed by the government to its citizenry.[18] Most recently, the High Court of Pakistan ordered the Pakistani government to implement its national climate change policy, noting that the threat posed by climate change calls for judicial 'protection of fundamental rights of the citizens of Pakistan, in particular, the vulnerable and weak segments of the society who are unable to approach this Court'.[19]

---

[15] See The Johannesburg Principles on the Role of Law and Sustainable Development www.unep.org/Documents.Multilingual/Default.asp?ArticleID=3115&DocumentID=259.

[16] U Narain and R Greenspan Bell, *Who Changed Delhi's Air? The Roles of the Court and the Executive in Environmental Policymaking* (Washington, DC, Resources for the Future, 2005).

[17] See *Mendoza Beatriz Silva et al v State of Argentina et al on damages (damages resulting from environmental pollution of Matanza/Riachuelo river)* (2008) File M 1569 XL, www.escr-net.org/docs/i/1469150; *Manila v Concerned Residents of Manila Bay* (2008) GR Nos 171947-48, http://sc.judiciary.gov.ph/jurisprudence/2011/february2011/171947-48.htm.

[18] *Urgenda v The Netherlands* (2015) C/09/456689 / HA ZA 13-1396 (English translation), http://uitspraken.rechtspraak.nl/inziendocument?id=ECLI:NL:RBDHA:2015:7196(*Urgenda*).

[19] See *Ashgar Leghari v Pakistan*, http://edigest.elaw.org/pk_Leghari.

In other countries, judges have been extremely reluctant to second-guess the environmental decisions of the legislative and executive branches of government. In the US for example, Wood argues that 'the judiciary has lost its potency as a third branch of government operating in the environmental realm' owing to its habitual deference to administrative decision-makers.[20] In many countries, inconsistencies and contradictions in judges' perceptions of their 'role and responsibilities' in environmental governance are apparent at all court levels. Within the Federal Court of Canada, for example, one can find both a cutting-edge application of the precautionary principle with respect to conservation of an Aboriginal fishery,[21] and a decision declining to require the federal government to even *attempt* compliance with a statutory requirement to curb greenhouse gas emissions in accordance with the Kyoto Protocol.[22]

It is evident, then, that both within and among the nations of the world, there is a need for greater clarity in the role and responsibilities of the judiciary in relation to environmental sustainability. I would argue that transformative environmental adjudication is an urgent imperative in the Anthropocene. In addition to their important role in interpreting environmental statutes and regulations, judges have a unique ability to protect the planet by developing and enforcing non-statutory environmental law, in particular: environmental civil actions; the public trust doctrine; constitutional environmental rights; and indigenous environmental law. I now consider each in turn below.

IV. Civil Actions

Environmental civil claims involve actions by private parties (and occasionally governments) to recover compensation for, or to prevent, environmental harms.[23] When properly adjudicated, environmental civil claims constitute a potentially transformative tool for environmental protection.[24] The law of environmental civil claims (also known as 'toxic torts' in the common law tradition) can function as radical environmental law[25] in a variety of ways. First, civil actions have the capacity to fundamentally alter the economic equation, making it cheaper to

---

[20] Wood (n 8) at 59–60.
[21] *Haida Nation v Canada (Fisheries and Oceans)*, 2015 FC 290.
[22] *Friends of the Earth v Canada (Governor in Council)*, 2008 FC 1183, 39.
[23] See generally L Collins and H McLeod-Kilmurray, *The Canadian Law of Toxic Torts* (Toronto, Thompson Reuters, 2014).
[24] ibid, 2–3; ADK Abelkop, 'Tort Law as an Environmental Policy Instrument' (2014) 92(2) *Oregon Law Review* 381; KN Hylton, 'When Should We Prefer Tort Law to Environmental Regulation?' (2002) 41 *Washburn Law Journal* 515.
[25] I use the term 'radical environmental law' to refer to environmental law that addresses the root causes of environmental degradation, in contrast to that which leaves the status quo unchallenged and merely attempts to mitigate (or justify) the inevitable environmental consequences of existing unsustainable systems.

protect than to pollute the environment. While statutory environmental law could theoretically impose meaningful economic consequences for environmentally harmful behaviour, it has generally failed to do so.[26] Civil actions, in contrast, can lead to very large awards, sometimes even bankrupting environmental wrongdoers.[27] Thus, judges adjudicating environmental civil claims have the power to decouple fiscal profit from environmental degradation, a challenge that has so far proved insurmountable to environmental regulators.

Second, civil claims empower those injured by environmental harm to seek redress directly from wrongdoers. Civil claims do not require governmental intervention and are available as a last resort to people who are economically and politically disenfranchised.[28] Where statutory environmental law has failed a given community or individual, the law of civil claims acts as a crucial 'safety net'.[29] Moreover, monetary awards arising from civil claims are paid directly to those who have been harmed, while fines from environmental prosecutions generally go to the public purse. Thirdly, in constitutional democracies, the law of civil claims is adjudicated by an independent judiciary that is not subject to the political agendas of any given government. Unlike regulators, who often become identified with the regulated community, viewing it as the 'client' of government ministries (a phenomenon known as 'agency capture'), judges can make decisions independent of political pressure.[30]

There are a number of examples of very significant environmental successes in the area of civil claims. Looking to history, Pontin argues persuasively that a series of nuisance claims brought by members of the British aristocracy during the nineteenth century were highly effective at preserving environmental quality in rural areas, protecting ecosystems, non-human animals and the majority of the English population from the environmental horrors of the Industrial Revolution.[31] In the late twentieth century, a massive wave of litigation arising from the toxic effects of asbestos effectively drove the industry out of business in North America.[32] Most recently, the Dutch court in the historic *Urgenda* case relied in part on a civil duty of care in ordering the Dutch government to substantially and quickly reduce greenhouse gas emissions.[33] It seems clear, then,

---

[26] See generally F Ackerman and L Heinzerling, *Priceless: On Knowing the Price of Everything and the Value of Nothing* (New York, New Press, 2004).

[27] See eg Queena Sook Kim, 'Firms Hit by Asbestos Litigation File for Bankruptcy to Escape' *Wall Street Journal* (21 December 2000) www.wsj.com/articles/SB97735349584304992,

[28] AM Linden, 'Tort Law as Ombudsman' (1973) 51 *Canadian Bar Review* 157.

[29] LM Collins, 'Evergreen? The Environmental Law of Torts (2014) 22 *Tort Law Review* 107.

[30] LM Collins, 'Tort, Democracy and Environmental Governance: Crown Liability for Environmental Non-Enforcement' (2007) *Tort Law Review* 107, 110–11.

[31] B Pontin, 'The Secret Achievements of Nineteenth Century Nuisance Law: *Attorney General v Birmingham Corporation* (1858-1895) in Context' (2007) 19 *Environmental Law and Management* 271; B Pontin, 'Nuisance Law and the Industrial Revolution: A Reinterpretation of Doctrine and Institutional Competence' (2012) 75(6) *Modern Law Review* 1010.

[32] Queena Sook Kim, 'Firms hit by Asbestos Litigation File for Bankruptcy to Escape' (n 27).

[33] *Urgenda* (n 18) at [4.35]–[4.83].

that judges can do much to protect our shared environment through progressive adjudication in environmental civil claims.

While civil claims are inherently anthropocentric and necessarily limited, the public trust doctrine has a more comprehensive potential for ensuring environmental sustainability where other branches of government have failed to do so.

V. The Public Trust Doctrine

The public trust doctrine provides that natural resources are held in trust by government for present and future generations of citizens and thus cannot be alienated or depleted to an extent that would undermine their long-term viability. The public trust doctrine may be viewed as a binding domestic mechanism for implementing the international concept of intergenerational equity, which posits the present generation of humans as simultaneously beneficiaries and trustees of a global environmental trust.[34] In the West, the public trust doctrine is thought to derive from Roman law under Justinian: '[b]y the law of nature these things are common to mankind—the air, running water, the sea'.[35] The French *Civil Code*, also historically recognised public ownership in navigable rivers, streams, beaches, ports and harbours.[36] The doctrine also survived into English common law, as noted by H de Bracton in his mid-thirteenth-century treatise: '[b]y natural law these are common to all: running water, air, the sea and the shores of the sea … All rivers and ports are public, so that the right to fish therein is common to all persons'.[37]

Outside the Western legal tradition, the public trust doctrine is equally well-grounded culturally and historically. Islamic law, for example, posits Muslims as trustees (or stewards) of the natural world with duties towards both current and future generations.[38] Asian philosophical and religious traditions also include notions of responsibility to future generations,[39] which in some cases are thought to include reincarnations of those currently living.[40] The Indian Supreme Court has recognised the public trust doctrine as consistent with ancient Indian spiritual

---

[34] The authoritative articulation of the doctrine of intergenerational equity remains E Brown Weiss, *In Fairness to Future Generations: International Law, Common Patrimony, and Intergenerational Equity* (Tokyo, UN University Press, 1989).

[35] TC Sandars, *The Institutes of Justinian* (1876), Book II, Title I, 158.

[36] *British Columbia v Canadian Forest Products Ltd*, [2004] 2 SCR 74, [75].

[37] *Bracton on the Laws and Customs of England* (Cambridge, MA, Harvard University Press, 1968) vol 2, 39–40.

[38] A Nanji, 'The Right to Development: Social and Cultural Rights and Duties to the Community' in *Proceedings of the Seminar on Islamic Perspectives on the Universal Declaration of Human Rights*, UN Doc HR/IP/SEM/1999/1 (pt II, s 2) (1999) at 346 (citing Qur'anic ayah 2:30).

[39] ibid, 20.

[40] ibid. See also JM Peek, 'Buddhism, Human Rights, and the Japanese State' (1995) 17(3) *Human Rights Quarterly* 527, 529.

teachings and has suggested that it dates back to the Chen dynasty in China.[41] Streams of African customary law also include a notion of ownership/stewardship of land by the collective, including future generations. One Ghanaian chief has explained that in this conceptualisation, 'land belongs to a vast family of whom many are dead, a few are living, and a countless host are still unborn'.[42] Similarly, in what is now known as North America, Haudenosaunee (or Iroquois) law explicitly requires decision-makers to take into account impacts extending seven generations into the future.[43]

Since the pivotal 1892 US Supreme Court decision in *Illinois Central Railroad Company v Illinois*,[44] judges in multiple countries around the world have used the public trust doctrine to protect vital natural resources against government misuse or inaction.[45] In *Illinois*, the Court held that the state could not alienate lakebed property to a private entity because it held title to these submerged lands 'in trust for the people of the State that they may enjoy the navigation of the waters, carry on commerce over them, and have liberty of fishing therein freed from the obstruction or interference of private parties'.[46] In the majority of American states, the public trust doctrine is limited to protecting navigable waters, shorelines and submerged lands, but some have extended the doctrine to protect non-navigable waters, parklands and wildlife, and to prevent hazardous pollution.[47] Babcock notes that American courts:

> have vigorously used the public trust doctrine to protect communal resources from inconsistent uses and have strictly scrutinized transfers of public trust resources to ensure that the transfers are in the public interest. Courts never lose their power to revoke a transfer that they later find is not in the public interest. The virtual effect of the public trust doctrine is to convert the private owners of trust resources into permanent custodians of those resources under an easement held by the government [in trust for the public].[48]

Given that the US constitutionally protects the right to hold private property, (and considering the significant role property rights have played in legitimising

---

[41] *Reliance Natural Res, Ltd*, (2010) INSC 374, pt IV, [98].

[42] Weiss, *In Fairness to Future Generations* (n 34) at 86. See also J Church, 'Sustainable Development and the Culture of Ubuntu' (2012) 45(3) *De Iure* 511–31.

[43] *The Great Law of Peace of the Longhouse People (Iroquois League of Six Nations)* (White Roots of Peace, Mohawk Nation at Akwesasne, Rooseveltown, NY 1973) ch 28.

[44] *Illinois Central Railroad Company v Illinois*, 146 U.S. 387, 435 (1892) (*Illinois*).

[45] MC Blumm and RD Guthrie, 'Internationalizing the Public Trust Doctrine: Natural Law and Constitutional and Statutory Approaches to Fulfilling the Saxon Vision' (2012) 45 *UC Davis Law Review* 741.

[46] *Illinois* (n 44) at 452.

[47] AB Klass, 'The Public Trust Doctrine in the Shadow of State Environmental Laws: A Case Study' (2015) 45 *Environmental Law* 431, 438–39. See generally MC Blumm and MC Wood, *The Public Trust Doctrine in Environmental and Natural Resources Law* (Durham, NC, Carolina Academic Press, 2013).

[48] HM Babcock, 'The Public Trust Doctrine: What a Tall Tale They Tell' (2015) 61 *South Carolina Law Review* 393, 397 (internal citations omitted).

socio-ecological destruction more generally) it is remarkable that the public trust doctrine has been held to supersede vested property interests in the US.[49]

In India, the Supreme Court first recognised the public trust doctrine in the 1997 case of *Mehta v Nath*.[50] In *Nath*, a private developer with ties to the Minister for Environment and Forests had been granted licences to land encroaching on a public forest and had diverted a streambed in order to protect its property from flooding. The Indian Supreme Court adopted the public trust doctrine (citing English common law, relevant US jurisprudence and Indian spiritual traditions) and used it to invalidate the leases and order ecological restoration to repair the damage resulting from the developer's activities. The Court subsequently situated the public trust doctrine within India's constitutional right to life and applied it to cases involving the construction and operation of an underground shopping centre in a public park,[51] and the exploitation of natural gas deposits in Indian waters.[52]

In the Philippines, the public trust doctrine can be found within that country's constitutional right to 'a balanced and healthful ecology in accord with the rhythm and harmony of nature' and various statutory provisions.[53] The Supreme Court of the Philippines has nonetheless played a pivotal role in enforcing the public trust doctrine and has even held that it derives from natural law and is thus independent of any written provisions. In the famous *Minors Oposa* case, in which a group of children challenged a series of timber licences, the Court recognised the environmental rights of future generations and further held:

> While the right to a balanced and healthful ecology is to be found under the Declaration of Principles and State Policies and not under the Bill of Rights, it does not follow that it is less important than any of the civil and political rights enumerated in the latter. Such a right belongs to a different category of rights altogether for it concerns nothing less than self-preservation and self-perpetuation [,] the advancement of which may even be said to predate all governments and constitutions. As a matter of fact, these basic rights need not even be written in the Constitution for they are assumed to exist from the inception of humankind.[54]

Though *Oposa* did not actually result in the cancellation of timber licences, it set an important legal precedent that ultimately resulted in a very positive outcome in the subsequent case of *Metropolitan Manila Development Authority v Concerned*

---

[49] ibid.

[50] *Mehta v Nath* (1997), 1 SCC 388 (India). See also PA Barresi, 'Mobilizing the Public Trust Doctrine in Support of Publicly Owned Forests as Carbon Dioxide Sinks in India and the United States' (2012) 23 *Colorado Journal of International Environmental Law and Policy* 56–57.

[51] *MI Builders v Sahu* AIR 1999 SC 2468.

[52] *Reliance Natural Resources Ltd v Reliance Industries* SCC Civ App No 4273 (7 May 2010).

[53] Constitution of the Republic of the Philippines, Art II, s 16, available at: www.gov.ph/constitutions/1987-constitution/#article-ii.

[54] See *Minors Oposa v Secretary of the Department of Environment and Natural Resources*, 30 July 1993, 33 ILM 173, 187.

Residents of Manila Bay. In the course of its extraordinary judgment, the Court explicitly referenced the trust concept:

> So it was in *Oposa v Factora*, the Court stated that the right to a balanced and healthful ecology need not even be written in the Constitution for it is assumed, like other civil and political rights guaranteed in the Bill of Rights, to exist from the inception of mankind and it is an issue of transcendental importance with intergenerational implications. Even assuming the absence of a categorical legal provision specifically prodding petitioners to clean up the bay, they and the men and women representing them cannot escape their obligation to future generations of Filipinos to keep the waters of the Manila Bay clean and clear as humanly as possible. Anything less would be a betrayal of the trust reposed in them.[55]

In Kenya, judicial leadership appears to have led to explicit constitutional recognition of the public trust doctrine. In its 2006 decision in *Waweru v Republic of Kenya*, a criminal case arising from the discharge of raw sewage into the Kiserian River, the High Court of Kenya recognised an implicit environmental right within Kenya's constitutional right to life. It further held that this environmental right included the public trust doctrine:

> [i]n the case of land resources, forests, wetlands and waterways…the Government and its agencies are under a public trust to manage them in a way that maintains a proper balance between the economic benefits of development with the needs of a clean environment.[56]

Further, 'the water table and the river courses affected are held in trust by the present generation for the future generations'.[57] In fashioning an appropriate remedy, the Court declared that 'the government itself is both under…statutory obligation[s]…and also under a public trust to provide adequate land for the establishment of treatment works' and issued an order in the nature of *mandamus* compelling the government to construct sewage treatment facilities.[58] Only a few years after the decision in *Waweru*, Kenya's 2010 Constitution explicitly incorporated public trust concepts in a number of its provisions. The new right to a healthy environment under Article 42, for example, includes the right 'to have the environment protected for the benefit of present and future generations through legislative and other measures'.[59] Article 61 provides that '[a]ll land in Kenya belongs to the people collectively as a nation, as communities and as individuals'.[60] Article 69 requires the State to 'ensure sustainable exploitation, utilisation, management and

---

[55] *Metro Manila Dev Auth v Concerned Residents of Manila Bay (Metro Manila)*, GR No 171947-48, 574 S.C.R.A. 661 (SC, 18 December 2008) (Phil.) available at: http://sc.judiciary.gov.ph/jurisprudence/2008/december2008/171947-48.htm [page/paragraph numbers unavailable].

[56] *Waweru v Republic*, (2006) 1 KLR 677, 692 (HCK) (Kenya), [42], available at: www.chr.up.ac.za/index.php/browse-by-subject/339-kenya-waweru-v-republic-2007-ahrlr-149-kehc-2006-.html.

[57] ibid, [48].

[58] ibid, [52].

[59] Constitution of Kenya, Art 42(a) available at: www.kenyaembassy.com/pdfs/the%20constitution%20of%20kenya.pdf.

[60] ibid, Art 61(1).

conservation of the environment and natural resources, and ensure the equitable sharing of the accruing benefits'.[61]

As the foregoing demonstrates, the public trust doctrine provides a space for effective environmental adjudication in the Anthropocene. Remedies include both prohibitive and mandatory injunctive relief, including—crucially—ecological restoration. Judicial recognition can lead to explicit incorporation of the doctrine in constitutional and statutory regimes, or can function as an independent system of environmental protection. Importantly, '[t]he judicial branch remains the ultimate guardian of the trust … [T]he public trust arena harbors a judicial 'veto' of extraordinary scope, unparalleled in other areas of the law'.[62]

VI. Constitutional Environmental Rights

Like the public trust doctrine, constitutional environmental rights are limits on government powers; they allow judges to override inadequate or unwise statutory provisions and executive or administrative decisions, thus remedying the serious structural limitations in our current systems of environmental regulation. Constitutionalised environmental rights also serve as meta-principles that guide and shape a nation's overall environmental policy, and as a result, have the potential to transform environmental governance and—crucially—environmental outcomes. Empirical data compiled by David Boyd and others demonstrates persuasively that constitutional environmental rights are a transformative tool for sustainability. Compared to countries that lack such protection, nations with constitutional environmental rights rank higher on multi-indicator assessments of environmental performance, have smaller ecological footprints (a comprehensive measurement of environmental impact) and have been more successful in reducing dangerous air pollution (including greenhouse gases).[63] These relative improvements apply whether nations are compared with all other countries around the globe or with only those in their own region (eg Africa, the Americas, Asia-Pacific, Europe and the Middle East/Central Asia). Moreover, the content and enforcement of environmental legislation and the outcome of environmental litigation tend to improve following constitutionalisation of environmental rights.[64] Judges have two crucial

---

[61] ibid, Art 69(1)(a). See also W du Plessis and M Faure, *Balancing of Interests in Environmental Law in Africa* (Pretoria, Pretoria University Law Press, 2011).

[62] Wood, 'Advancing the Sovereign Trust Part II' (n 1) at 75.

[63] DR Boyd, *The Environmental Rights Revolution: A Global Study of Constitutions, Human Rights, and the Environment* (Vancouver, UBC Press, 2012); JR May and E Daly, *Global Environmental Constitutionalism* (Cambridge, Cambridge University Press, 2014); C Jeffords and L Minkler, 'Do Constitutions Matter? The Effects of Constitutional Environmental Rights Provisions on Environmental Outcomes' Working papers 2014-16, University of Connecticut, Department of Economics, https://ideas.repec.org/p/uct/uconnp/2014-16.html.

[64] Boyd, *Environmental Rights Revolution* (n 63).

roles to play in securing the benefits of constitutional environmental rights for the nations of the world: first, by creating such rights through judicial interpretation, and, secondly, by enforcing them effectively.

National courts that have thus far refused to effectuate environmental protection through existing constitutional rights (notably in Canada and the US) could take inspiration from those that have seen fit to do so. As in the public trust area, the Supreme Court of India stands out as a leader in the creation of environmental rights through constitutional interpretation. In a series of famous cases, the Court has held that '[t]he right to life…includes the right of enjoyment of pollution-free water and air for full enjoyment of life'.[65] The Supreme Court of Pakistan has also constitutionalised environmental rights, holding that

> [a]ny action taken which may create hazards of life will be encroaching upon the person rights of a citizen to enjoy the life according to law.…In our view the word 'life' constitutionally is so wide that the danger and encroachment complained of would impinge [upon] fundamental rights of a citizen.[66]

The Supreme Court of Bangladesh has held that that country's constitutional right to life precluded the government from permitting the marketing of food contaminated with radiation.[67] In a case concerning risks associated with gas flaring, the Federal High Court of Nigeria held that the constitutional right to life 'inevitably' includes the right to a 'clean, poison-free, healthy environment'.[68] In the result, the Court struck down the regulations authorising gas flaring in the claimant's community and ordered the respondents to take immediate steps to stop all flaring in the relevant area. Unfortunately, however, the Court's decision was never enforced and gas flaring in Nigeria continues.[69]

In Canada and the US, courts have thus far declined to recognise environmental rights inherent in any existing constitutional provisions. In a series of cases beginning in the 1970s, litigants tried to convince American courts to recognise a right to environmental quality within the 'penumbra' of the Ninth Amendment, a

---

[65] *Subhash Kumar v State of Bihar et al*, WP (Civil) No 381 of 1988, D/-9-1-91 (Supreme Court of India); see also *M.C. Mehta v India*, WP (Civil) No 12739 of 1985 (Supreme Court of India); *Indian Council for Enviro-Legal Action v Union of India et al.*, [1996] 5 Supreme Court Cases 281, per Kuldip Singh J; J Razzaque, *Public Interest Environmental Litigation in India, Pakistan, and Bangladesh* (The Hague, Kluwer Law International, 2004) 87 ff.

[66] ibid.

[67] *Farooque v Bangladesh*, WP 92 of 1996 (1996.07.01).

[68] *Gbemre v Shell Petroleum Development Co Nigeria Ltd et al*, Order of the Federal High Court of Nigeria in the Benin Judicial Division Holden at Court Benin City, 14 November 2005. See KSA Ebeku, 'Constitutional Right to a Healthy Environment and Human Rights Approaches to Environmental Protection in Nigeria: *Gbemre v Shell* Revisited' (2008) 16(3)*Review of European, Comparative & International Environmental Law* 312.

[69] Indeed, the trial judge in *Gbemre* was transferred out of the district after ruling against Shell; E Ukala, 'Gas Flaring in Nigeria's Niger Delta: Failed Promises and Reviving Community Voices' (2011) 2 *Washington & Lee Journal of Energy, Climate, & the Environment* 97, 105–11. A similar non-enforcement problem has arisen at the regional level. See *SERAC v Nigeria*, Case No ACHPR/COMM/ A044/1, Afr Comm'n Hum & Peoples' Rights PP 51-53 (27 May 2002).

provision recognising (but not exhaustively enumerating) fundamental rights.[70] The American courts consistently rejected claims for the recognition of a substantive constitutional right to environment.[71] Claims for the environmental deprivation of the right to *equality* are at least theoretically viable in American constitutional law, despite significant evidentiary hurdles. Such claims may arise, for example, where a particular racial group is targeted for disproportionate exposure to environmental hazards such as toxic waste dumps.[72] Moreover, the possibility remains that a US court will soon recognise environmental deprivations of the right to life, liberty and/or property enshrined in the substantive due process clauses of the Fifth and Fourteenth Amendments. Eurick concludes that

> the continued recognition of the right to a healthful environment at the state and international level coupled with the Supreme Court's recent recognition of the theory of substantive due process supports the conclusion that the right can exist within the federal Constitution.[73]

Two recently filed actions will test this theory on very strong factual foundations—the first dealing with the knowing provision of contaminated drinking water to the citizens of Flint, Michigan;[74] and the second addressing harm to minors from climate change.[75]

In Canada, courts have dismissed cases asserting environmental violations of the constitutional rights to life, liberty and security of the person arising from cruise missile testing (allegedly increasing the risk of nuclear war),[76] fluoride in public drinking water,[77] a proposed waste incinerator,[78] and pollution from a landfill.[79] However, each of these cases was dismissed on either procedural or factual grounds and the courts did accept that state-sponsored environmental harm could result in a constitutional violation. Two ongoing cases are likely to lead to Canada's first judicial finding of an environmental violation of Canada's constitutional *Charter of Rights and Freedoms*.[80] In *Grassy Narrows First Nation*,

---

[70] See CL Gallagher, 'The Movement to Create an Environmental Bill of Rights: From Earth Day, 1970 to the Present' (1997) 9 *Fordham Environmental Law Journal* 107.

[71] ibid.

[72] See eg RJ Klee, 'What's Good for School Finance Should be Good for Environmental Justice: Addressing Disparate Environmental Impacts Using State Courts and Constitutions' (2005) 30 *Columbia Journal of Environmental Law* 135, 141 ff; JP Eurick, 'The Constitutional Right to a Healthy Environment: Enforcing Environmental Protection Through State and Federal Constitutions' (2011) 11 *International Legal Perspectives* 185.

[73] ibid, 188.

[74] *Mays v Snyder* available at: http://flintwaterstudy.org/wp-content/uploads/2015/11/Mays-vs.-Snyder-et-al.-Complaint-and-Jury-Demand-Final-1.pdf.

[75] *Juliana v United States of America*, 2016 WL 1442435 (8 April 2016).

[76] *Operation Dismantle v The Queen*, [1985] 1 SCR 441.

[77] *Millership v British Columbia* 2003 BCSC 82; *Locke v Calgary* (1993), 15 Alta LR 70 (QB).

[78] *Coalition for a Charter Challenge v Metropolitan Authority*, (1993), 10 CELR (NS) 257 (NS SC [In Chambers]), reversed (1993), 108 DLR (4th) 145 (NS CA) [*Coalition for a Charter Challenge*].

[79] *Manicom v Oxford County* (1985), 52 OR (2d) 137.

[80] Canadian Charter of Rights and Freedoms, pt I of the Constitution Act, 1982, being sch B to the Canada Act 1982 (UK) 1982, c 11.

an indigenous group is challenging the constitutionality of logging permits that would result in the release of toxic mercury into its traditional lands and waters. The application alleges that the permit violates the applicants' rights to life, liberty, security of the person and equality. With very sophisticated counsel and a strong factual record, the applicants in *Grassy Narrows* are very likely to succeed. The Supreme Court of Canada has just heard a second case, alleging violation of an indigenous group's freedom of religion through state-permitted development on a traditional sacred site.[81] Though the lower courts rejected the claim on its facts, both accepted that it would be possible to infringe freedom of religion by state-sponsored interference with an indigenous sacred site. The lower courts, however, failed to take into account the unique significance of sacred natural areas in indigenous spirituality and failed to have regard to relevant international law.[82] Given its demonstrated commitment to the project of reconciliation with Aboriginal peoples,[83] the Supreme Court of Canada is likely to take a more progressive approach.

In countries that still lack an explicit constitutional right to a healthy environment, recognising the constitutional dimension of environmental protection is perhaps the most meaningful contribution judges could make to sustainability in the Anthropocene. This would not require any addition or modification to existing rights; rather it requires judges to recognise that serious state-sponsored environmental harm may violate existing rights just as effectively as other means. Indeed,

> it may be as simple as recognizing that an individual who is killed by a state-permitted air emission is equally dead as one who is shot by state police. Both should be protected from the deprivation of life [though] the former death is mediated by environmental forces while the latter is not.[84]

Once a constitutional environmental right is created either by judicial interpretation or by codification in an explicit constitutional provision, judicial enforcement takes on a crucial role. Contrast the Nigerian case of *Gbemre*, in which the finding of a constitutional violation utterly failed to arrest the impugned harm from gas flaring, with the dramatically effective remedies provided by courts in other parts of the world. In Argentina, for example, the Supreme Court has made Herculean efforts to compel restoration and preservation of the Matanza-Riachuelo river basin; one of the most polluted watersheds in that nation. In orders in 2006 and 2007 the Court required the government, among other things,

---

[81] *Ktunaxa Nation v British Columbia*, 2015 BCCA 352, leave to appeal granted by the SCC 17 March 2016. See also N Bakht and L Collins, 'The Earth is our Mother: Freedom of Religion and the Preservation of Aboriginal Sacred Sites in Canada' (2017) *McGill Law Journal* (forthcoming).

[82] See eg *Mayagna (Sumo) Awas Tinga Community v Nicaragua Case* (2001), Inter-Am Ct HR (Ser C) No 79.

[83] See eg *Tsilhqot'in Nation v British Columbia*, [2014] 2 SCR 257.

[84] LM Collins, 'An Ecologically Literate Reading of the Canadian Charter of Rights and Freedoms' (2009) 26 *Windsor Journal Social & Legal Issues* 7, 8.

to conduct a comprehensive environmental assessment of the state of the river, to inspect all polluting facilities, close illegal dumps, clean up the river banks, improve storm-water, sewage treatment and wastewater systems, and develop a regional environmental health plan.[85] The orders included strict timelines, ongoing judicial oversight and daily fines against the regulator for non-compliance. The World Bank subsequently approved \$2 billion in financing for this project, which has already resulted in the provision of clean drinking water to one million people, a new sewage system serving half a million people, closure of 134 garbage dumps and the creation of 139 sampling points for air, water and soil quality monitoring.

In the Ecuadorian case of *República del Ecuador Asamblea Nacional, Comisión de la Biodiversidad y Recursos Naturales*,[86] the Second Court of Criminal Guarantees of Pichincha found that illegal mining violated the rights of nature guaranteed in Ecuador's Constitution. The Court enjoined the illegal mining and held that the 'armed forces of Ecuador and the national police should collaborate' to enforce the injunction 'including by destroying all of the items, tools and other utensils that constitute a grave danger to nature and that are found in the site where there is serious harm to the environment'.[87] This injunction was enforced by more than 500 members of the military who demolished mining equipment with explosives. While this is perhaps an extreme example, it illustrates that strong judicial remedies coupled with government enforcement can have a dramatic impact on the ground.

Constitutional environmental rights clearly are game-changing legal tools over which judges have substantial power. Indeed, in this field of law progressive adjudication can be the difference between environmental degradation and environmental transformation.

VII. Indigenous Environmental Law

Finally, judges around the world have the power to interpret and apply indigenous environmental law as they adjudicate environmental disputes of many kinds. As Borrows has argued, the adoption of indigenous law enriches the legal toolkit for environmental protection, appropriately posits indigenous peoples as legal subjects, and, most importantly, entails a paradigm shift away from modes of thought that have produced the Anthropocene and towards philosophical and legal structures that have the potential to support a sustainable inter-species

---

[85] Boyd (n 63) at 130–31.
[86] *República del Ecuador Asamblea Nacional, Comisión de la Biodiversidad y Recursos Naturales*, Acta de Sesión No 66 (15 June 2011).
[87] ibid.

community on Earth.[88] The Brundtland Commission in its pivotal 1989 report recognised that

> [tribal and indigenous] communities are the repositories of vast accumulations of traditional knowledge and experience that link humanity with its ancient origins. Their disappearance is a loss for the larger society, which could learn a great deal from their traditional skills in sustainably managing very complex ecological systems.[89]

While it is important to avoid romantic stereotypes that may essentialise or constrain indigenous peoples, there is no doubt much to be learned from indigenous approaches to environmental protection.[90] Moreover, the recognition and implementation of indigenous environmental law serves the twin purposes of environmental sustainability and reconciliation between indigenous and non-indigenous communities.[91] Indigenous perspectives have already had a major impact on legislative and constitutional provisions in countries such as Ecuador and New Zealand.[92] Similarly, judges around the world have the ability to draw wisdom from indigenous traditions to revitalise environmental law. There are two interrelated ways in which courts can give effect to indigenous environmental law. First, courts can consider, adopt and apply indigenous environmental law in their adjudication of domestic constitutional and statutory provisions. Secondly, in some circumstances courts can delegate particular environmental disputes to indigenous mechanisms of self-government; this goes beyond indigenous law into the realm of indigenous environmental governance.[93]

---

[88] J Borrows, *Canada's Indigenous Constitution* (Toronto, University of Toronto Press, 2010); J Borrows, 'Living Law on a Living Earth' in *Law and Religious Pluralism in Canada* (Vancouver, UBC Press, 2008); J Borrows, 'Living Between Water and Rocks: First Nations, Environmental Planning, and Democracy' (1997) 47 *University of Toronto Law Journal* 417; J Borrows, 'With or Without You: First Nations Law (in Canada)' (1996) 41 *McGill Law Journal* 629.

[89] World Commission on Environment and Development, *Our Common Future* (1987) 12, 114–15. See also F Berkes, *Sacred Ecology: Traditional Ecological Knowledge and Resource Management* (Philadelphia, Taylor & Francis, 1999).

[90] See BJ Richardson, 'The Ties that Bind: Indigenous Peoples and Environmental Governance' in BJ Richardson, S Imai and K McNeil (eds), *Indigenous Peoples and the Law: Comparative and Critical Perspectives* (Oxford, Hart Publishing, 2009) 337–70.

[91] See United Nations Subcommittee on the Prevention of Discrimination and the Protection of Minorities, *Study of the Problem of Discrimination against Indigenous Populations* UN Doc E/CN.4/Sub.2/1986:

> [A]ll indigenous communities have, and uphold, a complete code of rules of various kinds which are applicable to the tenure and conservation of lands as an important factor in the production process, the foundation of family life, and the territorial basis for the existence of their people as such.

[92] See Constitution of the Republic of Ecuador, Art 71, available at: http://pdba.georgetown.edu/Constitutions/Ecuador/english08.html; E Daly, 'The Ecuadorian Exemplar' (2012) 21(1) *Review of European, Comparative and International Environmental Law* 63; CJ Iorns Magallanes, 'Maori Cultural Rights in Aotearoa New Zealand: Protecting the Cosmology that Protects the Environment' (2015) 21(2) *Widener Law Review* 273.

[93] For an excellent explanation of the relationship between law and governance, see LJ Kotzé, *Global Environmental Governance* (Cheltenham, Edward Elgar, 2012) 995–98; see also P Orebech and others,

In the first scenario, domestic courts hearing environmental matters arising under particular constitutional or legislative provisions can seek guidance
from the indigenous legal position on the question at issue. In many cases,
this will require courts to revisit and revise long-established rules of evidence,
as Canadian courts have done since the landmark decision in *Delgamuukw
v British Columbia*,[94] where the Supreme Court accepted that oral histories could
be evidence of Aboriginal title. Indeed, Canada's highest court has shown some
leadership in this area. In a series of cases beginning in the 1990s, the Court affirmed
that indigenous legal perspectives must be taken into account in the adjudication
of Aboriginal rights claims.[95] Henderson opines that this jurisprudence 'ended the
legal dialectic between the familiar English system and the exoticised Aboriginal
difference' in Canada.[96] Most recently, the Supreme Court evinced an understanding and respect for indigenous environmental law by recognising that the environmental rights of Aboriginal title-holders include an intergenerational component.
In *Tsilhqot'in Nation v British Columbia*, the Court made history by sustaining a
claim for Aboriginal title over a large tract of land in British Columbia. Moreover,
it held that 'incursions on Aboriginal title cannot be justified if they would substantially deprive future generations of the benefit of the land',[97] and further that
Aboriginal title lands cannot be put to uses that would 'destroy the ability of the
land to sustain future generations of Aboriginal peoples'.[98] The notion of a binding obligation of ongoing sustainability is otherwise absent from Canadian law,
but is an organising principle in indigenous legal traditions in the territory now
known as Canada.[99] Thus, the Court would appear to be giving effect to indigenous law in this breakthrough decision.

In the second scenario, where the statutory framework is amenable, courts can
support indigenous environmental law and governance by recognising indigenous
decision-making jurisdiction over environmental matters. In *Wisconsin v EPA*,[100]
the state of Wisconsin challenged the federal Environmental Protection Agency's
devolution of regulatory power over water quality on reserve to a Chippewa
indigenous group. The Seventh Circuit Court of Appeal upheld the Chippewa's

---

The Role of Customary Law in Sustainable Development (Cambridge, Cambridge University Press,
2005); TA McClenaghan, 'Why Should Aboriginal Peoples Exercise Governance over Environmental
Issues?' (2002) 51 *University of New Brunswick Law Journal* 211.

[94] *Delgamuukw v British Columbia* [1997] 3 SCR 1010, [84]–[87].

[95] See also Borrows, 'With or Without You: First Nations Law (in Canada)' (n 88).

[96] J (S) Youngblood Henderson and others, *Aboriginal Tenure in the Constitution of Canada*
(Toronto, Carswell, 2000) 8.

[97] ibid, para 86.

[98] ibid, para 121.

[99] See eg L Little Bear, 'Relationship of Aboriginal People to the Land and the Aboriginal
Perspective on Aboriginal Title' in CD-ROM: *For Seven Generations: An Information Legacy of the Royal
Commission on Aboriginal Peoples* (Ottawa, Minister of Supply & Services, 1996). Indigenous law has
no binding force in Canada but courts have held that it should be taken into account in interpreting
the content of Aboriginal rights under the Canadian Constitution; see *Delgamuukw v British Columbia*
[1997] 3 SCR 1010.

[100] *Wisconsin v US Envtl Prot Agency*, 266 F3d 741 (7th Cir 2001) cert denied 535 US 1121.

right to regulate water quality on its reservation, including the right to set higher standards than those in place at the state level. The Court held that

> [b]ecause the Band has demonstrated that its water resources are essential to its survival, it was reasonable for the EPA, in line with the purposes of the *Clean Water Act*...to allow the tribe to regulate water quality on the reservation, even though that power entails some authority over off-reservation activities.[101]

Some 10 years after *Wisconsin v EPA*, the Indian Supreme Court recognised an indigenous group's right to regulate resource extraction in its traditional territory in *Orissa Mining Corp Ltd v The Union of India*.[102] In that case, the Supreme Court enforced provisions of the Forest Rights Act granting tribal peoples customary rights over their traditional territories. The case concerned a proposed bauxite mine in the 'Niyamgiri', an area considered sacred by the local Dongria Kondh indigenous people. After a number of illegal acts, including the failure to obtain consent from the Dongria Kondh, the proponent was denied the necessary permits and appealed to the courts. In 2013, the Supreme Court ordered the state government to seek consent for the proposed mine by referring the decision to the *gram sabhas* (or village councils) of the affected indigenous communities.[103] As Menon explains:

> every village of the 12 consulted rejected the proposal for mining. All villages unanimously resolved that the Niyamgiri, the abode of their god, was to be protected and that no permission for mining could be issued. Following this, the [state] issued an order 'finally rejecting' the company's application for environmental clearance.

To summarise, the adoption and enforcement of indigenous law is a transformative judicial tool for environmental sustainability and social equity in the Anthropocene epoch, which is ultimately characterised by troublingly deep inter- and intra-species injustices and inequalities of the type that indigenous peoples have experienced since the onset of colonisation.

VIII. Conclusion

In the modern regulatory state, many judges have come to see their role in environmental protection as marginal, habitually deferring to the administrative branch of government. Weaving together four doctrinally distinct areas of law, this chapter has attempted to show that the opposite is true. Judges have a central

---

[101] ibid, 750. See also EA Kronk Warner, 'Tribes as Innovative Environmental Laboratories' (2015) 86 *University of Colorado Law Review* 789.

[102] *Orissa Mining Corp Ltd v The Union of India* (2013) 6 SCC 476 (India).

[103] M Menon, 'India's First Environmental Referendum: How Tribal People Protected the Environment' (2015) 45 *Environmental Law Reporter News & Analysis* 10656.

role to play in transforming environmental law for the Anthropocene. Indeed, judges possess a powerful toolkit for ensuring the sustainability of our societies (and our species). They can change environmental economics, by requiring corporate actors to internalise the environmental costs of their conduct through damages awards in environmental civil claims. They can require governments to act as responsible stewards of crucial natural resources through the public trust doctrine. They can change an entire national legal order by recognising and implementing constitutional environmental rights. Judges can also give effect to time-tested systems of effective environmental governance by interpreting and applying indigenous law. Since we cannot rely solely on the executive and legislative authorities to mediate the human-environment interface in the Anthropocene, these and other progressive judicial initiatives will be necessary in order to protect our common future.

15

The Emergence of Transnational Environmental Law in the Anthropocene

JOLENE LIN

I. Introduction

In 2000, Paul Crutzen and Eugene Stoermer coined the term 'Anthropocene' to refer to a new geological epoch—one that is dominated by humans.[1] As to when the Holocene ended and the Anthropocene began, the answer is necessarily uncertain. Some suggest that the Anthropocene started with the Industrial Revolution when human activities started to expand at an exponential rate.[2] Others, like William Ruddiman, argue that the Anthropocene began five to eight thousand years ago when mankind first cleared forests and developed agriculture.[3] What is clear is that the Anthropocene is witnessing the exertion of significant pressure on the Earth's systems and further pressure could destabilise critical biophysical systems in adverse and harmful ways.[4] Having already crossed three of the nine planetary boundaries that define what Rockstrom and others describe as a 'safe operating space for humanity', it is critical that humanity collectively strives to avoid breaching more planetary boundaries.[5]

While there are individuals who question the utility of formalising the relationship between humankind and the environment in such a way, recognising the Anthropocene arguably serves an important purpose: it challenges us to reflect and ask hard questions about our existing social, political and economic structures. The Anthropocene could also serve to consolidate and create a common meaning

---

[1] PJ Crutzen and E Stoermer, 'The "Anthropocene"' *Global Change Newsletter* (Intl Geosphere-Biosphere Programme, Stockholm, Sweden, May 2000) 17–18.

[2] J Rockstrom and others, 'Planetary Boundaries: Exploring the Safe Operating Space for Humanity' (2009) 14 *Ecology and Society* 1, 3.

[3] WF Ruddiman, 'The Anthropogenic Greenhouse Era Began Thousands of Years Ago' (2003) 61 *Climatic Change* 261, 261.

[4] Rockstrom and others, 'Planetary Boundaries' (n 2) at 3.

[5] ibid, 27.

out of the numerous messages and arguments about the impact of humanity on the environment. As Kotzé puts it,

> the Anthropocene…could create a common understanding of the centrality of people in global earth systems change; could refocus the debate on ways to ameliorate this impact; could instill a common understanding of the global geographical, temporal and causal dimension of anthropogenic impacts and ecological crisis; and could promote a collective appreciation of the many different aspects surrounding possible socio-legal institutional change.[6]

Of particular importance to readers of this book, the concept of the Anthropocene invites us to think more critically about law and environmental governance and whether environmental law is well equipped to respond to the challenges of the Anthropocene. Kim and Bosselmann have argued that '[t]he current system of international environmental law and governance, with its maze of [multilateral environmental agreements (MEAs)], is considered to be unsuitable for navigating the Anthropocene'.[7] There are a number of reasons behind the perceived ineffectiveness of international environmental law—ranging from the propensity to manage environmental issues on a sectoral basis (instead of an integrated approach) to the tendency for MEAs to incorporate lowest common denominator standards in order to secure collective agreement by states.[8] In the exploration for alternative forms of governance to supplement traditional inter-state lawmaking, the concept of the 'transnational' has gained traction in environmental law scholarship. This chapter seeks to explore how a shift from international environmental law to transnational environmental law (TEL) may provide us with a more nuanced approach as we consider how we should deal with the effects of global human-induced environmental change, including how we can promote sustainable energy use and how we value and regulate the world's limited natural resources.

At this juncture, it would be helpful to briefly outline what TEL refers to. TEL is broader than, and includes, international environmental law. In a nutshell, '[TEL] encompasses all environmental law norms that apply to transboundary activities or that have effects in more than one jurisdiction'.[9] By focusing on the transnational features of norm development and implementation, rather than the international dimensions, the concept of TEL recognises that important environmental regulation takes place outside formal treaty regimes. At the same time, there is significant interaction between formal treaty regimes and these other forms of

---

[6] L Kotze, 'Rethinking Global Environmental Law and Governance in the Anthropocene' (2014) 32(2) *Journal of Energy and Natural Resources Law* 127.

[7] RE. Kim and K Bosselmann, 'International Environmental Law in the Anthropocene: Towards a Purposive System of Multilateral Environmental Agreements' (2013) 2 *Transnational Environmental Law* 285, 286.

[8] E Louka, *International Environmental Law: Fairness, Effectiveness, and World Order* (Cambridge, Cambridge University Press, 2006) 21; P Sands and J Peel, *Principles of International Environmental Law*, 3rd edn (Cambridge, Cambridge University Press, 2012) 894.

[9] GC Shaffer and D Bodansky, 'Transnationalism, Unilateralism and International Law' (2012) 1 *Transnational Environmental Law* 31, 32.

environmental governance such as voluntary certification schemes that provide consumers with some assurance that products such as timber and fish have been harvested according to sustainable practices, and transnational municipal networks that seek to diffuse norms and practices of sustainable development among cities around the world.[10] Furthermore, TEL recognises that in order to foster community responses to global environmental issues ranging from climate change to tackling illegal wildlife trafficking, it is necessary to involve non-state actors such as businesses, civil society and scientific experts, to name a few. In brief, TEL seeks to 'move beyond the state' and provide a theoretical framework for a more multi-actor, multi-level and normatively plural system of environmental law and governance. It recognises that the state is but one of the many actors that ought to be involved in governing human actions vis-à-vis the environment. It also recognises the important normative contributions made by non-state actors that operate at multiple levels and often in non-coercive ways.

Viewing global environmental law and governance through the lens of the Anthropocene highlights a number of key issues. First, the Anthropocene highlights the interconnectedness of Earth's natural processes.[11] This raises challenges for global environmental law and governance because these responses have to be holistic not only in terms of geography, but also in terms of time and scale. Secondly, the Anthropocene focuses attention on the overwhelming impact of humanity on the global environment. As environmental law and governance mediates the human-environment interface and shapes our institutional responses to environmental issues, the appreciation of the dominance of the human impact will force us to rethink the morality of the centrality of human beings in our relationship with the environment. Finally, given the complexities and uncertainties that characterise the Anthropocene, environmental law and governance will have to adjust: It has to become more dynamic and reflexive, operate at multiple levels and be capable of harnessing multi-actor responses. It is in relation to this final point that TEL offers the most promise. As a normative framework that has its roots in international relations theory that seeks to move away from the state as the central organising concept, TEL embraces the possibilities of multi-level, multi-actor governance. In the Anthropocene, as environmental problems and their political solutions become increasingly complex, TEL has the potential to offer a broader and richer analysis of the role of law in tackling environmental problems. This, in

---

[10] On voluntary certification schemes, see eg T Buthe and W Mattli, *The New Global Rulers: The Privatization of Regulation in the World Economy* (Princeton NJ, Princeton University Press, 2011); G Salmon, 'Voluntary Sustainability Standards and Labels (VSSLs): The Case for Fostering Them' (2002) Roundtable on Sustainable Development, OECD www.oecd.org/sd-roundtable/papersand-publications/39363328.pdf. On transnational municipal networks, see eg MM Betsill and H Bulkeley, 'Transnational Networks and Global Environmental Governance: The Cities for Climate Protection Program' (2004) 48 *International Studies Quarterly* 471; S Bouteligier, *Cities, Networks and Global Environmental Governance: Spaces of Innovation, Places of Leadership* (New York, Routledge, 2013).
[11] Rockstrom and others (n 2) at 23.

turn, can be the basis for more effective environmental governance in pursuit of ecological integrity and the maintenance of planetary boundaries.

To explore the potential of TEL to provide a more appropriate response to the complex challenges of the Anthropocene, this chapter uses the European Union's (EU) sustainable biofuels regulatory regime as a case study to illustrate how TEL is characterised by the involvement of public and private actors in cross-border standard-setting and implementation, and how the interactions between various actors across multiple levels of governance give rise to hybrid regulatory features. TEL also occasionally involves unilateralism.[12] In the case of the EU's sustainable biofuels policy, the EU's sustainability criteria create more stringent requirements for biofuels to be sold in the EU market. The result is to create pressure on non-EU producers to ensure that their production methods are sustainable if they wish to have non-restricted access to the EU market. TEL is created when EU standards have extraterritorial normative effect in the absence of an international agreement. This gives rise to two broad questions concerning legitimacy. The first question is whether it is legitimate for economically powerful states to use trade-based measures to unilaterally direct international policy. The second question is whether there are satisfactory responses to the claim that private regulation (eg by sustainability schemes and auditors) is non-democratic and therefore illegitimate. This chapter argues that unilateralism can be legitimate if due process and non-discrimination norms laid down in international law are adhered to. As for the second claim, this chapter takes the view that private regulation is not necessarily more undemocratic than international law. In the case of biofuels, the attempts by sustainability certification schemes to include stakeholders from various sectors of society in developed and developing countries are laudable pragmatic efforts to build legitimacy where there is no agreed-upon notion of 'democracy' in the transnational space.

Finally, the decision to examine biofuels policy as a case study is informed by the realisation that the creation of biofuels captures the essence of the Anthropocene: biofuels is a man-made product that is intended to be a silver bullet that addresses the objectives of mitigating climate change, enhancing energy security and supporting agriculture.[13] However, in pursuit of these objectives, biofuels also raise significant concerns such as their environmental sustainability from a 'field to pump' viewpoint and the pressure placed on food security and vulnerable communities.[14] To properly govern biofuels production and consumption requires a holistic, multi-actor approach at multiple levels of governance. It also requires a blend of private and public regulatory approaches. Finally, on a more sobering note, the case of biofuels is a reminder of our hubris in thinking that we can solve

---

[12] For discussion, see eg J Scott and L Rajamani, 'EU Climate Change Unilateralism' (2012) 23 *European Journal of International Law* 469.

[13] See discussion in pt III below.

[14] ibid.

environmental problems through more technological developments; an issue that will become increasingly pertinent as we move further into the Anthropocene.

Part II briefly sketches the concept of TEL. Part III analyses the EU's sustainable biofuels regulatory regime and advances the two arguments about legitimacy set out above. Part IV concludes with observations about how the emerging concept of TEL provides an alternative framework for environmental governance in the Anthropocene.

II. A Primer on Transnational Environmental Law

Transnationalism is well established in the field of international relations as the study of phenomena that bridge, extend or occur beyond state boundaries. By definition, transnational phenomena involve non-state and sub-state actors such as non-governmental organisations (NGOs), businesses, charities, religious orders and municipalities.[15] While international, intergovernmental and inter-state activities involve relations between states, transnational relations, in addition to the foregoing interactions, also occur between states and non-state actors as they interact across state borders.[16]

In the 1970s, in an attempt to challenge the dominant state-centric view of world affairs, Joseph Nye and Robert Keohane sought to bring attention to the transnational dimensions of world affairs. At that time, they indicated that 'when [transnational phenomena] have been recognized, they have often been consigned…to the environment of interstate politics, and relatively little attention has been paid to them or their connections with the interstate system'.[17] Defining 'transnational relations' as 'contacts, coalitions and interactions across state boundaries that are not controlled by the central foreign policy organs of governments', Nye and Keohane edited a special issue of *International Organization* devoted to theorising the impact of transnational relations on the inter-state system. It should be noted that in their conception of 'transnational interaction', non-governmental actors play a significant role. While transnational interactions may involve governments, they are not the exclusive actors; transnational interactions must involve at least one actor that is not an agent of a government or intergovernmental organisation.[18] They also advocated a world politics paradigm that broadens the

---

[15] H Bulkeley and others, *Transnational Climate Change Governance* (Cambridge, Cambridge University Press, 2014) 5. On religious organisations as transnational actors, see J Haynes, 'Transnational Religious Actors and International Politics' (2001) 22 *Third World Quarterly* 143. On cities as transnational actors, see M Acuto, 'Global Cities as Actors: A Rejoinder to Calder and de Freytas' (2009) 29 *SAIS Review of International Affairs* 175.

[16] Bulkeley and others, *Transnational* (n 15).

[17] JS Nye Jr and RO Keohane, 'Transnational Relations and World Politics: An Introduction' (1971) 25 *International Organization* 329, 330.

[18] ibid, 332.

conception of actors to include non-state actors and sub-state entities (such as
states within a federal system).[19]

By the end of the 1970s, however, the field of international relations reaffirmed
its commitment to a state-centric paradigm. In the 1980s and early 1990s, international regimes emerged as a major focus of theoretical debate and empirical study
in international relations.[20] In the mid-1990s, Thomas Risse-Kappen's volume
Bringing Transnational Relations Back In (1995) rekindled interest in the issues
that Nye and Keohane had explored in the 1970s. This 'second wave' of transnational relations scholarship had a prominent focus on transnational NGOs that
had gained ascendency on the international stage since the 1970s. This second
wave of scholarship also focused on demonstrating that transnational actors and
interactions were capable of influencing state behaviour.[21] However, a growing
number of scholars also began to examine transnational relations beyond their
impact on state behaviour. It was increasingly recognised that, apart from seeking to influence governmental policy, non-state actors and sub-state actors were
establishing norms and principles with normative impact across state boundaries.

Cities and local governments, for example, have started to organise themselves
as networks and formed organisations to increase their role and influence in
global governance.[22] Founded in 1990, the International Council for Local Environmental Initiatives (ICLEI) is one of the world's largest organisations of local
governments. Its membership in 2012 included 12 mega-cities, 100 super-cities
and urban regions, 450 large cities and 450 small and mid-sized cities in 84 countries.[23] ICLEI represents the environmental concerns of local government internationally by participating in major sustainability forums such as UN-Water, the
International Water Association and UN Habitat.[24] ICLEI also works to promote
biodiversity conservation and resource efficiency at the local level.[25] Its Cities Biodiversity Center works closely with the Convention on Biological Diversity secretariat to organise capacity-building events for cities and side-events parallel to the

---

[19] JS Nye Jr and RO Keohane, 'Transnational Relations and World Politics: A Conclusion' (1971) 25
International Organization 721. It should be noted that Keohane and Nye subsequently modified their
usage of terms for the sake of clarity. Hence, in RO Keohane and JS Nye, 'Transgovernmental Relations and International Organizations' (1974) 27 *World Politics* 39, 41, the term 'transnational' refers
to non-governmental actors and the term 'transgovernmental' refers to sub-units of governments on
those occasions when they act relatively autonomously from higher authority in international politics.
[20] S Haggard and BA Simmons, 'Theories of International Regimes' (1987) 41 *International Organization* 491.
[21] A seminal work in this wave of scholarship is ME Keck and K Sikkink, *Activists beyond Borders:
Advocacy Networks in International Politics* (Ithaca, NY, Cornell University Press, 1998).
[22] CF Alger, 'Expanding Governmental Diversity in Global Governance: Parliamentarians of States
and Local Governments' (2010) 16 *Global Governance* 59.
[23] ICLEI, *ICLEI—Local Governments for Sustainability Corporate Report 2011/12* (2012) 7, www.
iclei.org. Megacities are cities with a population of at least 10 million people. In ICLEI terminology, a
super-city has a population of 1 to 10 million people, a large city has a 100,000 to 1 million people, and
a city or town has up to 100,000 people.
[24] ICLEI, 'Who is ICLEI', http://www.iclei.org/iclei-global/who-is-iclei.html.
[25] ibid.

Conference of the Parties (COP) meetings. By implementing international norms and practices concerning biological diversity at the local level, and drawing on local practices to inform the further development and refinement of global practices, networks like ICLEI play an important role in transnational norm diffusion processes.

Scholars also began to observe how cities were beginning to claim political authority and develop independent policies in relation to foreign affairs and security as they seek to protect their inhabitants from threats such as terrorism and pandemics.[26] Cities are also engaging in diplomacy, traditionally seen to be the domain of states, in pursuit of global objectives such as conflict prevention.[27] The European Network of Local Authorities for Peace in the Middle East, for example, organises many lobbying activities such as election monitoring and seeks to keep the Middle East peace process on the international agenda.[28] As such, cities are '[demonstrating] how states and international organizations are no longer the only problem solving units in world politics'.[29]

Scholars like Anne-Marie Slaughter and Kal Raustiala built on Nye and Keohane's work on transgovernmental relations and theorised about the transgovernmental regulatory networks (TRNs) that had emerged in those areas of economic and trade activity where there are no international treaties and institutions to develop common rules and coordinate responses to crises caused by globalisation. Prominent examples include international finance and competition law.[30] In these networks, national regulators come together to exchange ideas, coordinate

---

[26] For discussion, see K Ljungkvist, *Global City 2.0: From Strategic Site to Global Actor* (London, Routledge, 2016) 77–78.

[27] The notion of 'parallel diplomacy' or 'paradiplomacy' reflects this thinking by creating an image of a central track of diplomacy on which state governments operate and a peripheral track for city actors. It can be argued that this view is an over-simplification of 21st-century statecraft. As van der Pluijm and Melissen put it, '[c]ontemporary diplomacy has…become…a web of interactions with a changing cast of state, city and other players, which interact in different ways depending on the issues, their interests and capacity to operate'; R van der Pluijm and J Melissen, *City Diplomacy: The Expanding Role of Cities in International Politics* (Clingendael Institute, 1 April 2007) 9.

[28] A Sizoo and A Musch, 'City Diplomacy: the Role of Local Governments in Conflict Prevention, Peace-building and Post-conflict reconstruction' in A Musch and others (eds), *City Diplomacy: The Role of Local Governments in Conflict Prevention, Peace-building, Post-conflict Reconstruction* (The Hague, VNG International, 2008) 17.

[29] M Acuto, 'City Leadership in Global Governance' (2013) 19 *Global Governance* 481, 495.

[30] In competition law, Cheng suggests that the abandonment of the Singapore agenda in the WTO (which included competition policy) led the international competition community to eschew formal harmonisation through international treaties and focus on voluntary convergence; TK Cheng, 'Convergence and Its Discontents: A Reconsideration of the Merits of Convergence of Global Competition Law' (2012) 12 *Chicago Journal of International Law* 433, 435. In international finance, Simmons describes regulation as 'diverse and ad hoc' whereby '[r]ule development has tended to involve small numbers of national regulators or supervisors, working briefly but intensively on relatively narrow issues, and producing nonbinding agreements'; BA. Simmons, 'The International Politics of Harmonization: The Case of Capital Market Regulation' (2001) 55 *International Organization* 589, 592. The most resounding advocacy for TRNs has come from A-M Slaughter, who argues in *A New World Order* that TRNs should be 'embraced' as 'the architecture of a new world order'; A-M Slaughter, *A New World Order* (Princeton, NJ, Princeton University Press, 2005) 213.

efforts and negotiate common standards.[31] They deal with each other directly rather than indirectly through foreign ministries.[32] In brief, an important contribution to this field in the past decade has been the development of an account of how transnational actors do not just pursue their objectives by lobbying states and intergovernmental organisations; but also pursue governance in their own right.[33]

What has been of growing interest to scholars of transnationalism in recent years is the emergence of novel, hybrid governance forms when non-state and substate actors come together in various configurations (for example, sustainability round-tables involving businesses, NGOs, members of the public and government officials). These transnational hybrid initiatives have been the subject of a flourishing body of scholarship, which needs to be understood against the background of a wider debate on the rise of 'private regulation' in social, economic and environmental governance.[34] The transnational governance scholarship also intersects with other debates and models on polycentric governance, experimentalist governance, regime complex and orchestration, to name a few.[35]

TEL is situated within this broader scholarship on transnational phenomena but its focus is limited to transnational law in the environmental domain. The concept of transnational law has been developed to address legal norms that do not fall neatly within the categories of domestic law or international law.[36] Shaffer argues that the term 'transnational law' can be divided into two concepts based on whether the focus is on the subject or the source of legal change in a domestic legal system.[37] If the focus is on the subject, then it can be said that TEL refers to the law that applies to transboundary situations whereby the relevant legal norms may derive from domestic legal systems, public international law, or private ordering

---

[31] P-H Verdier, 'Transnational Regulatory Networks and Their Limits' (2009) 34 *Yale Journal of International Law* 113, 114.

[32] Keohane and Nye, 'Transgovernmental Relations and International Organizations' (n 19) at 42.

[33] Bulkeley and others (n 15) at 7.

[34] S Ponte and C Daugbjerg, 'Biofuel Sustainability and the Formation of Transnational Hybrid Governance' (2015) 24 *Environmental Politics* 96, 100. On the rise of private regulation, see T Buthe and W Mattli, *The New Global Rulers: The Privatization of Regulation in the World Economy* (Princeton, NJ, Princeton University Press, 2011).

[35] On polycentric governance, see E Ostrom, 'A Polycentric Approach for Coping with Climate Change' (2014) 15 *Annals of Economics and Finance* 97. On experimentalist governance, see M Hoffmann, *Climate Governance at the Crossroads: Experimenting with a Global Response after Kyoto* (Oxford, Oxford University Press, 2011). On regime complex, see K Raustiala and DG Victor, 'The Regime Complex for Plant Genetic Resources' (2004) 58 *International Organization* 277. On orchestration, see KW Abbott and others (eds), *International Organizations as Orchestrators* (Cambridge, Cambridge University Press, 2015).

[36] Global law, on the other hand, refers to norms that may not have been produced by inter-state agreement but which claim to be universal in application or have universal validity. As Perez puts it, '[t]he globality of these systems stems from their (parallel) claim for universal validity, and from the cosmopolitan nature of their thematic horizon (which means that their normative effort is directed primarily at global issues'; see O Perez, 'Normative Creativity and Global Legal Pluralism: Reflections on the Democratic Critique of Transnational Law' (2003) 10 *Indiana Journal of Global Legal Studies* 25, 26.

[37] GC Shaffer (ed), *Transnational Legal Ordering and State Change* (Cambridge, Cambridge University Press, 2014) 5.

such as a mediated settlement between a polluter and the community harmed by the pollution damage.[38] If the focus is on the source of legal change, then TEL is about the study of (1) how legal norms are created and applied across state borders by public and private actors that seek to improve environmental performance in target states, industries and communities in close connection with the environmental resource at stake (for example, indigenous peoples and forests); (2) the outcomes of such patterns of norm creation and diffusion; and (3) normative concerns that arise from transnational hybrid legal ordering such as legitimacy.[39] Paraphrasing Shaffer's definition of transnational law, this second concept of TEL is not a doctrinal one

> but a *methodological* one that is used to assess empirically how transnational-induced legal change occurs and what type of effects it has. The concept, in other words, does not aim to delineate a particular body or field of law or legal doctrine, but cuts across fields of law and provides an analytic means for assessing transnationally induced change in a globalised world.[40]

This chapter adopts this latter concept of TEL.

The Anthropocene is characterised by increasing uncertainty in the functioning of the Earth system and greater recognition of the inter-connectedness of natural processes. This calls for more responsive governance than that provided by international treaty regimes that are top-down in nature and tend to be slow to respond to scientific discoveries and technological developments. TEL offers a conceptual framework for analysing how more responsive regulation involving multiple actors at various levels of governance occurs and the types of results that ensue. The following Part III examines the EU's sustainable biofuels regulatory system as an example of TEL in action and its regulatory potential in the Anthropocene.

III. The EU's Quest for Sustainable Biofuels

At the start of the twenty-first century, biofuels occupied a marginal position in the oil-and-gas dominated global energy market.[41] The development of biofuels

---

[38] Shaffer points out that this concept is a functional one that reflects a professional concern that, because both international and domestic laws are inadequate to address cross-border situations, a more accurate or useful concept is required to govern these situations; ibid.

[39] See eg N Craik, 'Deliberation and Legitimacy in Transnational Environmental Governance' IILJ Working Paper 2006/10 (Global Administrative Law Series); articles in 'Special Issue: Law, Expertise and Legitimacy in Transnational Economic Governance' (2010) 8 *Socio Economic Review*; D Szablowski, *Transnational Law and Local Struggles: Mining Communities and the World Bank* (Oxford, Hart Publishing, 2007). This conceptualisation is heavily influenced by Shaffer's concept of 'transnational law as transnational legal ordering'; Shaffer, *Transnational Legal Ordering and State Change* (n 37) at 6–7.

[40] Shaffer (n 37) at 7.

[41] In 2013, liquid biofuels met around 2.3% of total global transport fuel demand. This represented an increase in use of biofuels by a factor of three compared to 2004 levels; C Lins and others, *10 Years of Renewable Energy Progress (The First Decade: 2004–2014)* (REN21, Paris, France) 14.

had not gone beyond some small-scale experiments and short periods of national support in most countries except Brazil, where bioethanol has held a significant position in its domestic energy portfolio since the 1970s.[42] In the 2000s, a conflux of factors created the biggest window of opportunity for the commercial development of biofuels. These three factors are climate change, energy security and rural development. Touted as a 'triple-win' silver bullet that could help lower greenhouse gas emissions, enhance energy security and promote rural development, governments of developed and developing countries alike jumped on the biofuels bandwagon. It should be noted, however, that political and socio-economic factors dictate the relative weight that states attach to climate change mitigation, energy security and rural development and that this 'trio of benefits' is a glib sound bite which glosses over the policy contradictions that can arise from trying to achieve all three objectives simultaneously.[43] Every biofuels programme to date has been supported by extensive governmental intervention in the form of research grants, laws and regulations, subsidies and import tariffs because biofuels have historically been more expensive to produce compared to petroleum fuels.[44]

In the EU, the year 2003 witnessed the launch of more aggressive policies to encourage the development of the biofuels industry.[45] The focus during this period was on stimulating biofuels demand and supply, and little attention was paid to the environmental and socio-economic effects. Between 2005 and 2008, biofuels incentive programmes in the United States, the EU and some 24 other countries contributed to global food markets experiencing the largest price shocks in 30 years.[46] More information about the environmental and socio-economic problems associated with industrial-scale biofuels production also began to emerge. Also reflecting some of the markers of the Anthropocene, these problems include rampant deforestation and consequent biodiversity loss and ecological damage, 'land grabs' and displacement of rural communities and indigenous peoples from their homes, and the controversial possibility that the production

---

[42] CR Soccol and others, 'Bioethanol from Lignocelluloses: Status and Perspectives in Brazil' (2010) 101 *Bioresource Technology* 4820.

[43] See discussion in The Royal Society, *Sustainable Biofuels: Prospects and Challenges* (January 2008) Policy document 01/08 www.royalsociety.org.

[44] AM Bento, 'Biofuels: Economic and Public Policy Considerations' in RW Howarth and S Bringezu (eds), *Biofuels: Environmental Consequences and Interactions with Changing Land Use* (Proceedings of the Scientific Committee on Problems of the Environment (SCOPE) International Biofuels Project Rapid Assessment, Gummersbach, Germany, 22–25 September 2008) http://cip.cornell.edu/scope/1245782000; MB Charles, R Ryan, N Ryan and R Oloruntoba, 'Public Policy and Biofuels: The Way Forward?' (2007) 35 *Energy Policy* 5737, 5741; OECD, Trade and Agriculture Directorate, Committee for Agriculture, Working Party on Agricultural Policies and Markets, 'A Review of Policy Measures Supporting Production and Use of Bioenergy' (July 2008) Doc No TAD/CA/APM/WP(2007)24/FINAL http://www.oecd.org/dataoecd/37/43/41037609.pdf.

[45] C Charles and others, *Biofuels—At What Cost? Government Support for Ethanol and Biodiesel in the European Union* (Global Subsidies Initiative, 2013) 17, www.iisd.org/gsi/biofuel-subsidies/biofuels-what-cost.

[46] R Bailis and J Baka, 'Constructing Sustainable Biofuels: Governance of the Emerging Biofuel Economy' (2011) 101 *Annals of the Association of American Geographers* 827, 828.

of biofuels releases more greenhouse gases than the production of conventional transportation fuels like diesel and petroleum thereby fully running against one of the key policy rationales for promoting biofuels.[47]

The European Commission (EC) soon came under mounting pressure from scientists, environmental and human rights NGOs and some member states (eg Germany, Italy, France and the United Kingdom) to address the environmental and food security dimensions of biofuels production.[48] While there was general agreement that environmental criteria such as avoiding growing crops on land with high biodiversity value would be compliant with World Trade Organization (WTO) law, there was considerable doubt about whether social sustainability criteria such as non-violation of labour rights would breach WTO rules.[49] Eventually, in the negotiations between the Commission, the Council and Parliament that led to the adoption of the Renewable Energy Directive (RED), the European Parliament negotiators conceded on their demands for social sustainability criteria and accepted that the Commission would report on social sustainability issues every second year.[50] Thus, the 2009 RED only includes environmental 'sustainability criteria' for biofuels.[51] Briefly, these criteria specify that biofuels must provide at least 35 per cent greenhouse gas emission savings compared to fossil fuels and must not come from crops cultivated on land with a high biodiversity value or on former peat land.[52] While a type of biofuel can be imported into the EU even if it does not meet the sustainability standards, compliance is required in order for the biofuel in question to count towards attainment of EU or national renewable energy obligations or to be eligible for financial support.[53] Thus, the sustainability criteria are not legally mandatory requirements, but exporters that fail to meet these requirements will encounter restricted access to the EU market.

From a TEL perspective, the interesting features of the attempt to ensure that biofuels consumed within the EU meet some ecological sustainability requirements

---

[47] See *Towards Sustainable Production and Use of Resources: Assessing Biofuels* (UNEP, 2009); Nuffield Council on Bioethics, *Biofuels: Ethical issues* (April 2011) www.nuffieldbioethics.org; JM Melillo and others, *Unintended Environmental Consequences of a Global Biofuels Program*, MIT Joint Program on the Science and Policy of Global Change, Report No 168 (January 2009); C Mandil and A Shihab-Eldin, *Assessment of Biofuels Potential and Limitations* (International Energy Forum, February 2010); A Ajanovic, 'Biofuels versus Food Production: Does Biofuels Production Increase Food Prices?' (2011) 36 *Energy* 2070; T Searchinger and others, 'Use of US Croplands For Biofuels Increases Greenhouse Gases Through Emissions From Land Use Change' (2008) 319 *Science* 1238.

[48] A Mol, 'Environmental Authorities and Biofuel Controversies' (2010) 19 *Environmental Politics* 61, 72.

[49] Ponte and Daugbjerg, 'Biofuel Sustainability and the Formation of Transnational Hybrid Governance' (n 34) at 105.

[50] ibid, 107.

[51] Directive 2009/28/EC on the promotion of energy from renewable sources [2009] OJ L145/16.

[52] ibid, Art 17. For discussion of the complexities and contested meanings of 'sustainability' and how this carries through to biofuels governance, see Bailis and Baka, 'Constructing Sustainable Biofuels' (n 46).

[53] Directive 2009/28, Art 17(1).

lie in the compliance framework and the underlying policy commitment to greening market access. Our attention is drawn to how the sustainability criteria is found in an EU directive, implemented by the EC through a network of public, private or hybrid institutions and actors which diffuse these norms and induce regulatory action (that will lead to compliance with the sustainability criteria) by actors located outside the EU. In the Anthropocene, such governance arrangements offer a promising avenue for addressing complex global environmental problems that are beyond the regulatory reach of any single state and which demand multi-actor, cross-border and integrated solutions.

A. The Compliance Framework

The Commission does not directly ensure that a biofuel product satisfies the sustainability criteria.[54] The task of 'certifying' biofuels as being compliant is delegated to certification schemes that have been developed by business associations, non-profit organisations and governments usually working in partnership. These initiatives are usually labelled 'roundtables' or 'stewardship councils' to signal their multi-stakeholder nature.[55]

The Commission 'benchmarks' these certification schemes against the RED sustainability criteria to determine the extent to which a certification scheme addresses the sustainability criteria and the robustness of its verification system. Subsequently, a producer or importer (in the Commission's language, an 'economic operator') can rely on certification by a recognised scheme to demonstrate compliance with the RED sustainability criteria. To demonstrate independence and transparency, a certification scheme, in turn, relies on auditing by third-party entities such as accreditation bodies before it affixes its 'approved' seal on the biofuel product. As these accreditation bodies are separate entities from those involved in devising the rules and implementing the certification scheme, they are cast as independent arbiters of the verification process and therefore fit to 'regulate the regulators'.[56]

The responsibility of monitoring and verification is therefore divided among myriad actors to ensure that a biofuel is sustainable from the time the feedstock is produced in the fields to the time it reaches the consumer in the EU market. This form of regulation is also known as 'meta-standard regulation' whereby

> [i]nstead of requiring producers to be certified to the Meta-Standard [ie the RED sustainability criteria in this case] directly, compliance with the Meta-Standard can be

---

[54] For detailed discussion, see J Lin, 'Governing Biofuels: A Principal-Agent Analysis of the European Union Biofuels Certification Regime and the Clean Development Mechanism' (2012) 24 *Journal of Environmental Law* 43, 53.

[55] For discussion, see S Ponte, '"Roundtabling" Sustainability: Lessons from the Biofuel Industry' (2014) 54 *Geoforum* 261.

[56] M Hatanaka and L Busch, 'Third-party Certification in the Global Agrifood System: an Objective or Socially Mediated Governance Mechanism?' (2008) 48 *Sociologia Ruralis* 73. For an interesting

achieved through certification to existing standards which have proven to provide a sufficient guarantee that (most of) the…criteria of the Meta-Standard are complied with.[57]

B. The State as Orchestrator

TEL often involves the use of soft law (such as codes of conduct) and New Governance techniques, thus encompassing what Abbott and Snidal call 'Transnational New Governance'.[58] Building on Abbott and Snidal's ideas about the emergence of Transnational New Governance, this section looks at the sustainable biofuels compliance framework as an example of how the EU is proactively employing New Governance techniques at the transnational level to achieve desired regulatory goals.

At the domestic level, 'Old Governance' refers to the state governing regulated activities via 'command and control' and the main enforcement mechanism consists of top-down coercive sanctions. Old Governance relies on 'hard law' and the Old Governance view of societal actors is that they are self-interested and unaccountable, and therefore incapable of self-regulation or playing any meaningful role in state regulation.[59] At the international level, Old Governance comprises of treaty law ('hard law') and an array of issue-specific international organisations that are created and governed by their member states. Albeit to a lesser degree compared to the domestic level, international Old Governance also comprises of centralised governance by international organisations whose legitimacy is based on formal authority and bureaucratic expertise.[60]

On the other side of the spectrum, the New Governance model of regulation is difficult to define precisely, but can be understood to refer to a diverse range of innovative regulatory practices that stand in contrast to Old Governance.[61]

and enlightening discussion about the role of auditors in verifying compliance with land governance criteria in 2 biofuels certification schemes, Bonsucro (formerly the Better Sugarcane Initiative) and the Roundtable on Sustainable Biofuels, see E Fortin and B Richardson, 'Certification Schemes and the Governance of Land: Enforcing Standards or Enabling Scrutiny?' (2013) 10 *Globalizations* 141, 147–48, 151–52.

[57] Dehue and others, 'Towards a Harmonised Sustainable Biomass Certification Scheme' (2007) Ecofys, 4, www.assets.panda.org.

[58] K Abbott and D Snidal, 'Strengthening International Regulation through Transnational New Governance: Overcoming the Orchestration Deficit' (2009) 42 *Vanderbilt Journal of Transnational Law* 501.

[59] J Braithwaite, 'Responsive Regulation and Developing Economies' (2006) 34 *World Development* 884, 886–87.

[60] Abbott and Snidal, 'Strengthening International Regulation through Transnational New Governance' (n 58) at 534.

[61] Since L Salamon, 'The New Governance and the Tools of Public Action' (2001) 28 *Fordham Urban Law Review* 1611, the seminal work that introduced New Governance as 'the silent revolution', there has been a proliferation of scholarship on New Governance. See eg G de Burca and J Scott (eds), *Law and New Governance in the EU and the US* (Oxford, Hart Publishing, 2006); O Lobel, 'The Renew Deal: The Fall of Regulation and the Rise of Governance in Contemporary Legal Thought' (2004) 89 *Minnesota Law Review* 342.

The salient distinction between Old Governance and New Governance is the differing role that the state plays in regulation; all other characteristics flow from this primary distinction. The inability of the state to regulate many spheres of activity using Old Governance approaches is often seen to be the main reason for the rise of domestic New Governance.[62] New Governance incorporates a decentralised range of public and private institutions and actors into the regulatory system by, for example, encouraging self-regulation by industry, relying on this range of actors for regulatory expertise, and making use of 'soft law' to complement or substitute mandatory 'hard law'.[63] In New Governance, the state remains a significant actor but it behaves less as a 'commander' and more as an 'orchestrator' that facilitates and directs collaborative regulation by the network of actors.[64] The state often initiates New Governance programmes as it recognises New Governance as an important regulatory tool and uses it proactively.[65] Therefore, behind all New Governance programmes lurks the hand of the state as it can require private actors and institutions to abide by due process norms/administrative law and can retain the threat of introducing mandatory regulation should self-regulation prove to be unsatisfactory.[66]

Abbott and Snidal advance the normative argument that states and intergovernmental governmental organisations (IGOs) ought to promote Transnational New Governance to fill the gaps of Old Governance in the international regulatory domain. However, Transnational New Governance will take off only if states and IGOs provide the necessary 'orchestration and support'.[67] 'Orchestration includes a wide range of directive and facilitative measures designed to convene, empower, support, and steer, public and private actors engaged in regulatory activities'.[68] They point out that the greatest current weakness of Transnational New Governance is a lack of orchestration.[69] As the above description of the EU sustainable biofuels compliance framework shows, the EU (the equivalent of the 'state' in this instance) can be said to be engaging in 'directive orchestration'.[70] It is imposing conditions on public benefits and giving state endorsement to 'approved' schemes to bolster the practice of biofuels eco-labelling. By the meta-standard approach, the EU is also performing an important facilitative role of encouraging uniformity

---

[62] G de Burca and J Scott, 'Narrowing the Gap: Law and New Approaches to Governance in the European Union' (2007) 13 *Columbia Journal of European Law* 513, 513–14.

[63] J van der Heijden, 'Looking Forward and Sideways: Trajectories of New Governance Theory, Amsterdam Law School Legal Studies Research Paper No 2013-04, 4–6 http://papers.ssrn.com/sol3/papers.cfm?abstract_id=2204524.

[64] Abbott and Snidal (n 58) at 521.

[65] ibid, 523.

[66] I Ayres and J Braithwaite, *Responsive Regulation: Transcending the Deregulation Debate* (Oxford, Oxford University Press, 1992) 158.

[67] Abbott and Snidal (n 58) at 509–10.

[68] ibid.

[69] ibid, 545.

[70] ibid, 544.

of standards across competing biofuels certification schemes. This reduces excessive multiplicity which encourages 'forum-shopping' among biofuels producers and causes confusion on the part of consumers.[71]

The pressure to address the socio-economic problems associated with biofuels production did not go away after mandatory social sustainability criteria were excluded from the RED. Private regulation has provided an alternative regulatory pathway—many certification schemes include social sustainability criteria although their coverage differs widely. As Ponte and Daugbjerg point out, 'the private schemes fill a gap in the governance of biofuels that the EU considers difficult to address without breaching WTO trade rules'.[72] Viewed from another perspective, the EU's resort to Transnational New Governance has allowed it to overcome certain constraints on linking social and environmental standards to trade.[73]

Further, the EC can hardly claim to have the ability or the resources to police compliance with the sustainability criteria in plantations and production plants located outside the EU. The Commission accordingly had to experiment with new governance techniques to achieve its sustainable biofuels regulatory aims. This leads to another observation about TEL: Most scholars of the New Governance school favour a hybrid of Old Governance and New Governance, in which the state maintains a baseline of minimum mandatory regulation, regulates those actors which do not subscribe to New Governance, and uses New Governance to implement or supplement mandatory law.[74] This is an acknowledgement of the significant role that the state continues to play in regulation even though it is no longer the sole locus of authority. Similarly, while TEL eschews the state as its central organising concept, it does not discount the important role that the state continues to play in governing. It advocates regulatory innovation and involves the community, private individuals and the market in environmental governance.

C. Legitimacy

Inevitably, questions of the legitimacy of TEL are raised. In the context of the EU sustainable biofuels regime, two broad questions concerning legitimacy arise. The first question concerns the legitimacy of the EU using market access as a policy

---

[71] See discussion in JM Endres, 'Clearing the Air: the Meta-standard Approach to Ensuring Biofuels Environmental and Social Sustainability' (2010) 28 *Virginia Environmental Law Journal* 108–11.

[72] Ponte and Daugbjerg (n 34) at 107.

[73] As Krasner has argued, transnational private regulation can help governments to escape certain constraints; SD Krasner, 'Power Politics, Institutions, Transnational Relations' in T Risse-Kappen (ed), *Bringing Transnational Relations Back In: Non-State Actors, Domestic Structures and International Institutions* (Cambridge, Cambridge University Press, 1995).

[74] De Burca and Scott, 'Narrowing the Gap' (n 62) at 514–15; DM Trubek and LG Trubek, 'New Governance and Legal Regulation: Complementarity, Rivalry, and Transformation' (2007) 13 *Columbia Journal of Environmental Law* 539, 541–42.

mechanism to unilaterally impose environmental standards on their trading partners. The other question concerns the legitimacy of rulemaking, rule promotion
and adjudication of compliance by private authorities (ie the certification schemes
and auditors).[75] Both types of legitimacy concerns have prompted calls for a 'multilateral governance framework' for biofuels, the institutional design of which
seeks to promote public participation, transparency and deliberative decision-
making.[76] Lima, for example, argues that sustainability regulation in the form of
voluntary certification schemes and the EU sustainability criteria lack transparency and are 'a weak replacement for a structured multilateral legal framework as
demanded by the principle of the rule of law'.[77] Both sets of legitimacy concerns
will be addressed in turn below.

Given the socio-economic differences between developed countries and developing ones, the legitimacy of developed countries unilaterally directing international policy is questionable.[78] It can be argued that the EU's unilateral imposition
of environmental standards on other members of the international community
raises questions of political legitimacy, that is, the acceptance and justification of
shared rule by an aggregate international community of sorts.[79] In this regard,
legitimacy is 'the justification of actions to those whom they affect according to
reasons they can accept'.[80] Justification of authority is, in turn, deemed essential
to securing compliance or the obedience of the governed. However, this argument
could well be set aside as erroneously based on a misconception of what the EU
is trying to achieve through unilateral action. Scott has argued that the ultimate
goal of the EU's resort to trade-related environmental measures 'is not to enforce
compliance with EU rules on the part of operators situated abroad; it is rather
aimed at galvanising or incentivising regulatory or normative engagement elsewhere'.[81] This idea of using market access to influence the regulatory policies of
trading partners is not new. Vogel's *Trading Up*, published in 1995, is the seminal

---

[75] eg Chimni has argued that the worrisome aspect of 'global law without a state' is the absence
of transparency. Further, 'the deterritorialized legal order takes advantage of its well-honed internal
practices to subvert state legal orders, in particular in third world countries…global law without the
state [also] often does not take into account the socio-economic context in third world countries';
BS Chimni, 'International Institutions Today: An Imperial Global State in the Making' (2004) 15
European Journal of International Law 1, 18.

[76] MG Bastos Lima, 'Biofuel Governance and International Legal Principles: Is it Equitable and
Sustainable?' (2009) 10 *Melbourne Journal of International Law* 470.

[77] ibid, 492.

[78] Cultural imperialism, in that developed countries might impose inappropriate standards and
cultural values on developing countries, is another salient concern.

[79] S Bernstein, 'Legitimacy in Global Environmental Governance' (2005) 1 *Journal of International
Law and International Relations* 139.

[80] M Williams, 'Citizenship as Agency within Communities of Shared Fate' in S Bernstein and
WD Coleman (eds), *Unsettled Legitimacy: Political Community, Power, and Authority in a Global Era*
(Vancouver, University of British Columbia Press, 2009) 43.

[81] J Scott, 'The Multi-Level Governance of Climate Change' (2011) 1 *Carbon and Climate Law
Review* 25.

work on the concept of 'the lure of green markets'.[82] Vogel demonstrated how more stringent regulation in a large market led large companies to adapt to that regulation, providing them with a comparative advantage and creating incentives for these companies to lobby for more stringent regulation in other jurisdictions that have yet to do so. The result is what Vogel termed the 'California effect'—the dissemination of stricter environmental regulation across borders. Vogel thereby also demonstrated that unilateral regulatory action by a state exercising market power creates TEL (ie the creation and diffusion of norms across borders). To return to the point on legitimacy, it can be argued that such norm creation and diffusion processes do not amount to the imposition of rules against the will of the recipient state. A state trying to galvanise regulatory action abroad by leveraging on the size of its market is quite different from a state imposing its standards in a discriminatory manner. Further, if the diffusion of these norms results in improved environmental performance and respect for ecological sustainability, it can be argued that these outcomes justify a state's attempt to galvanise regulatory activity extraterritorially. In the Anthropocene, perhaps it is timely to consider the validity of environmental sustainability and ecological integrity concerns as justification for more robust transnational regulatory action akin to the EU's approach to governing biofuels.

Bernstein has demonstrated that what counts as a legitimate institution varies across inter-governmental and non-state institutions.[83] His research has shown that despite trenchant criticism levelled against it, the United Nations Framework Convention on Climate Change regime continued to be seen as the legitimate forum for global climate change governance. At the same time, non-state based forms of governance are held up to far more stringent requirements of accountability and transparency in order to be considered legitimate. Bernstein argues that a major reason for this difference in attitudes towards state-based and non-state based governance structures is that the Kyoto Protocol is based on state consent, which is the lynchpin of what legitimacy demands of a MEA.[84] In short, a treaty that is the product of agreement among equal sovereigns enjoys legitimacy and is therefore the ideal type according to Bernstein. It can be argued that, in comparing TEL that involves a state attaching conditions to market access in order to achieve an environmental objective with international environmental law(based on multilateral negotiations), the comparison is not between an imperfect institution and a perfect ideal. The comparison is between two imperfect institutional alternatives. To foster legitimacy, multilateral treaty negotiations require agreement by consensus. This permits a single state or a small group of states, especially when there are free rider or collective action issues at stake, to stall negotiations

---

[82] D Vogel, *Trading Up: Consumer and Environmental Regulation in a Global Economy* (Cambridge, MA, Harvard University Press, 1995) 261.

[83] S Bernstein, 'Legitimacy in Intergovernmental and Non-state Global Governance' (2011) 18 *Review of International Political Economy* 17.

[84] ibid, 31.

and delay action by the international community. Unilateral action that is applied in a principled manner (eg in a non-discriminatory manner and subject to due process constraints) may be an imperfect, but superior, alternative to the complete lack of action to promote environmental interests.[85] In the biofuels context, there has been little appetite for multilateral negotiations for a treaty-based governance framework because of uncertainty and the complicated nature of biofuels and their impacts.[86] TEL therefore offers some states a pathway for advancing environmental interests in the face of scientific uncertainty and the lack of appetite on the part of the international community to regulate.

It can further be argued that the idea of outright imposition of rules by one actor on another (which rightly gives rise to legitimacy concerns) is too simplistic. First, while recognising the vulnerability of export-driven economies to the demands of economically powerful markets such as the EU, the former are not entirely powerless and defenceless actors who have no choice but to submit in acquiescence. To reiterate the earlier point made by Scott, the use of market access to shape transnational environmental policy is to tap into the logic of free markets and rational behaviour to create incentives for regulatory action outside the EU when no incentives existed before.

Let us take the Indonesian Sustainable Palm Oil Scheme (ISPO) as a case in point. In 2010, the Indonesian government announced plans to develop a nationwide mandatory certification scheme for the palm oil sector.[87] The government gave two official reasons for this policy decision.[88] First, the conditions imposed by the EU sustainability criteria and, related to this, the need for Indonesian palm oil to remain competitive in the global commodity markets. By 2010, palm oil had gained a notorious international reputation. Transnational environmental activist groups like Greenpeace had conducted highly visible public campaigns against multinational companies whose well-known consumer products contain palm oil to raise awareness of the damage done to Indonesian tropical rainforests by industrial palm oil production. (Deforestation in Indonesia for palm oil and illegal logging is so rapid that it has been estimated that the country's forests might be destroyed by 2022).[89] These campaigns succeeded in pressuring some global

---

[85] For discussion of the critical role that international law plays in disciplining unilateral action as part of the broader TEL process, see Shaffer and Bodansky, 'Transnationalism, Unilateralism and International Law' (n 9) at 39–41.

[86] Naiki further argues that, for this reason, biofuels governance has taken the form of a regime complex instead of a core umbrella regime at the international level; Y Naiki, 'Trade and Bioenergy: Explaining and Assessing the Regime Complex for Sustainable Bioenergy' (2016) 27 *European Journal of International Law* 129, 145.

[87] As it is a nation-wide scheme, it will include the small-scale, palm oil growers who produce on a subsistence-like basis but contribute 40% of Indonesia's total output (Interview No 2 with sustainability manager of major biofuel producer firm, on file with author).

[88] R Suharto, 'Why Indonesia Needs ISPO' *The Jakarta Post* (12 February 2010) www.thejakartapost.com/news/2010/12/02/why-indonesia-needs-ispo.html.

[89] C Nellemann and others, 'The Last Stand of the Orangutan 'State of Emergency: Illegal Logging, Fire and Palm Oil in Indonesia's National Parks' (2007) United Nations Environment Programme, GRID-Arendal, Norway, www.grida.no/files/publications/orangutan-full.pdf. See eg the highly visible

brands to commit towards using only certified (sustainable) palm oil in their products and to suspend purchases from Indonesian producers which allegedly clear primary forests or peatland to set up palm oil plantations.[90] The Indonesian government recognised the Indonesian palm oil sector would lose its competitive advantage if it continued 'business as usual' and ignored the environmental and social issues caused by large-scale palm oil cultivation.[91]

Critics may point out that, given the prominence of the Roundtable on Sustainable Palm Oil (RSPO) certification scheme, it is curious that the Indonesian government elected to develop a new standard rather than promote RSPO certification.[92] These critics are likely to dismiss the ISPO as a state-backed effort to evade the more rigorous requirements for RSPO certification. However, there may be validity to the Indonesian government's claim that RSPO certification is expensive and requires extensive documentation.[93] It is out of reach for the thousands of illiterate small-scale farmers who sell their small output to the processing mills. Out of about 2000 plantations in Indonesia, less than 50 were certified by the RSPO in 2010. There was therefore real concern about whether Indonesia could produce enough certified palm oil.

Whether certification by the RSPO or the ISPO is effective in enforcing standards or merely enables scrutiny, is a valid question for more empirical study. For present purposes, the point that this chapter seeks to make is that the Indonesian government would not have introduced the ISPO if not for the regulatory pressure by transnational civil society and the EU biofuels scheme. The ISPO is not a

campaign launched by Greenpeace, 'Ask Nestle to Give Rainforests a Break', which led to Nestle announcing a new policy committed towards identifying and excluding companies in its supply chain that owe or manage plantations linked to deforestation, such as certain palm oil producers/processors; www.greenpeace.org/international/en/news/features/Sweet-success-for-Kit-Kat-campaign/.

[90] 'Indonesia Develops Rival Sustainable Palm Oil Scheme' *The Jakarta Post* (11 October 2010) www.thejakartapost.com/news/2010/11/10/indonesia-develops-rival-sustainable-palm-oil-scheme.html.

[91] The Netherlands, Italy, Germany and Spain are the 4 EU member states that are among the top 10 major destination countries for Indonesian crude palm oil, accounting for about 23% of total annual export (measured in tonnes) in 2008, 2009 and the first 6 months of 2010. India is the single largest importer of Indonesian crude palm oil. Exports to India accounted for 46% of the total exports between 2006 and June 2010. 'An Analysis of Indonesian Exports of Crude Palm Oil' (14 October 2010) TradeData International Analysis Report http://tradedata.net/files/1TQQ3XTKTI/Indonesian_exports_of_Crude_Palm_Oil_HS_Code_1511100000_.pdf.

[92] Ponte and Cheyns describe the RSPO as the most important and visible sustainability network in the palm oil industry; see S Ponte and E Cheyns, 'Voluntary Standards, Expert Knowledge and the Governance of Sustainability Networks' (2013) 13 *Global Networks* 459. For more discussion of the RSPO, see also E Cheyns, 'Multi-stakeholder Initiatives for Sustainable Agriculture: The Limits of the "Inclusiveness" Paradigm' in S Ponte, P Gibbon and J Vestergaard (eds), *Governing through Standards: Origins, Drivers and Limits* (Basingstoke, Palgrave, 2011) 210–35; WF Laurance and others, 'Improving the Performance of the Roundtable on Sustainable Palm Oil for Nature Conservation' (2010) 24 *Conservation Biology* 377; JF McCarthy, P Gillespie, and Z Zen, 'Swimming Upstream: Local Indonesian Production Networks in "Globalized" Palm Oil Production' (2012) 40 *World Development* 555; G Schouten and P Glasbergen, 'Creating Legitimacy in Global Private Governance: The Case of the Roundtable on Sustainable Palm Oil' (2011) 70 *Ecological Economics* 1891.

[93] Suharto, 'Why Indonesia Needs ISPO' (n 88).

response of weakness, of caving in to EU pressure. The ISPO is *domestic* regulation that, for all its flaws and weaknesses due to endemic problems of corruption and lax enforcement within the archipelago of a thousand islands, is created by a state (Indonesia) and tailored to meet its *domestic* circumstances. There is thus clear interaction between transnational norms and processes and domestic factors and needs that led to regulatory change in Indonesia. *That* is the essence of TEL. To argue that unilateralism is essentially economic bullying misses the point.

Scharpf has posited two main forms of legitimacy: input (process) and output (performance and effectiveness) legitimacy. From the viewpoint of output legitimacy, to the extent that a particular set of rules or standards promotes the common good, it should be seen to be legitimate; the process leading to the promulgation of a norm is not pertinent to its legitimacy, and democracy has no role to play in fostering legitimacy. Under this account, 'the question is rather which set of criteria constitutes the best expression of the common good'.[94] The role of experts in determining these standards (and defining what 'the common good' constitutes) and how private governance schemes build legitimacy through expertise has been the subject of numerous studies focusing on standards. Jacobsson argues that standard-setting organisations build legitimacy through presenting their standards as 'expert knowledge stored in the form of rules'.[95] Kerwer posits that a necessary (but not always sufficient) precondition for the effectiveness of standards is that the target audience believes that the expertise on which the standards are based is convincing.[96]

Perez argues that the declining trust in experts and their professed expertise has meant that the power of 'expert knowledge to provide privileged accounts of the common good and, hence, to serve as a source and arbiter of legitimacy' has also declined.[97] Instead, the conception of legitimacy that is gaining ascendency in contemporary global society is one that places emphasis on the process that leads to the production of a transnational norm, that is, input legitimacy: '[t]he legitimacy of transnational regimes is judged, increasingly, by the nature of the process that led to the regimes' creation, and by the public accountability of those who implement them'.[98] 'As such, democratisation' is often viewed as the solution to the 'legitimacy problem'.[99] Held has observed that '[d]emocracy seems to have scored

---

[94] Perez, 'Normative Creativity and Global Legal Pluralism' (n 36) at 28.

[95] B Jacobsson, 'Standardization and Expert Knowledge' in N Brunsson and B Jacobsson (eds), *A World of Standards* (Oxford, Oxford University Press, 2000) 41.

[96] D. Kerwer, 'Rules that many Use: Standards and Global Regulation' (2005) 18 *Governance* 611, 618; see also TA Loya and J Boli, 'Standardization in the World Polity: Technical Rationality over Power' in J Boli and GM Thomas (eds), *Constructing World Culture: International Nongovernmental Organizations since 1875* (Stanford University Press, 1999).

[97] Perez (n 36) at 28.

[98] ibid, 29.

[99] See eg D Bodansky, 'The Legitimacy of International Governance: A Coming Challenge for International Environmental Law' (1999) 93 *American Journal of International Law* 596; A Buchanan and RO Keohane, 'The Legitimacy of Global Governance Institutions' (2006) 20 *Ethics & International Affairs* 405; T Risse, 'Transnational Governance and Legitimacy' in A Benz and Y Papadopoulos (eds), *Governance and Democracy: Comparing National, European and International Experiences* (London, Routledge, 2012).

a historic victory over alternative forms of governance…[It] bestows an aura of legitimacy on modern political life: laws, rules and policies appear justified when they are "democratic"'.[100]

Yet, the meaning of the concept of 'democracy' in the transnational arena is highly contested. There is no consensus on what constitutes adequate participation and deliberation for a regulatory system to be deemed 'democratic' and hence 'legitimate'.[101] Bernstein's analytical framework highlights that a checklist of legitimacy requirements cannot be developed a priori because the concept of legitimacy is a shifting one, one that evolves over time and is also highly contingent on the interactions of power within the social structures of affected communities.[102] What many private authority schemes have sought to do is to include transparency and accountability mechanisms in their governance structures and rulemaking processes to promote representative and deliberative democracy and thereby increase their input legitimacy. Meidinger suggests that this is a form of anticipatory democracy at work as these regulatory programmes aim to anticipate emergent public values, institute mechanisms to advance them and thereby enhance authority.[103] The Forestry Stewardship Council (FSC) is often held up as the 'poster child' of treating transparency and stakeholder consultation as ends unto themselves.[104] However, there is a 'legitimacy trade off' which private authority schemes have to grapple with: high levels of participation and transparency increase support and buy-in, but also slow down decision-making processes and potentially impede timely action on policy problems.[105] Auld and Gulbrandsen's comparative study of the FSC and the Marine Stewardship Council shed light on how schemes may choose to design their institutional features differently to address this trade-off.[106]

Abbott and Snidal argue that the attempts by private authority schemes to incorporate transparency and accountability mechanisms in their governance structures are '[p]ragmatic steps [that] constitute sensible approaches to developing democracy in an arena where the very meaning of the concept is in doubt;

---

[100] D Held, *Democracy and the Global Order: From the Modern State to Cosmopolitan Governance* (Stanford University Press, 1995) 3.

[101] See also the discussion in Bernstein, 'Legitimacy in Intergovernmental and Non-state Global Governance' (n 83) at 21–23 on the assumed relationship between democracy and legitimacy in global governance.

[102] ibid, 42.

[103] E Meidinger, 'Competitive Supragovernmental Regulation: How Could it be Democratic' (2007) 8 *Chicago Journal of International Law* 513, 531–32.

[104] G Auld and LH Gulbrandsen 'Transparency in Nonstate Certification: Consequences for Accountability and Legitimacy' (2010) 10(3) *Global Environmental Politics* 97–119. For an excellent discussion of the FSC, see S Bernstein and B Cashore, 'Nonstate Global Governance: Is Forest Certification a Legitimate Alternative to a Global Forest Convention?' in J Kirton and MJ Trebilcock (eds), *Hard Choices, Soft Law: Voluntary Standards In Global Trade, Environment And Social Governance* (Aldershot, Ashgate Publishing, 2004).

[105] Bernstein (n 83).

[106] Auld and Gulbrandsen, 'Transparency in Nonstate Certification' (n 104).

over time, they could have significant consequences for global democracy'.[107] However, the jury is still out on this issue as more empirical evidence of how participation actually works in private regulatory schemes is needed.[108] One indication, by Ponte and Cheyns, is that 'sustainability networks are far less inclusive, transparent and participatory than they portray themselves to be' as they manipulate who gets to participate and use subtle techniques to drown the voices of politically weaker actors.[109] This chapter argues that the democratisation of TEL, for example, through the creation of inclusive models of deliberation and public participation is a laudable objective in pursuit of the genuine aspiration to subject transnational issues to deliberation by all who are affected. However, this is a work-in-progress in pursuit of a moving target (that is, the shifting and contested notion of democracy in the transnational context). It is premature to conclude that TEL is illegitimate on this ground. It is an imperfect institutional design, but nevertheless has the potential to fill the inadequacies of traditional multilateral rulemaking.

In the Anthropocene, as we grapple with increasingly complex and uncertain socio-ecological challenges and attempt to find ways to achieve more harmonious co-existence between *homo sapiens* and Earth's ecological systems, we are required to revisit the normative and regulatory institutions that govern the human-environment interface. As discussed in the foregoing, TEL is not a perfect institutional design, but it offers some advantages over traditional inter-state rulemaking. Its more flexible nature, embrace of multiple actors and levels of governance, and responsiveness to legitimacy concerns makes TEL worthy of further enquiry in the spirit of creative governance experimentation in the Anthropocene.

IV. Conclusion

This chapter has sought to demonstrate how the concept of TEL can offer a different set of lenses through which environmental issues and solutions can be understood in the Anthropocene. TEL places the emphasis on the need for an 'all hands on deck' approach to environmental protection, and not just heavy reliance on the state to develop and implement solutions. This is of particular salience in the Anthropocene, as we increasingly realise that the complexity of socio-ecological challenges requires multi-actor responses and the state is not equipped to deal with the challenges on its own. TEL also encourages experimentation as humanity seeks to find ways to fulfil the aspirations of millions who are currently denied access to electricity and basic needs while managing our collective environmental footprint.

---

[107] Abbott and Snidal (n 58) at 555.
[108] Meidinger, 'Competitive Supragovernmental Regulation' (n 103) at 533, makes the same point.
[109] Ponte and Cheyns, 'Voluntary Standards, Expert Knowledge and the Governance of Sustainability Networks' (n 92) at 19.

In the case of biofuels, we see experimentation at a number of levels. Biofuels were being explored as a carbon-friendly substitute for petroleum to mitigate climate change. The EU also experimented with delegating regulatory responsibilities to private certification schemes and inducing foreign biofuel feedstock producers to adhere to environmental standards that are absent in their home jurisdictions. Ultimately, the experiment also sought to galvanise the promulgation of similar sustainability criteria in biofuel feedstock-producing countries.

However, TEL has its limitations and raises questions of legitimacy. Northern interests and actors can dominate the development and implementation of TEL, and trade protectionism can be thinly disguised as unilateralism in pursuit of environmental goals. Recognising these limitations and potential for abuse (and what can be done to ameliorate these negative factors), this chapter has argued that TEL is not an 'either or' proposition. It is an imperfect alternative, but used in combination with other imperfect regulatory approaches, it may improve humanity's chances of protecting its safe operating space in the Anthropocene.

16

The End of European Union Environmental Law: An Environmental Programme for the Anthropocene

HAN SOMSEN*

I. Introduction

The impending arrival of the Anthropocene triggers simultaneous feelings of shock and enlightenment not unlike those experienced after a brutal medical diagnosis finally putting a name to disturbing symptoms that have kept us awake at night. The cruelty of the verdict resides in the fact that we can no longer choose to dismiss discomforting pains and fears that have made us restless for so long. The irreversible fact of the matter is that the human identity henceforth is that of someone mortally wounded, and that chances of survival depend on a physician's skills and the rate of medical progress before the day of reckoning when, without such fortune, the human project is set to expire. With this candour comes a curious sense of relief, however, as we finally understand what we are fighting, and hence no longer need to pain ourselves trying to guess the nature and magnitude of our challenge.

In this case, our newly acquired insight is that: (1) in the Anthropocene humankind has become the dominant force determining the fate of planet Earth and its inhabitants and that (2) without a dramatic turnaround in environmental policy or some technological break-through, humans are precariously close to extinguishing themselves.

It is this second limb of the diagnosis, which scientists have captured in the planetary boundaries hypothesis, that many will obviously find most alarming.[1]

* Professor of EU Law, School of Law, Tilburg University.
[1] J Rockström and others, 'A Safe Operating Space for Humanity' (2009) 461(24) *Nature* 472–75.

Nine inter-related critical planetary processes have been identified (climate change, rate of biodiversity loss, interference with the nitrogen and phosphorous cycles, stratospheric ozone depletion, ocean acidification, global freshwater use, change in land use, chemical pollution and atmospheric aerosol loading) which threaten fatally to disrupt the self-regulating capacity of the Earth system. It is now believed that transgressing critical thresholds that underlie these processes will trigger sudden, non-linear catastrophic change on a scale making human life on the planet impossible.[2] To continue relying on the current corpus of environmental law, notwithstanding the fact that it has presided over a well-observed steady slide towards dysfunctionality and ineffectiveness, would be to disregard the best available scientific evidence, and hence tantamount to giving up hope for survival.

Traumatic as all this may be, it settles firmly in the affirmative any lingering question whether the time has come for a renaissance of environmental law. On a scale inviting comparison with Galileo's *Dialogues*, the Anthropocene Working Group's findings compel humankind to redefine and reorganise its relation with its surroundings, and to prepare itself for an immediate future in which it must manage and assume final responsibility and control over the environment in ways that mirror its supreme power over and critical dependency on it.

A productive starting point for this critical endeavour is to lay bare the structural faults in those central paradigms, categorisations and regulatory instruments clearly exposed by the Anthropocene, but on which environmental law continues to be premised. To be sure, unlike a medical diagnosis leaving no choice but to accept as fatal something previously believed to be benign and operable, to put the finger on the causes of the planet's predicament amounts to an existential challenge to entrenched religious, political and economic powers and ideologies that dominate and pervade every single aspect of contemporary life. Realistically, the battle ahead is hence one which is unlikely to be won, and accepting defeat but enjoying the party while it lasts amounts to a sensible choice for some. Yet, unlike sufferers of life-threatening disease, or denialist business-, religious- and political leaders,[3] academic scholars do not have the luxury of such resignation.

The purpose of this chapter is to discuss fundamental disconnections between the foundational phenomenological, spatial, temporal and instrumental presumptions underpinning current environmental law on the one hand, and

---

[2] On the contested nature of these and other thresholds, see V Galaz, *Global Environmental Governance, Technology and Politics* (Cheltenham, Edward Elgar, 2014) 22–23.

[3] Michel Serres explicitly articulates the parallel with the Holy Inquisition on the occasion of Galileo's trial, at the end of which the accused uttered his famous defiant words '*Eppur si muove!*' (and yet it moves!). Serres frames contemporary denialism as a second trial:

> Science won all the rights three centuries ago now, by appealing to the Earth, which responded by moving. So the prophet became king. In our turn, we are appealing to an absent authority, when we cry, like Galileo, but before the court of his successors, former prophets turned kings: 'the Earth is moved.' The immemorial, fixed Earth, which provided conditions and foundations of our lives, is moving, the fundamental Earth is trembling.

M Serres, *The Natural Contract* (Ann Arbor, The University of Michigan Press, 1995) 86.

the realities that reveal themselves through the lens of the Anthropocene, on the other. That discussion will be situated within the context of the European Union, a *sui generis* polity which by virtue of its unique characteristics and well-developed environmental policy offers an apt illustration of the challenges and possible responses to them in this respect. Unlike the international legal order, in which state sovereignty, weak lawmaking processes and ineffective compliance mechanisms conspire to mount obstacles to a decisive and effective change of course, EU environmental law is not constrained by those obstacles to the same extent, and therefore offers an interesting and potentially inspiring perspective.

Section II summarily and in the abstract explains what is meant when it is asserted that the Anthropocene heralds new phenomenological, spatial, temporal and instrumental challenges for EU environmental policy. These are then further discussed in greater detail in sections III (phenomenological and spatial challenges) and IV (challenges of a temporal nature). Conclusions are articulated in section V.

II. Phenomenological, Spatial, Temporal and Instrumental Challenges for Environmental Policy

Phenomenologically the most violent tremor rocking conventional environmental law is the collapse of the human versus nature dichotomy that has always been at its core. In essence, the Anthropocene marks a point in Earth's history when anthropogenic impacts on the Earth system have become so profound and deleterious that nature has become human, and humans are coming dangerously close to succumbing to nature. Michel Serres frames this perplexing paradox as follows:

> If we judge our actions innocent and we win, we win nothing, history goes on as before, but if we lose, we lose everything, being unprepared for some possible catastrophe. Suppose that, inversely, we choose to consider ourselves responsible: if we lose, we lose nothing, but if we win, we win everything, by remaining the actors of history. Nothing or loss on one side, win or nothing on the other: no doubt as to which is the better choice.[4]

Once disentangled, this conundrum immediately raises questions about the *Grundnorm* underpinning environmental law; the foundational norm from which its rules have been derived and with which these rules have sought to be consistent.[5] More than anything else, what environmental law needs in the Anthropocene is a high-order norm fit to serve as backbone for what Serres termed a 'Natural Contract' simultaneously targeting ecological and social integrity, security and

---

[4] ibid, 5.

[5] R Kim and K Bosselmann, 'International Environmental Law in the Anthropocene: Towards a Purposive System of Multilateral Environmental Agreements' (2013) 2 *Journal of Transnational Environmental Law* 285.

justice.[6] Perhaps symptomatic of the tenacity of the human versus nature divide, that discussion has never matured beyond a politically charged and hopelessly misguided tangle of anthropocentric and eco-centric visions of environmental law. Admittedly, it is hard to find a high-order *Grundnorm* in, or even to distil one from, current EU environmental law, let alone one which is sufficiently unambiguous to explain EU law's failure to prevent the current malaise. Logically, however, the absolute nature of the human versus nature dichotomy implies that this norm is likely to represent something of a mirror-image of the *Grundnorm* we associate with being inherently part of the human reality, ie human dignity. Although human dignity is a contested notion, it is conceived here as empowering people to assume full control over their own lives and, as a corollary, preventing others from intruding into those lives, unless free and prior informed consent has been granted.[7] The *Grundnorm* for the environment, inversely, can hence be assumed to amount to a norm pursuant to which human intrusions in the environment, in any of its parts and regardless of their consequences, are mandated unless and until people themselves have chosen to limit their freedom to do so.[8]

In spatial terms, regulatory disconnections between the object of regulation and the regulatory modalities used occur in different ways.[9] Geographically, systemic ecological inter-relationships translating as complexities dictate that in the Anthropocene conceiving environmental challenges as local, national, regional or global is random and political, and obliterates chances for effective regulatory responses. To persist in such categorisations serves political and legal expediency, leaving intact a dysfunctional Westphalian state-centred global legal order, but ignores what we now know is the universal nature of even the seemingly most frivolous local environmental impact.

Perceived as *regulatory* spaces, more abstractly we can say that the act of classifying a problem such as climate change as an *environmental* issue, rather than as a problem reflecting, for example, poverty, gender inequality, global trade or energy policies, is similarly random and political.[10] It is random because we are all too well aware that climate change is a result of a combination of all of the above, and

---

[6] Serres, *The Natural Contract* (n 3).

[7] On the competing meanings of human dignity, see D Beyleveld and R Brownsword, *Human Dignity and Human Rights in Bioethics and Biolaw* (Oxford, Oxford University Press, 2002).

[8] Further explored by H Somsen, 'From Improvement towards Enhancement: A Regenesis of EU Environmental Law at the Dawn of the Anthropocene' in *The Oxford Handbook on the Law and Regulation of Technology* (Oxford, Oxford University Press, forthcoming) ch 16.

[9] On the issue of 'regulatory disconnection', see R Brownsword and H Somsen, 'Law, Innovation and Technology: Before we Fast Forward—a Forum for Debate' (2009) 1 *Law, Innovation and Technology* 1–73.

[10] See eg C Carlarne, 'Delinking International Environmental Law & Climate Change' (2015) 4 *Michigan Journal of Environmental & Administrative Law* 1–60; A Grear, 'Deconstructing Anthropos: A Critical Legal Reflection on "Anthropocentric" Law and Anthropocene "Humanity"' (2015) 26 *Law & Critique* 225–49; SH Baker, 'Adaptive Law in the Anthropocene' (2015) 90 *Chicago-Kent Law Review* 563–84.

it is political because any specific classification serves to privilege one paradigm and body of regulatory principles and instruments over competing others.

In temporal terms, the Anthropocene heralds an age of extraordinarily fast anthropogenic environmental change. As observed, these changes reflect a moment in history when humankind has effectively taken command of the planet, but without managing to assume control. Although the principles of prevention and precaution may at face value suggest otherwise, current environmental law is manifestly unfit for the purposes of assuming control, simply because it is uniquely retrospective in orientation. Thus, environmental law is firmly geared towards 'preserving' and 'protecting' the environmental status quo, or towards 'improving' the environment to status quo ante levels. This trilogy of retrospective duties is given further weight by the precautionary principle, which in effect codifies an a priori bias favouring the status quo over intentional environmental change. Yet the acknowledgement that the environmental status quo is or will soon become untenable in terms of its capability to support (human) life inevitably calls for an additional and different branch of environmental law that is prospective in orientation, and capable of guiding regulators that intentionally enhance the environment in pursuit of biodiversity and human life in ways that have no historical or ecological precedent.

Such initiatives do not constitute environmental 'regulation' in the conventional sense of the word, as they do not target the behaviour of regulatees, but instead seek directly to mould the environment in pursuit of human and ecological imperatives. Quite clearly, law is needed to regulate such initiatives. However, unlike conventional environmental law, those rules do not prescribe specific outcomes but instead regulate the process of enhancement. In EU law, legislation on genetically modified organisms represents the example most closely reflecting the regulation of such prospective ambitions.

III. The Human versus Nature Dichotomy in EU Environmental Law

The idea that humankind must articulate a 'Natural Contract' to reflect the indivisibility of nature and human beings was first articulated by the French philosopher Michel Serres.[11] In tandem with Bosselmann[12] and reflecting the Earth Charter,[13] it may be suggested that a legal *Grundnorm* for the Anthropocene should aspire to

---

[11] Serres (n 3).

[12] See R Kim and K Bosselmann, 'Operationalizing Sustainable Development: Ecological Integrity as a *Grundnorm* for International Law' (2015) 24 *Review of European, Comparative and International Environmental Law* 194–208.

[13] The Earth Charter is available on the internet at: http://earthcharter.org/virtual-library2/the-earth-charter-text.

maintaining ecological integrity, of which human beings form an integral part. As for a Natural Contract reflecting the most striking phenomenological, spatial and temporal ramifications of the Anthropocene articulated above, it may be posited that such a Contract should echo: the indivisibility of the human and the natural; the hierarchical parity between laws serving people and laws serving nature and; the universality and indivisibility of ecological systems (aquatic, terrestrial etc), local and global.

In the remainder of this section the focus is on the ways in which the human/nature dichotomy is legally expressed in the Charter of Fundamental Rights of the European Union and in primary EU environmental law.

A. The Charter of Fundamental Rights of the European Union

The Charter of Fundamental Rights of the European Union features high in the hierarchy of sources of EU law, and for that reason constitutes a suitable starting point for a legal conceptualisation of the relationship between human beings and nature as set out by EU law.[14] The Charter codifies rights derived from past case law of the Court of Justice of the European Union (CJEU), from the European Convention on Human Rights 1950, from the common constitutional traditions of EU member states and from an open-ended group of other international instruments that served as a source of inspiration. The Charter binds EU institutions and bodies as well as national authorities in so far as they act in their capacity as agents for the EU. Legislation adopted by the EU institutions and such member states that contravene the Charter's provisions will hence be struck down.

The preamble states that 'the Union is founded on the indivisible, universal values of human dignity, freedom, equality and solidarity'. The general structure and specific language of the Charter suggest that human dignity, operationalised through a number of articulated freedom, equality and solidarity rights, is the EU's foundational value.

The centrality of human dignity in the EU legal order is amplified by the preambular claim that the Union 'places the individual at the heart of its activities, by establishing the citizenship of the Union and by creating an area of freedom, security and justice' and that, '[e]njoyment of these rights entails responsibilities and duties with regard to other *persons*, to the *human* community and to *future generations*'.[15] Indeed, Article 1 of Title I of the Charter entitled 'Dignity', reflects the Charter's general predisposition: '[h]uman dignity is inviolable. It must be respected and protected'.

Unlike the boldly proclaimed but debatable universality and indivisibility of human dignity, freedom, equality and solidarity, the indisputable indivisibility of

---

[14] [1992] OJ C 326/391.The Charter of Fundamental Rights (The Charter') is available on the internet at http://ec.europa.eu/justice/fundamental-rights/charter/index_en.htm.

[15] Emphasis added.

human beings and the environment is not explicitly registered in the Charter.[16] Article 37 of the Charter, featuring as a manifestation of solidarity, provides that '[a] high level of environmental protection and the improvement of the quality of the environment must be integrated into the policies of the Union and ensured in accordance with the principle of sustainable development'.

It is true that the reference to the principles of integration and sustainable development goes some way towards acknowledging the inseparability of human and ecological imperatives. In subtle but systemic ways, however, these same principles serve the collateralisation of environmental imperatives. In particular, the principle of proportionality which adjudicates the inevitable conflicts that arise in the arena of integration operates so as to put a burden of proof on regulators pursuing environmental ends, and thereby translates into a structural bias favouring economic interests over ostensibly competing ecological imperatives. That bias evidently is consistent with the liberal EU legal order which, in its own words, 'places the individual at the heart of its activities'.[17] Quite irrespective of its lack of operational pedigree, a fundamental flaw underpinning the principle of sustainable development is its underlying assumption that critical environmental thresholds and impacts can be predicted with a degree of certainty, and that a balancing exercise between 'human' and 'natural' imperatives is therefore possible.

The foregoing analysis suggests that human dignity is the single most important principle on which the EU legal order rests, and that the freedoms and rights through which it is realised carry prima facie more weight than any imperative of ecological integrity. In fact, perhaps the most glaring evidence of the continued primacy of the human/nature dichotomy is the absence of an articulated principle of ecological integrity serving as a counterpart for human dignity. Although it undoubtedly is a challenge to arrive at a workable legal articulation of such a principle, that clearly is no excuse for not trying. By way of example and shadowing the Earth Charter's Preamble, a formulation in the Charter could read as follows: '[i]t is imperative that we, the peoples of Europe, declare our responsibility to one another, to the greater community of human and non-human life, and to future generations'. That declaration could be further concretised through the articulation of a general principle of non-degradation, which currently is only occasionally found in secondary legislation.[18] The prevailing paradigm remains far removed from such a proposal, as will be illustrated by an abstract examination of primary EU environmental law below.

---

[16] R Brownsword, 'What the World Needs Now; Techno-Regulation, Human Rights and Human Dignity in Human Rights: Global governance and the quest for justice' (Oxford, Hart, 2004) 203

[17] See more generally M Dawson, 'The Political Face of Judicial Activism: Europe's Law-Politics Imbalance' in M Dawson, B de Witte and E Muir (eds), *Judicial Activism at the European Court of Justice* (Cheltenham, Edward Elgar 2013) 11–31.

[18] See eg Art 4(1) of Directive 2000/60/EC [2000] OJ L 327/1 (Water Framework Directive). It provides: 'Member States shall implement the necessary measures to prevent deterioration of the status of all bodies of surface water, subject to the application of paragraphs 6 and 7 and without prejudice to paragraph 8'.

B. Primary EU Environmental Law

The term 'primary EU environmental law' covers all provisions in the Treaty on
the Functioning of the European Union (TFEU) and the Treaty on European
Union (TEU) that operationalise the EU's environmental policy. The rationale for
EU environmental policy is articulated in Article 191(1) of the TFEU as follows:

> Union policy on the environment shall contribute to pursuit of the following objectives:

— preserving, protecting and improving the quality of the environment,
— protecting human health,
— prudent and rational utilisation of natural resources,
— promoting measures at international level to deal with regional or worldwide environmental problems, and in particular climate change.

In view of the principle of integration enshrined in Article 11 of the TFEU,
besides these specific environmental provisions, primary EU environmental law also comprises other provisions of EU law through which sustainable
development is promoted.[19] This does not mean, however, that the principle of
integration dissolves the human/nature dichotomy in primary EU law. This is
because, to the extent that these various powers (environmental, health, transport, energy, internal market, etc) differ, they are mutually exclusive. No matter
the degree of symbiosis between those different concerns, because of these procedural and substantive differences a hard choice as to the applicable regulatory
regime (and hence logic) must be made. Such choices are hugely important as
they dictate the different paradigms that come to inform subsequent regulatory
action. For example, if the regulation of a certain type of waste is conceived as an
environmental matter, the principles of Article 191 of the TFEU apply, but if it
is deemed to be an issue primarily affecting the internal market in waste, Article
114 of the TFEU and its internal market logic put its mark on the matter.[20] This
certainly also applies to the Union's powers in the sphere of the environment
and human health. The former, according to Article 4(e) of the TFEU, involves
a shared competence, whilst the Union's health policy is confined to supporting,
coordinating or supplementing Member State actions.[21]

It is settled case law of the Court of Justice of the European Union (CJEU)
that the proper policy-base for any proposed initiative is dictated by the centre

---

[19] The principle of environmental integration has lost much if not all of its significance, however,
through the inclusion in the TFEU of competing principles of integration in Arts 7 (the general con-
sistency of all EU policies and activities), 8 (gender equality), 9 (employment, social protection, social
exclusion, education, training and human health), 10 (discrimination) and 12 (consumer protection).

[20] Just as Art 191 of the TFEU clarifies the EU's powers in the sphere of the environment, Art 114
of the TFEU grants powers to the EU to adopt legislation to establish and protect the internal market.

[21] TFEU, Art 168.

of gravity of the substance of that initiative, and that if an issue only incidentally touches on an adjacent policy area, this is not sufficient reason to rely on the correspondent legal basis for that policy.[22] The TFEU treats climate change as an issue of environmental law, so that climate policy is a shared competence in which the EU has come to assume a lead role. This is evidently sensible, given the transboundary nature of climate change and the pointlessness of uncoordinated national responses. However, as a matter of EU law, the scale of the problem is relevant only for settling the question whether any given EU competence should be exercised (the principle of subsidiarity);[23] it is not relevant for determining whether a competence exists in the first place. By the same token that it is questionable whether minimum quality standards for drinking water are a manifestation of environmental law rather than health law,[24] it is debatable whether the conceptualisation of climate change as an environmental problem is compatible with the centre of gravity test such as is prescribed by the CJEU.

The fact that the legal basis of such policies has not often become a matter of contention is due to the fact that Article 191(1) of the TFEU explicitly acknowledges that environmental policy aims to 'contribute to' human health. In the practice of EU environmental lawmaking, even in those cases when the protection of human health appeared to be the primary aim of a measure, as long as a degree environmental preservation, protection or improvement is required the EU appears to be acting within its prerogatives when it bases such measures on Article 191 of the TFEU. Indeed, it is only because of the explicit reference to human health in Article 191(1) of the TFEU that EU ambient air-quality standards, which clearly primarily target human health, have not been invalidated. It is also the explicit reference to human health in Article 191(1) which helps explain the migration of the precautionary principle mentioned to the realm of health policy.

A conflict between the two legal bases is bound to arise and a hard choice will therefore have to be made when health policy is pursued through the manipulation of the environment in ways that transcend the 'preserve, protect and improve' trilogy that is at the heart of Article 191 of the TFEU. For example, the emerging practice of intentional extinction or alterations through the genetic manipulation of disease-transmitting insects to root out dengue fever, zika, or malaria, cannot be said to involve environmental protection, and such efforts reside rather

---

[22] See eg Case C-70/88 *Parliament v Council* [1991] ECR I-4529, [17]; Case C-155/91 *Commission v Council* [1993] ECR I-939, [19]; Case C-187/93 *Parliament v Council* [1994] ECR I-2857, [25]; and Case C-84/94 *United Kingdom v Council* [1996] ECR I-5755, [45].

[23] See Art 5(3): '[u]nder the principle of subsidiarity, in areas which do not fall within its exclusive competence, the Union shall act only if and in so far as the objectives of the proposed action cannot be sufficiently achieved by the Member States, either at central level or at regional and local level, but can rather, by reason of the scale or effects of the proposed action, be better achieved at Union level'.

[24] Directive 98/83/EC on the quality of water intended for human consumption is based on Art 130s (now TFEU, Art 191) [1998] OJ L 330/32.

under Article 168 of the TFEU (health).[25] In contrast, the same techniques used to protect biodiversity must be based in Article 191 of the TFEU.[26]

The EU's environmental policy is hence in support of a mixture of human and environmental concerns, which superficially may be taken as reflecting the indivisibility of human and natural imperatives. We are reminded by the Charter, however, that it is *individuals* who are at the heart of the Union's activities, implying a clear hierarchy among the aims of Article 191 of the TFEU in a way entirely consistent with the liberal project that the EU represents. That hierarchy, prioritising individual aspirations (as reflected in individual rights and freedoms) and collective human ambitions (enshrined in equality and solidarity rights) over ecological integrity, needs to be rejected, however. It must be rejected not primarily or merely as a matter of moral principle, but also as a matter of empirical fact, since it perpetuates a human/nature duality we now see is false in the Anthropocene epoch. To deny this fallacy, in Einstein's words this 'optical delusion', is to abandon hope of avoiding catastrophe for the present and future generations.[27]

Most conspicuous by its absence in the Title on the Environment in the TFEU and anywhere else in the Treaties is therefore a high-order legal norm articulating that it is imperative for the Union and its member states to act to preserve, protect and improve not so much 'the environment' in the abstract but what the Earth Charter terms *environmental integrity*, of which human health forms an integral part.[28] Environmental integrity has been defined as 'the capacity of an ecosystem to support and maintain a balanced, integrated adaptive community of organisms having a species composition, diversity and functional organization comparable to that of similar, undisturbed ecosystems in the region'.[29]

As it is, Article 191(1) of the TFEU does not articulate any ambition with sufficient clarity to serve as a yardstick for pronouncing on the success or failure of

---

[25] See House of Lords Science and Technology Committee, *Genetically Modified Insects*, 1st Report (HL 2015–16, 68). Genetically modified mosquitos have been released in the Cayman Islands, Malaysia and Brazil to put an end to dengue fever without recourse to hazardous pesticides, with promising results; www.theatlantic.com/health/archive/2014/09/engineering-mosquitoes-to-stop-disease/379247/.

[26] See M Specter, 'Could Genetically Modified Insects Save Hawaii's Endangered Birds' *The New Yorker* (9 September 2016), available at www.newyorker.com/news/daily-comment/could-genetically-modified-mosquitoes-save-hawaiis-endangered-birds.

[27] A Einstein, letter of 1950, as quoted in the *New York Times* (29 March 1972) and the *New York Post* (28 November 1972:

> [a] human being is part of a whole, called by us 'universe', a part limited in time and space. He experiences himself, his thoughts and feelings as something separated from the rest ... a kind of optical delusion of his consciousness. This delusion is a kind of prison for us, restricting us to our personal desires and to affection for a few persons nearest to us. Our task must be to free ourselves from this prison by widening our circle of compassion to embrace all living creatures and the whole of nature in its beauty.

[28] See K Bosselmann, 'The Way Forward: Governance for Ecological Integrity' in L Westra, K Bosselmann and R Westra (eds), *Reconciling Human Existence with Ecological Integrity* (London, Earthscan, 2008) 319–32.

[29] As quoted by V Carrigan and MA Villard, 'Selecting Indicator Species to Monitor Ecological Integrity: A Review' (2002) 78 *Environmental Monitoring and Assessment* 45–61.

the Union's environmental policy. Rather, it outlines policy goals (to which 'it shall contribute') the broadness of which renders them legally meaningless beyond the fact that they imply that the EU's environmental competences are extensive. It is in any event obvious that the provisions in Title XX on the environment are not of a nature to make them amenable to actions for failure to act under Article 265 of the TFEU, a provision which has become something of a legal fossil.[30] No amount of ecological blindness or apathy on the part of the EU or its member states appears sufficient for EU citizens to trigger some procedure or process by which they can take their own and their children's fate in their own hands by forcing EU institutions to act, or by bypassing them altogether. Indeed, there is nothing in primary EU environmental law remotely comparable to the (directly effective) internal market provisions that have empowered market participants directly to enforce their rights. To be sure, in the absence of a legally relevant trigger for mandatory regulatory intervention, the EU institutions will continue to enjoy unfettered discretion to designate environments deemed worth preserving, protecting and improving and, concomitantly, to decide which elements of the biosphere are allowed to perish.[31]

That conclusion is not fundamentally tempered by the subsequent environmental provisions in Title XX. Article 191(2) reads:

> Union policy on the environment shall aim at a high level of protection taking into account the diversity of situations in the various regions of the Union. It shall be based on the precautionary principle and on the principles that preventive action should be taken, that environmental damage should as a priority be rectified at source and that the polluter should pay.

Quite apart from the fact that what constitutes 'a high level of protection' remains moot, the most fundamental omission in Article 191(2) of the TFEU again is the absence of a holistic operational notion and final purpose of EU environmental action, such as 'ecological integrity', through which environmental principles

---

[30] TFEU, Art 265 provides as follows:

Should the European Parliament, the European Council, the Council, the Commission or the European Central Bank, in infringement of the Treaties, fail to act, the Member States and the other institutions of the Union may bring an action before the Court of Justice of the European Union to have the infringement established. This Article shall apply, under the same conditions, to bodies, offices and agencies of the Union which fail to act.

The action shall be admissible only if the institution, body, office or agency concerned has first been called upon to act. If, within two months of being so called upon, the institution, body, office or agency concerned has not defined its position, the action may be brought within a further period of two months.

Any natural or legal person may, under the conditions laid down in the preceding paragraphs, complain to the Court that an institution, body, office or agency of the Union has failed to address to that person any act other than a recommendation or an opinion.

[31] See in more detail H Somsen, 'Towards a Law of the Mammoth? Climate Engineering in Contemporary EU Environmental Law' (2016) *European Journal of Risk Regulation* (special issue) 109–19.

acquire concrete meaning and significance. In the current constellation, it is perfectly possible for the EU to realise a high level of environmental protection (for example, in terms of standards for pesticides in drinking water), and at the same time allow the ecological integrity of its (aquatic) environment to be severely compromised.

The same applies to the principles of prevention and precaution. Both principles lower the barrier for EU regulatory intervention and for that reason are invaluable. But as long as EU environmental policy remains essentially devoid of an articulated higher holistic purpose, ie the protection or restoration of ecological integrity, their application remains random and thereby inherently disproportional.

IV. Temporal Challenges: The Retrospectivity of EU Environmental Law

The foregoing analysis has shown that the core of EU environmental policy as articulated in Article 191(1) of the TFEU consists of a discretionary commitment on the part of the Union to act to preserve, protect and improve the environment, thus also contributing to public health and the rational utilisation of natural resources. I have suggested that this commitment is set to remain discretionary for as long as the treaties do not contain a *Grundnorm* (or 'floor') triggering regulatory intervention, such as the maintenance of ecological integrity. At present, not even the imminent extinction of a species manifestly central to ecological integrity, such as the honey bee, compels the EU institutions to act.[32] In fact, individuals cannot force the EU institutions to act owing to the programmatic nature of the environmental provisions in Title XX, thereby ruling out reliance on them by citizens. Thus, as a general rule, within the EU legal order citizen individual empowerment vis-à-vis the EU is subject to the liberal precondition of direct and individual concern. This 'ecological blindness' is an inevitable feature of a legal order which, as proclaimed in the Charter, places human dignity at the core of all its activities without at the same time acknowledging the inseparability of the human and nature.[33]

Unlike EU citizens who by virtue of the mere fact that they are human have inherent human dignity and thereby enjoy the rights and freedoms articulated in the Charter that protect them against external interferences, there are no human

---

[32] The EU's policy on bees is explained on the EU's website at http://ec.europa.eu/food/animals/live_animals/bees_en.

[33] Bosselmann, 'The Way Forward' (n 26) at 323: '[f]irst, what is wrong with the dominant model of governance? The short answer is ecological blindness. By overlooking the ecological dimensions of human existence, conventional governance models are purely concerned with human welfare following economic rationality. The narrow anthropocentric view led to "economic governance" on the one hand and "environmental governance" on the other'.

interferences in ecological systems that primary EU environmental law deems ipso facto off limits. It is only after EU institutions have chosen to exercise their discretion to restrict EU citizens' freedom to destroy or manipulate nature that such limitations come to apply.

EU environmental law therefore is conditionally permissive in orientation; human interferences in the environment are permitted unless and until such interferences have been regulated. The precautionary principle does not counter this basic tenet of EU environmental law as it cannot trigger discrete EU duties to preserve, protect or improve the environment. Rather, the principle lowers the evidentiary threshold for regulatory action once such action is considered by the EU institutions, crucially allowing them to negotiate the hurdle of scientific uncertainty, which in the Anthropocene has become the normal state. It is true that the precautionary principle has been instrumental in occasionally apportioning a burden of proof on economic operators to show that a proposed activity is 'safe' before it is authorised (eg REACH),[34] but this occurs only in a context of secondary law, ie *after* the discretionary exercise of environmental powers granted by EU institutions.

The absence in EU environmental law of an ecological equivalent to human dignity (ecological integrity) implies boundless institutional discretion to preside over and acquiesce in the *destruction* of the environment. And it would also seem to imply that there is no principled deontological ceiling as to what the EU, its member states and citizens may aspire to in terms of intentionally *enhancing* the environment. Elsewhere I have defined environmental enhancement as follows:

> Intentional interventions to alter natural systems, resulting in unprecedented characteristics and capabilities deemed desirable or necessary for the satisfaction of human and ecological imperatives or desires.[35]

Descriptively, the Anthropocene shows that humankind has taken command of nature but without assuming control. Normatively, the Anthropocene implies that humankind must now confront this final responsibility through its regulatory institutions. Assuming control means that in addition to preserving, protecting and improving the environment, *enhancing* the environment becomes an inevitable additional aim of EU environmental policy.

Environmental enhancement might come in the form of genetically engineered insects to control the spread of the malaria mosquito due to global warming, solar radiation management and carbon dioxide removal to combat anthropogenic climate change, de-extinction technologies to restore biodiversity, etc. Some of these

---

[34] Regulation (EC) No 1907/2006 concerning the Registration, Evaluation, Authorisation and Restriction of Chemicals (REACH) [2006] OJ 96/1. See FM Fleurke and H Somsen, 'Precautionary Regulation of Chemical Risk: How REACH Confronts the Regulatory Challenges of Scale, Uncertainty, Complexity and Innovation' (2011) 48 *Common Market Law Review* 357–93.

[35] Somsen, 'From Improvement towards Enhancement' (n 8).

enhancement initiatives are currently still at the stage of development, but others are already being deployed.[36] Quite clearly, enhancement initiatives come into play only when (precautionary) policies to preserve and protect the ecological status quo of environments have failed, and attempts to improve such environments to status quo ante levels have proved fruitless (see Figure 16.1).

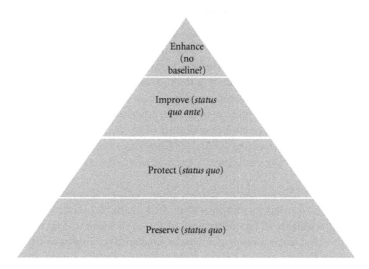

Figure 16.1: Hierarchy of Environmental Policy Initiatives

The absence in the treaties of a holistic high-order ecological norm that also captures environmental enhancement initiatives therefore is obviously of great practical significance. At first glance its implication appears to be that there is no principled constraint on EU or national enhancement initiatives, just as there is no indication of circumstances which could give rise to a prima facie duty to pursue them. By way of an (admittedly bizarre) thought-experiment: if dyeing EU waters white to reflect sunlight so as to cool down the planet proved technically possible without breaching any relevant pre-existing laws, Title XX would not appear to form an obstacle to such an initiative. Conversely, even if only through genetic techniques honey bees could be made resistant to pesticides, and as a result threats of extinction and ecological as well as human catastrophe could be averted, EU environmental law does not appear to impose an obligation to do so.

In the absence of a high-order ecological norm, constraints on the EU institutions in respect of environmental enhancement or, conversely, duties to initiate enhancement initiatives, if they exist, must be derived from something else. The next two sections focus on the temporal scope of Article 191(1) of the TFEU as a check on the Union's enhancement powers, and on the human right to

---

[36] Galaz, *Global Environmental Governance, Technology and Politics* (n 2); Somsen (n 8).

a clean environment, as a possible source of duties to enhance aspects of the environment.

A. EU Environmental Law: Static or Dynamic?

Do the powers enumerated in Article 191(1) of the TFEU 'to preserve, protect, and improve' the environment include powers intentionally to alter environments (possibly with unprecedented results), in order to satisfy human and ecological imperatives, ie powers to *enhance* the environment? The answer to this question depends on whether Article 191(1) of the TFEU espouses a dynamic or static vision of 'the environment'. When the reference point for environmental quality is derived from some fixed past point in time, or is territorially circumscribed, this translates into a static notion of the environment. Such a static concept of the environment suits the Holocene, the present geological epoch characterised by relative ecological stability and harmony, but clearly does not connect with the needs of the Anthropocene, a period in which radical environmental change is occurring. To entertain a static notion of the environment underpinning environmental law in the dynamic contemporary reality that marks the Anthropocene is tantamount to adhering to postal laws to regulate e-mail communication. The fact of the matter is that the EU must learn to preside over a dynamic environmental policy, at least if it is to have a realistic chance of successfully engaging with the unprecedented challenges that it will face now and in future. Yet a necessary precondition for the coherence and effectiveness of such a dynamic policy is that its outer contours are circumscribed by an overarching high-order norm of ecological integrity of sufficient clarity. Without such a *Grundnorm*, the EU's substantive environmental powers effectively become infinite, which is difficult to square with the principle of conferral,[37] and in any event would appear to require an amendment of the Treaties. Also, without a *Grundnorm* a dynamic environmental policy is bound to become random, incoherent and itself a source of ecological risk. By way of concrete example, high-order guidance on suitable candidates for de-extinction and the areas in which they are to be re-introduced is an imperative precondition for a dynamic wildlife conservation policy. Clearly, the fact that it appears technologically possible to bring back the mammoth from extinction does not mean that as a matter of wildlife conservation policy it ought to be done, or if it is to be done that the mammoth should be re-introduced in the territories where it went extinct 4,500 years ago.[38]

---

[37] See TEU, Art 5.

[38] B Shapiro, *How to Clone a Mammoth* (Princeton NJ, Princeton University Press, 2015). See also G Church, who argues that the goal of 'De-Extinction' should be 'deep ecological enrichment', interpreted as the restoration and enhanced resilience of ecosystems in the face of changing environmental conditions; G. Church, 'De–Extinction is a Good Idea' *Scientific American* (26 August 2013), quoted in PJ Seddon, A Moehrenschlager, J Ewen, 'Reintroducing Resurrected Species: Selecting DeExtinction Candidates' (2014) 29 *Trends in Ecology and Evolution* 1–8.

In summary, current EU environmental law is bound to be dysfunctional. This is so because if it is premised on a static notion of the environment it cannot engage the reality that in the Anthropocene ecological conditions are fluid and dynamic. If it allows for a dynamic environmental policy without the benefit of a higher-order norm, it is random, incoherent and ineffective. This disconcerting conclusion does not obviate the need to determine whether the orientation of EU environmental policy is static or dynamic, because the answer to that question is indicative of future reforms that are needed. It is a question that is not easy to answer, however, because the evidence emerging from primary and secondary EU environmental law is not unambiguous.

The primary provisions of EU environmental law to a large extent reflect the principles that were enshrined in the environmental action programmes dating back to the early 1970s, and hence do not reflect the insights of the Anthropocene Working Group, nor the technological prowess of the present day and age. Undoubtedly, therefore, the founding fathers of the EU's environmental law and policy regime had a decidedly static mind-set. 'Preserving' the environment accordingly involved keeping intact the status quo of environments that, on the basis of the criteria adopted by EU institutions, were singled out for preservation by member states. The duties to 'protect' and to 'preserve' the environment, as well as their scope, are conditioned by the duty to 'preserve', which is triggered only after the discretionary exercise of environmental powers by the EU. Put simply: member states must protect the integrity of environments that satisfy EU standards, and improve up to those same standards environments that have deteriorated. For example, in the sphere of nature conservation, Directive 2009/147/EC on the Conservation of Wild Birds,[39] in tandem with the 1992 Directive on the Conservation of Natural Habitats and of Wild Fauna and Flora,[40] constitutes a comprehensive nature conservation regime. On the basis of predominantly objective criteria amenable to judicial review, member states are under an obligation to protect listed species and to designate the most suitable areas for their protection. The designation of such areas in turn triggers duties to *preserve* the integrity of the area or specific species; to *protect* it against external interferences (such as economic development, hunting etc); and to *improve* the area to a favourable conservation status in cases where the protective regime had failed to uphold the integrity of the area. In temporal and spatial terms, the point of reference giving substance and meaning to the duties to preserve, protect and improve is the status quo at the time when the member states designated (or should have designated)[41] the area. In essence, the logic underpinning the directives hence betrays a static concept of nature.

---

[39] [2009] OJ L 20/7.
[40] [2002] OJ L 206/7.
[41] See Case C-355/90 *Commission v Spain* [1993] ECR I-4221.

The incompatibility of such a static temporal and spatial scope with the state of flux of the European environment very soon demanded a legal response, however, and has forced the CJEU to instil temporal and spatial dynamism in the regime. In particular, the CJEU has needed and will continue to need to pronounce on the temporal and spatial member state obligations in respect of populations[42] that have recently become extinct, populations that have been re-introduced but have gone extinct, and populations that have vanished but where re-introduction plans are possible.

It is impossible to predict with any degree of certainty how far the CJEU is pre-pared to go in its dynamic interpretation before it feels it has stretched the flexibil-ity of the EU's nature conservation regime to its limits. For example, how will the Court ultimately construe the obligation in Article 6(2) of the Habitats Directive to avoid 'significant disturbance'? It has already ruled that Article 6(2) includes a duty proactively to ensure that a population *recovers*, but could this possibly come to include obligations to resort to genetic manipulation or even to de-extinction programmes?[43]

The magnitude of the issues at stake implies that it should not be for the CJEU to determine the future shape and form of the European environment. Rather, the proper way forward is for primary EU law to add 'environmental enhancement' to Article 191(1) of the TFEU as an additional goal of EU environmental policy, which is to be resorted to (only) when this is necessary in pursuit of an articulated high-order principle of ecological integrity.

B. Discretionary Commitment to Improve or Obligation of Result to Enhance?

The previous section concluded that EU environmental policy in essence appears to be premised on a static notion of the environment. However, in the absence of a high-order principle of ecological integrity and in conjunction with the teleologi-cal mind-set of the CJEU, the door for a dynamic metamorphosis of EU environ-mental policy in which there is a place for environmental enhancement is clearly ajar. In this section I very briefly speculate on the question whether it is conceiv-able that duties arise which compel the EU and its member states to engage in enhancement policies.

---

[42] See the very interesting work currently undertaken by Arie Trouwborst in the context of the Ius Carnivoris project, www.tilburguniversity.edu/about/schools/law/about/departments/eip/research/carnivores/. Cases that directly relate to the temporal and spatial scope of the Habitats Direc-tive include Case C-117/00 *Commission v Ireland* [1992] ECR I-5356, Case C-418/04 *Commission v Ireland* [2004] ECR I-11000, Case C-258/11 *Sweetman* ECLI:EU:C:2013:220, Case C-521/12 *Briels* ECLI:EU:C:2014:330, Case C-301/12 *Cascina Tre Pini* ECLI:EU:C:2014:214, Case C-6/04 *Commission v United Kingdom* [2005] ECR I-9056, Case C-383/09 *Commission v France* ECLI:EU:C:2011:369.

[43] Case C-117/00 *Commission v Ireland*, Case C-418/04 *Commission v Ireland*.

At present, as has been shown, Article 191(1) of the TFEU establishes a discretionary EU commitment to preserve, protect and improve the environment, and the proposition that the EU and its member states could have *obligations* to *enhance* the environment is therefore not immediately self-evident. On the other hand, the notion that states have duties to respect, protect and fulfil environmental human rights is uncontroversial. If the enjoyment of environmental human rights becomes conditional upon interventions in the environment of a kind that deserves the label 'environmental enhancement', a duty to deploy environmental enhancement might arise.

Elsewhere, I have pointed out the degree of synergy between the three levels of duties that are at the heart of the United Nation's 'respect, protect and fulfil' human rights framework on the one hand, and the duties to preserve, protect and improve the environment as set out in Article 191(1) of the TFEU on the other.[44] The similarities (ie respect versus preserve; protect versus protect; fulfil versus improve) facilitate a fairly straightforward re-interpretation of Article 191(1) of the TFEU to reflect the UN framework. To do so is not only an acknowledgement of the collapse of the human/nature divide, it also reflects the fact that EU institutions are bound by human rights and must act in a manner consistent with them.

The UN human rights framework arose from debates regarding the substance of the right to food,[45] but its value extends to social and economic rights more generally and is therefore of particular relevance for the present purposes. Although the Respect Protect Fulfil framework is foremost a non-binding conceptual tool, it is one which the EU subscribes to.[46]

According to the framework, as regards social and economic rights, states have three levels of duties: duties to avoid depriving (to respect); duties to protect from deprivation (to protect); and duties to aid the deprived (to fulfil). State duties to pursue enhancement initiatives most likely arise in the context of duties to fulfil, or in the language of Article 191(1) of the TFEU, the duty to improve the environment. The duty to fulfil is a restorative duty towards people whose rights have already been violated. 'The duty of aid is ... largely a duty of recovery—recovery from failures in the performance of duties to respect and protect'.[47]

The arrival of environmental enhancement technologies such as genetic manipulation, synthetic biology and climate engineering opens up the possibility, for the first time in human history, of directly securing environmental rights that previously appeared to have been unattainable. At least as a matter of technological theory, species could be brought back from extinction and global warming

---

[44] Somsen (n 8).

[45] *The Right to Adequate Food as a Human Right*, report prepared by Mr A Eide, E/CN.4/Sub. 2/1983/25 (1983).

[46] See A Williams, *The Ethos of Europe: Values, Law and Justice in the EU* (Cambridge, Cambridge University Press, 2010); O de Schutter, *International Human Rights Law* (Cambridge, Cambridge University Press, 2010).

[47] H Shue, 'The interdependence of Duties' in P Alston and K Tomasevski (eds), *The Right to Food* (The Hague, Martinus Nijhoff, 1985) 86.

could be reversed. Moreover, such environmental enhancement initiatives will often represent a cheaper alternative to current mitigation policies.[48]

It is not altogether impossible, therefore, to envisage a time in which the EU and its member states will find themselves under a human rights based duty to deploy environmental enhancement technologies to secure environmental rights. In that respect, the fact that the CJEU has frequently referred to EU environmental provisions as bestowing 'environmental rights clearly is significant.[49]

V. Conclusion

The science that informs the Anthropocene and the intimately associated planetary boundaries hypothesis expose structural shortcomings in EU environmental policy and law that specialists in EU environmental law have long bemoaned. The fact that the Union's perspective on the environment is anthropocentric in its orientation has been a source of ongoing criticism, yet ultimately is not its most dysfunctional feature. Rather, it is the sharp dichotomy between people and nature formalised in the Treaties that is proving untenable and counter-productive. Scientists have shown that, as a matter of empirical fact, nature has become human, and that human beings are critically close to succumbing to nature, as it were. By implication, inconsistencies between legal competences and principles pertaining to the protection of human beings (eg the protection of human health) and those relating to the environment in Article 191 of the TFEU must be approached with a high degree of suspicion.

At present, EU environmental law sustains the human/nature dichotomy in various ways. Most fundamental is the fact that the principle of human dignity, which the EU Charter of Fundamental Rights elevates to the single most important organising principle of all EU activities, has no ecological counterpart in the form of a principle of ecological integrity. That omission is far from symbolic, as it translates into a systemic regulatory bias towards short-term individual human interests. It bestows unfettered discretion on the EU institutions about if, when and how to wield their considerable environmental powers, and it renders important principles such as precaution incoherent and directionless.

The absence of an ecological *Grundnorm* hinders the preservation and protection of the environmental status quo and/or the improvement and restoration of environments to status quo ante levels. However, it also means that

---

[48] See eg 'Cheap but Imperfect: Can Geoengineering Slow Climate Change?' *Spiegel Online* (20 November 2013) www.spiegel.de/international/world/scientist-david-keith-on-slowing-global-warming-with-geoengineering-a-934359.html.

[49] On the notion of EU environmental rights, see S Prechal and L Hancher, 'Individual Environmental Rights: Conceptual Pollution in EU Environmental Law?' (2001) 2 *Yearbook of European Environmental Law* 89.

emerging initiatives intentionally to enhance the environment in the furtherance of human or ecological imperatives can take place essentially without limits,
which is an alarming prospect. Hence, the fact that the proximity of humankind to
critical planetary boundaries may necessitate enhancement initiatives takes nothing away from the fact that such interventions must be legally disciplined. To that
end, the EU treaties may have to be amended to add 'enhancement' to the trilogy
of discretionary intentions enumerated in Article 191(1) of the TFEU. To be sure,
failure to do so would imply entrusting the EU institutions with powers they were
never intended to possess.

INDEX

Lightning Source UK Ltd.
Milton Keynes UK
UKHW01n0648020818
326610UK00009B/439/P